DHVANYALOKA
ध्वन्यालोक :

DHVANYĀLOKA
of
Ānandavardhana

Critically edited with
Introduction, Translation & Notes By
Dr. K. KRISHNAMOORTHY,

WITH A FOREWORD BY
Dr. K.R. SRINIVASA IYENGAR,

MOTILAL BANARSIDASS
Delhi :: Varanasi :: Patna

MOTILAL BANARSIDASS
Indological Publishers & Booksellers
Head Office : 41-U.A. Bungalow Road, Delhi-110 007
Branches : 1. Chowk, Varanasi-1 (U.P.)
2. Ashok Rajpath, Patna-4 (BIHAR)

First Edition : 1974
Second Edition : Delhi, 1982 , 2016

This book has been published on the paper supplied
through the Govt. of India at concessional rate

Printed in India
By Shantilal Jain, at Shri Jainendra press,
A-45, Phase I, Industrial Area, Naraina, New Delhi-110 028
Published by Narendra Prakash Jain, for Motilal Banarsidass,
Bungalow Road, Jawahar Nagar, Delhi-110 007.

CONTENTS

	Pages
Foreword by Dr. K. R. Srinivasa Iyengar	i–vii
Author's Preface	ix–x
Introduction	xi–xLi
Critical Text and English Translation of Dhvanyāloka	1–299
Notes	301–385
Glossary of technical terms and English equivalents	386–394
Index of *Kārikās*	395–398
Index of *Parikaraślokas*, etc. in the *Vṛtti*	399
Index of quotations	400–402
Index of authors and works	403–406
Errata	407

PREFACE

This edition is substantially a reprint of the first edition published by the Karnatak University, Dharwar, in 1974.

It has not been available for some time and I am happy that thanks to the kindness of Ms. Motilal Banarsidass, this de-luxe edition is within the reach of scholars and students interested in literature.

I have taken this opportunity to give at the end an appendix of 'Additions and Corrections' which incorporates the revisions rendered necessary in the light of reviews by esteemed scholars in different learned journals.

My thanks are due to my friend Sri Suresh Kulkarni for the cover design which brings out symbolically the ever-spreading waves of *dhvani*-resonance as well as the blooming lotus-hearts of responsive readers of poetry by the sunrise of the *Dhvanyaloka*.

Dharwar
21st December 1981

K. KRISHNAMOORTHY

FOREWORD

In acceding to Dr. K. Krishnamoorthy's request for a Foreword to his new critical edition of the *Dhvanyāloka*, with Notes and an English translation, I am not claiming any special knowledge of Sanskrit poetics or even a general acquaintance with Sanskrit, that may entitle me to speak with anything like authority. But I have known Dr. Krishnamoorthy rather intimately, and I have followed his career of scholarship with pride and admiration; and having myself for many long years pursued with indifferent success the profession of literary criticism, I am greatly interested in studies on the Sanskrit schools of poetics, and more particularly in the attempts of savants to trace the filiations between Western and Indian canons of aesthetic criticism. A new literature is invariably the product of a cross-fertilization of apparently alien cultures, as, for example, Elizabethan drama derived as much from the indigenous tradition as from the impact of classical literature, generally through translations. Indian literature today cannot deny the imperatives of our national tradition, which from Vedic times has run as a continuous stream, now broad and deep, now perhaps no more than a tenuous trickle, and at times indeed but a pure spring flowing under the sandy soil, invisible to the man who is in a hurry. On the other hand, the introduction of Western education into India in the 19th century opened new possibilities to the Indian writer, and accordingly new forms of literature, new modes of expression, new currents of ideas have been explored during the last hundred years or more in almost all our regional literatures. Even as the contemporary Indian creative writer is thus the heir to the two great traditions, the indigenous and the Western, the present day critic too—if he is to prove worthy of his vocation and rise to the height of his opportunities—must needs drink deep in the springs of both the Indian and Western traditions in criticism. A succession of great writers—Bharata, Bhāmaha, Daṇḍin, Ānandavardhana, Abhinavagupta, Mammaṭa, Jagannātha—have given us a body of critical thought as impressive in volume as it is invaluable as a guide to literary appreciation. The theories, evolved at first with reference to classical Sanskrit literature, were taken over by the critics of many of the new regional literatures, and so in course of time came to have a national currency. In the appreciation of literature, *rasa* or communicated sensibility is the deciding factor and *dhvani* or the richness of the undertones is the soul of poetry. Such in a nutshell was the *rasa-dhvani* theory, perhaps the most rewarding peak of all the Himalayas of Sanskrit treatises on poetics. No less rewarding to the modern Indian critic is the Western tradition in criticism beginning with Aristotle and Longinus and, notwithstanding diversions and periods of suspended animation, persisting till our own time of the New, Newer and Newest critics. The modern Indian critic should be ready to draw upon both these wells of living tradition, for only thus can he achieve a vigorous and fruitful play of his critical powers. There is here a great opportunity for him, and he can make the two opulent traditions of critical thought, the Indian and the European, meet in a new synthesis suggestive of the deeper unity of human aspiration and realisation through the ages.

There are, however, the usual difficulties incident to any new adventure, whether in the material world or in the more elusive world of ideas. Of the classics of Western criticism we have both definitive editions and also reliable translations in almost all European languages. Aristotle, Longinus, Horace, Dante, Boileau, Lessing, Coleridge, Arnold, Croce, I. A. Richards, Eliot, F. R. Leavis, Allen Tate, George Lukacs—they are easily accessible to us, and competent historical surveys of European criticism as well as monographs on individual critics are also available. As regards Indian poetics, the monumental labours of Dr. S. K. De and Mahāmahopādhyāya P.V. Kane, Krishna Chaitanya's survey, and the occasional but illuminating studies of scholars like the late M. Hiriyanna and Mahāmahopādhyāya Kuppuswami Sastri, and the meritorious work of Dr. Raghavan and Sankaran, have revealed to our gaze vista upon vista of critical enquiry and exegesis, and we still suffer as it were from a feeling of awe and bewilderment at the variegated richness of the prospect. Yet more needs to be done. The classics of Sanskrit criticism must be made available to the 'common reader' through translation in English and in the major regional languages of India. Comparative studies of the Indian and

Western schools of criticism, whether on a comprehensive scale or governed by a principle of resolved limitation to particular facets, would be no less welcome and would help to stimulate critical activity on the right lines. It is thus a matter of very real gratification to me that my esteemed friend, Dr. Krishnamoorthy has canalized his erudition and industry towards these essentially fruitful fields of activity.

In his thesis, *The 'Dhvanyāloka' and Its Critics*,—which, although completed when he was hardly twentyfive without effective guidance from a teacher, was approved *cum laude* for the Ph. D. degree of the Bombay University by two such savants as the late Mahāmahopādhyāya P. V. Kane and Professor H. D. Velankar — Dr. Krishnamoorthy boldly and with ample justification gave Ānandavardhana the central place in the history of Sankrit poetics. Besides outlining an account of the life and life-work of Ānandavardhana set in relation to his age and also the wider background of Sankrit poetics, Dr. Krishnamoorthy drew pointed attention to suggestive parallels between Indian and European critical thought. Self-contained chapters from Dr. Krishnamoorthy's thesis first appeared in learned journals, and its publication in its entirety, in 1968 won him the gratitude of students of Indian critical thought the world over. It brought him the Mysore University Golden Jubilee Award for Research. Of not less importance are Dr. Krishnamoorthy's Kannada renderings of the *Dhvanyāloka Kāvyālaṅkāra*, *Kāvyādarśa* and *Kāvyaprakāśa*, (winning him an award of the Karnatak State Sahitya Akademi 1973) as also his study of Kālidāsa (1972) published in New York, his monograph on Ānandavardhana's poetics in Kannada, his Sanskrit essay entitled *Alaṅkāra-Śāstre Kāvya-Vaividhya-Vāda-Vimarśaḥ* which was awarded the Navinam Ramanujacharya prize and has been published by the Mysore University and his *Essays in Sanskrit Criticism* which has been awarded the Rani Sethu Parvati Prize by the Kerala University — an impressive body of work that has elicited deservedly high praise from scholars. Now comes his excellent edition of the *Dhvanyāloka*, with a translation in English which I have no doubt will receive a ready welcome from the students of Indian and Western literature. Although others have written about the *Dhvanyāloka* or translated it in part, it is to Dr. Krishnamoorthy that we owe both the complete English translation of the *Kārikās* as well as the *Vṛtti*, and an orderly account of its current of ideas and an appreciation of the abiding value of its critical canons.

In the present edition of the *Dhvanyāloka*, Dr. Krishnamoorthy has collated readings from ten manuscripts as also the earlier editions, and has arrived at an almost definitive text of this great classic. The Notes are the fruit of his constant study of the subject for a period of over two decades. And he has taken advantage of this occasion and revised the English translation, which had first appeared in 1955, so as to make it at once close to the original and very readable in English. Whereas in his Kannada version of the *Dhvanyāloka* he has translated verse into verse, here in the English version his aim is only to provide a faithful and clear prose rendering of the verse portions of the original, though by resorting to italics and indented spacing, these passages are set strikingly apart from the main prose commentary. With a text like the *Dhvanyāloka* teeming with subtleties and intricacies and numerous illustrative quotations, what is needed is not a merely facile or free or readable paraphrase but a scrupulously exact translation, a version that reproduces with absolute fidelity the original text in its entirety. This ideal Dr. Krishnamoorthy has steadily kept before him, and it is all the more to his credit that his rendering of the *Dhvanyāloka* is fairly free from clumsy, clogging or twisted phrases or sentences, and thus raises no barrier between itself and the reader.

This is not, of course, the place to enter into a detailed discussion on Sanskrit poetics or on the particular topics covered by the *Dhvanyāloka*. Even as, try as we might, we cannot empty life of its mystery, we cannot, for all our analytical categories, explain away the whole mystery of poetic creation. Life is a complex of fact and fancy, logic, meaning and mystery and poetry as it were pierces life where it is most sensitive, and seeks to pluck the heart of the mystery—yet the mystery, something of it at least, must remain to tantalize or to silence us. What we ordinarily see of life is the veil of appearance, and to the extent we penetrate through it and touch the hidden centre, our apprehension is complete or final. The poet uses words in a metrical order to convey something of the mystery—the deeper significance—of life. But words too are mere appearance, and words have to be so charged with significant undertones that the poet may be able to convey through appearances the reality that lies behind them. We often refer to the poet's inspiration, the divine afflatus that is like a sudden surge of primordial poetic energy. But inspiration has to be turned into the currency of language before it can become poetry. We may likewise describe poetry at its purest as a "mystic incantation allied to prayer", or as soul communing with soul. When poetic expression approximates to the *mantra,* the effect on the hearer is far more profound than the mere words would seem to warrant: it is as though, leaping over the physical boundaries or the coils of intellectual cognition, the meaning intended by the poet lodges directly in the reader's soul. Words, grammatical organization, rhythmic arrangement, jugglings with sound, figures of speech, the operations of the intellect, the emotional excitement, the rule of current fashions and the pull of tradition—all have their part to play in determining the composition of a poem; yet without the soul-quality there is no poem, only a life-less mass of words, a temple without the installed deity, a statue without life. *Dhvani* in poetry is really this soul-quality which is at once the excuse and the explanation of the rest. Not the outer habiliments of form and diction, the riot of *śabdālaṅkāras,* and *arthālaṅkāras,* not the stern logic of the plot or the innate worth of the sentiments, but it is this reality within, the soul-quality, this undertone of seminal suggestion that constitutes the utter uniqueness of poetry.

Sanskrit rhetoricians mention the basic categories of *vastu* (matter, plot or form), *alaṅkāra* (embellishment, fullness of detail or diction) and *rasa* (sentiment, sensibility or emotional intensity); but Ānandavardhana rightly urges that in respect of all these, the reality within is of far greater consequence than the outer appearance. Not until the story or the plot is seized in terms of universality does it become poetic, nor until verbal expression becomes a new way, the only satisfying way in the context, of adequately conveying the writer's individual vision of life or character does such expression become poetic;

and likewise, not until the communicated sensibility is so laden with the undertones of significance as to kindle the soul to a new awareness of life's "deep magic" can such sentiment or sensibility be called truly poetic. In a word, only when a poem, instead of imprisoning or suffocating the reader within the granite walls of precise meaning, proves rather to be a magic casement opening on the foam of the endless oceans of ambrosial significance can it deserve the name of poetry. What we seek in a scientific statement is the sufficiency of the statement; in poetry we seek to pierce the *māyā* of visible or cognizable picture or statement, and touch or apprehend the intangible reality within. It would not do to apply to poetry the categories of analysis that might be valid with regard to a science or to a prose treatise. It would be like judging men—a Buddha, a Christ, a Gandhi, or even imaginative characters like Hamlet, Stavrogin and Tess—in terms of poundage, colour or height. Poetry not only tells us something, but *does* something to us. Tragedy effects the katharsis of the emotions of pity and terror, said Aristotle; great poetry *transports* us, said Longinus; and Ānandavardhana said—if not in so many words as Abhinavagupta did—that poetry is a means of cultivating the double vision so that we may be enabled to perceive the visible and invade the invisible, mark the immediate contours of Appearance, yet peer beyond them and glimpse the very image of splendorous Reality.

There is, then, the element of *pleasure* in poetry; and there is pleasure even in tragedy, even in Vālmīki's description of Rāma's banishment or Kālidāsa's presentation of the rejection of Śakuntalā. Pleasure, certainly, but of what kind? "A superior amusement...not an amusement for superior people", says T. S. Eliot. The pleasure that the sensitive reader—the *Sahṛdaya*—derives from poetry is not the sort of amusement or pleasure that is meant merely to "kill time"; on the contrary, it works almost a sea-change, and leaves upon him a permanent effect. We are not the same people after reading the poem that we were before. The words of the poet are verily like a dance of creative life, they are like unto a racing squadron of the spirit, and whereas the five senses open *without*, the sixth sense that poetry gives us opens *within*, and the undertones of

Dhvani carry us almost to the threshold of Reality. The pleasure is not denied, it is only transformed into a discipline in awareness, a deepening of consciousness, a realization of things undreamt of before. The *Rasa-Dhvani* theory of poetry is thus naturally affiliated to the main Vedantic tradition in philosophy, although the encrustation of multiple categories and hair-splitting differentiations may tend to obscure this fact. But that is no reason why, at this distance of time, we should miss the quintessential aspect of the *Rasa-Dhvani* theory in our excessive preoccupation with the burden of detail and the controversial fog, which have more a historical than an integral relation to the theory.

Be that as it may, Dr. Krishnamoorthy deserves our gratitude for his sustained attempts to popularise Indian aesthetics, not only as a unique discipline in poetic appreciation, but also as a springboard for comparative studies. The present edition of the *Dhvanyāloka* with Notes and a dependable and readable English translation comes as a natural climax to Dr. Krishnamoorthy's varied labours in the field of Sanskrit studies, and especially Sanskrit poetics. In recent years there has been a revival of Sanskrit studies in the country, and Sanskrit has been showing every sign of its amazing vitality as a living language and literature. It is, therefore, gratifying that dedicated scholars like Dr. Krishnamoorthy are giving their time so purposefully to promote the study and dissemination of Sanskrit literature. With the habits of the cloistered scholar, unattached to coteries or empire-builders, undaunted by difficulties or discouragement, Dr. Krishnamoorthy has long persevered in his chosen path, and has now won a position of authority and responsibility in the academic world as Professor and Head of the Department of Sanskrit at the Karnatak University. I do earnestly hope that with his learning and dedication, his sensibility and industry, he will be able in the years to come to build in his university a flourishing School of Comparative Aesthetics oriented towards the critical appreciation of the flowering new literature in the Indian subcontinent.

91, Kutchery Road,
Mylapore, Madras.
1 February 1973

K. R. Srinivasa Iyengar

PREFACE

This edition which embodies the result of my work for over a decade is being released with the hope that it is a substantial improvement on the bare English translation which appeared in the Poona Oriental Series in 1955 and which has been long out of print.

The text has been now critically edited for the first time by collating some fresh manuscripts which have not been used by previous editors of the *Dhvanyāloka*. The English translation itself has been rewritten in the light of valuable suggestions made by scholars of repute, Indian and foreign, while reviewing it in learned journals. I have endeavoured strictly to follow Abhinavagupta's explanations throughout this English translation. In the light of my experience as a post-graduate teacher of the *Dhvanyāloka* for twenty years, I have added copious notes which discuss the most crucial points from the standpoint of University students. A useful introduction has been added to this edition discussing text-readings and problems of authorship and literary theory, taking into account the research done up to date.

To facilitate reference, the Sanskrit original and the English translation are so arranged as to face each other. Lines have been numbered and the headings of chapters prominently provided on each page. No pains have been spared to provide as many indexes as possible; viz. of *kārikās*, *parikaraślokas*, illustrative verses and of works and authors. A glossary of Sanskrit and English equivalents is another useful feature of this edition. I have strictly avoided using material published by me elsewhere in this work.

I have to thank heartily Dr. K. R. Srinivasa Iyengar for taking the trouble of touching up his Foreword to suit this edition. I must thank Pandit K. Bhujabali Shastri for procuring for my use the palm-leaf manuscript of the *Dhvanyāloka* from the Dānashālā Math, Moodabidre. I am also thankful to the Director, Bhandarkar Oriental Research Institute, Poona for allowing me to consult the *Dhvanyāloka* manuscripts in his charge.

I am very grateful to the Karnatak University not only for enabling me to complete this research work but also for having arranged its publication. In this connection, the unfailing courtesy and keen interest evinced by Sri. C. S. Kanavi, Director of Publications and his staff deserves special mention.

It is my duty and pleasure to record various kinds of assistance rendered to me by colleagues, Dr. D. N. Shanbhag, Dr. B. R. Modak, and Vidwan M. C. Dixit at all levels of preparing this work and seeing it through the press.

I might utilise this occasion to announce that I look forward to bring out an edition of the *Locana* also on similar lines as a companion volume, in the near future.

It is hoped that this edition will be found useful by scholars and the general public interested in Sanskrit literature and criticism. The few misprints in the text noted in the Errata at the end may be rectified by readers. But it must be mentioned that the Aryabhushan Press has done its very best in the printing of this work for which thanks are due.

Dept. of Sanskrit,
Karnatak University,
Dharwar.
12–7–1974.

K. Krishnamoorthy

INTRODUCTION

THE TEXT OF THE *DHVANYĀLOKA*

The first notice of the manuscripts of the *Dhvanyāloka* was made in 1877 by G. Bühler in his detailed *Report* of a tour in search of Sanskrit manuscripts. The text of the *Dhvanyāloka* was first published in the Kāvyamālā Series by the Nirnaya Sagar Press Bombay in 1890 on the basis of three manuscripts, along with Abhinavagupta's Locana. In 1902 it was first completely translated into German by that great savant Hermann Jacobi of Bonn which appeared serially in Vols. LVI and LVII of the *Zeitschrift der Deutschen Morgenländischen Gesellschaft* during the years 1902-1903. In the old volumes (IX-X 1917) of the *Indian Thought* from Allahabad. Prof. K. Rama Pisharoti began on a very ambitious scale an English translation of both the text of the *Dhvanyāloka* and the *Locana*. But it is found to stop abruptly at Uddyota II, Kārikā 16 (immediately before the *Saṁgrahaślokas*; see p. 60 of the present edition). Meanwhile the NS Press issued subsequent revised editions, the fourth being issued in 1935 by Wasudev Laxman Shastri Paṇshikar.

A perusal of these will show how the readings were more often than not incorrect. Both Jacobi and Pisharoti have written numerous notes suggesting their reconstructed readings in view of the extremely confusing misreadings found in the NSP editions. My *paramaguru*, Prof. M. Hiriyanna of Mysore was recalling how he wrote the first ever thesis on the *Dhvanyāloka* for the M. A. degree of the Madras University as soon as the *editio princeps* appeared; but, though he got the degree, how he desisted from allowing its publication because the text itself was so corrupt.

In these circumstances the scholars had to be satisfied with the broad surveys of the Dhvani theory contained in the works of the pioneer-scholars; S. K. De, P. V. Kane and A. Shankaran which appeared between 1923 and 1929. The learned works of modern scholars[1] have indeed illuminated many a point in the Dhvanyāloka, but they avoid discussion of readings.

A number of subsequent editions of the Dhvanyāloka have appeared in India, sometimes with independent new commentaries in Sanskrit by modern editors[2]. The text of the Locana in the NSP edition was no better than that of the Dhvanyāloka itself and it was limited to the first three Uddyotas. These deficiencies were sought to be remedied on the basis of fresh Kerala manuscripts by Shri Ramashāraka. This edition of the Dhvanyāloka and complete Locana with Ramashāraka's Sanskrit com. called *Bālapriyā* [Abbreviated here as BP] (published in 1940, in the Kashi Sanskrit series, Benares) was published by Pattābhirāma Shastri. No doubt he has successfully recovered several improved readings in the text of both the Dhvanyāloka and the Locana, as Pattabhirama Shastri has demonstrated in his introduction to this edition. But this edition too suffers from one serious omission. It does not give variant manuscript readings anywhere. However, scholars are usually found citing the readings in this edition rather than the NSP edition.

In 1944, the Kuppuswami Shastri Research Institute, Madras brought out a critical edition of the *Dhvanyāloka, Locana, Kaumudī* by Uttungodaya (on the *Locana*), and *Upalocana* by Kuppuswami Shastri, on Uddyota–I based on some southern manuscripts. Though it is a very good edition as far as it goes, it does not go beyond Uddyota–I.

1. (i) V. Raghavan : *Bhoja's Śṛṅgāra Prakāśa*, Madras, 1963.
(ii) S. P. Bhattacharya : *Studies in Indian Poetics*, Calcutta, 1964.
(iii) Ramaranjan Mukherji : *Literary Criticism in Ancient India*, Calcutta, 1966.
(iv) J. L. Masson and M. V. Patwardhan : Śāntarasa and Abhinavagupta's philosophy of Aesthetics, Poona, 1969.
(v) Mukund Madhav Sharma : *Dhvani Theory in Sanskrit Poetics*, Varanasi, 1968.

2. E. g. *Dhvanyāloka*—1. with the *Didhiti* com. of Badrinath Sharma, Vārānasi, 1937; 2. with *Avadhāna* com. by Madhusūdana Mishra Sharma, Calcutta Sanskrit Series, 1938; though these do not contain the *Locana*, they virtually echo the *Locana* and do not help in deciding a correct reading of the text of the *Dhvanyāloka*.

Meanwhile, when the present editor took up this work for a detailed study in 1946, he wrote out for himself a working English translation to help him write the thesis entitled 'The Dhvanyāloka and its critics', which was awarded a Ph. D. degree by the Bombay University in 1947 (since published in 1968, Kāvyālaya, Mysore). The Poona Oriental Series was good enough to issue the English translation itself independently as No. 92, in 1955.

Mention must be made of other editions which have since appeared with English or Hindi translation and notes, though they do not bother themselves about problems of correct readings. One in English is by B. Bhattacharya, published by Firma K. L. Mukhopadhyāya, Calcutta; first Uddyota, 1956, (1965, II Ed.), and second Uddyota 1957. One in Hindi, is by Rama Sagar Tripathi, published by Motilal Banarasidass of Delhi, in 1963. These are of some help only to students preparing for their University examinations and do not serve the scholars interested in deciding the text.

My references to various manuscript catalogues show that there are scores of manuscripts of both the *Locana* and the *Dhvanyāloka* deposited in manuscript Libraries all over India, not to speak of Nepal, and Great Britain. They are in Sharada, Grantha, Malayalam, Telugu, Nevari and Kannada Scripts, besides the Devanāgari. In spite of my efforts over two decades. I could succeed in consulting only Poona manuscripts (ten in number. These are referred to by their numbers as recorded in the manuscript catalogue of the B. O. R. I.). But I was extremely lucky in securing for my use, a manuscript of the *Dhvanyālaka* with *Locana* (upto the end of the uddyota III) from the Dānashāla Math of Moodabidre in the South Kanara District of the Karnatak State. It is a palm-leaf manuscript in Kannada script and is about two hundred years old. The text is complete in 28 folios i. e. 55 pages and on the reverse of folio 28, begins the text of the Locana. Each folio measures 20″ × $2\frac{1}{4}$″. It has been designated as Kavyālokalankāra in the said collection. And it has been used fully for the first time here (referred to as MB). I was also able to check up some of these new readings which appear most appropriate with another very old plam leaf manuscript of the Dhvanyaloka and the Locana in Telugu Script displayed by the Andhra Sahitya Parishat, Kakinada at the Sanskrit Vishva Parishad Session at Bombay in 1961. But, unfortunately, I could not secure it for a second consultation as it is reported to be lost.

My purpose in the present edition has been to constitute an accurate and dependable text with all the available printed and manuscript material for select passages which required utmost attention in so far as they could not yield proper meanings. Hence I have not mechanically set out all the critical variants which did not materially alter the argument of the text. I have spared no pains to record the readings from not only MB and Poona manuscripts, but also from both the NSP (referred to as घ throughout the footnotes in this edition) and BP which are printed editions. The क, ख, and ग, variants noted by NSP are also recorded here. Another noteworthy feature of the present edition is the recording of readings as found in testimonial of later writers. The pride of place among them goes to the anonymous *Kalpalatāviveka* (abbreviated as KLV) recently published as No. XVII in the Lalbhai Dalpatbhai Bharateeya Samskriti Vidyamandir, Ahmedabad in 1968. It contains the bulk of the Locana and the Dhvanyāloka almost like a transcript. It is also interesting that it has some Kārikās not found in any other edition (See footnote on p. 98 of this edition).

IMPROVED READINGS IN THIS EDITION

An idea of the extent to which the present attempt has succeeded in reclaiming improved readings may be had by a look at the following table wherein only some outstanding instances are cited along with the readings found in other editions. It should be noted also that the BP which does not have an Errata contains a large number of misprints too, which are not taken into consideration here.

Readings adopted in this edition	Readings in other editions
P. 14 L. 13 स्वरश्रुत्यादिलक्षणमिवाप्रगीतानाम् ।	... मिव प्रगीतानाम् (NSP)
P. 24 L. 4 उपसर्जनीभावेन	उपसर्जनाभावेन (BP)

Reading adopted in this edition			Readings in other editions
P. 24	L. 12	ध्वनिसंभावनां निराकरोति।	ध्वनिसंभागनां करोति। (NSP)
P. 28	L. 3	तदप्रसिद्धालङ्कार°	तदत्र प्रसिद्धालङ्कार° (NSP)
P. 30	L. 1	मा चैतत्स्यात् भक्तिर्लक्षणं ध्वनेः।	तत्रैतत्स्यात् भक्तिर्लक्षणं ध्वनेः। (NSP)
P. 34	L. 10	समग्र एव लक्ष्यत इति।	समग्र एव लक्ष्यति इति। (NSP)
P. 62	L. 17	न प्राधान्येन।	प्राधान्येन। (NSP)
P. 64	L. 11	उपमाश्लेषस्य	श्लेषस्य (NSP) उपमा श्लेषस्य (BP)
P. 110	L. 14	मन्मथोन्माथकापादनावस्था°	मन्मथोन्माथकदनावस्था° (BP) मन्मथोन्मादकतापादनावस्थान° (NSP)
P. 112	L. 20	न विरोधी।	न विरोधि। (BP)
P. 114	L. 10	रसश्च्युतः	रसच्युतः (NSP, BP)
P. 124	L. 11	उत्तमदेवताविषयप्रतिषिद्धसंभोगशृंगार°	उत्तमदेवताविषयप्रसिद्धसंभोगशृंगार° (NSP, BP)
P. 124	L. 13	यथौचित्यत्यागः	यथौचित्यात्यागः (BP)
P. 168	L. 7	दुष्टत्वं नानुवादे	वानुवादे (BP)
P. 182	L. 12	सर्वाकारमहंकाररहितत्वे शान्तरसप्रभेदत्वम्।	सर्वाकारमहंकाररहितत्वेन शान्तरसप्रभेदत्वम् (NSP, BP)
P. 186	L. 2	क्षिप्रमेवावज्ञाविषयता	क्षिप्रमेवावज्ञानविषयता (NSP, BP)
P. 192	L. 10	तदवधारितप्रकरणानां	तदनवधारितप्रकरणानां (NSP, BP)
P. 220	L.	लिङ्गितया	लिङ्गतया (NSP, BP)
P. 226	L. 17	अमिअ	आमिअ (NSP, BP)
P. 230	L. 14	प्रतिपदपाठेनैव	प्रतिपादपाठेनैव (NSP, BP)

Readings adopted in this edition			Readings in other edition
P. 262	L. 13	सर्वस्वलक्षणविषयं	सर्वलक्षणविषयं (NSP, BP)
P. 278	L. 6	अंशिरूप°	अङ्गिरूप° (NSP, BP)
P. 276	L. 13	चशब्दः	च शब्दः (NSP, BP)
P. 284	L. 11	वा न प्रतिभासन्ते	प्रतिभासन्ते (NSP, BP)

It will be observed that in most of these, the existing readings are misreadings since they yield meanings inapplicable in the particular context. The present editor has avoided undue emendation and attempted to fix the text first on manuscript evidence and next on the evidence of the *Locana*. It is hoped that this will serve as a first step in the direction of a definitive text of Dhvanyāloka free from avoidable errors.

TITLE OF THE TEXT

Though all printed editions give, without exception, the title of the text as '*Dhvanyāloka*', this has not the support of even a single manuscript consulted by the present editor. Even when the Descriptive catologues of manuscripts describe the colophon as *Dhvanyāloka*, it has been found to be inaccurate on verification in the original manuscripts in question. The manuscripts mostly record the alternate titles 'Kāvyāloka' and 'Sahṛdayāloka' though some times the forms 'Sahṛdayahṛdayāloka' or 'Sahṛdayāvaloka' are also met with. It is interesting to observe in this connection that Abhinavagupta himself uses the form of only 'Kāvyāloka' in his *Locana*, while he uses the form 'Sahṛdayāloka' at least thrice in his *Abhinavabhāratī*.[1] Maheśvarānanda in his *Mahārthamañjarī* pays a tribute to the *Locana* and the *Kāvyāloka* in these words :—

साहित्याब्धौ कर्णधारोऽहमासम्
काव्यालोकं लोचनं चानुशील्य ।

1. (i) तच्चास्माभिः सहृयालोकलोचने तद्विवरणे विस्तरतो व्याख्यातम्...
Nāṭyaśāstra, Vol. I, GOS, Baroda, 1934, Pp. 299-300.
(ii) ...इति चिरन्तनैरेवोक्तम् ॥ यथा सहृदयालोककारः--संधिसंध्यङ्ग...
Ibid, Vol. III, 1954, P. 42.
(iii) ...निर्णीतमस्माभिः सहृदयालोकलोचने च । Ibid. Vol. IV, 1964

Even the commentators of *kāvyas* like Rāghavabhaṭṭa, Mallinātha and post-*dhvani* writers on poetics do not testify to the title ' *Dhvanyāloka* '.

The present editor was even wondering for some time whether, after all, the name Dhvanyāloka was a late fabrication by Durgaprasad or somebody. But his hesitation was allayed by a recent publication of Dr. Kunjunni Raja, who has edited for the first time with English translation and notes a small work, the *Dhvanyālokasaṅgraha* by an anonymous author, from a single palm-leaf manuscript[1]. The form ' Dhvanyāloka ' is thus attested by manuscript evidence much earlier than the 19th century. Dr. Raja (Op. cit. foreword, p. iv) also mentions that the previous portion of this palm-leaf manuscript contains the *Locana* text wherein also the name *Dhvanyāloka* occurs at the beginning, in the words—ध्वन्यालोकलोचनव्याख्याप्रारंभः ।

These facts have thrown an interesting sidelight on the different forms of the title of Ānandavardhana's work. The thesis of the duality of the authorship of the Dhvanyāloka advanced by Jacobi, De, Kane and others has been effectively disproved by the present writer elsewhere.[2] The earliest references to the author of the Dhvanyāloka are sometimes made by the expression सहृदयैः[3]. This led pioneers like Sovani and Kane to conclude that Sahṛdaya was the proper name of only the Kārikākāra and that Āloka was the name of only Ānandavardhana's Vṛtti thereon. These scholars ignore Abhinavagupta's own indisputable references to Kārikās of the *Dhvanyāloka* as of Ānandavardhana's authorship found in more than one place in his *Abhinavabhāratī*, a work written by him after the *Locana*.

1. Annals of Oriental Research, University of Madras, Vol. XXIV, Part II, 1973.
   P. 12.

2. K. Krishnamoorthy, *Dhvanyāloka and its critics*, Kāvyālaya, Mysore, 1968, Ch. III.

3. Cf. (i) Pratīhārenduraja–Kāvyālankāra–Sāra–Saṅgraha--laghu--Vṛtti, Ed. N. B. Banhatti, Bombay, 1925, P. 85 etc. (ii) Mukulabhaṭṭa's Abhidhāvṛttimātṛkā, Ed. R. P. Dwivedi, Chowkhamba, Benares, 1973, P. 66.

Eg. (i) एतमेवार्थं सम्यगानन्दवर्धनाचार्योऽपि विविच्य न्यरूपयत्—

ध्वन्यात्मभूते शृङ्गारे समीक्ष्य विनिवेशितः।
रूपकादिरलङ्कारवर्ग एति यथार्थताम् ॥

इत्युक्त्वा क्रमेण

विवक्षा तत्परत्वेन नाङ्गित्वेन कदाचन।
काले च ग्रहणत्यागौ नातिनिर्वहणैषिता ॥

इत्यादिना ग्रन्थसन्दर्भेण सोदाहरणेन। तच्चास्माभिः सहृदयालोकलोचने तद्विवरणे विस्तरतो व्याख्यातमिति तत्कुतूहलं तदेव गृह्णीयात्। — Nāṭyaśāstra, Vol. II. GOS, Baroda, 1934, Pp. 299-300.

(ii) यस्तु वेणीसंहारे भानुमत्या सह दुर्योधनस्य दर्शितो विलासः, स नायकस्य तादृशेऽवसरे अत्यनुचित इति चिरन्तनैरेवोक्तम्। यथा सहृदयालोककारः—

संधिसंध्यङ्गघटनं रसबन्धौ व्यपेक्षया।
न तु केवलया शास्त्रस्थितिसंपादनेच्छया ॥

एतच्च विवरण एवास्माभिर्वितत्य दर्शितम् ॥–Ibid. Vol. III, 1954, P-42.

(iii) कविर्हि सामाजिकतुल्य एव। तत एवोक्तम्—

शृङ्गारी चेत्कविः काव्ये जातं रसमयं जगत्।
स एव वीतरागश्चेन्नीरसं सर्वमेव तत् ॥

इत्यानन्दवर्धनाचार्येण। Ibid, Vol-I, 1956, P. 294.

These clinching references are enough to justify our holding that the careful distinction he actually made between the Vṛttikāra and the Kārikākāra in the course of his *Locana* was dictated by exegetical procedure and nothing else.

Even the work of Baṭṭanāyaka which was written to demolish *Dhvani* was called by the name हृदयदर्पण or सहृदयदर्पण. This raises the question regarding the exact significance of the attested titles सहृदयालोक and सहृदयदर्पण. I don't think that this question has been fully discussed. I secured transcripts of three unpublished commentaries on the *Locana* available at Tirupati and Madras MS. libraries. They are all anonymous. But the one fragment called काव्यालोकलोचनव्याख्या (obtained from Tirupati) which is a very learned and voluminous discussion of only the Maṅgalasloka of Abhinava, explains pointedly the significance of the word *sahṛdaya* therein as follows :—

सहृदयशब्देन तु सामान्यवाचिनापि सहृदयविशेष आनन्दवर्धनाचार्योऽत्र विवक्षितः। उक्तं ह्यमुनान्यत्र "विद्वत्कविसहृदयचक्रवर्तिन" इति। तस्य हि विद्वत्ता तत्त्वालोकादिग्रन्थप्रणयनेन प्रसिद्धा। विषमबाणलीलादिकाव्यरचनया च कवित्वम्; काव्यतत्त्वावबोधविदग्धतारूपं सहृदयत्वं किमुच्यते ध्वनिमार्गोपदेशप्रथमदेशिकस्य। अस्ति च तस्यैव श्लोकः —

"या व्यापारवती रसान्रसयितुं काचित्कवीनां न वा
दृष्टिर्या परिनिश्चितार्थविषयोन्मेषा च वैपश्चिती।
ते द्वेऽप्यवलम्ब्य विश्वमनिशं निर्वर्णयन्तो वयं
श्रान्ता नैव च लब्धमब्धिशयन त्वद्भक्तितुल्यं सुखम्॥

इति। अत्र च प्रथमश्लोकव्याख्यानान्ते वक्ष्यते — सहृदयचक्रवर्ती खल्वयं ग्रन्थकृदिति। (Page 29).

This brilliant summing up of Abhinavagupta's stand regarding the authorship of the *Dhvanyāloka* is from one whose mind is unprejudiced by the controversies of modern scholars. He states categorically that the word *sahṛdaya* is general in its connotation to apply to perceptive critics of poetry. But in the invocatory verse of Abhinava the expression सहृदय in the compound कविसहृदयाख्यं could also stand for the admittedly foremost of the *sahṛdayas*, viz. Ānandavardhana himself. This has been our contention all along. The word *Āloka* cannot be divested of its earlier part and made to refer exclusively to the *Vṛtti* as Kane chooses to do. The name *Āloka* is an essential part of the compound name and it should stand for both *Kārikā* and *Vṛtti*. This commentator has not failed to draw our attention to Abhinava's own testimony that Ānandavardhana was the doyen of not only poets but also perceptive critics or *sahṛdayas*.

Thus if it is accepted that the full title of the work is *Sahṛdayāloka* it would naturally mean the Light on Poetry shed by the best sahṛdaya, viz. Ānandavardhana, or for the benefit of sahṛdayas in general and thus would become significant. Any other way of understanding the compound would be forced and lacking in significance.

The procedure of Ānandavardhana himself in slyly hinting at his name is observed in so wording the first *Kārikā* (which is by the bye very poetic) that it contains the word सहृदयमनःप्रीति

which could be explained by the synonym आनन्द. This is truly in line with the concluding expression in the work viz. आनन्दवर्धन इति प्रथिताभिधानः। Thus understood, the title of its critique by Bhaṭṭanāyaka also becomes easy to follow as a sly reference to the *Dhvanyāloka* itself.

Even prior to Abhinava, the Candrikākāra quoted in the *Locana* had committed a slip in exegetical procedure by explaining the meaning of a *Kārikā* introducing new material from the *Vṛtti* though not expressly stated in the *Kārikā* itself. More than all, at the end of the first chapter, Abhinava writes an equivocal verse alluding to *Āloka* as the title of the whole work (i. e. both *Kārikā* and *Vṛtti*) and that both *Candrikā* and *Locana* were commentaries thereon :—

किं लोचनं विनालोको भाति चन्द्रिकयापि हि।
तेनाभिनवगुप्तोऽत्र लोचनोन्मीलनं व्यधात्॥

The significance is brought out by *Kaumudī* as follows :

लोचनं स्वकीयमेतदेव व्याख्यानम्। आलोकः व्याख्येयत्वेन प्रस्तूयमानः काव्यालोकग्रन्थः। चन्द्रिका अस्यैव अन्यकृतं व्याख्यानान्तरम्। — KSRI Edition, Madras, 1944, P. 302.

Another anonymous commentary on the *Locana* from Madras, (R 2680, Govt. Oriental Manuscripts Library, Madras-5), has the following explanation :—

लोचनं नेत्रं अयं व्याख्यानग्रन्थश्च। लोको भवनमालोकश्चायं ध्वनिग्रन्थः। चन्द्रिका ज्योत्स्ना ध्वनिव्याख्यानग्रन्थश्चान्यः।

The protagonists of the dual authorship theory labour under the misapprehension that *Āloka* is only the name of the *Vṛtti* and that *Dhvani* is the name of the *Kārikā*. These citations should dispel their doubts; for, Abhinava and others refer to the whole work by the partial name *Āloka* as much as others refer to it by the other partial name *Dhvani* when they talk of Dhvanikāra, Dhvanikṛt, etc. The name *Dhvani* itself is too specialised to be the name of any treatise. It could only be an abbreviated form of a fuller title, in this case, *Dhvanyāloka*. Just as रघुवंशकाव्यकार is referred to by the short form रघुकार,

Dhvanyālokagranthakāra can be popularly called ध्वनिकार. In this usage *Dhvani* is nothing but a shortened form of a longer title, such as Dhvanigrantha, Dhvaniśāstra and Dhvanyāloka. In any case all these refer both to the *Kārikā* and the *Vṛtti* written by Ānandavardhana himself.

The earliest references to the author or the work *Dhvanyāloka* also confirm the above conclusion. About 900 A.D. Jayantabhaṭṭa, the author of the *Nyāyamañjarī*, refers to a पण्डितंमन्य 'who took to (प्रपेदे) Dhvani to explain वाक्यार्थ' and ridicules him. This shows how he was aware of only one author and not two and proceeds to review an instance of *Dhvani* actually found in the *Vṛtti* and not in the *Kārikā*. Similarly Rajaśekhara, in one of his eulogistic *subhāṣitas* quoted in anthologies, talks of Ānandavardhana as establishing the poetic theory of Dhvani in a work called *Dhvani* and carved out glory for himself. An equally remarkable reference to the work by the short form Dhvani is that of Utpalācārya[1] in his *Spanda-pradīpikā*[2]. Commenting on the first *Spanda-kārikā* of Kallaṭa, Utpala explains a word by citing the Dhvanyāloka in these words — यत्तु 'शक्तिचक्रविभवप्रभवं' इति पदमुपन्यस्तं तदुद्देशार्थम् । साभिप्रायत्वान्महाकवेः । उक्तं च ध्वनौ—प्रतीयमानं पुनरन्यदेव वस्त्वस्ति वाणीषु महाकवीनाम् । यत्तत्प्रसिद्धावयवातिरिक्तं विभाति लावण्यमिवाङ्गनासु ।

In the B. O. R. I. collection of manuscripts there is a work called ध्वनिगाथापञ्जिका (MS. No. XII — 182). Its author was one Ratnākara of Kashmir and he uses the word *Dhvani* to mean ध्वन्यालोक or ध्वनिशास्त्र as he himself states at the beginning —

वाग्देवीं शिरसा नत्वा वाचो वैचित्र्यहेतवे ।
करोति कश्चिद्गाथानां ध्वनिशास्त्रस्य पञ्जिकाम् ॥

and also at the conclusion of the work —

गाथानां पञ्चिकां कृता ध्वनिशास्त्रस्य यन्मया ।
पुण्यं रत्नाकरेणापि विबुद्धः स्यात्ततो जनः ॥

---

1. His date is first half of the tenth century according to Bühler. See Bühler's 'Tour...', p. 79.

2. Edited by Vaman Shastri Islampurkar, Vizianagaram Sanskrit Series, Benares, Vol. XIV, 1898, p. 12.

The short form *Dhvani* in his usage covers the illustrative portion of the text also, and is a synonym for *Dhvaniśāstra* which is the meaning of the word *Dhvanyāloka* as we will see presently.

The general definition of Dhvani, viz,, यत्रार्थः शब्दो वा is quoted by the Ceylonese commentator Ratnaśrījñāna (931 A. D.) of Daṇḍin's *Kāvyādarśa* and he tries to bring it under *samāsokti*. [*Kāvyalakṣaṇa* of Dandin with com. of Ratnaśrījñāna, Mithila Research Institute, Darbhanga, 1957. He was domiciled in Magadha.] The Kannada *Kavirājamārga* of King Nṛpatuṅga (9th Century A. D.) alludes to *Dhvani* at the end of his treatment of *alaṅkāras*. Now all these early references envisage an acquaintance with Dhvani examples found only in the *Vṛtti* and not in *Kārikās*. Hence, we may conclude that in Indian tradition there is not a single shred of evidence to dispute Ānandavardhana's authorship of the *Kārikās* and the *Vṛtti* together called by the name *Dhvanyāloka* or *Kāvyāloka* or *Sahṛdayāloka*.

With this background the significance of the three titles can be clearly grasped. The word *āloka* which is an essential part of the title as we saw above has two senses, viz. (i) light and (2) sight. That this author had a special fancy for the word *āloka* is also evidenced by the title he gave to his philosophical treatise (unfortunately lost), namely, the *Tattvāloka*. The second meaning, of *āloka* makes it correspond to Darśana which is another name for a ' system of thought ' i. e. a Śāstra[1]. Possibly both the meanings were intended to be conveyed by the author. The title Kāvyāloka presents the least difficulty. It is a synonym of Kāvya-prakāśa, i. e. Light on Poetry or a systematic treatise on poetry. The word *Dhvanyāloka* could mean Light of Suggestion (in poetry) or a systematic treatise on suggestion (in poetry). The last title, namely Sahṛdayāloka, would carry the meanings of Light (or a systematic treatise) for the benefit of *Sahṛdayas*. As we saw above, it may also contain a veiled hint that Ānandavardhana, the author of the work, is himself a Sahṛdaya *par excellence*.

---

1. Cf. न्यायदर्शन, सांख्यदर्शन etc.

THE IMPORTANCE OF THE DHVANYĀLOKA

As pointed out by me elsewhere in detail,* the *Dhvanyāloka* is an epoch-making work in Sanskrit poetics. Ānandavardhana builds a new structure of poetic theory on the foundation of the thought of his predecessors viz. Bharata, Bhāmaha, Udbhaṭa and Vāmana. For the first time in the history of Indian Thought he asks basic questions relating to aesthetics and semantics and answers them systematically like a philosopher. This would be achievement enough for a writer. But he goes far beyond a mere philosophical theory. He gives us for the first time, again, in Indian poetics examples of literary analysis and practical criticism. Unlike his predecessors, Ānandavardhana gives a large number of illuminating examples from the best writers in Sanskrit literature and discusses with insight the reasons for their appeal to a man of taste. None can lay the charge that literary theory is considered in a vacuum in this work. He not only helps the reader to understand and appreciate poetry better, but he also offers valuable guidance to the poet by laying down for the first time the basic principles of poetic creation. Ānandavardhana is, thus, both the Aristotle and the Longinus of India.

One is really wonderstruck by the modernity of some of the fundamental ideas of this 9th century Indian author. It was Bergson who argued that by animating words with a life of their own, the poet suggests to us things that speech is not calculated to express. This was Ānandavardhana's finding on which he builds a whole superstructure. Similarly, we are reminded while reading this work of I. A. Richards' distinction between emotive language and referential language, John Crowe Ransom's 'structure' and 'texture' of poetry, the classical rule of the unity of action, and of the neo-classical organic

* See : K. Krishnamoorthy—

(i) The Dhvanyāloka and Its Critics, Kāvyālaya, Mysore, 1968.

(ii) Essays in Sanskrit Criticism, Karnatak University, Dharwar 1964.

(iii) Some thoughts on Indian Aesthetics and Literary Criticism, University of Mysore, 1968.

form. The modern ideas of 'ambiguity', 'implication', calculated complexity', 'irony', 'language of paradox' have their counterports in the different variations of Dhvani. Ezra Pound defines poetry as 'simply language charged with meaning to the utmost possible degree'. Hulme wants the poet 'to bend language to express the poet's unconventional vision, to break the stiff general patterns of language in which words tend to be used like dead counters. T. S. Eliot and others talk of the 'objective correlative' of the poet's vision in adequate metaphorical language. To the readers of the Dhvanyāloka the germs of such ideas appear to be already anticipated by Ānandavardhana in his own way.*

Ānandavardhana's novelty of approach is most evident in the third chapter where he gives for the first time detailed rules on the following :—

1. The relation of *Saṅghaṭanā* or phonetic patterns of diction to the psychological theme of *rasas*.

2. The canon of propriety which decides the success or failure of a poet.

3. The question of *aṅgāṅgibhāva* of *rasas* in whole works.

4. Deterrents of *rasa*.

5. Opposition and harmony between *rasas*.

6. The status of other aesthetic concepts viz. *alaṅkāra*, *guṇa*, *rīti* and *Vṛtti* vis-a-vis *rasa*.

7. The beauty of figurative meaning vis-a-vis suggested *rasas*.

Some of these correspondences are discussed by me at length in the article 'Some Aspects of T. S. Eliot's Critical Theory in the light of Sanskrit Poetics', published in '*Indian Response to Poetry in English*', Macmillan, Madras, 1970, pp. 34--43.
For an interesting attempt to evaluate Western poetry from the stand-point of *Dhvani*, see, Krishan Rayan, *Suggestion and Statement in Poetry*, London, 1972.
One of the most perceptive modern studies of *Rasa-dhvani* is by D. H. H. Ingalls, *An Anthology of Sanskrit Court Poetry*, Introduction, Cambridge Mass, 1965.

It will be observed that none of these considerations were worked out by any of his predecessors mentioned by Ānandavardhana. But some germs of these ideas are found to be present in Rudraṭa's *Kāvyālaṅkāra*. Rudraṭa's examples of *Bhāvālaṅkāra* and *Sūkṣmālaṅkāra*[1] remind us positively of *Vastudhvani*, while his treatment of *Virasa* as a *doṣa*[2] is reminiscent of Ānandavardhana's account of *anaucitya*. Further, the concluding verses of Rudraṭa (XVI, 37-41) clearly indicate the rules of decorum pertaining to the treatment of human characters which are further elaborated by Ānandavardhana in his account of *aucitya* and *anaucitya*. So also there are similarities between the two writers in the treatment of *rītis* and *vṛttis* in relation to *rasas*. What is much more striking is Rudraṭa's dictum regarding the naming of compound figures. (*Saṅkara* or *Saṁsṛṣṭi*) by the joint name of the constituents. In the whole range of Sanskrit poetics it is only Rudraṭa who sanctions such a compound usage[3]. Ānandavardhana uses at least two such compound expressions, viz. श्लेषव्यतिरेक and उपमाश्लेष. All these facts taken together point to the strong possibility that Ānandavardhana was familiar with Rudraṭa's text as we have it to day, though he has not cited him by name. Incidentally, it must be recorded that Abhinavagupta has actually quoted Rudraṭa's *Bhāvālaṅkāra* as implied in Ānandavardhana's account of *Guṇībhūta-vyaṅgyālaṅkāras*[4]. This is a matter which invites further investigation.

Equally intriguing is the correspondence of these ideas which we find in the *Śṛṅgāratilaka* of Rudrabhaṭṭa :—

विरसं प्रत्यनीकं च दुःसन्धानरसं तथा ।
नीरसं पात्रदुष्टं च काव्यं सद्भिर्न शस्यते ॥

1. Cf. Rudraṭa—*Kāvyālaṅkāra*, VII, 38–40, 98-99.

2. Ibid, XI-12-14.

3. Ibid, X-24. तन्नामानः is explained as follows by Namisādhu :— येषामलङ्काराणां मिश्रभावस्त एव मिलितास्तेषां नामेत्यर्थः। यदि सहोक्तेः समुच्चयस्य च संकरः तदा सहोक्तिसमुच्चय इति नाम ।

4. See *Locana*, p. 232, K. S. R. I. Edition.

विहाय जननीमृत्युशोकं मुग्धे मया सह ।
यौवनं मानय स्पष्टमित्यादि विरसं मतम् ॥
प्रबन्धे नीयते यत्र रस एको निरन्तरम् ।
महतीं वृद्धिमिच्छन्ति नीरसं तच्च केचन ॥ ...
अन्येष्वपि रसेष्वेते दोषा वर्ज्या मनीषिभिः ।
यत्संपर्कान्न यात्येव काव्यं रसपरम्पराम् ॥

[काव्यमाला Ed. Bombay, 1899, III–46–48 and 53].

A little earlier he also gives a list of contrary *rasas* (Vv. 21-23) even like Ānandavardhana. One cannot positively say that either Rudraṭa or Rudrabhaṭṭa (if they were different authors) was posterior to Ānandavardhana.

These ideas are also echoed by a number of Prakrit poets who were positively prior to Ānandavardhana. Haribhadra (730-830 A. D.) in his *Samarāicchakahā* refers to the three-fold division of *Kathās* into *Divya*, *Mānuṣa* and *Divya Mānuṣa* (alluded to in the Dhvanyāloka) :—

दिव्वं दिव्वमाणुसं माणुसं च । तत्थ दिव्वं नाम जत्थ केवलमेव दवचरियं वण्णिज्जइ । [Jacobi's Ed. P. 2]

Similarly, Kautūhala (circa 750 A. D.) in his *Līlāvatī* states—

तं जह दिव्वमाणुसी, माणुसी तहच्चेअ ।

The various kinds of *kathā* noted by Ānandavardhana have also their parallels in Uddyotanasūri's (778 A. D.) *Kuvalayamālā* :—

तासो पुण पंचकहावो । तं जहा—
सअलकहा, खंडकहा, उल्लावकहा, परिहासकहा,... [अनुच्छेद 7]

The above considerations strongly suggest that Ānandavardhana, himself a famous Prakrit poet, was very well aware of the different types of Prakrit *kathā* literature. He has made use of several ideas which were in the air at his time but which had found no clear systematisation in the works of earlier theorists.

Reverting to the earlier question of *angi-rasa* vis-a-vis *aṅga-rasas*, it is interesting to notice that Ānandavardhana himself has referred to two rival opinions on the part of interpreters of Bharata (Vide. p. 178 of the text, infra, lines 17-19); Ānandavardhana himself following the first view that one *rasa* can serve as a *vyabhicāri* or accessory of another; the second view being that *sthāyibhāvas* themselves are styled by the term *rasas* throughout by Bharata. Abhinavagupta in his *Locana* rightly cites Bharata's text :—

बहूनां समवेतानां रूपं यस्य भवेद्बहु ।
स मन्तव्यो रसः स्थायी शेषाः सञ्चारिणो मताः ॥

(Nāṭyaśāstra, G. O. S. Edn., Vol. I. p. 375)

He also records the view of one Bhāguri who openly admitted *Sthāyitā* and *sañcāritā* of *rasas* while commenting on this. This throws interesting sidelight on the pre-Abhinavagupta commentatorial tradition on the Nāṭyaśāstra, followed by Ānandavardhana Rudraṭa, Rudrabhaṭṭa etc. which bars one's rushing to any conclusion on the question of mutual borrowing, when taken in itself.

DHVANI THEORY AFTER ĀNANDAVARDHANA

Another intriguing question is that of pre-Abhinavagupta commentators on the *Dhvanyāloka*. the *Locana* abounds in references to previous commentators, though only one is specified by name as *Candrikākāra*.* The other name mentioned is that of Vivaraṇakṛt, which is too vague to decide whether a commentator of *Dhvanyāloka* is meant or Udbhaṭa, the author of the *Bhāmahavivaraṇa*. These references justify the conclusion that the *Dhvanyāloka* came to be studied with great enthusiasm within a century of its composition and that its study had spread to remote provinces like Magadha and Karnataka.

Even independent writers who differed from Ānandavardhana found it impossible to ignore him. In fact, Bhaṭṭanāyaka, Kuntaka, Mahimabhaṭṭa, Dhanañjaya, Bhoja, Pratīhārendurāja and Rājaśekhara have all restated as it were the essentials of

* Cf. *Locana*, KSRI Ed. Pp. 54, 60, 131, 184, 193, 213 etc. and NSP Ed. (1935), Pp. 109, 120, 150, 152, 161, 194, 260, 265, 269, 290, etc.

the new theory itself by adopting different terminologies. This is an indirect compliment indeed to the soundness of the facts behind the Dhvani theory. Later text-book writers of repute like Mammaṭa, Viśvanātha, Vidyādhara, Vidyānātha and Jagannātha make no bones about accepting the *Dhvani* theory as the last word in Indian poetics. For all this success of the *Dhvani* theory Abhinavagupta shares the credit with Ānandavardhana. It was Abhinavagupta indeed who refuted eloquently all the rival stands and vindicated the cause of *Dhvani.*

ĀNANDAVARDHANA'S SEMANTICS

Anandavardhana is the first writer in Indian poetics to attempt an enquiry into semantics. As a preliminary to his exposition of the essence of poetry, he distinguishes between the two well known usages of language, viz., use of language outside poetry on the one hand and the unique usage exclusive to poetry on the other. The first referential usage is a gift of convention and is well within the reach of everyone who knows the language. The second is the indirect use of language wherein the meaning may be either metaphorical or implicit. Ānandavardhana notes that meaning at this second level too is not very far from the first or conventional level. The first level of meaning is characterised as *vācyārtha* and the second as *bhākta.* Poetry too starts from these two levels of meaning only. But it does not stop there as in common parlance or scientific discourse. It uses them as a jumping-off ground to convey an entirely new meaning which is different not only in degree but often in kind also. This third meaning which is unique and exclusive to poetry is alone characterised as the essence of poetry. And it has its parallels in fine arts like music.

Combining in himself the triple rare attainments of poetic genius, impeccable scholarship and immaculate literary taste, Ānandavardhana succeeded not only in laying his finger on *rasa* as the soul of poetry but also in offering a scientific explanation of it as *Dhvani.* The theory was so formulated that it could assimilate the essence of all the traditional aesthetic categories while emphasising the claims of rasa.*

*For a fuller exposition of this see : K. Krishnamoorthy, Dhvani as the meeting-point of all principles of Sanskrit Literary Theory—*Principles of Indian Literary Criticism*, Delhi, 1969, Pp. 201–209.

'RASA' IN THE 'DHVANI' THEORY

In the history of Indian aesthetic thought, the concept of *Rasa* is the oldest since Bharata himself gives in his *Nāṭyaśāstra* some citations from earlier works which already refer to *rasa*. His greatness lay in giving it a vital and central place in his scheme of tenfold plays and explaining it in terms of *vibhāva*, *anubhāva* and *vyabhicāri-bhāva* schematically. It appears that all the elements in a play, viz., plot, characterization, style, setting and acting are governed by the dictates of *rasa*. His famous *rasa sūtra* led to diverse explanations at the hands of later philosophers, the chief of whom are Lollaṭa, Śankuka, Bhaṭṭa-Nāyaka and Abhinavagupta. We also know for certain that poets like Kālidāsa, Bāṇa, Bhavabhūti and Māgha were quite conversant with the general outlines of the *rasa* theory. Nor need we have any doubt that early theorists like Bhāmaha, Daṇḍin, Vāmana, Udbhaṭa and Rudraṭa accepted by and large the value of *rasa* in poetry too. In their rough and ready analysis of poetry which was by definition beautiful, they had only two heads:–*śabda* (sound) and *artha* (sense); and all aspects of beauty had to be subsumed uuder the one or the other head. Thus, beautiful sound comprised of *śabdālaṅkāras* involving the principles of alliteration and rhyme. The beauty of sense or meaning could primarily lie in the poet's artistic turn of thought or imaginative creation called *vakrokti* and a number of figures of speech were defined and illustrated. In such a scheme there is no wonder that the beauty of emotional content due to *rasa*, *bhāva*, etc. also came to be recognised only as certain *alaṅkāras*. viz. Rasavad, Preyas, Ūrjasvin, Udatta and Samāhita or as certain *guṇas*. In general terms, the ancient theorists also affirmed the desirability of infusing Mahākāvyas with all the *rasas* to sustain interest.

It will be seen that this broad idea of beauty in literature, analysable into *alaṅkāra* or *guṇa* is in no way adequate to explain the unique essence of all literature. If we want a dependable yardstick to distinguish gradations in poetic success, the *alaṅkāra*-cum-*guṇa* scheme cannot take us far. Even the doctrines of *mārga* or *rīti* or *saṅghaṭanā* will be found insufficient to arrive at precise literary estimates of poets of varying degrees of achievement. The more we study *alaṅkāras*, the more puzzled we become when asked whether they are merely means of ornamentation or form the resulting beauty itself. This is the famous distinction between *alaṅkāra* and *alaṅkārya* which we owe to the searching philosophy of *Dhvani*, formulated for the first time in the *Dhvanyāloka* by Ānandavardhana. The differentia of poetry cannot be rendered precise until it can mark off the boundaries of poetic language from the other uses of language. We have common parlance as well as scientific use of language We may utilise some *alaṅkāras* and *guṇas* in our daily conversation as well as scientific writing. Would our activity be really poetic on such occasions? In fact, we all know that while every educated man can understand ordinary human talk as well as scientific discourse, not all educated men can appreciate poetry. Again, what about the varying temperaments and moods of poets ? What exactly do they want to achieve by their work? and can we know when they have succeeded or when they have failed? Such are some of the considerations which prompted Ānandavardhana to reinterpret the earlier concepts and to propound the theory of *Dhvani* as the best and most adequate explanation of aesthetic experience or *rasa* in literature. The new principle of *dhvani* or suggestion is so formulated that it not only solves all these issues effectively but also meets with the approval of accredited experts in linguistics, logic and semantics.

It is Ānandavardhana's contention that only the *Dhvani* theory can logically explain all the facts of the poetic process to the satisfaction of the creative poet on the one hand and the appreciative critic on the other. When we say logic, we should not forget that the logic of poetry is not the same as logic in other fields; it is a magic indeed which eludes the logic we are used to outside poetry. But to establish it with unassailable arguments to the satisfaction of confirmed sceptics is no easy task and the several threads of argument that lie scattered in the *Dhvanyāloka* and *Locana* all converging to the one centre of *rasa* are more often than not missed even by a wary student. I propose to indicate some of them here.

Rasa indeed is the corner-stone of the arch of *Dhvani*. It is first and foremost, an aesthetic canon. *Rasa* is that which initially inspires the poet into creativity and ultimately ensures the aesthetic delight of the critic. In life there is ample joy and pain, but no *rasa* or pleasurable relish of them. Impersonal, disinterested and universal delight is exclusive to poetry and termed *rasa*. Even spiritual bliss, termed sometimes *rasa* in the Upaniṣadic language (cf. *Raso vai sah*) differs from *kāvyarasa* in so far as it does not follow any prescribed course of *yoga* but is more or less a result of inborn taste. If poetry is thus *sui generis*, it is only because of *rasa*; and it is this paramount status of *rasa* which has to be emphasized in any adequate analysis of poetic beauty. We shall see how only the theory of *Dhvani* answers to this description.

The thesis of the *Dhvani* theorist can be simply stated :— *'Dhvani' is the quintessence of poetry; and 'rasa' is the quintessence of 'dhvani'*. What then is *Dhvani*? *Dhvani* is an exclusively poetic feature concerned with exploiting the beauty of every element in the medium of language like *alaṅkāra*, *guṇa* and *rīti* to serve the ultimate artistic end of *rasa*. In other words, *Dhvani* is the name of the whole poetic process itself which, for want of a better equivalent in English, is usually rendered as 'suggestion'. This marks it off from the conventional capacity of language to give accepted meanings, i. e. meanings shared by all the community in their social or intellectual intercourse. It marks it off from the secondary or figurative usage of language too whose province does not include *rasa*. In other words, *dhvani* is that meaning in poetry which is appreciated by the critic as most beautiful, knowingly or unknowingly. The beauty of *vācyārtha* or explicit meaning and *lakṣyārtha* or implicit meaning is only an outer aspect of poetic beauty. Words and common meanings in poetry are no doubt used by the poet with an eye to beauty. This is exactly what is described by the ancient concepts of *alaṅkāra*, *guṇa* and *rīti* or *vṛtti*. But the soul or core essence of poetry is not adequately explained by any or all of them. The concept of *alaṅkāra* or embellishment demands an *alaṅkārya* or a subject to be embellished. The concept of *guṇa* too requires a subject which it qualifies. The doctrines of *rīti* and *vṛtti* too become meaningful only in relation to the essence of poetry and not otherwise. The ancients in their theorisings were getting gradually wiser about the special and unique status of *rasa*, but none pitched upon the only complete explanation, viz. *Dhvani*. Thus, to speak of *rasa* as an *alaṅkāra* of a special class called *rasavadādi* shows only a very vague awareness of the problem; regarding *rasa* as a *guṇa* is an improvement upon it. To associate it with *rīti* and *vṛtti* is certainly a further improvement, since both these are more abstract than *alaṅkāra* and *guṇa*. But the logical culmination of aesthetic theory is an open recognition of the inmost essence of poetry as exclusively *rasa*; and this is done only by the concept of *dhvani*.

If the task of the *dhvani*-theorist is rendered easy in a way by the concepts already in the field, it is also hampered in another way because the beauty already analysed has to be accommodated properly in the new explanation in a scientific manner. In the analytical method of the ancients, poetry is seen in its elements of *śabda* or sound and *artha* or sense. So *alaṅkāras* or *guṇas* are features, outer or inner, of only *śabda* or *artha* or both. All that their synthetic grasp could formulate was *rīti* or *racanā* or style and *vṛtti* or mode of acting in drama and mode of alliteration in poetry. The new theorist had to arrive at a new perspective to urge the claim of *rasa* to greater recognition in its own right, without underestimating the value of the earlier findings in the field. That the *Dhvani* theory meets the challenge boldly is indeed its best claim on our attention.

Unless this new perspective of *dhvani* is realised, we miss the very message of the *Dhvanyāloka*. What is wanted is a finer analysis in our general notion of beauty itself. That beauty or *cārutā* exists at many levels is the first theorem of Ānandavardhana. Grant this and the rest will follow as corollaries. The beauty of *vācakaśabda* and *vācyārtha* is no doubt explained by the concepts of *alaṅkāra* and *guṇa*; but this beauty is quite distinct from the beauty of *vyaṅgyārtha* whose most celebrated representative is *rasa*. We should not commit the mistake of thinking that the two are exclusive in the best passages of poetry. On the other hand, they mostly co-exist. But what is incumbent on the critic is the exercise of his aesthetic judgment in arriving at a clear decision about the relative prominence of the two kinds of beauty in any given passage. If the critic feels that the beauty of the expressed element (*vācya*) outshines the beauty of the suggested (*vyaṅgya*), it helps him to rate that passage as second-rate poetry. If on the other hand, he is convinced that the suggested beauty surpasses the beauty of the expressed, he will rate it as *dhvani-kāvya* or first-rate poetry. If the suggested element is almost negligible in appeal, it will be third-rate poetry (*citra-kāvya*).

It is only from such a perspective involving the criterion of *vyaṅgya-prādhānya* that the nature and scope of *rasa* can be realised fully in the *dhvani*-theory. Only when all the elements of *vācya-vācaka* charm stop attracting attention to themselves and participate generously in contributing to the supremacy of the *vyaṅga* effect, viz. *rasa*, we get real *dhvani* :—

" वाच्यवाचकचारुत्वहेतूनां विविधात्मनाम् ।
रसादिपरता यत्र स ध्वनेर्विषयो मतः ॥ " (II 4.)

Though theoretically sound, this canon involves some practical difficulties. When there is a clear recognition of diverse elements of beauty like *alaṅkāra* and *rasa*, it may go difficult to decide their relative superiority. So Ānandavardana gives us an unfailing guideline to show the way out :—

" प्रधानेऽन्यत्र वाक्यार्थे यत्राङ्गं तु रसादयः ।
काव्ये तस्मिन्नलङ्कारो रसादिरिति मे मतिः ॥ " (II. 5)

One need not despair that all *rasa*, *bhāva*, etc. are as a rule suggested and the suggested must be superior to the expressed beauty. Ānandavardhana says that *rasādis* also may be suggested and yet remain *aṅga* or subsidiary to the *aṅgin* or principal beauty of *vācya*. This is the famous *aṅga-aṅgi-bhāva* extended to the relation between *rasa* and *alaṅkāra* for the first time by Ānandavardhana. Before his time, theorists were aware of this relationship between two *alaṅkāras* only (as in *Saṅkara*) or between two *rasas* only. But in Ānandavardhana's system it can hold good between an *alaṅkāra* and *rasa* too.

The implications of this indeed are far-reaching. If *rasa* is principal, it is called *dhvani*; if *rasa* is subsidiary, it loses its claim to the title of *dhvani* and acquires the lower status of *rasavadalaṅkāra*. It means that *rasa* has a dual role in poetry. It may be both *dhvani* and *alaṅkāra* depending on the intention of the poet. From this follows the dictum that the status of an *alaṅkāra* is always lower than that of *dhvani*. This is the most intriguing and confusing part of the *Dhvani* argument. Again and again, we are told that what is suggested in poetry is more intrinsic and aesthetic than what is merely denoted, that *vyaṅgya-cārutva* is *ipso facto* superior to *vacyā-cārutva*. We are also told that *rasādis* are never *vācya* but exclusively *vyaṅgya*. How then can the beauty of *vyaṅgya rasa* be ever subordinated to any other ? Is it not a contradiction in terms to speak of *rasādis* as *alaṅkāra* which is only a *vācya-saundarya-prakāra* ?

Such an apparent contradiction is dictated by the exigencies of facts in poetry and cannot be rated merely by considerations of logic. If the intrinsic status of *rasa* is one thing, its functional status in poetry may be another. A mere presence or touch of suggestion (*vyaṅgya-saṁsparśa*) does not constitute *Dhvani* what constitutes *Dhvani* is that *vyaṅgya* which is also exclusively important in relation to other elements of beauty in the poem. It must be realised at the outset that various elements of beauty will be coexisting in any instance of good poetry. Some of them will be *vācya* and some of them may by *vyaṅgya*. The relative prominence of the *vācya* over the *vyaṅgya* or *vice versa* will alone be the decisive factor in deciding whether something is *alaṅkāra* or *dhvani*. Thus, we have a new philosophy of *alaṅkāra* also in the *dhvani* system which is different from that of the old school. Any element of beauty which subserves the beauty of another comes to be styled *alaṅkāra*. According to this new definition, *rasa* can be deemed *alaṅkāra* in examples like '*kṣipto hastāvalagnaḥ*...'. The mistake of the ancient theorists lay in the fact that they deemed even principally suggested *rasādis* as *alaṅkāras*, though logically they could only remain *alaṅkārya*, totally distinct from *alaṅkāras*.

Apart from *rasādis*, coming to the *vācya-alaṅkāras* themselves, it may be asked what their *alaṅkārya* is. This is a question raised by Ānandavardhana himself. His answer is that it is mostly *vastu* or idea intended by the poet. Every poem has a theme or a subject or an idea which is its *vastu*. This may be conveyed directly or figuratively, or suggestively. Thus, we can speak of *vācya*–, *lakṣya*– and *vyaṅgya*– *vastus*. It is not impossible that two or more of these coexist in a poem. What involves the exercise of the critic's judgment is the task of deciding which of them provides the final resting place (*saṁvid-viśrānti*) in his understanding of the poem. Now it may be the one, now the other. This freedom and impreciseness is of the very essence of poetry. It cannot be ordered to any logical rule. All that the *Dhvani* theory states is that the *vācya vastu* or *alaṅkāra*, howsoever beautiful in itself, must be reckoned as inferior to the *vyaṅgya-vastu* or *alaṅkāra* or *rasa* in respect of appeal to men of taste.

It will be seen how the *vyaṅgya* element is regarded as threefold as against the *vācya* element which is only two-fold. That is so because of the unique nature of *rasa* which can never be *vācya*. By reciting the names of *rasas* like Sṛṅgāra, Hāsya, Karuṇa, we do not feel love, mirth or sorrow. They can only be suggested by a proper manipulation of the antecedents, consequents and incidental moods of characters in a situation suited to the sentiments concerned. So, then, though *rasa* is never *vācya*, *vastu* and *alaṅkāra*, however, can be both *vācya* and *vyaṅgya*.

What we have in poetry is the varying juxtaposition of *vācya* and *vyaṅgya* elements. Let us look at the logical possibilities:— The two *vācya* elements and the three *vyaṅgya* ones make five in all. In all poetry, the first *vācya-vastu* must be invariably present. It may be associated with either a *vācya alaṅkāra* or a *vyaṅgya vastu* or a *vyaṅgya alaṅkāra* or a *vyaṅgya rasādi*. Now *vācya vastu*+*vācya alaṅkāra* is only *alaṅkāra* in the new system, because the two belong to the same functional order. But when the two orders are interposed, the resultant beauty demands the exercise of the critic's judgment. Thus, in *vācya alaṅkāra*+*vyaṅgya vastu* it will be regarded as *alaṅkāra* only if the beauty of the *vyaṅgya vastu* is subsidiary to the beauty of the *vācya*. This is known as the principle of *guṇībhūta-vyaṅgya* which adequately explains all the *alaṅkāras* without denying the suggested element in them. On this principle indeed *vyaṅgya rasa* too is regarded as *rasavadalaṅkāra*. But if the *vyaṅgya vastu* or *alaṅkāra* or *rasa* is not subsidiary to the *vācya*, but surpassing it in beauty, then these come to be raised to the highest state of *dhvani.* This is the functional philosophy underlying the three divisions of *vyaṅgyārtha* into *vastu-dhvani, alaṅkāra-dhavani* and *rasa-dhvani.* Unless something is exclusively and relatively all-important, it won't be classed as *dhvani.* However, of the three, the province of *Rasa-dhvani* is not only the largest but also the sweetest. Its nature is such that it cannot but colour every minute ingredient or aspect of poetry on the one hand and every class of *dhvani* on the other. In poetry, language is used uniquely because the poet endeavours to convey emotions, moods and feelings in addition to mere facts and actions. Even such hard and dry things like stones and bones become associated with some mental feeling like anguish; and therefore even in seemingly *rasa*-less passages of poetry, a perceptive and sensitive reader will experience some shade or the other of *rasādi.* So the logically distinct categories of *vastu-dhvani* and *alaṅkāra-dhvani* cannot be deemed to be totally exclusive of *rasa* any time. Once we theoretically admit that *dhvani* is the essence of best poetry to do full justice to the claims of *rasa*, we cannot rule out logically the application of that definition to *vastu-dhvani* and *alaṅkāra-dhvani* also. These latter too are definitely more aesthetic than their *vācya* counterparts and they also, in some measure at least, partake of the healing touch of *rasa* which is not however prominent enough to be classed as *rasa-dhvani.*

Such a wide theory embracing all varieties of *vastu-*, *alaṅkāra-*, and *rasa- dhvani* in the category of best poetry is also practically more serviceable than a theory restricted to *rasa.* In Prakrit folk- poetry abounding in examples of subtle wit and clear hints to love assignations, the canon of *rasa* cannot apply *in toto*, though their appeal to the intelligent reader is unquestioned. These are best explained as *vastu-dhvani* suggested by the unique nature of the characters and the situation in question. Similarly, great poets have shown their preference in leaving certain figurative ideas and images suggested instead of openly expressing them as in prose. Actually, the term *alaṅkāra-dhvani* is a misnomer. What is suggested now is only a *vastu* and it should be strictly called *vastu-dhvani* only. But to distinguish this *vastu* which is due to *kavisamaya* or *prauḍhokti* from other *vastus* we refer to its general status elsewhere as *alaṅkāra* and call it *alaṅkāra-dhvani* after the analogy of *Brāhmaṇa-Śramaṇa-nyāya* which is similar to our reference to some as Brahmin-Christians today.

Theoretically too, exclusion of *vastu-dhvani* and *alaṅkāra-dhvani*, would land us in a hopelessly miserable state in establishing the aesthetic value of *vyaṅgya* as superior to *vācya* when we are confronted in argument by learned logicians and grammarians and the like who can be presumed to understand only *vyaṅgya-vastu* as distinct from *vācya-vastu* and not also *vyṅgya-rasa*, because *vyaṅgya-rasa* is by definition something that can be felt only by the few gifted ones called *sahṛdayas* or *rasikas* and outside the reach of merely learned specialists. Hence, *vastu-dhvani* examples only are cited to convince such hard-headed sceptics and *rasa-dhvani* illustrations are avoided.

All this carries the implicit assumption that there is such a unique function of language as suggestion over and above the two well known functions called denotation and indication. The Mīmāṁsakas and other philosophers who are supposed to be experts in this matter have nowhere spoken of this function. Even in Bhartṛhari's philosophy of Sanskrit grammar, there is a sort of predilection to assume an almost mystical 'revealing power' to explain the evolution of all meaning from sound forms in terms of *sphoṭa* or *śabda-brahman*. If what is exclusive to poetry is a unique speciality, a speciality not figured out by all philosophers of language, there is no wonder at all; and that speciality can be none other than *rasa* or aesthetic experience of the reader as ably pointed out by Abhinavagupta while dismissing the *bhāktavāda*. The theory of secondary meaning is differently held by different schools and can be conveniently widened to include all meanings other than the conventional one; yet it cannot explain or cover the fact of *rasa-dhvani*, showing its inadequacy to explain literature. Even the best advocate of *lakṣaṇā* can only plead for some varieties of *vastu-dhvani* (viz. *avivakṣita-vācya*) as covered by forms of *lakṣaṇā*; but the vast bulk of literary charm lies outside that limited sphere.

While classifying *dhvani* varieties, Ānandavardhana gives such significant titles as remind us of the relative status of *vācya* all the time. Under this logical scheme *Rasādi-dhvani* comes to be styled *asaṁlakṣyakrama-vyaṅgya*. That is to say, the *vyaṅgya rasa* is felt almost simultaneously with the comprehension of the *vācyārtha.* The logical time-sequence between two becomes so thin as to escape notice. This is compared to the quick piercing of a hundred lotus leaves placed one above the other with a needle in the shortest span of one second. Abhinavagupta is our authority on aesthetic psychology and on the state of the reader during *rasāsvāda.* But Ānandavardhana spares us from any account of these. By the term *rasa* he refers not only to the reader's aesthetic response and to the poet's creative afflatus which are both subjective, but to the permanent states or *sthāyi-bhāvas* objectively embodied in the poem through characters and plot. The characters are the seat of such *rasas* and there can be opposition between two *rasas* like love and detachment when they are only *rasavad-alaṅkāra.* The fleeting mental states or *vyabhicāribhāvas* of Bharata are simply referred to as *bhāvas,* without any epithet. The other constituents of *rasādi* group are the *ābhāsas, uddīpana, praśama, sandhi, sabalatā,* etc. of the *rasas* and *bhāvas* with varying degrees of intermixture and pitch. We have no space to dwell on their details here.

Ānandavardhana criticises the summary treatment of *Rasavad Alaṅkāra* by the ancients. He hoists them on their own petard. It is their credo that the province of each *alaṅkāra* must be different without any room for overlapping and hence their definitions are carefully constructed from this point of view, guarding against the fallacies of Too Broad and Too Narrow. But when *rasa* is primarily felt in a passage replete with human emotional behaviour and it is characterised as *rasavad-alaṅkāra,* either they should mean that other figures like the simile have no scope there or if their coexistence is admitted, they will have to give up the postulate that figures like the simile have an exclusive field of their own. For, in literature, sentient emotional behaviour of some sort or the other will be attributed even to inanimate objects in nature and figures like the simile will have no scope at all left to them uncovered by *Rasavadalaṅkāra.* If, on the other hand, they deny such attributed sentiment the name of *Rasavadalaṅkāra,* they will be branding some of the best examples of *rasa* as *rasa*-less, exposing themselves to the charge that they are lacking in taste. They are thus cornered by the two horns of the dilemma. The only way out is to distinguish primarily beautiful *rasādi* which is *dhvani* from *rasādi* subserving another element in the poem and which is *rasavadalaṅkāra.* Thus, in the new scheme, even other *alaṅkāras* like *Preyas* of the early theorists will come to be designated as *rasavadalaṅkāra* only.

Such a realisation of the vital role of *rasādis* entitling them to the rank of *dhvani* will help immensely in the revaluation of other concepts also. It will at once stand out how *guṇas* stand apart from *alaṅkāras.* The *guṇas* though felt as inhering in *śabdārthas* really belong to *rasas* only in their variety. Some *rasas* like Śṛṅgāra and Karuṇa melt the hearts of readers and are styled *madhura* or soft and sweet. Some others like Vīra, Raudra and Bībhatsa rouse our hearts and are styled as characterised by '*ojas*' or brilliance. Besides these two, only one more *guṇa* is enough to explain the common effectiveness of all *rasas* and all *racanās* and that is *prasāda* or lucidity.

Ānandavardhana dwells on the *vyañjakatva* or suggestive charm of each minute element in poetry like syllable, base, affix, termination, word, gender, number, collocation of compounds or otherwise, sentence, paragraph, canto and whole work—only in relation to *rasa-dhvani.* From the minute attention of early theorists to parts of *vācya-vācaka,* he turns our attention to the much more profitable task of analysis of *vyaṅgya-vyañjaka,* from parts to the whole. He affirms that beauty so detected alone is the most significant aspect of beauty in poetry. If the *vācya* aspect is also taken into account, the only significant charm detected will be of *prasādaguṇa* or lucidity in addition. If we leave out *vācya* also from consideration, the only charm holding our attention would be alliteration and so forth : —

रसादिसमर्पणसामर्थ्यमेव नैसर्गिकं शब्दानां विशेष इति व्यञ्जकत्वाश्रय्येव तेषां मुख्यं चारुत्वम् । वाचकत्वाश्रयस्तु प्रसाद एवार्थापेक्षायां तेषां विशेषः । अर्थानपेक्षायां त्वनुप्रासादिरेव । (Vṛtti on III. 16; p. 158).

All this clarification by Ānandavardhana is meant to render more cogent Udbhaṭa's idea that particular words alone are suited for particular *rasas.* We are indebted to Abhinavagupta for citing *Bhāmahavivaraṇa* by name in this context (p. 358). To what extent Udbhaṭa had gone beyond the early theorisings in his *Bhāmahavivaraṇa* is unknown; but it is clear that Ānandavardhana was not fabricating anything preposterous or very new and which was not already hinted at in glimmering flashes by earlier thinkers.

Only the implications of this general theory on poetic creation and critical appreciation remain to be glanced at in conclusion. The testimony cited in the *Dhvanyāloka* of the most celebrated Ādikavi Vālmīki himself as unburdening his *śloka* or sentiment of pathos through the outlet of a spontaneous outburst, viz., *śloka* is more than clinching. It proves that the creative process is spurred into activity at all because of *rasāveśa.* The spell of *rasa* or overmastering passion is an aesthetic experience to the core and is to be carefully distinguished from raw personal emotion familiar to all in life. Vālmīki did not have the worldly and personal emotion of sorrow when he saw the surviving bird crying piteously and wallowing in the blood of its mate just killed by the hunter. In that case he would have just wept and acted like any one of us and not composed a rhythmic verse. This intense constructiveness of vision goes beyond objects of physical sight. In Blake's much quoted words, " it can see the world in a grain of sand and Heaven in a wild flower. But howsoever sombre the theme, it brings to the artist no grief in the usual sense of the word. For grief disables, but this kind of vision empowers. It has been said that God is a person who feels all the pain there is in the world without being disabled by it at all. And thus much of divineness there is in a great artist. "[1] We thus come to the conclusion that *Rasa* in poetry is *alaukika* or something quite unique, impersonal and super-normal, something all sweet and beautiful, an end in itself, aesthetically satisfying. Poets can wring out this *rasa* or joy even out of pain itself in the world. The poet's *pratibhā*' in other words, is directly conditioned by *rasāveśa* whose nature is creativity at once vivid and beautiful or रसावेशवैशद्यसौन्दर्यनिर्माणक्षमत्वम् in the words of Abhinavagupta. When the vision is clear and deep, the poet will effortlessly achieve the task of marshalling all his material towards the one goal of *rasa* and devises his plot, characters and style in due regard to the principle of unity of *rasa* in the midst of a variety of shifting *rasas* and *bhāvas.* Vālmīki's concentrated attention to the principal sentiment of

1. C. E. Montague, *A Writer's Notes on his Trade*, Penguin Books, London, 1930, p. 189.

Karuṇa or pathos and Vyāsa's all out emphasis on Śānta or tranquillity are instances in point. The main thread of *aṅgi-rasa* is never allowed to be lost in the midst of a thousand and one *aṅgas*. But they are epic sages. Even among later poets, Kālidāsa provides the best example of a *rasakavi* in his poems as well as in his plays. He never repeats himself or echoes his predecessors. What makes him truly himself is his devotion to the claims of *rasa* at evey step. Though a genius, he desists from the temptation of too many *alaṅkāras* and will keep various *aṅga-rasas* and *bhāvas* within the limits of propriety so that the *aṅgi-rasa* shines out in full splendour. The detection of this propriety or *aucitya* in the treatment of *rasa* by the poet is alone the primary business of the critic and not the labelling in terms of *alaṅkāras*. Even lapses will be ignored and his *rasa* admired by critics if the poet's genius is strong.

Thus, the philosophy of *dhvani* which gives the most adequate and searching explanation of *rasa* will be found to bear many a parallel in the thought of modern writers like I. A. Richards, Christopher Caudwell and Susan Langer. It touches the inmost depth of poetry on the one hand and illumines the most serviceable procedure for practical literary criticism on the other. The best supporters of Ānandavardhana are his worst critics because they all tacitly admit that *Rasa* is the soul of poetry though they demur to the new name *Dhvani*. Let me close with a nice tribute to him paid by Rājaśekhara :—

ध्वनिनातिगभीरेण काव्यतत्त्वनिवेशिना ।
आनन्दवर्धनः कस्य नासीदानन्दवर्धनः ॥

ध्वन्यालोकः

ध्वन्यालोकः

प्रथमोद्द्योतः

स्वेच्छाकेसरिणः स्वच्छस्वच्छायायासितेन्दवः[1] ।
त्रायन्तां वो मधुरिपोः प्रपन्नार्तिच्छिदो नखाः[2] ॥

काव्यस्यात्मा ध्वनिरिति बुधैर्यः समाम्नातपूर्व-
स्तस्याभावं जगदुरपरे भाक्तमाहुस्तमन्ये ।
केचिद्वाचां स्थितमविषये[3] तत्त्वमूचुस्तदीयं
तेन[4] ब्रूमः सहृदयमनःप्रीतये तत्स्वरूपम् ॥ १ ॥

बुधैः काव्यतत्त्वविद्भिः काव्यस्यात्मा ध्वनिरिति संज्ञितः, परम्परया यः समाम्नातपूर्वः[5] सम्यक् आ समन्तात् म्नातः प्रकटितः, तस्य सहृदयजनमनः-प्रकाशमानस्याप्यभावमन्ये जगदुः । तदभाववादिनां चामी विकल्पाः सम्भवन्ति । तत्र[6] केचिदाचक्षीरन् — ‘ शब्दार्थशरीरं तावत्काव्यम् । तस्य[7] च शब्दगता-श्चारुत्वहेतवोऽनुप्रासादयः प्रसिद्धा एव । अर्थगताश्चोपमादयः । वर्ण[8]सङ्घटना-धर्माश्च ये माधुर्यादयस्तेऽपि प्रतीयन्ते । तदनतिरिक्तवृत्तयो वृत्तयोऽपि याः कैश्चि[9]दुपनागरिकाद्याः प्रकाशिताः, ता अपि गताः श्रवणगोचरम् । रीतयश्च वैदर्भीप्रभृतयः । तद्व्यतिरिक्तः कोऽयं ध्वनिर्नामेति ’ ।

अन्ये ब्रूयुः । ‘ नास्त्येव ध्वनिः । प्रसिद्धप्रस्थानव्यतिरेकिणः काव्य-प्रकारस्य काव्यत्वहानेः । सहृदयहृदयाह्लादिशब्दार्थमयत्वमेव काव्यलक्षणम् । न चोक्तप्रस्थानातिरेकिणो[10] मार्गस्य तत्सम्भवति । न च तत्समयान्तःपातिनः

---

१. ‘ विजितेन्दवः ’ ग. २. ‘ वः प्रपन्नार्तिच्छिदो मधुरिपोर्नखाः ’ ग. ३. ‘ मविषयं ’ ग. ४. ‘ येन ’ ग. ५. समाम्नातः समाख्यातः तस्य – घ. ६. ‘ तत्र ’ क-ख-पुस्तकयोर्नास्ति. ७. तत्र-BP. ८. वर्ण omitted in MB. ९. ‘ काचि ’ ग. १०. ‘ तिक्रमिणो ’ ग.

THE LIGHT OF SUGGESTION

THE FIRST FLASH

May Lord Hari's claws preserve you
In his Lion's form self-adopted;
They outshine the moon in clear hue
And destroy the woes of the devoted.

Though the learned men of yore have declared time and again that the soul of poetry is suggestion, some would aver its non–existence, some would regard it as something (logically) implied and some others would speak of its essence as lying beyond the scope of words. We propose, therefore, to explain its nature and bring delight to the hearts of perceptive critics.1

The word learned men has the sense of those who know the truth about poetry. Through an unbroken tradition, these have taught that the soul of poetry has been named Suggestion. Although it is felt so by cultured critics in their minds (even to-day), others affirmed its non-existence. The following are the different views of those who believe in its non-existence :

According to some (of the objectors) : " Poetry is but that whose body is constituted by sound (or word) and meaning. Sources of charm through sound such as ' alliteration ' are well-known; and so are the sources of charm through meaning such as ' simile '. Merits or qualities of composition like ' sweetness ' are also familiar to us. Also we have heard of dictions such as the ' cultured ' propounded by some, though in truth their features are no different from qualities of style. We have further heard of styles like *Vaidarbhī*. But what could this concept of DHVANI (suggestion) be which is different from any of these ? "

Others assert thus : " ' Suggestion ' does not exist indeed; for a species of poetry opposed to all well-known canons will necessarily cease to be poetry. Poetry can only be defined as that which is made up of such words and meanings as will delight the mind of the critic. This will not be achieved by a route which excludes all the well-known canons mentioned. Even if the

सहृदयान् कांश्चित्परिकल्प्य तत्प्रसिद्ध्या[1] ध्वनौ काव्यत्वव्यपदेशः[2] प्रवर्तितोऽपि सकलविद्वन्मनोग्राहितामवलम्बते[3] ।'

पुनरपरे तस्याभावमन्यथा कथयेयुः । 'न सम्भवत्येव ध्वनिर्नामापूर्वः कश्चित्[4] । कामनीयकमनतिवर्तमानस्य तस्योक्तेष्वेव चारुत्व[5]हेतुष्वन्तर्भावात् । तेषामन्यतमस्यैव वा अपूर्वसमाख्यामात्रकरणे यत्किञ्चन कथनं[6] स्यात् ।

किञ्च वाग्विकल्पानामानन्त्यात्सम्भवत्यपि वा कस्मिंश्चित्काव्यलक्षण-विधायिभिः प्रसिद्धैरप्रदर्शिते[7] प्रकारलेशे ध्वनिर्ध्वनिरिति यदेतदलीकसहृदयत्व-भावनामुकुलितलोचनैर्नृत्यते तत्र हेतुं न विद्मः । सहस्रशो हि[8] महात्मभि-रन्यैरलङ्कारप्रकाराः[9] प्रकाशिताः प्रकाश्यन्ते च । न च तेषामेषा दशा श्रूयते । तस्मात्प्रवादमात्रं ध्वनिः । न त्वस्य क्षोदक्षमं तत्त्वं[10] किञ्चिदपि[11] प्रकाशयितुं शक्यम् । तथा चान्येन कृत एवात्र श्लोकः ।

यस्मिन्नास्ति न वस्तु किञ्चन मनःप्रह्लादि सालङ्कृति[12]
व्युत्पन्नै रचितं च नैव[13] वचनैर्वक्रोक्तिशून्यं च यत् ।
काव्यं तद्ध्वनिना समन्वितमिति प्रीत्या प्रशंसञ्जडो
नो विद्मो[14]ऽभिदधाति किं सुमतिना पृष्टः स्वरूपं ध्वनेः ॥'

भाक्तमाहुस्तमन्ये । अन्ये तं ध्वनिसंज्ञितं काव्यात्मानं गुणवृत्ति-रित्याहुः[15] । यद्यपि च ध्वनिशब्दसंकीर्तनेन काव्यलक्षणविधायिभिर्गुणवृत्तिरन्यो वा न कश्चित्प्रकारः प्रकाशितः, तथापि अमुख्यया[16]वृत्त्या काव्येषु व्यवहारं दर्शयता ध्वनिमार्गो मनाक्स्पृष्टोऽपि न लक्षित इति[17] परिकल्प्यैवमुक्तम्— 'भाक्तमाहुस्तमन्ये' इति ।

---

१. 'परिकल्पिततत्प्र'-घ २. ० व्यवहारः – MB ३. 'मेव लम्बते'-ग. ४. कश्चित्प्रकारः – MB. ५. काव्यशोभाहेतु ०– MB. ६. 'कथं न'-ख; 'कथितं'-ग. ७. प्रसिद्धैरदर्शिते-घ. ८. 'ऽपि'-क-ख. ९. ० रन्यैरलंकारकारैरलं – MB. १०. 'क्षोद-क्षमत्वं'-ग. ११. 'दस्ति'-क-ख. १२. 'नालंकृति'-ख, 'सोऽलंकृति'-ग. १३. यत्न-MB १४. 'भिदधातु'-ग.; विदधाति-MB. १५. ० वृत्तिमाहुः –MB १६. गुणवृत्त्या-घ. १७. 'मनाक्स्पृष्टो लक्ष्यत इति'-घ. मनाक्स्पृष्टो संलभ्यते-MB.

designation of poetry were to be accepted as applying to DHVANI on the unanimous support of a coterie of self-styled critics, it would fail to win the acceptance of all the learned."

Yet another opinion about its non-existence is : "It is indeed impossible that 'suggestion' can be something unknown before. Since it is not distinct from a source of charm, it gets naturally included in the causes of charm already enunciated. By coining a novel designation to just one of them nothing profound will have been stated. Moreover, since the ways of speech are endless, even if there should be an insignificant element left unexplained by the famous framers of the rules of poetry, we cannot understand the reason why persons should close their eyes under the self-assumed illusion of being 'perceptive critics' and dance about with joy saying that they have discovered DHVANI therein. Thousands of other great men have expounded, and are still expounding, figurative elements (of speech). But we do not hear of any such over-excitement on their part. Therefore, DHVANI is but a fabrication; and it would be impossible to demonstrate any truth about it which can bear scrutiny. In fact, a gentleman has already composed a verse to this effect :

> *Poetry, wherein there is nothing to delight the mind and no embellishment, which is destitute of felicitous words and artful turns, is praised so warmly by the dunce as being endowed with* DHVANI (*Suggestion*). *But we are at a loss to imagine what answer he would give when faced with a straight question by an intelligent critic about the nature of* DHVANI *itself* !"

Some others mention it as something (logically) implied. (To put it differently,) others declare that the soul of poetry, designated by the term Suggestion, is the same as a secondary usage of words. Although it is true that no literary theorist has ever shown any element like a secondary usage of words as being specifically identical with Suggestion by mentioning the word 'Suggestion' itself, we have noted here such a view because we can conclude that one who points out the secondary usage of words in poetry has slightly touched the fringe of the doctrine of Suggestion, though one does not define it.

केचित्पुनः लक्षणकरण[1]शालीनबुद्धयो ध्वनेस्तत्त्वं गिरामगोचरं सहृदयहृदयसंवेद्यमेव समाख्यातवन्तः ।

तेनैवंविधासु[2] विमतिषु स्थितासु सहृदयमनःप्रीतये तत्स्वरूपं ब्रूमः ।

तस्य हि ध्वनेः स्वरूपं सकलसत्कविकाव्योपनिषद्भूतमतिरमणीयमणीयसीभिरपि[3] चिरन्तनकाव्यलक्षणविधायिनां बुद्धिभिरनुन्मीलितपूर्वम्, अथ च रामायणमहाभारतप्रभृतिनि[4] लक्ष्ये सर्वत्र प्रसिद्धव्यवहारं लक्षयतां सहृदयानामानन्दो मनसि लभतां प्रतिष्ठामिति प्रकाश्यते ।

तत्र ध्वनेरेव[5] लक्षयितुमारब्धस्य भूमिकां रचयितुमिदमुच्यते—

योऽर्थः[6] सहृदयश्लाघ्यः काव्यात्मेति[7] व्यवस्थितः ।
वाच्यप्रतीयमानाख्यौ तस्य भेदावुभौ स्मृतौ ॥ २ ॥

काव्यस्य हि ललितोचितसन्निवेशचारुणः शरीरस्येवात्मा साररूपतया स्थितः[8] सहृदयश्लाघ्यो यो[9]ऽर्थस्तस्य वाच्यः प्रतीयमानश्चेति द्वौ भेदौ ।

तत्र वाच्यः प्रसिद्धो यः प्रकारैरुपमादिभिः ।
बहुधा व्याकृतः सोऽन्यैः

काव्यलक्ष्मविधायिभिः[10]

ततो[11] नेह प्रतन्यते ॥ ३ ॥

केवलमनूद्यते यथोपयोगमिति ।

प्रतीयमानं पुनरन्यदेव वस्त्वस्ति वाणीषु महाकवीनाम् ।
यत्तत्प्रसिद्धावयवातिरिक्तं विभाति[12] लावण्यमिवाङ्गनासु ॥४॥

---

१. करण omitted in MB. २. ० विधासु तिसृषु – MB. ३. ० रमणीयं मनीषिभिरपि – MB.; अपि ० omitted in घ. ४. ० प्रभृति–MB. ५. पुनर्ध्वनेरेव – घ. ६. अर्थः ० घ. KLV. ७. ० त्मा यो – घ, KLV. ८. 'स्मृतः' क-ख. ९. 'अ' क-ख. १०. 'धायिभिः भट्टोद्भटप्रभृतिभिः – MB. ११. 'भट्टोद्भटप्रभृतिभिस्ततो' – ग. १२. 'आभाति' – ग, MB, KLV.

Still others, not astute enough to frame a definition, rest content with saying that the true nature of suggestion is beyond all words and that it is discernible only to the minds of perceptive critics.

In view of the prevalence of so many conflicting opinions, we propose to elucidate the nature of Suggestion for the delight of the perceptive critics.

Suggestion itself is both the quintessence of the works of all first-rate poets and the most beautiful principle of poetry though it remained unnoticed even by the subtlest of the rhetoricians of the past. However, refined critics are certainly alive to its primary presence in literary works like the Rāmāyaṇa and the Mahābhārata; and with a view to placing their delight on a secure footing, we shall explain its nature (in detail).

The following is meant to serve as a groundwork for the theory of Suggestion which has been taken up for a detailed study :—

That meaning which wins the admiration of refined critics is decided to be the soul of poetry. The 'explicit' and the 'implicit' are regarded as its two aspects. 2

That meaning which wins the admiration of perceptive critics and which is of the very essence of poetry—even as the soul is of a body which is naturally handsome by the union of graceful and proper limbs—has two aspects, viz., the explicit and the implicit.

Of these, the explicit is commonly known and it has been already set forth in many ways through figures of speech such as the simile by other writers; hence it need not be discussed here at length. 3

The expression, '*other writers*', alludes to writers on poetics (like Bhaṭṭa Udbhaṭa.). '(*Hence it need not be discussed here at length*' should be taken to imply that) the conclusions of earlier writers will be freely quoted whenever a need arises for them.

But the implicit aspect is quite different from this. In the words of first-rate poets it shines supreme and towers above the beauty of the striking external constituents even as charm in ladies. 4

प्रतीयमानं पुनरन्यदेव वाच्याद्वस्त्वस्ति वाणीषु महाकवीनाम् । यत्तत्सहृदयसुप्रसिद्धं[1] प्रसिद्धेभ्योऽलङ्कृतेभ्यः प्रतीतेभ्यो वावयवेभ्यो[2] व्यतिरिक्तत्वेन प्रकाशते लावण्यमिवाङ्गनासु । यथा ह्यङ्गनासु लावण्यं पृथङ्निर्वर्ण्यमानं[3] निखिलावयवव्यतिरेकि किमप्यन्यदेव सहृदयलोचनामृतं तत्त्वान्तरं तद्वदेव सोऽर्थः ।

स ह्यर्थो वाच्यसामर्थ्याक्षिप्तं वस्तुमात्रमलङ्कारा[4] रसादयश्चेत्यनेकप्रभेदप्रभिन्नो दर्शयिष्यते । सर्वेषु च तेषु प्रकारेषु[5][6] तस्य वाच्यादन्यत्वम् । तथा ह्याद्यस्तावत्प्रभेदो वाच्याद्दूरं विभेदवान्[7] । स हि कदाचिद्वाच्ये विधिरूपे प्रतिषेधरूपः । यथा—

भम धम्मिअ वीसत्थो सो सुणओ अज्ज मारिओ देण ।
गोलाणईकच्छकुडङ्गवासिणा दरिअसीहेण ॥
[भ्रम धार्मिक विश्वस्तः स शुनकोऽद्य मारितस्तेन ।
गोदानदीकूललताकुञ्जवासिना दृप्तसिंहेन ॥ इति च्छाया]

कदाचिद्वाच्ये[8] प्रतिषेधरूपे विधिरूपो[9] यथा —

अत्ता एत्थ णिमज्जइ एत्थ अहं दिअसअं पलोएहि ।
मा पहिअ रत्तिअन्धअ सेज्जाए मह णि[10]मंज्जहिसि ॥
[श्वश्रूरत्र निमज्जति अत्राहं दिवसकं प्रलोकय ।
मा पथिक राज्यन्धक शय्यायामावयोर्माङ्क्षीः ॥ इति च्छाया]

क्वचिद्वाच्ये विधिरूपेऽनुभयरूपो यथा —

वच्च मह व्विअ एक्केइ होन्तु णीसाससरोइअव्वाइं ।
मा तुज्झ वि तीअ विणा दक्खिण[11]हअस्स जाअन्तु ॥

---

१. 'यत्तत्सहृदयहृदयसुप्रसिद्धं' – घ २. 'चावयवेभ्यः' – ख. ३. 'अपृथक्पृथङ्निर्वर्ण्यमा°' – ग. ४. अलंकाररसादय° — BP. ५. प्रकार° – MB. ६. प्रकारेषु omitted in MB. ७. 'दूरप्रविभेदवान्' – ग. ८. 'क्वचिद्वाच्ये' – घ.; BP. ९. क्वचित्प्रतिषेधे विधिरूपो – घ. foot notes. १०. महँण – घ. ११. दक्खिणण – घ., BP.

The implicit aspect is entirely different from the explicit aspect and it is found in the words of first-rate poets. It is most familiar to the minds of refined critics and it shines forth as being over and above the 'striking external constituents.' The expression 'striking' connotes not only what is 'adorned with figures' but also what is 'perceptible to the senses.' Charm in ladies is a simile in point. Just as charm in ladies exceeds the beauty of all the individual limbs observed separately, and delights like ambrosia the eye of the admirer in a most unique fashion, so also does this implict meaning. It will be shown in the sequel that this meaning embraces various divisions such as the bare idea, figures and sentiments, all implied by the inner power of the explicit. In all these varieties, it will be seen to differ from the explicit. To illustrate : even the first variety itself differs very widely from the explicit. Sometimes the implicit meaning will be of the nature of a prohibition when the explicit is of the nature of positive proposal; e. g.,

Ramble freely, pious man !
That dog to-day is killed
By the fierce lion that dwells
In Godā river dells.

Sometimes, though the explicit meaning is of the nature of a prohibition, the implicit will be of the nature of a positive proposal; e. g.,

Mother-in-law lies here, lost in sleep;
And I here; thou shouldst mark
These before it is dark.
O traveller, blinded by night,
Tumble not into our beds aright.

Sometimes, though the explicit meaning may be of the nature of a positive proposal, the implicit may be neither a definite prohibition nor a definite proposal; e. g.,

Get thee gone! I pray,
May all sighs and tears be mine, I say.

[व्रज ममैवैकस्या भवन्तु निःश्वासरोदितव्यानि ।
मा तवापि तया विना दाक्षिण्यहतस्य जनिषत ॥ इति च्छाया]

क्वचिद्वाच्ये प्रतिषेधरूपेऽनुभयरूपो यथा –

दे आ पसिअ णिवत्तसु मुहससिजोह्लाविलुत्ततमणिवहे ।[1]
अहिसारिआणॅ विग्घं करोसि अण्णाणं वि हआसे ॥

[प्रार्थये तावत्प्रसीद निवर्तस्व मुखशशिज्योत्स्नाविलुप्ततमोनिवहे ।
अभिसारिकाणां विघ्नं करोष्यन्यासामपि हताशे ॥ इति च्छाया]

क्वचिद्वाच्याद्विभिन्नविषयत्वेन व्यवस्थापितो यथा –

कस्स व ण होइ रोसो दट्ठूण पिआएँ सव्वणं अहरम् ।
सभमरपँ[2]उमग्घाइणि वारिअवामे सहसु एह्लिम् ॥

[कस्य वा न भवति रोषो दृष्ट्वा प्रियायाः सव्रणमधरम् ।
सभ्रमरपद्माघ्रायिणि वारितवामे सहस्वेदानीम् ॥ इति च्छाया]

अन्ये चैवंप्रकारा[3] वाच्याँ[4]द्विभेदिनः प्रतीयमानभेदाः सम्भवन्ति । तेषां दिङ्मात्रमेतत्प्रदर्शितम् ।

द्वितीयोऽपि प्रभेदो वाच्याद्विभिन्नः सप्रपञ्चमग्रे दर्शयिष्यते ।

तृतीयस्तु रसादिलक्षणः प्रभेदो वाच्यसामर्थ्याक्षिप्तः प्रकाशते,[5] न तु साक्षाच्छब्दव्यापारविषय इति वाच्याद्विभिन्न एव । तथा हि वाच्यत्वं तस्य स्व[6]शब्दनिवेदितत्वेन वा स्यात्, विभावादिप्रतिपादनमुखेन वा । पूर्वस्मिन्पक्षे स्वशब्दनिवेदितत्वाभावे रसादीनामप्रतीतिप्रसङ्गः । न च सर्वत्र तेषां स्वशब्दनिवेदितत्वम् ।[7] यत्राप्यस्ति तत्[8], तत्रापि विशिष्टविभावादिप्रतिपादनमुखेनैवैषां[9] प्रतीतिः[10] । स्वशब्देन सा[11] केवलमनूद्यते, न तु तत्कृता ।

---

१. 'तमणिवहे' – ख, ग. २. °उपमग्घा° – घ. ३. 'चैवंविधाः प्रकारा' – घ. ४. 'क्वचिद्वाच्याद्' – ग. ५. 'प्रकाश्यते' – क - ख. ६. 'स्व'-क-ख-पुस्तकयोर्नास्ति. ७. 'निवेद्यत्वम् । यत्रापि नास्ति'-क-ख. ८. तत्–घ पुस्तके नास्ति. ९. °मुखेन तेषां – MB. १०. 'अप्रतीतिः' – ग. ११. 'सा' क-ख-पुस्तकयोर्नास्ति.

Let them not be thine again
In false courtesy to me.

Sometimes, though the explicit meaning is of the nature of a prohibition, the implicit is neither a prohibition nor a proposal; e. g.,

Humbly I beg thee, please go back;
Indeed, O sweet, thou drivest all gloom
By the bright light of your moon-face.
A pity it is that thou dost harm
The journeys of other wantons
Seeking their lovers' arms.

Sometimes, the implicit meaning will relate to something entirely different from that to which the explicit is related. e. g.,

Who will not rise in rage
Seeing his beloved's lip wounded?
You heeded not my warning
And kissed the lotus hiding a bee.
Now rightly pay the penalty!

There are various other forms besides these in which the varieties of the implicit meaning appear distinct from the explicit. What has been demonstrated above should be taken only as a pointer in that direction.

That the second class of the implicit (viz. figures of speech) too differs from the explicit will be demonstrated in detail later on.

But the third class of the implicit, viz., sentiments etc., is seen to shine forth as a result of the latent power in the explicit. It never becomes an object of direct verbal denotation and hence it is decidedly distinct from the explicit. If at all it could be an object of the explicit, it might be so alleged either as being directly denoted by its proper names or as being denoted through the delineation of characters in a setting, etc. If the first alternative were true, there would be no possibility of an experience of sentiments etc., in instances where their proper names are not

विषयान्तरे तथा[1] तस्या अ[2]दर्शनात्। न हि केवलशृङ्गारादिशब्दमात्रभाजि विभावादिप्रतिपादनरहिते काव्ये मनागपि रसवत्त्वप्रतीतिरस्ति। यतश्च स्वाभिधानमन्तरेण केवलेभ्योऽपि विभावादिभ्यो विशिष्टेभ्यो[3] रसादीनां प्रतीतिः, केवलाच्च स्वाभिधानाद[4]प्रतीतिः, तस्मादन्वयव्यतिरेकाभ्यामभिधेयसामर्थ्याक्षिप्तत्वमेव रसादीनाम्, न त्वभिधेयत्वं कथञ्चिदिति तृतीयोऽपि प्रभेदो वाच्याद्भिन्न एवेति स्थितम्। वाच्येन त्वस्य सहैव[5] प्रतीतिरित्यग्रे [6]दर्शयिष्यते।

काव्यस्यात्मा स एवार्थस्तथा चादिकवेः पुरा।
क्रौञ्चद्वन्द्ववियोगोत्थः शोकः श्लोकत्वमागतः॥ ५॥

विविध[7]वाच्यवाचकरचनाप्रप[8]ञ्चचारुणः काव्यस्य स एवार्थः सारभूतः। तथा चादिकवेर्वाल्मीकेः[9]सन्निहितसहचरीविरहकातरक्रौञ्चाक्रन्दजनितः शोक एव श्लोकतया परिणतः।[10] शोको हि करुण[11]स्थायिभावः।[12] प्रतीयमानस्य चान्यभे[13]ददर्शनेऽपि रसभावमुखेनैवोपलक्षणं, प्राधान्यात्।

---

१. 'तथा' ग-पुस्तके नास्ति. २. 'दर्शनात्' -ग. ३. 'विशिष्टेभ्यो' ग-पुस्तके नास्ति. ४. 'स्वाभिधानमात्राद्'-क-ख. ५. सहैव - घ. ६. 'प्रदर्शयिष्यते' - ग. ७. 'विविधविशिष्टवाच्य'-घ. ८. 'प्रपञ्च' क-ख-पुस्तकयोर्नास्ति. Also not found in the citation made in KLV. p. 111. ९. °निहतसहचरी - BP.; °निहित.° MB. १०. After this घ cites the verse :

"मा निषाद प्रतिष्ठां त्वमगमः शाश्वतीः समाः।
यत्क्रौञ्चमिथुनादेकमवधीः काममोहितम्॥"

११. 'करुणरसे' - घ. १२. प्रतीयमानरूप एवेति प्रतिपादितम् (घ). १३. प्रभेद (घ).

employed. Never are they so denoted directly by their proper names. Even when proper names are present, the experience of sentiments etc. is not due to them but only due to the delineation of characters in a proper setting etc. The experience of sentiments etc. is only given a designation by the proper name and is not at all conditioned by it. In fact we do not have the experience (of sentiments etc.) in all the instances where proper names are used. Indeed, there is not even the slightest experience of the presence of sentiments in a composition which contains only their proper names such as the *Erotic* and which is destitute of all delineation of the characters in a setting and so forth. Since we can have the experience of sentiments etc. only through the characters in a setting etc. irrespective of their proper names and since we cannot have the experience only by the use of proper names, we may conclude on the basis of these considerations, both positive and negative, that sentiments etc. are only implied by the latent power of the explicit and in no way denoted explicitly. Thus it is established that even the third class of the implicit meaning is quite distinct from the explicit. It will be shown in the sequel, however, that its experience will appear to be almost simultaneous with the explicit.

That meaning alone is the soul of poetry; and so it was that, of yore, the sorrow of the First Poet (i. e. Vālmīki) at the separation of the curlew couple took the form of a distich. **5**

That meaning alone happens to be the quintessence of poetry whose outward charm is secured by the combination of varied and uncommon explicit meanings, expressions and art of arrangement. That is why the sorrow of the First Poet, on hearing the wail of the he-curlew afflicted with separation from its close mate, transformed itself into a distich. Sorrow indeed is the abiding emotion which is at the basis of the sentiment of pathos. As already explained, it is only of the nature of the implicit. Though one can discern other sub-species of the implicit, they can all be understood by the synecdoche of sentiments and emotions since these happen to be the most important representatives of the rest.

सरस्वती स्वादु तदर्थवस्तु निःष्यन्दमाना महतां कवीनाम् ।
अलोकसामान्यमभिव्यनक्ति[1] परिस्फुरन्तं[2] प्रतिभाविशेषम् ॥६॥

तत्[3] वस्तुतत्त्वं[4] निःष्यन्दमाना महतां कवीनां भारती[5] अलोकसामान्यं प्रतिभाविशेषं परिस्फुरन्तमभिव्यनक्ति । येनास्मिन्नतिविचित्रकविपरम्परावाहिनि[6] संसारे कालिदासप्रभृतयो द्वित्राः पञ्चषा वा महाकवय इति[7] गण्यन्ते ।

इदं चापरं प्रतीयमानस्यार्थस्य[8] सद्भावसाधनं प्रमाणम्—

शब्दार्थशासनज्ञानमात्रेणैव न वेद्यते ।
वेद्यते स तु काव्यार्थतत्त्वज्ञैरेव केवलम् ॥ ७ ॥

शब्दार्थशासनज्ञानमात्रेऽपि परैर्न वेद्यते सोऽर्थो[9] यस्मात्केवलं काव्यार्थतत्त्वज्ञैरेव ज्ञायते। यदि च[10] वाच्यरूप एवासावर्थः[11] स्यात्तद्[12]वाच्यवाचकरूप[13]परिज्ञानादेव तत्प्रतीतिः स्यात् । अथ च वाच्यवाचकलक्षणमात्रकृतश्रमाणां काव्यतत्त्वार्थ[14]भावनाविमुखानां स्वरश्रुत्यादि[15]लक्षणमिवाऽप्रगीतानां[16] गान्धर्वलक्षणविदामगोचर एवासावर्थः ।

एवं वाच्यव्यतिरेकिणो व्यङ्ग्य[17]स्य सद्भावं प्रतिपाद्य प्राधान्यं तस्यैवेति दर्शयति[18]—

सोऽर्थस्तद्व्यक्तिसामर्थ्ययोगी शब्दश्च कश्चन ।
यत्नतः प्रत्यभिज्ञेयौ तौ शब्दार्थौ महाकवेः ॥ ८ ॥

स[19] व्यङ्ग्योऽर्थस्तद्व्यक्तिसामर्थ्ययोगी[20] शब्दश्च कश्चन, न सर्वः,[21]

---

१. 'अवलोकसाम्यं प्रतिभाविशेषं परिस्फुरन्तं समभिव्यनक्ति'–क-ख. २. प्रतिस्फुरन्तं–घ. ३. तत् घ पुस्तके नास्ति. ४. 'वस्तुतत्त्वं' इत्यारभ्य 'व्यनक्ति' इति पर्यन्तं क–ख-पुस्तकयोर्नास्ति. ५. सरस्वती–घ. ६. 'न्नियति' क–ख. ७. 'इति'–ग-पुस्तके नास्ति. ८. 'हि'–घ, KLV. ९. 'शब्दार्थशासनज्ञानमात्रेऽपि परं न वेद्यते सोऽर्थो'–घ. १०. 'च' क-ख-पुस्तकयोर्नास्ति. ११. 'एवास्यार्थः'–ग. १२. 'तत्' क–पुस्तके नास्ति. १३. 'तद्वाचकरूप'–ग. वाचक स्वरूप–घ. १४. 'काव्यार्थतत्त्व' क–ख. १५. 'स्वलक्षण'–ग. १६. ०मिव प्रगीतानां–घ. १७. 'व्यङ्ग्यस्यार्थस्य'–ग. १८. 'प्रतिपादयति'–घ., 'प्रदर्शयति'–ग. १९. 'स' not found in BP. २०. 'अर्थस्तत्प्रकाशनसामर्थ्ययोगी'–घ. २१. न शब्दमात्रम्–ग, BP.

The speech of first-rate poets streaming forth that sweet content reveals clearly their extraordinary genius which is as unearthly as it is ever bright. 6

The speech of first-rate poets which streams forth such subjects as are full of the said meaning will reveal most clearly the extraordinary genius of the poets; a genius which not only appears unearthly but also ever bright. Hence it is that though the world of traditionally accepted poets is very wide and varied, only two to three or at the most five to six amongst them, such as Kālidāsa, are counted as first-rate poets.

Here is another evidence to prove the existence of the Implicit meaning :

It is not understood by a mere learning in grammar and in dictionary. It is understood only by those who have an insight into the true significance of poetry. 7

By a mere learning in rules of grammar and meanings recorded in lexicons, that meaning connot be grasped; for it can be grasped only by those who have an insight into the true significance of poetry. In case this meaning too were the same as the explicit, then it should have been quite possible to understand it merely by a knowledge of the nature of explicit meanings and expressions. But the fact is that that meaning (i. e. implicit meaning) remains beyond the understanding of persons with a grounding merely in the science of meanings and words but averse to aesthetic contemplation of the intrinsic significance of poetry, even as the true appreciation of notes and tones of music will remain beyond the reach of scholars in the science of music if they are not good musicians.

Thus after establishing the existence of the implicit meaning as distinct from the explicit, the over-riding superiority of that meaning is demonstrated in what follows :

That meaning, and that rare word which possesses the power of conveying it, only these two deserve the careful scrutiny of a first–rate poet. 8

‘ *that meaning* ’ refers to the implicit and ‘ *that rare word which possesses the power of conveying it* ’ points out that it is not any and every word (recorded in the dictionary). Such a

तावेव शब्दार्थौ महाकवेः प्रत्यभिज्ञेयौ । व्यङ्ग्यव्यञ्जकाभ्यामेव हि सुप्रयुक्ताभ्यां महाकवित्वलाभो महाकवीनां, न वाच्यवाचकरचनामात्रेण ।

इदानीं व्यङ्ग्यव्यञ्जकयोः प्राधान्येऽपि यद्वाच्यवाचकावेव प्रथममुपाददते कवयस्तदपि युक्तमेवेत्याह–

आलोकार्थी यथा दीपशिखायां यत्नवाञ्जनः ।
तदुपायतया तद्वदर्थे वाच्ये[1] तदादृतः ॥ ९ ॥

यथा ह्यालोकार्थी सन्नपि दीपशिखायां यत्नवाञ्जनो[2] भवति तदुपायतया । न हि दीपशिखामन्तरेणालोकः सम्भवति । तद्वद्व्यङ्ग्यमर्थं प्रत्यादृतो जनो वा[3]च्येऽर्थे यत्नवान् भवति । अनेन प्र[4]तिपादकस्य कवेर्व्यङ्ग्यमर्थं[5] प्रति व्यापारो दर्शितः ।

प्रतिपाद्यस्यापि तं दर्शयितुमाह –

यथा पदार्थद्वारेण वाक्यार्थः सम्प्रतीयते ।
वाच्यार्थपूर्विका तद्वत्प्र[6]तिपत्तस्य वस्तुनः ॥१०॥

यथा हि[7] पदार्थद्वारेण वाक्यार्थावगमस्तथा[8] वाच्यार्थप्रतीतिपूर्विका व्यङ्ग्यस्यार्थस्य प्रतिपत्तिः ।

इदानीं वाच्यार्थप्रतीतिपूर्वकत्वेऽपि तत्प्रतीतेर्व्यङ्ग्यस्यार्थस्य प्राधान्यं यथा न व्यालुप्यते[9] तथा दर्शयति –

---

१. 'अर्थो वाच्यो' – ग.; 'वाच्ये प्रति तमादृतः' No. 254 (BORI) २. 'जनो' क-ख-पुस्तकयोर्नास्ति. ३. 'वाच्यार्थे' – ख. ४. 'प्रतिपादिकस्य' – ख. ५. 'अर्थं' क-ख-पुस्तकयोर्नास्ति. ६. 'प्रतिपन्नस्य'.–क - ख; प्रतिपत्तव्य° – घ. ७. 'हि' क - ख पुस्तकयोर्नास्ति. ८. 'वाक्यार्थस्यावगमः' ग. ९. 'व्यालुप्येत' – घ. विलुप्यते No. 254 (BORI).

word and such a meaning – only these two deserve the careful recognition of a first–rate poet. The status of first–rate poets is achieved only by the effective employment of suggested meanings and suggestive expressions and not by a mere use of conventional meanings and conventional words.

It is shown below that poets are quite justified in availing themselves, at the outset, of the conventional meaning and conventional word even if the suggested meaning and the suggestive word happen to be far superior.

Just as a man interested in perceiving objects (in the dark) directs his efforts towards securing a lamp since it is a means to realise his end, so also does one who is ultimately interested in the suggested meaning proceed by first evincing interest in the conventional meaning. 9

Even though a man may ultimately be interested only in the perception of objects, he will (first) direct his efforts towards securing light as it serves as a means to achieve his end. In fact, without a lamp, there could be no perception possible. So also a man who is ultimately interested in the suggested meaning will first direct his efforts towards the conventional meaning. By this it is shown how a poet labours towards the suggested meaning.

That this is true of the reader also is shown below :

Just as the purport of a sentence is grasped through the meaning of individual words, the knowledge of that sense is got at only through the medium of the explicit sense. 10

Just as the purport of the sentence as a whole is known only through the medium of word-import, so also is the knowledge of the suggested sense gained through the medium of the conventional sense.

Now, even though the knowledge of the suggested sense is thus invariably preceded by a knowledge of the conventional sense, it is shown below how its importance does not grow less on that account :

स्वसामर्थ्यवशेनैव वाक्यार्थं प्रथयन्नपि[1] ।
यथा व्यापारनिष्पत्तौ पदार्थो न विभाव्यते ॥११॥

यथा स्वसामर्थ्यवशेनैव वाक्यार्थं प्रकाशयन्नपि पदार्थो व्यापारनिष्पत्तौ न विभाव्यते विभक्ततया –

तद्वत्सचेतसां सोऽर्थो वाच्यार्थविमुखात्मनाम् ।
बुद्धौ तत्त्वार्थदर्शिन्यां झटित्येवावभासते[2] ॥१२॥[3]

एवं वाच्यव्यतिरेकिणो व्यङ्ग्यस्यार्थस्य सद्भावं प्रतिपाद्य प्रकृत उपयोजयन्नाह[4] –

यत्रार्थः शब्दो वा तमर्थमुपसर्जनीकृतस्वार्थौ ।
व्यङ्क्तः काव्यविशेषः स ध्वनिरिति सूरिभिः कथितः ॥१३॥

यत्रार्थो वाच्यविशेषः वाचकविशेषः[5] शब्दो वा तमर्थं व्यङ्क्तः स काव्यविशेषो ध्वनिरिति । अनेन वाच्यवाचकचारुत्वहेतुभ्य उपमादिभ्योऽनुप्रासादिभ्यश्च विभक्त एव ध्वनेर्विषय इति दर्शितम् ।

यदप्युक्तम् – 'प्रसिद्धप्रस्थानातिक्रमिणो मार्गस्य काव्यत्वहानेर्ध्वनिर्नास्ति' इति तदप्ययुक्तम् । यतो लक्षणकृतामेव स केवलं न प्रसिद्धः, लक्ष्ये तु परीक्ष्यमाणे स एव सहृदयहृदयाह्लादकारि[6] काव्यतत्त्वम् । ततोऽन्यच्चित्रमेवेत्यग्रे[7] दर्शयिष्यामः ।

---

१. प्रतिपादयन् – BP. & KSS. Editions. २. 'झगिति' – ग, KLV. ३. यत्रा(त्रा)वभासते । (?) इति घपुस्तके वृत्तावधिकः । यत्रावभासते No. 254 (BORI). ४. प्रकृते ध्वनिलक्षणे उपयोगं गमयन्नाह – KLV. ५. 'वाचकविशेषः' क–ख पुस्तकयोर्नास्ति. ६. सहृदयाह्लादि काव्यम्. क–ख. ७. 'एव' क–ख-पुस्तकयोर्नास्ति.

Though by its own power the word-import is responsible for conveying the sentence-import, just as it escapes notice once its purpose is served — 11

While it is true that word–import itself conveys sentence-import through its own power, just as it does not at the same time appear as distinct from the sentence-import once this latter has been conveyed :—

So also that suggested meaning flashes suddenly across the truth–perceiving minds of perceptive critics when they turn away from the literal meaning. 12

So far, the existence of suggested meaning apart from the explicit has been set forth; and now it is made to serve the purpose on hand in the following text:

That kind of poetry, wherein the (conventional) meaning renders itself secondary or the (conventional) word renders its meaning secondary and suggests the (intended or) implied meaning, is designated by the learned as DHVANI or 'Suggestive Poetry'. 13

The kind of poetry wherein not only meaning, i. e., specific meaning but also word, i. e. specific word, goes to suggest only the said (implicit) meaning, is signified by the name DHVANI or Suggestive Poetry. By this it is shown how the province of Suggestive Poetry is quite distinct from that of the sources of charm in explicit meaning, such as the figure simile on the one hand, and from that of the sources of charm in distinctive sound, such as the figure alliteration on the other.

The *prima facie* view already mentioned, viz., "Suggestion does not exist indeed; for, a species of poetry opposed to all well-known canons will necessarily cease to be poetry", is unsound. The reason is that it is unfamilar only to writers on poetics and if one were to examine the best specimens of literature, it alone would emarge as the most intrinsic principle of poetry delighting all refined critics. We shall show later on that all else is only 'puzzling picture'.

यदप्युक्तम्[1] कामनीयकमनतिवर्तमानस्य [2]तस्योक्तालङ्कारादिप्रकारेष्वन्तर्भावः इति, तदप्यसमीचीनम्; यतो वाच्यवाचकमात्राश्रयिणि प्रस्थाने व्यङ्ग्यव्यञ्जकसमाश्रयेण व्यवस्थितस्य ध्वनेः कथमन्तर्भावः, वाच्यवाचकचारुत्वहेतवो हि[3] तस्याङ्गभूताः, न तु तदेकरूपा एवेति प्रतिपादयिष्यमाणत्वात्[4]।

परिकरश्लोकश्चात्र—

‘ व्यङ्ग्यव्यञ्जकसंबन्धनिबन्धनतया ध्वनेः ।
वाच्यवाचकचारुत्वहेत्वन्तःपातिता कुतः ॥ ’

ननु यत्र प्रतीयमानस्यो[5]ऽर्थस्य वैशद्येनाप्रतीतिः स नाम मा भूद्ध्वनेर्विषयः। यत्र तु [6]तत्प्रतीतिरस्ति, यथा समासोक्त्याक्षेपानुक्तनिमित्तविशेषोक्ति[7]पर्यायोक्तापह्नुतिदीपकसङ्करालङ्कारादौ, तत्र[8] ध्वनेरन्तर्भावो भविष्यतीत्यादि निराकर्तुमभिहितम्—‘ उपसर्जनीकृतस्वार्थौ ’ इति। अर्थो गुणीकृतात्मा, गुणीकृताभिधेयः[10] शब्दो वा यत्रार्थान्तरमभिव्यनक्ति स ध्वनिरिति। तेषु कथं तस्यान्तर्भावः। व्यङ्ग्यप्राधान्ये हि ध्वनिः। न चैतत्समासोक्त्यादिष्वस्ति। समासोक्तौ तावत्—

उपोढरागेण विलोलतारकं तथा गृहीतं शशिना निशामुखम्।
यथा समस्तं तिमिरांशुकं तया पुरोऽपि[11] रागाद्गलितं न लक्षितम्॥

१. ‘ उदितं ’-ग. २. तस्योक्तेष्वेव काव्यशोभाहेतुष्वन्तर्भावः – MB. ३. ‘ हि ’ क-ख. पुस्तकयोर्नास्ति. ४. प्रतिपिपादयिष्यमाणत्वात् – घ. ५. ‘ अप्यर्थस्य ’. – ग ६ तत् – omitted BP. ७. ‘ पर्यायापह्नुति ’. – ग. ८. ‘ ० सङ्करादौ ’. – ग., ० सङ्करालङ्काराप्रस्तुतप्रशंसादौ – MB. ९. ‘ तत्र तत्र ’ – ग. १० ० भिधेयश्च–घ ११. ‘ पुरोविरागात् ’ – ग.

The other objection, viz., "since it is not distinct from a source of charm, it naturally comes under the causes of charm already enumerated", is also fallacious. How can suggestion which is grounded on the relation of the suggested sense to the suggesting word be ever comprehended by a theory which is based on the relation of only the conventional sense to the denotative word ? It will be expounded later that the sources of beauty in conventional meanings and expressions can only be ancillary and never identical with it.

Here is a mnemonic verse :

Suggestion, indeed, is conditioned by only the relation between the suggested and the suggester; when such is the case, how can it ever be subsumed under the source of beauty in the expressed and the expression ?

Perhaps some might argue in the following strain : 'Such instances (of figures of speech) wherein no implicit meaning is clearly discernible may by all means be regarded as incapable of subsuming suggestion. But suggestion can certainly be subsumed under such figures of speech as Condensed Metaphor, Paraleipsis, Metonymy, Periphrasis, Fancied Denial, Ellipsis implying a Simile, and Merging of Figures, since we have a clear perception of the implicit meaning in these. It is in order to refute such an argument that the words, 'renders itself or its meaning secondary' etc., have been included in the text. The idea is that when in a work of poetry an explicit meaning renders itself secondary or when a word renders its own denotative meaning secondary and each of these suggests another sense, we call it Suggestive Poetry. How can this suggestion be brought under the said figures ? Suggestion is possible only when the suggested element is exclusively important. This is not so in Condensed Metaphor and the like. In an instance of Condensed Metaphor such as—

The twilight (heroine's face) with twinkling stars (shining pupils) was illumined (kissed) by the moon (the hero) glowing red (overcome by emotion) so suddenly (with such love) that the entire mass of darkness (black garment) disappearing in the east (slipping even in front), due to illumination (love) was not at all noticed.—

इत्यादौ व्यङ्ग्येनानुगतं वाच्यमेव[1] प्राधान्येन प्रतीयते, समारोपितनायिकानायकव्यवहारयोर्निशाशशिनोरेव वाक्यार्थत्वात् ।

आक्षेपेऽ[2]पि व्यङ्ग्यविशेषाक्षेपिणो वाच्यस्यैव चारुत्वं प्राधान्येन [3]वाक्यार्थ आक्षेपोक्तिसामर्थ्यादेव ज्ञायते । तथाहि [4]तत्र शब्दोपा[5]रूढो विशेषाभिधानेच्छया प्रतिषेधरूपो य आक्षेपः स एव व्यङ्ग्यविशेषमाक्षिपन्मुख्यं काव्यशरीरम् । चारुत्वोत्कर्षनिबन्धना[6] हि वाच्यव्यङ्ग्ययोः प्राधान्यविवक्षा । यथा —

अनुरागवती सन्ध्या दिवसस्तत्पुरस्सरः ।
अहो दैवगतिश्चित्रा[7] तथापि न समागमः ॥

अत्र सत्यामपि व्यङ्ग्यप्रतीतौ वाच्यस्यैव चारुत्वमुत्कर्षवदिति तस्यैव प्राधान्यविवक्षा ।

यथा च दीपकापह्नुत्यादौ व्यङ्ग्यत्वेनोपमायाः प्रतीतावपि प्राधान्येनाविवक्षितत्वान्न तया व्यपदेशस्तद्वदत्रापि द्रष्टव्यम् । अनुक्तनिमित्तायामपि विशेषोक्तौ—

आहूतोऽपि सहायैरोमित्युक्त्वा[8] विमुक्तनिद्रोऽपि ।
गन्तुमना अपि पथिकः सङ्कोचं नैव शिथिलयति ॥

इत्यादौ व्यङ्ग्यस्य प्रकरणसामर्थ्यात्प्रतीतिमात्रम् । न तु तत्प्र[9]तीतिनिमित्ता काचिच्चारुत्वनिष्पत्तिरिति न प्राधान्यम् ।

---

१. 'एव' – क – ख पुस्तकयोर्नास्ति. २. 'हि' – क – ख. ३. 'वाच्यार्थ' – ग.; काव्यार्थ No 254 (BORI). ४. 'तथाहि तत्र हि–ग. ५. शब्दोपारूढरूपो–घ. ६. 'निबन्धनाभिंदा' –ग. ७. कीदृक् BP. ८. 'सहायैरेमीत्युक्त्वा'.–घ. ९. 'तत्' क-ख-पुस्तकयोर्नास्ति.

it is the explicit meaning alone which appears as prominent and the suggested sense is only secondary to it. The main subjects of description are the night and the moon. And the behaviour of a heroine and that of a hero are attributed to them (only secondarily).

Even in Paraleipsis, we find beauty more in the explicit than in the particular idea it hints at. That the explicit is relatively more important than the implicit in this figure is brought out even by its title—'the pointer'. In an instance of Paraleipsis in poetry, that which stands out as the chief element is the very act of hinting at and it will be of the nature of a disavowal serving the purpose of conveying speciality; and it will be found expressed openly, in so many words, though all the while it will be hinting at the suggested idea. Between the expressed and the suggested, which of them is intended to be relatively more important can be settled only by determining the relative excellence of charm. For example—

Twilight is full of love (red colour),
And the day chases her face to face ;
But oh, look at the decree of Fate
The twain do never meet !

Though a suggested idea is understood here, charm is felt to exist only in the expressed. Hence that alone should be taken to be primarily intended.

Just as in figures like Ellipsis implying a simile and Fancied Denial, although we find a suggested simile, we do not designate these figures by that name because the explicit aspects in them are intended to be more important, so also in Paraleipsis the same consideration should be kept in sight.

The same is true of Metonymy in which (the effect alone is mentioned and) the cause is omitted :

The friends are calling outside;
' Coming ' is his reply form inside
All his sleep is gone by.
Still the traveller rolls in langour
Though with a mind to go.

In instances like this, we simply get at the suggested idea by force of context and we do not come across any charm therein. Hence the suggested idea is not of primary importance.

पर्यायोक्तेऽपि यदि प्राधान्येन व्यङ्ग्यत्वं तद्भवतु ना[1]म तस्य ध्वनावन्तर्भावः । न तु ध्वनेस्तत्रान्तर्भावः । तस्य महाविषयत्वेनाङ्गित्वेन च प्रतिपादयिष्यमाणत्वात्[2] । न पुनः पर्यायोक्ते भामहोदाहृतसदृशे व्यङ्ग्यस्यैव प्राधान्यम् । वाच्यस्य तत्रोपसर्जनीभावेनाविवक्षितत्वात् ।

अपह्नुतिदीपकयोः पुनर्वाच्यस्य प्राधान्यं व्यङ्ग्यस्य चा[3]नुयायित्वं प्रसिद्धमेव ।

सङ्करालङ्कारेऽपि यदालङ्कारोऽलङ्कारान्तरच्छायामनुगृह्णाति, तदा व्यङ्ग्यस्य प्राधान्येनाविवक्षितत्वान्न ध्वनिविषयत्वम् । अलङ्कारद्वयसम्भावनायां तु वाच्यव्यङ्ग्ययोः समं प्राधान्यम् । अथ वाच्योपसर्जनीभावेन व्यङ्ग्यस्य तत्रावस्थानं[4] तदा सोऽपि ध्वनिविषयोऽस्तु, न तु स एव ध्वनिरिति वक्तुं शक्यम् । पर्यायोक्तनिर्दिष्टन्यायात् । अपि च सङ्करालङ्कारस्य क्वचित् सङ्करोक्तिरेव ध्वनिसम्भावनां निराकरोति[5] ।

अप्रस्तुतप्रशंसायामपि यदा सामान्यविशेषभावान्निमित्तनिमित्तिभावाद्वा [6]अभिधीयमानस्याप्रस्तुतस्य प्रतीयमानेन प्रस्तुतेनाभिसम्बन्धः तदाभिधीयमानप्रतीयमानयोः सममेव प्राधान्यम् । यदा तावत्सामान्यस्याप्रस्तुतस्याभिधीयमानस्य प्राकरणिकेन विशेषेण[7] प्रतीयमानेन सम्बन्धस्तदा विशेषप्रतीतौ सत्यामपि[8] प्राधान्येन तस्य सामान्येनावि[9]नाभावात्सामान्यस्यापि प्राधान्यम् । यदापि विशेषस्य सामान्यनिष्ठत्वं तदापि सामान्यस्य प्रा[10]धान्ये सामान्ये सर्वविशेषा[11]णामन्तर्भावाद्विशेषस्यापि प्राधान्यम् । निमित्तनिमित्तिभावे चायमेव न्यायः ।

---

१. 'नाम'–ग. पुस्तके नास्ति. २. प्रातिपिपादिष्यमाणत्वात्–घ. ३. 'च'–घ-पुस्तके नास्ति. ४. 'तत्रापि व्यवस्थानं'–घ. ५. अपि च संकरालंकारस्य संकरोक्तिरेव ध्वनिसम्भावनां करोति – घ. ६. अभिधीयमानस्य इत्यारभ्य अभिधीयमान° इति पर्यन्तं घ-पुस्तके नास्ति. ७. 'विशेषणेन.'–ख. ८. 'सत्यां'–ग-पुस्तके नास्ति. ९. 'विनाभावात्'–क-ख. १०. 'प्राधान्येन'–क-ख. ११. 'विशेषणानां'–क-ख.

So also in Periphrasis, if the suggested idea were to be regarded as primarily important, it might by all means be brought under suggestion; but suggestion will not be subsumed under it. For not only the province of suggestion is wider but its importance also is greater (than that of the expressed) as it will be explained later. In the figure Periphrasis as illustrated by Bhāmaha, we do not have at all any exclusive importance attached to the suggested idea, since the expressed one is not intended there to be secondary.

So far as Fancied Denial and Ellipsis implying a simile are concerned, it is well known that the expressed element alone is primary therein and that the suggested element is secondary to it.

In Merging of Figures too, when one figure favours the shade of another figure, the suggested alone is not primarily intended and hence it cannot be reckoned to subsume suggestion. In instances where two figures may be said to exist simultaneously, the expressed and the suggested get equal importance. If in an instance the expressed is secondary and the suggested has primary importance, then it might, of course, be brought under suggestion. But it is not possible to say even then that it is itself identical with suggestion. The argument given in connection with Periphrasis is applicable here also. What is more, the very expression we use to signify this figure, viz., 'Merging of Figures' prevents often even our imagining that it might be the same as suggestion.

So also in the figure, Vicarious Reference, in instances where the expressed extraneous idea and the implied contextual idea are related to each other either as universal and particular or as cause and effect, the expressed and the implied get equal importance of course. In other words, when the expressed extraneous idea is a universal and it is related to the implied contextual idea which happens to be its particular, the universal itself gets equal importance since its relationship with the particular is one of inseparable inherence. Similarly, even when the extraneous particular happens to be related to the contextual universal, notwithstanding the importance accruing to the universal (by its sheer relevancy), the particulars are comprehended by the universal. The same logic applies also to instances where the expressed and the implied are related to each other

यदा तु सारूप्यमात्र[1]वशेनाप्रस्तुतप्रशंसायामप्रकृतप्रकृतयोः सम्बन्धस्तदाप्यप्रस्तुतस्य सरूपस्याभिधीयमानस्य [2]प्राधान्येनाविवक्षायां ध्वनावेवान्तर्भावः । इतरथात्वलङ्कारान्तरत्वमेव । तदयमत्र संक्षेपः –

(१) 'व्यङ्ग्यस्य यत्राप्राधान्यं वाच्यमात्रानुयायिनः ।
समासोक्त्यादयस्तत्र वाच्यालङ्कृतयः स्फुटाः ॥

(२) व्यङ्ग्यस्य प्रतिभामात्रे वाच्यार्थानुगमेऽपि वा ।
न ध्वनिर्यत्र वा तस्य प्राधान्यं न प्रतीयते ॥

(३) तत्परावेव शब्दार्थौ यत्र व्यङ्ग्यं प्रति स्थितौ ।
ध्वनेः स एव विषयो मन्तव्यः सङ्करोज्झितः ॥[3]

तस्मान्न ध्वनेरन्यत्रान्तर्भावः ।

इतश्च नान्तर्भावः; यतः काव्यविशेषोऽङ्गी ध्वनिरिति कथितः । तस्य पुनरङ्गानि – [4]अलंकारा गुणा वृत्तयश्चेति प्रतिपादयिष्यते । न चावयव एव पृथग्भूतोऽवयवीति प्रसिद्धः । अपृथग्भावे तु तदङ्गत्वं तस्य न तु तत्त्वमेव । यत्रापि वा तत्त्वं तत्रापि ध्वनेर्महाविषयत्वान्न[5] तन्निष्ठत्वमेव ।

'सूरिभिः कथित' इति विद्वदुपज्ञेयमुक्तिः, न तु यथाकथञ्चित्प्रवृत्तेति [6]प्रतिपाद्यते । प्रथमे हि विद्वांसो वैयाकरणाः, व्याकरणमूलत्वात्सर्वविद्यानाम् । ते[7] च श्रूयमाणेषु वर्णेषु ध्वनिरिति [8]व्यवहरन्ति । [9]तथैवान्यैस्तन्मतानुसारिभिः

---

१. 'वशेनान्यस्य' – क-ख. २. 'प्राधान्यस्य' – क-ख. ३. These three – परिकरश्लोकs have-been printed as कारिकाs in N. S. P. edn. ४. 'अलंकारो' – क-ख. ५. 'न' – क-ख-पुस्तकयोर्नास्ति. ६. 'प्रकाश्यते' – ग. ७. 'तेषु श्रूय°' – क-ख. ८. 'व्याहरन्ति' – ख. ९. 'तथैवान्यैः' इत्यारभ्य 'नातिक्रमणीयम्' इत्यन्तं क-ख-पुस्तकयोः नास्ति.

as cause and effect. Even in instances of Vicarious Reference where the relation is of similarity, if the extraneous expressed idea bearing similarity is not intended as primarily important, it comes, of course, under the category of suggestion. Otherwise (i.e. if it is intended as primarily important), it will just be one of the figures.

The following mnemonic verses sum up the position :—

1. *Wherever we find the implied meaning unimportant and merely ancillary to the expressed, we should clearly conclude that such instances contain only figures like the Condensed Metaphor.*
2. *In places where we have just a glimmer of the implied, or where the implied is just a handmaid to the expressed, or where its primary importance is not clearly discernible, there is no Suggestive Poetry.*
3. *Only those instances wherein we find both the word and the meaning solely directed towards the implied meaning should be regarded as real instances of Suggestive Poetry admitting of no confusion whatever.*

It is thus established that suggestion cannot be subsumed under other heads.

Another reason why it cannot be so subsumed is the statement that 'it is only the full-limbed species of poetry which gets the designation of DHVANI or Suggestive Poetry'. It will be explained hereafter that the limbs (of poetry) are figures, qualities, and varieties of diction. Looking upon each component part as the whole itself is quite unheard of. When considered collectively, it will be but a part of the whole and never identical with the whole. Even if identity were possible in some instances, Suggestive Poetry cannot be looked upon as conditioned by its limbs mentioned, since its sphere is very extensive.

The expression, " *is designated by the learned* " brings out the fact that this designation was first devised by the learned and that it has not gained currency in a haphazard fashion. The foremost among the learned are grammarians because grammar lies at the root of all studies. They indeed refer to articulate letters by the term DHVANI or Suggester. In the same way, since the element of suggestion is common (to both), not only the

सूरिभिः काव्यतत्त्वार्थदर्शिभिर्वाच्यवाचकसम्मिश्रः शब्दात्मा काव्यमिति व्यपदेश्यो व्यञ्जकत्वसाम्याद्ध्वनिरित्युक्तः। न चैवंविधस्य ध्वनेर्वक्ष्यमाणप्रभेदतद्भेदसङ्कलनया महाविषयस्य यत्प्रकाशनं तद[1]प्रसिद्धालङ्कारविशेषमात्रप्रतिपादनेन तुल्यमिति तद्भावितचेतसां युक्त एव संरम्भः। न च तेषु कथञ्चिदीर्ष्यया कलुषितशेमुषीकत्वमाविष्करणीयम्।

तदेवं ध्वनेस्तावदभाववादिनः प्रत्युक्ताः। अस्ति ध्वनिः।

स चासावविवक्षितवाच्यो विवक्षितान्यपरवाच्यश्चेति द्विविधः सामान्येन। तत्राद्यस्योदाहरणम् —

सुवर्णपुष्पां पृथिवीं चिन्वन्ति पुरुषास्त्रयः।
शूरश्च कृतविद्यश्च यश्च जानाति सेवितुम्॥

द्वितीयस्यापि —

शिखरिणि क्व नु नाम कियच्चिरं किमभिधानमसावकरोत्तपः।
तरुणि येन तवाधरपाटलं दशति बिम्बफलं शुकशावकः॥

यदप्युक्तं भक्तिर्ध्वनिरिति तत्प्रतिसमाधीयते —

भक्त्या बिभर्ति नैकत्वं रूपभेदादयं ध्वनिः।

अयमुक्तप्रकारो ध्वनिर्भक्त्या नैक[2]त्वं बिभर्ति, भिन्नरूपत्वात्। वाच्यव्यतिरिक्तस्यार्थस्य वाच्यवाचकाभ्यां तात्पर्येण प्र[3]काशनं यत्र व्य[4]ङ्ग्यप्राधान्ये स ध्वनिः। उपचारमात्रं तु[5] भक्तिः।

---

१. 'तदत्र'-घ. २. 'नैकतां'-ग. ३. अर्थप्रकाशनं-घ. ४. 'व्यङ्ग्यप्राधान्ये' -क-ख पुस्तकयोर्नास्ति. ५. 'तु'-क-ख पुस्तकयोर्नास्ति.

word and its meaning but its essential verbal power and also that which is usually referred to by the term poetry, has been given the same designation, viz., DHVANI by other learned men whose insight into the fundamental truth about poetry is profound and who are followers of the principles laid down by grammarians. A treatment, then, of such a comprehensive concept as suggestion, with all its divisions and subdivisions yet to be explained in the sequel, is not at all on a par with the enumeration of the well known, specific figures of speech and hence the enthusiasm of persons imbued in their minds with the value of suggestion is quite proper. None need display jealousy to show somehow that they are all men of deranged minds.

The advocates of the view that suggestion is non-existent have been thus refuted. Suggestion does exist.

Broadly considered, it will be two-fold : (1) with unintended literal import and (2) with intended but further-extending literal import. The following is an example of the first kind :

Three persons will gather
Flowers of gold from the earth :
The bold, the learned,
And he who knows how to serve.

The following illustrates the second :

On which mountain and for how long
Did this one perform penance ?
And what might be its name ?
For, the young parrot pecks
The fruit so red as your lips.

The counterview that metaphorical indication itself is suggestion is answered in what follows :—

Suggestion does not bear identity with indication because there is difference in nature between the two.

Suggestion which has been explained above does not bear identity with logical implication or indication since the two have different natures. Suggestion is the unidirectional communication of a sense other than the expressed by both the expressed sense and the expression while at the same time the

मा[1] चैतत्स्याद्भाक्तिर्लक्षणं ध्वनेरित्याह —

अतिव्याप्तेरथाव्याप्तेर्न चासौ लक्ष्यते तया ॥ १४ ॥

नैव[2] भक्त्या ध्वनिर्लक्ष्यते । कथम् ? अतिव्याप्तेरव्याप्तेश्च । तत्रातिव्याप्तिर्ध्वनिव्यतिरिक्तेऽ[3]पि विषये भक्तेः सम्भवात् । यत्र हि व्यंञ्जकत्वकृतं[4] महत्सौष्ठवं नास्ति तत्राप्युपचरितशब्दवृत्त्या प्रसिद्ध्यनुरोधप्रवर्तितव्यवहाराः कवयो दृश्यन्ते । यथा —

परिम्लानं पीनस्तनजघनसङ्गादुभयत-
स्तनोर्मध्यस्यान्तः परिमिलनम्[5]प्राप्य हरितम् ।
इदं व्यस्तन्यासं श्लथ[6]भुजलताक्षेपवलनैः
कृशाङ्ग्याः सन्तापं वदति बिसिनीपत्रशयनम् ॥

तथा[7] —

चुम्बिज्जइ सअहुत्तं[8] अवरुन्धिज्जइ सहस्सहुत्तं वि ।
रमिअ पुणो वि रमिज्जइ पिए जणे णत्थि पुणरुत्तम् ॥

[चुम्ब्यते शतकृत्वोऽवरुध्यते सहस्रकृत्वः ।
रन्त्वा पुनरपि रम्यते प्रिये जने[9] नास्ति पुनरुक्तम् ॥ इति च्छाया]

तथा[10] —

कुविआओ पसण्णाओ ओरण्णमुहीओ विहसमाणाओ ।
जह गहिआ तह हिअअं हरन्ति उच्छिन्तमहिलाओ ॥

[कुपिताः प्रसन्ना अवरुदितवदना विहसन्त्यः ।
यथा गृहीतास्तथा हृदयं हरन्ति स्वैरिण्यो महिलाः ॥ इति च्छाया]

१. 'तत्रैतत्स्याद्भाक्तिर्लक्षणं'-घ, KLV ननु मा भूद्भाक्तिर्ध्वनिरिति चैकं रूपं, भवतु भक्तिर्ध्वनेर्लक्षणमित्याह-MB. २. 'न च'-घ, KLV. ३. 'च'-ग. ४. 'व्यञ्जकत्वकृतं'-BP. ५. 'परिमलनमप्राप्य'-घ. ६. 'प्रशिथिलभुजाक्षेप'-घ. ७. 'यथा'-ग. ८. असहुत्तं-BP. ९. प्रियो जनो-घ. BP. १०. 'यथा',-ग.

implied sense will be exclusively important. But indication is merely metaphorical application.

One might perhaps urge—" Indication may not be identical with suggestion; but it can at least be regarded as a differentia of the latter ". This view is countered below :

Nor is this a differentia of that as both the fallacies of Too Wide and Too Narrow would result (if one were to hold such a view). 14

Nor is suggestion determined by indication, ' Why ' ? '*Because of the fallacy of Too Wide and also of the fallacy of Too Narrow*'. The fallacy of Too Wide is there inasmuch as indication can exist even in such instances as are devoid of suggestion. Even in instances where no excessive charm due to suggestion is present, poets are seen to employ words with metaphorical applications in pursuance of established usage as in the following example :

This bed of lotus–leaves ***bespeaks***
The torment of the damsel that slept thereon.
Faded at its two ends with pressure
Of her buxom breasts and burly hips.
The part that spanned her slender waist
Remains green without such pressure.
And here it is in disorder
By the movements of her drooping creeper-like arms.

To take another example :

The beloved one is kissed for the hundredth time,
Is embraced for the thousandth time,
And with but a brief pause, is fondled again;
Yet there is no ***tautology*** *for lovers.*

Here is another example :

Angry or pleased, in tears or in smiles,
In whatever state they are caught,
Wanton women ***steal*** *one's heart.*

तथा –

अज्जाएँ पहारो णवलदाए दिण्णो पिएण थणवट्टे ।
मिउओ वि दूसहो व्विअ जाओ हिअए सवत्तीणम् ॥
[भार्याया प्रहारो नवलतया दत्तः प्रियेण स्तनपृष्ठे ।
मृदुकोऽपि दुःसह इव जातो हृदये सपत्नीनाम् ॥ इति च्छाया]

तथा[1]—

परार्थे यः पीडामनुभवति भङ्गे[2]ऽपि मधुरो
यदीयः सर्वेषामिह खलु विकारोऽप्यभिमतः ।
न सम्प्राप्तो वृद्धिं यदि स भृशमक्षेत्रपतितः
किमिक्षोर्दोषो[3]ऽसौ न पुनरगुणाया मरुभुवः ॥

इत्य[4]त्रेक्षुपक्षेऽनुभवतिशब्दः । न चैवं[5]विधः कदाचिदपि ध्वनेर्विषयः ।

यतः –

उक्त्यन्तरेणाशक्यं[6] यत्तच्चारुत्वं प्रकाशयन् ।
शब्दो व्यञ्जकतां बिभ्रद्ध्वन्युक्तेर्विषयी भवेत् ॥१५॥

अत्र चोदाहृते विषये नोक्त्य[7]न्तराशक्यचारुत्वव्यक्तिहेतुः शब्दः ।

किञ्च–

[8]रूढा ये विषयेऽन्यत्र शब्दाः स्वविषयादपि ।
लावण्याद्याः प्रयुक्तास्ते न भवन्ति पदं ध्वनेः ॥१६॥

तेषु चोपचरितश[9]ब्दवृत्तिरस्तीति । तथाविधे च विषये क्वचित्सम्भवन्नपि ध्वनिव्यवहारः प्रकारान्तरेण प्रवर्तते । न तथाविधशब्दमुखेन । अपिच–

मुख्यां वृत्तिं परित्यज्य गुणवृत्त्यार्थदर्शनम् ।
यदुद्दिश्य फलं तत्र शब्दो नैव स्खलद्गतिः ॥ १७ ॥

---

१. ‘ यथा ’–ग. २. ‘ च ’–ग. ३. ‘ अयं ’–ग. ४. ‘ इत्यादाविक्षुपदेऽनुभूतिशब्दः ’–क-ख; इत्यत्रेक्षुपदेऽनुभूतिशब्दः – घ. ५. ‘ कदाचिद्ध्वनेर्विषयः । यतः ’–क–ख; कदाचिदपि ध्वनेर्विषयोऽभिमतः ।–घ. ६. ‘ णाशङ्क्य ’–ख. ७. ‘ नोक्त्यन्तरेणाशक्यं ’ –क-ख. ८. निरूढा ’ – ग. ९. ‘ शब्दप्रवृत्ति ’–ग.

This is also an example :

Though it was but a mild blow
Which the husband ***gave*** *with a fresh creeper*
On the bosom of his youngest wife,
It became a smarting blow as it were
On the hearts of his other wives.

The following is still another example :

If that which ***suffers*** *pain for others' sake*
And remains sweet though broke in twain,
If that whose various deformities too
Are held to be ever pleasing,
Falls on a barren soil and fails to grow,
Is it the mistake of the sugar-cane,
And not at all of the worthless desert ?

In this last example, the word ***suffers*** is an instance of indication. Such instances can never be regarded as instances of suggestion. For—

Only that word, which conveys a charm incapable of communication by any other expression and which is pregnant with suggestive force, becomes a fit instance for the title " Suggestive ". 15

In the illustrative examples given above the word does not become a source of suggesting any charm uncommunicable by other expressions. Moreover —

Words which signify by common usage meanings other than what they primarily denote, as for instance the word lāvaṇya, do not become instances of Suggestion. 16

But in such words anyway, there is metaphorical application. Even if the title ' Suggestion ' should be possible of application towards them, it would be on the basis of an entirely different consideration. Words of the kind mentioned will have nothing to do with it.

If one gives up the primary denotative power of a word and understands a sense (secondarily conveyed by it) through its indicative power, it is because of a purpose. In conveying this purpose, the word does not move falteringly at all (as it moves falteringly when indicating a meaning secondarily). 17

तत्र[1] हि चारुत्वातिशयविशिष्टार्थप्रकाशनलक्षणे[2] प्रयोजने कर्तव्ये यदि शब्दस्यामुख्यता तदा तस्य प्रयोगे दुष्टतैव स्यात् । तस्मात् –

वाचकत्वाश्रयेणैव गुणवृत्तिर्व्यवस्थिता ।
व्यञ्जकत्वैकमूलस्य ध्वनेः स्याल्लक्षणं कथम् ॥ १८ ॥

तस्मादन्यो ध्वनिरन्या च गुणवृत्तिः ।

अव्याप्तिरप्यस्य[3] लक्षणस्य । न हि ध्वनिप्रभेदो विवक्षितान्यपरवाच्यलक्षणः, अन्ये च बहवः प्र[4]कारा भक्त्या व्याप्यन्ते; तस्माद्भक्तिरलक्षणम्[5] ।

कस्यचिद्ध्वनिभेदस्य सा तु स्यादुपलक्षणम् ।

सा पुनर्भक्तिर्वक्ष्यमाणप्रभेदमध्यादन्यतमस्य भेदस्य यदि नामोपलक्षणतया संभाव्येत[6], यदि च गुणवृत्त्यैव ध्वनिर्लक्ष्यत इत्युच्यते, तदभिधाव्यापारेण तदितरोऽलङ्कारवर्गः[7] समग्र एव लक्ष्यत[8] इति प्रत्येकमलङ्काराणां लक्षणकरणवैयर्थ्यप्रसङ्गः[9] । किं च –

लक्षणेऽन्यैः कृते चास्य पक्षसंसिद्धिरेव नः ॥ १९ ॥

कृतेऽपि वा पूर्वमेवान्यैर्ध्वनिलक्षणे पक्षसंसिद्धिरेव नः; यस्माद् ध्वनिरस्तीति नः[10] पक्षः । स च प्रागेव संसिद्ध इत्ययत्नसंपन्नसमीहितार्थाः संवृत्ताः[11] स्मः ।

---

१. 'अत्र'–ग. २. 'लक्षणाप्रयोजने'–ग. ३. 'अव्याप्तिरस्य'–घ. ४. 'तद्भेदप्रकारा वक्ष्यमाणा भक्त्या'–ग. ५. °रलक्षणा । KLV. ६. 'संभाव्येत' BP. ७. 'तदितरालंकार'–ग. ८. लक्ष्यति–घ. ९. 'लक्षणकरणे'–घ. १०. 'वादिनः'–क-ख. ११. 'संपन्नाः'–घ.

In order to justify secondary usage, one will have to posit a purpose, namely, the communication of a meaning imbued with great charm. If the word were to convey this purpose too in a secondary way only, then the very employment of the word would be fallacious. But it is not so in fact.

Therefore—

The fact is that indication is grounded on the primary denotative force of words. How can it ever be a definition of suggestion whose sole support is suggestivity ? 18

Hence suggestion is one thing and indication another.

The definition (that suggestion is indication) contains the fallacy of *Too Narrow* also. Indication does not cover instances of suggestion like 'that with intended but further-extending literal import' as also numerous other instances. Hence, indication cannot be a definition of suggestion.

(At the most), it might serve as a pointer to one of the species of suggestion. 19 (a)

One could only fancy that indication might serve, if at all, as a pointer to just a single species from among the numerous varieties of suggestion pointed out in the sequel. With all this, if one were to assort dogmatically that suggestion is indeed defined by indication, that way, one might say that the act of defining individual figures is an utter waste since the primary denotation of words defines the entire group of all individual figures. What is more—

If one were to say that the definition of suggestion has already been propounded by others, it would only substantiate our own position. 19 (b)

Even if it be true that the definition of suggestion has already been propounded by earlier writers, it would only mean a substantiation of our own position. For, our position is that suggestion exists; and in case it has been established already, we should consider ourselves to be extremely fortunate inasmuch as our object has already been realised without any labour at all on our part.

येऽपि सहृदयहृदयसंवेद्यमनाख्येयमेव ध्वनेरात्मानमाम्नासिषुस्तेऽपि न परीक्ष्यवादिनः। यत उक्तया नीत्या वक्ष्यमाणया च ध्वनेः सामान्यविशेषलक्षणे प्रतिपादितेऽपि यद्यनाख्येयत्वं तत्सर्वेषामेव वस्तूनां प्रसक्तम्[1]। यदि पुनर्ध्वनेरतिशयोक्त्यानया काव्यान्तरातिशायि[2] तैः स्वरूपमाख्यायते तत्तेऽपि युक्ताभिधायिन एव।

इति [3]श्रीराजानकानन्दवर्धनाचार्यविरचिते सहृदयालोके[4]
प्रथमोद्द्योतः[5] ॥

१. 'तत्प्रसक्तम्' BP. २. 'अतिशयितं स्वरूपं'-ग. ३. 'श्रीमदानन्द°'-क-ख. ४. सहृदयहृदयालोके-Nepal Ms. 'काव्यालोके'-क. 'सहृदयालोकनाम्नि काव्यालंकारे'-ग. No Ms. gives 'ध्वन्यालोके'. ५. 'संकेतः'-ख.

Even those, who assert that the nature of suggestion is within the experience of only the perceptive critics and that it is inexpressible, betray only their lack of discernment. (The reason is not far to seek). We have already propounded the general definition of suggestion; and definitions of its several varieties will be set forth hereafter. If inspite of all these, it should be thought of as "inexpressible", then this would be true of everything in the world. If, on the other hand, they are only giving expression to the all-surpassing nature of suggestion by means of this exaggeration, then they also might be regarded as but stating the truth itself.

द्वितीयोद्द्योतः

एवमविवक्षितवाच्यविवक्षितान्यपरवाच्यत्वेन[2] ध्वनिर्द्विप्रकारः प्रकाशितः। तत्राविवक्षितवाच्यस्य प्रभेदप्रतिपादनायेदमुच्यते —

अर्थान्तरे सङ्क्रमितमत्यन्तं वा तिरस्कृतम् ।
अविवक्षितवाच्यस्य ध्वनेर्वाच्यं द्विधा मतम् ॥ १ ॥

तथाविधाभ्यां[3] च ताभ्यां व्यङ्ग्यस्यैव विशेषः[4] । तत्रार्थान्तरसङ्क्रमितवाच्यो यथा —

स्निग्धश्यामलकान्तिलिप्तवियतो वेल्लद्बलाका घना
वाताः शीकरिणः पयोदसुहृदामानन्दकेकाः कलाः ।
कामं सन्तु दृढं कठोरहृदयो रामोऽस्मि सर्वं सहे
वैदेही तु कथं भविष्यति हहा हा देवि धीरा भव ॥

इत्यत्र[5] रामशब्दः । अनेन हि व्यङ्ग्यधर्मान्तरपरिणतः[6] संज्ञी प्रत्याय्यते, न संज्ञि[7]मात्रम् ।

यथा च ममैव विषमबाणलीलायाम् —

ताला जाअन्ति गुणा जाला दे सहिअएहिं घेप्पन्ति ।
रइकिरणाणुग्गहिआइँ होन्ति कमलाइँ कमलाइं ॥
[तदा जायन्ते गुणा यदा ते सहृदयैर्गृह्यन्ते ।
रविकिरणानुगृहीतानि भवन्ति कमलानि कमलानि ॥ छाया ।]

इत्यत्र द्वितीयः कमलशब्दः ।

---

१. 'अविवक्षितार्थ°'–क–ख. २. वाच्यत्वे–घ. ३. वाच्याभ्यां–क–ख. ४. 'विशेष इति व्यङ्ग्यप्रकाशनपरस्य ध्वनेरेवायं प्रकारः, तत्रार्थान्तर–घ' ५. 'इत्यत्रानेन रामशब्देन हि'–क–ख. ६. '°रूपपरिणतः'–घ. ७. 'संज्ञा°–घ. ८. 'अत्र'–घ.

THE SECOND FLASH

So far, two varieties of suggestion, viz., 'that with unintended literal import' and 'that with intended but further-extending literal import' have been mentioned. Now the sub-varieties of the first are set forth in what follows :—

'Merged in the other meaning' and 'Completely lost'—these are the two kinds of the expressed in 'Suggestion with intended literal import'. 1

The first, viz., 'Merged in the other meaning' is instanced in the following :—

The quarters all are painted deep
With the glistening black of clouds,
And the cranes in circles fly (with excitement);
The breezes are moisture-laden
And these friends of clouds, the peacocks,
Send their joyous notes in the wind.
Let them all confront me !
I shall bear them all, as I am Rāma
Whose heart is adamant to be sure;
But how will Sītā fare !
Alas ! Alas ! My dear queen !
Be bold, I beseech thee.

The word Rāma in this example carries the suggestive force mentioned. The word does not merely denote an individual with that proper name but conveys the sense of a person endowed with various qualities by the force of suggestion. An illustration is also found in my own work, *Viṣamabāṇalīlā* :—

Merits become merits indeed
When critics of culture hold them so.
Lotuses will be lotuses
Only when sunshine shelters them.

Here the word 'lotuses' repeated a second time is an instance in point.

अत्यन्ततिरस्कृतवाच्यो[1] यथादिकवेर्वाल्मीकेः —

रविसंक्रान्तसौभाग्यस्तुषारावृतमण्डलः ।
निःश्वासान्ध इवादर्शश्चन्द्रमा न प्रकाशते ॥ इति[2] ।

अत्रान्धशब्दः । यथा च[3]

गअणं च मत्तमेहं धारालुलिअज्जुणाइँ अ वणाइँ ।
णिरहङ्कारमिअङ्का हरन्ति णीलाओ[4] वि णिसाओ ॥
[गगनं च मत्तमेघं धारालुलितार्जुनानि च वनानि ।
निरहङ्कारमृगाङ्का हरन्ति नीला अपि निशाः ॥ छाया ।]

अत्र मत्तनिरहङ्कारशब्दौ ।

असंलक्ष्यक्रमोद्द्योतः क्रमेण द्योतितः परः ।
विवक्षिताभिधेयस्य ध्वनेरात्मा द्विधा मतः ॥२॥

मुख्यतया प्रकाशमानो व्यङ्ग्योऽर्थो ध्वनेरात्मा । स च वाच्यार्थापेक्षया कश्चिदलक्ष्यक्रमतया तुल्यं प्रकाशते, कश्चित्क्रमेणेति द्विधा मतः । तत्र

रसभावतदाभासतत्प्रशान्त्यादिरक्रमः[5] ।
ध्वनेरात्माङ्गिभावेन भासमानो व्यवस्थितः ॥ ३ ॥

रसादिरर्थो हि सहे[6]व वाच्येनावभासते । स चाङ्गित्वेनाव[7]भासमानो ध्वनेरात्मा ।

इदानीं रसवदलङ्काराद[8]लक्ष्यक्रमद्योतनात्मनो ध्वनेर्विभक्तो विषय इति प्रदर्श्यते[9] —

---

१. 'वाच्यार्थे ध्वनिर्यथा'–ग. २. 'इति'–क-ख पुस्तकयोर्नास्ति. ३. 'यथा च श्लोकः–गअणं च'–ग., तथा च omitted in BP. & घ. ४. 'लीलाइ वि'-क-ख. ५. °भासभावशान्त्यादि° – MB. ६. 'सहैव'-घ. ७. 'अव' क-ख पुस्तकयोर्नास्ति. ८. 'अलंकारादौ'–क ख. ९. 'दर्श्यते' – KLV.

We can cite the following verse of the First Poet, Vālmīki, to illustrate the second variety, viz., 'Suggestion with completely lost literal import':—

All the charm to the sun hath fled
And the orb is hid in snow;
Like a mirror by breath blinded,
The moon now does not glow.

Here the word '*blinded*' contains the said suggestion. So also the following verse:—

The sky with dizzy cloud,
The Arjun woods with rain-drops dripping loud,
And nights with moons not proud,
Though black in hue,
They capture you.

Here the words '*dizzy*' and '*not proud*' are full of suggestion.

The nature of suggestion 'with intended literal import' is also two-fold: (i) 'of discernible sequentiality' and (ii) 'of undiscernible sequentiality.' 2

The nature of suggestion is the implied sense which is communicated prominently. A variety of it is grasped simultaneously with the expressed, since the sequentiality existing between the two is not discernible. Another variety of the same comes about when the sequentiality is discernible. Of these two,

Sentiment, emotion, the semblance of sentiment or mood and their (rise and) cessation etc., are all of 'undiscerned sequentiality'. It is decided that when we have the prominent presence of this variety, we are having the very soul of suggestion. 3

Categories like sentiment shine forth along with the literal import. If they shine also with prominence we have the very soul of suggestion.

It will be shown in what follows that the sphere of this suggestion 'of undiscerned sequentiality' is quite distinct from that of the figure of speech called *Rasavadalaṅkāra* or Figurative Sentiment:—

वाच्यवाचकचारुत्वहेतूनां विविधात्मनाम् ।
रसादिपरता यत्र स ध्वनेर्विषयो मतः ॥ ४ ॥

रसभावतदाभासतत्प्रशमलक्षणं मुख्यमर्थमनुवर्तमाना यत्र शब्दार्था[1]-लङ्कारा गुणाश्च परस्परं ध्वन्यपेक्षया विभिन्नरूपा व्यवस्थितास्तत्र काव्ये ध्वनिरिति व्यपदेशः ।

प्रधाने[2]ऽन्यत्र वाक्यार्थे यत्राङ्गं तु रसादयः ।
काव्ये तस्मिन्नलङ्कारो रसादिरिति मे मतिः ॥ ५ ॥

यद्यपि रसवदलङ्कारस्यान्यैर्दर्शितो[3] विषयस्तथापि यस्मिन् काव्ये प्रधानतयान्योऽर्थो वाक्यार्थीभूतस्तस्य चाङ्गभूता ये[4] रसादयस्ते रसादेरलङ्कारस्य विषया[5] इति मामकीनः[6] पक्षः । तद्यथा चाटुषु प्रेयोऽलङ्कारस्य वाक्यार्थत्वेऽपि रसादयोऽङ्गभूता दृश्यन्ते ।

स च रसादिरलङ्कारः शुद्धः संकीर्णो वा । तत्राद्यो यथा

किं हास्येन न मे प्रयास्यसि पुनः प्राप्तश्चिराद्दर्शनं
केयं निष्करुण प्रवासरुचिता केनासि दूरीकृतः ।
स्वप्नान्तेष्विति ते[7] वदन् प्रियतमव्यासक्तकण्ठग्रहो
बुद्ध्वा रोदिति रिक्तबाहुवलयस्तारं रिपुस्त्रीजनः ॥

इत्यत्र करुणरसस्य शुद्ध[8]स्याङ्गभावात्स्पष्टमेव रसवदलङ्कारत्वम् ।

१. 'शब्दालंकारा अर्थालंकारा गुणाश्च'-क-ख; KLV. २. प्राधान्ये — No. 254 (BORI). ३. 'अन्यैः'-ग पुस्तके नास्ति. ४. 'ये' ग पुस्तके नास्ति. ५. 'विषय'-घ. ६. 'मामकः'-ग; MB, KLV. ७. 'वो'-क-ख. ८. 'शुद्धस्य'-ग-पुस्तके नास्ति.

Only that, wherein all the several beautifiers of the expressed sense and the expression exist with the single purpose of conveying sentiment and so on, is to be regarded as coming under the scope of suggestion. **4**

The poem in which the chief category is of the nature of sentiment, emotion, their semblance or cessation and wherein all figures, both of sound and sense, and qualities come in only as handmaids of the chief category and remain as much distinct from what is suggested as from one another, gets the designation of Suggestive Poetry.

But if in a poem the chief purport of the sentence should relate to something else, and if sentiment and so on should come in only as auxiliaries to it, it is my opinion that sentiment and so on are figures of speech in such a poem. **5**

Although others have explained the scope of Figurative Sentiment (in quite a different way), still it is my view that only such sentiments etc. as become auxiliaries to some other purport of the sentence which happens to be much more important are to be regarded as figures. For instance, one can easily see how in hymns of praise, sentiments etc., appear as auxiliaries though they are generally regarded as instances of the figure of Affectionate Praise.

The Figurative Sentiment according to our view may be either pure or mixed. The following is an illustration of the first kind :—

> ' *Why this jest ?*
> *Thou shalt not certainly part again from me,*
> *Having returned after so long.*
> *O ruthless one ! whence this flair for travel ?* —
> *Thus in dreams do the wives of your enemy speak*
> *Clasping fast the necks of their beloved lords;*
> *But soon they awake*
> *To find empty their embraces*
> *And to lament loud.*

In this example the pure sentiment of pathos is an auxiliary (to the praise of the king) and hence it is clearly Figurative Sentiment.

एवमेवंविधे विषये रसान्तराणां स्पष्ट एवाङ्गभावः। संकीर्णो[1] रसादिरङ्गभूतो यथा —

क्षिप्तो हस्तावलग्नः प्रसभमभिहतोऽ[2]प्या[3]ददानोंऽशुकान्तं
गृह्णन् केशेष्वपास्तश्चरणनिपतितो नेक्षितः सम्भ्रमेण ।
आलिङ्गन्योऽवधूतस्त्रिपुरयुवतिभिः साश्रुनेत्रोत्पलाभिः
कामीवार्द्रापराधः स दहतु दुरितं शाम्भवो वः शराग्निः ॥

इत्यत्र त्रिपुररिपुप्रभावातिशयस्य वाक्यार्थत्वे ईर्ष्याविप्रलम्भस्य श्लेषसहितस्याङ्गभाव इति, एवंविध एव र[4]सवदलङ्कारस्य न्याय्यो विषयः। अत एव चेर्ष्याविप्रलम्भकरुणयोरङ्गत्वेन व्यवस्थानात्[5]समावेशो न दोषः । यत्र हि रसस्य वाक्यार्थीभावस्तत्र कथमलङ्कारत्वम्? अलङ्कारो हि चा[6]रुत्वहेतुः प्रसिद्धः; न[7] त्वसावात्मैवात्मनश्चारुत्वहेतुः ।

तथा[8] चायमत्र संक्षेपः —

रसभावादितात्पर्यमाश्रित्य विनिवे[9]शनम् ।
अलङ्कृतीनां सर्वासामलङ्कारत्वसाधनम् ॥

तस्माद्यत्र रसादयो वाक्यार्थीभूताः स स[10]र्वः न रसादेरलङ्कारस्य वि[11]षयः; स ध्वनेः प्रभेदः, तस्योपमादयोऽलङ्काराः। यत्र तु[12] प्राधान्येना[13]र्थान्तरस्य

---

१. 'संकीर्णे' -क-ख. २. 'तश्चा' -ग. ३. 'आदधानो' -क-ख. ४. 'रसवदाद्यलंकारस्य' -घ., रसवदादेरलंकारस्य - KLV. ५. 'समावेशे' क-ख, MB. ६. 'चारुत्वे सिद्धिहेतुः' -क-ख. ७. 'न त्वात्मैवात्मनः । तथा' -क-ख, KLV. ८. 'तथायमत्र' -ग. ९. 'विनिवेशितम्' -क-ख. १०. 'सर्वे ते न'-घ., 'सर्वे— विषयाः'-क-ख-पुस्तकयोर्नास्ति. ११. वा विषयाः-घ. १२. 'तु'क-ख. पुस्तकयोर्नास्ति. १३. 'अर्थान्तरवाक्यार्थी°' क-ख.

The mixed variety of auxiliary sentiment is instanced in the following :—

> *Let the fire of Śiva's shaft burn down our sins; a shaft that conducted itself in the manner of a lover who has given offence afresh to his beloved :—Though shaken off by the wives of Tripura with fearful eye-lilies, it would cling fast to their hands; though forcibly pushed out, it would hold on to the ends of t' eir skirts; though violently thrust aside by the hair (of its feather), it would fall at their feet and yet remain unnoticed because of their agitation; and though pushed back, it would hug them verily.*

Here, the main purport of the sentence is the extraordinary glory of Śiva. The sentiment of love-in-separation due to jealousy is conveyed by *double entendre* and this is made auxiliary to it (i. e. praise of glory.) Only such instances are proper illustrations of Figurative Sentiment. Hence it is that though the sentiments of love-in-separation due to jealousy and of pathos are mutually opposed, since they have been both rendered auxiliary (to the main purport, their inclusion in the same place does not become a defect. But in instances where sentiment itself happens to be the main purport) how can it ever be a figure ? It is well known that a figure is (nothing but) an enhancer of charm. It is indeed impossible that a thing can become an enhancer of its own charm.

The following verse sums up the position :—

> *It is only the employment of figures, one and all, in view of the main purport of sentiment, emotion, etc., that really justifies their being regarded as sources of charm.*

Therefore, none of those cases where sentiment etc. happen to be the main purport, become instances of Figurative Sentiment. On the other hand they will only form a species of suggestion. Simile etc. are all enhancers of its charm alone. But in cases where the main purport happens to be some other meaning and

वाक्यार्थीभावे रसादिभिश्चारुत्वनिष्पत्तिः क्रियते, स रसादेरलङ्कारताया[1] विषयः ।

एवं ध्वनेरुपमादीनां रसवदलङ्कारस्य च विभक्त[2]विषयता भवति ।

यदि तु चेतनानां वाक्यार्थीभावो रसाद्यलङ्कारस्य विषय इत्यु[3]च्यते [4]तर्ह्युपमादीनां प्रविरलविषयता निर्विषयता वाभिहिता स्यात् । यस्मादचेतनवस्तुवृ[5]त्ते वाक्यार्थीभूते पुनश्चेतनवस्तुवृ[6]त्तान्तयोजनया यथाकथञ्चिद्भवितव्यम् । अथ सत्यामपि तस्यां यत्राचेतनानां वाक्यार्थीभावो नासौ रसवदलङ्कारस्य विषय इत्युच्यते । तन्महतः काव्यप्रबन्धस्य रसनिधानभूतस्य नीरसत्वमभिहितं स्यात् । यथा—

तरङ्गभ्रूभङ्गा क्षुभितविहगश्रेणि[7]रशना
विकर्षन्ती फेनं वसनमिव संरम्भशिथिलम् ।
यथाविद्धं याति स्खलितमभिसन्धाय बहुशो
[8]नदीरूपेणेयं ध्रुवमसहना सा परिणता ॥

यथा वा—

तन्वी मेघजलार्द्रपल्लवतया धौताधरेवाश्रुभिः
शून्येवाभरणैः स्वकालविरहाद्विश्रान्तपुष्पोद्गमा ।
चिन्तामौनमिवाश्रिता मधुकृतां शब्दैर्विना [9]लक्ष्यते
चण्डी मामवधूय पादपतितं जातानुतापेव सा ॥

---

१. 'अलंकारताविषयः'-क-ख. २. 'विविक्त'-ग. ३. 'इति'-ग पुस्तके नास्ति. ४. 'तदुपमा'-क-ख; KLV. ५. 'वृत्तान्ते'-क-ख. ६. 'वृत्तान्त'-क-ख पुस्तकयोर्नास्ति, ७. 'नयना'-क-ख. ८. 'नदीभावेनेयं'-क-ख. ९. 'दृश्यते'-ग.

when its beauty is enhanced by sentiment etc., we get proper instances of Figurative Sentiment.

Thus understood, the distinct spheres of suggestion, figures like simile and Figurative Sentiment become clearly demarcated.

If one were to assert that the treatment of sentient subjects alone serves to exemplify Figurative Sentiment, it would mean that figures like simile would either be left with very little scope or no scope at all. For even when the theme happens to be the behaviour of an insentient object, the behaviour of a sentient object also will in one way or another be superimposed upon it. Again, even when such a superimposition is present, one would have to say that it is not an instance of Figurative Sentiment in case the insentient ones alone form the main theme of description. And this would be tantamount to an assertion that the vast bulk of literature which happens to be really the golden treasury of sentiments is without any sentiment. Here is an example :

Frowning with its waves as with brows,
Girdled with the line of fluttering birds,
Throwing off its foam as a garment slipped in anger,
Hurrying in devious ways with far too tumbling steps
Surely, here is my jealous beloved,
*Changed into the form of the stream.**

This is another example :

There standest thou creeper,
All slender, thy poor sad leaves are moist with rain.
Thou silent, with no voice of honey-bees
Upon the drooping boughs; as from thy lord
The season separated, leaving off
Thy habit of bloom. Why I might think I saw
My passionate darling penitent
With tear-stained face and body unadorned
*Thinking in silence how she spurned my love.**

---

* *Translation Sri Aurobindo's.*

[1]यथा वा—

तेषां गोपवधूविलाससुहृदां राधारहःसाक्षिणां
क्षेमं भद्र कलिन्दशैलतनयातीरे लतावेश्मनाम् ।
[2]विच्छिन्ने स्मरतल्पकल्पनमृदुच्छेदोपयोगेऽधुना
ते जाने जरठीभवन्ति विगलन्नीलत्विषः पल्लवाः ॥

इत्येवमादौ विषयेऽचेतनानां वाक्यार्थीभावेऽपि [3]चेतनैवस्तुवृत्तान्तयोजनास्त्येव । [4]अथ यत्र चेतनवस्तुवृत्तान्तयोजनास्ति तत्र रसादिरलङ्कारः; तदेवं सत्युपमादयो निर्विषयाः प्रविरलविषया वा स्युः । यस्मान्नास्त्येवासावचेतनवस्तुवृत्तान्तो यत्र चेतनवस्तुवृत्तान्तयोजना नास्ति, अन्ततो [5]विभावत्वेन । [6]तस्मादङ्गत्वेन च रसादीनामलङ्कारता । यः पुनरङ्गी रसो भावो वा सर्वाकारमलङ्कार्यः स ध्वनेरात्मेति । किञ्च—

तमर्थमवलम्बन्ते येऽङ्गिनं ते गुणाः स्मृताः[7] ।
अङ्गाश्रितास्त्वलङ्कारा मन्तव्याः कटकादिवत् ॥ ६ ॥

ये तमर्थं रसादिलक्षणमाङ्गिनं सन्तमवलम्बन्ते ते गुणाः शौर्यादिवत् । वाच्यवाचकलक्षणान्यङ्गानि ये पुनराश्रितास्तेऽलङ्कारा मन्तव्याः कटकादिव[8]त् । [9]तथाच—

शृङ्गार [10]एवं मधुरः परः प्रह्लादनो रसः ।
तन्मयं[11] काव्यमाश्रित्य माधुर्यं प्रतितिष्ठति ॥ ७ ॥

१. 'यथा वा'-ग पुस्तके नास्ति. २. संत्यक्ते-MB. ३. 'सचेतन'-क-ख.
४. 'अत्र यत्र'-ग. ५. 'विभातत्वेन'-क-ख. ६. 'तस्मादङ्गत्वेन च'-ग पुस्तके नास्ति.
७. 'योऽङ्गिनं ते गुणाश्रिताः'-ग. ८. 'कुण्डलादिवादिति'-ग., KLV; 'कटकादिवादिति'-घ.
९. यथा च-क. १०. 'एको'-ग. ११. 'तद्रूपं'-ग.

Or, to take a still another example :

How do they do, those bower-huts, O friend,
On the bank of the river Jamunā ?
Those companions of the sports of cowherdesses
And those witnesses of Rādhā's amours ?
Now that none will pluck them soft
To turn them into beds of love,
I am afraid that all those fresh green leaves
Do lose their greenness and become old.

In these examples, though insentient objects happen to be themes of description, the attribution of sentient behaviour to them is quite obvious. Perhaps it might be argued that one may accept the presence of Figurative Sentiment in instances of this type wherein one finds attribution of sentient behaviour. At that rate, figures like simile will be left with no scope at all or, at the most, with very little scope. For, there is no such insentient theme at all in poetry in which the attribution of sentient behaviour is wholly absent; it will be found at least in the form of (a sentimental description of) the setting or situation. Hence, only sentiments that are secondary in importance should be regarded as figures. If one finds a sentiment or emotion with paramount importance, it will serve only as the object for beautification by other figures etc. and is of the very essence of suggestion. Furthermore—

Those which inhere in this principal element are regarded as qualities. And figures are to be known as those that are associated with its parts even like ornaments such as the bracelet. 6

Those that ever inhere in the principal element (of poetry) viz. sentiment etc., are qualities like the quality of valour and so forth (in the world). On the other hand, those that relate to its component parts only, viz., the expressed sense and the expression, are to be regarded as figures or ornaments like the bracelet and so on (in the world). So also—

The Erotic indeed, is the sweetest and the most delectable of all sentiments. The quality of sweetness is grounded securely on poetry which is full of this sentiment. 7

शृङ्गार एव रसान्तरापेक्षया मधुरः प्रह्लादहेतुत्वात् । तत्प्रकाशनपर-शब्दार्थतयां[1] काव्यस्य स माधुर्यलक्षणो गुणः । श्रव्यत्वं[2] पुनरोजसोऽपि साधारणमिति ।

शृङ्गारे विप्रलम्भाख्ये करुणे च प्रकर्षवत् ।
माधुर्यमार्द्रतां याति यतस्तत्राधिकं मनः[3] ॥ ८ ॥

विप्रलम्भशृङ्गारकरुणयोस्तु माधुर्यमेव प्रकर्षवत् । सहृदयहृदया-वर्जनातिशयनिमित्तत्वादिति[4] ।

रौद्रादयो रसा दीप्त्यां लक्ष्यन्ते काव्यवर्तिनः ।
तद्व्यक्तिहेतू शब्दार्थावाश्रित्यौजो व्यवस्थितम् ॥ ९ ॥

रौद्रादयो हि रसाः परां दीप्तिमुज्ज्वलतां जनयन्तीति लक्षणया त एवं[6] दीप्तिरित्युच्यन्ते[7] । तत्प्रकाशनपरः शब्दो दीर्घसमासरचनालङ्कृतं वाक्यम् । यथा—

चञ्चद्भुजभ्रमितचण्डगदाभिघात-
संचूर्णितोरुयुगलस्य सुयोधनस्य ।
स्त्यानावबद्धघनशोणितशोणपाणि-
रुत्तंसयिष्यति कचांस्तव देवि भीमः ॥

तत्प्रकाशनपरश्चार्थो[8]ऽनपेक्षितदीर्घसमासरचनः प्रसन्नवाचकाभिधेयः । यथा—

---

१. 'प्रह्लादहेतुत्वात्प्रकाशनपरः । शब्दार्थयोः '-च. २. 'श्राव्यत्वं '-ग. ३. 'मतः'-ग. ४. 'इति-'ग. पुस्तके नास्ति. ५. 'दीप्ता'-क-ख. ६. 'लक्षणया त एव '-क-ख-पुस्तकयोर्नास्ति. ७. °त्युच्यते-BP, घ. °त्युच्यन्ते is acc. to MB. ८. 'तत्प्रकाशितश्चार्थो '-क-ख.

The Erotic shines indeed as sweeter and more delectable than every other sentiment. 'Sweetness' is a quality which relates to word and meaning of compositions (imbued with this sentiment) and not to mere sound–harmony. For, sound–harmony is found alike in forcefulness too (and is not a differentia of sweetness).

In sentiments viz., Love-in-separation and the Pathetic, sweetness will be uppermost. It is so because the mind is moved very much in such instances. 8

The quality of sweetness alone is uppermost in the sentiments of Love–in–separation and the Pathetic as it causes great delectation in the minds of refined critics.

Sentiments like the Furious are characterised by great exciting power in poetry. The quality of forcefulness is that which inheres in sound and sense which produce this effect. 9

Indeed sentiments like the Furious produce excessive excitement (in the readers). Hence, by secondary usage, one might refer to the sentiments themselves by the term 'excitement'. The sound which produces this effect is none other than a sentence adorned by lengthy compound constructions. As for instance :

cañcad-bhuja-bhramita-caṇḍa-gadābhighāta-
saṁcūrṇitoru-yugalasya suyodhanasya ।
styānāvabaddha-ghana-śoṇita-śoṇa-pāṇi-
ruttaṁsayiṣyati kacāṁstava devi bhīmaḥ ॥
(O Queen ! this Bhīma shall himself bind
Your scattered curls with his hands
Reddened by the profuse and coagulated puddles
Of Suyodhana's blood as he lies low
With thighs pulverised by hard blows
From this terrible mace
Swung by these redoubtable arms of mine.)

The sense which produces this effect of forcefulness does not stand in need of lengthy compound constructions; it may contain simple constructions only. As for instance :—

योयः शस्त्रं बिभर्ति स्वभुजगुरुमदः पाण्डवीनां चमूनां
यो यः पाञ्चालगोत्रे शिशुरधिकवया गर्भशय्यां गतो वा ।
यो यस्तत्कर्मसाक्षी चरति[1] मयि रणे यश्च यश्च प्रतीपः
क्रोधान्धस्तस्य तस्य स्वयमपि जगतामन्तकस्यान्तकोऽहम् ॥

°इत्यादौ तयो[2]रोजस्त्वम् ।

समर्पकत्वं काव्यस्य यत्तु सर्वरसान् प्रति ।
स प्रसादो गुणो ज्ञेयः सर्वसाधारणक्रियः ॥ १० ॥

प्रसादस्तु स्वच्छता शब्दार्थयोः[3] । स च सर्वरससाधारणो गुणः सर्वरचनासाधारणश्च[4] व्यङ्ग्यार्थापेक्षयैव मुख्यतया[5] व्यवस्थितो मन्तव्यः ।

श्रुतिदुष्टादयो दोषा अनित्या ये च दर्शिताः ।
ध्वन्यात्मन्येव शृङ्गारे ते हेया इत्युदाहृताः ॥ ११ ॥

अनित्यदोषाश्च ये श्रुतिदुष्टादयः सूचितास्तेऽपि न वाच्ये अर्थमात्रे[6], न च व्यङ्ग्ये शृङ्गारव्यतिरेकिणि शृङ्गारे[7] वा ध्वनेरनात्मभूते[8] । किं तर्हि[9] ? ध्वन्यात्मन्येव शृङ्गारेऽङ्गितया व्यङ्ग्ये ते[10] हेया इत्युदाहृताः । अन्यथा[11] हि तेषामनित्यदोषतैव[12] न स्यात् ।

---

१. 'चलति'-क-ख. २. द्वयोः-BP. ३. 'शब्दार्थयोरिति'-क-ख. ४. 'साधारणश्चेति'-घ. ५. 'मुख्यतया द्रष्टव्यः'-ग, MB. ६. 'तेऽपि वाच्येऽर्थमात्रे'-क-ख; तेऽपि न वाच्यार्थमात्रे-घ. ७. 'शृङ्गारे'-घ पुस्तके 'व्यङ्ग्ये' शब्दस्य अनन्तरमस्ति । also in MB. ८. ध्वनेरनात्मभावे-घ. ९. ध्वन्यात्मभूते किं तर्हि'-क-ख. १०. 'ये ते'-क-ख. ११. 'तथाहि'-ग. १२. '°नित्यत्वदोषमेव'–क-ख. °नित्यदोषत्वमेव-MB.

yo yaḥ śastraṁ bibharti svabhujagurumadaḥ pāṇḍavīnāṁ
camūnāṁ
yo yaḥ pāñcālagotre śiśuradhikavayā garbhaśayyāṁ gato vā
yo yastatkarmasākṣī carati mayi raṇe yaśca yaśca pratīpaḥ
krodhāndhastasya tasya svayamapi jagatāmanta-
kasyāntako'haṁ

(*Whosoever with over weening pride of his strong arms*
Bears weapons in Pāṇḍavas' battalions,
Whosoever is sprung from Pāñcāla clan—
Whether child, grown-up or embryo,
Whosoever has been a silent witness of that ghastly deed
And whosoever will cross my way as I move in the
battle-field,
I, in my blinding rage, shall prove a Destroyer
Of each one of them and of even Yama himself !)

Thus sound and sense can both become imbued with forcefulness.

That quality in poetry by which poetry throws itself open to the entry of all sentiments may be taken as perspicuity. Its applicability is universal. 10

Perspicuity is just the lucidity in sound as well as in sense. It is a quality common to all sentiments and all kinds of composition. Hence this quality should be understood as primarily relating to the suggested sense only.

Defects like ' indelicacy ' which have been shown to be impermanent (by the ancient writers) have been in fact illustrated as blemishes only with reference to the erotic sentiment when its nature is suggestion. 11

Impermanent defects like ' indelicacy ' which have been mentioned by earlier writers do not become defects at all when they are found in instances of expressed sense only; or even in instances of suggested erotic sentiment, if the suggested sentiment is also not of the utmost importance therein, or in instances of sentiments other than the erotic. That the defects are to be avoided as such only when the erotic happens to be principally suggested, becomes clear by the illustrations given (by the ancient writers themselves). If this were not so, they would not at all be impermanent defects.

एवमयम[1]संलक्ष्यक्रमोद्द्योतो[2] ध्वनेरात्मा प्रदर्शितः सामान्येन ।

तस्याङ्गानां प्रभेदा ये प्रभेदाः स्वगताश्च ये ।
तेषामानन्त्यमन्योन्यसम्बन्धपरिकल्पने ॥ १२ ॥

अङ्गितया व्यङ्ग्यो रसादिर्विवक्षितान्यपरवाच्यस्य ध्वनेरेक आत्मा य उक्तस्तस्याङ्गानां वाच्यवाचकानुपातिनामलङ्काराणां ये प्रभेदा निरवधयः[3], ये च स्वगतास्तस्याङ्गिनोऽर्थस्य रसभावतदाभासतत्प्रशमलक्षणा विभावानुभावव्यभिचारिप्रतिपादनसहिता अनन्ताः स्वाश्रयापेक्षया निःसीमानो विशेषास्तेषामन्योन्यसम्बन्धपरिकल्पने क्रियमाणे कस्यचिदन्यतमस्यापि रसस्य प्रकाराः परिसङ्ख्यातुं न शक्यन्ते किमुत सर्वेषाम् । तथा हि शृङ्गारस्याङ्गिनस्तावदाद्यौ[4] द्वौ[5] भेदौ— सम्भोगो विप्रलम्भश्च । सम्भोगस्य च परस्परप्रेमदर्शनसुरतविहरणादि[6]लक्षणाः प्रकाराः[7] । विप्रलम्भस्याप्यभिलाषेर्ष्याविरहप्रवासविप्रलम्भादयः । तेषां च प्रत्येकं[8] विभावानुभावव्यभिचारिभेदाः[9] । तेषां च देशकालाद्याश्रया[10]वस्थाभेद इति स्वगतभेदापेक्षयैकस्य[11] तस्यापरिमेयत्वम्, किं पुनरङ्गप्रभेदकल्पनायाम्[12] । ते ह्यङ्गप्रभेदाः प्रत्येकमङ्गिप्रभेदसम्बन्धपरिकल्पने क्रियमाणे सत्यानन्त्यमेवोपयान्ति ।

---

१. 'अयं' क-ख पुस्तकयोर्नास्ति. २. 'क्रमद्योतो' क-ख; क्रमोद्योत्य-घ. ३. 'निरवयवा'-ग. ४. 'शृङ्गारस्य तावदाद्यौ' –ग; 'शृङ्गारस्यैवाङ्गिनस्तावदाद्यौ-घ. KLV. ५. 'द्वौ'–क-ख पुस्तकयोर्नास्ति. ६. 'विरहणादि'-ग. ७. 'प्रकारा लक्षणाः' क-ख. ८. प्रत्येक–ग पुस्तके नास्ति ९. 'भेदः'-BP. १०. 'कालाश्रया-क-ख. ११. 'भेद इति स्वगतापेक्षयैतस्य' ग; भेदा इति स्वगतभेदापेक्षयैव तस्य'-घ, KLV. १२. 'कल्पनया'-घ., KLV.

So far we have explained in general terms the nature of 'suggestion of undiscerned sequentiality'.

The sub-divisions of its parts and its own sub-divisions become endless indeed if one were to take into account their mutual permutations also. 12

It has been pointed out that the soul of suggestion with intended but further-extending literal import, is such sentiment etc. as is principally suggested. The external parts of this suggestion are the figures which relate to sound and sense. Now if the endless sub-divisions of these figures and the divisions of its intrinsic soul, viz., sentiment, abiding emotion, the semblance and cessation of these — which once again become endless by contact with different stimuli of setting, responses, and passing moods — and all the mutual relationships possible between each other amongst them be added up and reckoned, it would be clear that the entire varieties of even a single sentiment will baffle all counting, not to mention the impossibility of counting all varieties of all the sentiments. We may thus take the instance of the erotic sentiment which happens to be principally suggested in a work. First of all, it falls under a two-fold division :— (i) love-in-union and (ii) love-in-separation. Love-in-union can be further divided into (i) exchange of love-glances, (ii) dalliance, (iii) honeymoon and so forth. So also love-in-separation embraces such classes as (i) desire, (ii) jealousy, (iii) separation, (iv) journey and so forth. Every one of these classes will get different associations of stimuli of setting, emotional responses, passing moods and so on. These subclasses too become still more different by differences of circumstance such as place and time. Thus it will be impossible to count exhaustively all the varieties and sub-varieties of a single sentiment itself. What need we say then of counting exhaustively all varieties of suggestion when we take into account the different varieties of its external parts also ? And if we should set about considering the permutations and combinations of each of the varieties of the external parts with each of the varieties of intrinsic sentiments too, there can be no doubt at all that their number will be limitless.

दिङ्मात्रं तूच्यते येन व्युत्पन्नानां सचेतसाम् ।[1]
बुद्धिरासादितालोका सर्वत्रैव भविष्यति ॥ १३ ॥

दिङ्मात्रकथनेन[2] हि व्युत्पन्नानां सहृदयानामेकत्रापि रसभेदे[3] सहालङ्कारैरङ्गाङ्गिभावपरिज्ञानादासादितालोका बुद्धिः सर्वत्रैव भविष्यति । तत्र—

शृङ्गारस्याङ्गिनो यत्नादेकरूपानुबन्धनात्[4] ।
सर्वेष्वेव प्रभेदेषु नानुप्रासः प्रकाशकः ॥ १४ ॥

अङ्गिनो हि शृङ्गारस्य ये उक्ताः प्रभेदास्तेषु सर्वेष्वेक[5]प्रकारानुबन्धितया प्रबन्धेन प्रवृत्तोऽनुप्रासो[6] न व्यञ्जकः । अङ्गिन[7] इत्यनेनाङ्गभूतस्य शृङ्गारस्यैकरूपानुबन्ध्यनुप्रासनिबन्धने कामचारमाह ।

ध्वन्यात्मभूते शृङ्गारे यमकादिनिबन्धनम् ।
शक्तावपि प्रमादित्वं विप्रलम्भे विशेषतः ॥ १५ ॥

ध्वनेरात्मभूतः[8] शृङ्गारस्तात्पर्येण वाच्यवाचकाभ्यां प्रकाश्यमानस्तस्मिन्यमकादीनां यमकप्रकाराणां निबन्धनं दुष्करशब्द[9]भङ्गश्लेषादीनां शक्तावपि प्रमादित्वम् । 'प्रमादित्व'मित्यनेनैतद्दर्श्यते[10] – काकतालीयेन कदाचित्कस्यचिदे[11]कस्य यमकादेर्निष्पत्तावपि भूम्नालङ्कारान्तरवद्रसाङ्गत्वेन

---

१. There is a lacuna from here up to तत् स्थितमेव under Kārikā 26 in No. 254 of BORI. २. 'कल्पनेन '-ग. ३. 'रसभेदेऽङ्गाङ्गिभाव '-ग; रसभेदे कर्तव्येऽलंकारेऽङ्गाङ्गिभाव '-घ. रसप्रभेदे-KLV. ४. 'बन्धवान् '-BP. ५. सर्वेष्वेव प्रभेदेष्वेक '-क-ख. ६. 'प्रवृत्तानुप्रासो '-ग. ७. अङ्गिरूपस्य शृङ्गारस्य '-क-ख. ८. 'ध्वनेरात्मभूतः '-गपुस्तके नास्ति. ९. 'दुष्टम् । शब्द '–ग. १०. 'दृश्यते '-ग. ११. 'कस्यचित् '-गपुस्तके नास्ति.

Hence their broad indication only will be given here. But it should be enough to educate refined critics. Their minds will have received the light which would enable them to guess aright everywhere. 13

Refined critics can indeed be educated even by a mere indication of the direction. If their mind has been illumined in such a way that it can correctly discriminate between what is extrinsic and what is intrinsic when they are to employ figures to beautify any single sentiment, the mind will certainly be able to judge properly in every other instance too. The point is this :—

In none of the varieties of the principal erotic sentiment does alliteration become a source of suggestion since it involves great effort at achieving similarity. 14

In none of the varieties mentioned above of the principal erotic sentiment does alliteration become a partaker of suggestion, because it will proceed with the exclusive purpose of achieving similarity (in sound). The employment of the adjective 'principal' in the text serves to point out that when the erotic sentiment is only secondary in importance, the use of such alliterations abounding in similarity of sounds is left to the option of the writer.

Even if the poet should be an expert in the use of figures like assonance, his employment of them in the erotic sentiment which is of the nature of suggestion, and particularly in that of love-in-separation, would amount only to a lapse on his part. 15

In instances where we find the erotic sentiment as of the nature of suggestion, i. e. as that which is principally suggested by both sound and sense, it would be a lapse indeed on the part of a poet if he were to employ various kinds of assonance and difficult verbal puns involving the splitting of words in different ways, however skilful he might be in devising these. The following is the point made out by the expression "would indicate only a lapse on his part" : Though assonance etc. can be used once or twice in an accidental way, they should not be pressed into the

निबन्धो न कर्तव्य इति। 'विप्रलम्भे विशेषत' इत्यनेन विप्रलम्भे[1] सौकुमार्यातिशयः ख्याप्यते[2]। तस्मिन्द्योत्ये यमकादेरङ्गस्य[3] निबन्धो नियमान्न कर्तव्य इति[4]।

अत्र[5] युक्तिरभिधीयते—

रसाक्षिप्ततया यस्य बन्धः शक्यक्रियो भवेत्।
अपृथग्यत्ननिर्वर्त्यः सोऽलङ्कारो ध्वनौ मतः॥ १६॥

निष्पत्तावाश्चर्यभूतोऽपि[6] यस्यालङ्कारस्य रसाक्षिप्ततयैव[7] बन्धः शक्यक्रियो भवेत्सोऽस्मिन्नलक्ष्यक्रमव्यङ्ग्ये ध्वनावलङ्कारो मतः। तस्यैव रसाङ्गत्वं मुख्यमित्यर्थः। यथा—

कपोले पत्राली करतलनिरोधेन मृदिता
निपीतो निःश्वासैरयममृतहृद्योऽधररसः।
मुहुः कण्ठे लग्नस्तरलयति बाष्पः स्तनतटीं[8]
प्रियो मन्युर्जातस्तव निरनुरोधे न तु वयम्॥

रसाङ्गत्वे[9] च तस्य लक्षणमपृथग्यत्ननिर्वर्त्यत्वमिति[10] यो[11] रसं बन्धुमध्यवसितस्य[12] कवेरलङ्कारस्तां[13] वासनामत्यूह्य यत्नान्तरमास्थितस्य निष्पद्यते स[14] न रसाङ्गमिति। यमके च प्रबन्धेन बुद्धिपूर्वकं[15] क्रियमाणे नियमेनैव यत्नान्तरपरिग्रह आपतति शब्दविशेषान्वेषणरूपः। अलङ्कारान्तरेष्वपि तत्तुल्यमिति चेत्, नैवम्। अलङ्कारान्तराणि हि निरूप्यमाणदुर्घटनान्यपि रससमाहितचेतसः प्रतिभानवतः कवेरहम्पूर्विकया परापतन्ति। यथा कादम्बर्यां कादम्बरीदर्शनावसरे; यथा च मायारामशिरोदर्शनेन[16] विह्वलायां[17] सीतादेव्यां सेतौ[18]। युक्तं

१. 'विप्रलम्भशृङ्गारे'-ग. विप्रलम्भशृङ्गारस्य-MB. २. 'ख्याप्यते प्रकाश्यते'-ग. ३. 'यमकस्याङ्गभूतस्य'-ग. ४. 'इति'-क-ख पुस्तकयोर्नास्ति. ५. 'तत्र'-क. ६. 'अपि'-ग पुस्तके नास्ति. ७. 'साक्षितया'-ख. ८. 'तटम्'-घ. ९. 'रसाअनत्वे'-क-ख. १०. 'लक्षणमक्षुण्णमपृथग्यत्नं निर्वर्त्यत इति'-घ. अक्षुण्ण–ग पुस्तके नास्ति. °निर्वर्त्यमिति – MB. ११. यो-घ पुस्तके नास्ति. १२. 'रससंबन्धमध्य'-ग. १३. 'कवयोऽलंकारः'-क-ख. १४. 'स'-घ पुस्तके नास्ति. १५. 'बुद्धिपूर्वके'-क-ख. १६. 'रामाद्रि'-घ; 'राम' क-ख पुस्तकयोर्नास्ति. १७. 'दर्शनविह्वलायां'-घ. १८. 'इति.' क-ख. सेतौ सेतुबन्धकाव्य इत्यर्थः. -marginalia.

service of sentiments quite in the same profusion as one might turn the other figures of speech to such use. The expression, "particularly in that of love-in-separation", explains the excessive tenderness of that sentiment and when it is to be delineated, assonance etc. should never be employed as a rule.

The reason for this is given below :—

> **Only that is admitted as a figure of suggestive poetry whose employment is rendered possible just by the emotional suffusion of the poet and which does not require any other extra effort on his part. 16**

Though in the result it might appear very amazing, that figure, whose employment is due only to the poet's over-mastering emotion, is regarded as a figure of 'suggestive poetry of undiscerned sequentiality'. The idea is that it alone serves as the best vehicle of sentiment.

For example :—

The paintings on the cheeks are faded
By the pressure from the palm of your hand;
This juice of lips, so sweet as nectar
Is quaffed by your sighs;
The tear that clasps the neck so often
Has made the edge of your bosom throb
O hard-hearted one !
Anger has become your darling, *not I.*

The figure which can be a promoter of sentiment usually bodies itself forth in all its completeness without any extra effort on the part of the poet. Hence if one were to find that the figure indicates an extra effort of the poet in its employment rather than his concentration in the sole delineation of sentiment, though this latter alone is his avowed object, one can conclude that it cannot serve as a promoter of sentiment. In the pertinacious and deliberate employment of assonance on a poet's part, one can see invariably his extra effort in the choice of select words. If one were to state that this fact is equally applicable to other figures too, it would be wrong. The other figures will come (spontaneously) swarming at the beck and call of a poet concentrated upon sentiment and gifted with (a rich) imagination and will compete with one another for

चैतत्, यतो रसा वाच्यविशेषैरेवाक्षेप्तव्याः । तत्प्रतिपादकैश्च शब्दैस्तत्प्रकाशिनो वाच्यविशेषा एव रूपकादयोऽलङ्काराः । तस्मान्न तेषां बहिरङ्गत्वं[1] रसाभिव्यक्तौ; यमकदुष्करमार्गेषु तु तत्[2]स्थितमेव[3] । यत्तु रसवन्ति कानिचिद्य[4]मकादीनि दृश्यन्ते, तत्र रसादीनां[5]मङ्गता; यमकादीनां त्वङ्गितैव । रसाभासे[6] चाङ्गत्वमप्यविरुद्धम् । अङ्गितया तु व्यङ्ग्ये[7] रसे नाङ्गत्वं, पृथक्प्रयत्ननिर्वर्त्यत्वाद्यमकादेः । अस्यैवार्थस्य सङ्ग्रहश्लोकाः —

रसवन्ति हि वस्तूनि सालङ्काराणि कानिचित् ।
एकेनैव प्रयत्नेन निर्वर्त्यन्ते[8] महाकवेः ॥
यमकादिनिबन्धे तु पृथग्यत्नोऽस्य जायते ।
शक्तस्यापि रसेऽङ्गत्वं तस्मादेषां न विद्यते[9] ॥
रसाभासाङ्गभावस्तु यमकादेर्न वार्यते ।
ध्वन्यात्मभूते शृङ्गारे त्वङ्गता[10] नोपपद्यते ॥

इदानीं ध्वन्यात्मभूतस्य शृङ्गारस्य[11] व्यञ्जकोऽलङ्कारवर्ग आख्यायते --

ध्वन्यात्मभूते शृङ्गारे समीक्ष्य विनिवेशितः ।
रूपकादिरलङ्कारवर्ग एति यथार्थताम् ॥ १७ ॥

---

१. 'तस्मात्तेषां किं न बाहि°'–ग. २. 'तत्' -ग पुस्तके नास्ति. ३. 'एव बहिरङ्गत्वम्' -क-ख. ४. 'कानिचिद्वस्तूनि यम°' -क-ख. ५. 'रसानां'–क-ख. ६. 'रसाभावे'-क-ख. ७. 'व्यङ्ग्येन' -क-ख. 'आङ्गिना तु व्यङ्ग्ये'-घ. ८. 'निवर्तन्ते'-क-ख. ९. 'जायते'–. No. 254 (BORI). १०. 'ह्यङ्गता'–क–ख. ११. 'शृङ्गारस्य'– घ पुस्तके नास्ति.

their first preference at his hands, though outwardly they might appear to involve great labour on his part. We may cite as instances the description in *Kādambarī* of the moment of Kādambarī's sight (by the hero) and the description of the vexed Sītā at the sight of the severed head of Māyā-Rāma in the poem *Setubandha.* Indeed it is quite natural this should be so. For, sentiments have to be conveyed only by way of particular primary senses. And figures like metaphor are just the kind of primary senses that serve to convey sentiments by means of their own expressive words. Hence they are never extraneous to the delineation of sentiment. But a *tour de force* such as a complicated assonance can never be anything but an extraneous element to it. Even in stray instances of assonance which show a touch of sentiment etc., the sentiment should be regarded only as subsidiary, and it is the assonance alone which is primary in importance. But so far as suggested sentiment is concerned, these intricate rhymes can never become its vehicles since they invariably acquire supreme prominence for themselves by reason of the extra effort necessitated in their employment.

This idea is summed up in the following words:—

1. *Most emotional themes are adorned with figures also by a single effort of the first-rate poet.*

2. *However proficient a poet might be in the employment of figures, extra effort on his part will be called forth in devising assonance etc. Hence intricate rhymes cannot serve as vehicles of sentiments.*

3. *This does not, however, prevent assonance etc. from being made vehicles of semblance of sentiment. But in the erotic sentiment, which is of the nature of suggestion, they cannot be regarded as accessories.*

The group of figures that enters into the suggestion of the erotic sentiment, intrinsic to *dhvani* will be set forth below:—

The galaxy of figures like metaphor becomes truely significant (i. e. will be real ornaments) when they are employed with great discrimination in instances of the Erotic Sentiment which is intrinsic to dhvani. **17**

अलङ्कारो हि बाह्यालङ्कार[1]साम्यादङ्गिनश्चारुत्वहेतुरुच्यते । वाच्यालङ्कारवर्गश्च रूपकादिर्यावानुक्तो वक्ष्यते च[2] कैश्चित् अलङ्काराणामनन्तत्वात्स[3] सर्वोऽपि[4] यदि समीक्ष्य विनिवेश्यते तदलक्ष्यक्रमव्यङ्ग्यस्य ध्वनेरङ्गिनः सर्व[5]स्यैव चारुत्वहेतुर्निष्पद्यते ।

एषा[6] चास्य विनिवेशने समीक्षा[7] —

विवक्षा तत्परत्वेन नाङ्गित्वेन कदाचन[8] ।
काले च ग्रहणत्यागौ नातिनिर्वहणैषिता ॥ १८ ॥
निर्व्यूढावपि चाङ्गत्वे यत्नेन प्रत्यवेक्षणम् ।
रूपकादेरलङ्कारवर्गस्याङ्गत्वसाधनम् ॥ १९ ॥

रसबन्धेष्वत्यादृतमनाः[9][10] कविर्यमलङ्कारं तदङ्गतया विवक्षति ।

यथा—

चलापाङ्गां दृष्टिं स्पृशसि बहुशो वेपथुमतीं
रहस्याख्यायीव स्वनसि मृदु कर्णान्तिकचरः ।
करौ[11] व्याधु[12]न्वत्याः पिबसि रतिसर्वस्वमधरं
वयं तत्त्वान्वेषान्मधुकर हतास्त्वं खलु कृती ॥

अत्र हि भ्रमरस्वभावोक्तिरलङ्कारो रसानुगुणः ।

'नाङ्गित्वेने' ति[13] [14]न प्राधान्येन । कदाचिद्र[15]सादितात्पर्येण विवक्षितोऽपि ह्यलङ्कारः कश्चिदङ्गित्वेन[16] विवक्षितो दृश्यते ।

---

१. 'बाह्यालंकारस्याङ्गिनश्च'–क-ख. २. 'वा'–ग. ३. 'स.'– घ पुस्तके नास्ति. ४. अपि–क-ख पुस्तकयोर्नास्ति. ५. 'सर्व एव'–घ. ६. 'या चास्य'-क. 'यस्य चास्य'–ख. ७. 'समीक्षा सा चास्य प्रकाश्यते'–क-ख–MB. ८. 'कथंचन'–घ. ९. 'रसबन्धे ध्वन्यध्वन्यादृत'–ग. १०. 'गनः'–क-ख. ११. 'करं'-घ. १२. 'व्याधुन्वन्त्याः'–घ. १३. 'इति'–क-ख पुस्तकयोर्नास्ति. १४. 'न'–घ पुस्तके नास्ति. १५. 'केनाचित्'–क-ख. १६. 'अङ्गित्वेन दृष्टः'–क-ख.

An *alaṅkāra* (lit. 'ornament') or figure is regarded as a beautifier of the principal element in poetry in the same way as an external ornament is regarded as a cause of beauty in one's whole personality. The principal element of poetry in 'suggestion with undiscerned sequentiality' and all the figures of speech defined by the ancients such as metaphor—and even the figures yet to be defined, since the number of figures is legion—will serve as promoters of its beauty if they are employed with proper discrimination.

The following is the nature of discrimination to be exercised by the poet in the employment of figures :—

The sole consideration that it is only a means to the delineation of sentiment and never an end in itself, the necessity of employing it at the right time and of abandoning it at the right time; the absence of over-enthusiasm on the poet's part in pressing it too far, and finally, his keen watchfulness in making sure that it remains a secondary element only—these are the various means by which figures like metaphor become accessories (of suggested sentiment). **18 & 19**

Here is an example of the utilisation of a figure of speech as an accessory to sentiment by a poet who is bent upon delineating sentiments only:—

'Her moving corner'd eye
Trembling as in pain, thou touchest oft and oft;
Like secret-whisperer,
Tenderly thou hummest, flitting by her ear;
She waving both her hands,
Thou doest drink her lip, be-all of pleasure soft;
We, searching for the truth,
Are undone, O drone ! thou, yea, art lucky here !'[1]

The realistic description of the bee's behaviour in the above verse is in keeping with the sentiment. "Consideration that it is never an end in itself" implies that though a figure may be utilised as an accessory to sentiment in an instance, it should not at the same time be also intended as pre-eminent.

---

1. Roby Datta's translation.

यथा–

चक्राभिघातप्रसभाज्ञयैव चकार यो राहुवधूजनस्य ।
आलिङ्गनोद्दामविलासवन्ध्यं[1] रतोत्सवं चुम्बनमात्रशेषम् ॥

अत्र हि पर्यायोक्तस्याङ्गित्वेन विवक्षा रसादितात्पर्ये सत्यपीति । अङ्गत्वेन[2] विवक्षितमपि यमवसरे[3] गृह्णाति नानवसरे ।

अवसरे गृहीतिर्यथा—

उद्दामोत्कलिकां विपाण्डुररुचं प्रारब्धजृम्भां क्षणा-
दायासं श्वसनोद्गमैरविरलैरातन्वतीमात्मनः ।
अद्योद्यानलतामिमां समदनां नारीमिवान्यां ध्रुवं
पश्यन् कोपविपाटलद्युति मुखं देव्याः करिष्याम्यहम् ॥

इत्यत्र उपमा[4]-श्लेषस्य ।

गृहीतमपि च यमवसरे त्यजति तद्रसानुगुणतयालङ्कारान्तरापेक्षया ।

यथा —

रक्तस्त्वं नवपल्लवैरहमपि श्लाघ्यैः प्रियाया गुणै-
स्त्वामायान्ति शिलीमुखाः स्मरधनुर्मुक्तास्तथा[5] मामपि ।
कान्तापादतलाहतिस्तव मुदे तद्वन्ममाप्यावयोः
सर्वं तुल्यमशोक केवलमहं धात्रा सशोकः कृतः ॥

---

१. 'शून्यं'-क-ख. २. अङ्गत्वेन–ग पुस्तके नास्ति. 'अङ्गित्वेना°'-घ. ३. 'इयमवसरे' -क-ख. ४. 'उपमा'-घ पुस्तके नास्ति. उपमा श्लेषस्य–BP. ५. '°स्सखे'-घ.

For example,

He is indeed the Lord
Who, by his brisk order to his discus to smite,
Made the amorous sport of Rāhu's wives,
Devoid of its wild frolic of embraces,
And confined to kisses forsooth.

Here, periphrasis is indeed intended as pre-eminent though there is the idea that it should serve as an accessory to the sentiment.

It is not enough if the poet intends his figure to be secondary; he must make sure of its timely employment also. The following is an instance of a figure so employed with regard to propriety of circumstance :—

To-day I shall make the Queen's face purple with anger
Gazing upon this garden-creeper as upon a mistress
That in a moment has displayed buds profuse (powerful longing),
Has a complexion pale with opening buds (has commenced to yawn),
And manifests the disturbance (anguish) felt
By the ceaseless puffs of wind (by constant heavings of sighs).[1]

In this instance the *double entendre* based on simile is most appropriate.

The following is an instance of abandoning half-way even a figure of speech already taken up for treatment in favour of other figures which are more helpful in revealing sentiments :—

Red thou art by fresh tendrils;
And so (i. e. fascinated) am I by thy sweet virtues.
Bees do swarm towards you;
So do they (i. e. arrows) come towards me,
Shot by the bow of the God of Love.
A blow from the darling's sole will delight you;
And so does it delight me too.
Thus O Sorrowless Tree, one in all respects are we;
But I am consigned to sorrow by God !

---

1. Translation based on that of M. R. Kale.

अत्र हि प्रबन्धप्रवृत्तोऽपि श्लेषो व्यतिरेकविवक्षया त्यज्यमानो रसविशेषं पुष्णाति। नात्रालङ्कारद्वयसन्निपातः, किं तर्हि? अलङ्कारान्तरमेव श्लेषव्यतिरेकलक्षणं नरसिंहवदिति चेत्—न; तस्य प्रकारान्तरेण व्यवस्थापनात्[1]। यत्र हि श्लेषविषय एव शब्दे प्रकारान्तरेण व्यतिरेकप्रतीतिर्जायते[2] स तस्य विषयः। यथा—

'स हरिर्नाम्ना देवः सहरिर्वरतुरगनिवहेन'

इत्यादौ।

अत्र ह्यन्य एव शब्दः श्लेषस्य[3] विषयोऽन्यश्च व्यतिरेकस्य। यदि चैवंविधे विषयेऽलङ्कारान्तरत्वकल्पना क्रियते तत्संसृष्टेर्विषयापहार[4] एव स्यात्। श्लेषमुखेनैवात्र व्यतिरेकस्यात्मलाभ इति नायं संसृष्टेर्विषय इति चेत्, न; व्यतिरेकस्य प्रकारान्तरेणापि दर्शनात्। यथा—

नो कल्पापायवायोरदयरयदलत्क्ष्माधरस्यापि शम्या
गाढोद्गीर्णोज्ज्वलश्रीरहनि न रहिता नो तमः कज्जलेन।
प्राप्तोत्पत्तिः पतङ्गान्न पुनरुपगता मोषमुष्णत्विषो वो
वर्तिः सैवान्यरूपा सुखयतु निखिलद्वीपदीपस्य दीप्तिः॥

---

१. व्यवस्थानात्–MB. No. 254, BORI. २. 'क्रियते'–क, ख. ३. 'शब्दश्लेषस्य'–घ. ४. 'क्रियेत ततः संसृष्टेर्विषयापरभार'–ग.

The *double entendre* in the initial part of the above verse has been given up half-way in order to make room for another figure viz. poetic contrast. As such, it intensifies the sentiment in question. The two figures do not merge into each other in this instance. Then how exactly are the two related ? If one were to say that they are related like the Man-Lion (an avatār of Viṣṇu) inducing the impression of a new figure altogether though consisting of two clearly different parts, viz., that of *double entendre* and poetic contrast, it would be wrong. For, the nature of Merging of Figures has been defined differently. If we find one and the same word giving rise to both *double entendre* and poetic contrast, we may regard it is an instance of Merging of Figures.

For example :

> ' *sa harir nāmnā devaḥ, saharir varaturaganivahena* '
> *That Viṣṇu is Hari only by name;*
> *But the King is similar to Hari*
> *And also a possessor of the best of steeds,*
> *Thus deserving the title* ' *Sahari* '
> *Better than the real Hari.*

But in the instance at issue the words that contain *double entendre* and poetic contrast respectively are quite different ones. If even in instances like this, only a different figure (i. e. Merging of Figures) is supposed to exist, then it would mean robbing Collocation of Figures of all its scope. It is indeed a pointless argument that this cannot be an instance of Collocation of Figures in as much as the existence of poetic contrast is achieved only through the agency of *double entendre*. For poetic contrast is often instanced in other ways also; e. g. :—

> *May the light of the lamp of all lands,*
> *With its wick so unique, bring us delight;*
> *It is not put out even by the force of terrible gales*
> *That blow at the time of the deluge*
> *To rend even mighty mountains in twain;*
> *It spreads an intense and brilliant light*
> *Even by day all round;*
> *It is never sullied by slightest soot;*
> *Though it is brought forth by the firefly (also, the sun),*
> *It never gets dim by the rise of the sun.*

अत्र हि साम्यप्रपञ्चप्रतिपादनं[1] विनैव व्यतिरेको दर्शितः। नात्र श्लेषमात्राच्चारुत्वप्रतीतिरस्तीति श्लेषस्य व्यतिरेकाङ्गत्वेनैव विवक्षितत्वात्[2] न स्वतोऽलङ्कारतेत्यपि[3] न वाच्यम्। यत एवंविधे विषये साम्यमात्रादपि सुप्रतिपादिताच्चारुत्वं दृश्यत एव। यथा—

आक्रन्दाः स्तनितैर्विलोचनजलान्यश्रान्तधाराम्बुभि-
स्तद्विच्छेदभुवश्च शोकशिखिनस्तुल्यास्तडिद्विभ्रमैः।
अन्तर्मे दयितामुखं तव शशी वृत्तिः समैवावयो-
स्तत्किं मामनिशं सखे जलधर त्वं दग्धुमेवोद्यतः॥

इत्यादौ।

रसनिर्वहणैकतानहृदयो[4] यं च[5] नात्यन्तं निर्वोढुमिच्छति।

यथा—

कोपात्कोमललोलबाहुलतिकापाशेन बध्वा दृढं
नीत्वा वासनिकेतनं दयितया सायं सखीनां पुरः।
भूयो नैवमिति स्खलत्कलगिरा संसूच्य दुश्चेष्टितं
धन्यो हन्यत एव निह्नुतिपरः प्रेयान्रुदत्या हसन्॥

अत्र हि रूपकमाक्षिप्तमनिर्व्यूढं[6] च परं रसपुष्टये[7]।

निर्वोढुमिष्टमपि यं[8] यत्नादङ्गत्वेन प्रत्यवेक्षते यथा—

---

१. प्रतिपादनप्रपञ्चं'–ग. २. 'विवक्षितत्वम्'–घ. ३. 'ऽलंकारत्वेनेत्यपि–'घ. ४. हृदयश्च–घ. ५. 'यश्च'–ग. ६. 'अनिर्व्यूढः'–ग. ७. 'संपरिपुष्टये'–ग., रसपरिपुष्टये –MB; No. 254 (BORI). ८. 'यद्यत्नादङ्गत्वेन'–घ.

In this example, poetic contrast is used without any reference to the points of similarity between the things described. Nor would it be right to think that in the earlier example, *double entendre* is not intended as individually important, that it is intended only as an accessory to poetic contrast and that we do not have any feeling of beauty due exclusively to *double entendre*. For poetic contrast can be rendered beautiful even by a good description of mere similarity (i. e. even without the assistance of *double entendre*) as in the following example :

Similar are my moans to your rumbles,
And my tears to your ceaseless showers;
The flames of sorrow within me in her separation
Are like the flashes of your lighting withal;
My darling's face is there within me
And within you the moon is found.
Thus alike we are in all respects ;
Yet my friend ! O cloud ! tell me,
Why are you so intent upon burning me down ?

The following is an example which illustrates how a poet bent upon the sole object of delineating sentiments will desist from carrying a figure too far :—

He is indeed a lucky lover who is bound fast
By the noose of his beloved's creeperlike arms
So soft and tense in her mounting anger,
Then to the bed-chamber is led in the evening
Even as the confidants are looking on,
Is warned not to do it again with an allusion
To his love-offence in a faltering and sweet tone,
And is beaten by the weeping beloved
As he tries to hide his fault smilingly.

The metaphor (of binding the lover) in this verse which has been allowed to be implied only (in the latter lines) and not carried into every detail contributes to the full delineation of sentiment.

The following example illustrates how the poet looks to it carefully that the accessory nature of the figure is not disturbed even when he intends to utilise the figure in detail so as to heighten the sentiment :—

श्यामास्वङ्गं चकितहरिणीप्रेक्षणे[1] दृष्टिपातं
गण्ड[2]च्छायां शशिनि शिखिनां बर्हभारेषु केशान् ।
उत्पश्यामि प्रतनुषु नदीवीचिषु भ्रूविलासान्
हन्तैकस्थं क्वचिदपि न ते भीरु[3] सादृश्यमस्ति ॥

इत्यादौ ।

स एवमुपनिबध्यमानोऽलङ्कारो रसाभिव्यक्तिहेतुः कवेर्भवति । उक्तप्रकारातिक्रमे तु नियमेनैव रसभङ्गहेतुः सम्पद्यते । लक्ष्यं च तथाविधं[4] महाकविप्रबन्धे[5]ष्वपि दृश्यते बहुशः । तत्तु सूक्तिसहस्रद्योतितात्मनां[6] महात्मनां[7] दोषोद्घोषणमात्मन एव दूषणं भवतीति न विभज्य दर्शितम् । किं तु रूपकादेरलङ्कारवर्गस्य येयं व्यञ्जकत्वे[8] रसादिविषये लक्षणे[9]दिग्दर्शिता तामनुसरन् स्वयं चान्यल्लक्षणमुत्प्रेक्षमाणो यद्यलक्ष्यक्रमप्रति[10]भमनन्तरोक्तमेनं[11] ध्वनेरात्मानमुपनिबध्नाति सुकविः समाहितचेतास्तदा तस्या[12]त्मलाभो भवति महीयानिति ।

क्रमेण प्रतिभात्यात्मा योऽस्यानुस्वानसन्निभः ।
शब्दार्थशक्तिमूलत्वात्सोऽपि द्वेधा व्यवस्थितः ॥ २० ॥

अस्य विवक्षितान्यपरवाच्यस्य ध्वनेः संलक्ष्य[13]क्रमव्यङ्ग्यत्वानुरणनप्रख्यो य आत्मा सोऽपि शब्दशक्तिमूलोऽर्थशक्तिमूलश्चेति द्विप्रकारः ।

---

१. 'हरिण'–क. ख. २. 'वक्त्र'–ग. ३. 'चण्डि'–ग. ४. 'तथाविधमपि'–घ. ५. 'अपि'–घ पुस्तके नास्ति. ६. '°सहस्रसंभावितात्मनां'–MB. ७. 'महतां'–क. ख. ८. 'व्यञ्जकत्वेन'–क. ख. ९. लक्षणा°–घ. १०. 'क्रमपतितम°'–घ.; क्रमप्रतिभासम° No. 254 (BORI). ११. 'एवं'–घ. १२. 'चेतास्तदस्या°'–घ. १३. 'सक्रमव्यङ्ग्यत्वाद्'–घ.

'In the Priyaṅgu do I trace thy limbs,
In eyes of startled antelope thy glance;
Thr moon recalls thy radiant countenance,
The peacock's tails thy shining tresses;
While tiny ripples in the streamlets view
To imitate the archings of thy brows,
Yet alas, O jealous one, in none of these
Is there the whole likeness of thee ![1]

A figure of speech thus utilized by a poet will succeed in revealing sentiments. In case the conditions laid down be transgressed, it invariably becomes a destroyer of sentiment. Even this is seen amply illustrated in the works of great poets. But it has not been shown in detail here since a loud exposure of the defects of great men who have the bright light of a thousand good sayings about them would amount to a censure of the critic himself. But it deserves to be reiterated that the poet will have best fulfilled his purpose only when he exercises concentration in infusing his work with the soul of suggestion 'with undiscerned sequentiality' described above, follows faithfully the mentioned ways in which the galaxy of figures like metaphor can be harmonised with delineation of sentiment and imagines for himself the other details left unsaid herein.

The other element of this suggestion manifests itself in the same way as resonance and the temporal sequentiality of the two meanings will be discernible. It is also two-fold :—'that which is based on the power of word' and 'that which is based on the power of sense.' **20**

This suggestion 'with intended but further-extending literal import' contains an element which is similar to resonance in so far as it is suggested in such a way that one can notice temporal sequentiality (between the expressed and suggested senses). It is further subdivided into 'that which is based on the power of word', and 'that which is based on the power of sense'.

One might raise an objection at this juncture to this effect : 'If one were to consider every instance where a new sense is conveyed by the power of word as a variety of suggestion, then

1. Translation Rooke's.

ननु शब्दशक्त्या यत्रार्थान्तरं प्रकाशते स यदि ध्वनेः प्रकार उच्यते तदिदानीं श्लेषस्य विषय एवापहृतः स्यात्, नापहृत इत्याह—

आक्षिप्त एवालङ्कारः शब्दशक्त्या प्रकाशते[1] ।
यस्मिन्ननुक्तः शब्देन शब्दशक्त्युद्भवो हि सः ॥ २१ ॥

यस्मादलङ्कारो, न वस्तुमात्रं, यस्मिन् काव्ये शब्दशक्त्या प्रकाशते स[2] शब्दशक्त्युद्भवो ध्वनिरित्यस्माकं विवक्षितः[3] । वस्तुद्वये च शब्दशक्त्या प्रकाशमाने[4] श्लेषः । यथा—

येन ध्वस्तमनोभवेन बलिजित्कायः पुरास्त्रीकृतो
यश्चोद्वृत्तभुजङ्गहारवलयो गङ्गां च योऽधारयत् ।
यस्याहुः शशिमच्छिरो हर इति स्तुत्यं च नामामराः
पायात्स स्वयमन्धकक्षयकरस्त्वां सर्वदोमाधवः ॥

नन्वलङ्कारान्तरप्रतिभायामपि श्लेषव्यपदेशो भवतीति[5] दर्शितं भट्टोद्भटेन, तत्पुनरपि शब्दशक्तिमूलो ध्वनिर्निरवकाश[6] इत्याशङ्क्येदमुक्तं 'आक्षिप्त' इति । तदयमर्थः—यत्र शब्दशक्त्या साक्षादलङ्कारान्तरं[7] वाच्यं सत्प्रतिभासते स

१. प्रकाश्यते–MB. २. स एव–घ. ३. 'विवक्षितम्'–BP. ४. प्रकाश्यमाने–MB.
५. 'श्लेषस्य व्यपदेश इति'–क. ख.; श्लेषव्यपदेश एवेति No. 254 (BORI).
६. निरवकाशः'–घ;ग. पुस्तके नास्ति. ७. साक्षादलंकारं–घ.

the figure *double entendre* would be completely robbed of its scope ! ' The following text points out that it is not so.

Only that instance wherein is present a figure that is not expressed directly by any word but conveyed solely by the suggestive power of the word itself, should be regarded as suggestion based on the power of the word. 21

For, only a figure which is conveyed by the power of the word is intended by us to form an instance of suggestion based on the power of the word and not all ideas so conveyed are instances of this suggestion. If two ideas are manifest (simultaneously) as a result of the power of the word, we have only an instance of *double entendre*. For example :—

Meaning that relates to Hara :

He by whom the god of Love was destroyed,
By whom the very body of Bali's enemy (*i. e. Hari*)
was turned into a shaft,
Whose neklaces and bracelets are serpents forsooth,
Who bore the Celestial River on his head,
And whose holy title, 'the moon-crested Hara',
Is praised by all the gods;
May that slayer of Andhaka
And the spouse of Pārvatī preserve thee !

Meaning that releates to Hari :

He, the Unborn, by whom the Demon of the Cart was destroyed,
Whose body that triumphed over Bali was into a feminine form changed,
Who slew the proud serpent Kāliṅga,
Who held aloft the mountain as well as the earth,
Whose holy name, 'the beheader of Dragon's Head',
Is glorified by all the gods,
And who was himself the cause
Of the destruction of Yādavas—
May that all-giver Mādhava preserve thee !

In fact, Bhaṭṭa Udbhaṭa has pointed out that the name *double entendre* can apply to such instances too wherein we get the idea of another figure through the particular figure present

सर्वः श्लेषविषयः[1]। यत्र तु शब्दशक्त्या सामर्थ्याक्षिप्तं वाच्यव्यतिरिक्तं व्यङ्ग्यं[2]-मेवालङ्कारान्तरं प्रकाशते स ध्वनेर्विषयः। शब्दशक्त्या साक्षादलङ्कारान्तर-प्रतिभा यथा—

तस्या विनापि हारेण निसर्गादेव हारिणौ।
जनयामासतुः कस्य विस्मयं न पयोधरौ॥

अत्र शृङ्गारव्यभिचारी विस्मयाख्यो भावः साक्षाद्विरोधालङ्कारश्च प्रतिभासते[3] इति विरोधच्छायानुग्राहिणः श्लेषस्यायं विषयः, न त्वनुस्वानोपमव्यङ्ग्यस्य ध्वनेः। अलक्ष्यक्रम[4]व्यङ्ग्यस्य[5] तु ध्वनेर्वाच्येन श्लेषेण विरोधेन[6] वा व्यञ्जितस्य विषय एव। यथा ममैव—

श्लाघ्याशेषतनुं सुदर्शनकरः सर्वाङ्गलीलाजित-
त्रैलोक्यां चरणारविन्दललितेनाक्रान्तलोको हरिः।
बिभ्राणां मुखमिन्दुरूपमखिलं चन्द्रात्मचक्षुर्दध-
त्स्थाने यां स्वतनोरपश्यदधिकां सा रुक्मिणी वोऽवतात्॥

---

१. 'श्लेषः'—क. ख. २. 'अव्यङ्ग्यं'—ग. ३. 'भातीति'—क-ख. ४. 'क्रम-प्रतिभासस्य'—ग. ५. 'व्यङ्ग्यप्रतिभासस्य'—घ. ६. श्लेषविरोधेन—No. 254 (BORI).

there. In view of this, one might again doubt whether suggestion based upon the power of the word can be left with any independent scope at all. It is in order to remove such a doubt that the word 'suggestive' has been used in the text. Hence this is the idea : All instances wherein, through the power of the word, only an expressed figure is conveyed by another expressed figure, should be brought under the province of *double entendre.* But such instances where a new figure is conveyed by the suggestive power of the word only, a figure which appears thus to be quite different from an expressed one, will come under the scope of suggestion based upon the power of the word. The following is an example of an expressed figure conveyed directly (i. e. not suggestively) by the power of the word :—

Her bosoms without a garland though,
Garlanded (also, ravishing) by nature were;
Whom would they not amaze !

The mood of 'surprise' described here happens to be a passing mood related to the erotic sentiment. Alongside of it we also find the figure of paradox. Hence this should be regarded only as an instance of *double entendre* which assists in conveying a shade of paradox; and not as an instance of suggestion based on the power of the word. All the same, the Erotic sentiment conveyed here by the use of the expressed figures *double entendre* or paradox can of course be regarded as an instance of suggestion with undiscerned sequentiality. Here is another example taken from one of my own works :—

The entire body of Rukmiṇī is praiseworthy
While Hari's hand alone is handsome (*also, he holds a discus called* '*The Handsome*' *in his hand*) ;
She has triumphed over the three worlds
By the graces of all her limbs,
While Hari has measured out the worlds
By the grace of his lotus-foot alone;
Her whole face is of the form of the moon
While he is but moon-eyed.
Thus indeed did Hari find
Her person far superior to his own ;
May that Rukmiṇī protect us.

अत्र वाच्यतयैव व्यतिरेकच्छायानुग्राही[1] श्लेषः प्रतीयते[2] । यथा च

भ्रमिमरतिमलसहृदयतां प्रलयं मूर्च्छां तमः शरीरसादम्[3] ।
मरणं च जलदभुजगजं प्रसह्य कुरुते विषं वियोगिनीनाम् ॥

यथा वा—

चमहिअमाणसकञ्चणपङ्कअणिम्महिअपरिमला जस्स ।
अखण्डिअदाणपसारा बाहुप्पलिहा च्चिअ गइन्दा ॥
(खण्डितमानसकाञ्चनपङ्कजानिर्मथितपरिमला यस्य ।
अखण्डितदानप्रसरा बाहुपरिघा इव गजेन्द्राः ॥ (छाया)

अत्र रूपकच्छायानुग्राही[4] श्लेषो वाच्यतयैवावभासते । स चाक्षिप्तोऽलङ्कारो यत्र पुनः शब्दान्तरेणाभिहितस्वरूपस्तत्र न[5] शब्दशक्त्युद्भवानुरणनरूपव्यङ्ग्यध्वनिव्यवहारः । तत्र[6] वक्रोक्त्यादिवाच्यालङ्कारव्यवहार एव । यथा—

दृष्ट्या केशव गोपरागहृतया[7] किञ्चिन्न दृष्टं मया
तेनैव स्खलितास्मि नाथ पतितां किं नाम नालम्बसे ।
एकस्त्वं विषमेषु खिन्नमनसां सर्वाबलानां गति-
र्गोप्यैवं गदितः सलेशमवताद्गोष्ठे हरिर्वश्चिरम् ॥

---

१. °यानुगृहीतः-MB. २. 'प्रतीयत एव'-क-ख. ३. 'सादं च'- क-ख.
४. °नुगृहीतः-MB. ५. न-घ पुस्तके नास्ति. ६. किन्तु वाच्यश्लेषालंकार-KLV.
७. 'हतया'-ग.

The *double entendre* which assists in the communication of Paradox happens only to be expressed in this verse. Here is another instance :—

Reeling, jadedness, and laziness;
Sinking, swoon and stupor;
Slenderness of body and death itself—
All these are perforce brought upon wives in separation
By the poison (also, water) of cloud-like snakes
(also, of snake-like clouds).

To give a still another example :—

Laden with the scent of golden lotuses,
Squeezed by them in the Mānasa lake (also, laden with the glory of smashing out the fond dreams of his enemies)
And shining with unimpaired abundance of ichor (also gifts),
The mighty elephants are just like his arm-bolts.

Here also the *double entendre* which assists in the use of the metaphor happens to be expressed only.

Even a suggested figure will not become an instance of resonant suggestion based on the power of the word if it also gets expressed at the same time by other expressions. In such instances we will find only an expressed figure like Evasive Speech. The following is an example in point :—

O Krishna, nothing was seen by me,
Blinded as I was by the dust raised by cows
(also, as I was drawn by love for the cow-herd.)
Hence I have stumbled (also, strayed away from morality);
And why don't you, O lord, give support to a fallen person ?
(also, why don't you behave like a hunband towards me ?)
Are you not the only succour for the frail women
Whose minds are troubled by uneven paths (also, whose minds are troubled by the five-arrowed Cupid) ?
Thus in the cow-pen was Hari addressed
By the cowherdess with equivocal words;
May he preserve us for long.

एवञ्जातीयकः सर्व एव भवतु कामं वाच्यश्लेषस्य विषयः। यत्र तु सामर्थ्याक्षिप्तं सदलङ्कारान्तरं शब्दशक्त्या प्रकाशते स सर्व एव ध्वनेर्विषयः। यथा——

अत्रान्तरे कुसुमसमययुगमुपसंहरन्नजृम्भत ग्रीष्माभिधानः फुल्लमल्लिकाधवलाट्टहासो महाकालः'।

यथा च——

उन्नतः प्रोल्लसद्धारः कालागुरुमलीमसः।
पयोधरभरस्तन्व्याः[1] कं न चक्रेऽभिलाषिणम्॥

यथा वा——

दत्तानन्दाः प्रजानां समुचितसमयाकृष्टसृष्टैः[2] पयोभिः
पूर्वाह्णे विप्रकीर्णा दिशि दिशि विरमत्याह्नि संहारभाजः।
दीप्तांशोर्दीर्घदुःखप्रभवभवभयोदन्वदुत्तारनावो
गावो वः पावनानां परमपरिमितां प्रीतिमुत्पादयन्तु॥

एषूदाहरणेषु[3] शब्दशक्त्या प्रकाशमाने सत्यप्राकरणिकेऽर्थान्तरे वाक्यस्यासम्बद्धार्था[4]भिधायित्वं मा प्रसाङ्क्षीदित्यप्राकरणिकप्राकरणिकयोरर्थयोरुपमानोपमेयभावः कल्पयितव्यः[5] सामर्थ्यादित्यर्थाक्षिप्तोऽयं[6] श्लेषो न शब्दोपारूढ इति विभिन्न एव श्लेषादनुस्वानोपमव्यङ्ग्यस्य ध्वनेर्विषयः।

---

१. 'तस्याः' – ग. २. 'क्लिष्टसृष्टैः–घ, BP. ३. 'एतेषु' क-ख. ४. 'संबन्धा' –ग,…संबद्धाभिधायित्वं-KLV. ५. कल्पनीयः-MB. ६. 'इत्याक्षिप्तोऽयं' क-ख.

Instances of this kind may, by all means, be objects of expressed *double entendre.* But passages where another figure is conveyed only by the suggestive power of the word deserve to be regarded only as instances of suggestion. As for instance:—

> *In the meanwhile appeared (also, yawned) the Terrible Time (also Lord Siva) of the name ' Summer ' putting an end to the two flowering months (also, bringing an end of the aeons) and with radiant laughter in the form of mansions festooned with blooming jasmines (also, with boisterous laughter white like full-blown jasmines).*

Another instance :—

> *Buxom (also, louring), and adorned with a garland*
> *(also, showering a downpour),*
> *And dark as the black aloe,*
> *Whom would not the lady's heavy breasts (also, the heavy clouds)*
> *Make passionately amorous ?*

To take a still another instance :

> *Bringing delight to the public by sucking*
> *And showering down water (also, milk) at proper times,*
> *Scattering wide in every quarter in the forenoon*
> *And receding back at the close of day,*
> *Those veritable ships that ferry one across*
> *The ocean of rebirth's terror and suffering,*
> *May such rays (also, cows) of the blazing Sun*
> *Bring us delight, holy and limitless.*

In all these examples, an extra meaning is conveyed by the power of the word and in order that the two meanings might not appear as entirely disconnected, we will have to postulate the relation of the standard of comparison and the object compared as existing between the two since there is justification also for doing so. Thus the *double entendre* we see here is not grounded on words only as it is the case when it happens to be an expressed figure. But it is a figure suggested by the special suggestive power of the word. Thus the examples of *double entendre* and resonance-like suggestion are entirely different from one another.

अन्येऽपि चालङ्काराः शब्दशक्तिमूलानुस्वानरूपव्यङ्ग्ये ध्वनौ सम्भवन्त्येव। तथा हि विरोधोऽपि शब्दशक्तिमूलानुस्वानरूपो दृश्यते[1]। यथा स्थाण्वीश्वराख्यजनपदवर्णने भट्टबाणस्य—

'यत्र च मत्तमातङ्गगामिन्यः शीलवत्यश्च गौर्यो विभवरताश्च श्यामाः पद्मरागिण्यश्च धवलद्विजशुचिवदना मदिरामोदिश्वसनाश्च[2] प्रमदाः'।

अत्र हि वाच्यो विरोधस्तच्छायानुग्राही[3] वा श्लेषोऽयमिति न शक्यं वक्तुम्। साक्षाच्छब्देन विरोधालङ्कारस्याप्रकाशितत्वात्। यत्र हि साक्षाच्छब्दावेदितो विरोधालङ्कारस्तत्र हि श्लिष्टोक्तौ वाच्यालङ्कारस्य विरोधस्य श्लेषस्य वा विषयत्वम्।

यथा तत्रैव[4]—

'समवाय इव विरोधिनां पदार्थानाम्। तथाहि—सन्निहितबालान्धकारोऽपि भास्वन्मूर्तिः[5]' इत्यादौ। यथावा ममैव—

सर्वैकशरणमक्षयमधीशमीशं धियां हरिं कृष्णम्।
चतुरात्मानं निष्क्रियमरिमथनं नमत चक्रधरम्॥

अत्र हि शब्दशक्तिमूलानुस्वानरूपो विरोधः स्फुटमेव प्रतीयते। एवंविधो व्यतिरेकोऽपि[7] दृश्यते। यथा ममैव—

१. 'दृश्यत एव'–क-ख, KLV. २. 'श्वसनाश्च' इत्यतः परं–'(चन्द्रकान्तवपुषः शिरीषकोमलाङ्ग्यश्च अभुजंगगम्याः कञ्चुकिन्यश्च पृथुकलत्रश्रियो दरिद्रमध्यकलिताश्च लावण्यवत्यो मधुरभाषिण्यश्च अप्रमत्ताः प्रसन्नोज्वलरागाश्च अकौतुकाः प्रौढाश्च')–ध. ३. 'विरोधच्छाया'–क-ख., विरोध इति तच्छायानुग्राही श्लेषोऽयमिति – KLV. ४. हर्षचरिते – ख. ५. अपि शब्दः – घ पुस्तके नास्ति. ६. मूर्तिश्च–ख. ७. 'एवं विरोधव्यतिरेकोऽपि – क. ख.

Other figures are also possible in this suggestion which is based upon the power of the word and which is of the nature of resonance. For instance, the figure of Paradox becomes a promoter of this suggestion. An example is found in Bāṇa's description of the country of Sthāṇvīśvara:—

> *Where women are outcaste-seekers* (*also, elephant-gaited*) *and yet chaste, Gaurīs* (*also, white in complexion*) *and yet enamoured of persons other than Śiva* (*also, riches*), *dark* (*also, beautiful*) *and yet red in complexion* (*also, possessing rubies*), *with mouths as clean as those of the best Brahmins* (*also, sparkling and clean teeth*), *yet breathing out the odour of wine.*

It is not possible to state here definitely either that the primarily expressed figure is Paradox or that it is *double entendre* helping the idea of Paradox. The reason lies in the fact that the figure of Paradox has not been conveyed expressly by the words. But in instances where Paradox is expressly conveyed by words, if we find *double entendre* also, we will have either the expressed figure Paradox or the expressed figure *double entendre*. Here is an instance from the *Harṣacarita*:—

> *It was just like a meeting-place of opposite things. Thus for instance, it not only had the proximity of rising darkness* (*also, the blackness of hair*), *but it was the embodiment of the Sun* (*also, its body was luminous*). . . .

For the suggested Paradox, an instance can be cited from my own work:—

> *Bow down, you all, to that god*
> *Who is the only refuge for all, while he is deathless*
> (*also, homeless*),
> *Who is the supreme ruler* (*also, not the lord of*
> *intelligence as also the lord of intelligence*),
> *Who is Hari* (*also, green*) *as well as Kṛṣṇa*
> (*i. e. dark and also remover of sins*),
> *Who is four-fold in form* (*also, who is a clever person*)
> *and also inactive,*
> *And who is the destroyer of enemies* (*also, breaker of*
> *wheels*),
> *While he holds a wheel in his hand.*

खं येऽत्युज्ज्वलयन्ति[1] लूनतमसो ये वा नखोद्भासिनो
ये पुष्णन्ति सरोरुहश्रियमपि क्षिप्ताब्जभासश्च ये ।
ये मूर्धस्ववभासिनः[2] क्षितिभृतां ये चामराणां शिरां-
स्याक्रामन्त्युभयेऽपि ते दिनपतेः पादाः श्रिये[3] सन्तु वः[4] ॥

एवमन्येऽपि शब्दशक्तिमूलानुस्वानरूपव्यङ्ग्यध्वनिप्रकाराः[5] सन्ति[6], ते सहृदयैः स्वयमनुसर्तव्याः । इह तु ग्रन्थविस्तरभयान्न तत्प्रपञ्चः[7] कृतः ।

अर्थशक्त्युद्भवस्त्वन्यो यत्रार्थः संप्रकाशते[8] ।
यस्तात्पर्येण वस्त्वन्यद्[9] व्यनक्त्युक्तिं[10] विना स्वतः ॥ २२ ॥

यत्रार्थः स्वसामर्थ्यादर्थान्तरमभिव्यनक्ति शब्दव्यापारं विनैव सोऽर्थशक्त्युद्भवो नामानुस्वानोपमव्यङ्ग्यो ध्वनिः । यथा—

एवं वादिनि देवर्षौ पार्श्वे पितुरधोमुखी ।
लीलाकमलपत्राणि गणयामास पार्वती ॥

अत्र हि लीलाकमलपत्रगणनमुपसर्जनीकृतस्वरूपं शब्दव्यापारं विनै-

---

१. येऽभ्युज्ज्वलयन्ति – KLV. २. 'मूर्धनि' – ग. ३. 'श्रियै' – ग., KLV. ४. 'नः' – क-ख ५. 'रूपा ध्वनिप्रकाराः' – क-ख. ६. 'संभवन्ति' – क-ख; MB. ७. 'तत्'–क-ख पुस्तकयोर्नास्ति. ८. After this KLV adds a *Kārikā*, *vṛtti* and illustration not found in any other MS. just preceding *Kārikā* 22 :—

किञ्च—
वस्तुमात्रमपि व्यङ्ग्यं शब्दशक्त्या प्रधानतः ।
शब्दशक्त्युद्भवस्यास्य ध्वनेः स्याद् गोचरः क्वचित् ॥

वस्तुमात्रमपीति । यद्वस्तुमात्रं प्रतीयमानमस्य ध्वनेरप्रयोजकमुक्तं तदपीत्यर्थः । क्वचिदिति वस्तुमात्रप्रतीतौ यत्र श्लेषव्यपदेशस्तद्व्यतिरिक्तोऽस्य विषय इत्यर्थः । यथा—

पंथिय । न एत्थ सत्थरमत्थि मणं पत्थरत्थले गामे ।
उग्गयपओहरं पेक्खिऊण जइ वससि ता वससु ॥
पथिक ! नात्र संस्तरोऽस्ति मनाक प्रस्तरस्थले ग्रामे ।
उद्गतपयोधरं प्रेक्ष्य यदि वससि तद् वस ॥ [छाया]

संस्तरस्तृणादिशय्या । प्रस्तराः पाषाणः । एवमपि चेन्मेवभयं तद्वस । व्यङ्ग्यं तु प्रहरचतुष्टयमप्युपभोगेन नात्र निद्रां कर्तुं लभ्यते । सर्वे ह्यत्राविदग्धाः । तदुन्नतपयोधरां मामुपभोक्तुं यदि वससि तदाऽऽस्वेति । अत्र वाच्यबाधेन व्यङ्ग्यस्य स्थितत्वात्तयोर्नोपमेयभावः । The above Prakrit Verse is No. 879 in Weber's ed. of Gāthāsaptaśatī and is quoted in Kāvyaprakāśa IV. 58 (Zalkikar's ed.). ९. स प्रकाशते –BP, KLV. १०. 'ध्वनाति'–ग.

In this example, of course, Paradox based upon the suggestive power of words and of the nature of resonance is most transparent.

We find in the same way poetic contrast too conveyed suggestively as for instance in the following verse of mine:—

May both those feet (also, rays) of the Sun to your welfare conduce;

Both they that dispel darkness (also, sin)

And they that profusely illumine the sky (also, the different senses);

They that partake of (or enhance) the beauty of lotuses,

They that shine on the heads of earth-supporting mountains (or kings);

Also they that rest on the heads of heavenly gods (or the tips of chowries).

Similarly, there are also other varieties of this suggestion based upon the power of the word and of the nature of resonance. They should all be understood by perceptive critics in their own wisdom. They have not been recorded in detail here for fear of the work's growing too voluminous.

The other variety of suggestion is based upon the power of sense and it is instanced in places where the second meaning is conveyed only by way of implication by the first meaning and not by the expressed words at all. **22**

That instance where one meaning gives rise to another through its own power of implication and not through the denotative power of words becomes an example of suggestion based upon the power of meaning and similar to resonance. The following is an example :

As the divine sage said this,
The down-faced Pārvatī by her father's side
Counted the petals of the toy-lotus
She held in her hand.

Here, the idea of counting lotus petals is conveyed expressly and it (i. e. the expressed meaning) subjugates itself in communicating the second idea, namely, bashfulness, one of the

वार्थान्तरं व्यभिचारिभावलक्षणं प्रकाशयति । न चायमलक्ष्यक्रमव्यङ्ग्यस्यैव ध्वनेर्विषयः । यतो यत्र साक्षाच्छब्दनिवेदितेभ्यो विभावानुभावव्यभिचारिभ्यो रसादीनां प्रतीतिः, स तस्य केवलस्य मार्गः । यथा कुमारसम्भवे मधुप्रसङ्गे वसन्तपुष्पाभरणं वहन्त्या देव्या आगमनादिवर्णनं मनोभवशरसन्धानपर्यन्तं शम्भोश्च परिवृत्तधैर्यस्य चेष्टाविशेषवर्णनादि साक्षाच्छब्दनिवेदितम्[1] । इह तु सामर्थ्याक्षिप्तव्यभिचारिमुखेन रसप्रतीतिः । तस्मादयमन्यो ध्वनेः प्रकारः ।

यत्र च शब्दव्यापारसहायोऽर्थोऽर्थान्तरस्य व्यञ्जकत्वेनोपादीयते स नास्य ध्वनेर्विषयः । यथा—

सङ्केतकालमनसं विटं ज्ञात्वा विदग्धया ।
हसन्नेत्रार्पिताकूतं लीलापद्मं निमीलितम् ॥

अत्र हि लीलाकमलनिमीलनस्य व्यञ्जकत्वमुक्त्यैव निवेदितम् । तथा च—

शब्दार्थशक्त्या[2]क्षिप्तोऽपि व्यङ्ग्योऽर्थः कविना पुनः ।
यत्राविष्क्रियते स्वोक्त्या सान्यैवालङ्कृतिर्ध्वनेः ॥ २३ ॥

शब्दशक्त्यार्थशक्त्या शब्दार्थशक्त्या वाक्षिप्तोऽपि व्यङ्ग्योऽर्थः कविना पुनर्यत्र स्वोक्त्या प्रकाशीक्रियते सोऽस्मादनुस्वानोपमव्यङ्ग्या[3]द्ध्वनेरन्य एवालङ्कारः[4] । अलक्ष्यक्रमव्यङ्ग्यस्य वा ध्वनेः सति सम्भवे स तादृगन्योऽलङ्कारः ।

---

१. ‘निवेशिनेभ्यः’ – क - ख. २. ‘शक्त्यापि क्षिप्तो’ – ग. शक्त्या वाक्षिप्तो–घ. ३. व्यङ्ग्याख्याद्ध्वनेः ... KLV. ४. ‘एव क्रमः’ क - ख.: एवाक्रमः No. 254 (BORI).

passing moods, without taking the assistance of the denotative words at all. This cannot be regarded as an instance of suggestion with undiscerned sequentiality. Only those contexts where Sentiments, etc are made known by the descriptions of the situational stimuli, responses and the passing moods which are themselves expressed by so many words will serve as proper instances of this suggestion. The description of Pārvatī adorned with flowers of spring up to the point of Cupid's discharge of his arrow in the description of spring in the *Kumārsambhava* and also the description of the several responses of Śiva at a time when his mind was perturbed (in the same poem) will show us how they are all expressed by words directly. But here sentiment is made known to us in a quite different way; and that is through the passing mood suggested by the power of implication (in primary sense). Hence this should be regarded as another variety of suggestion. But a context wherein one meaning is made to suggest another by taking the assistance of denotative power will not be an instance of this type of suggestion. The following is an example in point :

Knowing the mind of the paramour
Seeking the time of assignation,
The clever maid closed her toy-lotus
With a smiling glance telltale.

The fact that the closing of the lotus is suggestive has also been expressed in so many words in this example.

Moreover,

A context wherein even an idea suggested by the power of the word and sense is again expressed directly in so many words by the poet, will instance only a figure far removed from suggestion. **23**

When a poet expresses again directly in so many words what has already been suggested either by the power of the word or of sense or of both, we get only a figure quite different from this resonance-like suggestion. In case it happens to be an instance of suggestion with undiscerned sequentiality, we may say that such a procedure will serve as a new figure.

तत्र शब्दशक्त्या यथा :

वत्से मा गा विषादं श्वसनमुरुजवं सन्त्यजोर्ध्व[1]प्रवृत्तं
कम्पः को वा गुरुस्ते भवतु बलभिदा जृम्भितेनात्र याहि ।
प्रत्याख्यानं सुराणामिति भयशमनच्छद्मना कारयित्वा
यस्मै लक्ष्मीमदाद्वः स दहतु दुरितं मन्थमूढां[2] पयोधिः ॥

अर्थशक्त्या यथा—

अम्बा शेतेऽत्र वृद्धा परिणतवयसामग्रणीरत्र तातो
निःशेषागारकर्मश्रमशिथिलतनुः कुम्भदासी तथात्र ।
अस्मिन् पापाहमेका कतिपयदिवसप्रोषितप्राणनाथा
पान्थायेत्थं तरुण्या कथितमवसरव्याहृतिव्याजपूर्वम् ॥

उभयशक्त्या यथा ‘ दृष्ट्या केशव गोपरागहृतया ’ इत्यादौ ।

प्रौढोक्तिमात्रनिष्पन्नशरीरः सम्भवी स्वतः ।
अर्थोऽपि द्विविधो ज्ञेयो वस्तुनोऽन्यस्य दीपकः ॥ २४ ॥

अर्थशक्त्युद्भवानुरणनरूपव्यङ्ग्ये[3] ध्वनौ यो व्यञ्जकोऽर्थ उक्तस्तस्यापि

१. ‘ संवृणूर्ध्व ’–ग. २. ‘ मन्थमुग्धः ’–ग. ३. ‘ व्यङ्ग्यध्वनौ ’–क-ख.

The following is an instance where what is suggested by the power of the word is expressed also :—

> ' *O my daughter dear ! don't court misery (also,*
> *the poison-eater, viz., Śiva).*
> *Give up your deep sigh (also, fast-moving Windgod)*
> *issuing forth so high (also, the up-stretching Firegod).*
> *Why do you tremble so (also, why should you bother*
> *about Varuṇa or Bṛhaspati) ?*
> *Enough of yawns (also, Kubera) that drain away*
> *your strength (also, the enemy of Bala, viz., Indra)*
> *You please come this way with me'—*
> *Arranging thus for the rejection of the gods*
> *Under the guise of allaying her fears,*
> *The Ocean indeed did give away Lakṣmī,*
> *Agitated at the churning, to Viṣṇu.*
> *May he remove our sin !*

The following is an instance where what is suggested by the power of sense is expressed also :—

> ' *Here my old mother sleeps,*
> *And here my father, the oldest of the old;*
> *Here it is that the house-maid stretches her body,*
> *So tired and jaded by her ceaseless chores !*
> *Here I am, woe is me, all alone;*
> *Even my husband went on a journey a few days ago'—*
> *Thus did the young woman speak to the traveller*
> *Under the guise of welcoming words.*

The example already quoted, " O Kṛṣṇa " serves as an instance where what is suggested by the power of both the word and sense is expressed also.

The sense which suggests another sense is also two-fold :

1. Existing only in ornate expression and 2. Naturally existing. **24**

The sense which has been pointed out as the suggester of a second sense in suggestion (of the form of resonance based upon the power of sense) is also of two kinds. The first is that whose

द्वौ प्रकारौ— कवेः कविनिबद्धस्य वा वक्तुः[1] प्रौढोक्तिमात्रनिष्पन्नशरीर एकः, स्वतस्सम्भवी च द्वितीयः । कविप्रौढोक्तिमात्रनिष्पन्नशरीरो यथा—

सज्जेहि सुरहिमासो ण दाव अप्पेइ जुअइजणलक्खमुहे ।
अहिणवसहआरमुहे णवपल्लवपत्तले अणङ्गस्स शरे ॥
[सज्जयति सुरभिमासो न तावदर्पयति युवतिजनलक्ष्यमुखान् ।
अभिनवसहकारमुखान्नवपल्लवपत्रलाननङ्गस्य शरान् ॥ च्छाया]

कविनिबद्धवक्तृप्रौढोक्तिमात्रनिष्पन्नशरीरो यथोदाहृतमेव — "शिखरिणि ...." इत्यादि[3] ।

यथा वा—

साअरविइण्णजोव्वणहत्थालम्बं समुण्णमन्तेहिम् ।
अब्भुट्ठाणं विअ मम्महस्स दिण्णं तुह थणेहिम् ॥
[सादरवितीर्णयौवनहस्तालम्बं समुन्नमद्भ्याम् ।
अभ्युत्थानमिव मन्मथस्य दत्तं तव स्तनाभ्याम् ॥ इति च्छाया]

स्वतःसम्भवी य औचित्येन बहिरपि[4] सम्भाव्यमानसद्भावो न केवलं भणितिवशेनैवाभिनिष्पन्नशरीरः । यथोदाहृतम्— 'एवं वादिनि....' इत्यादि ।

यथा वा—

सिहिपिञ्छकण्णऊरा जाआ[6] वाहस्स गव्विणी भमइ ।
मुत्ताफलरइअपसाहणाणँ मज्झे सवत्तीणम् ॥
[शिखिपिच्छकर्णपूरा जाया व्याधस्य गर्विणी भ्रमति ।
मुक्ताफलरचितप्रसाधनानां मध्ये सपत्नीनाम् ॥ इति च्छाया]

अर्थशक्तेरलङ्कारो यत्राप्यन्यः प्रतीयते ।
अनुस्वानोपमव्यङ्ग्यः स प्रकारोऽपरो ध्वनेः ॥ २५ ॥

वाच्यालङ्कारव्यतिरिक्तो यत्रान्योऽलङ्कारोऽर्थसामर्थ्यात्प्रतीयमानोऽवभासते सोऽर्थशक्त्युद्भवो नामानुस्वानरूपव्यङ्ग्यो[7]ऽन्यो[8] ध्वनिः ।

---

१. 'वस्तु'–ग. २. 'निष्पन्नो यथा'–ग. ३. इत्यादौ–घ. ४. 'बहिरपि'–ग पुस्तके नास्ति. ५. 'अभि'–क-ख. पुस्तकयोर्नास्ति. ६. 'बहुआ'–ग. ७. अनुरणनरूपो व्यङ्ग्यो' क-ख. ८. 'अन्यो'–ग. पुस्तके नास्ति.

existence is real only in the ornate expression either of the poet himself or of a character created by the poet. The second exists naturally.

The following is an example of suggestive sense whose existence is real only in the ornate expression of the poet;

The month of spring keeps ready but does not fling
The arrows of Cupid, with sharp heads
Of new mango buds and feathers of fresh leaves,
At young women, that targets are.

The example already given, viz., '*On which mountain etc.*' will serve as an instance of suggestive sense which is real only in the ornate expression of the character created by a poet; or, here is another example :

By your rising breasts, so fondly
Served by the handmaid, youth,
Cupid seems welcomed warmly
Through gesture of rising in courtesy.

The naturally existing is that sense which can possibly exist in fact in the world of reality also. It does not owe its existence only to the ornateness of poetic expression. Examples of this are had in illustrations already cited viz. *As the divine sage, etc.* The following may be taken as another example :

Decking her ears with peacock's plumes,
The wife of the hunter moves in pride
In the midst of all her rivals
With their ornaments of pearls.

Contexts where a new figure of speech is seen to result from the mere power of sense and is suggested in the form of resonance should be deemed as instances of another variety of suggestion. **25**

When we find a new figure conveyed by the power of sense itself, a figure which is quite distinct from the ordinarily expressed figure, we should regard it as another variety of resonance-like suggestion based on the power of sense.

तस्य[1] प्रविरलविषयत्वमाशङ्क्येदमुच्यते—

रूपकादिरलङ्कारवर्गो यो वाच्यतां श्रितः ।
स सर्वो गम्यमानत्वं बिभ्रद्भूम्ना प्रदर्शितः ॥ २६ ॥

अन्यत्र[2] वाच्यत्वेन प्रसिद्धो यो रूपकादिरलङ्कारः[3] सोऽन्यत्र प्रतीयमानतया बाहुल्येन प्रदर्शितस्तत्रभवद्भिर्भट्टोद्भटादिभिः । तथा च ससन्देहादिषु[4]पमारूपकातिशयोक्तीनां[5] प्रकाशमानत्वं प्रदर्शितमित्यलङ्कारान्तरस्या[6]लङ्कारान्तरे[7] व्यङ्ग्यत्वं न यत्नप्रतिपाद्यम्[8] ।

इयत्पुनरु[9]च्यत एव[10]—

अलङ्कारान्तरस्यापि प्रतीतौ यत्र भासते ।
तत्परत्वं न वाच्यस्य[11] नासौ मार्गो ध्वनेर्मतः[12] ॥ २७ ॥

अलंकारान्तरेषु त्वनुरणनरूपालङ्कार[13]प्रतीतौ सत्यामपि यत्र वाच्यस्य व्यङ्ग्यप्रतिपादनौन्मुख्येन चारुत्वं न प्रकाशते नासौ ध्वनेर्मार्गः । तथा च दीपकादावलङ्कारे[14] उपमाया गम्यमानत्वेऽपि तत्परत्वेन चारुत्वस्याव्यवस्थानान्न[15] ध्वनिव्यपदेशः । यथा[16]—

चन्दमऊएहिँ णिसा णलिनी कमलेहिँ कुसुमगुच्छेहिँ लआ ।
हंसेहिँ सरअसोहा कव्वकहा सज्जनेहिँ करइ गरुई ॥

[चन्द्रमयूखैर्निशा नलिनी कमलैः कुसुमगुच्छैर्लता ।
हंसैश्शारदशोभा काव्यकथा सज्जनैः क्रियते गुर्वी ॥ च्छाया]

इत्यादिषूपमागर्भत्वे[17]ऽपि सति वाच्यालङ्कारमुखेनैव चारुत्वं व्यवतिष्ठते न व्यङ्ग्यालङ्कारतात्पर्येण । तस्मात्तत्र वाच्यालङ्कारमुखेनैव काव्यस्य[18] व्यपदेशो न्याय्यः । यत्र तु व्यङ्ग्यपरत्वेनैव वाच्यस्य व्यवस्थानं[19] तत्र व्यङ्ग्यमुखेनैव व्यपदेशो युक्तः ।

---

१. 'तत्र'-क-ख. २. 'अन्यवाच्यत्वेन'-ग. ३. ... रलङ्कारवर्गः-KLV. ४. 'संदेहादिषु'-BP. ५. यौक्त्यादीनां-MB, KLV. ६. अलंकारान्तरत्वे'-क-ख. ७. ...लङ्कारान्तरेण-KLV. ८. 'प्रतिपाद्यमिति'-ग. ९. 'पुनरुक्तं'-क-ख. १०. 'एव'-क-ख. पुस्तकयोर्नास्ति. ११. 'काव्यस्य'-क-ख., MB.; No. 254 (BORI), KLV. १२. 'ध्वनौ'-क-ख. १३. 'अलंकारान्तरस्य रूपकादेरलंकार°'-घ. १४. 'दीपकालंकारे' १५. 'अवस्थानात्'-ग. १६. 'तथाहि' क-ख. १७. 'उपमालंकारगर्भत्वे सत्यपि'-ग., उपमागर्भत्वे सत्यपि-KLV. १८. 'काव्यव्यपदेशो BP, KLV. १९. 'काव्यस्य व्यवस्थापनं' क-ख., काव्यस्य व्यवस्थानं-KLV.

The following is said in order to remove a plausible doubt that the scope of this variety may be quite a limited one.

It has been shown effectively (even by the ancient writers) that the assemblage of figures like metaphor though generally found to be expressed only, also become suggested quite often.26

It has already been shown conclusively by emiment writers like Bhaṭṭa Udbhaṭa that figures like metaphor which are commonly found to be expressed in many instances will also be conveyed by suggestion in quite a large number of instances.

Thus in the figure of Poetic Doubt etc. they have pointed out the suggestion of other figures viz., simile, metaphor and exaggeration. Hence there is no need at all for laboriously explaining how one figure may be suggested by another. Still this much deserves to be recorded :—

Even if there should be found a suggested figure, unless there is also a singleness of aim towards it on the part of the expressed, it cannot be considered as a mode of suggestion. 27

Even if in the figure expressed there should be a resonance-like suggestion of other figures, it will not merit the title of a mode of suggestion unless the expressed one shows also extra beauty in its principally hinting at the other ones. So it is that though simile is hinted at in figures like Ellipsis, we don't call the suggested simile by the name of suggestion since there is not beauty solely contributed by it. The following is an example :—

To night is greatness brought by moon-beams
And to the lotus-plant by flowers;
And to the glory of autumn by swans;
And so it is to poetic works
At the hands of good critics.

In this and such other instances, though the figure simile is implicit, all the beauty is centred only in the expressed figure and not in the singleness of aim directed towards the suggested figure. Hence such instances of poetry should properly be described as containing only expressed figures. But instances where the expressed is utilized as wholly directed towards the communication of the suggested alone, may be called after the suggested figures.

यथा—

प्राप्तश्रीरेष कस्मात्पुनरपि मयि तं मन्थखेदं विदध्या-
न्निद्रामप्यस्य पूर्वामनलसमनसो नैव सम्भावयामि ।
सेतुं बध्नाति भूयः किमिति च सकलद्वीपनाथानुयात-
स्त्वय्यायाते वितर्कानिति दधत इवाभाति कम्पः पयोधेः ॥

यथा[1] वा ममैव—

लावण्यकान्तिपरिपूरितादिङ्मुखेऽस्मि-
न्स्मेरेऽधुना तव मुखे तरलायताक्षि ।
क्षोभं यदेति न मनागपि तेन मन्ये
सुव्यक्तमेव जलराशिरयं पयोधिः ॥

इत्येवंविधे विषयेऽनुरणनरूप[2]रूपकाश्रयेण काव्यचारुत्वव्यवस्थानाद्रूपकध्वनिरिति व्यपदेशो न्याय्यः ।

उपमाध्वनिर्यथा—

वीराणं रमइ घुसिणारुणम्मि ण तहा पिआथणुच्छङ्गे ।
दिट्ठी रिउगअकुम्भत्थलम्मि जह बहलसिन्दूरे ॥
[वीराणां रमते घुसृणारुणे न तथा प्रियास्तनोत्सङ्गे ।
दृष्टी रिपुगजकुम्भस्थले यथा बहलसिन्दूरे ॥ छाया]

यथा वा ममैव विषमबाणलीलायामसुरपरा[3]क्रमणे कामदेवस्य—

तं ताण सिरिसहोअररअणाहरणम्मि हिअअमेक्करसम् ।
बिम्बाहरे पिआणं णिवेसिअं कुसुमबाणेन ॥
[तत्तेषां श्रीसहोदररत्नाहरणे हृदयमेकरसम् ।
बिम्बाधरे प्रियाणां निवेशितं कुसुमबाणेन ॥ छाया ॥]

आक्षेपध्वनिर्यथा—

स वक्तुमखिलान् शक्तो हयग्रीवाश्रितान् गुणान् ।
योऽम्बुकुम्भैः परिच्छेदं ज्ञातुं शक्तो[4] महोदधेः ॥

---

१. No. 254 (BORI) has this additional example :—

यथा च—
ज्योत्स्नापूरप्रसरधवले सैकतेऽस्मिन्सरय्वा
वादद्यूतं सुचिरमभवत् सिद्धयूनोः कयोश्चित् ।
एकः प्राह प्रथमनिहतं केशिनं कंसमन्यः
स त्वं तत्त्वं कथय भवता को हतस्तत्र पूर्वम् ॥

२. अनुरणनरूपकाश्रयेण-घ. ३. °सुरपुराक्रमे-MB. ४. शक्तो ज्ञातुं-KLV.

The following is an instance in point :—

Already he possesses Lakṣmī
Wherefore should he trouble me by churning ?
I fancy not he likes to sleep anon
Since his mind is never relaxed.
Or does he build a bridge across me once again ?
What use can it serve at all
To him recognised as a sovereign Emperor,
Over all the lands far and near.
The shuddering Ocean at your very approach
Seems to harbour such conjectures.

or to give another instance :—

Filling all space with the light of beauty
And smiling when your face doth remain,
O sweet-eyed one, since the sea doesn't swell,
I am sure it is only a mass of water (also, inertness).

In the above example since the beauty of the verses is due to metaphor which is suggested like resonance, we should properly regard them as instances of Suggested Metaphor.

Here is an instance of Suggested Simile :—

The eyes of heroes will not so delight
In their beloveds' red-anointed breasts
As in the temples of enemies' elephants,
Painted deep in red minium.

The following is another example selected from my own work *Viṣamabāṇalīlā* and the context is the conquest of Cupid over demons :—

Robbing the gems born with Lakṣmī
Had been their sole desire so far;
But now had Cupid put in its stead,
Their beloved's reddish lips.

The suggested figure of Paraleipsis is illustrated in the following verse :—

He alone can possibly recount
Hayagrīva's merits in full,
Who by single pots can measure out
The capacity of the mighty main.

अत्रातिशयोक्त्या[1] हयग्रीवगुणानामवर्णनीयताप्रतिपादनरूपस्यासाधारणतद्विशेषप्रकाशनपरस्याक्षेपस्य प्रकाशनम्[2]।

अर्थान्तरन्यासध्वनिः शब्दशक्तिमूलानुरणनरूपव्यङ्ग्योऽर्थशक्तिमूलानुरणनरूपव्यङ्ग्यश्च सम्भवति। तत्राद्यस्योदाहरणम्—

देव्वाएत्तम्मि फले किं कीरइ एत्तिअं पुणा भणिमो[3]।
कङ्किल्लपल्लवाः पल्लवाणँ अण्णाण ण सरिच्छा॥
[दैवायत्ते तु फले किं क्रियतामेतावत्पुनर्भणामः।
रक्ताशोकपल्लवाः पल्लवानामन्येषां न सदृशाः॥ च्छाया]

पदप्रकाशश्चायं ध्वनिरिति वाक्यस्यार्थान्तरतात्पर्येऽपि सति न विरोधः। द्वितीयस्योदाहरणं यथा—

हिअअट्ठाविअमण्णुं अवरुण्णमुहं हि मं पसाअन्त।
अवरद्धस्स वि ण हु दे पहुजाणअ रोसिउं सक्कम्॥
[हृदयस्थापितमन्युमपरोषमुखीमपि मां प्रसादयन्।
अपराद्धस्यापि न खलु ते बहुज्ञ रोषितुं शक्यम्॥ च्छाया]

अत्र हि वाच्यविशेषेण सापराधस्यापि बहुज्ञस्य कोपः कर्तुमशक्य इति समर्थकं सा[4]मान्यमन्वितमन्यत्तात्पर्येण प्रकाशते।

व्यतिरेकध्वनिरप्युभयरूपः सम्भवति। तत्राद्यस्योदाहरणं प्राक्प्रदर्शितमेव। द्वितीयस्योदाहरणं यथा—

जाएज्ज वणुद्देसे खुज्ज व्विअ पाअवो गडिअवत्तो[5]।
मा माणुसम्मि लोए ताएक्करसो दरिद्दो अ॥
[जायेय वनोद्देशे कुब्ज एव पादपो गलित[6]पत्रः।
मा मानुषे लोके त्यागैकरसो दरिद्रश्च॥ च्छाया]

अत्र हि त्यागैकरसस्य दरिद्रस्य जन्मानभिनन्दनं त्रुटित[7]कुब्ज[8]पादप-

---

१. अत्रातिशयोक्त्या निदर्शनया वा–KLV. २. प्रकाशनात्–KLV. ३. 'भणामि' ख-ग. ४. अर्थसामान्य°–घ. ५. घडिअवत्तो–घ. सडियपत्तो–KLV. ६. घटितपत्रः,–घ. ७. घटित°–MB. शटितपत्रकुब्ज–KLV. ८. 'त्रुटितपत्रकुब्ज'–घ.

Paraleipsis which describes the merits of Hayagrīva as indescribable and which thus brings out his extraordinary greatness is suggested in the above example by means of the expressed exaggeration.

The suggested figure of Illustration may take the form of both resonance-like suggestion based on power of the word and that based on power of sense. The following is an example of the former :—

When the fruit is left to Fate,
It cannot be helped;
Yet this we do repeat—
The red Aśoka's tender leaves
Are not the same as other leaves.

The suggested Illustration here is conveyed by a word (viz., fruit) and hence there is no contradiction involved when the sentence as a whole is taken as implying a general idea.

The following is an example of the latter :—

I conceal my anger in my heart
And show no sign of wrath upon my face;
Yet, O clever man, as you cajole me,
I cannot be angry with thee
Though you might an offender be.

The general statement that it is impossible to be angry with clever men though they might have given offence, is got at by exclusive suggestiveness of the expressed; and it illustrates the particular statement expressed herein.

In the same way the suggested Contrast also is two-fold. The first can be illustrated in the example already cited; and the following is an example of the second :—

I would rather be born as a tree,
Stunted and shorn of leaves, in the forest,
Than as a generous but poor person
In this world of men.

The expressed ideas in this example are —censure of the life of a generous-hearted poor person and praise of the life of

जन्माभिनन्दनं च साक्षाच्छब्दवाच्यम् । तथाविधादपि पादपात्ताद्दशस्य पुंस उपमानोपमेय[1]त्वप्रतीतिपूर्वकं शोच्यतायामाधिक्यं तात्पर्येण प्रकाशयति । उत्प्रेक्षाध्वनिर्यथा—

चन्दनासक्तभुजगनिःश्वासानिलमूर्च्छितः ।
मूर्च्छयत्येष पथिकान्मधौ मलयमारुतः ॥

अत्र हि मधौ मलयमारुतस्य पथिकमूर्च्छाकारित्वं[2] मन्मथोन्माथ[3]-दायित्वेनैव । तत्तु चन्दनासक्तभुजगनिःश्वासानिलमूर्च्छितत्वेनोत्प्रेक्षित[4]मित्युत्प्रेक्षा साक्षादनुक्तापि वाक्यार्थसामर्थ्यादनुरणनरूपा[5] लक्ष्यते । न चैवंविधे विषये इवादिशब्दप्रयोगमन्तरेणासंबद्धतैवेति[6] शक्यते[7] वक्तुम्, गमकत्वादन्यत्रापि तदप्रयोगे तदर्थावगतिदर्शनात् । तथा—

ईसाकलुसस्स वि तुह मुहस्स णं एस पुण्णिमाचन्दो ।
अज्ज सरिसत्तणं पाविऊण अङ्गे विअ ण माइ ॥

[ईर्ष्याकलुषस्यापि तव मुखस्य नन्वेष पूर्णिमाचन्द्रः ।
अद्य सदृशत्वं प्राप्याङ्ग एव न माति ॥ च्छाया]

यथा वा —

त्रासाकुलः परिपतन् परितो निकेतान्
पुंभिर्न कैश्चिदपि धन्विभिरन्वबन्धि ।
तस्थौ तथापि न मृगः क्वचिदङ्गनाभि-
राकर्णपूर्णनयनेषुहतेक्षणश्रीः ॥

---

१. 'उपमानोपमेयभावं'-क.-ख. २. 'करणत्वं'-क.-ख....कारणत्वं-KLV. ३. °थोन्माथकदायि-KLV. ४. ... तत्वेनोत्प्रेक्ष्यत इत्युत्प्रेक्षा-KLV. ५. 'रूपव्यङ्ग्या' -क.-ख-KLV. ६. 'सबद्धैवेति'-घ. ७. 'शक्यं'-घ., KLV. ८. इव-घ.

a bare and stunted tree. But it is arrived at by suggestion that a comparison is intended between the tree so described and the man so stated, and that the latter deserves far more pity than the former. In fact this Fancied Contrast is exclusively suggested.

The following is an example of suggested Poetic Fancy:—

The stuporous Southern Wind
Wafting the breaths of snakes entwined to sandal trees
Is causing stupor in travellers
In this season of spring.

Since the verse describes the season of spring, the Southern Wind can cause stupor in travellers only in so far as it excites the passion of love in them, And the Wind itself is poetically fancied as stuporous because of its carrying the breaths of snakes entwining sandal trees. This fancy is not expressed clearly by words (like "as though"), but is conveyed suggestively by the power of sense of the sentence itself just like resonance. It is not possible to say that, in the absence of express words like "as though", such instances have no connection at all with Poetic Fancy; for there is clear evidence for it. We find other examples too of Poetic Fancy where words expressing it are absent; e. g.

Obtaining at last similarity to your face
Sullied by jealousy though,
This full-orbed moon has outgrown
The limits of his own body in joy.

To give another instance:

Though no bowmen pursued the frightened deer,
Fleeing past houses (in the street),
The deer did not stop its flight anywhere,
Because its lovely eyes were shot at by arrows—
The full and sidelong glances of ladies.

शब्दार्थव्यवहारे च प्रसिद्धिरेव प्रमाणम् । श्लेषध्वनिर्यथा —

रम्या इति प्राप्तवतीः पताकाः रागं[1] विविक्ता इति वर्धयन्तीः ।
यस्यामसेवन्त नमद्वलीकाः समं वधूभिर्वलभीर्युवानः ॥

अत्र वधूभिः सह वलभीरसेवन्तेति वाक्यार्थप्रतीतेरनन्तरं वध्व इव वलभ्य इति श्लेषप्रतीतिरशब्दाप्यर्थसामर्थ्यान्मुख्यत्वेन वर्तते[2] । यथासंख्यध्वनिर्यथा —

अङ्कुरितः पल्लवितः कोरकितः पुष्पितश्च सहकारः ।
अङ्कुरितः पल्लवितः कोरकितः पुष्पितश्च[3] हृदि मदनः ॥

अत्र हि यथोद्देशमनूद्देशे[4] यच्चारुत्वमनुरणनरूपं मदनविशेषणभूताङ्कुरितादिशब्दगतं तन्मदनसहकारयोस्तुल्ययोगितासमुच्चयलक्षणाद्वाच्यादति[5]रिच्यमानमालक्ष्यते । एवमन्येऽप्यलङ्कारा यथायोगं योजनीयाः ।[6]

एवमलङ्कारध्वनिमार्गं व्युत्पाद्य तस्य प्रयोजनवत्तां ख्यापयितुमिदमुच्यते—

शरीरीकरणं येषां वाच्यत्वे न (वाच्यत्वेन) व्यवस्थितम् ।
तेऽलङ्काराः परां छायां यान्ति ध्वन्यङ्गतां गताः ॥ २८ ॥

ध्वन्यङ्गता चोभाभ्यां प्रकाराभ्यां व्यञ्जकत्वेन व्यङ्ग्यत्वेन च । तत्रेह प्रकरणाद्व्यङ्ग्यत्वेनेत्यवगन्तव्यम् । व्यङ्ग्यत्वेऽप्यलङ्काराणां प्राधान्य-

---

१. कामं–घ. २. विवर्तते–घ. ३. 'कुसुमितः'–ग. ४. 'अनुद्देशे'–क-ख–KLV. ५. 'अनति'–क-ख. ६. At this point KLV adds what appears like Kārikā–किञ्च

वाच्यालङ्कारशक्तेस्तु वस्तु यत्र प्रतीयते ।
अनुस्वानोपमव्यङ्ग्यो मन्तव्यः सोऽपि च ध्वनिः ॥

This is not found in any of the manuscripts.

Convention alone is the authority for all such usages of words and senses.

The following illustrates a suggested *double entendre* :

The youths in the town enjoyed
Terraces along with women;
For they were lovely with flags (also fame) aloft
In seclusion (also, symmetrical in limbs)
and swelling redness (also, love);
With arched ridges (also, the three folds on the
feminine belly) too.

As soon as we get the idea that the youths enjoyed the terraces of their houses with their women, we also get an idea of the *double entendre* that the terraces were like women. Though the words do not directly convey the *double entendre* (since the surface-meaning of words is enough to make the sentence meaningful), it happens to be principally suggested (as reinforcing the implied simile).

The following is an example of suggested Relative

Enumeration :—

The mango tree put forth sprouts,
Turned into leaf, budded and blossomed;
Love in the heart too put forth sprouts,
Turned into leaf, budded and blossomed.

Here, the resonance-like charm due to the adoption of the same order in predicating about Love and the mango tree far outshines the charm to the expressed figures—'Combination of Equals' and 'Conjunction of things with common actions.'

In the same way readers should find out for themselves instances of other suggested figures also. Having thus enunciated the way of suggested figures, the following is said in order to proclaim its usefulness:—

Those very figures which do not possess invariably even the capacity of forming the body of poetry when they appear in their expressed state, will be found to assume extraordinary beauty when they become participants of suggestion. 28

Participation in suggestion is possible in two ways: (i) through the suggesters and (2) through the suggested. In

विवक्षायामेव सत्यां ध्वनावन्तःपातः । इतरथा तु गुणीभूतव्यङ्ग्यत्वं प्रतिपादयिष्यन्ते[3] । अङ्गित्वेन व्यङ्ग्यतायामपि ।

अलङ्काराणां द्वयी गतिः – कदाचिद्वस्तुमात्रेण व्यज्यन्ते, कदाचिदलङ्कारान्तरेण[1] । तत्र —

व्यज्यन्ते वस्तुमात्रेण यदा[2]लङ्कृतयस्तदा ।

ध्रुवं ध्वन्यङ्गता तासां

अत्र हेतुः – **काव्यवृत्तेस्[3]तदाश्रयात् ॥ २९ ॥**

यस्मात्तत्र तथाविधव्यङ्ग्यालङ्कारपरत्वेनैव काव्यं प्रवृत्तम् । अन्यथा तु तद्वाक्यमात्रमेव स्यात् । तासामेवालङ्कृतीनाम् —

अलङ्कारान्तरव्यङ्ग्यभावे

पुनः[4] **ध्वन्यङ्गता भवेत् ।**

चारुत्वोत्कर्षतो व्यङ्ग्यप्राधान्यं यदि लक्ष्यते ॥ ३० ॥

उक्तं ह्येतत् – चारुत्वोत्कर्षनिबन्धनौ[5] वाच्यव्यङ्ग्ययोः प्राधान्यविवक्षा इति । वस्तुमात्रव्यङ्ग्यत्वे चालङ्काराणामनन्तरोपदर्शितेभ्य एवोदाहरणेभ्यो विषय उन्नेयः[6] । तदेवमर्थमात्रेणालङ्कारविशेषरूपेण वार्थेनार्थान्तरस्या[7]लङ्कारस्य वा प्रकाशने चारुत्वोत्कर्षनिबन्धने सति प्राधान्येऽर्थशक्त्युद्भवानुरणनरूपव्यङ्ग्यो ध्वनिरवगन्तव्यः ।

एवं ध्वनेः प्रभेदान् प्रतिपाद्य तदाभासविवेकं कर्तुमुच्यते —

१. 'अलङ्कारेण'-BP-त्र. २. ':यत्र'-क-ख. ३. °वृत्तिस्तदाश्रया-BP.
४. 'पुनः' क-ख पुस्तकयोर्नास्ति. ५. °न्धना हि-MB. ६. 'उन्नेतव्यः'-ग.
७. 'वस्त्वन्तरस्य'-क-ख.

this context it should be taken that the second kind of participation is meant. Even when figures are suggested, they will come under suggestion only if the suggested element is also intended as principal. Otherwise they will be of the form of subordinate suggested sense only as will be pointed out later. The same is true of instances also wherein, though there is a suggested figure, the expressed figures alone appear as principal in importance.

Figures have a two-fold course : (1) Sometimes they are suggested by the idea itself; (2) at other times they are suggested by figures. Of these,

> **When figures are suggested only by the idea itself, they are invariably participants of suggestion; for the very procedure of poetry is dependent upon it. 29**

The last quarter of the text adduces a reason in support of the statement made earlier. The reason is that poetry proceeds only by way of incorporating such suggested figures; otherwise it would be just an ordinary discourse.

> **If other figures are suggested they will become participants of suggestion in case the principal importance of the suggested is dicernible in respect of extraordinary charm. 30**

The phrase, ' even by expressed figures ,' is to be understood in the text after ' if other figures are suggested .'

It has already been remarked that the relative importance or otherwise of the expressed and the suggested depends solely upon the degree of beauty brought about by the two. Figures suggested by the idea itself may also be easily illustrated with examples already cited. Thus in fine, we may conclude that in instances where by means of either the idea (or sense) itself or a figure contained in the idea, another idea or another figure is suggested in such a way that the principal beauty is centred only in the latter, we will get resonance-like suggestion based upon the power of sense.

Having thus explained the varieties of suggestion, the following is said in order to distinguish between suggestion and its semblance :—

यत्र प्रतीयमानोऽर्थः प्रक्लिष्टत्वेनं[1] भासते ।
वाच्यस्याङ्गतया वापि नास्यासौ गोचरो ध्वनेः ॥ ३१ ॥

द्विविधोऽपि प्रतीयमानः स्फुटोऽस्फुटश्च । तत्र य एव स्फुटः शब्दशक्त्यार्थशक्त्या वा प्रकाशते स एव ध्वनेर्मार्गो नेतरः । स्फुटोऽपि योऽभिधेयस्याङ्गत्वेन प्रतीयमानोऽवभासते सोऽस्यानुरणनरूपव्यङ्ग्यस्य ध्वनेरगोचरः । यथा—

कमलाअरा ण मलिआ हंसा उड्डाविआ ण अ पिउच्छा ।
केण वि गामतडाए अब्भं उत्ताणअं फलिहम्[2] ॥
[कमलाकरा न मलिता हंसा उड्डायिता न च पितृष्वसः ।
केनापि ग्रामतटाकेऽभ्रमुत्तानितं क्षिप्तम् ॥ छाया]

अत्र हि प्रतीयमानस्य मुग्धवध्वा जलधरप्रतिबिम्बदर्शनस्य वाच्याङ्गत्वमेव । एवंविधे विषयेऽन्यत्रापि यत्र व्यङ्ग्यापेक्षया वाच्यस्य चारुत्वोत्कर्षप्रतीत्या प्राधान्यमवसीयते, तत्र व्यङ्ग्यस्याङ्गत्वेन प्रतीतेर्[3]ध्वनेरविषयत्वम् । यथा—

वाणीरकुडङ्गोड्डीणसउणिकोलाहलं सुणन्तीए ।
घरकम्मवावडाए बहुए सीअन्ति अङ्गाइं ॥
[वेतसलताकुञ्जोड्डीनशकुनिकोलाहलं शृण्वन्त्याः ।
गृहकर्मव्यापृताया वध्वाः सीदन्त्यङ्गानि ॥ छाया]

एवंविधो हि[4] विषयः प्रायेण गुणीभूतव्यङ्ग्यस्योदाहरणत्वेन निर्देक्ष्यते । यत्र तु प्रकरणादिप्रतिपत्त्या निर्धारितविशेषो वाच्योऽर्थः पुनः प्रतीयमानाङ्गत्वेनैवावभासते सोऽस्यैवानुरणनरूपव्यङ्ग्यस्य ध्वनेर्मार्गः । यथा –

उच्चिणसु पडिअं कुसुमं मा धुण सेहालिअं हलिअसुह्णे ।
अह दे विसमविरावो[6] ससुरेण सुओ वलअसद्दो ॥
[उच्चिनु पतितं कुसुमं मा धुनीः शेफालिकां हालिकस्नुषे ।
एष ते विषमविरावः श्वशुरेण श्रुतो वलयशब्दः ॥ छाया]

---

१. 'प्रश्लिष्टत्वेन '–क; प्रम्लिष्टत्वेन–BP, No. 254 (BORI), KLV. २. 'व्यूढं' इति गाथासप्तशतीधृतः पाठः । ३. प्रतीतौ ध्वने° KLV. ४. 'हि '–क. पुस्तके नास्ति. ५. 'व्यङ्ग्यत्वस्य '–ग. ६. Locana has rendered this in Sanskrit as विषमविपाकः possibly suggesting the reading विसमविवाओ; but हेमचन्द्र reads अवसाणविरसो under I. 19. of Kāvyānuśāsana.

If in an instance the implied sense is such that it can be caught only with great difficulty or if it is only subordinate to the expressed sense, in either case, it will not be an instance of suggestion. **31**

The implied sense is two-fold: (1) clear and (2) vague. Of these two, only the first kind belongs to the way of suggestion when it is conveyed by the power of either the word or the sense and not the second. Even if it should be clear, if the implied sense appears as subordinate to the expressed, it will be outside the scope of this resonance-like suggestion. For instance.

The lotuses have not been crushed,
Nor have the swans flown away, O aunt;
Some one has thrown the cloud itself
Into our village-tank upside down.

Here the implied idea is that the guileless woman saw a reflection of the cloud, and it is subordinate to the expressed idea. In this and such other instances where we find greater beauty in the expressed than in the suggested element and can conclude therefore that the expressed is more important than the implied, we cannot see suggestion instanced because it happens to be subordinate only. To take an example :—

As she hears the twitter of birds,
Flying away from the shrubs of water-reeds,
The limbs of the daughter-in-law
Busy in her chores
Droop (all too suddenly).

It will be pointed out in the sequel that examples like the above illustrate subordinate suggested poetry. But on the other hand, resonance-like suggestion is present in instances, where, even after determining all the implications of the expressed sense in view of the context and so forth, we find that the expressed appears only as subsidiary to the suggested. For example :—

Pick the fallen flowers only,
Don't shake the plant,
O village-chief's daughter-in-law,
For, the loud jingle of your bangles
Is heard by your father-in-law!

अत्र ह्यविनयपतिना सह रममाणा सखी बहिःश्रुतवलयकलकलया सख्या प्रतिबोध्यते । एतदपेक्षणीयं वाच्यार्थप्रतिपत्तये । प्रतिपन्ने च वाच्ये[1]ऽर्थे तस्याविनयप्रच्छादनतात्पर्येणाभिधीयमानत्वात्पुनर्व्यङ्ग्याङ्गत्वमेवे[2]त्यस्मिन्ननुरणनरूपव्यङ्ग्यध्वनावन्तर्भावः ।

ए[3]वं विवक्षितवाच्यस्य ध्वनेस्तदाभासविवेके प्रस्तु[4]ते सत्यविवक्षितवाच्यस्यापि तं कर्तु[5]माह–

अव्युत्पत्तेरशक्तेर्वा निबन्धो यः स्खलद्गतेः ।
शब्दस्य स च न ज्ञेयः सूरिभिर्विषयो ध्वनेः ॥ ३२ ॥

स्खलद्गतेरुपचरितस्य शब्दस्या[6]व्युत्पत्तेरशक्तेर्वा निबन्धो यः स च न ध्वनेर्विषयः । यत[7]ः—

सर्वेष्वेव प्रभेदेषु स्फुटत्वेनावभासनम् ।
यद्व्यङ्ग्यस्याङ्गिभूतस्य तत्पूर्णं ध्वनिलक्षणम् ॥ ३३ ॥

तच्चोदाहृतविषयमेव ॥

इति श्री रा[8]जानकानन्दवर्धनाचार्यविरचिते सहृदयालोके द्वितीय उद्योतः ॥

---

१. 'वाच्यार्थे' – क-ख. 'अर्थे' – घ. पुस्तके नास्ति. २. 'व्यङ्गत्वमेव' –क-ख. ३. 'एवंविधवाच्यस्य' –ग. ४. कृते–KLV. ५. 'तत्कर्तुं' – क-ख. ६. 'अशक्तेरव्युत्पत्तेः' – क-ख. ७. 'यतश्च' –घ. ८. 'श्रीमदानन्द°' – क-ख. ९. 'काव्यालोके' – क-ख; सहृदयहृदयालोके No. 254 (BORI).

Here a lady dallying with a rude paramour is warned by her confidant who hears the loud sound of her bangles outside. We have to understand so much in order to grasp the expressed sense itself fully. After this is understood, when we catch the hidden hint that the confidant is trying to conceal the crudeness of the paramour at the same time, the verse once again becomes a participant in suggestion and deserves to be classed as an instance of resonance-like suggestion.

Having thus distinguished between the real and the apparent forms of suggestion with intended expressed sense, the author now proceeds to distinguish the real and apparent forms of suggestion with unintended expressed sense :—

The usage of a word with faltering denotation either because of the poet's want of education or because of his lack of genius, should not be regarded by the learned as a way of suggestion. 32

Usage of words with only a metaphorical application due to either inadequate education or want of genius will not come within the scope of suggestion.

The full definition of suggestion in all its varieties includes clarity of mainfestation and principal importance of the suggested element. 33

This has been abundantly illustrated by now.

तृतीयोद्द्योतः

एवं व्यङ्ग्यमुखेनैव[1] ध्वनेः प्रदर्शिते सप्रभेदे स्वरूपे पुनर्व्यञ्जकमुखेनैतत्[2]प्रकाश्यते —

अविवक्षितवाच्यस्य पदवाक्यप्रकाशता ।
तदन्यस्यानुरणनरूपव्यङ्ग्यस्य च ध्वनेः ॥ १ ॥

अविवक्षितवाच्यस्यात्यन्ततिरस्कृतवाच्ये प्रभेदे[3] पदप्रकाशता यथा महर्षेर्व्यासस्य

सप्तैताः समिधः श्रियः[4]

यथा वा कालिदासस्य —

कः सन्नद्धे विरहविधुरां त्वय्युपेक्षेत जायाम्

यथा वा[5] —

किमिव हि मधुराणां मण्डनं नाकृतीनाम्[6]

एतेषूदाहरणेषु 'समिध' इति 'सन्नद्ध' इति 'मधुराणामि'ति च पदानि व्यञ्जकत्वाभिप्राये[7]णैव कृतानि । तस्यैवार्थान्तरसंक्रमितवाच्ये यथा —

रामेण प्रियजीवितेन तु कृतं प्रेम्णः प्रिये नोचितम्[8] ।

अत्र रामेणेत्येतत्पदं साहसैकरसत्वादिव्यङ्ग्याभिसंक्रमित[9]वाच्यं व्यञ्जकम् ।

यथा वा—

एमेअ जणो तिस्सा देउ कवोलोपमाइ ससिबिम्बम् ।
परमत्थविआरे उण चन्दो चन्दो विअ वराओ ॥
[एवमेव जनस्तस्या ददाति कपोलोपमायां शशिबिम्बम् ।
परमार्थविचारे पुनश्चन्द्रश्चन्द्र इव वराकः ॥ छाया]

---

१. व्यङ्ग्यमुखेन-MB. २. मुखेन तत्प्रकाश्यते-घ. ३. 'स्वप्रभेदे'-घ. ४. धृतिः क्षमा दया शौचं कारुण्यं वागनिष्ठुरा । मित्राणां चानभिद्रोहः सप्तैताः समिधः श्रियः ॥ MB. ५. 'यथा वा'-ग-पुस्तके नास्ति; 'यथा वा तस्यैव'-घ. ६. सरसिजमनुविद्धं शैवलेनापि रम्यम् । मलिनमपि हिमांशोर्लक्ष्म लक्ष्मीं तनोति ॥ इयमधिकमनोज्ञा वल्कलेनापि तन्वी किमिव... ॥ MB. ७. 'व्यञ्जकाभिप्रायेणैव'-घ. MB. ८. MB. cites full verse as given in लोचन. ९. 'व्यङ्ग्यार्थसंक्रामित'-क-ख.

THE THIRD FLASH

So far the nature and varieties of suggestion have been pointed out in detail from the standpoint of the suggested. Now the same shall be set forth from the standpoint of the suggester:

Both the varieties of suggestion with unintended literal import and reasonance-like suggestion are suggested by individual words and by whole sentences. 1

Here are some examples for suggestive words which convey suggestion of the sub-class "with the expressed sense completely lost," under the class of "unintended expressed sense."

1 ...*These seven are the faggots of wealth.*

2 *When you have come well equipped,*
Who can any more neglect his wife ?

3 *What will not be an ornament to figures*
Which are by nature comely.

In these examples, the words, *faggots*, *equipped* and *comely* are used with exclusive suggestive force.

An example of a suggestive word carrying suggestion of the sub-class, 'with expressed sense merged in another' is furnished in the following:—

Nothing worthy of your love has been done, O sweet,
By Rāma whose love for his own life is greater.

Here the expressed sense of the word Rāma merges itself in the suggested ideas of unique valour, etc. and hence the word carries a suggestive force.

The following is another instance:—

Thus do the folk quote the moon
As a fitting comparison to her cheeks;
But if one were to reflect aright,
The moon is but a poor fellow like the moon.

The word 'moon' used for a second time in the above instance is a conveyer of suggestion 'with expressed sense merged in another.'

अत्र द्वितीयश्चन्द्रशब्दोऽर्थान्तरसंक्रमितवाच्यः ।

अविवक्षितवाच्यस्यात्यन्ततिरस्कृतवाच्ये प्रभेदे वाक्यप्रकाशता यथा—

‘ या निशा सर्वभूतानां तस्यां जागर्ति संयमी ।
यस्यां जाग्रति भूतानि सा निशा पश्यतो मुनेः ॥

अनेन हि वाक्येन[1] न निशार्थो न च जागरणार्थः कश्चिद्विवक्षितः । किं तर्हि ? तत्त्वज्ञानावहितत्वमतत्त्वपराङ्मुखत्वं च मुनेः प्रतिपाद्यत इति तिरस्कृतवाच्य[2]स्य व्यञ्जकत्वम् । तस्यैवार्थान्तरसंक्रमितवाच्यस्य वाक्यप्रकाशता यथा—

विसमइओ च्चिअ काण वि काण वि वोलेइ अमिअणिम्माओ ।
काण वि विसामिअमओ काण वि अविसामओ कालो ॥
[विषमय इव केषामपि केषामपि प्रयात्यमृतनिर्माणः ।
केषामपि विषामृतमयः केषामप्यविषामृतः कालः ॥ इति च्छाया]

अत्र हि वाक्ये विषामृतशब्दाभ्यां दुःखसुखरूपसंक्रमितवाच्याभ्यां व्यवहार इत्यर्थान्तरसंक्रमित[3]वाच्य[4]स्य व्यञ्जकत्वम् ।

विवक्षिताभिधेयस्यानुरणनरूपव्यङ्ग्यस्य शब्दशक्त्युद्भवे प्रभेदे पद-प्रकाशता यथा—

प्रातुं[5] धनैरर्थिजनस्य वाञ्छां दैवेन सृष्टो यदि नाम नास्मि ।
पथि प्रसन्नाम्बुधरस्तडागः कूपोऽथवा किं न जडः कृतोऽहम् ॥

अत्र हि जड इति[6] पदं निर्विण्णेन वक्त्रात्मसमानाधिकरणतया प्रयुक्त-मनुरणनरूपतया कूपसमानाधिकरणतां स्वशक्त्या प्रतिपद्यते[7] ।

---

१. ‘ वाक्यार्थेन ’–ग. २. वाच्यस्यास्य–घ-B. P., KLV. ३. ‘ संक्रान्त ’–क-ख. ४. वाच्यस्यास्य – घ. ५. ‘ त्रातुं ’–क - ख, दातुं – MB. ६. ‘ इत्येतत् ’ – क - ख. ७. प्रतिपाद्यते–MB. No. 254 (BORI).

An example of a suggestive sentence of this sub-class of suggestion itself under the class of ' that with unintended expressed sense is the following:—

When it is night for all creatures.
The saint doth keep vigil;
When the creatures are awake,
It will be night for the wise seer.

The sentence does not intend as its purport either the idea of night or the idea of waking state. What else is it then? The idea intended is being alive to the knowledge of Reality and averse to unreality on the part of a sage. Hence the expressed sense of the sentence is completely given up and the sentence is suggestive.

Here is an example of a suggestive sentence conveying the sub-class of suggestion, viz., ' that with expressed sense merged in another ':—

To some it passes like nectar indeed.
To some both poison and nectar;
And to some neither poison nor nectar.

Here the words ' poison ' and ' nectar ' are used in such a way as to merge in the sense of ' miserable ' and ' happy. ' Hence these words possess the suggestivity of the type mentioned.

The following illustrates the suggestivity of a word in the sub-class of resonance-like suggestion based upon the word under the class of suggestion with intended expressed sense:—

Granting I was not created by Fate
To fulfil the wishes of suppliants,
Why was I not made insentient,
Say, a limpid lake on the roadside,
Or even a well for that matter ?

The word ' insentient ' is used by the despondent speaker to apply to himself; but it also applies to the lake and the well by its own verbal force.

तस्यैव वाक्यप्रकाशता यथा हर्षचरिते सिंहनादवाक्येषु–

‘ वृत्ते[1]ऽस्मिन्महाप्रलये धरणीधारणायाधुना त्वं शेषः । ’

एतद्धि वाक्यमनुरणनरूपमर्थान्तरं शब्दशक्त्या स्फुटमेव प्रकाशयति[2] ।

अस्यैव कविप्रौढोक्तिमात्रनिष्पन्नशरीरस्यार्थशक्त्युद्भवे प्रभेदे पदप्रकाशता यथा हरिविजये–

चूअंकुरावअंसं छणपसरमहग्घणमणहरसुरामोअम्[3] ।
असमप्पिअं[4] पि गहिअं कुसुमसरेण महुमासलच्छिमुहम् ॥
[चूताङ्कुरावतंसं क्षणप्रसरमहार्घमनोहरसुरामोदम् ।
असमर्पितमपि गृहीतं कुसुमशरेण मधुमासलक्ष्मीमुखम् ॥ छाया]

अत्र असमर्पितमपि कुसुमशरेण मधुमासलक्ष्म्या मुखं गृहीतमित्यसमर्पितमपीत्येतदर्थाभिधायिपदमर्थशक्त्या कुसुमशरस्य बलात्कारं प्रकाशयति[5] ।

अत्रैव प्रभेदे वाक्यप्रकाशता यथोदाहृतं प्राक् ‘ सज्जेहि सुरहिमासो ’ इत्यादि । अत्र सज्जयति सुरभिमासो न तावदर्पयत्यनङ्गाय शरानित्ययं वाक्यार्थः[6] कविप्रौढोक्तिमात्रनिष्पन्नशरीरो मन्मथोन्माथकृतापादनावस्थां[7] वसन्तसमयस्य सूचयति ।

स्वतःसंभवि[8]शरीरार्थशक्त्युद्भवे प्रभेदे पदप्रकाशता यथा–

वाणिअअ हत्थिदन्ता कुत्तो अम्हाण वाघकित्ती अ ।
जाव लुलिआलअमुही घरम्मि परिसक्कए सुण्हा ॥
[वाणिजक हस्तिदन्ताः कुतोऽस्माकं व्याघ्रकृत्तयश्च ।
यावल्लुलितालकमुखी गृहे परिष्वक्कते स्नुषा ॥ छाया]

---

१. प्रवृत्ते॰ MB. २. ‘ लक्षयति ’–क-ख. ३. छणपसरमहं घणमहुरामोअम्–घ. ४. अपणामअं वि.–क–ख. ५. लक्षयति–क - ख. ६. No. XII 184 (BORI) and No. XII 185 (BORI) stop at this and omit the rest up to सूचयति । ७. ‘ वस्थानात् ’–क - ख; मन्मथोन्माथकदनावस्थां – BP.; No. 254 (BORI). ८. ‘ संभवितार्थ॰ ’ - ग., MB.

An example of suggestive sentence coming under this very class of suggestion is found in the sentences of Siṁhanāda in the *Harṣacarita*:—

When this joy-ending incident has befallen, you are the only person left to assume the burden of state (just as the Primeval Serpent alone is capable of bearing the burden of the earth when the great deluge is raging).

This sentence clearly conveys the resonance-like suggested sense by its verbal force alone.

The following quotation from *Harivijaya* (of Sarvasena) is an example of suggestive word in the sub-class of suggestion based upon the power of sense, viz., that which exists only in the ornate expression of the poet:—

Though unoffered, Lord Cupid caught
The face of the goddess of Spring,
Whose ears were bedecked with mango-sprouts
And perfume profoundly sweet.

In the statement, ' though unoffered, the face of the goddess of Spring was caught by Cupid ', the word ' unoffered ' which denotes only a circumstance, suggests, by the power of sense, the use of force on the part of Cupid.

In this variety of suggestion itself, an example of a suggestive sentence is furnished in the illustration already cited, viz., ' The spring gets ready ' etc. In that example the purport of the sentence that ' the spring keeps ready but does not yet fling the arrows of Cupid ' is existent only in the ornate expression of the poet and it suggests the passion-exciting nature of spring.

The following is an instance of word-suggestiveness of the sub-class of suggestion viz., ' naturally existing ', under the class of suggestion based upon the power of sense:—

O merchant, how can we have
Elephant-tusks or tiger-skins,
So long as the daughter-in-law here
Moves with curls fluttering on her face ?

अत्र लुलितालकमुखीत्येतत्पदं व्याधवध्वाः स्वतःसम्भावितशरीरार्थशक्त्या सुरतक्रीडासक्तिं सूचयंस्तदीयस्य[1] भर्तुः सततसंभोगक्षामतां प्रकाशयति ।

तस्यैव वाक्यप्रकाशता यथा —

सिहिपिञ्छकण्णऊरा बहुआ वाहस्स गव्विरी भमइ ।
मुत्ताफलरइअपसाहणाणं मज्झे सवत्तीणम् ॥
[शिखिपिच्छकर्णपूरा भार्या व्याधस्य गर्विणी भ्रमति ।
मुक्ताफलरचितप्रसाधनानां मध्ये सपत्नीनाम् ॥ छाया]

अनेनापि[2] वाक्येन व्याधवध्वा शिखिपिञ्छकर्णपूराया नवपरिणीतायाः कस्याश्चित्सौभाग्यातिशयः प्रकाश्यते[3] । तत्सं[4]म्भोगैकरसो[5] मयूरमात्रमारणसमर्थः पतिर्जात इत्यर्थप्रकाशनात् तदन्यासां चिरपरिणीतानां मुक्ताफलरचितप्रसाधनानां दौर्भाग्यातिशयः ख्याप्यते । तत्सम्भोगकाले स एव व्याधः करिवरवधव्यापारसमर्थ आसीदित्यर्थप्रकाशनात्[6] ।

ननु काव्यविशेषो ध्वनिरित्युक्तं तत्कथं तस्य पदप्रकाशता । काव्यविशेषो हि विशिष्टार्थप्रतिपत्तिहेतुः शब्द[7]सन्दर्भविशेषः । तद्भावश्च पदप्रकाशत्वे नोपपद्यते । पदानां स्मारकत्वेनावाचकत्वात् । उच्यते — स्यादेष दोषः यदि वाचकत्वं प्रयोजकं ध्वनिर्व्यवहारे स्यात् । न त्वेवम्; तस्य व्यञ्जकत्वेन व्यवस्थानात्[8] । किं च काव्यानां शरीरि[9]णामिव संस्थान[10]विशेषावच्छिन्नसमुदायसाध्यापि चारुत्वप्रतीतिरन्वयव्यतिरेकाभ्यां भागेषु कल्प्यत इति पदानामपि व्यञ्जकत्वमुखेन व्यवस्थितो ध्वनिव्यवहारो न विरोधी ।

अनिष्टस्य श्रुतिर्यद्वदापादयति दुष्टताम् ।
श्रुतिदुष्टादिषु व्यक्तं तद्वदिष्टश्रुति[11]र्गुणम्[12] ॥

---

१. 'सूचयति तदीयस्य' - ग. २. 'अपि'—क-ख. पुस्तकयोर्नास्ति. ३. 'प्रख्याप्यते' -ग. ४. तत्संभोग इत्यारभ्य 'ख्याप्यते' इति पर्यन्तं घ-पुस्तके नास्ति. ५. ० रथो - Bl'. ६. 'प्रदर्शनात्' - ग. ७. शब्द omitted in No 185 XII (BORI). ७. न ध्वनिव्यवहारे-घ. ८. एवं छलेन परिहृत्य वस्तुवृत्तेनोपसंहरति। This additional sentence occurs after this in XII 185 (BORI) which occurs only as marginalia in XII 184 (BORI). ९. शरीरिणामिव - घ. & No. 254 (BORI). १०. 'संस्थिति' - ग. ११. श्रुतिः- क-ख. १२. गुणः- ग.

The word 'with curls fluttering on her face' can possibly apply to the hunter's wife and at the same time it conveys by the power of sense her great passion for dalliance and the consequent weakness of her husband due to his sexual indulgence.

An example of sentence-suggestiveness in the same variety of suggestion is the illustration–*Adorning her ear with peacock's plumes, etc.*, already cited (under III. 24). This sentence too illustrates the great conjugal felicity of a hunter's newly wedded wife whose ears are bedecked with peacock's plumes. Besides, since it is hinted at that the husband's strength, which once was great enough to kill down mightiest elephants and bring many rare pearls to his wives who used them as ornaments, has now been reduced to such an extent by constant dalliance with her that he can kill only peacocks, the conjugal misfortune of the first wives is also suggested.

One might raise the following objection at this juncture :— 'Suggestion has been defined earlier as a species of poetry.' How can such a species be suggested by a word ? A species of poetry can mean only that composition of words which enables one to understand a specific meaning. This fact will be inapplicable to it when it is held that it is suggested by a word; for, words are only reminders of such a suggested meaning and not at all denoters.

Here is our answer to the objection :— the alleged defect would have tainted our assertion if it were true that denotation was the criterion for deciding the existence of suggestion. But it is not true. It has already been established that suggestiveness alone is the criterion in question. In life also, we often speak of the presence or absence of beauty in the individual limbs of persons though in fact it is only the combined beauty of all the graceful and symmetrical limbs that can really be present or absent in a person's body as a whole. In the same way, there is no contradiction involved in one's regarding the individual words also as suggesters of beauty which is really occasioned by the combination of different words and in referring to them by the word *suggestion*. These ideas are summed up in the following aphorisms :—

1. *Just as reminiscence of something undesired clearly becomes a blemish in defects like "Indelicacy", so also the reminiscence of something desired should be regarded as an excellence,*

पदानां स्मारकत्वेऽपि पदमात्रावभासिनः ।
तेन ध्वनेः प्रभेदेषु सर्वेष्वेवास्ति रम्यता ॥
विच्छित्तिशोभिनैकेन भूषणेनेव कामिनी ।
पदद्योत्येन सुकवेर्ध्वनिना भाति भारती ॥

इति परिकरश्लोकाः ।

यस्त्वलक्ष्यक्रमव्यङ्ग्यो ध्वनिर्वर्णपदादिषु ।
वाक्ये सङ्घटनायां च स प्रबन्धे[1]ऽपि दीप्यते ॥ २ ॥

तत्र वर्णानामनर्थकत्वाद्द्योतकत्वमसम्भव[2]वीत्याशङ्क्येदमुच्यते—

शषौ सरेफसंयोगो[3] ढकारश्चापि भूयसा ।
विरोधिनः स्युः शृङ्गारे ते न वर्णा रसश्च्युतः[4] ॥ ३ ॥

त एव तु निवेश्यन्ते बीभत्सादौ रसे यदा ।
तदा तं दीपयन्त्येव तेन वर्णा रसश्च्युतः[5] ॥ ४ ॥

श्लोकद्वयेनान्वयव्यतिरेकाभ्यां वर्णानां द्योतकत्वं दर्शितं भवति । पदे चालक्ष्यक्रमव्यङ्ग्यस्य द्योतनं[6] यथा—

उत्कम्पिनी भयपरिस्खलितांशुकान्ता
  ते लोचने प्रतिदिशं विधुरे क्षिपन्ती ।
क्रूरेण दारुणतया सहसैव दग्धा
  धूमान्धितेन[7] दहनेन न वीक्षितासि ॥

अत्र हि "ते" इत्येतत्पदं रसमयत्वेन स्फुटमेवावभासते सहृदयानाम्[8] ।

---

१. प्रबन्धोऽभिधीयते: -क, ख. २. 'न संभवति'-ग., MB. ३. संयोगौ-घ. ४. रसच्युतः-घ, BP. ५. रसच्युतः-घ, BP. ६. द्योतकत्वं-घ. ७. 'धूमान्धितेन'-क-ख. ८. 'सहृदयानां'-क-ख पुस्तकयोर्नास्ति.

2. *Though words are only reminders, there is certainly charm therefrom in all the varieties of suggestion that manifests itself through the individual words.*

3. *Just like a damsel who appears charming by just a single ornament full of beauty, so also the work of a good poet will appear to advantage when adorned by suggestion even in one word.*

Suggestion with undiscerned sequentiality will flash forth in letter, word etc., sentence, composition, and finally the work as a whole. **2**

The objection that letters cannot be suggestive because they are meaningless by themselves is answered below :—

The (Sanskrit) letters 'ś', and 'ṣ' letters conjunct with 'r' and 'ḍh'-all these become deterrents of the erotic sentiment. Hence those letters are not conducive to a particular sentiment. **3**

When these very letters are employed in relation to the sentiment of disgust and so forth, they will only intensify them. Hence also letters suggest sentiments. **4**

The above aphorisms show negatively and positively tha letters do possess suggestiveness.

Suggestiveness of word in 'suggestion with undiscerned sequentiality' is illustrated below :—

There thou stood, trembling all over
With the hem of thy garment slipping down in fear
And throwing those distressed glances
In each and every direction;
Oh ! you were burnt down so soon
By the cruel fire fiercely;
You could not be seen by him surely,
Since he was blinded by his own smoke.

That the word *those* in this example is suggestive of sentiment can be clearly discerned by receptive critics. Another example :

यथा वा

झगिति कनकचित्रे तत्र दृष्टे कुरङ्गे
रभसविलसितास्ते दृष्टिपाताः प्रियायाः ।
पवनविलुलितानामुत्पलानां पलाश-
प्रकरमिव किरन्तः स्मर्यमाणा दहन्ति ॥*

पदावयवेन द्योतनं यथा —

व्रीडा[1]योगान्नतवदनया सन्निधाने गुरूणां
बद्धोत्कम्पं कुचकलशयोर्मन्युमन्तर्निगृह्य ।
तिष्ठेत्युक्तं किमिव न तया यत्समुत्सृज्य बाष्पं
मय्यासक्तश्चकितहरिणीहारिनेत्रत्रिभागः ॥

इत्यत्र "त्रिभाग"शब्दः ।

वाक्यरूपश्चालक्ष्यक्रमव्यङ्ग्यो ध्वनिः शुद्धोऽलङ्कारसङ्की[2]र्णश्चेति द्विधा मतः । तत्र शुद्धस्योदाहरणं यथा रामाभ्युदये – 'कृतककुपितैः—' इत्यादि श्लोकः । एतद्धि वाक्यं परस्परानुरागं परिपोषप्रा[3]प्तं प्रदर्शयत्सर्वत एव परं रसतत्त्वं प्रकाशयति ।

*This verse is not commented upon in the Locana.

१. क-ख – पुस्तकयोश्चतुर्थचरण एवास्य श्लोकस्यास्ति. २. ०ऽलङ्कारान्तरसङ्कीर्ण° – MB; No. 254 (BORI) ३. 'परस्परानुबद्धरागपरिपोषकतया प्राप्त°'–क-ख.

The sight of the deer of wondrous gold,
Suddenly brought into my beloved's looks
Such a fine glimmer and sweetness
—Even like the petals of the dark lily
Blown about by a sudden breeze—
That even a recollection of those looks
Brings me scorching pain.

Suggestiveness of a part of a word is instanced in the following :—

With her shy face bent down in the presence of elders.
Suppressing her great sorrow
Which made her bosoms heave,
Did she not almost tell me "remain" !
When through her tears she fixed on me
Her one-third glance so lovely
As that of a frightened fawn ?

Here the part of the word viz., 'one-third' is suggestive. A suggestive sentence in 'suggestion with undiscerned sequentiality' is two-fold : (1) Pure and (2) Mingled with another figure. The following quotation from *Rāmābhyudaya* is an example of the first :—

He, whom you followed even into the forest
With feigned anger, tears and piteous looks;
Though stopped lovingly by mother so much,
That very beloved of yours, O sweet,
Lives indeed with a heart of adamant,
Even when he is parted from you,
And even though he sees the quarters
Darkened by the new rain-clouds.

This sentence as a whole exquisitely conveys fullness of sentiment showing as it does the height of mutual love (in the hero and the heroine).

अलङ्कारान्तरसङ्कीर्णो यथा – 'स्मरनवनदीपूरेणोढाः'[1] इत्यादिश्लोकः। अत्र हि रूपकेण यथोक्तव्यङ्ग्यव्यञ्जकलक्षणानुगतेन प्रसाधितो[2] रसः सुतरामभिव्यज्यते ।

अलक्ष्यक्रमव्यङ्ग्यः सङ्घटनायां भासते ध्वनिरित्युक्तम्, तत्र सङ्घटनास्वरूपमेव तावन्निरूप्यते[3]–

असमासा समासेन मध्यमेन च भूषिता ।
तथा दीर्घसमासेति त्रिधा सङ्घटनोदिता ॥ ५ ॥

कैश्चित् ।

तां केवलमनूद्येदमुच्यते--

गुणानाश्रित्य तिष्ठन्ती माधुर्यादीन्व्यनक्ति सा ।
रसान्–

सा[4] सङ्घटना रसादीन् व्यनक्ति गुणानाश्रित्य तिष्ठन्तीति । अत्र च विकल्प्यं गुणानां सङ्घटनायाश्चैक्यं व्यतिरेको वा । व्यतिरेकेऽपि द्वयी गतिः[5]। गुणाश्रया सङ्घटना, सङ्घटनाश्रया वा गुणा इति । तत्रैक्यपक्षे सङ्घटनाश्रयगुणपक्षे च गुणानात्मभूतानाधेयभूतान्वाश्रित्य तिष्ठन्ती सङ्घटना रसादीन् व्यनक्तीत्ययमर्थः । यदा तु नानात्वपक्षे[6] गुणाश्रयसङ्घटनापक्षः[7] तदा गुणानाश्रित्य तिष्ठन्ती[8] गुणपरतन्त्रस्वभावा न तु गुणरूपैवेत्यर्थः । किं पुनरेवं विकल्पनस्य[9] प्रयोजनमित्यभिधीयते ।

यदि गुणाः सङ्घटना चेत्येकं[10] तत्त्वं सङ्घटनाश्रया वा गुणाः, तदा सङ्घटनाया इव गुणानामनियतविषयत्वप्रसङ्गः[11] । गुणानां हि माधुर्यप्रसाद-

---

1. Locana gives the whole stanze as follows :—

स्मरनवनदीपूरेणोढाः पुनर्गुरुसेतुभि-
र्यदपि विधृताः तिष्ठन्त्यारादपूर्णमनोरथाः ।
तदपि लिखितप्रख्यैरङ्गैः परस्परमुन्मुखा
नयननलिनीनालानीतं पिबन्ति रसं प्रियाः ॥

२. 'प्रसाङ्गिनः' क-ख. No. 184 & No. 185 XII (BORI). ३. नात्रत्यथपं निरूप्यते - MB, No. 254 (BORI) - KLV. ४. 'सा' -घ पुस्तके नास्ति ५. गतिर्बोद्धव्या - घ. ६. नानात्वपक्षो KLV. ७. °पक्षश्च - MB. KLV ८. तिष्ठन्तीति - घ. ९. विकल्पस्य - MB. १०. 'चैकं' ग. ११. गुणानामप्यनियत° - MB.

The following is an example of the second variety :—

Buoyed up by the flooded river of new love,
But obstructed by the mighty dams (or elders like dams),
Though the lovers have to stay still
With their desires unfulfilled
Like so many figures with painted limbs,
Yet they remain facing one another
And drink the nectar of love
Through pipes of eye-lotuses.

The sentiment is beautifully suggested here by the suggestive figure, metaphor.

It has been mentioned that 'suggestion with undiscerned sequentiality' can relate to 'texture' or composition also. The nature of 'texture' itself is explained below :—

'Texture' is said to be of three kinds: (1) without compounds (2) with medium-sized compounds and (3) with long compounds. 5

'By others' is to be understood in the text. It is only quoted here and will be commented upon in what follows :—

Composition or texture is grounded in qualitites like Sweetness and suggests sentiments.

'Composition or texture is grounded in qualities and suggests sentiments'. Here a doubt may arise (a) whether there is identity between qualities and texture or (b) whether there is difference. In case there were difference between them, once again there would be scope for these two alternatives: (c) qualities may be the substratum of texture or (d) texture may itself be the substratum of qualities. Of these, in the alternatives of (a) and (d) the text would mean that texture is grounded in qualities which are either identical with itself or the nature of its attributes and that it suggests sentiments. But in the other alternatives of (b) and (c) 'grounded in qualities' will mean 'depending upon qualities', and not 'identical with qualities'. If one were to ask — "what is the use of such alternative explanations ?"—here is our reply :—

In the views (a) and (d) qualities too will come to be as variable as texture itself (though in fact they are constant).

प्रकर्षः करुणविप्रलम्भशृङ्गारविषय एव। रौद्राद्भुतादिविषयमोजः। माधुर्यप्रसादौ रसभावतदाभासविषयावेवेति विषयनियमो व्यवस्थितः, सङ्घटनायास्तु स[1] विघटते। तथा हि शृङ्गारेऽपि दीर्घसमासा दृश्यते[2] रौद्रादिष्वसमासा चेति।

तत्र शृङ्गारे दीर्घसमासा यथा – 'मन्दारकुसुमरेणुपिञ्जरितालका' इति। यथा वा –

अनवरतनयनजललवनिपतनपरिमुषितपत्रलेखं ते[3]।
करतलनिषण्णमबले वदनमिदं कं न तापयति॥ इत्यादौ।

तथा रौद्रादिष्वप्यसमासा[4] दृश्यते, यथा – 'यो यः शस्त्रं बिभर्ति स्वभुजगुरुमदः' इत्यादौ। तस्मान्न[5] सङ्घटनास्वरूपाः, न च सङ्घटनाश्रया गुणाः।

ननु यदि सङ्घटना गुणानां नाश्रयस्तत्किमालम्बना एते परिकल्प्यन्ताम्[6]। उच्यते – प्रतिपादितमेवैषामालम्बनम्।

तमर्थमवलम्बन्ते येऽङ्गिनं ते गुणाः स्मृताः।
अङ्गाश्रितास्त्वलङ्कारा मन्तव्याः कटकादिवत्॥ इति[7]।

अथवा भवन्तु शब्दाश्रया एव गुणाः, न चैषामनुप्रासादितुल्यत्वम्। यस्मादनुप्रासादयोऽनपेक्षितार्थ[8]शब्दधर्मा एव प्रतिपादिताः[9]। गुणास्तु व्यङ्ग्यविशेषावभासिनो वाच्यप्रतिपादनसमर्थाः शब्दधर्मा एवं[10]। शब्दधर्मत्वं चैषामन्याश्रयत्वेऽपि शरीराश्रयत्वमिव[11] शौर्यादीनाम्।

---

१. 'असौ'–क–ख. न संघटते – MB. २. दृश्यन्ते – घ. ३. पत्रलेखान्तम् – घ. ४. °समासो – घ. ५. तस्मान्न गुणाः – घ. ६. 'परिकल्प्यन्ते' – घ; परिकल्पन्ताम् – ग. ७. इत्यत्रान्तरे No. 254 (BORI), KLV. ८. ०तार्थविस्ताराः – घ. ०वस्तुविस्ताराः – No. 254 (BORI), No 185 (BORI). ९. 'प्रतिपादिताः'–घ पुस्तके नास्ति। १०. 'गुणास्तु' इत्यारम्य 'एवं' इतिपर्यन्तं–घ. पुस्तके नास्ति। ११. शरीराश्रितत्वमिव MB. (BORI), KLV.

Among qualities, Sweetness and Perspicuity are constantly present in abundance only when the Erotic sentiment of love-in-separation is delineated. Similarly, Forcefulness is related to sentiments of the Furious and Wonderment. Once again, Sweetness and Forcefulness are found only in instances expressive of sentiment, emotion, mood or their semblance. But there is no such conformity to any rule regarding the varieties of texture. Thus we find a texture with long compounds even in the Erotic sentiment and one without compounds even in the Furious sentiment.

The following is an example of texture with long compounds in the Erotic sentiment :— *mandāra-kusumareṇupiñjaritālakā.*

The woman with her curls variegated by the pollen of mandāra flowers.

Or to give another example :—

anavarata-nayana-jala-lava-
nipatana-parimuṣita-patralekhāntaṁ |
kara-tala-niṣaṇṇamabale
Vadanamidaṁ kaṁ na tāpayati ||

Whom does not your face torment, tender maid,
With all its drawings on the cheek wiped out
By the fall of incessant tears from the eyes,
And resting in the palm of your hand ?

For an illustration of the furious sentiment in which there is texture without compounds, we may mention the instance already cited — 'Whoever bears weapons' etc. Hence qualities are not identical with texture in their form. Nor are they attributes of texture.

One might urge as follows :— 'If texture is not a substratum of qualities, then what other substratum can be imagined for these ? Our reply is that we have already explained their substratum' (in II.6).

One might even accept that qualities are verbal. But even so they will not become similar to verbal figures like alliteration. For, even the ancient writers have declared that alliteration etc. are purely verbal characteristics having nothing to do with sense. But qualities can become characteristics of only such words whose primary meanings have the capacity of unique suggestiveness. Just as we regard qualities like valour as characteristics

ननु यदि शब्दाश्रया गुणास्तत्सङ्घटनारूपत्वं तदाश्रयत्वं[1] वा तेषां प्राप्तमेव। न ह्यसङ्घटिताः शब्दा अर्थविशेषप्रतिपाद्यरसाद्याश्रितानां[2] गुणानामवाचकत्वादाश्रया[3] भवन्ति।

नैवम्; वर्णपदव्यङ्ग्यत्वस्य रसादीनां प्रतिपादितत्वात्[4]।

अभ्युपगते वा वाक्यव्यङ्ग्यत्वे रसादीनां नियता न काचित्सङ्घटना तेषामाश्रयत्वं प्रतिपद्यत इत्यनियतसङ्घटनाः शब्दा एव गुणानां व्यङ्ग्यविशेषानुगता[5] आश्रयाः। ननु माधुर्ये यदि नामैवमुच्यते[6] तदुच्यताम्; ओजसः पुनः कथमनियतसङ्घटनाशब्दाश्रयत्वम्[7]। न ह्यसमासा सङ्घटना कदाचिदोजस आश्रयतां प्रतिपद्यते[8]।

उच्यते[9]—यदि न प्रसिद्धिमात्रग्रहदूषितं चेतस्तदत्रापि न न ब्रूमः[10]। ओजसः कथमसमासा[11] सङ्घटना नाश्रयः। यतो[12] रौद्रादीन् हि प्रकाशयतः काव्यस्य दीप्तिरोज[13] इति प्राक्प्रतिपादितम्। तच्चौजो यद्यसमासायामपि सङ्घटनायां[14] स्यात्तत्को दोषो भवेत्। न चाचारुत्वं सहृदयहृदयसंवेद्यमस्ति। तस्मादनियतसङ्घटनाशब्दाश्रयत्वे गुणानां न काचित्क्षतिः। तेषां तु चक्षुरादीनामिव यथास्वं विषयनियमितस्य स्वरूपस्य न कदाचिद्व्यभिचारः।

---

१. 'तदाश्रितत्वं' क-ख. No. 254 (BORI). KLV. २. ० रसाश्रितानां – MB. KLV. ३. ° वाचकादाश्रया – MB; अर्थविशेषं प्रतिपाद्य रसाद्याश्रितानां° – घ, ०.अवाचका आश्रया – No. 254 (BORI). ४. रसादीनां प्राति प्रतिपादितत्वात् – घ. ५. °षानुगतानां – No. 254 (BORI). ६. 'नामैतदुच्यते' ग. ७. °सङ्घटन-शब्दा° – BP. घ., No. 254 (BORI), KLV. ८. 'प्रतिपाद्यते' ग. ९. 'उच्यते च' ग. १०. ० त्रापि न ब्रूमः – घ. ११. 'असमाससंघटनाश्रयः' क-ख. १२. 'यतः' क-ख. पुस्तकयोर्नास्ति. १३. 'ओजोगुणः' – क-ख. १४. घटनायां – घ.

of the body, though in fact they are only characteristics of the soul, so also one might speak of qualities as characteristics of the word though they really relate to other things (viz. sentiments).

The objector might argue further as follows :—

'If qualities are verbal, it practically amounts to saying that they are either identical with texture or its attributes. For words which are not 'textured' can never become substrata of sentiments, etc. and are suggested only by specific factors mentioned above. They can never become substrata, because they are not at all capable of denoting qualities.

The argument is fallacious. As it has been explained earlier, sentiments etc. can be conveyed by letters as well as individual words.

Furthermore, even in instances of sentiment etc. suggested by a sentence, we do not have any constant texture which serves as the substratum of qualities. Hence such words only, as do not have any constant texture but as are enlivened by a touch of specific suggested elements, deserve to be regarded as substrata of qualities.

The objector might continue his argument like this :— 'If you say this about the quality of Sweetness, you might say so by all means. But how can Forcefulness be said to have a substratum in words whose composition is inconstant ? Will the quality of Forcefulness ever arise from words without the texture of long compounds ?

Our reply is this :— 'If your mind is possessed by the ghost of blind faith in convention, we cannot say anything. Otherwise, we will ask you why it should not be so ? Why should not the texture without long compounds be a substratum of Forcefulness ? We have already explained that Forcefulness is nothing but the brilliance in poetry which is suggestive of sentiments like the Furious, etc. What would be wrong with it if it should be found even in a texture without long compounds ? There is indeed no blemish which can be discerned by receptive critics. Therefore, nothing is lost if we regard qualities as attributes of words which do not possess a constant texture. Just as the objects of perception for the different senses such as the eye are clearly demarcated from one another, so also the objects

तस्मादन्ये गुणा अन्या च सङ्घटना। न च सङ्घटनामाश्रिता गुणा इत्येकं दर्शनम्; अथवा सङ्घटनारूपा एव गुणाः।

यत्तूक्तम् — "सङ्घटनावद्गुणानामप्यनियतविषयत्वं[1] प्राप्नोति, लक्ष्ये व्यभिचारदर्शनात्" इति। तत्राप्येतदुच्यते:—यत्र लक्ष्ये परिकल्पितविषयव्यभिचारस्तद्विरूपमेवास्तु। कथमचारुत्वं तादृशे[2] विषये सहृदयानां नावभातीति[3] चेत्? कविशक्तितिरोहितत्वात्। द्विविधो हि दोषः कवेरव्युत्पत्तिकृतोऽशक्तिकृतश्च। तत्राव्युत्पत्तिकृतो दोषः शक्तितिरस्कृतत्वात्कदाचिन्न लक्ष्यते। यस्त्वशक्तिकृतो दोषः सः झटिति प्रतीयते। परिकरश्लोकश्चात्र —

"अव्युत्पत्तिकृतो दोषः शक्त्या संव्रियते कवेः।
यस्त्वशक्तिकृतस्[4]तस्य[5] झटित्येवावभासते॥"

तथा हि—[6]महाकवीनामप्युत्पत्तिकृतमप्युत्तमदेवताविषयप्रतिषिद्धसंभोगशृङ्गारनिबन्धनाद्यनौचित्यं[7] शक्तितिरस्कृतत्वात्[8] ग्राम्यत्वेन न प्रतिभासते यथा कुमारसम्भवे देवीसम्भोगवर्णनम्। एवमादौ च विषये यथौचित्यत्यागस्तथा[9] दर्शितमेवाग्रे। शक्तितिरस्कृतत्वं चान्वयव्यतिरेकाभ्यामवसीयते। यथा हि शक्तिरहितेन कविना एवंविधे विषये[10] शृङ्गार उपनिबध्यमानः स्फुटमेव दोषत्वेन प्रतिभासते[11]।

---

१. 'अप्यविषयत्वं' क-ख. २. 'तादृशेऽपि' ग. तादृशविषये–घ. ३. प्रतिभातीति –घ, KLV. ४. 'कृतो दोषः' ग. ५. स झटित्यवभासते BP. ६. Text acc. to MB.; महाकवीनामप्युत्तमदेवताविषयप्रसिद्ध° –घ, BP. ७. 'अनौचित्यमुत्तमदेवविषयं' क-ख. ८. तिरस्कृतं ग्राम्यत्वेन–घ. ९. यथौचित्यात्याग° – BP. १०. विषये- घ पुस्तके नास्ति। ११. 'अवभासते' ग.

of different qualities (viz., sentiments) are clearly demarcated from one another and do not admit of even a single exception. Hence qualities and texture are entirely distinct from one another. This is not the same thing as saying that qualities have texture for their substratum, or even that qualities are of the nature of texture itself.

The objector has also remarked :—" If texture were to be inconstant in its application, qualities too would be equally inconstant in view of the several exceptions we find to this general rule. " To this we reply in the following manner :—If in a solitary instance you find an exception so imagined by you, let such exceptions exist by all means. If the objector should ask again " How is it that, in the instance pointed out by me, absence of charm escapes the observation of perceptive critics? ", we would give him the reply that any such supposed lack of charm remains concealed because of the poet's genius. Defect is of two kinds :—(1) Born of the poet's ignorance and (2) Born of the poet's lack of genius. Of these, the first will often escape notice as it will be concealed by the genius of the poet. But the defect due to ignorance attracts the critic's attention at once. The following aphorism sums up this very idea :—

A poet's defect resulting from ignorance will be hidden from view by his genius; but a defect due to his want of genius will attract one's attention immediately.

This may be illustrated now. Even first-rate poets have delineated indecent Erotic sentiment in relation to divine characters and yet this impropriety does not srike one as vulgar because the indecorum has been camouflaged by the poet's genius. The description of Goddess Pārvatī's amours in the Kumārsambhava is an explicit instance. How there is indecorum in this and such other examples is brought out in the sequel. Whether genius has really camouflaged the defect or not is decided on the strength of positive and negative grounds. Thus for instance, in any other poet (except Kālidāsa) such a delineation of the Erotic sentiment would certainly strike one as a clear blemish.

नन्वस्मिन् पक्षे ‘ यो यः शस्त्रं बिभर्ति ’ इत्यादौ किमचारुत्वम् ? अप्रतीयमानमेवारोपयामः[1] । तस्माद्गुणव्यतिरिक्तत्वे गुणरूपत्वे च सङ्घटनाया[2] अन्यः[3] कश्चिन्नियमहेतुर्वक्तव्य इत्युच्यते ।

तन्नियमे हेतुरौचित्यं वक्तृवाच्ययोः ॥ ६ ॥

तत्र वक्ता कविः कविनिबद्धो वा[4], कविनिबद्धश्चापि रसभावरहितो रसभावसमन्वितो वा, रसोऽपि कथानायकाश्रयस्तद्विपक्षाश्रयो वा, कथानायकश्च धीरोदात्तादिभेदभिन्नः पूर्वस्तदनन्तरो[5] वेति[6] विकल्पाः । वाच्यं च ध्वन्यात्मरसाङ्गं रसाभासाङ्गं वा, अभिनेयार्थमनभिनेयार्थं वा उत्तमप्रकृत्याश्रयं तदितराश्रयं वेति बहुप्रकारम् । तत्र यदा कविरपगतरसभावो[7] वक्ता तदा रचनायाः कामचारः । यदापि कविनिबद्धो वक्ता रसभावरहितस्तदा[8] स एव; यदा तु कविः कविनिबद्धो वा वक्ता रसभावसमन्वितो रसश्च प्रधानाश्रितत्वाद्[9] ध्वन्यात्मभूतस्तदा[10] नियमेनैव तत्रासमासामध्यमसमासे एव सङ्घटने । करुणविप्रलम्भशृङ्गारयोस्त्वसमासैव सङ्घटना । कथमिति[11] चेत्, उच्यते—रसो यदा प्राधान्येन प्रतिपाद्यस्तदा तत्प्रतीतौ व्यवधायका विरोधिनश्च सर्वात्मनैव परिहार्याः[12] । एवं च दीर्घसमासा सङ्घटना समासानामनेकप्रकारसम्भावनया कदाचिद्रसप्रतीतिं व्यवदधातीति तस्यां

---

१. ‘ प्रतीयमानं ’ ग. २. ‘ संघटनायां ’ क-ख. ३. नान्यः No. 254 (BORI) ४. वा कश्चित्-घ. ५. तदितरो KLV. ६. ‘ °रश्चेति ’ ग. ७. अपरसभावो KLV. ८. ‘ तदापि ’ क-ख. ९. ‘ प्रधानभूतत्वाद् ’-घ. १०. तदापि-घ. ११. ‘ कथं चेत् ’ -ग. १२. ‘ परिभाव्याः ’-ग.

According to the view that qualities are identical with textures one might very well ask what absence of beauty is there in instances like *Whoever bears weapons, etc.* ? We submit that it is such as is incorrigible. Therefore, whether texture is different from Qualities or whether it is identical with Qualities, some other rule which governs the employment of texture will have to be given out. Hence it will be explained hereafter :

The propriety or decorum of the speaker and the spoken is the consideration which governs it. 6

The speaker may be either the poet or a character created by the poet. The latter may also be further divided into one who is unaffected by sentiment and emotion or one who is affected by sentiment and emotion. Sentiment, again, may relate to the hero of the story or to his rival. The hero is of different kinds as 'the high-spirited', etc., and also 'major' and 'minor' and so forth.

'The spoken' too may be subsidiary either to the suggested sentiment or to the suggested semblance of sentiment; may be meant to be staged or may not be so meant; may relate to high characters or only to low characters.

In these various alternatives, there is full freedom of choice of the texture when the speaker happens to be devoid of sentiment and emotion. Even when the character created by the poet is devoid of sentiment and emotion, the above will apply. But when the poet or a character created by him happens to be 'a speaker' suffused with sentiment and emotion, and sentiment itself is principally intended and as such of the nature of suggestion, then as a rule, we will have only two kinds of texture, viz., that without compounds and that with medium-sized compounds. So far as the sentiments, viz., the Pathetic and Love-in-seperation are concerned, the texture will be only the one without compounds. If one were to ask why, we would give the following reply :—When sentiment is to be primarily delineated, all possible impediments and deterrents to its comprehension should be avoided in every way. In these circumstances, an excessive fondness for employing the said texture may impede the comprehension of sentiment since compounds lend themselves to various kinds of interpretations.

नात्यन्तमभिनिवेशः शोभते। विशेषतोऽभिनेयार्थे काव्ये, ततोऽन्यत्र[1] च विशेषतः करुणविप्रलम्भशृङ्गारयोः। तयोर्हि सुकुमारतरत्वात्स्वल्पायामप्यस्वच्छतायां[2] शब्दार्थयोः प्रतीतिर्मन्थरीभवति। रसान्तरे पुनः प्रतिपाद्ये रौद्रादौ मध्यमसमासा सङ्घटना कदाचिद्धीरोद्धतनायकसम्बन्ध[3]व्यापाराश्रयेण[4] दीर्घसमासापि वा[5] तदाक्षेपाविनाभाविरसोचितवाच्यापेक्षया न विगुणा भवतीति सापि नात्यन्तं परिहार्या। सर्वासु च सङ्घटनासु प्रसादाख्यो गुणो व्यापी। स हि सर्वरससाधारणः सर्वसङ्घटनासाधारणश्चेत्युक्तम्। प्रसादातिक्रमे ह्यसमासापि सङ्घटना करुणविप्रलम्भशृङ्गारौ न व्यनक्ति। तदपरित्यागे च मध्यमसमासापि न न प्रकाशयति[6]। तस्मात्सर्वत्र प्रसादोऽनुसर्तव्यः। अत एव च "यो यः शस्त्रं बिभर्ति" इत्यादौ यद्योजसः स्थितिर्नेष्यते तत्प्रसादाख्य एव गुणो न माधुर्यम्। न चाचारुत्वम्; अभिप्रेतरसप्रकाशनात्। तस्माद्गुणाव्यतिरिक्तत्वे गुणव्यतिरिक्तत्वे[7] वा[8] सङ्घटनाया यथोक्तादौचित्याद्विषयनियमोऽस्तीति तस्या अपि रसव्यञ्जकत्वम्। तस्याश्च रसाभिव्यक्तिनिमित्तभूताया योऽयमनन्तरोक्तो नियमहेतुः स एव गुणानां नियतो विषय इति गुणाश्रयेण व्यवस्थानमप्यविरुद्धम्।

विषयाश्रयमप्यन्यदौचित्यं तां नियच्छति।
काव्यप्रभेदाश्रयतः स्थिता भेदवती हि सा॥ ७॥

---

१. 'तत्रान्यत्र'-ग, KLV. २. 'स्वेच्छतायां'–क-ख. ३. °सम्बन्धि°–MB. ४. 'व्यापारक्षये'–ख. ५. 'समासाश्रयापि'–क-ख. ६. 'समासापि प्रकाशयति'–घ; न प्रकाशयति – क, ग., No. 254 (BORI). ७. 'गुणोतिरिक्तत्वे' – ग. ८. 'व्यतिरेकत्वे वा'–क-ख.

This is particularly true of literature meant for the stage and even in other forms of literature when the sentiments, viz., the Pathetic and Love-in-separation happen to be delineated. Since these two sentiments are most delicate, even the slightest obscurity in word or meaning will impede their comprehension. When other sentiments like the Furious are to be delineated, there is no need for eschewing middle-sized texture entirely: sometimes when the exploits of a " brave and braggart " hero are to be described, it is not essential that even the texture with long compounds should be completely forsaken. For even such textures are in no way inferior to the expressed meanings which suggest sentiments.

To all these textures, the quality of Perspicuity is uniformly applicable. It has been already remarked that it is common to all sentiments as well as all textures. If perspicuity should be abandoned, even textures without compounds will not be able to suggest the sentiments of Pathos and Love-in-separation. On the other hand, if it is not so abandoned, even textures of middle-sized compounds can suggest them. Hence Perspicuity deserves incorporation everywhere. So if one does not like to regard an instance like *Whoever bears weapons... etc.* as containing Forcefulness one should at least consider it as an instance of the quality, viz., Perspicuity and not of Sweetness. No loss of charm will result (in the example even if one should regard it like this), since the intended sentiment will be suggested anyway. Therefore whether one holds that texture is identical with qualities or that it is different from qualities, it is indeed suggestive of sentiments since its scope is governed by the rule of decorum explained above. The same rule of decorum which we described so long as applicable to textures suggestive of sentiment, will invariably govern the aim of qualities too ; and hence even if one were to decide that texture depends on the support of qualities, it would not contradict our position.

Another consideration which governs the usage of a texture is its decorum with regard to the literary medium adopted. Texture thus becomes different in different forms of literature. 7

वक्तृवाच्यगतौचित्ये सत्यपि विषयाश्रयमन्यदौचित्यं[1] सङ्घटनां नियच्छति । यतः काव्यस्य प्रभेदाः — मुक्तकं संस्कृतप्राकृतापभ्रंशनिबद्धम्, सन्दानितकविशेषककलापक[2]कुलकानि, पर्यायबन्धः, परिकथा, खण्डकथासकलकथे[3], सर्गबन्धोऽभिनेयार्थमाख्यायिकाकथे[4] इत्येवमादयः । तदाश्रयेणापि सङ्घटना विशेषवती भवति । तत्र मुक्तकेषु रसबन्धाभिनिवेशिनः कवेस्तदाश्रयमौचित्यम् । तच्च दर्शितमेव । अन्यत्र[5] कामचारः ।

मुक्तकेषु[6] प्रबन्धेष्विव रसबन्धाभिनिवेशिनः कवयो दृश्यन्ते । तथाह्यमरुककवेर्मुक्तकाः शृङ्गाररसस्यन्दिनः[7] प्रबन्धायमानाः प्रसिद्धा एव । सन्दानितकादिषु तु विकटनिबन्धनौचित्यान्[8]मध्यमसमासादीर्घसमासे एव रचने[9]। प्रबन्धाश्रयेषु[10] यथोक्तप्रबन्धौचित्यमेवानुसर्तव्यम् । पर्यायबन्धे[11] पुनरसमासामध्यमसमासे एव सङ्घटने । कदाचिदर्थौचित्याश्रयेण दीर्घसमासायामपि सङ्घटनायां परुषा ग्राम्या च वृत्तिः परिहर्तव्या । परिकथायां[12] कामचारः, तत्रेतिवृत्तमात्रोपन्यासेन नात्यन्तं रसबन्धाभिनिवेशात् । खण्डकथासकलकथयोस्तु[13] प्राकृतप्रसिद्धयोः कुलकादिनिबन्धनभूयस्त्वाद्दीर्घसमासायामपि न

---

१. 'विषयाश्रयगतमनौचित्यं' ग., 'विषयाश्रयमन्दौचित्यं' – घ. २. कालापक–घ. ३. परिकथा सकलकथा खण्डकथा – घ. ४. °माख्यायिका कथेत्येवमादयः – घ. ५. 'अन्यत्र तु' क-ख. ६. 'मुक्तकेषु हि – घ. ७. °स्यंदिनः प्रत्येकं – MB. ८ 'बन्धौचित्यात्' - ग. ९. 'संघटने' - घ. १०. 'पद्यप्रबन्धाश्रितेषु' – क - ख. ११. 'पद्यबन्धेषु' क – ख. १२. '°कथायां तु' क - ख. १३. कथयोः – च.

In addition to decorum of speaker and the spoken, decorum of the literary medium also governs the choice of texture. Literature in Sanskrit, Prakrit and Apabhraṁśa has various forms such as '*pearls*' (*muktakas* i. e., single stanzas forming a self-contained unit) or run-on verses of two, three, four or more stanzas in the same metre forming a single unit, stanzas in one or more metres describing a single topic, didactic stories in verse, full-fledged fiction in verse, short stories in verse, epics, dramatic works, historical novels in prose and romantic novels in prose. Texture becomes varied due to differences in their literary forms also. Of these, a poet who is intent on delineation of sentiment in *Pearls* will be guided by the considerations of decorum relating to sentiment. This decorum has already been explained. In *Pearls* where the poet has no such intent, he is free to employ any texture he likes.

Poets are, however, mostly seen to be intent on delineating sentiment even in *Pearls* as in full-fledged literary works. Thus the *Pearls* of the poet Amaru are famous for their profusion in the Erotic sentiment; and they are regarded as good as full-fledged works in point of charm. In run-on verses of two stanzas etc., affected and involved construction itself becomes proper and therefore we will have textures of medium-sized and long compounds. But if these run-on verses occur as parts of another whole poem, then the decorum towards a whole poem, indicated already, will apply to it. In works dealing with a single theme and containing verses in one or more metres, the textures to be employed should be only those without compounds and with medium-sized compounds, Sometimes, though the texture of long compounds might occur in view of decorum of content, 'harsh' and 'pallid' dictions will have to be avoided therein. But there is no such rule so far as didactic stories in verse are concerned. The reason is that there will just be a narration of the story and no intention of delineating sentiment. Full-fledged stories and short stories in verse are common only in the Prakrit language and they abound in run-on verses up to more than five stanzas. Therefore, the use of texture with long compounds also will not be wrong in them. The decorum of diction should always be decided in view of the sentiments to be delineated.

विरोधः । वृत्त्यौचित्यं तु यथारसमनुसर्तव्यम् । सर्गबन्धे तु रस[1]तात्पर्ये यथारसमौचित्यमन्यथा तु कामचारः[2]; द्वयोरपि मार्गयोः सर्गबन्धविधायिनां[3] दर्शनाद्रसतात्पर्यं साधीयः । अभिनेयार्थे तु सर्वथा रसबन्धेऽभिनिवेशः कार्यः । आख्यायिकाकथयोस्तु गद्यनिबन्धनबाहुल्याद्गद्ये छन्दोबन्धभिन्नप्रस्थानत्वा[4]दिह नियमे हेतुरकृतपूर्वोऽपि मनाक् क्रियते ।

एतद्यथोक्तमौचित्यमेव तस्यां[5] नियामकम् ।
सर्वत्र गद्यबन्धेऽपि च्छन्दोनियमवर्जिते ॥ ८ ॥

यदेतदौचित्यं वक्तृवाच्यगतं सङ्घटनाया नियामकमुक्तमेतदेव गद्ये छन्दोनियमवर्जितेऽपि विषयापेक्षं नियमहेतुः । तथा[6] ह्यत्रापि यदा कविः कविनिबद्धो वा वक्ता रसभावरहितस्तदा कामचारः । रसभावसमन्विते तु वक्तरि पूर्वोक्तमेवानुसर्तव्यम् । तत्रापि[7] च विषयौचित्यमेव[8] । आख्यायिकायां तु भूम्ना मध्यमसमासादीर्घसमासे एव सङ्घटने । गद्यस्य विकटबन्धाश्रयेण[9] च्छायावत्वात् । तत्र च तस्य प्रकृष्यमाणत्वात् । कथायां तु विकटबन्धप्राचुर्येऽपि गद्यस्य रसबन्धोक्तमौचित्यमनुसर्तव्यम् ।

रसबन्धोक्तमौचित्यं भाति सर्वत्र संश्रिता ।
रचना विषयापेक्षं तत्तु किञ्चिद्विभेदवत् ॥ ९ ॥

अथवा पद्यवद्गद्यबन्धेऽपि रसबन्धोक्तमौचित्यं सर्वत्र संश्रिता रचना भवति[10] । तत्तु विषयापेक्षं किञ्चिद्विशेषवद्भवति, न तु सर्वाकारम् । तथा हि

---

१. 'रस°' क-ख-पुस्तकयोर्नास्ति; 'रसतात्पर्येण'-घ. २. 'कामचारात्'-ग. ३. 'बन्धायिनां'-ग. ४. 'विभिन्नप्रस्थाने निबन्धनत्वात्'-क-ख. ५. 'नस्मात्'-क-ख, No. 254 (BORI). ६. 'यथा तच्चात्रापि'-ग. ७. 'अत्रापि'-क-ख, KLV, तत्रापि वा-घ. ८. 'एतत्'-क-ख, KLV. ९. विकटनिबन्धा°-घ, KLV. १०. 'भाति'-घ.

If an epic should be intent upon delineating sentiments, the decorum of sentiment will govern its use of texture. Otherwise, it is left to the free choice of the poet. We can see writers of epics who have composed works in both these ways; but of the two, the works that are intent upon sentiment should be regarded as superior. In dramatic works, anyway, there should be a sole intent of delineating sentiment. So far as historical novels and romantic novels are concerned, they are found mostly in prose only and their method differs from that of metrical works. Since the ancients have not given any specific rules concerning these, we shall frame them here in brief :

The considerations of decorum detailed above will also govern all prose works which are not governed by the rules of metre. **8**

Though prose works are not governed by rules of metre, the considerations of decorum mentioned above, viz., that of the speaker, the spoken and the literary medium, govern them. Here too, the poet is free to employ any texture he likes when the speaker is a poet or a character invented by a poet devoid of all sentiment and emotion. But if the speaker happens to be suffused with sentiment and emotion, the mentioned principles of decorum should be applied. And among them also decorum of the literary medium is of the highest importance. In the historical novel we find mostly textures with medium-sized and long compounds. The reason lies in the fact that literary prose attains beauty through the assistance of affected and involved construction. But in the romantic novel, though there is preference for involved construction, decorum of sentiment should be retained.

Texture with decorum in the delineation of sentiments will shine out wherever it might be found. It will, however, assume a shade of variation coupled with the decorum of literary medium. **9**

In other words, texture with decorum in delineating sentiments will shine out everywhere — in prose-works as well as in metrical ones. But due to decorum of particular literary media it acquires slightly different shades, but does not transform itself entirely.

गद्यबन्धेऽप्यतिदीर्घसमासा रचना न विप्रलम्भशृङ्गारकरुणयोराख्यायिकायामपि शोभते । नाटकादावप्यसमासैव[1] न[2] रौद्रवीरादिवर्णने । विषयापेक्षं त्वौचित्यं प्रमाणतोऽपकृष्यते प्रकृष्यते च । तथा ह्याख्यायिकायां नात्यन्तमसमासा स्वविषयेऽपि नाटकादौ नातिदीर्घसमासा चेति सङ्घटनाया दिगनुसर्तव्या ।

इति काव्यार्थविवेको योऽयं चेतश्चमत्कृतिविधायी ।
सूरिभिरनुसृतसारैरस्मदुपज्ञो न विस्मार्यः[3] ॥

इदानीमलक्ष्यक्रमव्यङ्ग्यो ध्वनिः प्रबन्धात्मा रामायण[4]महाभारतादौ प्रकाशमानः प्रसिद्ध एव । तस्य तु यथा प्रकाशनं तत्प्रतिपाद्यते । —

विभावभावानुभावसञ्चार्यौचित्यचारुणः ।
विधिः कथा[5]शरीरस्य वृत्तस्योत्प्रेक्षितस्य वा ॥ १० ॥

इतिवृत्तवशायातां[6] त्यक्त्वाननुगुणां स्थितिम् ।
उत्प्रेक्ष्या[7]प्यन्तराभीष्टरसोचितकथोन्नयः ॥ ११ ॥

सन्धिसन्ध्यङ्गघटनं रसाभिव्यक्त्यपेक्षया ॥
न तु केवलया शास्त्रस्थितिसम्पादनेच्छया ॥ १२ ॥

---

१. °समासैव घटना – घ. २. 'न' – घ पुस्तके नास्ति. ३. इय-मार्या – क – ख पुस्तकयोर्नास्ति: '– ग पुस्तके KLV, M.B पुस्तके चास्ति । ४. 'ध्वनिप्रबन्धौ रामायण' – घ. ५. 'तथा' – ग. ६. 'वशायत्तां' – ख. ७. उत्प्रेक्ष्यो – घ.

For instance, even in prose works, and even if there should be a historical novel amongst them, texture with long compounds will not be beautiful when the sentiments of Love-in-separation and Pathos are being delineated. So also in dramas etc., even while portraying the Furious and the Heroic sentiments, only the texture without compounds is utilised. The decorum of literary medium is both greater and smaller in degree than the decorum of sentiment (from different points of view). In the historical novel, we do not have texture without compounds even while depicting sentiments of Love-in-separation and Pathos. So also in dramas etc. we do not get texture with very long compounds even while depicting the Furious and such other sentiments. In this way one should understand the direction in which texture is employed.

'Suggestion with undiscerned sequentiality' relating to a whole work is quite well known in such works as the *Rāmāyaṇa* and the *Mahābhārata*. How it is suggested therein is explained below :—

Construction of only such a plot, either traditional or invented, as is charming with its decorum of (the accessories of sentiment, viz.,) stimuli of setting, abiding emotions, emotional responses, and passing moods; 10

Thus we have enunciated for the first time such principles of literature as will illumine the minds of readers. Learned men who are given to gathering intrinsic excellences from others should never forget these.

If, in a theme, adapted from a traditional source, the poet is faced with situations conflicting with the intended sentiment, his readiness to leave out such incidents and inventing in their place even imaginary incidents with a view to delineating the intended sentiment : 11

The construction of divisions and sub-dividions of the plot only with a view to delineating sentiments and not at all with a desire for mere conformity to rules of poetics : 12

उद्दीपनप्रशमने यथावसरमन्तरा[1] ।
रसस्यारब्धविश्रान्तेरनुसन्धानमङ्गिनः ॥ १३ ॥
अलङ्कृतीनां शक्तावप्यानुरूप्येण योजनम् ।
प्रबन्धस्य रसादीनां व्यञ्जकत्वे निबन्धनम् ॥ १४ ॥

प्रबन्धोऽपि रसादीनां व्यञ्जक इत्युक्तं तस्य व्यञ्जकत्वे निबन्धनम् । प्रथमं तावद्विभावभावानुभावसञ्चार्यौचित्यचारुणः कथाशरीरस्य विधिर्यथायथं प्रतिपिपादयिषित[2]रसभावाद्यपेक्षया य उचितो विभावो भावोऽनुभावः सञ्चारी वा तदौचित्यचारुणः कथाशरीरस्य विधिर्व्यञ्जकत्वे निबन्धनमेकम् । तत्र विभावौचित्यं तावत्प्रसिद्धम् । भावौचित्यं तु प्रकृत्यौचित्यात् । प्रकृतिर्ह्युत्तममध्यमाधमभावेन[3] दिव्यमानुषादिभावेन च विभेदिनी । तां यथायथमनुसृत्यासङ्कीर्णः स्थायी भाव उपनिबध्यमान औचित्य[4]भाग् भवति । अन्यथा तु केवलमानुषाश्रयेण दिव्यस्य[5] केवलदिव्याश्रयेण वा केवल[6]मानुषस्यो[7]त्साहादय उपनिबध्यमाना अनुचिता भवन्ति[8] । तथा च केवलमानुषस्य राजादेर्वर्णने सप्तार्णवलङ्घनादिलक्षणा व्यापारा उपनिबध्यमानाः सौष्ठवभृतोऽपि नीरसा एव नियमेन भवन्ति, तत्र त्वनौचित्यमेव हेतुः ।

ननु नागलोकगमनादयः सातवाहनप्रभृतीनां श्रूयन्ते, तदलोकसामान्यप्रभावा[9]तिशयवर्णने किमनौचित्यं सर्वोर्वीभरणक्षमाणां क्षमाभुजामिति ।

---

१. 'यथा वा रसमन्तरा' – क-ख. २. 'प्रतिपिपादयिष्यते' – ख. ३. 'ह्युत्तमाधमभावेन' – ग. ४. औचित्यवान् – घ. ५. 'दिव्यस्योत्तम' – ग. ६. केवल° घ-पुस्तके नास्ति. ७. 'मनुष्यस्य' – ख, केवलमनुष्यस्य – ग. ८. भान्ति – घ. ९. °प्रभावादति° – घ.

Bringing about both the high tide of sentiment and its low ebb appropriately in the work; preserving the unity of the principal sentiment from begining to end : 13

A discreet use of figures of speech even when the poet is capable of using them in any number; such are the conditions which underlie the suggestiveness of a whole work of liter ture in regard to sentiments, etc. 14

It has been already observed that a whole work of literature may also be suggestive of sentiments, etc. The conditions that underlie such suggestiveness are (enlisted here) :—

(1) The first condition is the construction of a beautiful plot, beautiful because of decorum in the use of stimuli of setting, emotions, emotional responses and passing moods with a view to the sentiments and emotions primarily intended to be delineated. Of these, the decorum of stimuli of setting is well known. The decorum of abiding emotions results from the decorum relating to the nature of characters Nature of characters can be divided into (1) High (2) Middle and (3) Low from one point of view and (1) Divine and (2) Human from another. Whatever the nature of the character delineated, the adoption of such an abiding emotion as is peculiar to the one chosen (without scope for confusion) will ensure decorum. Otherwise indecorum will result if one were to attribute 'divine' (i. e. super-human) high-spiritedness to characters who are but human or to attribute 'human' highspiritedness to characters who are divine. Thus it is that the description of supernatural exploits like jumping across the seven seas on the part of kings etc. who are only human, will appear devoid of sentiment in spite of their intrinsic worth. The reason for this is indecorum and nothing else.

At this point one might raise the following objection :— Indeed legendary kings like Sātavāhana have been credited with superhuman exploits like going to the netherworld of serpents etc. (in the well-known stories about them). How can there be any indecorum in even an exaggerated description of superhuman powers etc. on the part of kings who are supreme emperors of the entire earth ?

नैतदस्ति; न वयं ब्रूमो यत्प्रभावातिशयवर्णनमनुचितं राज्ञाम्, किं तु केवल-मानुषाश्रयेण योत्पाद्यवस्तुकथा क्रियते तस्यां दिव्यमौचित्यं न योजनीयम्। दिव्यमानुष्यायां[1] तु कथायामुभयमौचित्ययोजनमविरुद्धमेव। यथा पाण्डवादि[2]-कथायाम्। सातवाहनादिषु तु येषु यावदपदानं[3] श्रूयते तेषु[4] तावन्मात्रमनुगम्यमानमनुगुणत्वेन प्रतिभासते। व्यतिरिक्तं तु तेषामेवोपनिबध्यमानमनुचितम्। तदयमत्र परमार्थः—

अनौचित्यादृते नान्यद्रसभङ्गस्य कारणम्।
प्रसिद्धौचित्यबन्धस्तु रसस्योपनिषत्परा[5]॥

अत एव च भरते प्रख्यात[6]वस्तुविषयत्वं प्रख्यातोदात्तनायकत्वं च नाटकस्यावश्यकर्तव्यतयोपन्यस्तम्। तेन हि नायकौचित्यानौचित्यविषये कविर्न[7] व्यामुह्यति[8]। यस्तूत्पाद्यवस्तु नाटकादि कुर्यात्तस्य प्रसिद्धानुचितनायक-स्वभाववर्णने महान् प्रमादः।

ननु यद्युत्साहादिभाववर्णने कथञ्चिद्दिव्यमानुष्याद्यौचित्यपरीक्षा क्रियते तत्क्रियताम्, रत्यादौ तु किं तया प्रयोजनम्? रतिर्हि भारतवर्षोचितेनैव व्यवहारेण दिव्यानामपि वर्णनीयेति स्थितिः। नैवम्; तत्रौचित्यातिक्रमेण सुतरां दोषः। तथा ह्यधमप्रकृत्यौचित्येनोत्तमप्रकृतेः शृङ्गारोपनिबन्धने का भवेन्नोपहास्यता। त्रिविधं[9] प्रकृत्यौचित्यं भारतवर्षेऽप्यस्ति शृङ्गारविषयम्। यत्तु

१. मानुष्यायां–BP. २. पाण्डवादि°–MB. ३. 'अपादानं'–ग. ४. 'तदेव'–क-ख. ५. 'काव्यस्योपनिषत्'–Poona Mss. (BORI, XII, No. 186 and No. 183). ६. प्रबन्धप्रख्यात°–घ. ७. 'विषये कर्तव्ये कविर्न'–घ ८. 'विमुह्यति'–घ. ९. 'विविधं'–घ.

The objection does not apply to what we have said. We do not say that any and every exaggerated description of the powers of human kings is improper. What we say is that while a new plot is being invented by the poet with a human being as the hero, divine characteristics should not be depicted in him. But if the plot happens to be one chosen from a well known legend in which both the divine and human elements are already found interfused, the poet can, by all means, bring in these elements into his own plot without being open to the charge of indecorum. The stories of Pāṇḍavas, etc. provide good examples. Even in stories of Sātavāhana, etc. an inclusion of just such superhuman elements as possess the authority of legends would be advisable. Description of other superhuman elements which do not possess such authority would be certainly improper. Hence the following should be deemed as the quintessence of the matter.

There is no other cause for a breach in sentiment except indecorum. The greatest secret about sentiment is conformity to well known considerations of decorum.

This is indeed the reason why Bharata has laid the strict rule that in a drama *par excellence* only a well known plot and a well known noble hero should appear. If this rule is followed, a poet can never go wrong in the matter of decorum in relation to the hero with impossible superhuman characteristics when writing a drama with a plot invented by himself.

There is scope at this point for another objection :—" We can agree to your making a distinction between 'human' and 'superhuman' decorum so far as abiding emotions like 'high-spiritedness' are concerned; but what is the use of making this distinction in decorum when abiding emotions like love are involved? The fact is that we can describe even divine love only in terms of love familiar to us in kings of our own land, viz., Bhāratavarṣa ".

It is not so. Transgression of decorum would indeed be a grave defect even in the other emotions. Would it not be ridiculous if the love of a low character is depicted after the manner of a high character? Even in our own land there is thus a different decorum to be observed in regard to each of the three-

दिव्यमौचित्यं[1] तत्त्रानुपकारकमेवेति[2] चेत्--न वयं दिव्यमौचित्यं शृङ्गारविषयमन्यत्किञ्चिद् ब्रूमः। किं तर्हि? भारतवर्षविषये यथोत्तमनायकेषु राजादिषु शृङ्गारोपनिबन्धस्तथा[3] दिव्याश्रयोऽपि शोभते। नच राजादिषु ग्राम्यशृङ्गारोपनिबन्धनं[4] प्रसिद्धं नाटकादौ, तथैव देवेषु तत्परिहर्तव्यम्[5]। नाटकादेरभिनेयार्थत्वाद्[6]भिनयस्य[7] च सम्भोगशृङ्गारविषयस्यासभ्यत्वात्तत्र[8] परिहार इति चेन्न; यद्यभिनयस्यैवंविषयस्यासभ्यता[9] तत्काव्यस्यैवंविषयस्य सा केन निवार्यते? तस्मादभिनेयार्थेऽनभिनेयार्थे वा[10] काव्ये यदुत्तमप्रकृते राजादेरुत्तमप्रकृतिर्नायिकाभिः[11] सह ग्राम्यसम्भोगवर्णनं तत्पित्रोस्सम्भोगवर्णनमिव सुतरामसभ्यम्[12]। तथैवोत्तमदेवतादिविषयम्।

न च सम्भोगशृङ्गारस्य सुरतलक्षण एवैकः प्रकारः, यावदन्येऽपि प्रभेदाः[13] परस्परप्रेमदर्शनादयः सम्भवन्ति, ते कस्मादुत्तमप्रकृतिविषये[14] न वर्ण्यन्ते? तस्मादुत्साहवद्रतावपि प्रकृत्यौचित्यमनुसर्तव्यम्। तथैव विस्मयादिषु। यत्त्वेवंविधे विषये महाकवीनामप्यसमीक्ष्यकारिता लक्ष्ये दृश्यते स दोष एव। स तु शक्तितिरस्कृतत्वात्तेषां न लक्ष्यत इत्युक्तमेव। अनुभावौचित्यं तु भरतादौ प्रसिद्धमेव।

---

१. 'यत्त्वन्यद्दिव्यमौचित्यं'–घ. २. त(द्)त्रानुपकार°–घ. ३. 'शृङ्गार उपनिबद्धः'–क.–ख. ४. प्रसिद्धग्राम्य°-घ., BP; 'अप्रसिद्धग्राम्यसंभोगशृङ्गार'–क.–ख. ५. 'परिहातव्यम्-क. ६. 'अभिनेयार्थत्वात्तत्र परिहार'–ग, अभिनेयत्वाद°–घ. ७. '°दभिनेयस्य'–घ. ८. विषयत्वात्तत्र–घ. ९. '°सभ्यता'–क-ख, °सह्यता'–घ. १०. तस्मादभिनेयार्थे च काव्ये–घ. ११. 'उत्तमस्त्रीभिः सह.-ग. १२. 'वर्णनमिव सुतरामसह्यम्'–घ. वर्ण नवत्सुतरामसभ्यम्–क-ख. १३. 'यावदन्ये च परस्परप्रेमदर्शनादयः प्रभेदाः सन्ति'-ख. १४. 'तस्मात्'–ग.

fold types of characters in delineating the Erotic sentiment. If one were to say that decorum relating to divine characters is extraneous, we would say in reply that we affirm no such thing at all as a different decorum with regard to the Erotic sentiment which is unique to divine characters. On the other hand, we would affirm that the delineation of the Erotic sentiment in divine characters also will become delightful only when it is done after the manner of the Erotic sentiment in kings and such other high characters in our land. In dramas etc. one does not usually come across any delineation of vulgar erotic sentiment in the high characters such as kings. Along the same lines, this should be avoided in depicting the love of divine characters also. Even if one were to say that dramas are only meant to be enacted and, since an enacting of physical erotic sentiment would be indecent, it is eschewed only in dramas, we would ask back why the same indecency as relates to their enacting should not also relate to their description in poetry. Hence the truth is that both in dramas meant to be represented on the stage and in poems meant only to be read, any description of vulgar Erotic sentiment with reference to high characters like royal heroes and heroines would be as much impolite as a detailed account of the sexual act of one's own parents. The same is true also of its description with reference to divine characters who are of a high stature.

Nor is dalliance the only form of the Erotic sentiment. It includes other forms, too, like mutual love, sight, etc. Why should not they be delineated with reference to high characters? Thus we can conclude that decorum in the nature of characters is as much applicable to emotions like love as to high-spiritedness. The same is true of emotions like surprise. While it is true that in these matters even first-rate poets have erred and shown indiscretion, still their defect does not appear glaringly as a defect because it is covered up by their genius, as mentioned already.

Decorum relating to the depiction of emotional responses has been treated at length in the well known works of Bharata and others.

इयत्तूच्यते – भरतादिविरचितां स्थितिं वानुवर्तमानेन महाकविप्रबन्धान्वा पर्यालोचयता स्वप्रतिभां वानुसरता कविनावहितचेतसा भूत्वा विभावाद्यौचित्यभ्रंशपरित्यागे परः प्रयत्नो विधेयः औचित्यवतः[1] कथाशरीरस्य वृत्तस्योत्प्रेक्षितस्य वा ग्रहो व्यञ्जक इत्यनेनैतत्प्रतिपादयति – यदितिहासादिषु कथासु रसवतीषु विविधासु सतीष्वपि यत्तत्र विभावाद्यौचित्यवत्कथाशरीरं तदेव ग्राह्यं नेतरत्। वृत्तादपि[2] न कथाशरीरादुत्प्रेक्षिते विशेषतः प्रयत्नवता भवितव्यम्। तत्र[3] ह्यनवधानात्स्खलतः[4] कवेरव्युत्पत्तिसम्भावना महती भवति। परिकरश्लोकश्चात्र—

कथाशरीरमुत्पाद्य[5] वस्तु कार्यं तथातथा।
यथा रसमयं सर्वमेव तत्प्रतिभासते[6]॥

तत्र चाभ्युपायः सम्यग्विभावाद्यौचित्यानुसरणम्। तच्च दर्शितमेव।

किञ्च—

सन्ति सिद्धरसप्रख्या ये च रामायणादयः।
कथाश्रया[7] न तैर्योज्या स्वेच्छा रसविरोधिनी॥

तेषु हि कथाश्रयेषु तावत्स्वेच्छैव न योज्या। यदुक्तम्—'कथामार्गे न चातिक्रमः'। स्वेच्छापि वा यदि योज्यते, रसविरोधिनी न योज्या।

इदमपरं प्रबन्धस्य रसाभिव्यञ्जकत्वे निबन्धनम्[8]। इतिवृत्तवशायातां कथञ्चिद्रसाननुगुणां स्थितिं त्यक्त्वा पुनरुत्प्रेक्ष्याप्यन्तराभीष्टरसोचितकथोन्नयो[9]

१. 'औचित्यवता' – क-ख. २. 'तां स्थितिं वानुवर्तमानेन वृत्तादपि कथा' – क-ख. ३. नहि तत्र – घ. ४. 'हि' घ – पुस्तके नास्ति ५. 'शरीरात्' – क-ख. ६. एतत्प्रतिभासते – । ७. 'कथाश्रयान्तु' – क-ख. ८. 'निदर्शनम्' – क-ख. ९. कथोन्नेयो – घः

We shall content ourselves with saying only this much :— Every poet who is not only obedient to the rules laid down by Bharata and others but who has critically studied the literary works of first-rate poets and who also follows the dictates of his own creative imaginaiton, should direct all his efforts with great concentration towards the avoidance of indecorum in the matter of stimuli of setting, etc.

The statement in the text that it is the adoption of a plot endowed with decorum — whether historical or invented — which will become suggestive, indicates this : Though in chronicles etc. there may be several sentimental stories, only that in which there is decorum of setting etc. should be selected by the poet as his theme and not any other. He will have to show greater care in the construction of an invented plot than in that of a historical one. For, if the poet were to stumble in that due to his carelessness, it would make one conclude that the poet's want of education is very great. These ideas are summed up in the following aphorism :—

When constructing an invented plot, one should so arrange every individual part that the whole becomes full of sentiment.

Conformity to the rules of decorum of setting etc. is the means towards achieving it; and it has already been explained. Moreover,

The sentiments of works like the Rāmāyaṇa and the Mahābhārata are indeed fixed as it were. The poet's liberty should not go to the extent of violating these fixed sentiments in plots based upon such works.

When such works happen to be sources of the plot, the poet's freedom of invention should not find any scope at all. Even the ancients have declared : "There should not be any transgression in the construction of a well known traditional story". If at all the poet's freedom should find scope, it should be such as will not go against the original sentiment.

(2) The second condition which governs the suggestive power of a whole work of literature is this : If, in a plot adopted from a well known source, the poet is faced with situations

विधेयः, यथा कालिदासप्रबन्धेषु। यथा च सर्वसेनविरचिते हरिविजये। यथा च मदीय एवार्जुनचरिते महाकाव्ये। कविना काव्यम्[1]उपनिबध्नता सर्वात्मना रसपरतन्त्रेण भवितव्यम्। तत्रेतिवृत्ते यदि रसाननुगुणां स्थितिं पश्येत्तां भङ्क्त्वापि स्वतन्त्रतया रसानुगुणं कथान्तरमुत्पादयेत्। न हि कवेरितिवृत्तमात्रनिर्वहणेन किञ्चित्प्रयोजनम्, इतिहासादेव तत्सिद्धेः।

रसादिव्यञ्जकत्वे प्रबन्धस्य चेदमन्यन्मुख्यं निबन्धनं, यत्सन्धीनां मुखप्रतिमुखगर्भावमर्शनिर्वहणाख्यानां तदङ्गानां चोपक्षेपादीनां घटनं रसाभिव्यक्त्यपेक्षया, यथा रत्नावल्याम्; न तु केवलं शास्त्रस्थितिसम्पादनेच्छया। यथा वेणीसंहारे विलासाख्यस्य प्रतिमुखसन्ध्यङ्गस्य प्रकृतरसनिबन्धाननुगुणमपि द्वितीयेऽङ्के भरतमतानुसरणमात्रेच्छया घटनम्।

इदं चापरं प्रबन्धस्य रसव्यञ्जकत्वे निमित्तं यदुद्दीपनप्रशमने यथावसरमन्तरा रसस्य[2], यथा रत्नावल्यामेव। पुनरारब्धविश्रान्ते रसस्याङ्गिनोऽनुसन्धिश्च यथा तापसवत्सराजे।

प्रबन्धविशेषस्य च नाटकादे रसव्यक्तिनिमित्तमिदं[3] चापरमवगन्तव्यं यदलंकृतीनां शक्तावप्यानुरूप्येण योजनम्। शक्तो हि कविः कदाचिदलङ्कारनिबन्धने तदाक्षिप्ततयैवानपेक्षितरसबन्धः प्रबन्धमारभते तदुपदेशार्थमिदमुक्तम्। दृश्यन्ते च कवयोऽलङ्कारनिबन्धनैकरसा[4] अनपेक्षितरसाः प्रबन्धेषु। किञ्च —

---

१. प्रबन्धमुपनिबध्नता – घ. २. 'यथावसरमन्तरा रसस्य' क-ख– पुस्तकयोर्नास्ति.
३. 'परमवगन्तव्यम्' – ग., चावगन्तव्यं – घ. ४. 'रसानपेक्षाः' – क-ख.

conflicting with the intended sentiment, he should be prepared to leave out such incidents inventing in their place even imaginary ones in conformity to the intended sentiment. Kālidāsa's works provide us very good illustrations (of this condition) : and so does the *Harivijaya* of Sarvasena. An example may also be found in my own epic poem — *Arjunacarita.* A poet writing a whole work should be entirely bound by the demands made by sentiment. If he finds, therefore, in a historical source an element which is inappropriate to the sentiment, he should not hesitate to break away from it freely and to invent a new episode in its place which will be appropriate to the sentiment. The poet achieves no purpose indeed by blind fidelity to the story in sources, for this will have already been accomplished by the chronicles themselves.

(3) Another important condition which governs the suggestiveness of works is this :— The divisions of plot, viz., Opening, Enlargement, Complication, Deliberation and Conclusion and their sub-divisions such as the 'sowing of the seed,' etc., should be constructed only with a view to the delineation of sentiment, as in *Ratnāvalī;* and not with any desire for achieving conformity to rules (just for the sake of conformity) as in *Veṇīsaṁhāra*, where Merriment, a sub-division of the division of plot, viz., Enlargement, has been included in the Second Act though it is most inappropriate to the main sentiment, only because of the keenness of the author in obeying the rules laid down by Bharata.

(4) Another condition governing the suggestiveness of works is the proper portrayal of the rise and fall of the relevant sentiment. This is also found illustrated in the *Ratnāvalī*. Similarly, preservation of the unity of the principal sentiment is also important and this can be seen in *Tāpasavatsarāja.*

(5) There is also another condition which governs the suggestiveness of specific works like the drama and it is the discreet use of figures of speech even when the poet is capable of using them in plenty. A poet who is an adept in the employment of figures often becomes so much engrossed in them that he will compose his work in utter disregard of the delineation of sentiment. This rule has been laid down here for the edification of such a person. We commonly come across such instances of poets

अनुस्वानोपमात्मापि प्रभेदो य उदाहृतः ।
ध्वनेरस्य प्रबन्धेषु भासते सोऽपि केषुचित् ॥ १५ ॥

अस्य विवक्षितान्यपरवाच्यस्य ध्वनेरनुरणनरूपव्यङ्ग्योऽपि यः प्रभेद उदाहृतो द्विप्रकारः सोऽपि प्रबन्धेषु केषुचिद्द्योतते । तद्यथा मधुमथनविजये पाञ्चजन्योक्तिषु । यथा वा कामदेवस्य सहचरसमागमे विषमबाणलीलायाम् । यथा च गृध्रगोमायुसंवादादौ महाभारते ।

सुप्तिङ्वचनसम्बन्धैस्तथा कारकशक्तिभिः ।
कृत्तद्धितसमासैश्च द्योत्योऽलक्ष्यक्रमः क्वचित् ॥ १६ ॥

अलक्ष्यक्रमो ध्वनेरात्मा रसादि[1]ः सुब्विशेषैस्तिङ्विशेषैर्वचनविशेषैः सम्बन्धविशेषैः कारकशक्तिभिः कृद्विशेषैस्तद्धितविशेषैः समासैश्चेति चशब्दान्निपातोपसर्गकालादिभिः प्रयु[2]क्तैरभिव्यज्यमानो दृश्यते । यथा—

न्यक्कारो ह्ययमेव मे यदरयस्तत्राप्यसौ तापसः
सोऽप्यत्रैव निहन्ति राक्षसकुलं जीवत्यहो रावणः ।
धिग्धिक् शक्रजितं प्रबोधितवता किं कुम्भकर्णेन वा
स्वर्गग्रामटिकाविलुण्ठनवृथोच्छूनैः किमेभिर्भुजैः ॥

अत्र हि श्लोके भूयसा सर्वेषामप्येषां[3] स्फुटमेव व्यञ्जकत्वं दृश्यते । तत्र ‘मे यदरयः’ इत्यनेन सुप्सम्बन्धवचनानामभिव्यञ्जकत्वम् । ‘तत्राप्यसौ

१. रसादिभिः–घ.　२. प्रयुक्ते –घ.　३. ‘अमीषां’–ग.

whose only ambition is the use of the figures to the utter neglect of sentiments. Moreover,

Of this suggestion, the variety which is of the form of resonance and which has been already illustrated is found often in entire works of literature also. 15

In fact suggestion which is of the form of resonance and which includes two sub-classes has been illustrated under this form of suggestion, viz., Suggestion 'with intended but further extending literal import.' Here it is added that it will be found often in entire works of literature also. The words of Pāñcajanya in *Madhumathanavijaya* furnish a good illustration. So does the situation of Kāmadeva's meeting with his friends in my own work *Viṣamabāṇalīlā*. The words of the Vulture and Jackal etc. in the *Mahābhārata* are also illustrations in point.

Case-terminations, conjugational terminations, number, relation, accidence, primary affixes, secondary affixes, and also compounds—all these become conveyers of suggestion with undiscerned sequentiality. 16

The essence of suggestion with undiscerned sequentiality, i. e. of sentiment etc. is conveyed even by the speciality in case-terminations and cojugational terminations, in number, relation and accidence, in primary affixes, secondary affixes and compounds. The conjunction 'also' in the text indicates that even prepositions and tenses might become suggestive. Here is an example :—

That my enemies exist is insulting enough to me,
But more so that he is an anchorite !
He too kills down the race of demons even in my own place
And forsooth Rāvaṇa is still alive !
Fie, fie upon Indrajit ! Or what use is there in
waking up Kumbhakarṇa either ?
Of what avail are these arms of mine though fattened
By pillaging the hamlet of a heaven ?

Every element in this verse is full of clear, suggestive force. In 'that my enemies exist' the case-termination, relation,

तापस' इत्यत्र तद्धितनिपातयोः । 'सोऽप्यत्रैव निहन्ति राक्षसकुलं जीवत्यहो रावणः' इत्यत्र तिङ्कारकशक्तीनाम् । 'धिग्धिक् शक्रजितम्' इत्यादौ श्लोकार्धे कृत्तद्धितसमासोपसर्गाणाम् । एवंविधस्य[1] व्यञ्जकभूयस्त्वे च घटमाने काव्यस्य सर्वातिशायिनी बन्धच्छाया[2] समुन्मीलति । यत्र हि व्यङ्ग्यावभासिनः पदस्यैकस्यैव तावदाविर्भावस्तत्रापि काव्ये कापि बन्धच्छाया[3] किमुत यत्र तेषां बहूनां समवायः । यथात्रानन्तरोदिते[4] श्लोके । अत्र हि 'रावण' इत्यस्मिन् पदेऽर्थान्तरसंक्रमितवाच्येन ध्वनिप्रभेदेनालङ्कृतेऽपि पुनरनन्तरोक्तानां व्यञ्जकप्रकाराणामुद्भासनम् । दृश्यन्ते च महात्मनां प्रतिभाविशेषभाजां बाहुल्येनैवंविधा बन्धप्रकाराः । यथा महर्षेर्व्यासस्य—

अतिक्रान्तसुखाः कालाः प्रत्युपस्थितदारुणाः ।
श्वः श्वः पापीयदिवसाः पृथिवी गतयौवना ॥

अत्र हि कृत्तद्धितवचनैरलक्ष्यक्रमव्यङ्ग्यः, 'पृथिवी गतयौवना' इत्यनेन चात्यन्त[5]तिरस्कृतवाच्यो ध्वनिप्रकारः प्रकाशितः ।

एषां[6] च सुबादीनामेकैकशः समुदितानां च व्यञ्जकत्वं महाकवीनां प्रबन्धेषु प्रायेण दृश्यते[7] । सुबन्तस्य व्यञ्जकत्वं यथा —

तालैः शिञ्जद्वलयसुभगैः कान्तया नर्तितो मे ।
यामध्यास्ते दिवसविगमे नीलकण्ठः सुहृद्वः ॥

१. 'एवंविध'-क. २. कापि समुन्मीलति-MB. ३. 'बन्धार्द्धिः'-क-ख. ४. 'यथात्रैवानन्तरोदाहृते'-क.-ख. ५. 'च पदेनात्यन्त°'-क.-ख. ६. 'तेषां'-क-ख. ७. ऽन्यत्रापि दृश्यते-घ.

and number are suggestive. In 'but more so that he is an anchorite (*tāpasa*)', we have a suggestive secondary affix as well as an indeclinable. In 'he too kills down the race of demons in my own place; and forsooth, Rāvaṇa is still alive', we have the suggestive force of conjugational termination and accidence. In the second half of the verse we have suggestiveness of primary affix, secondary affix, compound and preposition. An all-surpassing beauty of construction will be manifest in a poem where numerous suggestive elements combine as in this instance. A rare beauty of construction will result in poetry even by the presence of a solitary suggestive word. When such is the case, what need we say about the combination of numerous suggestive elements ? The example given above illustrates this very strikingly. In the word "Rāvaṇa" we not only find the charm due to suggestion with the expressed sense merged in another, but also the charm due to various elements of suggestiveness described above. Such constructions are found in abundance in the works of great writers who are gifted with extraordinary genius. The following is an instance taken from the great sage Vyāsa :—

Past are their delights
And times do present more and more terrors.
Each morrow, the days become
More evil; Earth, alas, has lost her youth.

In this instance suggestion with undiscerned sequentiality is conveyed by primary affix and number and suggestion 'with the expressed completely given up' in the expression "Earth, alas, has lost her youth."

These case-terminations etc. are generally pregnant with suggestion both individually and collectively in the works of first-rate poets. Here is an example of suggestive case-termination :—

..*Made to dance by my dear wife*
With her rhythmic claps, so sweet
By the sound of gingling bangles,
Our friend, the peacock, will resort
To the golden perch at the close of day....

तिङन्तस्य यथा —

अवसर रोउं चिअ णिम्मिआइँ मा पुंस मे हअच्छीइं ।
दंसणमेत्तुम्मत्तेहिं जेहिँ हिअअं तुह ण णाअम् ॥
[अवसर रोदितुमेव निर्मिते मा पुंसय हते अक्षिणी मे ।
दर्शनमात्रोन्मत्ताभ्यां याभ्यां तव हृदयमेवंरूपं न ज्ञातम् ॥
[इति च्छाया]

यथा वा —

मा पन्थं रुन्धीओ अवेहि बालअ अहोसि अहिरीओ ।
अम्हेअ णिरिच्छाओ सुण्णघरं रक्खिदव्वं णो ॥
[मा पन्थानं रुधः अपेहि बालक अप्रौढ अहो असि अह्रीकः ।
वयं परतन्त्रा यतः शून्यगृहं मामकं रक्षणीयं वर्तते ॥ इति च्छाया]

सम्बन्धस्य यथा —

अण्णत्त वच्च बालअ ह्णाअन्तिं[1] किं मं पुलोएसि एअम्[2] ।
भो जाआभीरुआणं तडं विअ ण होई[3] ॥
[अन्यत्र व्रज बालक स्नान्तीं किं मां प्रलोकय°स्येवम् ।
भो जायाभीरुकाणां तटमेव न भवति ॥ इति च्छाया]

कृतकप्रयोगेषु प्राकृतेषु तद्धितविषये व्यञ्जकत्वमावेद्यत एव । अवज्ञातिशये कः[4] । समासानां च वृत्त्यौचित्येन विनियोजने ।

निपातानां व्यञ्जकत्वं यथा—

अयमेकपदे तया वियोगः प्रियया चोपनतः सुदुः[5]सहो मे ।
नववारिधरोदयो[6]दहोभिर्भवितव्यं च निरातपत्व[7]रम्यैः ॥

१. अण्हा – घ. २. किसमलहेसिएअम् (!) – घ. ३. हो जाआभीरुआण तुह …विअणु होई ॥ (?) – घ. ४. 'अवज्ञानिशये…समासानां' – ग., 'अवज्ञातिशये कः ।' – घ. पुस्तके नास्ति । ५. 'अतिदुःसहः' –,ग. ६. 'वारिधरोदयैः' – ग. ७. निरानपार्धरम्यैः – BP.

The following is an example of suggestive conjugational termination :—

Get away from here,
Don't exasperate my hapless eyes
Made as it were only to weep;
For they didn't see through thy heart
But became crazy at thy first sight.

To give another example :—

Don't stand in the way; get away O boy !
Oh, how shameless indeed thou art !
We are not at all free as we have a duty
To guard the deserted house.

A suggestive relation is illustrated in the following :—

Go elswhere, O boy !
Why do you look at me so when I bathe ?
Indeed, you should know—
The bank is not at all the place
For those who fear their wives.

In Prakrit, words which are derivatively formed from nouns by the addition of the affix '*ka*' (such as "*bhīruka*" in the above instance) are clearly suggestive of contempt.

Compounds also become suggestive when words are compounded in deference to the principles of diction. The suggestiveness of indeclinable conjunctions etc. is illustrated in the following verse :—

All too suddenly has this separation come
And that too from my beloved; so unbearable it is !
And now that the new rain-clouds have also appeared,
I believe the beauty of days will be halved
For want of any sunshine.

इत्यत्र चशब्दः । यथा वा—

मुहुरङ्गुलिसंवृताधरौष्ठं प्रतिषेधाक्षरविक्लवाभिरामम् ।
मुखमंसविवर्ति पक्ष्मलाक्ष्याः कथमप्युन्नमितं न चुम्बितं तु ॥

अत्र तुशब्दः । निपातानां प्रसिद्धमपीह द्योतकत्वं रसापेक्षयोक्तमिति द्रष्टव्यम् । उपसर्गाणां व्यञ्जकत्वं यथा—

नीवाराः शुकगर्भकोटरमुखभ्रष्टास्तरूणामधः
प्रस्निग्धाः क्वचिदिङ्गुदीफलभिदः सूच्यन्त एवोपलाः ।
विश्वासोपगमादभिन्नगतयः शब्दं सहन्ते मृगा–
स्तोयाधारपथाश्च वल्कलशिखानिष्यन्दलेखाङ्किताः ॥[1]

इत्यादौ । द्वित्राणां चोपसर्गाणामेकत्र पदे यः प्रयोगः सोऽपि रसव्यक्त्यनुगुणतयैव निर्दोषः । यथा—'प्रभ्रश्यत्युत्तरीयत्विषि तमसि समुद्वीक्ष्य वीतावृतीन्द्राग्जन्तून्' इत्यादौ । यथा वा[2]—'मनुष्यवृत्त्या समुपाचरन्तम्' इत्यादौ ।

निपातानामपि तथैव । यथा—'अहो बतासि स्पृहणीयवीर्यः' इत्यादौ । यथा वा—

---

१. एतदनन्तरम्—

मदमुखरकपोतमुन्मयूरं प्रविरलवामनवृक्षसंनिवेशम् ।
वनमिदमवगाहमानभीमं व्यसनमिवोपरि दारुणत्वमेति ॥

अत्र प्रशब्दस्योच्छब्दस्य च रसव्यञ्जकत्वमधिकं द्योतते ।

इति घ– पुस्तकेऽस्ति ।

२. 'यथा वा' क-ख पुस्तकयोर्नास्ति.

Here the conjunction 'too' is suggestive. In the same way, the conjunction 'but' in the following example is suggestive :—

The face of my sweet-browed beloved,
With lips covered frequently by the fingers,
Lovely with indistinct no's
And resting upon her shoulders
Was somehow raised up by me;
But kissed it could not be.

Suggestiveness of indeclinables is quite well known; but we are thinking here only of suggestiveness of sentiment.

Suggestive prepositions are found in the following example:—

Beneath the trees are seen wild rice
Fallen from the mouths of crevices
Wherein parrots do nestle.
Stones so oily and shining indicate
They have been used in cracking wild nuts.
With great confidence the deer wander free
And are unvexed by the din (of the chariot);
The roads to the rivers are marked by water streaks
Dripping from the tips of bark-garments.

The preposition "*pra*" in the Sanskrit verse is suggestive.

Sometimes two or three prepositions are prefixed to a single word and if this does not savour of a blemish, it is because of suggestiveness of sentiment alone; e. g.—

(1) '*prabhraṣyatyuttarīyatviṣi tamasi samudvīkṣya vītāvṛtīn drāg jantūn......*' (when darkness was drawing to a close with its hue of an upper garment, seeing all creatures getting up...)

(2) "*manuṣyavṛttyā samupācarantaṁ......*" (enacting as you do the behaviour of men...)

The same is true of indeclinables etc. also:—

(1) '*Aho batāsi spṛhaṇīyavīryaḥ......*' (Indeed your valour is covetable, I say !)

ये जीवन्ति न मान्ति ये स्मे[१] वपुषि प्रीत्या प्रनृत्यन्ति च[२]
प्रस्यन्दिप्रमदाश्रवः पुलकिता[३] दृष्टे गुणिन्यूर्जिते ।
हा धिक्कष्टमहो क्व यामि शरणं तेषां जनानां कृते
नीतानां प्रलयं शठेन[४] विधिना साधुद्विषः[५] पुष्यता ॥

इत्यादौ ।

पदपौनरुक्त्यं च व्यञ्जकत्वापेक्षयैव कदाचित्प्रयुज्यमानं शोभामावहति । यथा —

यद्वञ्चनाहितमतिर्बहु[६]चाटुगर्भं
कार्योन्मुखः खलजनः कृतकं ब्रवीति ।
तत्साधवो न न विदन्ति विदन्ति किन्तु
कर्तुं वृथा प्रणयमस्य न पारयन्ति ॥

इत्यादौ ।

कालस्य व्यञ्जकत्वं यथा—

समविसमणिव्विसेसा समन्तओ मन्दमन्दसंआरा ।
अइरा होहिन्ति पहा मणोरहाणं पि दुल्लङ्घाः ॥

[समविषमनिर्विशेषाः समन्ततो मन्दमन्दसञ्चाराः ।
अचिराद्भविष्यन्ति पन्थानो मनोरथानामपि दुर्लङ्घ्याः ॥ इति च्छाया]

अत्र ह्यचिराद्भविष्यन्ति पन्थान इत्यत्र भविष्यन्तीत्यस्मिन् पदे प्रत्ययः कालविशेषाभिधायी रसपरिपोषहेतुः प्रकाशते । अयं हि गाथार्थः प्रवासविप्रलम्भशृङ्गारविभावतया विभाव्यमानो रसवान् । यथात्र प्रत्ययांशो व्यञ्जकस्तथा क्वचित्प्रकृत्यंशोऽपि दृश्यते । यथा—

१. स्व – घ. २. ये – घ. ३. पुलकिनः – ग. ४. 'शनैश्च' – ग. ५. 'सा विद्विषा' – ग. ६. 'भुवि' – ग.

(2) *They who are revived,*
Who do not contain themselves with joy
and who dance about shedding tears of joy
With bodies thrilled at the very sight
Of a virtuous person;
They have now, alas ! been led to ruin by wicked Fate
Who favours only enemies of the good;
And woe is me ! alas !
Where can I now turn for help
For the relief of those persons ?

Repetition of words also becomes agreeable when such repetition is resorted to only in view of suggestiveness, e. g,:—

It is not that the good are not aware,
They are aware that the wicked one speaks
False words brimming with sweetest praise
Only because he is intent on cheating
And is selfish to a degree ;
And yet they cannot bring themselves
To betray his false affection.

Suggestiveness of tense is illustrated in the following :—

Ups and downs in the roads will all be levelled,
Journeys everywhere become slow and slower still;
Before long, they will exceed the reach
Even of one's mind-chariots.

The future tense in the verb ' will exceed ' is highly suggestive of sentiment in this example. The sentiment will become clear if one understands that the purport of the verse is nothing but the portrayal of a setting that serves as a stimulus for the sentiment of Love-in-separation due to journey. Just as the termination part of a word shows suggestive force in the above example, so also the basic part of a word may become suggestive as in the following:—

तद्गेहं नतभित्ति मन्दिरमिदं लब्धावगाहं दिवः
सा धेनुर्जरती चरन्ति करिणामेता घनाभा घटाः ।
स क्षुद्रो मुसलध्वनिः कलमिदं सङ्गीतकं योषिता-
माश्चर्यं दिवसैर्द्विजोऽयमियतीं भूमिं समारोपितः ॥

अत्र श्लोके दिवसैरित्यस्मिन् पदे प्रकृत्यंशो द्योतकः । सर्वनाम्नां च व्यञ्जकत्वं यथानन्तरोक्ते[1] श्लोके । अत्र च सर्वनाम्नामेव व्यञ्जकत्वं हृदि व्यवस्थाप्य कविना क्वेत्यादिशब्दप्रयोगो न कृतः । अनया दिशा सहृदयैरन्येऽपि व्यञ्जकविशेषाः स्वयमुत्प्रेक्षणीयाः । एतच्च सर्वं पदवाक्यरचनाद्योतनोक्त्यैव गतार्थमपि वैचित्र्येण व्युत्पत्तये पुनरुक्तम् ।

ननु[2] चार्थसामर्थ्याक्षेप्या रसादय इत्युक्तम्, तत्र सुबादीनां व्यञ्जकत्व वैचित्र्यकथनमनन्वितमेव । उक्तमत्र पदानां व्यञ्जकत्वोक्त्यवसरे । किञ्चार्थविशेषाक्षेप्यत्वेऽपि रसादीनां तेषामर्थविशेषाणां व्यञ्जकशब्दाविनाभावित्वाद्यथाप्रदर्शितं व्यञ्जकस्वरूपपरिज्ञानं विभज्योपयुज्यत एव । शब्दविशेषाणां चान्यत्र[3] च चारुत्वं यद्विभागेनोपदर्शितं तदपि तेषां व्यञ्जकत्वेनैवावस्थितमित्यवगन्तव्यम् ।

[4]यत्रापि न तत् संप्रतिभासते तत्रापि व्यञ्जके रचनान्तरे यदृष्टं सौष्ठवं तेषां[5] प्रवाहपतितानां तदेवाभ्यासादपोद्धृतानामप्यवभासत इत्यवसातव्यम्[6] ।

---

१. यथात्रैवानन्तरोक्ते – घ. २. न तु-च. ३. तत्रान्यत्र-घ. ४. यत्रापि तत्संप्रति न प्रति° – BP. ५. 'तेषां तेषां'–घ. ६. अवभासते इत्यवस्थातव्यम्–घ.

That was a hut with broken walls
And this is a mansion touching heavenly heights;
That was an aged cow,
And such herds of elephants, dark like clouds,
Are now moving hereabout.
How awakward was the thud of the pestle then !
But now I hear sweet music of lovely women.
What a wonder it is that the poor Brahmin
Has been raised in a few days to such a state !

Here the basic element in the word '*divasaiḥ*' (' within a few days ') is suggestive. The suggestiveness of pronouns also can be discerned in the above example itself. It is because of the suggestive force of the demonstrative pronouns that the poet has not made use of express words like ' where ' (in order to bring out the contrast). Along these lines, perceptive critics should imagine for themselves the suggestiveness of other types also (unmentioned here). Though all this was implied certainly in the statement that suggestiveness is found in word, sentence and texture, yet they have been set forth in detail so that critics might be edified in diverse ways.

At this stage, one might object as follows:—' Formerly it was declared that sentiments etc. are suggested only by the power of sense; now, will not this statement contradict the present statement that case-terminations etc. can also be suggestive in different ways. We have already given our reply to such objections while proving the suggestivity of words. Moreover, even supposing that sentiments etc. can be suggested only by specific senses, a classified treatment of suggestive elements given above would still be useful, since specific senses are inseparably connected with suggestive words. The classification proposed in other works regarding the charm attained by particular kinds of words in particular contexts also becomes justifiable only when we understand it to be based on the suggestiveness of words.

It might be urged that often such suggestiveness of sentiments is not found in specific words. But one will have to grant that a kind of charm is discernible even in such instances. For we will have appreciated the suggestive charm of specific words, etc.

कोऽन्यथा तुल्ये वाचकत्वे शब्दानां चारुत्वविषयो विशेषः स्यात् । अन्य एवासौ सहृदयसंवेद्य इति चेत्, किमिदं सहृदयत्वं नाम ? किं रसभावानपेक्षकाव्याश्रितसमयविशेषाभिज्ञत्वम्, उत रसभावादिमयकाव्यस्वरूपपरिज्ञाननैपुण्यम् ? पूर्वस्मिन् पक्षे तथाविधसहृदयव्यवस्थापितानां शब्दविशेषाणां चारुत्वनियमो न स्यात् । पुनः समयान्तरेणान्यथापि व्यवस्थापनसम्भवात् । द्वितीयस्मिंस्तु पक्षे रसज्ञतैव सहृदयत्वमिति । तथाविधैः सहृदयैः संवेद्यो रसादिसमर्पणसामर्थ्यमेव नैसर्गिकं शब्दानां विशेष इति व्यञ्जकत्वाश्रय्[1]येव तेषां मुख्यं चारुत्वम् । वाचकत्वाश्रयस्तु[2] प्रसाद[3] एवार्थापेक्षायां तेषां विशेषः । अर्थानपेक्षायां त्वनुप्रासादिरेव ।

एवं रसादीनां व्यञ्जकस्वरूपमभिधाय तेषामेव विरोधिरूपं लक्षयितु[4]मिदमुपक्रम्यते ।—

प्रबन्धे मुक्तके वापि रसादीन्बन्धुमिच्छता ।
यत्नः कार्यः सुम[5]तिना परिहारे विरोधिनाम् ॥ १७ ॥

प्रबन्धे मुक्तके वापि रस[6]भावनिबन्धनं प्रत्यादृतमनाः कविर्विरोधिपरिहारे परं[7] यत्नमादधीत । अन्यथा त्वस्य रसमयः श्लोक एकोऽपि सम्यङ्न सम्पद्यते ।

कानि पुनस्तानि विरोधीनि यानि यत्नतः कवेः परिहर्तव्यानीत्युच्यते—

१. व्यञ्जकत्वाश्रय एव –घ. २. वाचकत्वाश्रयाणां तु सोऽस्तु –ग. ३. After प्रसाद MB has उपमादिः. ४. 'लक्षयितुमुपक्रमते-क-ख. ५. सुकविना –MB. ६. रसाभाव –घ. ७. परं प्रयत्नं –MB.

at least in other works of first-rate poets abounding in suggestion of sentiment; and by constant appreciation of charm in such words found in a different context, we imperceptibly fall into the habit of fancying the same charm in these words by association even when they are found separately in other works. If it were not so, it would be impossible to explain the distinction that exists in words in point of denotation. If one were to dismiss it by the glib statement that the divergence is perceptible only to refined critics, we will have to put this counter-question to them:—What constitutes a refined critic? Is it a mere knowledge of certain conventional canons of literary criticism irrespective of sentiments and emotions; or is it a skill in appreciation of literature imbued with sentiments, emotions, etc.? If the first alternative be true, no beauty can be present as a rule in all instances of words advocated by these so-called refined critics, for it is quite possible to establish another coterie of critics and advocate the absence of beauty in such instances. And according to the second alternative, the definition of a refined critic will be nothing but sensitivity to sentiments. The natural uniqueness in particular words, which such critics find is none other than the power of infusing sentiments, etc. And hence their beauty is principally based on the suggestiveness of words. From the standpoint of denotation, the only uniqueness of charm discernible in them would just be the quality of Perspicuity. If sense too should be left out of account, only Alliteration, etc. would constitute the said uniqueness.

So far, the suggestiveness of sentiments, etc., has been explained. The following text begins an account of the circumstances that run counter to these :

Whether it is the whole work or a single stanza, a good poet who is desirous of incorporating sentiments etc. in what he writes should take pains to avoid hindrances to them. 17

A poet who is intent upon incorporating sentiments and emotions in his works, whether they be big or small, should turn all his efforts towards avoiding impediments. Otherwise he will not succeed in composing even a single verse full of sentiment. The following verses answer the question, 'what, then are these impediments which deserve to be carefully avoided by the poet ?'

विरोधिरससम्बन्धिविभावादिपरिग्रहः ।
विस्तरेणान्वितस्यापि वस्तुनोऽन्यस्य वर्णनम् ॥ १८ ॥

अकाण्ड एव विच्छित्तिरकाण्डे च प्रकाशनम् ।
परिपोषं गतस्यापि पौनःपुन्येन दीपनम् ।
रसस्य स्याद्विरोधाय वृत्त्यनौचित्यमेव च ॥ १९ ॥

प्रस्तुतरसापेक्षया विरोधी यो रसस्तस्य सम्बन्धिनां विभावानुभावव्यभिचारिणां परिग्रहो रसविरोधहेतुकः सम्भावनीयः । तत्र विरोधिरसविभावपरिग्रहो यथा शान्तरसविभावेषु तद्विभावतयैव निरूपितेष्वनन्तरमेव शृङ्गारादिविभा[1]ववर्णने । विरोधिरसभावपरिग्रहो यथा प्रियं प्रति प्रणयकलहकुपितासु कामिनीषु वैराग्यकथाभिरनुनये । विरोधिरसानुभावपरिग्रहो यथा प्रणयकुपितायां प्रियायामप्रसीदन्त्यां नायकस्य कोपावेशविवशस्य रौद्रानुभाववर्णने ।

अयं चान्यो रसभङ्गहेतुर्यत्प्रस्तुतरसा[2]पेक्षया वस्तुनोऽन्यस्य कथञ्चिदन्वितस्यापि विस्तरेण कथनम् । यथा विप्रलम्भशृङ्गारे नायकस्य कस्यचिद्वर्णयितुमुपक्रान्ते[3] कवेर्यमकाद्यलङ्कारनिबन्धनरसिकतया महता प्रबन्धेन पर्वतादिवर्णनम् । अयं चापरो रसभङ्गहेतु[4]रवगन्तव्यो यदकाण्ड एव विच्छित्तिः रसस्याकाण्डे[5] एव च प्रकाशनम् । तत्रानवसरे विरामो रसस्य[6] यथा नायकस्य

---

१. शृङ्गारादिवर्णने – घ. २. ‘रसाद्यपेक्षया’ – ग. ३. ‘उपक्रान्तस्थ’ – घ, अनुक्रान्ते – ग. ४. ‘भङ्गहेतुमावहति’ – ग; ५. ‘अकाण्ड एव प्रकाशनम्’ – ग. ‘°काण्डे च प्रथनम्’ – घ. ६. ‘रसस्य’ घ – पुस्तके नास्ति.

Sketching the setting etc., of an opposite sentiment, describing something whose connection with the subject on hand is only very remote, **18**

Stopping the delineation of sentiment abruptly as also elaborating it when not required; over-elaborating it again and again though it has already received sufficient elaboration, and indecorum in respect of behaviour—all these hinder the course of sentiment. **19**

(1) The first impediment to sentiment is the sketching of setting, emotional responses and passing moods which belong to a sentiment not only other than but opposed to the sentiment in hand. For instance, if after portraying a person as spiritual-minded (i. e. as substratum of the sentiment viz, tranquillity in its own proper setting), the poet makes the same person appear in the role of a romantic lover abruptly, (i. e. in the role of a substratum in a setting of the Erotic sentiment), the intended sentiment is hindered. An example of sketching the abiding emotion of an opposed sentiment is had when the hero tries to humour his wives who are angry because of lovers' quarrels by stories in praise of renunciation of worldly pleasures. Similarly, an example of an opposed sentiment is seen if the hero is discribed as getting wild with rage and putting forth gestures of fury when his sweetheart feigning love-anger does not yield to his importunities.

(2) The second impediment to sentiment is the lengthy description of a subject whose connection with the sentiment on hand is only a very distant one. This is illustrated in an instance where the poet who has begun a description of the hero, goes off at a tangent to describe mountains, etc. at an inordinate length.

(3) The third impediment to sentiment is unwarranted stoppage of the delineation of sentiment and elaboration of it at the wrong place. Unwarranted stoppage of it is instanced when, after portraying the rise of mutual love between the hero and the heroine, instead of describing their endeavours at union, the poem proceeds to dwell upon their other irrelevant activities. Elaboration of it at the wrong place is had when a god-like

कस्यचित्स्पृहणीयसमागमया नायिकया कयाचित्[1]परां परिपोषपदवीं प्राप्ते शृङ्गारे विदिते च परस्परानुरागे समागमोपायचिन्तोचितं[2] व्यवहारमुत्सृज्य स्वतन्त्रतया व्यापारान्तरवर्णने। अनवसरे च प्रकाशनं रसस्य[3] यथा प्रवृत्ते[4] प्रवृद्धविविधवीरसङ्क्षये[5] कल्पसङ्क्षयकल्पे सङ्ग्रामे देवप्रायस्यापि तावन्नायकस्य अनुपक्रान्तविप्रलम्भशृङ्गारस्य निमित्तमुचितमन्तरेणैव शृङ्गारकथायामवतारवर्णने। न चैवंविधे विषये दैवव्यामोहितत्वं कथापुरुषस्य परिहारो यतो रसबन्ध एव कवेः प्राधान्येन प्रवृत्तिनिबन्धनं युक्तम्। इतिवृत्तवर्णनं[6] तदुपाय एवेत्युक्तं प्राक् 'आलोकार्थी यथा दीपशिखायां यत्नवाञ्जनः' इत्यादिना।

अत एव चेतिवृत्तमात्रवर्णनप्राधान्येऽङ्गाङ्गि[7]भावरहितरसभावनिबन्धने च कवीनामेवंविधानि स्खलितानि भवन्तीति रसादिरूपव्यङ्ग्यतात्पर्यमेवैषां युक्तमिति यत्नोऽस्माभिरारब्धो न ध्वनिप्रतिपादनमात्राभिनिवेशेन। पुनश्चायमन्यो रसभङ्गहेतुरवधारणीयो यत्परिपोषं गतस्यापि रसस्य पौनःपुन्येन दीपनम्। उपभुक्तो हि रसः स्वसामग्रीलब्धपरिपोषः पुनः पुनः परामृश्यमाणः[8] परिम्लानकुसुमकल्पः कल्पते। तथा वृत्तेर्व्यवहारस्य यदनौचित्यं तदपि रसभङ्गहेतुरेव। यथा नायकं प्रति नायिकायाः कस्याश्चिदुचितां भङ्गिमन्तरेण स्वयं सम्भोगाभिलाषकथने। यदि वा वृत्तीनां भरतप्रसिद्धानां कैशिक्यादीनां काव्यालङ्कारान्तरप्रसिद्धानामुपनागरिकाद्यानां वा यदनौचित्यमविषये[9] निबन्धनं तदपि रसभङ्गहेतुः। एवमेषां रसविरोधिनामन्येषां चानया दिशा स्वयमुत्प्रेक्षितानां परिहारे सत्कविभिरवहितैर्भवितव्यम्। परिकरश्लोकाश्चात्र —

---

१. कयाचित्सह परां—क-ख, MB. २. 'चिन्तितोचितं'—क-ख. ३. 'रसस्य'—घ—पुस्तके नास्ति. ४. प्रवृत्त°—BP. ५. स्वप्रवृत्ति—घ. ६. °वर्णनं तु—MB. ७. 'चाङ्गाङ्गि'—ग. ८. 'पुनः पुनरामृष्यमाणः'—ख. ९. °चित्यमाविषये निबन्धनं—MB. १०. उचिताङ्गभाङ्गि—घ.

hero as Rāma is, for no reason at all, shown as getting interested in activities of love when a terrific battle is raging at its height spelling death of the greatest heroes (as at the time of universal destruction), though there has been absolutely no previous occasion leading up to even the sentiment of love-in-separation at that time. Nor can such a procedure be justified on the ground that the character is shown there only as a victim of delusion due to Destiny. For it is proper that the poet should write only with a view to delineating sentiment. The plot is only a means towards that end as observed in I·9 and so forth.

Such mistakes are committed by poets when they become primarily interested in describing the plot for its own sake and delineate sentiments without discriminating between principal and subsidiary ones. Hence our effort has all along been to make it clear that the poets do well to have the sole intention of infusing suggested sentiments etc. into their works and not merely to exhibit our enthusiasm in propounding a novel doctrine of suggestion.

(4) The fourth impediment to sentiment is its over-elaboration again and again, though it has already received sufficient elaboration. A sentiment which has received full elaboration in the shape of a description of its various constituents, and brings enjoyment will itself look like a faded flower if it is pressed far to much again and again.

(5) Indecorum in respect of behaviour is also another impediment to sentiment. For instance, if the heroine throwing aside decorum conveys openly to the hero her desire for dalliance, we get this defect. The word *Vṛtti* in the Text may mean either *Kaiśikī* (the graceful) etc. which are laid down by Bharata or the *Upanāgarikā* (The Urban) etc. laid down by other writers on Poetics. Indecorum in respect of the one or the other will be equally an impediment to sentiment.

Good poets must be very attentive in steering clear of these impediments to sentiment and also of other similar hindrances which can be imagined along these lines by the poets themselves. The following lines sum up the points :—

मुख्या व्यापारविषयाः सुकवीनां रसादयः ।
तेषां निबन्धने भाव्यं तैः सदैवाप्रमादिभिः ॥
नीरसस्तु प्रबन्धो[1] यः सोऽपशब्दो महान् कवेः ।
स तेनाकविरेव स्यादन्येनास्मृतलक्षणः ॥
पूर्वे विशृङ्खलगिरः कवयः प्राप्तकीर्तयः ।
तान्समाश्रित्य न त्याज्या नीतिरेषा मनीषिणा ॥
वाल्मीकिव्यासमुख्याश्च ये प्रख्याता[2]ः कवीश्वराः ।
तदभिप्रायबाह्योऽयं नास्माभिर्दर्शितो नयः ॥ इति ।

विवक्षिते रसे लब्धप्रतिष्ठे तु विरोधिनाम् ।
बाध्यानामङ्गभावं वा प्राप्तानामुक्तिरच्छला ॥ २० ॥

स्वसामग्र्यां[3] लब्धपरिपोषे तु विवक्षिते रसे विरोधिनां विरोधिरसाङ्गानां बाध्यानामङ्गभावं वा प्राप्तानां सतामुक्तिरदोषः[4] । बाध्यत्वं हि विरोधिनां शक्याभिभवत्वे सति नान्यथा । तथा च[5] तेषामुक्तिः प्रस्तुतरसपरिपोषायैव सम्पद्यते ।[7] अङ्गभावं प्राप्तानां च तेषां विरोधित्वमेव[6] निवर्तते । अङ्गभावप्राप्तिर्हि तेषां[8] स्वाभाविकी समारोपकृता वा । तत्र येषां नैसर्गिकी तेषां[8] तावदुक्तावविरोध एव । यथा विप्रलम्भशृङ्गारे तदङ्गानां व्याध्यादीनां, तेषां[9] च तदङ्गानामेवादोषो नातदङ्गानाम् । तदङ्गत्वे च सम्भवत्यपि मरणस्योपन्यासो

१. 'हि निबन्धो' –ग. MB. २. प्रख्याता–घ. ३. 'स्वसामग्री'–घ. ४. 'निर्दोषा' –ग., MB. ५. तथाच–घ पुस्तके नास्ति । ६. तावदुक्तावविरोध एव–घ. ७. अङ्गभावं प्राप्तानां च तेषां–घ. ८. 'स्वभाविकी' इत्यारभ्य 'नैसिर्गिकी तेषां' इति पर्यन्तं –घ. पुस्तके नास्ति. ९. तेषांच –घ. पुस्तके नास्ति.

Sentiments etc. are the most important ends for the activity of poets; hence poets should always be very attentive in delineating them.

A work devoid of sentiment is the most unpardonable solecism on the part of a poet. It will brand him as a poetaster with nothing but oblivion in store for him.

Time was when poets could win fame by their words unfettered by any rule; but the wise should not take them as their models and depart from the principles laid down above.

As a matter of fact, we have shown nothing here which is against the opinions of the most celebrated first-rate poets like Vālmīki and Vyāsa.

After the intended leading sentiment has been established on a secure footing, there will be no defect in including even hindrances provided that these come either as foils or as ancillaries. 20

After a full development of the intended leading sentiment as a result of its accessories, it would not at all be a defect to portray even the hindrances in case these serve as only foils or ancillaries of the intended leading sentiment. Hindrances will serve as foils only when they are positively overshadowed by the intended leading sentiments, not otherwise. Hence an account of the foils only enhances the development of the intended leading sentiment. If hindrances should come in as ancillaries, they will have lost their very hindering power. Hindrances can come in as ancillaries, either in a natural way or in an imagined way. In a description of natural ancillaries there is no scope at all for any hindrance. For example, there is no defect involved only in describing disease etc. while delineating the sentiment of Love-in-separation (because disease is a natural ancillary of love-in-separation) ; but it would be a defect if one were to describe therein things which are not ancillaries (such as death, for instance). Even if one were to think that death also is a possible ancillary of Love-in-separation, a mention of death

न न्याय्य[1]ः। आश्रयविच्छेदे रसस्यात्यन्तविच्छेदप्राप्तेः। करुणस्य तु तथाविधे विषये परिपोषो भविष्यतीति चेत् न; तस्याप्रस्तुतत्वात्, प्रस्तुतस्य च विच्छेदात्। यत्र तु करुणरसस्यैव[2] काव्यार्थत्वं तत्राविरोधः। शृङ्गारे वा मरणस्यादीर्घकालप्रत्यापत्तिसम्भवे कदाचिदुपनिबन्धो नात्यन्तविरोधी। दीर्घकालप्रत्यापत्तौ तु तस्यान्तरा प्रवाहविच्छेद एवे[3]त्येवंविधेतिवृत्तोपनिबन्धनं रसबन्धप्रधानेन कविना परिहर्तव्यम्।

तत्र लब्धप्रतिष्ठे तु विवक्षिते रसे विरोधिरसाङ्गानां बाध्यत्वेनोक्तावदोषो यथा—

क्वाकार्यं शशलक्ष्मणः क्व च कुलं भूयोऽपि दृश्येत सा
दोषाणां प्रशमाय मे श्रुतमहो कोपेऽपि कान्तं मुखम्।
किं वक्ष्यन्त्यपकल्मषाः कृतधियः स्वप्नेऽपि सा दुर्लभा
चेतः स्वास्थ्यमुपैहि कः खलु युवा धन्योऽधरं पास्यति॥

यथावा पुण्डरीकस्य महाश्वेतां प्रति प्रवृत्तनिर्भरानुरागस्य द्वितीयमुनिकुमारोपदेशवर्णने। स्वाभाविक्यामङ्गभावप्राप्तावदोषो यथा—

भ्रमिमरतिमलसहृदयतां प्रलयं मूर्च्छां तमः शरीरसादम्।
मरणं च जलदभुजगजं प्रसह्य कुरुते विषं वियोगिनीनाम्॥

---

१. ज्यायान्–BP. २. 'करुणस्यैव'–घ. ३. एव भवतीत्येवं°–MB.

would be improper, since a rupture of the substratum itself invariably brings about a rupture of sentiment also. One might aver that the portrayal of death lends greater beauty to the delineation of the Pathetic sentiment. But Pathos is not only irrelevant to the sentiment of Love-in-separation which is relevant here, but the relevant sentiment itself is broken up. It (portrayal of death) will not be a hindrance only when pathos itself happens to be the principal sentiment, or we might say this much :—on very rare occasions, mention of death will not appear as a very great hindrance to the Erotic sentiment, provided there is a prospect of this separation due to death coming to a speedy end by reunion (in another form). If a long period of time should intervene between death and such reunion, death would once again be a hindrance, since the even flow of the current of love would be stopped by it abruptly in the middle itself. Hence, a poet intent upon delineating sentiments should avoid such episodes in the plot.

How hindrances too do not appear as defects when they serve as foils of the intended leading sentiment is illustrated in the following example :—

Where is misdeed and where the spotless race of the moon ?
Would that I see her again !
My learning should resist all evil;
But how lovely is her face even in anger !
What will the pure and wise ones say about this ?
Ah, she is not to be had by me even in dream !
Take courage, my heart !
Which youth will be so lucky
As to drink (*the honey*) *of her lips* ?

Similarly, the advice of the ascetic's companion to Puṇḍarīka deeply fallen in love with Mahāśvetā is another instance.

The following is an example where a hindrance does not appear so because of its being ancillary to the intended leading sentiment in the natural course of things :—

Reeling, jadedness and laziness etc. (*supra, p.* 77)

इत्यादौ । समारोपितायामप्यविरोधो यथा 'पाण्डु क्षामं' इत्यादौ ।[1] यथावा– "कोपात्कोमललोलबाहुलतिकापाशेन"[2] इत्यादौ । इयं चाङ्गभावप्राप्तिरन्या यद[3]धिकारिकत्वात्प्रधान एकस्मिन् वाक्यार्थे रसयोर्भावयोर्वा परस्परविरोधिनोर्द्वयोरङ्गभावगमनं तस्यामपि न दोषः । यथा 'क्षिप्तो हस्तावलग्नः'[4] इत्यादौ । कथं तत्राविरोध[5] इति चेत्, द्वयोरपि तयोरन्यपरत्वेन व्यवस्था[6]नात् । अन्यपरत्वेऽपि विरोधिनोः कथं विरोधनिवृत्तिरिति चेत्, उच्यते–विधौ विरुद्धसमावेशस्य दुष्टत्वं नानुवादे । यथा—

एहि गच्छ पतोत्तिष्ठ वद मौनं समाचर ।
एवमाशाग्रहग्रस्तैः क्रीडन्ति धनिनोऽर्थिभिः ॥

इत्यादौ । अत्रहि विधिप्रतिषेधयोरनूद्यमानत्वेन समावेशे न विरोधस्तथेहापि भवति[7] । श्लोके ह्यस्मिन्नीर्ष्याविप्रलम्भशृङ्गारकरुणवस्तुनोर्न-

१. Compare p. 76, supra. २. See p. 68, supra. ३. यदधिकारि°–ब. ४. See p. 44, supra. ५. 'चात्र' क–ख. ६. व्यवस्थापनात्–घ. ७. भाविष्यति –BP.

In the following examples we have the use of hindrances not appearing as defects, because of their being ancillary to the intended sentiment in an imagined way:—

1. *Your pallid and sunken face,*
   Your passionate heart and sluggish body
   Declare loudly, O friend,
   The disease of consumption
   Rankling within your heart.
2. *It is indeed a lucky lover, etc.*

A hindrance can become subsidiary (to the intended sentiment) in another way also. Two sentiments or emotions mutually opposed may both be made ancillary to another idea which happens to be the principal import in the sentence by force of its contextual importance. The hindrance due to opposed sentiments will cease to be a defect in that case. Verses like '*Let the fire of Śiva's shaft* etc.' illustrate this. It might be asked how there is no opposition between the two sentiments therein. The reply is that both of them are definitely subsidiary to the main import. Once again it might be asked how the natural opposition between two opposite things disappears. We answer that such opposition will appear a defect only in positive statements and not in mere quotations. For example in the following verse :—

> "*Hither* ! .... *Away* !
> *You may sit* !....*no, get up* !
> *Speak up* ! .... *Silence* ! "
>
> *Thus do the wealthy persons play*
> *With suppliants possessed by desire.*

There is no real opposition though both positive injunctions and prohibitions are found side by side, because they are only quotations. In the same way we can understand that there is no opposition in the verse referred to (viz., *Let the fire of Śiva's shaft*, etc.). Neither the element of Love-in-separation due to jealousy nor that of Pathos is positively affirmed in this verse. Its main import is the extraordinary glory of Śiva as the

विधीयमानत्वम् । त्रिपुररिपुप्रभावातिशयस्य वाक्यार्थत्वात्तदङ्गत्वेन च तयोर्व्यवस्थानात्[1] ।

न च रसेषु विध्यनुवादव्यवहारो नास्तीति शक्यं वक्तुम्, तेषां वाक्यार्थत्वेनाभ्युपगमात् । वाक्यार्थस्य च वाच्यस्य यौ विध्यनुवादौ तौ तदाक्षिप्तानां रसानां केन वार्येते । यैर्वा साक्षाद्रसादीनां काव्यार्थता नाभ्युपगम्यते, तैस्तेषां तन्निमित्तता तावदवश्यमभ्युपगन्तव्या[2] । तथाप्यत्र श्लोके न विरोधः । यस्मादनूद्यमानाङ्ग[3]निमित्तोभयरसवस्तुसहकारिणो विधीयमानांशाद्भावविशेषप्रतीतिरुत्पद्यते ततश्च न कश्चिद्[4]विरोधः । दृश्यते हि विरुद्धोभयसहकारिणः कारणात्कार्यविशेषोत्पत्तिः । विरुद्धफलोत्पादन[5]हेतुत्वं हि युगपदेकस्य कारणस्य विरुद्धं[6] न तु विरुद्धोभयसहकारित्वम् । एवंविधं[7]विरुद्धपदार्थविषयः कथमभिनयः प्रयोक्तव्य इति चेत्, अनूद्यमानैवंविधवाच्यविषये या वार्ता सात्रापि भविष्यति । एवं विध्यनुवादनयाश्रयेणात्र श्लोके परिहृतस्तावद्विरोधः ।

किं च नायकस्याभिनन्दनीयोदयस्य कस्यचित्प्रभावातिशयवर्णने तत्प्रतिपक्षाणां यः करुणो रसः स परीक्षकाणां वैक्लव्यं नादधाति प्रत्युत प्रीत्यतिशयनिमित्ततां प्रतिपद्यत[8] इत्यतस्तस्य कुण्ठ[9]शक्तिकत्वात्तद्विरोधविधा-

---

१. 'स्थापनात्'- क-ख. २. 'गमनीया' - क - ख. ३. 'मानोऽङ्ग' - ग. ४. 'कश्चन' - क. ख. ५. 'फलोपादान' - क. ख. ६. विरुद्धत्वं - ७. 'एवं विधं' -ग. विध - घ. पुस्तके नास्ति । ८. प्रतिपद्यते-घ. ९. 'अकुण्ठ' -ग.

destroyer of Tripuras. The two elements of sentiment just now mentioned are clearly mainfest as subsidiary to this main import.

Nor is it posible to say that the procedure of direct assertion and indirect narration is not found in sentiments. The reason is that every one accepts them as imports of sentences. When purport of sentence and expressed sense can both contain the procedure of direct assertion and indirect narration, who can prevent the sentiments from containing these since sentiments are also suggested only by them? Even those who do not accept that s ntiments themselves can be the main import of poetry will have to concede that at least they are conveyed by the main import. Even then, there will be no opposition in the verse in question (viz., *Let the fire of Śiva's shaft*, etc.). There is no scope at all for any opposition because we get the idea mainly of the extraordinary greatness of Śiva as the directly asserted element in the verse and it is this element which is reinforced by the indirectly narrated elements of the other two sentiments (viz., Love-in-separation and Pathos). That particular effects are produced by the agency of two causes opposed to each other, yet co-operating in the production of effect, is a matter of common observation. Opposition would be there only when it is held that the same cause gives rise to two opposite effects simultaneously and not when it is said that two causes opposed to each other are contributing simultaneously towards the production of a single effect. It might be asked how such subjects involving opposite elements would have to be represented on the stage. The answer is that what applies to the representation of similar expressed subjects when they are indirectly narrated also applies to these indirect and suggested elements. Thus the opposition in the verse has been got over by the assistance of the analogous principle of direct assertion and indirect narration.

Furthermore, while the extraordinary greatness of a hero who is at the height of his admirable powers is made the main subject of description, the pathetic sentiment in respect of his enemies does not cause any sorrow in the minds of critics; on the other hand it serves to produce great delight. Since the power of the pathetic sentiment will thus have been practically

यिनो[1] न कश्चिद्दोषः। तस्माद्वाक्यार्थीभूतस्य रसस्य भावस्य वा विरोधी रसविरोधीति[2] वक्तुं न्याय्यः, न त्वङ्गभूतस्य कस्यचित्।

अथवा वाक्यार्थीभूतस्यापि कस्यचित्करुणरसविषयस्य[3] तादृशेन शृङ्गारवस्तुना भङ्गिविशेषाश्रयेण संयोजनं रसपरिपोषायैव[4] जायते। यतः प्रकृतिमधुराः[5] पदार्थाः शोचनीयतां प्राप्ताः प्रागवस्थाभाविभिः संस्मर्यमाणैर्विलासैरधिकतरं शोकावेशमुपजनयन्ति[6]। यथा——

अयं स रशनोत्कर्षी पीनस्तनविमर्दनः।
नाभ्यूरुजघनस्पर्शी नीवीविस्रंसनः करः॥[7]

इत्यादौ। तदत्र त्रिपुरयुवतीनां शाम्भवः शराग्निरार्द्रापराधः कामी यथा व्यवहरति स्म[8] तथा व्यवहृतवानित्यनेनापि प्रकारेणास्त्येव निर्विरोधत्वम्। तस्माद्यथा यथा निरूप्यते तथा तथात्र दोषाभावः। इत्थं च —

१. 'दायिनः' – क. ख. २. यो रसः स रसविरोधीति–घ. ३. 'विशेषस्य' – क. ख. ४. 'परिपोषमावहति–ग. ५. 'रमणीयाः' – क. ख. ६. शोकावेगं – घ. ७. B. O. R. I. Ms. No. 254 of 1875-76 (New No. 28) (Des. Cat. Vol. XII. No. 183) ends here. ८. स्म – घ – पुस्तके नास्ति.

stultified, no fault would be committed if one were to delineate its opposite sentiment also (i. e. the Erotic) in the place. Therefore, only that sentiment deserves to be termed as a hindrance to sentiment, which hinders either a sentiment or an emotion that happens to be the main import of the sentence in question and not at all the one which hinders only another ancillary sentiment or emotion.

The opposition in the verse may be got over in another way also :—Suppose the primarily intended import in the verse (viz., *Let the fire of Śiva's shaft*, etc.) is looked upon as an element of the sentiment of Pathos itself. In that case, the element of Erotic sentiment will have to be considered as conveyed in an indirect manner. If we thus consider that the Erotic element is subsidiary to the Pathetic element, the Pathetic sentiment will only acquire added significance. For, the sight of naturally lovely objects reduced to a pitiable state evokes greater sorrow (than the sight of objects without such loveliness) in the onlooker due to the reminiscences called up in his mind of all their past beauty. The following provides an instance:—

This is that hand which used to draw out our girdles,
And which used to caress our bosoms;
Which used to touch lovingly
Our navels, thighs and pubes
And untie the waist-knots of our lower garments !

In the same way, we can understand in the verse under consideration that the fire of Śiva's shaft conducted itself like a lover who has given offence but lately, and even thus considered, the seeming opposition therein will disappear. Thus from whatever standpoint we consider the verse, the opposition can be explained as unreal. On the analogy of this, all such instances as the following should be regarded as devoid of the defect of opposition :--

क्रामन्त्यः क्षतकोमलाङ्गुलिगलद्रक्तैः[1] सदर्भाः स्थलीः
पादैः पातितयावकैरिव पतद्बाष्पाम्बुधौताननाः ।
भीता भर्तृकरावलम्बितकरास्त्वद्वैरिनार्योऽधुना
दावाग्निं परितो भ्रमन्ति पुनरप्युद्यद्विवाहा इव ॥

इत्येवमादीनां सर्वेषामेव निर्विरोधत्वमवगन्तव्यम् । एवं तावद्रसादीनां विरोधिरसादिभिः समावेशासमावेशयोर्विषयविभागो दर्शितः ।

इदानीं तेषामेकप्रबन्धविनिवेशने न्याय्यो यः क्रमस्तं प्रतिपादयितुमुच्यते —

प्रसिद्धेऽपि प्रबन्धानां नानारसनिबन्धने ।
एको रसोऽङ्गीकर्तव्यस्तेषामुत्कर्षमिच्छता ॥ २१ ॥

प्रबन्धेषु महाकाव्यादिषु नाटकादिषु वा विप्रकीर्णतयाङ्गाङ्गिभावेन[2] बहवो रसा उपनिबध्यन्त[3] इत्यत्र प्रसिद्धौ सत्यामपि यः प्रबन्धानां छायातिशययोग[4]मिच्छति तेन तेषां रसानामन्यतमः कश्चिद्विवक्षितो रसोऽङ्गित्वेन विनिवेशयितव्य इत्ययं युक्ततरो मार्गः ।

ननु रसान्तरेषु बहुषु प्राप्तपरिपोषेषु सत्सु कथमेकस्याङ्गिता न विरुध्यत इत्याशङ्क्येदमुच्यते —

रसान्तरसमावेशः प्रस्तुतस्य रसस्य यः ।
नोपहन्त्यङ्गितां सोऽस्य स्थायित्वेनावभासिनः ॥ २२ ॥

प्रबन्धेषु प्रथमतरं प्रस्तुतः सन् पुनः पुनरनुसन्धीयमानत्वेन स्थायी यो रसस्तस्य सकलबन्धव्यापिनो[5] रसान्तरैरन्तरालवर्तिभिः समावेशो यः स नाङ्गितामुपहन्ति । एतदेवोपपादयितुमुच्यते—

---

१. °वलद्रक्तैः BP. २. भावेन वा–घ. ३. उपनिबध्यन्ते–घ. ४. 'छायायोगं' ग., 'छायातिशयमिच्छति'–घ. ५. '°संधिव्यापिन'–क. ख., MB. '°रसव्यापिनो'–घ.

Stepping on grounds over-grown with hard grass,
With blood gushing out of their tender toes,
Causing their feet to appear
As if they were painted with lac,
With faces washed in streams of flowing tears,
Overcome by fright and holding the hands of their husbands,
Your enemies' wives go round and round wildfires
As though they are going through
The ceremony of a wedding once over !

Thus far, we have pointed out the distinction where sentiments can be delineated side by side with the sentiments opposed to them and where they should not be so delineated. We shall explain in what follows the proper order to be followed in the delineation of such sentiments in one and the same work :—

Though there is a convention that more than one sentiment should find a place in entire works of literature, one of them alone should be made principal by the poet who aims at greatness in his works. 21

Though in fact the convention is that, in epics etc. as well as in dramas etc., several sentiments should be delineated with either equal importance to each or differing importance, the better procedure is that a poet who is intent upon adorning his work with abundant beauty should make it a rule to give principal importance to only one intended sentiment amongst them.

It might be asked how any single sentiment can be rightly made principal when several other sentiments too have received fullness of treatment. The following text answers the objection :—

The importance of an intended sentiment which is shining throughout the work abidingly cannot be marred by the inclusion of other sentiments. 22

When a sentiment happens to be intended as primary in a work and is kept up constant by being delineated again and again, its importance cannot be marred at all by the inclusion of other passing sentiments since it underlies all the rest. The reason why it is so is explained in the following :—

कार्यमेकं यथा व्यापि प्रबन्धस्य विधीयते ।
तथा रसस्यापि विधौ विरोधो नैव विद्यते ॥ २३ ॥

सन्ध्यादिमयस्य प्रबन्धशरीरस्य यथा कार्यमेकमनुयायि व्यापकं कल्प्यते[1] न च तत्कार्यान्तरैर्न[2] सङ्कीर्यते, न च तैः सङ्कीर्यमाणस्यापि तस्य प्राधान्यमपचीयते[3] तथैव रसस्याप्येकस्य सन्निवेशे क्रियमाणे विरोधो न कश्चित् । प्रत्युत प्रत्युदितविवेकानामनुसन्धानवतां सचेतसां तथाविधे विषये प्रह्लादातिशयः प्रवर्तते ।

ननु येषां रसानां[4] परस्पराविरोधः यथा — वीरशृङ्गारयोः शृङ्गारहास्ययोः रौद्रशृङ्गारयोर्वीराद्भुतयोर्वीररौद्रयो रौद्रकरुणयोः शृङ्गाराद्भुतयोर्वा तत्र भवत्वङ्गाङ्गिभावः । तेषां तु स कथं भवेद्येषां पस्स्परं बाध्यबाधकभावः[5] । यथा – शृङ्गारबीभत्सयोर्वीरभयानकयोः शान्तरौद्रयोः शान्तशृङ्गारयो[6]र्वा इत्याशङ्क्येदमुच्यते —

अविरोधी विरोधी वा रसोऽङ्गिनि रसान्तरे ।
परिपोषं न नेतव्यस्तथा स्यादविरोधिता ॥ २४ ॥

अङ्गिनि रसान्तरे शृङ्गारादौ प्रबन्धव्यङ्ग्ये सति अविरोधी विरोधी वा रसः परिपोषं न नेतव्यः । तत्रा[7]विरोधिनो रसस्याङ्गिरसापेक्षयात्यन्तमाधिक्यं न कर्तव्यमित्ययं प्रथमः परिपोषपरिहारः । उत्कर्षसाम्येऽपि तयो[8]र्विरोधासम्भवात् । यथा—

एकन्तो रुअइ पिआ अण्णन्तो समरतूरणिग्घोसो ।
णेहेण रणरसेण अ भडस्स दोलाइअं हिअअम् ॥
[एकतो रोदिति प्रिया अन्यतः समरतूर्यनिर्घोषः ।
स्नेहेन रणरसेन च भटस्य दोलायितं हृदयम् ॥ इति च्छाया]

१. कल्पते–घ, परिकल्प्यते–MB. २. 'तच्च कार्यान्तरैः'–क. ख. ३. 'अपनीयते. –ग. ४. 'रसादीनां' – क. ख. ५. 'भाव एव' – क. ख. ६. शान्तशृङ्गारयोः शृङ्गार-रौद्रयोर्वा–MB. ७. 'तत्राह' – ग., तत्राविरोधि°–घ. ८. तयोरविरोध°–MB.

Just as one plot is made to remain major in a work as a whole, so also one sentiment can be made to remain major and it will not at all lead to a discrepancy. 23

Just as one plot consisting of several parts is made to progress uniformly and pervade the work as a whole and just as it never gets mixed up with minor plots, and even if it should get mixed up, just as its importance does not suffer, so also when a single sentiment among several other minor ones is made as the major one in a whole work, there is not any discrepancy involved. On the contrary, such a procedure will bring abundant delight to refined critics whose discriminative power is sharp and appreciation vast.

Perhaps one might object to this as follows :—

'The relation of principal and subsidiary may hold good at best to such sentiments which are not opposed to each other, e. g. : The Heroic and the Erotic, the Erotic and the Marvellous, the Heroic and the Furious, the Furious and the Pathetic or the Erotic and the Marvellous. But how can it ever hold good in the case of sentiments that are mutually opposed such as— the Erotic and the Disgustful, the Heroic and the Terrible, Quietude and the Furious, Quietude and the Erotic ? '

Our reply to the objection is given below :—

When a sentiment is delineated in a work as the principal one, no other sentiment, whether unopposed or opposed to it, should be treated elaborately. This will ensure one that no opposition between them will remain any more. 24

When any single sentiment like the Erotic happens to be principal in a work, no other sentiment, whether unopposed or opposed, should be treated fully at the same time. Full treatment of the other sentiments can be avoided in the following ways :—

(1) Even an unopposed sentiment should not be given importance greater than that of the principal sentiment. Even if the two should get equal importance, there will be no scope for any opposition between them. e. g. :—

On one side cries the beloved
And the war-drum dins on the other;
The heart of the soldier oscillates
Between love and lust for fight.
Or–

यथावा—

कण्ठा[1]च्छित्वाक्षमालावलयमिव करे हारमावर्तयन्ती
कृत्वा पर्यङ्कबन्धं विषधरपतिना मेखलाया गुणेन ।
मिथ्यामन्त्राभिजापस्फुरदधरपुटव्यांञ्जताव्यक्तहासा
देवी सन्ध्याभ्यसूयाहसितपशुपतिस्तत्र दृष्टा तु वोऽव्यात् ॥

इत्यत्र ।

अङ्गिरसविरुद्धानां व्यभिचारिणां प्राचुर्येणा[2]निवेशनम्, निवेशने वा क्षिप्रमेवाङ्गिरसव्यभिचार्यनुवृत्तिरिति द्वितीयः । अङ्गत्वेन पुनः पुनः प्रत्यवेक्षा परिपोषं नीयमानस्याप्यङ्ग[3]भूतस्य रसस्येति[4] तृतीयः । अनया दिशान्येऽपि प्रकारा उत्प्रेक्षणीयाः । विरोधिनस्तु रसस्याङ्गिरसापेक्षया कस्यचिन्न्यूनता सम्पा[5]दनीया । यथा शान्तेऽङ्गिनि शृङ्गारस्य शृङ्गारे वा शान्तस्य । परिपोषरहितस्य रस[6]स्य कथं रसत्वमिति चेत्—उक्तमत्राङ्गिरसापेक्षयेति । अङ्गिनो हि रसस्य यावान् परिपोषस्तावांस्तस्य न कर्तव्यः; स्वतस्तु सम्भवी[7] परिपोषः केन वार्यते । एतच्चापेक्षि[8]कं प्रकर्षयोगित्वमेकस्य रसस्य[9] बहुरसेषु प्रबन्धेषु रसानामङ्गाङ्गिभावमनभ्युपगच्छ[10]तांप्यशक्यप्रतिक्षेपमित्यनेन प्रकारेणाविरोधिनां विरोधिनां च रसानामङ्गाङ्गिभावेन समावेशे प्रबन्धेषु स्यादविरोध[11]: । एतच्च सर्वं येषां रसो रसान्तरस्य व्यभिचारीभवति इति द[12]र्शनं तन्मतेनोच्यते । मतान्तरे तु[13] **रसानां** स्थायिनो भावा उपचाराद्रसशब्देनोक्तास्तेषामङ्ग[14]त्वं निर्वि[15]रोधमेव ।

१. 'कण्ठं च्छित्त्वाक्षम लेन्याद्दिश्लोके'–क. ख., कर्णे कृत्वाक्ष°–MB. २. प्राचुर्येण निवेशनम्–घ. ३. 'अपि त्वङ्ग'.–ग. ४. 'रस यैवेति'–क. ख. ५. न सम्पादनीया–घ. ६. रसस्य–घ. पुस्तके नास्ति. ७. स्वगतस्तु संभवि–घ. ८. 'एतच्चापेक्षिनं'–ग. ९. रसय।–घ. १०. °गच्छतामप्य°–MB. ११. 'अविरोधिना'–क. ख. १२. निदर्शनं–घ. १३. मतान्तरेऽपि–घ. १४. °मङ्गत्वे–घ. १५. निर्विरोधित्वमेव–घ.

Telling the beads of her necklace,
snatched off the neck, like a rosary, in her hand,
Turning the girdle like a snake into a knot of yogic pose,
Showing her smile with throbbing lips
muttering faked magical spells,
The goddess was seen sending Śiva into
a smile at her envy of Sandhyā.
May she preserve you !

(2) Passing moods which are opposed to the principal sentiment should not be described at length, and if described at all, there should be an immediate reversion to the passing moods of the principal sentiment. (3) Even when a subsidiary sentiment is being treated fully, it should be at all events kept only as a subsidiary one by constant care. Other ways could be imagined by readers themselves along the lines indicated.

If the subsidiary sentiment happens to be an opposed one, it should be carefully depicted only as being lesser than the principal sentiment; for example, if Quietude is the principal sentiment, the Erotic should be lesser in importance; so also, if the Erotic is the principal sentiment, Quietude should become lesser. The words, "than the principal sentiment", have been included in the gloss in order to silence the objection that there can be no sentiment at all, properly speaking, in the absence of full treatment. The idea is that the subsidiary sentiment should not be given the same degree of full treatment as is given to the principal sentiment. Who can ever deny the natural treatment which even a subordinate sentiment might receive (in the usual course of things)? Thus no one — not even those who do not accept the principal and subsidiary relation of sentiments—can ever deny that a single sentiment will have principal importance in spite of the fact that the work may contain several sentiments also alongside of it. Thus too, the opposition of sentiments can be avoided in works by portraying such unopposed or opposed sentiments with due deference to the principal and subsidiary relationship. The above has been written from the standpoint of those who hold that one sentiment can become an accessary of another as a passing mood. Since in the opinion of others, the abiding emotions themselves are metaphorically designated by the term 'sentiment', there is no difficulty at all in sentiments becoming ancillaries.

एवमविरोधिनां विरोधिनां च प्रबन्धस्थेनाङ्गिना रसेन समावेशे साधारणमविरोधोपायं प्रतिपाद्येदानीं विरोधिविषय[1]मेव तं प्रतिपादयितुमिदं[2]मुच्यते ।

विरु[3]द्धैकाश्रयो यस्तु विरोधी स्थायिनो भवेत् ।
स विभिन्नाश्रयः कार्यस्तस्य पोषेऽप्यदोषता ॥ २५ ॥

ऐकाधिकरण्यविरोधी नैरन्तर्यविरोधी चेति द्विविधो[4] विरोधी । तत्र प्रबन्धस्थेन स्थायिनाङ्गिना रसेनौचित्यापेक्षया विरुद्धैकाश्रयो यो विरोधी, यथा वीरेण भयानकः, स विभिन्नाश्रयः कार्यः । तस्य वीरस्य य आश्रयः कथानायकस्तद्विपक्षविषये सन्निवेशयितव्यः । तथा सति च तस्य, विरोधिनोऽपि यः परिपोषः स निर्दोषः । विपक्षविषये हि[5] भयातिशयवर्णने[6] नायकस्य नयपराक्रमादिसम्पत्सुतरामुद्योतिता भवति । एतच्च मदीयेऽर्जुनचरितेऽर्जुनस्य पातालावतरणप्रसङ्गे वैशद्येन प्रदर्शितम् ।

एवमैकाधिकरण्यविरोधिनः प्रबन्धस्थेन[7] स्थायिना रसेनाङ्गभावगमने निर्विरोधित्वं यथा तथा दर्शितम् । द्वितीयस्य तु तत्प्रतिपादयितुमुच्यते—

एकाश्रयत्वे निर्दोषो नैरन्तर्ये विरोधवान्[8] ।
रसान्तरव्यवधिना रसो व्यङ्ग्यः सुमेधसा[9] ॥२६॥

१. विरोधिविषये-घ. २. 'इदं' ग. पुस्तके नास्ति. ३. विरोधै-ब. ४. 'द्विधा'-ग. ५. 'वा' ग. ६. '°कथने' ग. ७. 'प्रबन्धे'-क. ख. ८. 'विरोधिनाम्'-क-ख. ९. व्यङ्ग्यः (न्यस्यः) सुमेधसा-घ.

Hitherto we have explained such general means of overcoming opposition between sentiments, as are commonly applicable to the resolution of opposition between the principal sentiment and the unopposed subsidiary sentiments as well as that between the principal sentiment and the opposed subsidiary sentiments. In what follows, the specific means of overcoming opposition between two opposed sentiments is set forth.

If a sentiment opposed to the principal one happens to occur in the same substratum as that of the latter itself, the opposed sentiment should be given a different substratum; (once this is done) there will be no defect even if it should be treated in full. 25

The Opposite is of two types :—(1) 'Opposite of another in the same substratum' and (2) 'Opposite of another coming beside it'. So far as the principal sentiment is concerned, if another sentiment also is found in the same substratum, i. e. acquires equal importance with it—e. g. when the Heroic is the principal sentiment, the occurrence of the Terrible along with it in one and the same character—we will have an instance of the first type of the Opposite and in such places, the substratum of the other sentiment should be varied : The terrible sentiment should be delineated only with reference to the enemy of the hero who is the substratum of the Heroic sentiment. When this is done, there would be no fault in even treating the opposed sentiment at length. By describing great terror on the part of the enemy, the extraordinary glory of the hero in point of his policy as well as prowess will only be thrown into a bolder relief. This has been very well illustrated in the description of Arjuna's descent to the netherworld in my own work, *Arjunacarita.*

The manner of avoiding the opposition caused by a conflicting sentiment in the same substratum and of making it subsidiary to the principal sentiment in the work has been pointed out in the above text. The same is pointed out below with reference to the opposite of the second variety :—

A sentiment which has no opposition due to the sameness of substratum but which becomes an opposite of another (i. e. principal) sentiment coming closely beside it, should be so conveyed by the intelligent poet that a third sentiment will intervene between these conflicting ones. 26

यः पुनरेकाधिकरणत्वे निर्विरोधो नैरन्तर्ये तु विरोधी स रसान्तरव्यवधानेन प्रबन्धे निवेशयितव्यः। यथा शान्तशृङ्गारौ नागानन्दे[1] निवेशितौ।

शान्तश्च तृष्णाक्षयसुखस्य यः परिपोषस्तल्लक्षणो रसः प्रतीयत एव। तथा[2] चोक्तम्—

यच्च कामसुखं लोके यच्च दिव्यं महत्सुखम्।
तृष्णाक्षयसुखस्यैते नार्हतः षोडशीं कलाम्॥

इति। यदि नाम सर्वजनानुभवगोचरता तस्य नास्ति नैतावतासावलोक[3]-सामान्यमहानुभावचित्तवृत्तिविशेषः[4] प्रतिक्षेप्तुं शक्यः। न च वीरे तस्यान्तर्भावः[5] कर्तुं युक्तः। तस्याभिमानमयत्वेन व्यवस्थापनात्[6]। अस्य चाहङ्कारप्रशमैकरूपतया स्थितेः। तयोश्चैवंविधविशेषसद्भावेऽपि यद्यैक्यं परिकल्प्यते तद्वीररौद्रयोरपि तथा प्रसङ्गः। दयावीरादीनां च चित्तवृत्तिविशेषाणां सर्वाकारमहङ्काररहितत्वे[7] शान्तरसप्रभेदत्वम्, इतरथा तु वीरप्रभेदत्वमिति व्यवस्थाप्यमाने न कश्चिद्विरोधः। तदेवमस्ति शान्तो रसः। तस्य चाविरुद्धरसव्यवधानेन प्रबन्धे विरोधिरससमावेशे सत्यपि निर्विरोधत्वम्, यथा प्रदर्शिते विषये।

एतदेव स्थिरीकर्तुमिदमुच्यते—

रसान्तरान्तरितयोरेकवाक्यस्थयोरपि।
निवर्तते हि रसयोः समावेशे विरोधिता॥ २७॥

---

१. नागानन्दने – घ. २. 'तथेत्यारभ्य कलामित्यन्तं क. ख. पुस्तकयोर्नास्ति. ३. 'सर्वलोक'–ग. ४. विशेषवत्–घ. ५. 'न च वीरेतरस्यान्तर्भावः'–ग., वीरे च तस्या–घ. ६. व्यवस्थानात्--MB. ७. °रहितत्वेन–BP.& घ. The reading given in the text is from MB.

Though a sentiment may be free from opposition conditioned by the sameness of substratum, if it should be found to conflict with another closely occurring sentiment, it should be introduced into one's work only after making a third sentiment intervene between them. The delineation of the sentiment of Quietude and the Erotic in the play *Nāgānanda* affords an illustration of this.

We state emphatically that there is a sentiment of Quietude and its nature is delineation of the joy due to the decline of desire. So it is that the ancients have also said :—

Both the passionate joy of this world
And the boundless joy in Heaven cannot come
To the level of even a sixteenth fraction
Of this joy due to decline of desire.

Even granting that this joy is above the experience of many individuals, one will not be justified at all in dissenting to its constituting a unique experience of some extraordinary personages. Nor is it right to include it under the category of the heroic sentiment itself. For, it is an established fact that the heroic (sentiment) is full of egotism; while this (Quietude) exists only when there is absence of egotism. If one were to imagine identity between the two notwithstanding this difference, one might at that rate imagine even the heroic and the furious as identical. Hence the best way of avoiding the difficulty would be to decide that specific states of mind like 'heroism in compassion' which are singularly free from egotism form varieties of the sentiment of Quietude and the same states of mind will form varieties of the heroic sentiment at other times (when there is a touch of egotism about them). Thus it is established that the sentiment of Quietude exists. A sentiment opposed to it may also be delineated in a work containing it without incurring any fault provided a third sentiment unopposed to it is made to intervene between the two as in the example already mentioned.

This very idea is reinforced in the following :—

By the intervention of another sentiment, even the opposition of two sentiments in the same sentence will disappear. 27

रसान्तरव्यवहितयोरेकप्रबन्धस्थयोर्वि[1]रोधिता निवर्तत इत्यत्र न काचिद्भ्रान्तिः । यस्मादेकवाक्यस्थयोरपि रसयोरुक्तया नीत्या विरुद्धता निवर्तते । यथा—

भूरेणुदिग्धान्नवपारिजातमालारजोवासितबाहुमध्याः ।
गाढं शिवाभिः परिरभ्यमाणान्सुराङ्गनाश्लिष्टभुजान्तरालाः ॥
सशोणितैः क्रव्यभुजां स्फुरद्भिः पक्षैः खगानामुपवीज्यमानान् ।
संवीजिताश्चन्दनवारिसेकैः सुगन्धिभिः कल्पलतादुकूलैः ॥
विमानपर्यङ्कतले निषण्णाः कुतूहलाविष्टतया तदानीम् ।
निर्दिश्यमानांल्ललनाङ्गुलीभिर्वीराः स्वदेहान् पतितानपश्यन् ॥

इत्यादौ । अत्रहि शृङ्गारबीभत्सयोस्तदङ्गयोर्वा वीररसव्यवधानेन समावेशो न विरोधी ।

विरोधमविरोधं च सर्वत्रेत्थं निरूपयेत् ।
विशेषतस्तु शृङ्गारे सुकुमार[2]तमो ह्यसौ ॥ २८ ॥

यथोक्तलक्षणानुसारेण विरोधाविरोधौ सर्वेषु रसेषु प्रबन्धेऽन्यत्र च निरूपयेत्सहृदयः; विशेषतस्तु शृङ्गारे । स हि रतिपरिपोषात्मकत्वाद्रतेश्च स्वल्पेनापि निमित्तेन भङ्गसम्भवात्सुकुमार[3]तमः सर्वेभ्यो रसेभ्यो मनागपि विरोधिसमावेशं न सहते ।

अवधानातिशयवान् रसे तत्रैव सत्कविः ।
भवेत्तस्मिन् प्रमादो हि झ[4]टित्येवोपलक्ष्यते ॥ २९ ॥

---

१. °विरुद्धयोर्विरोधिता – घ. २. सुकुमारतरो – घ. ३. सुकुमारतरः – ब.
४. 'झगित्ये°' – घ.

It cannot indeed be a delusion that the opposition between two sentiments in a work will disappear by the intervention of a third sentiment. For, it is seen that even the opposition of sentiments in the same sentence will disappear in deference to the principle laid down. The following is an illustration:—

The heroes comfortably seated in aeroplanes,
Saw below with wonder their own corpses
Pointed out by heavenly nymphs;
Their chests were scented with heavenly perfume now
While the bodies below were soiled by the earthly dust;
They were now embraced by the heavenly nymphs,
While the bodies below were clasped by she-jackals;
They were now being fanned by the barks of the heavenly tree
Sprinkled with scent of sandal–wood juice
While their bodies below were fanned by the flapping wings
Of flesh-eating vultures, smeared with blood.

In this illustration the heroic sentiment intervenes between the sentiments or the accessories of the sentiments of the Erotic and the Disgustful; and hence there is no opposition.

The opposition and non-opposition of sentiments should be clearly noticed in the above manner, particularly so in the Erotic sentiment, for it happens to be the most delicate of all (sentiments). 28

The perceptive critic should notice carefully the opposition and non-opposition of sentiments in whole works and other instances in accordance with the principles laid down above. He must particularly do so in the Erotic sentiment. For the Erotic sentiment is brought about by a full treatment of the emotion of love; and the nature of love is such that it will be marred by the slightest slip. Hence the Erotic sentiment is the most delicate of all sentiments and will not easily bear the inclusion of opposed sentiments even to the slightest extent.

A good poet should be extremely careful so far as that sentiment is concerned. Otherwise, the slightest inattention (or lapse) on his part will appear glaring at once. 29

तत्रैव च रसे सर्वेभ्योऽपि रसेभ्यः सौकुमार्यातिशययोगिनि कविरवधानवान् प्रयत्नवान्स्यात् । तत्र हि प्रमाद्यतस्तस्य सहृदयमध्ये क्षिप्रमेवावज्ञाविषयता भवति । शृङ्गाररसो हि संसारिणां नियमेनानुभवविषयत्वात्सर्वरसेभ्यः कमनीयतया प्रधानभूतः ।

एवं च सति—

विनेयानुन्मुखीकर्तुं काव्यशोभार्थमेव वा ।
तद्विरुद्धरसस्पर्शस्तदङ्गानां न दुष्यति ॥ ३० ॥

शृङ्गारविरुद्धरसस्पर्शः शृङ्गाराङ्गाणां यः स न केवलमविरोधलक्षणयोगे सति न दुष्यति यावद्विनेयानुन्मुखीकर्तुं काव्यशोभार्थमेव वा क्रियमाणो न दुष्यति । शृङ्गाररसाङ्गैरुन्मुखीकृताः सन्तो हि विनेयाः सुखं विनयोपदेशान् गृह्णन्ति । सदाचारोपदेशरूपा हि नाटकादिगोष्ठी विनेयजनहितार्थमेव मुनिभिरवतारिता ।

किं च शृङ्गारस्य सकलजनमनोहराभिरामत्वात्तदङ्गसमावेशः काव्ये शोभातिशयं पुष्यतीत्यनेनापि प्रकारेण विरोधिनि रसे शृङ्गाराङ्गसमावेशो न विरोधी । ततश्च—

सत्यं मनोरमा रामाः सत्यं रम्या विभूतयः ।
किं तु मत्ताङ्गनापाङ्गभङ्गलोलं हि जीवितम् ॥

इत्यादिषु नास्ति रसविरोधदोषः ।

विज्ञायेत्थं रसादीनामविरोधविरोधयोः ।
विषयं सुकविः काव्यं कुर्वन्मुह्यति न क्वचित् ॥ ३१ ॥

---

१. 'प्रयतः' – क-ख. २. प्रमाद्यस्तस्य –घ. ३. °मेवावज्ञानविषयता – घ; BP. Text acc. to MB. ४. 'भविष्यति' – क-ख. ५. सर्वसंसारिणां – क-ख. ६. °पदेशं – घ. ७. 'मनोभिरामत्वात्' – ग. ८. काव्यशोभा° – घ. ९. 'शृङ्गारविरोधिनि रसे' – क-ख., विरोधि रसे – घ.

The poet should be very attentive in regard to that sentiment as it is more delicate than every other sentiment. If he should carelessly falter in this sentiment, he will at once become a butt of contempt in the circle of refined critics. As the Erotic sentiment is invariably within the experience of all persons, it is not only the most charming but also the most important sentiment.

In these circumstances,

Either for the sake of winning the attention of people who deserve to be instructed or for the sake of endowing the work with unique charm, a touch of the opposite sentiments may be brought into the accessories of the Erotic sentiment. It will not then be a fault. **30**

The touch of opposite sentiments will not mar the accessories of the Erotic sentiment, not merely when the principles relating to non-opposition of sentiments are followed, but also when the purpose of winning the attention of people who deserve instruction or that of endowing the work with unique charm is present. People who deserve instruction will grasp the moral instruction happily only after their attention has been won. Sages brought entertainment parties such as the drama into vogue only for the propagation of moral instruction in a pleasing way to those who deserve to be so instructed. The inclusion of the accessories of the Erotic sentiment in opposed sentiments is justifiable on another ground also. It is the fact that the Erotic sentiment has the power to delight the minds of one and all. Hence there is no defect due to the employment of an opposed sentiment in instances like the following :—

It is true that women are winsome
And true it is that riches attract;
But life itself is ever so fleeting
As the fickle glances of a tipsy dame !

When a good poet composes his poem bearing in mind these concepts of non-opposition and opposition of sentiments etc., he shall never blunder. **31**

इत्थमनेनानन्तरोक्तेन प्रकारेण रसादीनां रसभावतदाभासानां परस्परं विरोधस्याविरोधस्य च विषयं विज्ञाय[1] सुकविः काव्यविषये प्रतिभातिशययुक्तः काव्यं कुर्वन्न क्वचिन्मुह्यति ।

एवं रसादिषु विरोधाविरोधनिरूपणस्योपयोगित्वं प्रतिपाद्य व्यञ्जक-वाच्यवाचकनिरूपणस्यापि तद्विषयस्य तत्प्रतिपाद्यते—

वाच्यानां वाचकानां च यदौचित्येन योजनम् ।
रसादिविषयेणैतत्कर्म[2] मुख्यं महाकवेः ॥ ३२ ॥

वाच्यानामितिवृत्तविशेषाणां वाचकानां च तद्विषयाणां रसादिविषयेणौ-चित्येन यद्योजनमेतन्महाकवेर्मुख्यं कर्म । अयमेव हि महाकवेर्मुख्यो व्यापारो यद्रसादीनेव मुख्यतया काव्यार्थीकृत्य तद्व्यक्त्यनुगुणत्वेन शब्दानामर्थानां चोपनिबन्धनम् ।

एतच्च रसादितात्पर्येण काव्यनिबन्धनं भरतादावपि सुप्रसिद्धमेवेति प्रतिपादयितुमाह—

रसाद्यनुगुणत्वेन व्यवहारोऽर्थशब्दयोः ।
औचित्यवान्यस्ता एता वृत्तयो द्विविधाः[3] स्थिताः ॥३३॥

व्यवहारो हि वृत्तिरित्युच्यते[4] । तत्र रसानुगुण औचित्यवान्वाच्याश्रयो यो व्यवहारस्ता एताः कैशिक्याद्या[5] वृत्तयः । वाचकाश्रयाश्चोपनागरिकाद्याः । वृत्तयो हि रसादितात्पर्येण संनिवेशिताः कामपि नाट्यस्य काव्यस्य च[6] च्छायामावहन्ति । रसादयो हि द्वयोरपि तयोर्जीवभूताः; इतिवृत्तादि तु शरीरभूतमेव ।

---

१. 'परिज्ञाय' – ग. २. 'रसादिविशेषेण' – ग. ३. विविधाः स्मृताः – ब. ४. 'वृत्तिरुच्यते' – ग. ५. कैशिक्यादयः' – ग. ६. 'वा' – क–ख.

When a poet gifted with extraordinary genius bears in mind, while he composes his work, the concept of opposition and non-opposition of sentiments, emotions, their semblances, etc., in the manner indicated above, he can never go wrong.

The usefulness of the treatment of opposition and non-opposition of sentiments has been explained above. In the following, the usefulness of the treatment of the expressed and the expressions also as are suggestive of sentiment is indicated:—

The main task of a first-rate poet lies in a proper marshalling of all the contents and the expressions in the direction of sentiments etc. 32

The main business of a first-rate poet is none other than the proper marshalling of both contents, i. e. plots, and expressions used in setting them forth, in the direction of sentiments, etc. In other words, the main function of the poet lies only in making one sentiment principal throughout the poem and in employing both words and senses only in such a way that the sentiment is suggested clearly.

The following text shows how this idea of writing a poem only with the main intention of suggesting sentiments etc., is a well known concept even in ancient treatises such as that of Bharata :—

Vṛttis (lit. Modes) are said to be of two kinds only because they relate to appropriate employment of senses and sound in keeping with sentiments, etc. 33

Modes of employment are themselves given the designation of "Mode". The mode of employing senses in conformity to sentiment as well as to the considerations of decorum underlies the various (dramatic) Modes such as *Kaiśikī* etc. Similarly that which relates to sounds underlies the (figurative) Modes such as *Upanāgarikā* (the urban) etc. Thus mode, properly employed with the sole intention of coveying sentiments etc., will lend charm to dramatic as well as poetic works. Sentiments, etc. constitute the life-essence of both these Modes; plots, etc. serve only as the body.

अत्र केचिदाहुः—" गुणगुणिव्यवहारो रसादीनामिति वृत्तादिभिः सह युक्त[1]ः, न तु जीवशरीरव्यवहारः। रसादिमयं हि वाच्यं प्रतिभासते न तु रसादिभिः पृथग्भूतम्। " इति। अत्रोच्यते—यदि रसादिमयमेव वाच्यं यथा गौरत्वमयं शरीरम्; एवं सति यथा शरीरे प्रतिभासमाने नियमेनैव गौरत्वं प्रतिभासते सर्वस्य तथा वाच्यत्वेन सहैव रसादयोऽपि सहृदयस्यासहृदयस्य च प्रतिभासेरन्। न चैवम्; तथा चैतत्प्रतिपादितमेव प्रथमोद्द्योते।

स्यान्मतम्; रत्नानामिव जात्यत्वं प्रतिपत्तृविशेषतः संवेद्यं वाच्यानां वाच्येन रसादिरूपत्वमिति। नैव[2]म्; यतो यथा जात्यत्वेन प्रतिभासमाने रत्ने रत्नस्वरूपानतिरिक्तत्वमेव तस्य लक्ष्यते तथा रसादीनामपि विभावा[3]नुभावादिरूप-वाच्याव्यति[4]रिक्तत्वमेव लक्ष्ये[5]त। न चैवम्; न हि विभावानुभावव्यभिचारिण एव रसा इति कस्यचिदवगमः। अत एव च विभावादिप्रतीत्यविनाभाविनी रसादीनां प्रतीतिरिति तत्प्रतीत्योः कार्यकारणभावेन व्यवस्थाना[6]त्क्रमोऽवश्यम्भावी। स तु लाघवान्न प्रकाशत इति ' अलक्ष्यक्रमा एव सन्तो व्यङ्ग्या रसादयः ' इत्युक्तम्।

ननु शब्द एव प्रकरणाद्यवच्छिन्नो वाच्यव्यङ्ग्ययोः सममेव प्रतीतिमुपजनयतीति किं तत्र क्रमकल्पनया। न हि शब्दस्य वाच्यप्रतीतिपरामर्श एव

---

१. 'युक्तः'—घ. पुस्तकेनास्ति. २. 'तत्रैवम्' क, 'तन्नैवम्'—ख. ३. रसानां विभाव—घ. ४. 'वाच्यानाति'—ग. ५. लक्ष्यते—घ. ६. 'व्यवस्थापनात्'—क-ख.

Some might raise the following objection :— 'Sentiments, etc. are related to plots, etc., by the quality-substance relation and not by the life-body relation. One can perceive the expressed only as full of sentiment but never the expressed as an entity separate from sentiment.' Here is our reply: Is the expressed sense full of sentiment in the same way as the body is full of whiteness ? If it were true, just as a sight of the body will be invariably accompanied by the perception of its whiteness also on the part of one and all, so also sentiments, etc., would have to be perceived by all critics, refined or otherwise, along with the perception of the expressed sense itself. But such is not the fact. That has been explained in the FIRST FLASH itself.

There is scope for this view also :— 'Just as the quality of preciousness in diamonds is discernible only to select connoisseurs, so also the presence of sentiments, etc., in the expressed sense is discernible only to select critics.' This view also is untenable. If it were correct, just as the preciousness in diamonds of quality will be discerned as not being different form the very nature of their being diamonds, so also sentiments would have to be discerned as not being different from the nature of the expressed situations, emotional responses, etc. But it is not so. No one gets the idea that the setting, the emotional responses and passing moods are themselves sentiments. The apprehension of the setting, etc. is only an invariable condition of all apprehension of sentiments etc.; hence we might posit a cause-effect relation to exist between the two apprehensions. There is, therefore, bound to be some temporal sequentiality also between the two. But this sequentiality is not noticed since it is minute. Hence it is that we mentioned above that sentiments are suggested only through undiscerned sequentiality.

This is another possible objection :— 'Since the word itself aided by the context, etc., produces the apprehension of the expressed as well as the suggested meanings at the same time, is there any point in imagining temporal sequentiality to exist at all between them ? There is no such rule that a word can become suggestive only when there is a conscious apprehension of the

व्यञ्जकत्वे निबन्धनम् । तथाहि गीतादिशब्देभ्योऽपि रसा[1]भिव्यक्तिरस्ति । न च तेषामन्तरा वाच्यपरामर्शः[2] । अत्रापि ब्रूमः— प्रकरणा[3]द्यवच्छेदेन व्यञ्जकत्वं शब्दानामित्यनुमतमेवैतदस्माकम् । किं तु तद्व्यञ्जकत्वं तेषां कदाचित्स्वरूपविशेष[4]निबन्धनं कदाचिद्वाचकशक्तिनिबन्धनम् । तत्र येषां वाचकशक्तिनिबन्धनं तेषां यदि वाच्यप्रतीतिमन्तरेणैव स्वरूपप्रतीत्या निष्पन्नं[5] तद्भवेन्न तर्हि वाचकशक्तिनिबन्धनम् । अथ तन्निबन्धनं तन्नियमेनैव वाच्यवाचकभावप्रतीत्युत्तरकालत्वं व्यङ्ग्यप्रतीतेः प्राप्तमेव ।

स तु क्रमो यदि लाघवान्न लक्ष्यते तत्किं क्रियते । यदि च वाच्यप्रतीतिमन्तरेणैव प्रकरणाद्यवच्छिन्नशब्दमात्र[6]साध्या रसादिप्रतीतिः स्यात्तदवधारित[7]प्रकरणानां[8] वाच्यवाचकभावे च स्वयमव्युत्पन्नानां प्रतिपत्तॄणां काव्यमात्रश्रवणादेवासौ भवेत् । सहभावे च वाच्यप्रतीतेरनुपयोगः, उपयोगे वा न सहभावः । येषामपि स्वरूपविशेषप्रतीतिनिमित्तं व्यञ्जकत्वं यथा गीतादिशब्दानां[9] तेषामपि स्वरूपप्रतीतेर्व्यङ्ग्यप्रतीतेश्च[10] नियमभावी क्रमः[11] । तत्तु[12] शब्दस्य क्रियापौर्वापर्यमनन्यसाध्यतत्फलघटनास्वाशुभाविनीषु वाच्येनाविरोधिन्य[13]भिधेयान्तरविलक्षणे रसादौ न प्रतीयते ।

---

१. रसाद्यभि°-घ. रसादि प्रतीतिरस्ति - MB. २. वाच्यप्रतीतिपरामर्शः -MB ४. ३. ' कारणाद्यव '-ख. ४. ' विषय '- क-ख. ५. ' प्रतीत्यनुनिष्पन्नं '- क-ख. ६. ' प्रकाराद्यवच्छिन्नमात्र '- क-ख. ७. °दनवधारित°-घ.B.P. ८. ' प्रकाराणां ' -क-ख. ९. गीतशब्दानां-घ. १०. ' व्यङ्ग्यप्रतीतेश्च '-ग-पुस्तके नास्ति. ११. नियमभावक्रमः-घ. १२. तत्र तु - घ. १३. ' वाच्यविरोधिनी '-क-ख.

expressed sense. For example, suggestion of sentiments, etc. is certainly achieved even from sounds in music and so forth; and there is no intervening apprehension of expressed sense at all between the sounds and the suggested sentiments.' The following is our reply :— We also agree that only such words as are aided by context etc., become suggestive. But this suggestiveness is sometimes due to their specific nature itself and sometimes due to the denotative power of words. In instances where suggestiveness is due only to the specific nature of sounds and where apprehension of expressed meanings does not play any part at all, it would be tantamount to saying that suggestiveness is not governed by the denotative power of words at all. But if suggestiveness is to be governed at all by the denotative power of words, the conclusion becomes irresistible that the apprehension of suggested sense can only be later in time than the apprehension of expressed sense and words that denote it.

If that temporal sequentiality is so brisk that it escapes notice, what is to be done ? If in truth the apprehension of sentiments were possible just by words aided by context etc. without any need of the apprehension of expressed sense, then every reader acquainted with the context, including those who are quite ignorant of the denotation of words, should have had the apprehension of sentiment by merely hearing a poem. If the apprehension of the expressed and the suggested were simultaneous, there would be no use at all for the apprehension of the expressed. On the contrary, if there should be any use for the apprehension of the expressed, it is possible that the two can co-exist. It is true that in music we have suggestiveness due to the perception of the specific nature of sound alone. But even there we do have, invariably, temporal sequentiality between the apprehension of the nature of sounds and the apprehension of suggested sentiments. But this temporal sequentiality in the two functions of sounds cannot be noticed when sentiments are suggested; because sentiments are neither opposed to the expressed sense nor appear as similar to the other senses; they are not capable of being conveyed by aught else and all their accessories work together with lightning quickness.

क्वचित्तु लक्ष्यत एव, यथानुरणनरूपव्यङ्ग्यप्रतीतिषु । तत्रापि कथमिति चेदुच्यते — अर्थशक्तिमूलानुरणनरूपव्यङ्ग्ये ध्वनौ तावदभिधेयस्य तत्सामर्थ्याक्षिप्तस्य चार्थस्याभिधेयान्तरविलक्षणतयात्यन्तविलक्षणे ये प्रतीती तयोरशक्यनिह्नवो निमित्तनिमित्तिभाव इति स्फुटमेव तत्र पौर्वापर्यम् । यथा प्रथमोद्योते प्रतीयमानार्थसिद्ध्यर्थमुदाहृतासु गाथासु । तथाविधे च विषये वाच्यव्यङ्ग्ययोरत्यन्तविलक्षणत्वाद्यैव एकस्य प्रतीतिः सैवेतरस्येति न शक्यते वक्तुम् । शब्दशक्तिमूलानुरणनरूपव्यङ्ग्ये तु ध्वनौ——

गावो वः पावनानां परमपरिमितां प्रीतिमुत्पादयन्तु

इत्यादावर्थद्वयप्रतीतौ शाब्द्यामर्थद्वयस्योपमानोपमेयभावप्रतीतिरुपमावाचकपदविरहे सत्यर्थसामर्थ्यादाक्षिप्तेति, तत्रापि सुलक्ष्यमभिधेयव्यङ्ग्यालङ्कारप्रतीत्योः पौर्वापर्यम् ।

पदप्रकाशशब्दशक्तिमूलानुरणनरूपव्यङ्ग्ये[3]ऽपि ध्वनौ विशेषणपदस्योभयार्थसम्बन्धयोग्यस्य योजकं पदमन्तरेण योजनमशाब्दमप्यर्थादवस्थितमित्यत्रापि पूर्ववदभिधेयतत्सामर्थ्याक्षिप्तालङ्कारमात्रप्रतीत्योः[4] सुस्थितमेव पौर्वापर्यम् । आर्थ्यपि च प्रतिपत्तिस्तथाविधे विषये उभयार्थसम्बन्धयोग्यशब्दसामर्थ्यप्रसावि[6]तेति शब्दशक्तिमूला[7] कल्प्यते ।

---

१. 'विलक्षणस्य ये प्रतीती' क-ख. २. सुलक्ष° – BP. ३. 'अपि ध्वनौ'-ग पुस्तके नास्ति. ४. 'प्रतिपत्त्योः'-ग. ५. योगा – घ. ६. °प्रतिप्रसवभूतेति – घ. ७. 'शब्दमूला' – ग.

But in some contexts, the sequentiality is noticeable also; instances where we find apprehension of resonance-like suggestion may be cited as examples. One might ask us 'how is it so ?' and here is our reply :—There will be apprehension of two senses in resonance-like suggestion based on the power of senses viz., (1) the expressed sense and (2) the sense suggested by the power of sense but quite distinct from the other expressed sense. Since no one can conceal the cause-effect relation between the apprehensions of the two senses, the temporal sequence between them is obvious. Prakrit stanzas quoted in the FIRST FLASH for establishing the existence of the implied sense serve as illustrations of this also. Since in those instances the difference between the expressed and the suggested is very great, it is impossible to affirm that the apprehension of the one is identical with that of the other. Even in resonance-like suggestion based upon the power of sound– as, for instance, *Bringing delight to the public* etc. where we have the apprehension of two senses from the same words, similitude between the two senses will be found suggested. Since we do not have any word openly expressing similitude, we will have to agree that it is suggested only by the power of sound. Thus it is clear that there is temporal sequence between the apprehension of the expressed sense and the suggested figure even in that type of suggestion.

Similarly, the temporal sequentiality between the apprehensions of the expressed sense and the suggested figure is patent also in the specific variety of resonance-like suggestion based upon the power of sound, viz., that which shines out in individual words. The fact is that the adjective will be equivocal. Instead of understanding another word for denoting the second sense, we apprehend the second sense also by virtue of the same word. Since the second sense is not conveyed by a specific word, we will have to hold that it is conveyed only through the power of sense. Though the apprehension of the suggested is thus produced by sense alone, it is still regarded as based on the power of the equivocal word itself.

अविवक्षितवाच्यस्य तु ध्वनेः प्रसिद्धस्वविषयवैमुख्यप्रतीतिपूर्वकमे-वार्थान्तरप्रकाशनमिति नियमभावी क्रमः । तत्राविवक्षित[1]वाच्यत्वादेव वाच्येन सह व्यङ्ग्यस्य क्रमप्रतीतिविचारो न कृतः । तस्मादभिधानाभिधेय-प्रतीत्योरिव वाच्यव्यङ्ग्यप्रतीत्योर्निमित्तनिमित्तिभावान्नियमभावी क्रमः । स तूक्तयुक्त्या[2] क्वचिल्लक्ष्यते क्वचिन्न लक्ष्यते ॥

तदेवं व्यञ्जकमुखेन ध्वनिप्रकारेषु निरूपितेषु कश्चिद्ब्रूयात्—किमिदं[3] व्यञ्जकत्वं नाम? व्यङ्ग्यार्थप्रकाशनं हि व्यञ्जकत्वम् । तद् व्यङ्ग्यत्वं चार्थस्य व्यञ्जकसिद्ध्यधीनम्; व्यङ्ग्यापेक्षया च व्यञ्जकत्वसिद्धिरित्यन्योन्य-संश्रयादव्यवस्थानम् । ननु वाच्यव्यतिरिक्तस्य व्यङ्ग्यस्य सिद्धिः प्रागेव प्रतिपादिता तत्सिद्ध्यधीना च व्यञ्जकसिद्धिरिति कः पर्यनुयोगावसरः ।

सत्यमेवैतत्; प्रागुक्तयुक्तिभिर्वाच्यव्यतिरिक्तस्य वस्तुनः सिद्धिः कृता, स त्वर्थो व्यङ्ग्यतयैव कस्माद्व्यपदिश्यते । यत्र च प्राधान्येनावस्थानं तत्र वाच्यतयैवासौ व्यपदेष्टुं युक्तः । तत्परत्वाद्वाक्यस्य । अतश्च तत्प्रकाशिनो वाक्यस्य वाचक[4]-त्वमेव व्यापारः । किं तस्य व्यापारान्तरकल्पनया? तस्मात्तात्पर्यविषयो योऽर्थः स तावन्मुख्यतया वाच्यः । या त्वन्तरा तथाविधे विषये वाच्यान्तरप्रतीतिः सा

१. 'तत्र त्वाविवक्षित'–क-ख. तत्रापि विवक्षित–घ. २. 'युक्तः'–ग. ३. किमिदं व्यञ्जकत्वं नाम व्यङ्ग्यार्थ प्रकाशनम् (।–घ), नहि व्यञ्जकत्वं व्यङ्ग्यत्वं चार्थस्य (चार्थस्यापि–घ.) व्यञ्जकसिद्ध्यधीनं व्यङ्ग्यत्वम्, (।–घ.) व्यङ्ग्यापेक्षया च व्यञ्जकत्वासिद्धिरित्य°–BP. घ. Text according to M. B. ४. वाचकत्वस्य–घ.

Even in suggestion based upon unintended expressed sense, since the apprehension of the suggested sense comes only after the apprehension that the conventional meaning of the word is inapplicable (in the context), temporal sequentiality is present as a rule. Since the expressed sense therein happens to be unintended, the question whether there is temporal sequentiality or not between the expressed and the suggested senses, was not taken up before. It is clear, therefore, that even as the apprehensions of denotative word and denoted sense involve a cause-effect relation and consequently temporal sequentiality, so also the apprehensions of the expressed and the suggested involve a cause-effect relation as well as temporal sequentiality. As already illustrated, sometimes it is noticed and sometimes it is not.

Some might object as follows to our procedure of dividing suggestion into various kinds from the standpoint of suggestiveness :—" What is this suggestiveness? The power of conveying the implied sense need not be designated by the name ' suggestiveness ' at all. The existence of the suggested sense is dependent upon the existence of the suggestive word; so also is the existence of the suggestive word dependent upon the existence of the suggested sense. As the definition thus moves in a vicious circle, nothing definite will have been established about either. " We would put them a counter-question: when we have already established the existence of suggested sense as distinct from the expressed (by other arguments), what scope for objection is there if suggestiveness were made to follow from the existence of the suggested?

The objector might argue further as follows : ' It is true that the existence of the suggested sense as distinct from the expressed has been established by the arguments already given. But why should that sense be called by the name " suggested " alone? It is right that we should designate it as " expressed " itself wherever it happens to be primarily important since it is primarily intended to be conveyed by the sentence as a whole. Thus the sentence which conveys that sense has only one function and that is denotation. What is the use of attributing a new function to it? Thus the sense which happens to be the main purport of a sentence can only be primarily " expressed. "

तत्प्रतीतिरुपायमात्रं पदार्थप्रतीतिरिव वाक्यार्थप्रतीतेः ।

अत्रोच्यते—यत्र शब्दः स्वार्थमभिदधानोऽर्थान्तरमवगमयति तत्र यत्तस्य स्वार्थाभिधायित्वं यच्च तदर्थान्तरावगमहेतुत्वं तयोरविशेषो विशेषो वा । न तावदविशेषः, यस्मात्तौ द्वौ व्यापारौ भिन्नविषयौ भिन्नरूपौ च प्रतीयेते एव । तथाहि वाचकत्वलक्षणो व्यापारः शब्दस्य स्वार्थविषयः गमकत्वलक्षणस्त्वर्थान्तरविषयः । न च स्वपरव्यवहारो वाच्यव्यङ्ग्ययोरपह्नोतुं शक्यः, एकस्य सम्बन्धित्वेन प्रतीतेरपरस्य सम्बन्धिसम्बन्धित्वेन । वाच्यो ह्यर्थः साक्षाच्छब्दस्य सम्बन्धी तदितरस्त्वभिधेयसामर्थ्याक्षिप्तः सम्बन्धिसम्बन्धी । यदि च स्वसम्बन्धित्वं साक्षात्तस्य स्यात्तदार्थान्तरत्वव्यवहार एव न स्यात् । तस्माद्विषयभेदस्तावत्तयोर्व्यापारयोः सुप्रसिद्धः । रूपभेदोऽपि प्रसिद्ध एव । न हि यैवाभिधानशक्तिः सैवावगमनशक्तिः । अवाचकस्यापि गीतशब्दादे रसादिलक्षणार्थावगमदर्शनात् । अशब्दस्यापि चेष्टादेरर्थविशेषप्रकाशनप्रसिद्धेः । तथाहि 'व्रीडायोगान्नतवदनया' इत्यादिश्लोके चेष्टाविशेषः सुकविनार्थप्रकाशनहेतुः प्रदर्शित एव । तस्माद्भिन्नविषयत्वाद्भिन्नरूपत्वाच्च स्वार्थाभिधायित्वमर्थान्तरावगमहेतुत्वं च शब्दस्य यत्तयोः स्पष्ट एव भेदः । विशेषश्चेन्न तर्हीदानीमवगमनस्याभिधेयसामर्थ्याक्षिप्तस्यार्थान्तरस्य वाच्यत्वव्यपदेश्यता । शब्द-

---

१. ततः – ख. २. वाच्यगम्ययो – ख. ३. °तुपशक्यः – ख. ४. °र्थान्तरव्यवहार – ख. ५ °र्थाविशेष – ख. ७. शब्दस्य । – ख. ७. 'अवगमनीयस्य' – क-ख.

Apprehension of other senses from the sentence prior to the apprehension of word-meaning is only a means to the knowledge of sentence-purport.'.

We shall now reply to the objection thus : Let us take an instance where a word conveys another meaning after having conveyed its primary meaning earlier. Is there any difference or no difference at all between the two functions of the word, viz. the denotation of primary meaning and the implication of another sense? The view that there is no difference at all between the two is untenable. For, not only the scopes of the two functions are different, but their natures are also different. To illustrate: the scope of the function of denotation in a word is confined to its primary sense; while the scope of the function of implication includes a sense other than the primary one. It is not possible to deny that the expressed is "its own" sense of a word while the implied sense is "one belonging to another". The apprehension of the implied will be remotely related to the word through the medium of the expressed sense. While the expressed sense is directly related to the word, the implied sense is related to that which in its turn is related to the word since it is implied by the power of expressed sense. If the implied sense too were directly related to the word, then there would be no need at all for referring to it as another sense. Thus the difference in scope between the two functions is clear.

In the same way, their difference in nature too is obvious. The function of denotation itself cannot be the same as the function of implication since we find suggestiveness of sentiments etc. even in words of music. It is well known too that gestures, etc. which are not even sounds, possess the function of suggesting specific ideas. In the illustration '*With her face bent down*' etc., the specific gesture (viz. side-glance) of the heroine has been described by the great poet in a way suggestive of unique charm. Since the scope and natures of the two functions are thus quite different, it is clear that the denotative function of words and the implying function of words are quite different from each other. When the separate individuality of the two functions is accepted, it will not be possible to give the designation

व्यापारगोचरत्वं[1] तु तस्यास्माभिरिष्यत एव, तत्तु व्यङ्ग्यत्वेनैव न वाच्यत्वेन । प्रसिद्धाभिधानान्तरसम्बन्धयोग्यत्वेन च तस्यार्थान्तरस्य प्रतीतेः[2] शब्दान्तरेण[3] स्वार्थाभिधायिना यद्विषयीकरणं तत्र प्रकाशनोक्तिरेव युक्ता ।

न च पदार्थवाक्यार्थन्यायो वाच्यव्यङ्ग्ययोः । यतः पदार्थप्रतीति[4]रसत्यैवेति कैश्चिद्विद्वद्भिरास्थितम् । यैरप्यसत्यत्वमस्या नाभ्युपेयते तैर्वाक्यार्थ[5]पदार्थयोर्घटतदुपादानकारणन्यायोऽभ्युपगन्तव्यः । तथाहि घटे निष्पन्ने तदुपादानकारणानां न पृथगुपलम्भस्तथैव वाक्ये तदर्थे वा प्रतीते पदतदर्थानां तेषां तदा विभक्ततयोपलम्भे वाक्यार्थबुद्धिरेव दूरीभवेत् । नत्वेष वाच्यव्यङ्ग्ययो[6]र्न्यायः । न हि व्यङ्ग्ये प्रतीयमाने वाच्यबुद्धिर्दूरीभवति, वाच्यावभासाविनाभावेन तस्य प्रकाशनात् । तस्माद्घटप्रदीपन्यायस्तयोः; यथैव हि प्रदीपद्वारेण घटप्रतीतावुत्पन्नायां न प्रदीपप्रकाशो निवर्तते तद्वद्व्यङ्ग्यप्रतीतौ वाच्यावभासः । यत्तु प्रथमोद्योते 'यथा पदार्थद्वारेण' इत्याद्युक्तं तदुपायत्वमात्रात्[7]साम्यविवक्षया ।

१. 'विषयत्वं'–क-ख. २. च प्रतीतेः – घ. ३. 'श्लेषान्तरेण'–क. ४. प्रतीतिरसत्येवेति – घ. ५. 'वाक्य-वाक्यार्थ' – क-ख. ६. 'व्यङ्ग्यवाच्ययोः' – क-ख. ७. °साम्यमात्रस्य° – घ.

of " the expressed " to that other meaning which is only implied by the power of the expressed sense. But we would quite agree that the other sense too comes within the power of words. But at the same time we would say that the meaning is conveyed only by way of suggestion and not by way of denotation. If a word which is capable only of denoting its primary meaning directly is also seen actually conveying another meaning, directly denoted not by this word but by some other word only, then we would be right in regarding it as an instance of suggestiveness of word.

The analogy of word-import and sentence-purport too does not quite apply to the Expressed and Suggested senses since in the opinion of some philosophers, the very apprehension of sense from individual words is unreal. Even those who do not hold that it is unreal will have to agree that the analogy of the relation between the pot and its material cause will explain better the relation between sentence-purport and word-import. Just as the material causes of a pot cannot be recognised separately after the pot has come into being, so also word and its sense are not recognised separately after the sentence and its purport have been apprehended as a whole. If they could be recognised separately, the very apprehension of the whole sentence-purport would have to be driven away to a distance. But this principle does not hold good with reference to the expressed and suggested senses. When the suggested sense is apprehended, the expressed sense is not driven away to a distance since the apprehension of the suggested is inseparably occasioned by the apprehension of the expressed. Hence the analogy of the pot and the lamp would fit them best. Just as the light of the lamp will not recede as soon as the perception of the pot is brought home to the observer, so also, the expressed sense will continue to shine out even after the apprehension of the suggested sense has been achieved. In the light of these considerations, it should be understood that the remark made in the FIRST FLASH–*Just as the purport of a sentence* etc. (No. 10)–aims only at pointing out the similarity between the two in respect of their being means to some other and (and that the analogy) is not intended to be pursued to the last detail.

नन्वेवं युगपदर्थद्वययोगित्वं वाक्यस्य प्राप्तं तद्भावे च तस्य वाक्यतैव[1] विघटते, तस्या ऐकार्थ्यलक्षणत्वात् ; नैष दोषः; गुणप्रधानभावेन तयोर्व्यवस्थानात्[2]। व्यङ्ग्यस्य हि क्वचित्प्राधान्यं वाच्यस्योपसर्जन[3]भावः क्वचिद्वाच्यस्य प्राधान्यमपरस्य गुणभावः[4]। तत्र व्यङ्ग्यप्राधान्ये ध्वनिरित्युक्तमेव; वाच्यप्राधान्ये तु प्रकारान्तरं निर्देक्ष्यते। तस्मात्स्थितमेतत् — व्यङ्ग्यपरत्वेऽपि काव्यस्य[5] न व्यङ्ग्यस्याभिधेयत्वमपि तु व्यङ्ग्यत्वमेव।

किं च व्यङ्ग्यस्य प्राधान्येनाविवक्षायां वाच्यत्वं तावद्भवद्भिर्नाभ्युपगन्तव्यमतत्परत्वाच्छब्दस्य। तदस्ति तावद्व्यङ्ग्यः शब्दानां कश्चिद्विषय इति। यत्रापि तस्य[6] प्राधान्यं तत्रापि किमिति तस्य स्वरूपमपह्नूयते[7]। एवं तावद्वाचकत्वादन्यदेव व्यञ्जकत्वम्; इतश्च वाचकत्वाद्व्यञ्जकत्वस्यान्यत्वं[8] यद्वाचकत्वं शब्दैकाश्रयमितरत्तु शब्दाश्रयमर्थाश्रयं च शब्दार्थयोर्द्वयोरपि व्यञ्जकत्वस्य प्रतिपादितत्वात्।

गुणवृत्तिस्तूपचारेण लक्षणया चोभयाश्रयापि[9] भवति। किन्तु ततोऽपि व्यञ्जकत्वं स्वरूपतो विषयतश्च भिद्यते। रूप[10]भेदस्तावदयम्—यदमुख्यतया व्यापारो गुणवृत्तिः प्रसिद्धा। व्यञ्जकत्वं तु मुख्यतयैव शब्दस्य व्यापारः। न ह्यर्थाद्व्यङ्ग्यत्रयप्रतीतिर्या तस्या अमुख्यत्वं मनागपि लक्ष्यते।

---

१. 'वाक्यतयैव घटते' – क-ख. २. 'स्थापनात्' – क-ख. ३. 'सर्जनी' – क-ख. ४. 'गुणीभावः' – क-ख, च गुणभावः – घ. ५. 'वाक्यस्य' – ग. ६. 'एतस्य' – क-ख. ७. 'अपाह्नियते' – ग. ८. 'व्यञ्जकत्वसामान्यत्वं' – घ. ९. चोभयाश्रिता – MB. १०. स्वरूप° – MB.

Some might say :—' At this rate a sentence will have to possess two senses simultaneously. If that should be the case, its very nature as a sentence will be upset. For, a sentence can only be that which conveys a single sense. ' But there is no fallacy in our argument. For, we decide that one of these senses is primary and the other secondary. In some instances, the suggested will be primary and the expressed secondary. In other instances the expressed itself will be primary and the suggested will be secondary. We have already declared that the designation of "suggestion" is to be given only when the suggested sense happens to be primary. When the expressed itself is primary it comes under one of the varieties of poetry to be explained in the sequel. Hence this much is certain :— When poetry intends the suggested sense, the latter can never be expressed, but only suggested.

What is more, in instances where the suggested is not intended as primary, you (i. e. the objector) will not be able to regard it even as expressed, since the word does not intend it at all. This also adds support to our conclusion that there is some definite scope for suggested senses of words. And where it happens to be intended as primary, why should its existence be gainsaid ? Hence suggestiveness is positively different from denotation. Another reason which supports the same conclusion is this :— Denotation is based upon words only, while suggestiveness is based not only upon words but also upon senses; since suggestiveness, as already pointed out, relates to words as well as senses.

Indication also is based upon both metaphorical application and secondary sense. But suggestiveness differs from it too both in respect of nature and of scope. This is the difference in scope: it is well known that indication is the name given to a verbal function which does not proceed principally. But suggestiveness is a verbal function which proceeds principally. The apprehension of the three-fold suggested sense from the expressed does not in the least appear to be subordinate.

अयं चान्यः स्वरूपभेदः — यद्गुणवृत्तिरमुख्यत्वेन व्यवस्थितं[1] वाचकत्वमेवोच्यते। व्यञ्जकत्वं तु वाचकत्वादत्यन्तं[2] विभिन्नमेव। एतच्च प्रतिपादितम्। अयं चापरो रूपभेदो यद्गुणवृत्तौ यदार्थो[3]ऽर्थान्तरमुपलक्षयति, तदोपलक्षणीयार्थात्मना[4] परिणत एवासौ सम्पद्यते। यथा "गङ्गायां घोषः" इत्यादौ। व्यञ्जकत्वमार्गे तु यदार्थोऽर्थान्तरं द्योतयति[5] तदा स्वरूपं प्रकाशयन्नेवासावन्यस्य प्रकाशकः प्रतीयते प्रदीपवत्। यथा—'लीलाकमलपत्राणि गणयामास पार्वती' इत्यादौ। यदि च यत्रा[6]तिरस्कृतस्वप्रतीति[7]रर्थोऽर्थान्तरं लक्षयति तत्र लक्षणाव्यवहारः क्रियते, तदेवं सति लक्षणैव मुख्यः शब्दव्यापार इति प्राप्तम्। यस्मात्प्रायेण[8] वाक्यानां वाच्यव्यतिरिक्ततात्पर्यविषयार्थावभासित्वम्।

ननु त्वत्पक्षेऽपि यदार्थो व्यङ्ग्यत्रयं प्रकाशयति तदा शब्दस्य कीदृशो व्यापारः। उच्यते—प्रकरणाद्यवच्छिन्नशब्दवशेनैवार्थस्य तथाविधं व्यञ्जकत्वमिति शब्दस्य तत्रोपयोगः कथमपह्नूयते।

विषयभेदोऽपि गुणवृत्तिव्यञ्जकत्वयोः स्पष्ट[9] एव। यतो व्यञ्जकत्वस्य रसादयोऽलङ्कारविशेषा व्यङ्ग्यरूपावच्छिन्नं वस्तु चेति त्रयं विषयः[10]। तत्र रसादिप्रतीतिर्गुणवृत्तिरिति न केनचिदुच्यते, न च शक्यते वक्तुम्। व्यङ्ग्यालङ्कारप्रतीतिरपि तथैव। वस्तु[11]चारुत्वप्रतीतये स्वशब्दानभिधेयत्वेन यत्प्रतिपादयितु[12]मिष्यते तद् व्यङ्ग्यम्। तच्च न सर्वं गुणवृत्तेर्विषयः[13], प्रसिद्ध्यनुरोधाभ्याम[14]पि गौणानां शब्दानां प्रयोगदर्शनात्। तथोक्तं प्राक्। यदपि च गुण[15]वृत्तेर्विषयस्तदपि च व्यञ्जकत्वानुप्रवेशेन। तस्माद्गुणवृत्तेरपि व्यञ्जकत्वस्यात्य-

---

१. व्यवहितं – घ. २. वाचकादत्यन्तं – घ. ३. पदार्थो – घ. ४. 'लक्षणीयात्परिणत' – क-ख. ५. 'बोधयति' – ख. ६. 'यत्रातितिरस्कृत' – ख. ७. स्वरूपप्रतीति° – घ. ८. यस्मात्प्रायेणैव – घ. ९. 'स्फुटः' – ग. १०. अस्खलद्गतित्वं समयानुपयोगित्वं पृथगवभासित्वं चेति त्रयम्।' इदं वाक्यं – घ. पुस्तकेऽधिकमस्ति। ११. वस्तुचारुत्वं° BP. घ. inserts the full stop before तथैव. १२. यत्प्रतिपिपादयितुं – BP. १३. °विषयः। – घ. १४. °धादाभ्यामपि – MB. १५. गुणवृत्तेः – घ. पुस्तके नास्ति।

This is another difference is respect of their natures :— Indication is practically denotation itself with this difference that it is a subordinate verbal function. But on the other hand, suggestion has been proved to be quite different from denotation. Still another difference between the two functions is this. When another sense is conveyed by a sense through indication, the first sense merges itself with the second and becomes one with it, as for instance in the sentence — *The Hamlet* (*is*) *in the Ganges.* But when one sense conveys another through suggestion, the first sense retains its individuality while conveying the other just like a lamp. *Pārvatī counted the petals of her play-lotus, etc.* are illustrations in point. If the name 'indication' were to be given to those instances also where one sense conveys another without losing its own importance, then it would be tantamount to saying that indication itself is the primary verbal function. For in general, every sentence possesses the power of conveying a purport over and above the expressed senses of individual words.

The following question may be put to us :— 'Well, even granting the truth of what you say, what is the precise verbal function involved when a sense conveys the three-fold suggested content ?' Here is our reply :— The sense therein acquires the said suggestiveness only because of the words aided by context etc. Hence how can anyone deny the use of words in such suggestion ?

The difference in the scope of indication and suggestiveness is also obvious. The scope of suggestiveness is three-fold, viz., (1) sentiments etc., (2) specific figures of speech and (3) suggested ideas. Of these, none will or can say that the apprehension of sentiments etc. is identical with indication. The same is true of suggested figures also. So far as suggested idea is concerned, that alone is suggested therein which is especially intended to be conveyed by the poet by a process other than denotation, when he finds that the beauty he wants to endow to the idea on hand cannot be achieved by means of denotation itself. All this cannot be included in the scope of indication since we can see several examples of indication based merely on convention or usage. This has been already explained. If at all there is any touch of beauty instanced in indication, it will be entirely due to the entry of the suggestive element therein.

न्तविलक्षणत्वम् । वाचकत्वगुणवृत्तिविलक्षणस्यापि च तस्य तदुभयाश्रयत्वेन व्यवस्थानम् ।

व्यञ्जकत्वं हि क्वचिद्वाचकत्वाश्रयेण व्यवतिष्ठते, यथा विवक्षितान्यपरवाच्ये ध्वनौ । क्वचित्तु गुणवृत्त्याश्रयेण यथा[1] अविवक्षितवाच्ये ध्वनौ । तदुभयाश्रयत्वप्रतिपादनायैव च ध्वनेः प्रथमतरं द्वौ प्रभेदावुपन्यस्तौ । तदुभयाश्रितत्वाच्च[2] तदेकरूपत्वं तस्य न शक्यते[3] वक्तुम् । यस्मान्न तद्वाचकत्वैकरूपमेव, क्वचिल्लक्षणाश्रयेण वृत्तेः । न च लक्षणैकरूपमेवान्यत्र वाचकत्वाश्रयेण व्यवस्थानात् । न चोभयधर्मत्वेनैव तदेकैकरूपं न भवति । यावद्वाचकत्वलक्षणादिरूपरहितशब्द[4]धर्मत्वेनापि[5] । तथाहि गीतध्वनीनामपि व्यञ्जकत्वमस्ति रसादिविषयम् । न च तेषां वाचकत्वं लक्षणा वा कथञ्चिल्लक्ष्यते । शब्दादन्यत्रापि[6] विषये व्यञ्जकत्वस्य[7] दर्शनाद्वाचकत्वादिशब्दधर्मप्रकारत्वमयुक्तं[8] वक्तुम् । यदि च[9] वाचकत्वलक्षणादीनां शब्दप्रकाराणां प्रसिद्धप्रकारविलक्षणत्वेऽपि व्यञ्जकत्वं प्रकारत्वेन परिकल्प्यते तच्छब्दस्यैव प्रकारत्वेन कस्मान्न परिकल्प्यते ।

तदेवं शाब्दे व्यवहारे त्रयः प्रकाराः—वाचकत्वं गुणवृत्तिर्व्यञ्जकत्वं च । तत्र व्यञ्जकत्वे यदा व्यङ्ग्यप्राधान्यं तदा ध्वनिः[10], तस्य चाविवक्षितवाच्यो विवक्षितान्यपरवाच्यश्चेति द्वौ प्रभेदावनुक्रान्तौ प्रथमतरं तौ सविस्तरं निर्णीतौ ।

अन्यो ब्रूयात्—ननु विवक्षितान्यपरवाच्ये ध्वनौ गुणवृत्तिता नास्तीति

---

१. 'यथास्मिन्'–क·ख. २. 'तदुभयाश्रयत्वाच्च'–क-ख, MB. ३. 'शक्यं'–ग. ४. 'शब्दाधिकत्वेन'–ग. ५. °नापि दर्शनात्–MB. ६. च विषये–घ. ७. व्यञ्जकत्वस्यापि–घ. ८. 'अशक्यं'–ग. ९. च–घ. पुस्तके नास्ति. १०. °ध्वनेस्तस्य–घ.

Hence indication and suggestiveness are widely different from each other. The truth is that suggestiveness not only differs from denotation on the one hand and indication on the other; on the contrary, it is actually based upon each of them also.

In suggestion with intended but further-extending expressed sense, suggestiveness gets assistance from denotation, in suggestion with unintended expressed sense, it gets assistance from indication. These two varieties of suggestion were proposed at the outset itself with a view to bringing out the fact that suggestiveness is assisted by both denotation and indication. It is not possible to regard suggestiveness which is assisted by both these to be identical with either. Since it sometimes derives assistance from indication, it cannot be identical with denotation alone; since it gets assistance sometimes from denotation, it cannot be identical with indication alone. Thus it cannot be comprehended by either since it partakes of the characteristics of both. Besides this, it also partakes of the characteristics of sound which is devoid of both the verbal powers of denotation and indication. Thus the sounds of music do possess suggestiveness in respect of sentiments, etc., and they are never seen to possess either denotation or indication.

Furthermore, since we can see suggestiveness in instances which are not even sounds, it is wrong to consider it as a form of verbal functions like denotation. Though suggestiveness is thus different from the well-known functions, viz., denotation and indication of words, if it should be still regarded as another form of verbal function itself, why should not one regard it at that rate as a form of word itself ?

Thus it is clear that the functions of words are three-fold — (1) Denotation, (2) Indication and (3) Suggestiveness. When the suggested sense itself happens to be the principal one also in an instance of suggestiveness, it deserves the title of suggestion. This suggestion may be divided into two important categories, viz., (1) that with unintended expressed sense and (2) that with intended but further-extending expressed sense. These have been treated elaborately at the outset itself.

The objector might argue as follows :— ' You are right when you say that there is no element of indication in suggestion

यदुच्यते तद्युक्तम् । यस्माद्वाच्यवाचकप्रतीतिपूर्विका यत्रार्थान्तरप्रतिपत्तिस्तत्र कथं गुणवृत्तिव्यवहारः ? न हि गुणवृत्तौ यदा निमित्तेन केनचिद्विषयान्तरे शब्द आरोप्यते अत्यन्ततिरस्कृतस्वार्थः यथा – 'अग्निर्माणवकः' इत्यादौ, यदा वा स्वार्थमंशेनापरित्यजंस्तत्सम्बन्धद्वारेण[1] विषयान्तरमाक्रामति, यथा – 'गङ्गायां घोषः' इत्यादौ, तदाविवक्षितवाच्यत्वमुपपद्यते[2] । अत एव च विवक्षितान्यपरवाच्ये ध्वनौ वाच्यवाचकयोर्द्वयोरपि स्वरूपप्रतीतिरर्थावगमनं च दृश्यत इति व्यञ्जकत्वव्यवहारो युक्त्यनुरोधी । स्वरूपं प्रकाशयन्नेवं[3] परावभासको व्यञ्जक इत्युच्यते । तथाविधे विषये वाचकत्वस्यैव व्यञ्जकत्वमिति गुणवृत्तिव्यवहारो नियमेनैव न शक्यते[4] कर्तुम्[5] । अविवक्षितवाच्यस्तु ध्वनिर्गुणवृत्तेः कथं भिद्यते । तस्य प्रभेदद्वये गुणवृत्तिप्रभेदद्वयरूपता लक्ष्यत एवं[6] यतः ।

अयमपि न दोषः । यस्मादविवक्षितवाच्यो ध्वनिर्गुणवृत्तिमार्गाश्रयोऽपि भवति न तु गुणवृत्तिरूप एव । गुणवृत्तिर्हि व्यञ्जकत्वशून्यापि दृश्यते । व्यञ्जकत्वं च यथोक्तचारुत्वहेतुं[7] व्यङ्ग्यं विना न व्यवतिष्ठते । गुणवृत्तिस्तु वाच्यधर्माश्रयेणैव व्यङ्ग्यमात्राश्रयेण चाभेदोपचाररूपा सम्भवति, यथा 'तीक्ष्णत्वादग्निर्माणवकः', 'आह्लादकत्वाच्चन्द्र[8] एवास्या मुखमित्यादौ । यथा च 'प्रिये[9] जने नास्ति पुनरुक्तम्' इत्यादौ । यापि लक्षणरूपा गुणवृत्तिः साप्युपलक्षणीयार्थसंबन्धमात्राश्रयेण चारुरूपव्यङ्ग्यप्रतीतिं विनापि सम्भवत्येव, यथा–'मञ्चाः क्रोशन्तीत्यादौ' विषये ।

---

१. 'संशयेन परित्यजन्' – ख. २. तदा विवक्षित – घ. ३. 'एव हि परावभासमानो' – क-ख. ४. 'नियमेन वै शक्यते – क-ख. ५. वक्तुम् – घ. ६. एव । यतोऽयमपि – घ. ७. 'हेतुकं' – क-ख. ८. 'आह्लादहेतुत्वात्' – ग. ९. 'प्रयोजने' – क-ख.

with intended but further-extending expressed sense. For it is impossible to speak of indication where a second meaning is apprehended over and above the apprehension of the expressed sense. There are two forms of indication :— (1) Usage of a word to convey a second meaning because of some reason and in such a way that the primary meaning is entirely concealed as in the example :—' *The student is a veritable fire.* ' (2) Usage of a word in such a way that its primary meaning is retained in part while another meaning also is conveyed as in the example ' *There is a hamlet in the Ganges.* ' In both these forms of indication, the primary sense is not intended in full. Therefore, it stands to reason that in suggestion with intended but further-extending expressed sense where the primary sense is fully intended and the denotative word itself conveys another sense also, one should speak of suggestiveness. Indeed, that which illumines itself along with shedding light upon other objects is regarded as suggester. In the instances mentioned, denotation itself possesses suggestiveness also and it is not at all possible to speak of indication as being applicable to them. But what difference is there between suggestion with unintended expressed sense and Indication ? ' The same two forms of indication described above constitute the two forms of this suggestion also. '

The fact is that there is no defect involved even in this state of affairs. Though suggestion with unintended expressed sense might operate in the wake of indication, it does not assume the form of indication itself. For, it is possible to come across indication which is completely devoid of the suggested content which is a source of beauty. This has been already pointed out. The first form of indication, viz., metaphorical attribution of identity, takes its stand in the characteristics of the expressed sense. For instance, the student is referred to as veritable fire because of his fire or short temper. The face of the heroine is spoken of as the moon itself because of its pleasing nature. Similarly, other examples are '......*there is no tautology for lovers*.' The second form of indication, viz., secondary sense also is possible if there is just a connection with the secondarily indicated sense though there is no apprehension of suggested content full of beauty: ' *cots creak* ' etc. are examples.

यत्र तु सा चारुरूपव्यङ्ग्यप्रतीतिहेतुस्तत्रापि व्यञ्जकत्वानुप्रवेशेनैव वाचकत्ववत् । असम्भविना चार्थेन यत्र व्यवहारः, यथा 'सुवर्णपुष्पां पृथिवीम्' इत्यादौ तत्र चारुरूपव्यङ्ग्यप्रतीतिरेव प्रयोजिकेति तथाविधेऽपि विषये गुणवृत्तौ सत्यामपि ध्वनिव्यवहार एव युक्त्यनुरोधी, तस्मादविवक्षितवाच्ये ध्वनौ द्वयोरपि प्रभेदयोर्व्यञ्जकत्वविशेषविशिष्टा[1] गुणवृत्तिर्न तु तदेकरूपा सहृदयहृदयाह्लादिनी प्रतीयमाना[2] । प्रतीतिहेतुत्वाद्विषयान्तरे तद्रूपशून्यायाश्च[3] दर्शनात् । एतच्च सर्वं प्राक्सूचितमपि स्फुटतरप्रतीतये पुनरुक्तम् ।

अपि च व्यञ्जकत्वलक्षणो यः शब्दार्थयोर्धर्मः स प्रसिद्धसम्बन्धानुरोधीति न कस्यचिद्विमतिविषयतामर्हति । शब्दार्थयोर्हि प्रसिद्धो यः सम्बन्धो वाच्यवाचकभावाख्यस्तमनुरुन्धान एव व्यञ्जकत्वलक्षणो व्यापारः सामग्र्यन्तरसम्बन्धादौपाधिकः प्रवर्तते । अत एव वाचकत्वात्तस्य विशेषः । वाचकत्वं हि शब्दविशेषस्य नियत आत्मा व्युत्पत्ति[4]कालादारभ्य तदविनाभावेन तस्य प्रसिद्धत्वात् । स त्वनियतः, औपाधिकत्वात् । प्रकरणाद्यवच्छेदेन तस्य प्रतीतिरितरथा त्वप्रतीतेः । ननु यद्यनियतस्तत्किं तस्य स्वरूपपरीक्षया । नैष दोषः; यतः शब्दात्मनि तस्यानियतत्वम्, न तु स्वे विषये व्यङ्ग्य[5]लक्षणे । लिङ्गत्व[6]न्यायश्चास्य व्यञ्जकभावस्य लक्ष्यते; यथा[7] लिङ्गत्वमाश्रयेष्व[8]नियताव-

---

१. 'विशेषणाविष्टा' – क-ख. २. प्रतीयमाना प्रतीति° – BP. ३. °शून्याया – BP.
४. 'संबन्धव्युत्पत्ति' – क-ख. ५. 'व्यञ्जक' – क. ६. लिङ्गलिङ्गिन्याय° – MB.
७. तथा हि – घ. ८. °माश्रयेषु नियता° – घ.

Of course, in some instances, indication becomes a source of the apprehension of the suggested content full of beauty; but it is entirely due to its touch of suggestiveness as in the case of denotation. In instances where we have a treatment of improbable events, e. g. *Three persons will gather*..., the treatment can be justified only in view of the apprehension of suggested beauty; and hence it stands to reason that we should regard them as instances of suggestion only, though indication might also be present therein. Thus in both the divisions of suggestion with unintended expressed sense, we will find indication tinged with a shade of suggestiveness. This will not appear identical with indication but quite separate from it and brings great delight to the minds of refined critics. Though all this has been indicated already, it has been repeated with the object of making the point clear.

Furthermore, the fact is indisputable that the suggestive power of words follows only in the wake of wellknown convention. The suggestive power of words follows the track of the wellknown conventional relation of word to meaning which is given the designation of the denoter-denoted relationship. But it becomes coloured by its association with other adventitious circumstances. That is where suggestiveness differs from denotation The denotation of every word is constant because, right from childhood when one first picks up the language, the meaning of each word remains quite unchanged throughout one's life. But the suggestiveness of words is not so constant. The reason is that it is adventitious. Its apprehension is there only when all circumstances such as context combine in conveying it, otherwise it will not be apprehended at all. It might be argued : 'What is the use of examining the nature of such an adventitious concept?' The examination of its nature is not at all a defect, in so far as its adventitiousness is seen only from the standpoint of suggested sense which happens to be its main province. The analogy of *probans* in an inference is well applicable to suggestiveness. Since inference is dependent upon

भासम्, इच्छाधीनत्वात्[1]; स्वविषयाव्यभिचारि च । तथैवेदं यथा दर्शितं व्यञ्जकत्वम् । शब्दात्मन्यनियतत्वादेव[2] च तस्य वाचकत्वप्रकारता[3] न शक्या कल्पयितुम् । यदि हि वाचकत्वप्रकारता तस्य भवेत्तच्छब्दात्मनि नियततापि स्याद्वाचकत्ववत् । स च तथाविध औपाधिको धर्मः शब्दानामौत्पत्तिक-शब्दार्थसम्बन्धवादिना वाक्यतत्त्वविदा पौरुषापौरुषेययोर्वाक्ययोर्विशेषमभिदधता नियमेनाभ्युपगन्तव्यः, तदनभ्युपगमे हि तस्य शब्दार्थसम्बन्धनित्यत्वे सत्यप्य-पौरुषेयपौरुषेययोर्वाक्ययोरर्थप्रतिपादने निर्विशेषत्वं स्यात् । तदनभ्युपगमे तु पौरुषेयाणां वाक्यानां पुरुषेच्छानुविधानसमारोपितौपाधिकव्यापारान्तराणां[4] सत्यपि स्वाभिधेयसम्बन्धापरित्यागे मिथ्यार्थतापि भवेत् ।

दृश्यते हि भावानामपरित्यक्तस्वस्वभावानामपि सामग्र्यन्तरसम्पात-सम्पादितौपाधिकव्यापारान्तराणां विरुद्धक्रियत्वम् । तथा हि—हिममयूख-प्रभृतीनां निर्वापितसकलजीवलोकं शीतलत्वमुद्वहतामेव प्रियाविरहदहनदह्यमान-मानसैर्जनैरालोक्यमानानां सतां सन्तापकारित्वं प्रसिद्धमेव । तस्मात्पौरुषेयाणां वाक्यानां सत्यपि नैसर्गिकेऽर्थसम्बन्धे मिथ्यार्थत्वं समर्थयितुमिच्छता वाचकत्व-व्यतिरिक्तं किंचिद्रूपमौपाधिकं व्यक्तमेवाभिधानीयम् । तच्च व्यञ्जकत्वादृते नान्यत् । व्यङ्ग्यप्रकाशनं हि व्यञ्जकत्वम् । पौरुषेयाणि च वाक्यानि

---

१. 'इच्छाविषयत्वात्' – ग. २. शब्दात्मनि नियततयैव – ब. ३. 'वाचकत्वाप्रकारता' – ग. ४. 'रोपितोपाधिव्यापार°' – ग. रोपितोपाधिकव्यापारा° – ब. व्यञ्जकत्वम्° MB.

one's desire, when there is no such desire to infer on a person's part, the existence of the quality of *probans* in anything is far from constant from the man's point of view of the *probandum*. Suggestiveness also is exactly like this. Though from the standpoint of word, it might be inconstant, one should not rush to the conclusion that it is a variety of denotation. If it were really a variety of denotation, it too should have been as constant as denotation itself in respect of word. An adherent of the Mīmāṁsā school of philosophy will have to accept perforce the conclusion that words have an adventitious power of the nature of suggestiveness. For he is a believer in the theory that not only there is a natural and eternal relation between word and its sense but also that there is difference between sentences uttered by men and those revealed in the Vedas. If he does not accept this adventitious power of words, the result would be that human utterance and superhuman revelations would both be on a par, since the relation between word and its sense is acknowledged to be eternal in both the cases. But if he should accept this adventitious power, he can easily count for the possibility of falsity in human utterances. For, though one might hold that the relation between sentences and their purport is eternal, there will also be room left to attribute adventitious drawbacks such as delusion due to the fleeting desires of the speaker.

Instances too can be found in nature of objects which produce effects opposite to their nature due to their contact with adventitious cirumstances though their nature itself is not completely lost on that account. For example, even the cool-rayed moon and such other cool objects which allay the heat of the entire universe by their refreshing coolness are seen to cause intense pain to onlookers who are afflicted by the burning pangs of separation from their beloveds. One who likes, therefore, to uphold the doctrine that the relation of word to its meaning is natural or eternal, will have to affirm obviously some adventitous element at least which belongs to words and which is distinct from denotation if he should explain properly the falsity of human utterances. And it cannot be anything other than suggestiveness. Suggestiveness is the same as the communication of what is suggested. All human utterances primarily communicate the intention of the speaker. That intention is

प्राधान्येन पुरुषाभिप्रायमेव प्रकाशयन्ति । स च व्यङ्ग्य एव न त्वभिधेयः, तेन सहाभिधानस्य वाच्यवाचकभाव[1]लक्षणसम्बन्धाभावात् ।

नन्वनेन न्यायेन सर्वेषामेव[2] लौकिकानां वाक्यानां ध्वनिव्यवहारः प्रसक्तः । सर्वेषाम[3]प्यनेन न्यायेन व्यञ्जकत्वात् । सत्यमेतत्; किं तु वक्त्रभिप्रायप्रकाशनेन[4] यद्[5] व्यञ्जकत्वं तत्सर्वेषामेव लौकिकानां वाक्यानामविशिष्टम् । तत्तु[6] वाचकत्वान्न भिद्यते, व्यङ्ग्यं हि तत्र नान्तरीयकतया व्यवस्थितम्; न तु विवक्षितत्वेन[7] । यस्य[8] तु विवक्षितत्वेन व्यङ्ग्यस्य स्थिति[9]: तद्व्यञ्जकत्वं ध्वनिव्यवहारस्य प्रयोजकम् । यत्त्वभिप्रायविशेषरूपं व्यङ्ग्यं शब्दार्थाभ्यां[10] प्रकाशते तद्भवति विवक्षितं तात्पर्येण प्रकाश्यमानं[11] सत्[12] । किन्तु तदेव केवलमपरिमितविषयस्य ध्वनिव्यवहारस्य न प्रयोजकमव्याप[13]कत्वात् । तथा[14] दर्शितभेदत्रयरूपं तात्पर्येण द्योत्यमानमभिप्रायरूपमनभिप्रायरूपं च सर्वमेव ध्वनिव्यवहारस्य प्रयोजकमिति यथोक्तव्यञ्जकत्वविशेषे ध्वनि[15]लक्षणे नातिव्याप्तिर्न चाव्याप्तिः । तस्माद्वाक्यतत्त्वविदां मतेन[16] तावद्व्यञ्जकत्व[17]लक्षणः शाब्दो व्यापारो न[18] विरोधी प्रत्युतानुगुण एव लक्ष्यते ।

परिनिश्चितनिरपभ्रंशशब्दब्रह्मणां विपश्चितां मतमाश्रित्यैव प्रवृत्तोऽयं ध्वनिव्यवहार इति तैः[19] सह किं विरोधाविरोधौ चिन्त्येते । कृत्रिमशब्दार्थसम्बन्धवादिनां तु युक्तिविदामनुभवसिद्ध एवायं व्यञ्जकभावः शब्दानामर्थान्तराणामिवावि[20]रोधश्चेति न प्रतिक्षेप्यपदवीमवतरति ।

वाचकत्वे हि तार्किकाणां विप्रतिपत्तयः प्रवर्तन्ताम्, किमिदं स्वाभाविकं

१. वाचकतालक्षण° – घ. २. सर्वेषामिवालौकिकाना°:– घ. ३. सर्वेषामेवानेन – घ. ४. 'वक्त्रभिप्रायविस्पष्टार्थप्रतिपादनेन' – ख. ५. 'यदिदं' – ख., यदि. – घ. ६. ननु – घ. ७. 'न तुविवक्षितत्वेन' – घ, पुस्तके नास्ति. ८. न – घ. ९. व्यवस्थितिः । – घ. १०. 'शब्दार्थाभ्यामेव' – क.ख. ११. 'प्रकाशमानं' – क-ख. १२. यत् – घ. १३. प्रयोजकम् । व्यापकत्वात् – घ. १४. 'ननु यथा दर्शित°' – क-ख. १५. °विशेषध्वनि° – घ. १६. मते न – घ. १७. व्यञ्जकलक्षणः – घ. १८. (न) – घ. १९. यैः – BP. २०. निर्विरोधश्चेति – घ.

suggested but not denoted since the relation of denoter-denoted does not apply at all to the intention and the word.

As for the objection that at this rate all sentences in the world will have to be designated as suggestive since all sentences in the world do contain suggestiveness (of intention), we say that the objection is valid in a way. It is a fact that suggestiveness of the speaker's intention is common to all human utterances in the world. But the thing is that this suggestiveness is in no way different from denotation itself. The suggested and the expressed are so organically bound up with each other therein and the suggested is not at all intended as exclusively important, which consideration alone entitles a content to get the designation of suggestion. If the speaker's intention which shines through words and meanings should be intended as important, it is only when it is directed towards the communication of the suggested alone exclusively. Nor can we think that even this suggestiveness is enough to explain all instances which come under the province of suggestion. For, the province of suggestion is unlimited while that of the said suggestiveness is but limited. Hence the conclusion is established that whether it be of the nature of speaker's intention or not, if the three-fold suggested content should be principally manifest, it will provide sufficient ground for the designation of suggestion. This definition of suggestion which takes into account suggestiveness as explained above cannot be tainted by the fallacies of *too wide* or *too narrow*. Thus the verbal power of suggestiveness will be found to be in agreement with the views of the experts on the theory of sentences (i. e. Mīmāṁsakas) far from conflicting with their doctrines.

So far as the system of grammar is concerned, the question whether the theory of suggestion is compatible with that system or not, does not arise at all; for the very expression ' suggestion ' has been borrowed (into the field of poetics) from the grammarians who maintain that sound in its eternal form of *SPHOṬA* (lit. Burst) is identical with Ultimate Reality itself (and that it is only suggested and never expressed).

Turning to the rationalistic system of logicians, it will be seen that the theory of suggestion cannot clash with their views

शब्दानामाहोस्वित्सामयिकमित्याद्याः। व्यञ्जकत्वे तु[1] तत्पृष्ठभाविनि भावान्तर[2]-साधारणे लोकप्रसिद्ध एवानुगम्यमाने :को विमतीनामवसरः ? अलौकिके ह्यर्थे तार्किकाणां विमतयो निखिलाः प्रवर्तन्ते[3] न तु लौकिके। न हि नीलमधुरादिष्वशेष-लोकेन्द्रियगोचरे बाधारहिते तत्त्वे परस्परं विप्रतिपन्ना दृश्यन्ते। न हि बाधारहितं नीलं नीलमिति ब्रुवन्नपरेण प्रतिषिध्यते नैतन्नीलं पीतमेतदिति । तथैव व्यञ्जकत्वं वाचकानां शब्दानामवाचकानां च गीतध्वनीनामशब्दरूपाणां च चेष्टादीनां यत्सर्वेषामनुभवसिद्धमेव[4] तत्केनापह्नूयते[5] । अशब्दमर्थं रमणीयं हि सूचयन्तो व्यवहारास्तथा[6] व्यापारा निबद्धाश्चानिबद्धाश्च[7] विदग्धपरिषत्सु विविधा विभाव्यन्ते । तान्[8]उपहास्यतामात्मनः परिहरन् कोऽतिसन्दधीत[9] सचेताः ।

अथ ब्रूयात्[10], अस्त्यतिसन्धानावसरे[11][12]: व्यञ्जकत्वं शब्दानां गमकत्वं तच्च लिङ्गत्वमतश्च :व्यङ्ग्यप्रतीतिर्लिङ्गिप्रतीतिरेवेति लिङ्गिलिङ्ग[13]भाव एव तेषां व्यङ्ग्यव्यञ्जकभावो[14] नापरः कश्चित्। अतश्चैतदवश्यमेव बोद्धव्यं यस्माद्वक्त्रभि-प्रायापेक्षया व्यञ्जकत्वमिदानीमेव त्वया प्रतिपादितं वक्त्रभिप्रायश्चानुमेयरूप एव।

---

१. 'हि' –ग. २. भावान्तरसाधारणे –घ. ३. 'तार्किकाणां निवेशः प्रवर्तते' –ग. 'तार्किकाणामभिनिवेशाः प्रवर्तन्ते' –घ. ४. एव –घ. पुस्तके नास्ति। ५. 'द्रूयते –ग., :" तत्केनाभिश्रूयते (पह्नूयते ?) –घ. ६. 'व्यवहारास्तथा व्यवहारा निबद्धाश्चा-निबद्धाश्च' –क-ख. ७. °निबन्धाश्च –घ. ८. तामुपहास्य° –घ. ९. 'इति संदधीत –ग. 'परिहरन्कथमभिसंदधीत' –घ. १०. (ब्रुयात्) –घ. ११. अभिसन्धाना° –घ. १२. अवसरे –घ. १३. लिङ्गलिङ्गिभाव –घ. १४. 'भावेनः परः' क–ख.

either. Indeed they hold that the relationship between a word and its meaning is conventional or man-made. So they also admit that suggestiveness is within our experience and that it is seen not only in meanings but also in words. Hence there is no need at all for refuting their views. The logicians indeed may hold divergent views so far as denotation is concerned, e. g. 'Is this a natural power or a man-made one? But there is no scope at all for any conflicting opinion so far as suggestiveness is concerned, because suggestiveness follows in the wake of denotation, and is found to be present even in other places (where denotation is absent) and its experience is pretty universal. All the controversies of logicians relate only to imperceptible objects and never to perceived ones. Logicians are never seen to hold conflicting views about such subjects of common and doubtless perception as — 'This is black' and 'This is sweet'. When one logician perceives an object as black without the association of any contradictory circumstances and says — 'This is black', another logician does not proceed to challenge him and assert — 'This is not black; this is yellow'. So also when suggestiveness is found by experience to exist in words which are denotative, in sounds of music etc. which are not even denotative, and finally in gestures and so forth too which are not words at all, no one can gainsay it. Various turns of speech both in verse and prose which are suggestive of non-denoted beautiful meanings are commonly met with in the gatherings of wits. Which man of taste can be deaf to their implications without becoming a butt of ridicule?

But the logicians might bring forward the following objection: It is true that in the instance mentioned, one does catch the implication of spoken words for they certainly possess suggestiveness. But in fact this suggestiveness is none other than implication; and implication is the same as the state of an inferential *probans*. The apprehension of the suggested idea is thus identical with the inferential knowldge of the *probandum*. In other words the relation of suggester - suggested is none other than the relation of probans - probandum. There is also another reason which substantiates this conclusion: you have yourself explained just now that words possess suggestiveness directed to the speaker's intention and it is our conviction that the speaker's intention is only inferable.

अत्रोच्यते[1]—नन्वेवमपि यदि नाम स्यात्तत्किं नश्छिन्नम्? वाचकत्वगुणवृत्तिव्यतिरिक्तो व्यञ्जकत्वलक्षणः[2] शब्दव्यापारोऽस्तीत्यस्माभिरभ्युपगतम्। तस्य चैवमपि न काचित् क्षतिः। तद्धि व्यञ्जकत्वं लिङ्गत्वमस्तु अन्यद्वा। सर्वथा प्रसिद्धशाब्दप्रकारविलक्षणत्वं शब्दव्यापारविषयत्वं च तस्यास्तीति नास्त्येवावयोर्विवादः। न पुनरयं परमार्थो यद्व्यञ्जकत्वं लिङ्गत्वमेव सर्वत्र व्यङ्ग्यप्रतीतिश्च लिङ्गिप्रतीतिरेवेति।

यदपि स्वपक्षसिद्धयेऽस्मदुक्तमनूदितं त्वया वक्त्रभिप्रायस्य व्यङ्ग्यत्वेनाभ्युपगमात्तत्प्रकाशने शब्दानां लिङ्गत्वमेवेति तदेतद्यथास्माभिरभिहितं तद्विभज्य प्रतिपाद्यते; श्रूयताम् — द्विविधो विषयः शब्दानाम् — अनुमेयः प्रतिपाद्यश्च। तत्रानुमेयो विवक्षालक्षणः। विवक्षा च शब्दस्वरूपप्रकाशनेच्छा शब्देनार्थप्रकाशनेच्छा चेति द्विप्रकारा। तत्राद्या न शाब्दव्यवहाराङ्गम्[3]। सा हि प्राणित्वमात्रप्रतिपत्तिफला। द्वितीया तु शब्दविशेषावधारणावसितव्यवहितापि[4] शब्दकरणव्यवहारनिबन्धनम्[5]। ते तु द्वे अप्यनुमेयो विषयः शब्दानाम्। प्रतिपाद्यस्तु प्रयोक्तुरर्थप्रतिपादनसमीहाविषयीकृतोऽर्थः।

स च द्विविधः—वाच्यो व्यङ्ग्यश्च। प्रयोक्ता हि कदाचित्स्व-

१. 'अत्रोच्यते' घ - पुस्तके नास्ति. २. व्यञ्जकलक्षणः - घ. ३. This and the following paragraph are found quoted in Sāhityacūḍāmaṇi, a commentary on Kāvyaprakāśa by Bhaṭṭa Gopāla. (KP. TSS Edn. p. 276) ४. '°सितान्यवहितामपि' - क-ख. ५. 'निबन्धनी' - क-ख.

To this, our rejoinder is as follows: even if the alleged view be true, there is nothing lost. Our only purpose is to establish the fact that suggestiveness is a verbal power, over and above two other powers, viz., denotation and indication. And this position of ours will not suffer in the least even if we should accept your allegation. It might be called by the name of suggestiveness, or that of an inferential *probans* or by any other name for that matter. But whatever the name by which we might call it, the fact remains that we will have admitted that there is no cause at all for any real dispute between us. But the truth is that suggestiveness is not identical with the state of an inferential *probans* nor is all apprehension of the suggested idea identical with inferential knowledge.

You have indeed made a clever use of our own words in substantiating your position. You have remarked glibly that the speaker's intention is certainly implied and added that such implication is the same as the state of an inferential *probans* We shall therefore explain in greater detail the real meaning of our statement for your benefit. The scope of words is two-fold : (1) Inferable and (2) denotative. Of these, the inferable is always of the nature of the speaker's intention. This intention of the speaker, once again, is two–fold : (1) desire to utter words for their own sake and (2) desire to convey meaning through words. Between these, the first type of speaker's intention does not play any part in verbal discourse. It only serves to distinguish an animal from a non-animal. But the second type of speaker's intention plays the part of a proximate cause in verbal discourse though it is rendered rather remote due to several other intervening factors between the utterance of the word and the apprehension of its meaning. And both these types of speaker's intention are inferable from words.

But the denotative scope of words relates to meaning itself which happens to be the aim of the speaker's intention to convey meaning. It is also two-fold : (1) the expressed and (2) the suggested. The speaker may use words with a view to conveying

शब्देनार्थं प्रकाशयितुं समीहते कदाचित्स्वशब्दानभिधेयत्वेन प्रयोजनापेक्षया कयाचित्। स तु द्विविधोऽपि प्रतिपाद्यो विषयः शब्दानां[1] न लिङ्गितया स्वरूपेण प्रकाशते, अपि तु कृत्रिमेणाकृत्रिमेण वा सम्बन्धान्तरेण। विवक्षा विषयत्वं हि तस्यार्थस्य शब्दैर्लिङ्गितया[2] प्रतीयते न तु स्वरूपम्। यदि हि लिङ्गतया[3] तत्र शब्दानां व्यापारः[4] स्यात्तच्छब्दार्थे सम्यङ्मिथ्यात्वादि-विवादा एव न प्रवर्तेरन्[5] धूमादिलिङ्गानुमितानुमेयान्तरवत्। व्यङ्ग्यश्चार्थो वाच्यसामर्थ्याक्षिप्ततया वाच्यवच्छब्दस्य सम्बन्धी भवत्येव। साक्षादसाक्षाद्भावो हि सम्बन्धस्याप्रयोजकः। वाच्यवाचकभावाश्रयत्वं च व्यञ्जकत्वस्य[6] प्रागेव दर्शितम्। तस्माद्वक्त्रभिप्रायरूप एव व्यङ्ग्ये[7] लिङ्गतया शब्दानां व्यापारः। तद्विषयीकृते तु प्रतिपाद्यतया। प्रतीयमाने तस्मिन्नभिप्रायरूपेऽनभिप्रायरूपे[8] च वाचकत्वेनैव व्यापारः सम्बन्धान्तरेण वा। न तावद्वाचकत्वेन यथोक्तं प्राक्। सम्बन्धान्तरेण व्यञ्जकत्वमेव। न च व्यञ्जकत्वं लिङ्गत्वरूपमेव आलोकादिष्वन्यथा दृष्टत्वात्। तस्मात्प्रतिपाद्यो विषयः शब्दानां न लिङ्गित्वेन[9]

---

१. 'शब्दात्' – ग. २. °लिङ्गतया – घ. ३. लिङ्गितया – BP. & – घ. ४. व्यवहारः – घ. ५. प्रवर्तेरन्। – घ. ६. 'व्यङ्ग्यव्यञ्जकत्वस्य' – क-ख. ७. 'व्यङ्ग्यो' – क-ख, – अभिप्रायरूपव्यङ्ग्ये – घ. ८. 'अनभिप्रायरूपे' – घ पुस्तके नास्ति. ९. लिङ्गत्वेन – घ.

his meaning directly by means of them (and then we have the expressed meaning), or he may use words which do not directly convey his meaning, with a view to achieving some purpose (and then we have the suggested meaning). Both these aspects of the denotative scope of words are far from appearing as *probandum* of any inference based on words. On the other hand, the relationship between word and such denotative content is one other than inference whether it be a conventional or an unconventional relationship. It is only the aspect of intention on the part of a speaker to employ words or meaningful words that is inferable and not the meaning itself conveyed by his words. If it were true that the meaning itself could form the *probandum* of an inference having words for its *probans*, there should be no scope for doubts at all whether any meaning is right or wrong. For instance, when the probandum viz., fire, is inferred from the *probans* viz., smoke, there is indeed no room for any doubt about the existence of fire. Since the suggested meaning is conveyed by the power of the expressed itself, it, too, is related to the word just as the expressed meaning is related to the word. Directness or remoteness is not the differentiating condition of a relationship. That suggestiveness is related to denotation has been already shown. The conclusion is thus indisputable that words will have the state of an inferential probans only while implying the intention of the speaker and that the meanings themselves which are signified by the words are due to the verbal power of denotation and not inference. Now we may take instances of meanings which are suggested by a word. These may be of the nature of intention and may not be as well. Can we say that all such meanings are conveyed by the power of denotation alone in words? Or should we postulate some other function? It has been already shown that the power of denotation alone cannot explain the suggested meaning. Hence we will have to admit another function and that function itself is called suggestiveness by us. The nature of suggestiveness is not co-extensive with the nature of an inferential *probans*, since the former exists in objects like light where the latter is absent. Just as the denoted content of words is not

सम्बन्धी वाच्यवत् । यो हि लिङ्गित्वेन तेषां सम्बन्धी[1] यथा दर्शितो विषयः स[2] न वाचकत्वेन प्रतीयते, अपि तूपाधित्वेन[3] । प्रतिपाद्यस्य च विषयस्य लिङ्गित्वे तद्विषयाणां विप्रतिपत्तीनां[4] लौकिकैरेव क्रियमाणानामभावः प्रसज्येतेति । एतच्चोक्तमेव ।

यथा च वाच्यविषये प्रमाणान्तरानुगमेन[5] सम्यक्त्वप्रतीतौ क्वचित्क्रियमाणायां तस्य प्रमाणान्तरविषयत्वे सत्यपि न शब्दव्यापारविषयताहानिस्तद्व्यङ्ग्यस्यापि । काव्य[6]विषये च व्यङ्ग्य[7]प्रतीतीनां सत्यासत्यत्वनिरूपणस्याप्रयोजकत्वमेवेति तत्र प्रमाणान्तरव्यापारपरीक्षोपहासायैव सम्पद्यते । तस्माल्लिङ्गिप्रतीतिरेव सर्वत्र व्यङ्ग्यप्रतीतिरिति न शक्यते[9] वक्तुम् ।

यत्त्वनुमेयरूप[10]व्यङ्ग्यविषयं शब्दानां व्यञ्जकत्वं तद्ध्वनिव्यवहारस्याप्रयोजकम् । अपि तु व्यञ्जकत्वलक्षणः शब्दानां व्यापार औत्पत्तिकशब्दार्थसम्बन्धवादिनाप्यभ्युपगन्तव्य इति प्रदर्शनार्थमुपन्यस्तम् । तद्धि व्यञ्जकत्वं कदाचिल्लिङ्गत्वेन कदाचिद्रूपान्तरेण शब्दानां वाचकानामवाचकानां च सर्ववादिभिरप्रतिक्षेप्यमित्ययमस्माभिर्यत्न आरब्धः । तदेवं गुणवृत्तिवाचकत्वा-

---

१. लिङ्गत्वेन सम्बन्धी – घ. २. 'असौ' – ग. ३. त्वौपाधिकत्वेन – घ. ४. विप्रतिपत्तीनां लौकिकानां – घ. ५. 'गमनेन' – क-ख. ६. 'कार्य' – ग. ७. 'वाच्यं-व्यङ्ग्य' – क-ख. ८. 'सत्यत्वासत्यत्वनिरूपणाप्रयोजक' – ग. ९. 'शक्यं' – क-ख १०. °नुमेयरूपं – घ.

identical with the probandum of an inference, so also the suggested content is not identical with it. Contrariwise, that which becomes the object of an inferred *probandum* as shown above, does not constitute what is denoted but constitutes only an adventitious attribute of what is denoted. If the denoted meaning too were to be inferable as probandum, there could be no occasion at all for any differences of opinion regarding it in the world. But such differences are within our common knowledge and this has also been explained already.

It is no doubt true that sometimes one does resort to inference or other Instruments of Knowledge while deciding the truth of even an expressed meaning. Though it thus falls within the scope of other Instruments of Knowledge, its being at the same time an object of the verbal power of denotation does not suffer in the least. The same is true of suggested meaning also. As a matter of fact, the question of logical truth and falsity in regard to suggested meaning is entirely futile. Such being the case, it would be nothing but ridiculous if one were to indulge in discussions regarding different Instruments of Knowledge applicable therein. In short, we can wind up the discussion by saying that it is impossible to identify the apprehension of the suggested meaning with the apprehension of the inferred *probandum* in every case.

Though it is true that we have affirmed above the existence of an implied aspect in words (viz., speaker's intention) which is also inferable, and that it can also be called by the name of suggestiveness, we never believe that it is a conclusive factor at all in deciding about the designation of suggestion to be given to particular instances.

The reason why we made that remark is quite a different one; it was put forward by us only as an argument to elicit the support of even philosophers holding the doctrine of eternal relationship between word and sound to the fact that suggestiveness is a unique function of words. That suggestiveness, as a matter of fact, co-exists sometimes with the state of inferential *probans* of words, and sometimes shines through denotative words as well as non-denotative words. We have laboured this point at length just to show that no scholastic

दिभ्यः शब्दप्रकारेभ्यो नियमेनैव तावद्विलक्षणं व्यञ्जकत्वम्। तदन्तःपाति-त्वेऽपि तस्य हठादभिधीयमाने तद्विशेषस्य[1] ध्वनेर्यत्प्रकाशनं विप्रतिपत्तिनिरासाय सहृदयव्युत्पत्तये वा तत्क्रियमाणमनतिसन्धेयमेव[3]। न हि सामान्यमात्रलक्षणे-नोपयोगिविशेषलक्षणानां प्रतिक्षेपः शक्यः कर्तुम्। एवं हि सति सत्तामात्र-लक्षणे कृते सकलसद्वस्तुलक्षणानां पौनरुक्त्यप्रसङ्गः। तदेवम्—

विमतिविषयो य आसीन्मनीषिणां सततमविदितसतत्त्वः।
ध्वनिसञ्ज्ञितः प्रकारः काव्यस्य व्यञ्जितः सोऽयम्॥

प्रकारोऽन्यो गुणीभूतव्यङ्ग्यः काव्यस्य दृश्यते।
यत्र व्यङ्ग्यान्वये वाच्यचारुत्वं स्यात्प्रकर्षवत्॥ ३४॥

व्यङ्ग्योऽर्थो ललनालावण्यप्रख्यो यः प्रतिपादितस्तस्य प्राधान्ये ध्वनिरित्युक्तम्। तस्य तु[6] गुणीभावेन वाच्यचारुत्वप्रकर्षे गुणीभूतव्यङ्ग्यो नाम काव्यप्रभेदः प्रकल्प्यते। तत्र वस्तुमात्रस्य व्यङ्ग्यस्य तिरस्कृतवाच्येभ्यः[7] प्रतीयमानस्य कदाचिद्वाच्यरूपवाक्यार्थापेक्षया गुणीभावे सति गुणीभूत-व्यङ्ग्यता।

यथा —

---

१. "पातित्वेऽपि तस्य ग्रहादभिधेयमानं तद्विशेषस्य ध्वनेः"–क-ख. पातित्वेनापि–घ. २. तस्य ग्रहादभिधीयमानमेतद्विशेषस्य–घ. ३. 'अभिसंधेयमेव'–क-ख. ४. 'अभि-प्रायविशेष' क–ख. ५. संज्ञकः KLV. ६. 'च' ग., तस्यैव – घ. ७. वाच्येभ्यः शब्देभ्यः – घ.

objection should be raised by any of the controversialists, adherents as they might be of different systems of thought. Hence we might conclude that suggestiveness is a power of words, quite different from all other powers like indication and denotation. Notwithstanding all this, controversialists might still persist in asserting dogmatically that it is included under them only; but our doctrine of suggestiveness which attempts at explaining the speciality of suggestiveness, at disarming all divergences of opinion and at educating the taste of critics will not certainly deserve any censure. It is not indeed possible to belittle the usefulness of detailed definitions of particulars, simply because general definitions are already there. If one should belittle them, it would be no better than saying that the definitions of all particular concepts in philosophy are just so many repetitions in view of the fact that the general definition of the *Summum genus* itself, viz., Reality, has been propounded at the very outset. Thus——

The variety of poetry designated as suggestion, which had become a source of controversy for long, because its real nature had eluded even persons of the best intellect, has now been explained.

We can see another variety of poetry viz. poetry of subordinated suggestion, wherein the artistic excellence of the expressed is greater than that of the suggested, though the latter also happens to be present alongside of the former. **34**

The suggested sense has been compared to the composite charm of lovely women and it has already been mentioned that when it happens to be exclusively important, we get the type of poetry which merits the designation of DHVANI. When the same happens to become secondary and the expressed alone shines forth prominently, we get another type of poetry which can be regarded as GUṆĪBHŪTA-VYAṄGYA or 'Poetry of subordinated suggestion'. In this variety, once again, a bare idea conveyed by such words as have lost their conventional denotation might be the suggested element and it might become secondary to the purport of the sentence as a whole got at by its component denotative words, as in the following example :—

लावण्यसिन्धुरपरैव हि केयमत्र यत्रोत्पलानि शशिना सह सम्प्लवन्ते ।
उन्मज्जति द्विरदकुम्भतटी च यत्र यत्रापरे कदलिकाण्डमृणालदण्डाः ॥

अतिरस्कृतवाच्येभ्योऽपि शब्देभ्यः प्रतीयमानस्य व्यङ्ग्यस्य कदाचिद्वाच्यप्राधान्येन काव्यचारुत्वापेक्षया[1] गुणीभावे सति गुणीभूतव्यङ्ग्यता, यथोदाहृतम् — 'अनुरागवती सन्ध्या' इत्येवमादि। तस्यैव स्वयमुक्त्या प्रकाशीकृतत्वेन गुणीभावः[2] यथोदाहृतम्—'सङ्केतकालमनसम्' इत्यादि । रसादिस्वरूप[3]व्यङ्ग्यस्य गुणीभावो रसवदलङ्कारे[4] दर्शितः[5]; तत्र च तेषामाधि[6]कारिकवाक्यापेक्षया गुणीभावो विवहनप्रवृत्त[7]भृत्यानुयायिराजवत् । व्यङ्ग्यालङ्कारस्य गुणीभावे[8] दीपकादिर्विषयः ।

तथा —

प्रसन्नगम्भीरपदाः काव्यबन्धाः सुखावहाः ।
ये च तेषु प्रकारोऽयमेवं[9] योज्यः सुमेधसा ॥ ३५ ॥

ये चैतेऽपरिमितस्वरूपा[10] अपि प्रकाशमानास्तथाविधार्थ[11]रमणीयाः सन्तो विवेकिनां सुखावहाः काव्यबन्धास्तेषु सर्वेष्वेवायं प्रकारो गुणीभूतव्यङ्ग्यो नाम योजनीयः । यथा—

लच्छी दुहिदा[12] जामाउओ हरी तंस घरिणिआ गङ्गा ।
अमिअमिअङ्का अ सुआ अहो कुडुम्बं महोअहिणो ॥
लक्ष्मीर्दुहिता जामाता हरिस्तस्य गृहिणी गङ्गा ।
अमृतमृगाङ्कौ च सुतावहो कुटुम्बं महोदधेः ॥ [इति च्छाया]

१. चारुत्वापेक्षया -घ २. गुणभावः -घ. ३. रसादिरूपव्यङ्ग्यस्य - घ. ४. गुणीभावे रसवदलङ्कारो -घ. ५. 'रसवदलंकारविषयः प्राक्प्रदर्शितः' क-ख. ६. 'तत्र च रसानामाधि' क-ख. ७. विवाहप्रवृत्त° -घ. ८. गुणीभावो -घ. ९. प्रकारोऽयमेवं -घ. १०. परिमितस्वरूपा -घ. ११. 'प्रकाशमानविततार्थ' क-ख. प्रकाशमानास्तथा रमणीयाः -घ. १२. 'पूआ' क-ख.

Who could be this new ocean of charm
With dark lilies floating beside the moon;
With twin temples of elephants merged
Beside plantain-stems and lotus-stalks ?

Even when words other than those whose expressed sense is concealed are employed, if only the suggested sense conveyed by them should be secondary to their expressed meaning, we find sometimes this variety of poetry with subordinated suggestion. Instances quoted already such as *Twilight is blushing etc.*, will serve as examples.

If what is suggested is also expressed again by other words, we should consider it too as an instance of subordinated suggestion. Examples of this have been already given : e. g. *Knowing that her paramour, etc.* If the suggested element happens to be of the nature of sentiment etc., and if it is also secondary to the expressed, we would consider it as an instance of Figurative sentiment as already demonstrated. The subordination of sentiment, etc., to the main purport of the sentence in such instances can be likened to the circumstantial subordination of a king who has to walk behind his own servant when the latter is a bridegroom taken in procession When a suggested figure is secondary to the expressed, we have instances of figures like Ellipsis implying a simile, etc.

In all poetic compositions that look delightful by reason of their lucid and elegant words, only this variety of poetry should be recognised by the intelligent critic. 35

Despite the fact that poetic compositions which look lovely and bring delight to discriminating critics appear unlimited, this very variety, viz., poetry of subordinated suggestion, should be recognised in all of them. For example :—

Lakṣmī is his daughter,
Hari himself the son-in-law
And wife no less than Gaṅgā;
Verily, Amṛta and the Moon are his two sons,
Ah, what a family indeed this Mighty Ocean has !

वाच्यालङ्कारवर्गोऽयं व्यङ्ग्यांशानुगमे सति ।
प्रायेणैव परां छायां बिभ्रल्लक्ष्ये निरीक्ष्यते ॥ ३६ ॥

वाच्यालङ्कारवर्गोऽयं व्यङ्ग्यांशस्यालङ्कारस्य[1] वस्तुमात्रस्य वा[2] यथायोगमनुगमे सति च्छायातिशयं बिभ्रल्लक्षणकारैरेकदेशेन दर्शितः । स तु तथारूपः प्रायेण सर्व एव परीक्ष्यमाणो लक्ष्ये निरीक्ष्यते । तथा हि—दीपक-समासोक्त्यादिवदन्येऽप्यलङ्काराः प्रायेण व्यङ्ग्यालङ्कारान्तरवस्त्वन्तरसंस्प-र्शिनो[3] दृश्यन्ते । यतः प्रथमं तावदतिशयोक्तिगर्भता सर्वालङ्कारेषु शक्यक्रिया । कृतैव च सा महाकविभिः कामपि काव्यच्छविं पुष्यति[4], कथं ह्यतिशययोगिता स्वविषयौचित्येन क्रियमाणा सती काव्ये नोत्कर्षमावहेत् । भामहेनाप्यतिश-योक्तिलक्षणे यदुक्तम्—

सैषा सर्वैव वक्रोक्तिरनयार्थो विभाव्यते ।
यत्नोऽस्यां कविना कार्यः कोऽलङ्कारोऽनया विना ॥ इति ॥

तत्रातिशयोक्तिर्यमलङ्कारमधितिष्ठति कविप्रतिभावशात्तस्य चारुत्वाति-शययोगो[6]ऽन्यस्य त्वलङ्कारमात्रतैवेति सर्वालङ्कारशरीरस्वीकरणयोग्यत्वेनाभेदो-पचारात्सैव[7] सर्वालङ्काररूपेत्ययमेवार्थोऽवगन्तव्यः । तस्याश्चालङ्कारान्तर-संकीर्णत्वं कदाचिद्वाच्यत्वेन कदाचिद्व्यङ्ग्यत्वेन । व्यङ्ग्यत्वमपि कदाचित्प्रा-धान्येन कदाचिद्गुणभावेन । तत्राद्ये पक्षे वाच्यालङ्कारमार्गः । द्वितीये तु ध्वना-वन्तर्भावः । तृतीये तु गुणीभूतव्यङ्ग्यरूपता ।

अयं च प्रकारोऽन्येषामप्यलङ्काराणामस्ति, तेषां तु[8] न सर्वविषयः । अतिशयोक्तेस्तु सर्वालङ्कारविषयोऽपि सम्भवतीत्ययं विशेषः । येषु चालङ्कारेषु

---

१. 'व्यङ्ग्यस्यांशस्यालंकारस्य वा यथायोगं' ग. २. वा – घ पुस्तके नास्ति। ३. 'व्यङ्ग्यालंकारान्तरसंस्पर्शि' क-ख. व्यङ्ग्यालंकारवस्त्वन्तरसंस्पार्शिनो–घ. ४. पुष्यतीति –घ. ५. सर्वत्र–घ. ६. अतिशययोगे°–घ. ७. 'सैवालंकार'–क-ख. ८. 'तु'–घ पुस्तके नास्ति ।

The whole host of figures is seen in many an instance to put on a new charm when it is brought into touch with the suggested element. 36

The earlier writers on Poetics have themselves shown how a few of the figures of sense acquire a new charm when they get into touch with the suggested element consisting of either a figure or a bare idea. But a scrutiny of instances will reveal that this is true of all the figures. To illustrate : Just like the figure Ellipsis implying a simile and condensed metaphor, all the other figures too are seen generally to contain a touch of either another figure or another idea which happens to be suggested. For, in the first place, one can posit at least a touch of exaggeration in figures one and all. In fact the greatest poets have amply incorporated exaggeration into their works with a view to endowing them with a unique shade of charm. When such exaggeration is utilized in a work in keeping with principles of decorum, how can it ever fail to cause delight ? Bhāmaha, indeed, has given the following definition of Exaggeration :—

This (Exaggeration) is itself the artistic turn of speech and it is by this that poetic content is made manifest. A poet should strive after this in particular and what figure can be there without it ?

This should be understood to convey the following sense only :—Only that figure in which Exaggeration reigns supreme, acquires abundant beauty due to the poet's genius. Others are ornamental figures only in name. Hence all figures deserve to be regarded as so many bodies (whose soul is exaggeration) only and by a metaphorical application of identity between them, (one might say that) exaggeration is itself the same as the host of all figures.

This sometimes merges with other figures expressly (1), and suggestively at other times. Its suggestibility too may be optionally principal (2), or secondary (3). In the first case, we have the well known expressed Figures. In the second case it comes under DHVANI or suggestive poetry. In the third case it will be poetry of subordinated suggestion. This characteristic is no doubt found in figures other than Exaggeration also.

सादृश्यमुखेन तत्त्वप्रतिलम्भः यथा रूपकोपमातुल्ययोगितानिदर्शनादिषु तेषु गम्यमानधर्ममुखेनैव यत्सादृश्यं तदेव शोभातिशयशालि भवतीति ते सर्वेऽपि चारुत्वातिशययोगिनः सन्तो गुणीभूतव्यङ्ग्यस्यैव विषयाः[1]। समासोक्त्याक्षेपपर्यायोक्तादिषु तु गम्यमानांशाविनाभावेनैव तत्त्वव्यवस्थानाद्[2]गुणीभूतव्यङ्ग्यता निर्विवादैव। तत्र च गुणीभूतव्यङ्ग्यतायामलङ्काराणां केषाञ्चिदलङ्कारविशेषगर्भतायां नियमः। यथा व्याजस्तुतेः प्रेयोलङ्कारगर्भत्वे। केषाञ्चिदलङ्कारमात्रगर्भतायां नियमः। यथा सन्देहादीनामुपमागर्भत्वे। केषाञ्चिदलङ्काराणां परस्परगर्भतापि सम्भवति। यथा दीपकोपमयोः। तत्र दीपकमुपमागर्भत्वेन प्रसिद्धम्। उपमापि कदाचिद्[3]दीपकच्छायानुयायिनी। यथा मालोपमा। तथा हि 'प्रभामहत्या शिखयेव दीपः' इत्यादौ[4] स्फुटैव दीपकच्छाया लक्ष्यते[5]।

तदेवं व्यङ्ग्यांशसंस्पर्शे सति चारुत्वातिशययोगिनो रूपकादयोऽलङ्काराः[6] सर्व एव गुणीभूतव्यङ्ग्यस्य मार्गः। गुणीभूतव्यङ्ग्यत्वं च तेषां तथाजातीयानां सर्वेषामेवोक्तानुक्तानां[7] सामान्यम्। तल्लक्षणे सर्वे एवैते सुलक्षिता भवन्ति। एकैकस्य स्वरूप[8]विशेषकथनेन तु सामान्यलक्षणरहितेन प्रतिपदपाठेनैव[9] शब्दा न शक्यन्ते तत्त्वतो निर्ज्ञातुम्, आनन्त्यात्। अनन्ता हि वाग्विकल्पास्तत्प्रकारा

१. विषयः -घ. २. '°स्थापनात्' -क-ख. ३. 'काचित्' -ग. ४. 'इत्यादौ विषये' -ग. ५. 'उपलक्ष्यते' -क-ख. ६. 'रूपकाद्यलंकाराः' -ग. ७. 'उक्तानां' -ख; 'उक्तानुयुक्तानां' -ग. ८. रूपविशेषकथनेन -घ. ९. °पाठेनैव -घ. प्रतिपाद° -BP. घ.

But these other figures do not have an all-inclusive reference to the whole host of figures. The uniqueness of Exaggeration lies in this that it is pervasive of every figure of speech.

In figures like Metaphor, Simile, Combination of Equals, Corroboration, etc., wherein similarity is the chief justification for their being styled as ornaments, the idea of similarity which is manifest only through implication attains excessive charm and hence they all come within the purview of poetry of subordinated suggestion. So far as figures like condensed Metaphor, Paraleipsis and Periphrasis are concerned, since the suggested element in them happens to provide invariably the justification for their being styled as ornaments, there can be no dispute regarding their claims to be brought under poetry of subordinated suggestion. But with regard to some figures under this class of poetry, their capacity to get a touch of other figures will be restricted only to particular ones. Veiled praise, for instance, involves only the figure 'Sweet Flattery.' In other figures, the said scope is further limited to suggestion of figures only (as against ideas). For instance, in Fancied Doubt, etc., only Simile is involved. Yet other figures may be found to be mutually involved, e. g. Ellipsis implying a Simile and Simile. That the figure Ellipsis involves simile is widely known. (Though not so well-known), even Simile may involve a shade of Ellipsis, as for instance—a Wreath of Similes. Thus in an example such as—*Like a lamp in union with radiant light*, etc., the shade of Ellipsis is quite clear.

All figures, then, which contain a touch of suggestion and at the same time owe their excessive charm due to that touch, deserve to be brought within the compass of Poetry of subordinated suggestion. The only feature shared in common by all the figures, mentioned as well as unmentioned here, is thus the element of subordinated suggestion. And hence by proper understanding of the latter's nature, all the characteristics of the former will become clear automatically. The procedure (of rhetoricians) who refrain from attempting a general definition of ornaments and give details only of individual figures cannot lead one to an apprehension of the truth about them

एव चालङ्काराः । गुणीभूतव्यङ्ग्यस्य च प्रकारान्तरेणापि व्यङ्ग्यार्थानुगमलक्षणेन[1] विषयत्वमस्त्येव । तदयं ध्वनिनिष्यन्द[2]रूपो द्वितीयोऽपि महाकविविषयोऽतिरमणीयो लक्षणीयः सहृदयैः । सर्वथा नास्त्येव सहृदयहृदयहारिणः काव्यस्य स प्रकारो यत्र न प्रतीयमानार्थसंस्पर्शेन सौभाग्यम् । तदिदं[3] काव्यरहस्यं परमिति सूरिभिर्भावनीयम्[4] ।

मुख्या महाकविगिरामलङ्कृ[5]तिभृतामपि ।
प्रतीयमानच्छायैषा भूषा लज्जेव योषिताम् ॥ ३७ ॥

अनया सुप्रसिद्धोऽप्यर्थः[6] किमपि कामनीयकमानीयते ।

तद्यथा—

विस्रम्भोत्था मन्मथाज्ञाविधाने ये मुग्धाक्ष्याः केऽपि लीलाविशेषाः[7] ।
अक्षुण्णास्ते चेतसा केवलेन स्थित्वैकान्ते सन्ततं भावनीयाः ॥

इत्यत्र केऽपीत्यनेन पदेन वाच्यमस्पष्टमभिदधता प्रतीयमानं[8] वस्त्व[9]क्लिष्टमनन्तमर्पयता का छाया नोपपादिता ।

अर्थान्तरगतिः काक्वा या चैषा परिदृश्यते ।
सा व्यङ्ग्यस्य गुणीभावे प्रकारमिममाश्रिता ॥ ३८ ॥

या चैषा काक्वा क्वचिदर्थान्तरप्रतीतिर्दृश्यते सा व्यङ्ग्यस्यार्थस्य गुणीभावे सति गुणीभूतव्यङ्ग्यलक्षणं[10] काव्यप्रभेदमाश्रयते । यथा— "स्वस्था

---

१. लक्षणेव – घ. २. निष्पंद° – घ. ३. 'तद्धि'–ग. ४. 'भावनीयमिति'–क.ख- ५. 'अलंकार'–ग. ६. 'काव्यार्थः'–क-ख. ७. लीलाविलासाः–घ. ८. 'प्रतीयमानत्वं'–क-ख. ९. 'वस्तु' घ –पुस्तके नास्ति. १०. 'गुणीभावव्यङ्ग्यलक्षणमिमं' – क-ख.

just as a bare enumeration of individual words cannot lead to the truth about all words possible in the world. The reason is that they are infinite. Indeed, the variations of human speech are infinite and the figures of speech in poetry too are equally infinite. But subordinated suggestion has a wider range of application, in so far as it can enter into relationship with suggested elements also. Therefore, this second manifestation of suggestion too should be recognised by refined critics as a beautiful avenue for first-rate poets. Certainly, there is not a single variety of poetry holding out an appeal to the hearts of refined critics which does not attain artistic excellence by the slightest touch of suggested sense. The learned should deem this as the greatest secret of poetry.

> **Even for such expressions of poets as are already adorned by figures, this shade of suggestion will be a most important ornament even as bashfulness will be for women.** 37

By this shade, even a common place will be invested with unique charm as for instance in the following :—

> *The indefinite graces of the bride with guileless looks*
> *Are so uncommon as they spring*
> *From her implicit obedience to Cupid's behests*
> *That one can only contemplate them*
> *In some solitary spot.*

The word 'indefinite' (original : *ke'pi*) conveys the expressed sense very vaguely and at the same time offers itself to be flooded with infinite suggested feeling most easily, and in so doing, is there any shade of beauty left uncontributed by it to the passage as a whole ?

> **Of course we see the communication of a new meaning by the agency of Ironic Tone. Even this will come within this variety of poetry so long as the suggested element happens to remain secondary.** 38

The communication of a new meaning through Ironic Tone also comes within the scope of this variety of poetry, viz., poetry of subordinated suggestion.

भवन्ति मयि जीवति धार्तराष्ट्राः ''। यथा वा—

आम असइओ ओरम पइव्वए ण तुएँ मलिणिअं सीलम्।
किं उण जणस्स जाअ व्व चन्दिलं तं ण कामेमो॥

[आम असत्यः उपरम पतिव्रते न त्वया मलिनितं शीलम्।
किं पुनर्जनस्य जायेव नापितं तं न कामयामहे॥ [इति च्छाया]

शब्दशक्तिरेव हि स्वाभिधेयसामर्थ्याक्षिप्तकाकुसहाया सत्यर्थविशेषप्रतिपत्तिहेतुर्न काकुमात्रम्। विषयान्तरे स्वेच्छाकृतात्काकु[1]मात्रात्तथाविधार्थप्रतिपत्त्यसम्भवात्। स चार्थः काकुविशेषसहायशब्दव्यापारोपारूढो[2]ऽप्यर्थसामर्थ्यलभ्यं[3] इति व्यङ्ग्यरूप एव। वाचकत्वानुगमेनैव तु यदा तद्विशिष्टवाच्य[4]प्रतीतिस्तदा गुणीभूतव्यङ्ग्यतया तथाविधार्थद्योतिनः काव्यस्य व्यपदेशः। व्यङ्ग्यवि[5]शिष्टवाच्याभिधायिनो हि गुणीभूतव्यङ्ग्यत्वम्।

प्रभेदस्यास्य विषयो यश्च युक्त्या प्रतीयते।
विधातव्या सहृदयैर्न तत्र ध्वनियोजना॥ ३९॥

सङ्कीर्णो हि कश्चि[6]द्ध्वनेर्गुणीभूतव्यङ्ग्यस्य च लक्ष्ये दृश्यते मार्गः। तत्र[7] यस्य[8] युक्तिसहायता तत्र[9] तेन व्यपदेशः कर्तव्यः। न सर्वत्र ध्वनिरागिणा भवितव्यम्। यथा—

---

१. 'कृतकाकु'–ग. २. 'व्यापारोऽप्यर्थरूढो'–क-ख. ३. 'सामर्थ्याल्लभ्यते'–ग. ४. 'वाच्यार्थ°'–क-ख. ५ व्यङ्ग्यस्य विशिष्ट–घ. ६. 'क्वचित्'–ग. ७. 'तत्र' –ग. पुस्तके नास्ति'. ८. यद्यस्य–घ, KLV. ९. 'तदनेन'–क-ख.

For example :—

Without worry will the sons of Dhṛtarāṣṭra
Remain as long as I live. (?)

To take another example :—

Yes, we are unchaste; but please stop scolding,
O paragon of chastity !
You have never sullied your morals truly;
But like the wife of a commoner
I am not in love with a barber.

It is not merely the Ironic Tone which is responsible for conveying the second sense but the power of words only which takes assistance from Ironic Tone suggested by its own power of denoted sense. For in other instances, where we resort to Ironic Tone at our will, it is not found that specific senses are communicated. The specific sense so communicated is suggested only in as much as it results only by the power of expressed sense though it is ingrained also in the power of word itself deriving assistance from specific Ironic Tone. When the apprehension of the expressed sense associated with suggested sense occurs in such a way that the latter is definitely subordinate to the former, we have indeed subordinated suggestion and instances of poetry containing it should be designated by this name. The characteristic of subordinated suggestion is indeed none other than denotation of the expressed sense in association with the suggested.

Instances which can reasonably be brought under this class of poetry should not be classed under DHVANI by refined critics. 39

The pathways of Dhvani or *primarily* suggestive poetry and poetry of subordinated suggestion often merge into each other in individual instances. Whether it is the one or the other name which the instance deserves should be decided only on the basis of stronger arguments in favour of the one or the other. One should not be unduly biased in favour of *Dhvani* everywhere. For instance,

पत्युः शिरश्चन्द्रकलामनेन स्पृशेति सख्या परिहासपूर्वम् ।
सा रञ्जयित्वा चरणौ कृताशीर्माल्येन तां निर्वचनं जघान ॥

यथा[1] च—

प्रयच्छतोच्चैः कुसुमानि मानिनी विपक्षगोत्रं दयितेन लम्भिता ।
न किञ्चिदूचे चरणेन केवलं लिलेख बाष्पाकुललोचना भुवम् ॥

इत्यत्र ' निर्वचनं जघान ', ' न किञ्चिदूचे ', इति प्रतिषेधमुखेन व्यङ्ग्यस्यार्थस्योक्त्या किञ्चि[2]द्विषयीकृतत्वाद्गुणीभा[3]व एव शोभते । यदा[4] वक्रोक्तिं विना व्यङ्ग्योऽर्थस्तात्पर्येण प्रतीयते[5] तदा तस्य प्राधान्यम् । यथा— ' एवं वादिनि देवर्षौ ' इत्यादौ । इह पुनरुक्तिर्भङ्ग्यास्तीति वाच्यस्यापि प्राधान्यम् । तस्मान्नात्रानुरणनरूपव्यङ्ग्यध्वनिव्यपदेशो[6] विधेयः ।

प्रकारोऽयं गुणीभूतव्यङ्ग्योऽपि ध्वनिरूपताम् ।
धत्ते रसादितात्पर्यपर्यालोचनया पुनः ॥ ४० ॥

गुणीभूतव्यङ्ग्योऽपि काव्यप्रकारो रसभावा[7]दितात्पर्यालोचने[8] पुनर्ध्व[9]निरेव सम्पद्यते । यथा[10]त्रैवानन्तरोदाहृते श्लोकद्वये ।

यथा च—

दुराराधा राधा सुभग यदनेनापि मृजत[11]-
स्तवैतत्प्राणेशाजघनवसनेनाश्रु पतितम् ।

१. ' तथा ' – क-ख. २. ' न किंचित् ' – ग. ३. ' गुणभाव ' – ग. ४. ' तस्माद्यत्रोक्तिं विना ' – क-ख. ५. ' प्रकाशते तत्र ' – क-ख. ६. ' भ्रमः ' – क-ख. ७. ' रसभावतात्पर्य ' – क-ख. ८. ' पर्यालोचने स पुनः – क-ख. ९. ' पुनरेव ध्वनिः ' – ग. १०. यथा तत्रैवोदाहृते ' – ग. ११. ' सृजतः ' – क-ख.

After painting her feet red,
The handmaid wished laughingly—
'May you touch the crescent moon
On your husband's head with this !'
At this, Pārvatī gave her a blow
With her garland without a word.

To cite another example :—

When her sweet partner addressed her
Unwittingly by her rival's name
While handing her flowers above her reach,
She did not say anything;
She only drew lines on the earth with her foot
And her eyes were bedewed with tears.

The suggested content has been to some extent expressed also by the negative statement–' without a word ' and ' did not say ' in the above examples. Hence it is better that we regard them as instances of subordinated suggestion only. It is only when suggested content is exclusively conveyed without any touch of indirect denotation that we might regard it as principal as in the example— ' *when the divine sage spoke thus......* '. But in the examples in hand, the suggested content is found repeated in an indirect way and hence the expressed content also is as important as the suggested itself. Therefore, one should not give it the name of poetry with resonance–like suggestion.

This class of poetry viz., that with subordinated suggestion will also assume the form of DHVANI or that with principal suggestion if one views it from the standpoint of exculsive purport of sentiments etc. 40

When viewed from the standpoint of purport, viz., sentiment, etc., even poetry with subordinated suggestion will become poetry with principal suggestion itself. The two examples just now quoted illustrate this. The following is another instance :—

'O gallant, Rādhā indeed is too stubborn;
She goes on shedding tears though you have
Wiped them with the waist-garment of your dearest sweet-heart.

कठोरं स्त्रीचेतस्तदलमुपचारैर्विरम हे
क्रियात्कल्याणं वो हरिरनुनयेष्वेवमुदितः ॥

एवं स्थिते च 'न्यक्कारो ह्ययमेव' इत्यादिश्लोक[1]निर्दिष्टानां पदानां व्यङ्ग्यविशिष्टवाच्यप्रतिपादनेऽप्येतद्वाक्यार्थीभूतरसापेक्षया व्यञ्जकत्वमुक्तम् । न तेषां[2] पदानामर्थान्तरसंक्रमितवाच्यध्वनिभ्रमो विधातव्यः, विवक्षितवाच्यत्वात्तेषाम् । तेषु हि व्यङ्ग्यविशिष्टत्वं वाच्यस्य प्रतीयते न तु व्यङ्ग्यरूपपरिणतत्वम् । तस्माद्वाक्यं तत्र ध्वनिः, पदानि तु गुणीभूतव्यङ्ग्यानि । न च केवलं[3] गुणीभूतव्यङ्ग्यान्येव पदान्यलक्ष्यक्रमव्यङ्ग्यध्वनेर्व्यञ्जकानि यावदर्थान्तरसंक्रमितवाच्यानि ध्वनिप्रभेदरूपाण्यपि[4] । यथात्रैव श्लोके रावण इत्यस्य प्रभेदा[5]न्तररूप[6]व्यञ्जकत्वम् । यत्र तु वाक्ये रसादितात्पर्यं नास्ति गुणीभूतव्यङ्ग्यैः पदैरुद्भासितेऽपि तत्र गुणीभूतव्यङ्ग्यतैव समुदायधर्मः । यथा—

राजानमपि सेवन्ते विषमप्युपयुञ्जते[7] ।
रमन्ते च सह स्त्रीभिः कुशलाः खलु[8] मानवाः ॥

१. श्लोके – घ. २. 'न त्वेषां पदार्थानां' क-ख. ३. 'न च केवलपदान्यलक्ष्य' ग. ४. 'अपि तु' – ग. ५. ध्वनिप्रभेद – घ, KLV. ६. °न्तररूपस्य व्यञ्जकत्वम्–घ. ७१. °पभुञ्जते – घ. ८. 'हन्त' – ग.

The heart of a woman is indeed adamant;
So you may stop these attempts at allaying her anger;
May Hari who was addressed thus
During his conciliations preserve us.

Now it will be remembered that the different words found in the example– '*That I have foes is sufficient shame......*' have been spoken of as suggestive from this standpoint only, i. e. from that of sentiment etc, which happens to be the purport of the sentence as a whole, though in fact we have a communication there of the expressed also in association with the suggested content. One should not commit the mistake of regarding those words as instances of suggestion with expressed content merged in the unexpressed; for the truth is that all of them have an expressed content which is intended (as important). The expressed content in them is no doubt associated with the suggested, but in no way can we say that it has transformed itself into the suggested. Therefore, the sentence therein is Dhvani or container of principal suggestion, while the words are all examples of subordinated suggestion. Nor need one think that only words with subordinated suggestion can become revealers of the suggested content with undiscerned temporal sequentiality; for, words instancing other types of suggestion also such as that with the expressed merged in the unexpressed, can become its revealers in the same way. For example, in the illustration under consideration, the word Rāvaṇa which belongs to a type of suggetion other than subordinated suggestion, we have suggestiveness. But in a sentence where there is no primary purport of sentiment, etc, even if there should be the presence of words with subordinated suggestion, the sentence as a whole will come only under the category of subordinated suggestion (and not under that of principal suggestion). The following and such other instances might be cited as examples :

Even a king they serve,
They make use of even poison,
And they dally with women too ;
How clever of mankind all !

इत्यादौ । वाच्यव्यङ्ग्ययोः[1] प्राधान्याप्राधान्यविवेके परः प्रयत्नो विधातव्यः, तेन[2] ध्वनिगुणीभूतव्यङ्ग्ययोरलङ्काराणां चासङ्कीर्णो विषयः सुज्ञातो भवति । अन्यथा तु प्रसिद्धालङ्कारविषय एव व्यामोहः प्रवर्तते । यथा[3]—

लावण्यद्रविणव्ययो न गणितः क्लेशो महान् स्वीकृतः[4]
स्वच्छन्दस्य[5] सुखं जनस्य वसतः चिन्तानलो दीपितः ।
एषापि स्वयमेव[6] तुल्यरमणाभावाद्वराकी हता
कोऽर्थश्चेतसि वेधसा विनिहितस्तन्व्यास्तनुं तन्वता ॥

इत्यत्र[7] व्याजस्तुतिरलङ्कार इति व्याख्यायि केनाचित्, तन्न चतुरस्रम्; यतोऽस्याभिधेयस्यैतदलङ्कारस्वरूपमात्रपर्यवसायित्वे[8] न सुश्लिष्टता । यतो न तावदयं रागिणः कस्यचिद्विकल्पः । तस्य 'एषापि स्वयमेव तुल्यरमणाभावाद्वराकी हता' इत्येवंविधोक्त्यनुपपत्तेः । नापि नीरागस्य; तस्यैवंविधविकल्पपरिहारैकव्यापारत्वात् । न चायं श्लोकः क्वचित्प्रबन्ध इति श्रूयते, येन तत्प्रकरणानुगतार्थतास्य परिकल्प्यते । तस्मादप्रस्तुतप्रशंसेयम् । यस्मादनेन वाच्येन गुणीभूतात्मना निःसामान्य[9]गुणावलेपाध्मातस्य निजमहिमोत्कर्षजनित-

१. °व्यङ्ग्ययोश्च – घ.　२. येन – घ.　३. तथा हि – घ.　४. अर्जितः – घ. ५. 'स्वच्छन्दस्य सखीजनस्य वसताश्चिन्तानलो दीपितः' – क-ख.; स्वच्छन्दं चरतो जनस्य हृदये चिन्ताज्वरो निर्मितः – घ.　६. 'स्वगुणानुरूपरमाणाभावात्' – ग.　७. इत्ययं श्लोको व्याजस्तुत्यलंकार° तन्न चैतत् चतुरस्रम्' – ग.　८. °सायित्वेन – घ.　९. निः-सामान्य – घ.

Great attention should be paid in the matter of deciding the principal or subordinate nature of the expressed and suggested contents. It is only thus that the distinct scopes of principal suggestion, subordinated suggestion and figures of speech can be clearly grasped without confusing the one for the other. Otherwise, confusion will arise even in regard to well known figures themselves as in the following :—

No heed was paid to the lavish expense
Of the stuff of loveliness
And great pains were taken upon himself;
But in the result, only a torch of misery has been lit
In people who were so long living happy and free;
Even this luckless lady herself
Has been drowned in despair
For want of a befitting spouse.
What might have been the idea in the Creator's mind
When he brought the body of this charming lady into being?

A critic has remarked that the figure of speech in this example is Veiled Praise. But the remark is not proper. For, if it were true that the purport of this sentence is exhausted in the nature of this figure alone, there will be no complete agreement between the various parts of the sentence. Certainly, the alternatives found in the example cannot be looked upon as coming from the mouth of any passionate lover. For, no lover would ever say anything in the strain of — ' Even this luckless lady herself has been drowned in despair due to the absence of a befitting spouse '. Nor could they be from the mouth of an ascetic since the sole activity of an ascetic consists in avoiding such alternatives (relating to passion). We do not also know the original source from which this verse has been selected. Had we known the source, perhaps we might have been able to understand by it a sense in keeping with the context in which it occurred. For all these reasons, the figure instanced herein is indirect narration (in our opinion). By so looking upon it as an indirect narration we would clearly understand the fact that it is nothing but a lament on the part of a person who is puffed up with the

समत्सरजनज्वरस्य[1] विशेषज्ञमात्मनो न कञ्चिदेवापरं पश्यतः परिदेवितमेतदिति प्रकाश्यते । तथा चायं धर्मकीर्तेः श्लोक इति प्रसिद्धिः । सम्भाव्यते च तस्यैव । यस्मात्—

अनध्यवसितावगाहनमनल्पधीशक्तिना–
प्यदृष्टपरमार्थतत्त्वमधिकाभियोगैरपि ।
मतं मम जगत्यलब्धसदृशप्रतिग्राहकं
प्रयास्यति पयोनिधेः पय इव स्वदेहे जराम् ॥

इत्यनेनापि श्लोकेनैवंविधोऽभिप्रायः प्रकाशित एव । अप्रस्तुतप्रशंसायां च यद्वाच्यं तस्य कदाचिद्विवक्षितत्वं, कदाचिदविवक्षितत्वं, कदाचिद्विवक्षिताविवक्षितत्वमिति त्रयी बन्धच्छाया । तत्र विवक्षितत्वं यथा—

परार्थे यः पीडामनुभवति भङ्गेऽपि मधुरो[2]
यदीयः सर्वेषामिह खलु विकारोऽप्यभिमतः ।
न सम्प्राप्तो वृद्धिं यदि स भृशमक्षेत्रपतितः
किमिक्षोर्दोषोऽसौ न पुनरगुणाया मरुभुवः ॥

यथा वा ममैव—

अमी ये दृश्यन्ते ननु सुभगरूपाः सफलता
भवत्येषां यस्य क्षणमुपगतानां विषयताम् ।
निरालोके लोके[3] कथमिदमहो चक्षुरधुना
समं जातं सर्वैर्न सममथवान्यैरवयवैः ॥

अनयोर्हि द्वयोः श्लोकयोरिक्षुचक्षुषी विवक्षितस्वरूपे एव न च[4] प्रस्तुते । महागुणस्याविषयपतितत्वादप्राप्तपरभागस्य कस्यचित्स्वरूपमुपवर्णयितुं द्वयोरपि श्लोकयोस्तात्पर्येण प्रस्तुतत्वात् । अविवक्षितत्वं यथा—

---

१. 'समस्तसमत्सरज्वरस्य'–क-ख. २. 'मधुर इत्यादि'–ग–पुस्तके एतावदेवास्ति, न तु संपूर्णं पद्यम्. ३. 'देशे'–क-ख. ४. तु –घ.

pride of matchless merits in himself, who has brought fever upon jealous rivals by the excess of greatness achieved by him and who cannot find a single critic of sound judgement able to appreciate him fully. There is also a tradition which ascribes this verse to Dharmakīrti. It is most plausib e that it is really his composition. For the same idea has been adumbrated by him in other verses of his like the following one :—

With depth unfathomed
Even by one whose intelligence is vast,
With its essence ungrasped
Even by those of great industry,
My doctrine, alas, will grow old in my own body
Like the ocean's water,
Since it can never obtain a worthy recipient.

The expressed in Indirect Narration will reveal a threefold shade of construction :—(1) Intended (2) Unintendod and (3) Both intended and unintended at the same time. The first, viz., Intended is instanced in '*If that which suffers pain for other's sake*' etc., or in the following verse of mine :—

The things of beauty which are commonly seen
Find their fulfilment only when they become
Objects of sight at least for a trice.
But if the world should become void of light,
How can the eye see things any more ?
It will only be on a par with all other limbs
Or, perhaps, not even on a par with other limbs.

In the two verses just now referred to, the sugercane and the eye are intended in fact though they do not constitute the main subject of description. The main subject of description for both the verses is the pitiable state of a very meritorious person who does not receive any recognition of his merits by others owing to the undeserved environment into which he has been driven. The following is an instance of the second, viz., Unintended :—

कस्त्वं भोः कथयामि दैवहतकं मां विद्धि शाखोटकं
　　वैराग्यादिव वक्षि साधु विदितं कस्मादिदं कथ्यते ।
वामेनात्र वटस्तमध्वगजनः सर्वात्मना सेवते
　　न च्छायापि परोपकारकरिणी[2] मार्गस्थितस्यापि मे ॥

न हि वृक्षविशेषेण सहोक्तिप्रत्युक्ती सम्भवत इत्यविवक्षिताभिधेयेनैवानेन श्लोकेन समृद्धासत्पुरुषसमीपवर्तिनो[3] निर्धनस्य कस्याचिन्मनस्विनः परिदेवितं तात्पर्येण वाक्यार्थीकृतमिति प्रतीयते । विवक्षितत्वाविवक्षितत्वं यथा —

उप्पहजाआएँ असोहिणीएँ फलकुसुमपत्तरहिआए ।
वेरीएँ वइं देन्तो पामर हो ओहसिज्जिहासि ॥
उत्पथजाताया अशोभनायाः फलकुसुमपत्ररहितायाः ।
बदर्या वृत्तिं ददत् पामर भो अवहसिष्यसे ॥ [इति च्छाया]

अत्र हि वाच्यार्थो नात्यन्तं सम्भवी न चासम्भवी[4] । तस्माद्वाच्यव्यङ्ग्ययोः प्राधान्याप्राधान्ये यत्नतो निरूपणीये ।

प्रधानगुणभावाभ्यां व्यङ्ग्यस्यैवं व्यवस्थिते ।
काव्ये उभे ततोऽन्यद्यत्तच्चित्रमभिधीयते ॥ ४१ ॥

चित्रं शब्दार्थभेदेन द्विविधं च व्यवस्थितम् ।
तत्र किञ्चिच्छब्दचित्रं वाच्याचित्रमतः परम् ॥ ४२ ॥

व्यङ्ग्यस्यार्थस्य प्राधान्ये ध्वनिसंज्ञितः काव्यप्रकारः, गुणभावे तु गुणीभूतव्यङ्ग्यता । ततोऽन्यद्रसभावादितात्पर्यरहितं व्यङ्ग्यार्थविशेषप्रकाशन-

---

श्रूयताम्' -ग.　२. 'करणे' -क-ख.　३. 'वासिनो' -क-ख.　४. न चासम्भवी -ध. पुस्तके नास्ति ।　५. 'तु' -ग.

'Ho ! who may'st be thou ?'
'Well, listen—take me to be a luckless tree of ill-omen',
'Why, you seem to talk in a strain of disgust (with Life) !'
'Quite so !' 'what for ?' 'I shall tell you presently :—
Look at yonder banyan tree;
All the travellers flock to it for refuge.
Though I stand by the roadside,
Even my shade is not doing good to men'.

Since conversation with a tree is impossible, the verse with its unintended expressed content conveys by implication the purport, viz., that it is the lament of a self-respecting person who is in penury though he is a henchman of a very rich patron, because of the latter's wicked nature.

The following is an example of the expressed content which is both intended and unintended :—

You will become a butt of ridicule, O boor,
If you go on fencing (or nourishing) this thorny shrub
Which has sprung up in an out-of-the-way corner,
Which is so ugly and bereft
Of all fruits, flowers and leaves !

The expressed content in this verse is neither quite possible nor quite impossible.

We may conclude therefore by saying that the principal or subordinate nature of the expressed and the suggested contents should be carefully noted.

These two classes of poetry are decided thus on the principle of importance or unimportance of the suggested content. That which is other than both is given the name of Portrait (CITRA). 41

Portrait-like poetry is also seen to be two-fold inasmuch as it is based either on word or on meaning. The first variety is word-portrait and the second, meaning-portrait. 42

If the suggested content is all important, we get the class of poetry called *Dhvani* or poetry with principal suggestion; if the same is subordinate, we get the second class of poetry

शक्तिशून्यं च काव्यं केवलवाच्यवाचकवैचित्र्यमात्राश्रयेणोपनिबद्धमालेख्य[1]प्रख्यं यदाभासते तच्चित्रम् । न तन्मुख्यं काव्यम् । काव्यानुकारो ह्यसौ । तत्र किञ्चिच्छब्दचित्रं यथा दुष्करयमकादि । वाच्यचित्रं[2] शब्दचित्रादन्यद्व्यङ्ग्यार्थसंस्पर्शरहितं प्राधान्येन वाक्यार्थतया स्थितं रसादितात्पर्यरहितमुत्प्रेक्षादि ।

अथ किमिदं चित्रं नाम ? यत्र न प्रतीयमानार्थसंस्पर्शः । प्रतीयमानो ह्यर्थस्त्रिभेदः प्राक्प्रदर्शितः । तत्र यत्र वस्त्वलङ्कारान्तरं वा व्यङ्ग्यं नास्ति स नाम चित्रस्य कल्प्यतां विषयः । यत्र तु रसादीनामविषयत्वं स काव्यप्रकारो न सम्भवत्येव । यस्मादवस्तुसंस्पर्शिता काव्यस्य[3] नोपपद्यते[4] । वस्तु च सर्वमेव जगद्गतमवश्यं कस्यचिद्रसस्य भावस्य वा[5] अङ्गत्वं[6] प्रतिपद्यते, अन्ततो[7] विभावत्वेन[8] । चित्तवृत्तिविशेषा हि रसादयः, न च तदस्ति वस्तु किञ्चिद्यन्न चित्तवृत्तिविशेषमुपजनयति तदनुत्पादने[9] वा कविविषयतैव तस्य न स्यात् कविविषयश्च चित्रतया कश्चिन्निरूप्यते ।

अत्रोच्यते — सत्यं न तादृक्काव्यप्रकारो[10]ऽस्ति यत्र रसादीनामप्रतीतिः[11] । किं तु यदा रसभावादिविवक्षाशून्यः कविः शब्दालङ्कारमर्थालङ्कारं-

---

१. 'आलेख्यमिवं' – ग. २. ततः शब्द° – BP. & घ. ३ 'तावत्काव्यस्य' – ग. ४. 'नापाद्यते' – क-ख. ५. 'भावस्य वा' घ – पुस्तके नास्ति । ६. 'वाङ्गत्वं' – ग. ७. अन्ततो घ – पुस्तके नास्ति । ८. 'अतो विभावत्वेन' – क-ख. ९. 'तदुपादाने च' – ग. १०. 'काव्यवाक्प्रकारः' – क-ख. ११. विप्रतिपत्तिः – घ.

called *Guṇībhūta-vyaṅgya* or poetry with subordinate suggestion; that class of poetry which is seen to differ from either, and which is destitute of purport relating to sentiments and emotions, etc., which is devoid of the power to reveal any suggested content and which owes its construction only to the strikingness of the expressed meanings and expressions denoting them, gets the name of *citra* or Portrait. It is not poetry at all, strictly speaking. It is only an imitation of poetry. One of the sub-divisions of this poetry of portraiture is word-portrait such as Rhyming Repetition and so on whose employment involves much labour. The second subdivision differs from word–portrait and may be called meaning–portrait. It will also be devoid of even a touch of the suggested content and will be wanting in the purport of sentiments etc. Poetic Fancy and such other figures are illustrations of this.

An objector may argue as follows :—

" Now what is this portrait–like poetry ? That in which were is not a touch of suggested content. The suggested content has been already shown to be three-fold. Of these three types, instances where the first two types of suggested content, viz., ideas and figures are absent, may by all means be imagined as instances of Portrait-like poetry. But indeed no class of poetry is possible in which sentiments etc., are not involved. For, we cannot of course regard poetry as devoid of content itself. And all subjects in the universe become ultimately connected with some sentiment or emotion, at least in the form of stimulii. Sentiments are indeed so many states of mind; and nothing in the world can be imagined which does not bring about a particular state of mind in man. In case a thing does not have any effect on one's state of mind, it cannot become a subject at all for the poet's activity. When something has become a subject for the poet's activity, how can we speak of it as portrait ?"

This is what we would say in reply : It is no doubt true that no species of poetry exists which absolutely does not convey sentiment. But all the same, if the poet is seen

वोपनिबध्नाति तदा तद्विवक्षापेक्षया रसादिशून्यतार्थस्य परिकल्प्यते । विवक्षोपारूढ एव हि काव्ये शब्दानामर्थः । वाच्यसामर्थ्यवशेन[1] च कविविवक्षाविरहेऽपि तथाविधे विषये रसादिप्रतीतिर्[2]भवन्ती परिदुर्बला भवतीत्यनेनापि प्रकारेण नीरसत्वं परिकल्प्य चित्रविषयो व्यवस्थाप्यते । तदिदमुक्तम्—

" रसभावादिविषयविवक्षाविरहे सति ।
अलङ्कारनिबन्धो यः स चित्रविषयो मतः ॥
रसादिषु विवक्षा तु स्यात्तात्पर्यवती यदा ।
तदा नास्त्येव तत्काव्यं ध्वनेर्यत्तु[3] न गोचरः ॥ "

एतच्च[4] चित्रं कवीनां विशृङ्खलगिरां[5] रसादितात्पर्यमनपेक्ष्यैव[6] काव्यप्रवृत्तिदर्शनादस्माभिः परिकल्पितम् । इदानीन्तनानां तु न्याय्ये काव्यनयव्यवस्थापने क्रियमाणे नास्त्येव ध्वनिव्यतिरिक्तः काव्यप्रकारः । यतः परिपाकवतां कवीनां रसादितात्पर्यविरहे व्यापार एव न शोभते । रसादितात्पर्ये न च[7] नास्त्येव तद्वस्तु यदभिमतरसाङ्गतां नीयमानं प्रगुणीभवति । अचेतना अपि हि भावा यथायथमुचितरसविभावतया[8] चेतनवृत्तान्तयोजनया वा न सन्त्येव ते ये यान्ति न रसाङ्गताम् । तथा चेदमुच्यते —

---

१. 'सामर्थ्येन कवि' - ग. २. 'रसभावप्रतीतिः' - क - ख. ३. 'यत्तु' - ग. ४. 'यतश्च' - क-ख. ५. 'विशृङ्खलं नितरां' ग. ६. 'अनवेक्ष्यैव' ग. ७. 'साति' - क-ख. ८. भावतया - घ.

without any exclusive intention of conveying sentiments, emotions, etc., and is more keen on employing figures only, either of sound or sense, we may take it (for all practical purposes) that the content is devoid of sentiments etc., in view of the keenness on employment of figures. The content of words in poetry is based only upon the poet's intention. Though some sort of apprehension of sentiments etc. is possible by force of the expressed sense itself even in instances wherein no such keen intention towards them is present on the poet's part, still it will be negligibly slender and from this standpoint also, one might justify the existence of a scope for Portrait-like Poetry. This is summed up in the following aphorisms :—

1. *The employment of figures in the absence of intention towards the purport of sentiments, emotions, etc., should be regarded as an illustration of Portrait-like Poetry.*

2. *If on the other hand, there exists a sole intention towards sentiments, etc., no poetry can remain outside the sphere of Dhvani or poetry of principal suggestion.*

This class of Poetry, i. e., Portrait-like poetry, has been noted at all by us because of the practice of poets who recognise no laws in their usage of words and who go about composing poems without any intention of incorporating sentiments, etc., therein. But if we should strictly apply the new principle of poetry laid down here, there can be no class of poetry other than *Dhvani* or poetry with principal suggestion. For, in the absense of whole-hearted intention towards sentiments etc., the very activity of poets will not appear charming; and contrariwise, in the presence of whole–hearted intention towards sentiments etc., there will be no subject which will not attain exceeding charm by being made an accessory of the intended sentiment. Even amongst insentient objects, there are none which will not become accessories of sentiment either by acting as stimuli towards the intended sentiment or at least by a metaphorical application of the behaviour of sentient objects to themselves. Hence it is that we say—

“ अपारे काव्यसंसारे कवि[1]रेकः प्रजापतिः ।
यथास्मै रोचते विश्वं तथेदं परिवर्तते ॥
शृङ्गारी चेत्कविः काव्ये जातं रसमयं जगत् ।
स एव वीतरागश्चेन्नीरसं सर्वमेव तत् ॥
भावानचेतनानपि चेतनवच्चेतनानचेतनवत् ।
व्यवहारयति यथेष्टं सुकविः काव्ये स्वतन्त्रतया ॥ ”

तस्मान्नास्त्येव तद्वस्तु यत्सर्वात्मना रसतात्पर्यवतः कवेस्तदिच्छया तदभिमतरसाङ्गतां न धत्ते । तथोपनिबध्यमानं वा न चारुत्वातिशयं पुष्णाति । सर्वमेतच्च महाकवीनां काव्येषु दृश्यते । अस्माभिरपि स्वेषु काव्यप्रबन्धेषु यथायथं दर्शितमेव । स्थिते चैवं सर्व एव काव्यप्रकारो न ध्वनिधर्मतामतिपतति; रसाद्यपे[2]क्षायां कवेर्गुणीभूतव्यङ्ग्यलक्षणोऽपि प्रकारस्तदङ्गतामवलम्बत इत्युक्तं प्राक्[3] । यदा तु चाटुषु देवतास्तुतिषु वा रसादीनामङ्गतया व्यवस्थानं हृदयवतीषु च षट्प्रज्ञादि[4]गाथासु कासुचिद्व्यङ्ग्यविशिष्टवाच्ये[5] प्राधान्यं तदपि गुणीभूतव्यङ्ग्यस्य ध्वनिनिष्यन्दभूतत्वमेवेत्युक्तं प्राक् । तदेवमिदानींतनकविकाव्यनयोपदेशे क्रियमाणे प्राथमिकानामभ्यासार्थिनां यदि परं चित्रेण व्यवहारः, प्राप्तपरिणतीनां तु ध्वनिरेव काव्य[6]मिति स्थितमेतत् । तदयमत्र संग्रहः —

यस्मिन् रसो वा भावो वा तात्पर्येण प्रका[7]शते ।
संवृत्त्या[8]भिहितं वस्तु यत्रालङ्कार एव वा ॥
काव्या[9]ध्वनि ध्वनि[10]र्व्यङ्ग्यप्राधान्यैकनिबन्धनः ।
सर्वत्र तत्र वि[11]षयी ज्ञेयः सहृदयैर्जनैः ॥

---

१. कविरेव – घ. २. रसाद्यपेक्षया – घ. ३. अवलम्बते प्राक् – घ. ४. षट्-प्रज्ञकगाथासु – BP. ५. वाच्यात् – घ. ६. प्राधान्येन काव्यमिति – घ. ७. प्रकाश्यते – घ. ८. भिहितौ – BP. ९. काव्याद्ध्वनिः – घ. १०. ध्वनेर्व्यङ्ग्यं – घ. ११. ‘ विजयी ’ .ग.

In the boundless realm of poetry, the poet alone is the creator, and as it pleaseth him, so doth this world revolve.

If the poet be intent upon the erotic sentiment in his poem, the whole world will be suffused with that sentiment. But if he be void of emotion (in his poem), the world too will be devoid of sentiment. A good poet will freely design even insentient objects to act as sentient ones and sentient objects to act as insentient ones.

Thus it is clear that there is absolutely no such subject which does not become an accessory of the intended sentiment by the poet's desire so long as his concern is solely with sentiment. Nor does it ever fail to acquire exceeding charm when so handled. All this is seen in the works of first–rate poets. In our own poetic compositions too, we have tried to illustrate these principles as far as possible. Thus viewed, all classes of poetry will come only within the sphere of *Dhvani* or poetry with principal suggestion. From this standpoint of sentiment etc. on the part of the poet, even the class designated by the name of 'poetry of subordinated suggestion' will come only under the sphere of *Dhvani*, as we already said. It has also been said that in quatrains of affectionate praise and devotional hymns, if sentiments etc. are regarded as subordinate and that in Prakrit verses known as *Hr̥dayavatīs* and in some gnomic verses of worldly–wise men, if the expressed sense itself with an undercurrent of suggested content strikes us as important, the reason is to be sought in the fact that the poetry of subordinated suggestion too is a derivative of *Dhvani* itself. Thus, when we strictly apply the new principle of poetry enunciated here, we can speak of Portrait–like Poetry only in a loose way, only as an aid to the understanding of beginners in the study of poetry. So far as persons with well–developed intellects are concerned, *Dhvani* or poetry with principal suggestion alone will deserve the title of Poetry. So, the following sums up the position :—

Refined critics should understand that Dhvani whose sole condition is the principal nature of the suggested content embraces all instances of poetry wherein is found a purposively conveyed sentiment or at least an idea or figure conveyed in a covert fashion.

सगुणीभूतव्यङ्ग्यैः सालङ्कारैः सह प्रभेदैः[1] स्वैः ।
सङ्करसंसृष्टिभ्यां पुनरप्युद्द्योतते बहुधा ॥ ४३ ॥

तस्य च ध्वनेः स्वप्रभेदैर्गुणीभूतव्यङ्ग्येन वाच्यालङ्कारैश्च[2] सङ्करसंसृष्टिव्यवस्थायां क्रियमाणायां बहुप्रभेदता लक्ष्ये दृश्यते । तथाहि स्वप्रभेदसङ्कीर्णः, स्वप्रभेदसंसृष्टो गुणीभूतव्यङ्ग्यसङ्कीर्णो गुणीभूतव्यङ्ग्यसंसृष्टो वाच्यालङ्कारान्तरसङ्कीर्णो वाच्यालङ्कारान्तरसंसृष्टः संसृष्टालङ्कारसङ्कीर्णः संसृष्टालङ्कारसंसृष्टश्चेति[3] बहुधा ध्वनिः प्रकाशते ।

तत्र स्वप्रभेदसङ्कीर्णत्वं कदाचिदनुग्राह्यानुग्राहकभावेन । यथा 'एवंवादिनि देवर्षौ' इत्यादौ । अत्र ह्यर्थशक्त्युद्भवानुरणनरूपव्यङ्ग्यध्वनिप्रभेदेनालक्ष्यक्रमव्यङ्ग्यध्वनिप्रभेदोऽनुगृह्यमाणः ।

खणपाहुणिआ देअर एसा जाआएँ किंपि दे भणिदा ।
रुअइ पडोहरवलहीघरम्मि अणुणिज्जउ वराई ॥
[क्षणप्राघुणिका देवर एषा जायया किमपि ते भणिता ।
रोदिति शून्यवलभीगृहेऽनुनीयतां वराकी ॥ [इति च्छाया ।]

अत्र ह्यनुनीयतामित्येतत्पदमर्थान्तरसङ्क्रमितवाच्यत्वेन विवक्षितान्यपरवाच्यत्वेन च सम्भाव्यते । न चान्यतरपक्षनिर्णये[4] प्रमाणमस्ति । एकव्यञ्जकानुप्रवेशेन[5] तु व्यङ्ग्यत्वमलक्ष्यक्रमव्यङ्ग्यस्य[6] स्वप्रभेदान्तरापेक्षया बाहुल्येन

---

१. प्रभेदः – BP. २. 'वाच्यालङ्कारान्तरैश्च' –क-ख. ३. 'संकीर्णालंकारसंसृष्टश्चेति' – ग. ४. 'निश्चये' – क-ख. ५. 'कदाचिद्द्विभिन्नयोरेकश एकव्यञ्जकानु'. ग. ६. 'व्यञ्जकत्वं' – क-ख.

It shines in divers ways with its several varieties of subordinated suggestion, Figures, its own sub-varieties, their inter-mingling and collocation. 43

If one should take into account the permutations and combinations of the different types of *Dhvani* itself and the varieties of subordinated suggestion and Figures of sense, their resulting number would be many. Thus to name some of the major manifestations of Dhvani—(1) Merged with its own varieties, (2) Co-existing with its own varieties, (3) Merged with subordinated suggestion, (4) Co-existing with subordinated suggestion, (5) Merged with other figures of sense, (6) Co-existing with other figures (7) Merged with other co-existing figures (8) Co-existing with other mutually co-existing figures.

The first manifestation will sometimes involve the relationship of the governor–governed as in—'*As the divine sage*' *etc.* Here the variety of Dhvani, viz., resonance–like suggestion based upon the power of sense governs the other variety of *Dhvani*, viz., suggestion with undiscerned sequentiality.

Sometimes the relationship existing between the two may be one of doubt that both are simultaneously applicable as in the following example :—

O Brother-in-law ! this lady
Just came out to see the procession,
When your wife said something in her ear;
And she is weeping so loud.
Pray, you comfort the piteous lady
In the empty terraced-house close by.

The expression—" Pray, comfort her " may be imagined both as an instance of suggestion with its expressed content merged in the unexpressed and as an instance of suggestion with the expressed content intended but further–extending. There is no positive ground for deciding one way or the other.

Often we see that several varieties of suggestion with undiscerned sequentiality do all enter into a single suggestive word as in the verse—'*The quarters are smeared*' etc. 'Co-existence with its own varieties' is also instanced in this verse itself. Here

सम्भवति । यथा—‘ स्निग्धश्यामल ’ इत्यादौ । स्वप्रभेदसंसृष्टत्वं च यथा पूर्वोदाहरण एव । अत्र ह्यर्थान्तरसंक्रामितवाच्यस्यात्यन्ततिरस्कृतवाच्यस्य च संसर्गः । गुणीभूतव्यङ्ग्यसङ्कीर्णत्वं यथा– ‘ न्यक्कारो ह्ययमेव मे यदरयः ’ इत्यादौ । यथा वा —

कर्ता द्यूतच्छलानां जतुमयशरणोद्दीपनः सोऽभिमानी
कृष्णाकेशोत्तरीयव्यपनयनपटुः पाण्डवा यस्य दासाः ।
राजा दुःशासनादेर्गुरुरनुजशतस्याङ्गराजस्य मित्रं
क्वास्ते दुर्योधनोऽसौ कथयत न रुषा द्रष्टुमभ्यागतौ स्वः ॥

अत्र ह्यलक्ष्यक्रमव्यङ्ग्यस्य वाक्यार्थीभूतस्य व्यङ्ग्यविशिष्टवाच्याभिधायिभिः पदैः सम्मिश्रता । अत एव च पदार्थाश्रयत्वे गुणीभूतव्यङ्ग्यस्य वाक्यार्थाश्रयत्वे च ध्वनेः सङ्कीर्णतायामपि न विरोध[2]ः स्वप्रभेदान्तरवत् । यथाहि[3] ध्वनिप्रभेदान्तराणि परस्परं सङ्कीर्यन्ते पदार्थवाक्यार्थाश्रयत्वेन च न विरुद्धानि ।

किं चैकव्यङ्ग्याश्रयत्वे तु प्रधानगुणभावो विरुध्यते न तु व्यङ्ग्यभेदापेक्षया ततोऽप्यस्य न विरोधः । अयं च सङ्करसंसृष्टिव्यवहारो बहूनामेकत्र वाच्यवाचकभाव इव व्यङ्ग्यव्यञ्जकभावेऽपि निर्विरोध एव मन्तव्यः । यत्र[4] तु पदानि कानिचिदविवक्षितवाच्यान्यनुरणनरूपव्यङ्ग्यवाच्यानि वा तत्र

१. संक्रमिता – घ.　　२. संकीर्णतायामविरोधः – घ.　　३. ‘ तथा हि ’ – क-ख.
४. ‘ यत्तु ’ – ग.

indeed we find a collocation of two varieties of suggestion viz., that with its expressed content merged in the unexpressed and that with its expressed content wholly lost. '*That there are enemies*', etc. illustrate the mingling of *Dhvani* with subordinated suggestion. Here is another example :—

Do tell us where that Duryodhana is,
That designer of the gambling ruse,
That burner of the lac-dwelling,
That self-conceited one,
That expert in undraping Draupadī
And loosing her braids of hair,
That master whose slaves are Pāṇḍavas,
That "King", that eldest of a hundred brothers
like Duśśāsana,
And that friend of Karṇa;
We have come here to see him truly,
And not out of anger.

In this example the suggested content with undiscerned sequentiality conveyed by the sentence as a whole is found mixed up with words that denote the expressed with an undercurrent of the suggested. Though there is thus an intermingling of the subordinated suggestion got through word- content, and principal suggestion got through sentence–purport, there is no opposition between them just as no opposition will be involved in the intermingling of two varieties of *Dhvani* itself. Just as varieties of Dhvani can intermingle without opposition, so also can other manifestations of suggestion based upon word-content and sentence-content intermingle without any opposition.

Furthermore, opposition between the principal and subordinate elements is possible only when the suggested content of the two happens to be one and the same, not when the suggested contents of the two are different from each other. Hence it should be understood that as in the case of denoted-denoter relationship, so in the case of suggested-suggester relationship also, the expressions 'intermingling' and 'collocation do not involve any opposition.

ध्वनिगुणीभूतव्यङ्ग्ययोः संसृष्टत्वम् । यथा — ‘ तेषां गोपवधूविलाससुहृदाम् ’ इत्यादौ । अत्र हि ‘ विलाससुहृदां ’ ‘ राधारहःसाक्षिणाम् ’ इत्येते पदे ध्वनिप्रभेदरूपे; ‘ ते ’, ‘ जाने ’ इत्येते च पदे गुणीभूतव्यङ्ग्यरूपे ।

वाच्यालङ्कारसङ्कीर्णत्वमलक्ष्यक्रमव्यङ्ग्यापेक्षया रसवति सालङ्कारे[1] काव्ये सर्वत्र[2] सुव्यवस्थितम् । प्रभेदान्तराणामपि कदाचित्सङ्कीर्णत्वं भवत्येव । यथा ममैव—

या व्यापारवती रसान् रसयितुं[3] काचित्कवीनां नवा
दृष्टिर्या परिनिष्ठितार्थ[4]विषयोन्मेषा च[5] वैपश्चिती ।
ते द्वे अप्यवलम्ब्य विश्वमनिशं निर्वर्णयन्तो वयं
श्रान्ता नैव च लब्धमब्धिशयन त्वद्भक्तितुल्यं सुखम् ॥

इत्यत्र विरोधालङ्कारेणार्थान्तरसंक्रमितवाच्यस्य ध्वनिप्रभेदस्य सङ्कीर्णत्वम्[6] ।

वाच्यालङ्कारसंसृष्टत्वं च पदापेक्षयैव । यत्र हि कानिचित्पदानि वाच्यालङ्कारभाञ्जि कानिचिच्च ध्वनिप्रभेदयुक्तानि । यथा—

दीर्घीकुर्वन् पटु मदकलं कूजितं सारसानां[7]
प्रत्यूषेषु स्फुटितकमलामोदमैत्रीकषायः ।
यत्र स्त्रीणां हरति सुरतग्लानिमङ्गानुकूलः
सिप्रावार्तः[8] प्रियतम इव प्रार्थनाचाटुकारः ॥

---

१. रसालङ्कारे च -घ. २. सर्वत्रैव -घ. ३. ‘ ग्रसयितुं ’ ग. ४. ‘ परिनिश्चितार्थ ’ -क-ख. ५. ‘ अस्ति ’ -ग. ६. ‘ असंकीर्णत्वम् ’ ग. ७. ‘ सारसीनां ’ -ग. ८. ‘ शिप्रावातः ’ -ग.

Examples where some of the words have unintended expressed content or an expressed content implying resonance-like suggested content, will instance Collocation of principal suggestion and subordinated suggestion. '*How do they do*', etc. are examples. In this example the expressions—'those companions of the sports' and 'those witnesses of Rādhā's amours' carry principal suggestion while the words 'all those' and 'I am afraid' carry subordinated suggestion.

The intermingling of figures of sense and suggestion with undiscerned sequentiality is most commonly met with in all poetry which is full of sentiments and adorned by figures. Other varieties of suggestion too can intermingle with figures as in the following verse of my own composition :

That fresh outlook of poets
Whose activity suceeds in enjoying sentiments all,
And that learned outlook which proceeds
Towards probing the truth of objects verily—
Both these outlooks we have tried to utilize
In figuring out the world so long
And we have become exhausted in the attemptt
O Lord, reclining on the sea,
We never obtained in any of these,
Happiness comparable to devotion to Thee.

In this example, the figure paradox is found intermingled with the variety of suggestion, viz., that with the expressed content merged in the unexpressed.

Collocation of Suggestion with figures of sense is possible only in regard to words. In examples of this kind, some of the words will contain figures of sense while some others will contain varieties of suggestion. For instance—

Lengthening artfully the sweet and excited notes of the cranes,
And perfumed all over by friendship with the scent of new-blown lotuses at dawn,
The wind over Siprā, so agreeable to the body,
Will remove the women's fatigue of limbs due to amorous sports
As if he were a dear lover
Proficient in the art of coaxing.

अत्र हि मैत्रीपदमविवक्षितवाच्यो ध्वनिः। पदान्तरेष्वलङ्कारान्तराणि। संसृष्टालंकारान्तरसंकीर्णो ध्वनिर्यथा—

दन्तक्षतानि करजैश्च विपाटितानि
प्रोद्भिन्नसान्द्रपुलके भवतः शरीरे।
दत्तानि रक्तमनसा मृगराजवध्वा
जातस्पृहैर्मुनिभिरप्यवलोकितानि॥

अत्र हि समासोक्तिसंसृष्टेन विरोधालंकारेण संकीर्णस्यालक्ष्यक्रमव्यङ्ग्यस्य ध्वनेः प्रकाशनम्[1]। दयावीरस्य परमार्थतो वाक्यार्थीभूतत्वात्[2]। संसृष्टालङ्कारसंसृष्टत्वं च ध्वनेर्यथा —

अहिणअपओअर[3]सिएसु पहिअसामाइएसु दिअहेसु।
सोहइ पसारिअगिआणं णच्चिअं मोरवन्दाणम्॥
[अभिनवपयोदरसितेषु पथिकश्यामायितेषु दिवसेषु।
शोभते प्रसारितग्रीवाणां (गीतानां) नृत्तं मयूरवृन्दानाम्॥ '
[इति च्छाया]

अत्र ह्युपमारूपकाभ्यां शब्दशक्त्युद्भवानुरणनरूपव्यङ्ग्यस्य ध्वनेः संसृष्टत्वम्।

एवं ध्वनेः प्रभेदाः प्रभेदभेदाश्च केन शक्यन्ते।
संख्यातुं दिङ्मात्रं तेषामिदमुक्तमस्माभिः॥ ४४॥

अनन्ता हि ध्वनेः प्रकाराः; सहृदयानां व्युत्पत्तये तेषां[4] दिङ्मात्रं कथितम्।

१. 'प्रकाशनेन' - क-ख. २. 'भूतत्वम' - क-ख. ३. °अररासिएसु - घ.
४. 'ते स्वयमुत्प्रेक्षणीयाः' - क-ख.

Principal suggestion which we have defined hitherto should be attentively studied not only by all the poets who aspire after writing good poetry but also by all the critics who aspire after understanding it well. 45

It is only by their skill in recognising principal suggestion defined above that good poets and good critics attain abiding glory in matters relating to poetry.

Those who were unable to explain properly this essential principle of poetry as they had only a glimmer of it (and nothing more), have brought into vogue the theory of styles. 46

We have explained above the fundamental principle of poetry by using the term DHVANI. Since only vague glimmerings of this principle were had by ancient writers, they could not explain it exhaustively and thus did they bring into vogue the theory of three Styles, Viz., *Vaidarbhī*, *Gauḍī* and *Pāñcālī*. While the theorists of style show only vague flashes of this very principle of poetry, we have very clearly demonstrated it in all its bearings and hence there is nothing for us to consider seriously about the theory of styles.

Once this theory of poetry is fully understood, even the so-called " Modes " relating to the nature of sounds as well as to the nature of meanings will become intelligible. 47

When this theory of poetry involving a discrimination of the suggested-suggester relationship is grasped, other categories like literary modes, viz., those relating to sound such as *Upanāgarikā* as well as those relating to sense such as *Kaiśikī* will become quite intelligible (even in the same way as the styles). Otherwise, Modes will remain only incredible like unseen objects, and will not come within the range of personal experience (though there might be testimony of the ancients to that effect). Therefore, the nature of principal suggestion should be understood clearly.

The definition of *Dhvani* by another critic, viz. ' it is that kind of poetry wherein some indefinable charm is brought about both in words and in meanings, a charm which is discernible only to select critics even like the preciousness of rare gems ', does not deserve consideration here as it is untenable. For, the uniqueness in the very nature of words which distinguishes one word from another is nothing but the absence of unintelligibility and tautology. Similarly, the positive excellences of words are harmony, and suggestivity. The unique excellences of meanings are perspicuity, suggestiveness and association with the suggested element. These unique characteristics of both words and meanings are quite definable and in fact they have been defined in several ways. If one should still imagine that there is some other indefinable uniqueness in words and meanings, it will only indicate that the man has taken leave of his good sense. For indefinability in the sense of 'inexpressibility by all words' is never indeed possible logically; since at least the word 'indefinable' itself will have ultimately expressed it, if not any other. If one should modify the notion of 'indefinability' to mean 'indeterminate or general experience of something which eludes specific usage of words', this view also agrees only with the unique charm of gems and not with the charm of poetry, since the latter has been explained by several writers on poetics quite determinately unlike the former whose values are never fixed only by general considerations. There is of course similarity between the two in the fact that their worth can be recognised only by select connoisseurs. There is not scope for any conflict of opinion at all in regard to the fact that only jewellers can recognise the worth of gems and that refined critics alone can appreciate the sentiments in poems.

As regards the well-known theory of the Buddhists that every thing-as-such in the world is indefinable, we shall take it up for discussion in our other work concerned with a review of Buddhist theories. It is not taken up here because of our fear that any exhibition here of our learning in other works might only offend the minds of the refined critics. We will only say that our definition of DHVANI will be at least on a par with the definitions of perception, etc., proposed by the Buddhist philosophers themselves.

Thus it might be taken that the definition of Dhvani propounded here is valid since no other definition will hold good for it and since it is not subsumed by the conventional meanings of words. The following sums up the conclusion :—

Indefinable manifestation is not a definition of Dhvani since its content can be defined. The definition given already should be deemed as the correct one.

चतुर्थोद्द्योतः

एवं ध्वनिं सप्रपञ्चं विप्रतिपत्तिनिरासार्थं व्युत्पाद्य तद्व्युत्पादने प्रयोजनान्तरमुच्यते —

ध्वनेर्यः सगुणीभूतव्यङ्ग्यस्याध्वा प्रदर्शितः।
अनेनानन्त्यमायाति कवीनां प्रतिभागुणः ॥ १ ॥

य एष ध्वनेर्गुणीभूतव्यङ्ग्यस्य च मार्गः[1] प्रकाशितः, तस्य फलान्तरं कविप्रतिभानन्त्यम्।

कथमिति चेत् —

अतो ह्यन्यतमेनापि प्रकारेण विभूषिता।
वाणी नवत्वमायाति पूर्वार्थान्वयवत्यपि ॥ २ ॥

अतो[2] ध्वनेरुक्तप्रभेदमध्यादन्यतमेनापि प्रकारेण विभूषिता सती वाणी पुरातनकविनिबद्धार्थसंस्पर्शवत्यपि नवत्वमायाति।

तथाह्यविवक्षितवाच्यस्य ध्वनेः प्रकारद्वयसमाश्रयणेन[3] नवत्वं पूर्वार्थानुगमेऽपि[4] यथा—

स्मितं किञ्चिन्मुग्धं तरलमधुरो दृष्टिविभवः
परिस्पन्दो वाचामभिनवविलासोर्मिसरसः[5]।
गतानामारम्भः किसलयितलीलापरिमलः[6]
स्पृशन्त्यास्तारुण्यं किमिव हि न रम्यं मृगदृशः ॥

---

१. अध्वा.–ग. २. अतो हि–घ. ३. श्रयेण–क–ख. ४. पूर्वोक्तानुगमेऽपि–क–ख. ५. विलासोक्ति°–घ. ६. °परिकरः–घ.

THE FOURTH FLASH

The theory of principal suggestion has been propounded thus far in all its bearings with a view to clearing up conflicting opinions. In what follows, the other practical uses to which such a theory might be put is explained :—

By the ways of principal suggestion as also subordinated suggestion shown thus far, the quality of creative imagination in poets will assume endlessness. 1

Endlessness of creative imagination in poets will be another outcome of the theory of principal and subordinated suggestion laid down already.

If one should ask—' how is it ? ', (here is our reply :)

By a mere touch of even a single variety of suggestion (among the many that have been enumerated), the poet's expression will acquire novelty though it might perhaps embody only a trite idea. 2

The expression of a poet will appear quite novel though it might embody an idea already found in an earlier poet, if it is adorned by at least a single variety of suggestion from among the many varieties that have been mentioned.

How a touch of the two varieties of suggestion with unintended expressed content endows novelty even to themes corresponding to those known already is illustrated in the following :—

Her gentle smile is winsome
And the grace of her looks tremulous and sweet,
Her utterance of words is ebullient with novel arts and emotion;
The course of her movements is like the sweet perfume
That spreads out of an opening bud.
Indeed as the deer-eyed lady steps into her youth,
Is there anything that does not look lovely ?

इत्यस्य—

सविभ्रमस्मितोद्भेदा लोलाक्ष्यः प्रस्खलद्गिरः ।
नितम्बालसगामिन्यः कामिन्यः कस्य न प्रियाः ॥

इत्येवमादिषु श्लोकेषु सत्स्वपि तिरस्कृतवाच्यध्वनिसमाश्रयेण अपूर्वत्वमेव प्रतिभासते ।

तथा —

यः प्रथमः प्रथमः स तु तथाहि हतहस्तिबहलपललाशी ।[1]
श्वापदगणेषु सिंहः सिंहः केनाधरीक्रियते ॥

इत्यस्य[2],

स्वतेजःक्रीतमहिमा केनान्येनातिशय्यते ।
महद्भिरपि मातङ्गैः सिंहः किम[3]भिभूयते ॥

इत्येवमादिषु श्लोकेषु सत्स्वपि अर्थान्तरसङ्क्रमितवाच्यध्वनिसमाश्रयेण नवत्वम् ।[4]

विवक्षितान्यपरवाच्यस्याप्युक्तप्रकारसमाश्रयेण नवत्वं यथा[5] —

निद्राकैतविनः प्रियस्य वदने विन्यस्य वक्त्रं वधूः
बोधत्रासनिरुध्दचुम्बनरसाप्याभोगलोलं स्थिता ।
वैलक्ष्याद्विमुखीभवेदिति पुनस्तस्याप्यनारम्भिणः
साकाङ्क्षप्रतिपत्ति नाम हृदयं यातं तु पारं रतेः ॥

---

१. तथाभिहतहस्ततर्पितपलाशी – ग. २. अस्य – ग. ३. केनाभिभूयते – घ.
४. एतद्वाक्यं – क. ख. पुस्तकयोर्नास्ति. ५. तत्रालक्ष्यक्रमप्रकारसमाश्रयेणान्यथात्वम् । यथा – घ.

This verse has acquired a novelty all its own thanks to the touch of suggestion with unintended expressed content, notwithstanding the existence of an earlier verse embodying the same idea. Here is the earlier verse :—

To whom are women not dear,
With their graceful smiles and tremulous looks,
With their faltering words and lingering steps
Under the weight of heavy hips ?

So also the following verse (1) appears novel because of its association with suggestion in which the expressed content is merged in the unexpressed despite the existence of an earlier verse (viz., 2) unfolding the same idea :—

1 *He that is first is first indeed;*
Among the host of beasts,
He that subsists upon the profuse flesh
Of elephants by himself killed,
Is the lion in truth;
By whom will the lion be baffled then ?

2 *Can one who has won glory by the wealth of his own valour*
Be outshone by anyone else ?
Will ever the lion be defeated
Even by the mightiest elephant ?

Novelty is seen in the same way by a touch of these varieties of suggestion with intended but further-extending expressed content; the first is the new verse and the second an old one embodying the same idea :—

1 *The bride placed her face over her lover's,*
Feigning sleep as he lay,
And stayed so for a while close to his forehead,
Her eagerness to kiss him being halted
By her fear that he might wake up.
He too would not make a move
Fearing that she might turn away her face
Because of bashfulness.
His heart in that acute suspense
Reached the acme of delight !

इत्यादेः[1] श्लोकस्य —

शून्यं वासगृहं विलोक्य शयनादुत्थाय किञ्चिच्छनै-
र्निद्राव्याजमुपागतस्य सुचिरं निर्वर्ण्य पत्युर्मुखम् ।
विस्रब्धं परिचुम्ब्य जातपुलकामालोक्य गण्डस्थलीं
लज्जानम्रमुखी प्रियेण हसता बाला चिरं चुम्बिता ॥

इत्यादिषु श्लोकेषु[2] सत्स्वपि नवत्वम् ।

यथा वा—' तरङ्गभ्रूभङ्गा ' इत्यादिश्लोकस्य ' नानाभङ्गिभ्रमद्भ्रूः ' इत्यादिश्लोकापेक्षयान्यत्वम् ।

युक्त्यानया[3]नुसर्तव्यो रसादिर्बहुविस्तरः[4] ।
मितो[5]ऽप्यनन्ततां याति[6] काव्यमार्गो यदाश्रयात् ॥ ३ ॥

बहुविस्तारोऽयं रसभावतदाभासतत्प्रशम[7]लक्षणो मार्गो यथास्वं विभावानुभावप्रभेदकलनया[8] यथोक्तं प्राक् । स सर्व एवानया युक्त्या[9]नुसर्तव्यः । यस्य रसादेराश्रयादयं काव्यमार्गः पुरातनैः कविभिः सहस्रसंख्यैरसंख्यैर्वा बहुप्रकारं क्षुण्णत्वान्मितो[10]ऽप्यनन्ततामेति । रसभावादीनां हि प्रत्येकं विभावानुभावव्यभिचारिसमाश्रयादपरिमितत्वम् । तेषां चैकैकं[11]प्रभेदापेक्षयापि तावज्जगद्वृत्तमुपनिबध्यमानं सुकविभिस्तदिच्छावशादन्यथा स्थितमप्यन्यथैव विवर्तते । प्रतिपादितं चैतच्चित्रविचारावसरे । गाथा चात्र कृतैव[12] महाकविना—

अतहट्ठिए वि तहसण्ठिए व्व हिअअम्मि जा णिवेसेइ ।
अत्थविसेसे सा जअइ विकडकइगोअरा वाणी ॥

[अतथास्थितानपि तथासंस्थितानिव हृदये या निवेशयति ।
अर्थविशेषान् सा जयति विकटकविगोचरा वाणी ॥ [इति च्छाया]

१. अस्य. – ग. इत्यस्य –घ. २. श्लोकेषु –घ. पुस्तके नास्ति । ३. दिशानया° –घ. ४. रसादिर्बहुविस्तरः –घ. ५. मिथोऽ° – BP. ६. प्राप्तः BP. °न्ततामेति – MB. ७. प्रशमन°–घ. ८. °प्रभेदकतया – ग. ९. दिशानु° – घ. १०. मिथो – BP. ११. चैषामेकैक° – ग. १२. तथा च गाथात्र कृता – क-ख.

2 *Seeing the sleeping chamber secluded,*
The young wife gently rose a bit from her bridal bed
And went on feasting her eyes for long
On the face of her husband feigning sleep;
She then kissed his face without hesitation
And finding that his cheeks were thrilled at her kiss,
She bent down her head abashed.
Then it was that the laughing husband
Kissed her long in turn.

Another example, equally striking, is the verse :

'*Frowning with its waves as with brows*', etc. Despite the existence of verses like—*nānābhaṅgī-bhramadbhrūḥ*.

The sentiments etc. whose scope is very wide should be followed along the said course. The otherwise limited range of poetry has become so unlimited only because of their influence. **3**

The scope of sentiments, emotions, their semblances, and their cessations is indeed very vast in view of the numerous varieties of stimuli and responses that are possible in regard to each of them. This has indeed been shown already. And all of them should be followed only along the said course (of suggestion). It is indeed because of the influence of sentiments, etc. that the field of poetry which has been narrowed down in several ways by the works of a thousand poets, or to be precise, of innumerable poets in the past, can still hold out infinite possibilities (for present as well as future poets). Sentiments and emotions, etc. become infinite indeed because of the association of each one of them with different stimuli, responses and passing moods. Even if the poet handles a subject taken from life in deference to the demands of any single sub-division of these, the subject becomes infused with characteristics quite unknown to it in life. This has already been set forth in our treatment of Portrait-like Poetry. A celebrated poet has indeed written a sententious verse conveying this fact :—

Homage to the Muse of the gifted poets
Which makes us feel in our hearts
As though things that are quite unreal
Are very real forsooth.

तदित्थं रसभावाद्याश्रयेण काव्यार्थानामानन्त्यं सुप्रतिपादितम् ।

एतदेवोपपादयितुमुच्यते —

दृष्टपूर्वा अपि ह्यर्थाः काव्ये रसपरिग्रहात् ।
सर्वे[1] नवा इवाभान्ति मधुमास इव द्रुमाः ॥ ४ ॥

तथा हि[2] विवक्षितान्यपरवाच्यस्यैव शब्दशक्त्युद्भवानुरणनरूपव्यङ्ग्य[3]-प्रकारसमाश्रयेण नवत्वम् । यथा—'धरणीधारणायाधुना त्वं शेषः' इत्यादौ ।

शेषो हिमगिरिस्त्वं च महान्तो गुरवः स्थिराः ।
यदलङ्घितमर्यादाश्चलन्तीं बिभ्रते भुवम् ॥[4]

इत्यादिषु सत्स्वपि ।

तस्यैवार्थशक्त्युद्भवानुरणनरूपव्यङ्ग्यसमाश्रयेण[5] नवत्वं यथा — 'एवं वादिनि देवर्षौ' इत्यादिश्लोकस्य

कृते वरकथालापे कुमार्यः पुलकोद्गमैः ।
सूचयन्ति स्पृहामन्तर्लज्जयावनताननाः ॥

इत्यादिषु सत्सु । अर्थशक्त्युद्भवानुरणनरूपव्यङ्ग्यस्य कविप्रौढोक्ति-निर्मित[6]शरीरत्वेन नवत्वं यथा — 'सज्जेइ सुरहिमासो' इत्यादेः

सुरभिसमये प्रवृत्ते सहसा प्रादुर्भवन्ति रमणीयाः ।
रागवतामुत्कलिकाः सहैव सहकारकलिकाभिः ।

इत्यादिषु सत्स्वप्यपूर्वत्वमेव ।

१. सर्वे नवत्वमायान्ति मधुमासे द्रुमा इव – MB. २. हि–घ पुस्तके नास्ति ३. °रणनव्यङ्ग्यरूप°–ग. ४. बिभृथः क्षितिम्–क-ख. ५. °श्रयणेन – ग. ६. °प्रौढोक्तिमात्रनिर्मित° – ग. प्रौढोक्तिनिष्पन्न° – MB.

The unlimitedness lent to poetic themes due to their association with sentiments, emotions, etc. has been demonstrated hitherto. This is accounted for in the following :—

Even trite subjects in poetry will put on a new freshness if they get into touch with sentiment just as the same trees appear quite new with the advent of spring. 4

The following illustrates how novelty is achieved by a commonplace theme due to the influence of resonance-like suggestion based upon the power of word under the class of suggestion with intended but further-extending expressed content:—

1 *Now you alone are left with (also, the primeval*
Serpent) for bearing the burden of the earth.

2 *The Primeval Serpent, Mount Himālaya, and you —*
Are all great, mighty and constant;
For the moving earth is borne by all the three
Without overstepping the self-apportion'd limits.

The second is the older verse.

An illustration of novelty due to the influence of resonance-like suggestion based upon the power of sense is found in the verse—'*As the divine sage*', etc. despite the existence of verses like—

When the talk about the bridegroom is going on,
Girls bend their faces in bashfulness
And betray the eagerness within their hearts
By their bristling thrills outside.

In the instance '*The spring keeps ready*', etc, we have novelty due to the touch of the same variety of suggestion with a subject which is real only in the ornate expression of the poet despite the existence of verses like—

At the advent of spring.
Do come forth at once
Longings in lovers' hearts
And buds in the mango tree.

अर्थशक्त्युद्भवानुरणनरूपव्यङ्ग्यस्य कविनिबद्धवक्तृप्रौढोक्तिमात्रनिष्पन्नशरीरत्वेन[1] नवत्वं यथा[2] — 'वाणिअअ हत्थिदन्ता' इत्यादिगाथार्थस्य

करिणीवेहव्वअरो मह पुत्तो एक्ककाण्डविणिवाइ ।
हअ सोन्हाएँ तह कहो जह कण्डकरण्डअं वहइ ॥

[करिणीवैधव्यकरो मम पुत्र एककाण्डविनिपाती ।
हतस्नुषया तथा कृतो यथा काण्डकरण्डकं वहति ॥ [इति च्छाया]

एवमादिष्वर्थेषु सत्स्वप्यनालीढतैव[3] ।

यथा[4] व्यङ्ग्यभेदसमाश्रयेण ध्वनेः काव्यार्थानां नवत्वमुत्पद्यते[5], तथा व्यञ्जकभेदसमाश्रयेणापि । तत्तु ग्रन्थविस्तरभयान्न लिख्यते, स्वयमेव सहृदयैरभ्यूह्यम् । अत्र च पुनःपुनरुक्तमपि सारतयेदमुच्यते —

व्यङ्ग्यव्यञ्जकभावेऽस्मिन् विविधे सम्भवत्यपि ।
रसादिमय एकस्मिन्[6] कविः स्यादवधानवान् ॥ ५ ॥

अस्मिन्नर्थानन्त्यहेतौ व्यङ्ग्यव्यञ्जकभावे विचित्रे[7] शब्दानां[8] सम्भवत्यपि कविरपूर्वार्थलाभार्थी[9] रसादिमय एकस्मिन्[10] व्यङ्ग्यव्यञ्जकभावे यत्नादवदधीत । रसभावतदाभासरूपे हि व्यङ्ग्ये तद्व्यञ्जकेषु च यथानिर्दिष्टेषु[11] वर्णपदवाक्यरचनाप्रबन्धेष्ववहितमनसः कवेः सर्वमपूर्वं काव्यं सम्पद्यते ।

तथा च रामायणमहाभारतादिषु संग्रामादयः पुनःपुनरभिहिता अपि नवनवाः प्रकाशन्ते । प्रबन्धे चाङ्गी रस एक एवोपनिबध्यमानोऽर्थविशेषलाभं

---

१. °शरीरत्वे सति –घ.

२. साअरविइण्णजोव्वणहत्थालम्बं समुण्णमन्तेहिं ।
अब्भुट्ठाणम्मिव मम्महस्स दिण्णं तुह थणेहिं ॥

अस्य हि गाथार्थस्य
उदिह...कआमोआ जह जह थणआ विणन्ति बालाणम् ।
तह तह लद्धावासो व्व मम्महो हिअअमाविसइ ॥

एतद्गाथार्थेन न पौनरुक्त्यम् । यथा वा—घ.

३. इत्येवमादिषु सत्स्वप्यनालीढतैव –क. ख. ४. यथा च–घ. ५. अपृथगर्थत्वमुत्पद्यते–ग.
६. एतस्मिन् – क-ख. ७. विचित्रं – BP. ८. शब्दानामिति नास्ति – घ.
९. कविरपूर्वलाभार्थे – घ. १०. एतस्मिन् – क-ख. ११. यथामाति – ग.

In the instance '*O merchant*' etc., we have novelty due to the touch of the same variety of suggestion with a subject which is real only in the ornate expression of a character invented by a poet despite the presence of verses like—

My son who brought widowhood to cow-elephants
By shooting just a single shaft,
Has now been reduced to such a state
By this wretched daughter-in-law
That he must carry a bundle of shafts.

Novelty is produced in poetic themes not only by their union with the varieties of suggested content, but also by their contact with the varieties of the suggestive elements. But we will not record it here lest the work should grow too voluminous. Refined critics may very well imagine it for themselves.

Though it has been reiterated again and again, still the following is said once more since it happens to be the very essence of the matter on hand :

Though several varieties of the suggested-suggester relationship are possible, the poet should be most intent upon one of them in particular, viz., that relating to the delineation of sentiments etc. 5

Though words involving the relation of suggested-suggester are possible in various ways, the poet desirous of securing novel poetic themes should be most intent upon one of them only, viz., suggestion of sentiments, etc. So long as the poet exercises undeflected concentration regarding the suggested contents, viz., sentiment, emotion, its semblance, and the suggesters previously explained, viz., letter, word, sentence, and texture, and the work as a whole, the poet's entire work will become strikingly novel. That is why in epics like the *Rāmāyaṇa* and the *Mahābhārata*, the subjects of 'battle' etc., appear quite new though they are described again and again.

In a work as a whole the delineation of a single sentiment as the predominant one will endow not only novelty of content but also abundance of charm. If one should ask for examples,

छायातिशयं च पुष्णाति। कस्मिन्निवेति चेत्—यथा रामायणे यथा वा[1] महाभारते। रामायणे हि करुणो रसः स्वयमादिकविनासूत्रितः[2] 'शोकः श्लोकत्वमागतः' इत्येवंवादिना। निर्व्यूढश्च स एव सीतात्यन्तवियोगपर्यन्तमेव स्वप्रबन्धमुपरचयता। महाभारतेऽपि शास्त्ररूपे काव्यच्छायान्वयिनि[3] वृष्णिपाण्डवविरसावसानवैमनस्यदायिनीं समाप्तिमुपनिबध्नता महामुनिना वैराग्यजननतात्पर्यं प्राधान्येन स्वप्रबन्धस्य दर्शयता मोक्षलक्षणः पुरुषार्थः शान्तो रसश्च मुख्यतया विवक्षाविषयत्वेन सूचितः। एतच्चांशेन विवृतमेवान्यैर्व्याख्याविधायिभिः। स्वयमेव चैतदुद्गीर्णं[4] तेनोदीर्णमहामोहमग्नमुज्जिहीर्षता लोकमतिविमलज्ञानालोकदायिना लोकनाथेन —

यथा यथा विपर्येति लोकतन्त्रमसारवत्।
तथा तथा विरागोऽत्र जायते नात्र संशयः॥

इत्यादि बहुशः कथयता। ततश्च शान्तो रसो रसान्तरैः, मोक्षलक्षणः पुरुषार्थः पुरुषार्थान्तरैः तदुपसर्जनत्वेनानुगम्यमानोऽङ्गित्वेन विवक्षाविषय इति महाभारततात्पर्यं सुव्यक्तमेवावभासते।

अङ्गाङ्गिभावश्च यथा रसानां[5] तथा प्रतिपादितमेव।

पारमार्थिकान्तस्तत्त्वानपेक्षया शरीरस्येवाङ्गभूतस्य रसस्य पुरुषार्थस्य च स्वप्राधान्येन चारुत्वमप्यविरुद्धम्।

---

१. यथा च-क-ख. २. स्वयमादिमुनिना सूचितः-ग. ३. शास्त्ररूपपूर्वकाव्यावस्थान्वयिनि-ग. शास्त्रकाव्यरूपच्छायान्वयिनि -घ. ४. स्वयं चोद्गीर्णं-घ. ५. रसादीनाम्.-क. ख. ६. पारमार्थिकान्तस्तत्त्वानपेक्षया शरीरस्यैवा° -ग.

we would say in reply that the *Rāmāyaṇa* is itself one example and that the *Mahābhārata* is another. Into the Rāmāyaṇa indeed, the First Poet himself has incorporated the sentiment of pathos as is clear by his own declaration—" *Sorrow has taken the turn of a stanza* ". It has in fact been kept up as predominant till the very end of the work in view of his concluding the work at the point of the eternal loss of Sītā by Rāma.

In the *Mahābhārata* too, which combines both the elements of instruction and poetry in one, it will be seen that its conclusion in a note of despair consequent on the miserable deaths of Vṛṣṇis as well as Pāṇḍavas, as constructed by the great sage, reveals his primary intention of preaching the moral of renunciation through his work and throws light upon the fact that he intended final emancipation as the foremost of human values and Peace as the most predominant sentiment in the whole work. This has been partially brought out even by the other commentators on the *Mahābhārata*. Even the reverend sage himself whose foremost desire was the rescue of his fellowmen from the deep abyss of ignorance in which they were weltering by vouchsafing to them the light of supreme knowledge, has declared in no uncertain terms :—

'Just (as much) as wordly pursuits
Turn out to be unavailing,
One's sense of aversion to them will become firm;
There is no doubt at all'.

and so on in the same strain more than once. It stands out most clearly that the main purport of the *Mahābhārata* is the communication of the fact that Peace is to be regarded as the most prominent sentiment, the others being secondary to it and that final emancipation is the most prominent of human values, the other values being only subsidiary to it. The principal-subordinate relationship of sentiments has been set forth already.

Just as the body might be invested with prominence though it is only secondary when the really prominent soul is not taken into consideration. so also a secondary sentiment as well as a secondary value might be justly regarded as prominent in itself and beautiful.

ननु महाभारते यावान् विवक्षाविषयः, सोऽनुक्रमण्यां सर्वमेवानुक्रान्तो न चैतत्तत्र दृश्यते, प्रत्युत सर्वपुरुषार्थप्रबोधहेतुत्वं सर्वरसगर्भत्वं च महाभारतस्य तस्मिन्नुद्देशे स्वशब्दनिवेदितत्वेन प्रतीयते।

अत्रोच्यते। सत्यं शान्तस्यैव रसस्याङ्गित्वं महाभारते मोक्षस्य च सर्वपुरुषार्थेभ्यः प्राधान्यमित्येतन्न स्वशब्दाभिधेयत्वेनानुक्रमण्यां[1] दर्शितं, दर्शितं तु व्यङ्ग्यत्वेनः—'भगवान् वासुदेवश्च कीर्त्यतेऽत्र सनातनः' इत्यस्मिन् वाक्ये। अनेन[2] ह्ययमर्थो व्यङ्ग्यत्वेन विवक्षितो यदत्र महाभारते पाण्डवादिचरितं यत्कीर्त्यते[3], तत्सर्वमवसानविरसमविद्याप्रपञ्चरूपञ्च, परमार्थसत्यस्वरूपस्तु भगवान् वासुदेवोऽत्र कीर्त्यते[4]। तस्मात्तस्मिन्नेव परमेश्वरे भगवति भवत भावितचेतसो, मा भूत विभूतिषु निःसारासु रागिणो, गुणेषु वा नयविनयपराक्रमादिष्वमीषु केवलेषु केषुचित् सर्वात्मना प्रतिनिविष्टधियः। तथा चाग्रे—पश्यत निःसारतां संसारस्ये[5]त्यमुमेवार्थातिशयं द्योतयन्[6] स्फुटमेवावभासते व्यञ्जकशक्त्य[7]नुगृहीतश्च[8]शब्दः। एवंविधमेवार्थं[9] गर्भीकृतं सन्दर्शयन्तोऽनन्तरश्लोका लक्ष्यन्ते—'स हि सत्यम्' इत्यादयः।

अयं च निगूढरमणीयोऽर्थो महाभारतावसाने हरिवंशवर्णनेन समाप्तिं विदधता तेनैव कविवेधसा कृष्णद्वैपायनेन सम्यक्स्फुटीकृतः। अनेन चार्थेन संसारातीते तत्त्वान्तरे भक्त्यातिशयं प्रवर्तयता सकल एव सांसारिको व्यवहारः पूर्वपक्षीकृतो न्यक्षेण प्रकाशते।[10] देवतातीर्थतपःप्रभृतीनां च

१. अनुक्रमण्या – BP. २. अनेन इति नास्ति – घ. ३. संकीर्त्यते – ग. ४. तत्सर्वमित्यारभ्य कीर्त्यते इति पर्यन्तं-घ पुस्तके नास्ति. ५. निःसारतां सर्वस्यास्य संसारव्यवहारस्य – क-ख. ६. द्योतयत् – घ. ७. शक्त्यानु° – घ. ८. व्यञ्जकत्वानुगृहीतश्च – क-ख. शक्त्यानुगृहीतश्च शब्दः – घ. °तश्च शब्दः – BP. ९. एवं विधमेव चार्थं – घ. १०. न्यक्षेण प्रकाश्यते – ग. °पक्षीकृतोऽध्यक्षेण प्रकाशते – घ.

It might be urged by some that all the points sought to be conveyed in the *Mahābhārata* have been enumerated exhaustively in the Introduction itself while the above point is conspicuous by its absence in the Introduction. They might add that, on the other hand, Vyāsa expressly claims in the Introduction that his work throws light on all the human values and that it contains all the sentiments.

Here is our answer to the objection : though it is true that nowhere in the Introduction we come across an express statement to the effect that in the *Mahābhārata*, Peace is intended to be the most prominent of all sentiments and that final emancipation is intended to be the most prominent of all human values, it is also true that this has been conveyed in a suggestive way through the sentence—

> *Herein, forsooth, will be glorified*
> *Lord Vāsudeva too, the Eternal.*

The idea implied in this sentence is that all the other subjects described in the *Mahābhārata* such as the exploits of the Pāṇḍavas end only in tragedy and belong only to the realm of ignorance while the only eternal and truly abiding subject glorified here is Lord Vāsudeva. Therefore (suggests Vyāsa). ' be devoted in heart only to that supreme Lord; don't remain attached to empty pleasures and don't be too intent upon excellences even like statesmanship, modesty, and valour just for their own sakes ' ! It is to suggest the utter futility of worldly existence indeed that *ca* (' too ') figures last in that sentence. The verses that immediately follow, viz., ' *He alone is Real* ', are also imbued with this very significance.

By appending *Harivaṁśa* at the end of the *Mahābhārata* the great Poet-Creator Kṛṣṇa Dvaipāyana has made this inner and beautiful significance abundantly clear. By propagating the cause of whole-hearted devotion in that Absolute Reality beyond the realm of worldly existence, he appears definitely to have regarded the entire activities of worldly existence to be of the nature of a *prima facie* case (deserving refutation). He indulges in lengthy descriptions of the greatness of deities, sacred spots.

प्रभावातिशयवर्णनं तस्यैव परब्रह्मणः प्राप्त्युपायत्वेन तद्विभूतित्वेनैव देवताविशेषाणामन्येषां च[2]। पाण्डवादिचरितवर्णनस्यापि वैराग्यजननतात्पर्याद्वैराग्यस्य च मोक्षमूलत्वान्मोक्षस्य च भगवत्प्राप्त्युपायत्वेन मुख्यतया गीतादिषु प्रदर्शितत्वात् परब्रह्मप्राप्त्युपायत्वमेव। परम्परया वासुदेवादिसंज्ञाभिधेयत्वेन चापरिमितशक्त्यास्पदं परं ब्रह्म गीतादिप्रदेशान्तरेषु तदभिधानत्वेन लब्धप्रसिद्धि माथुरप्रादुर्भावानुकृतसकलस्वरूपमंशिरूपं[3] विवक्षितं, न तु माथुरप्रादुर्भावांश एव, सनातनशब्दविशेषितत्वात्[4]। रामायणादिषु चानया संज्ञया भगवन्मूर्त्यन्तरे व्यवहारदर्शनात्। निर्णीतश्चायमर्थः[5] शब्दतत्त्वविद्भिरेव।

तदेवमनुक्रमणीनिर्दिष्टेन वाक्येन भगवद्व्यतिरेकिणः सर्वस्यान्यस्यानित्यतां प्रकाशयता[6] मोक्षलक्षण एवैकः परः पुरुषार्थः शास्त्रनयेन, काव्यनयेन च तृष्णाक्षयसुखपरिपोषलक्षणः शान्तो रसो महाभारतस्याङ्गित्वेन विवक्षित इति सुप्रतिपादितम्। अत्यन्तसारभूतत्वाच्चायमर्थो व्यङ्ग्यत्वेनैव दर्शितो न तु वाच्यत्वेन। सारभूतो[7] ह्यर्थः स्वशब्दानभिधेयत्वेन प्रकाशितः

---

१. तत्तद्विभूतित्वेनैव वा – घ. २. च – घ पुस्तके नास्ति। ३. स्वरूपमङ्गिरूपम् – ग. सकल स्वरूप शंसिरूपं – घ. Reading is clearly अंशिरूपं in No. XII 186 and No. 255 of BORI. ४. विशेषकत्वात् – ग. ५. °अंशः – घ. ६. प्रकाशयतो–घ. ७. साररूपो – ग.

asceticism, etc., only because they serve, in his opinion, as the channels of realising that Supreme Reality ; other particular gods also are glorified only as so many manifestations of His Supreme glory. The description of the exploits of Pāṇḍavas etc. is also meant to produce a sense of renunciation; renunciation, in its turn, is the very basic instrument of final emancipation; and final emancipation itself has been shown in the *Bhagavadgītā* and other works to be a sure means towards the attainment of the Supreme Reality. Thus, indirectly, even the description of the exploits of Pāṇḍavas etc., might be regarded as a means towards the attainment of the Supreme Reality. Instead of referring to the Supreme Reality by the very word Supreme Reality, Vyāsa uses a synonym, viz. Vāsudeva. By this word Vāsudeva we should consider as intended the meaning of Supreme Reality only, which is the abode of boundless power, because in several contexts like the Gītā, this word has been widely used to convey the meaning of Supreme Reality itself. It should not be understood to mean only the human form born as son of Vāsudeva in Mathurā but wholly the Supreme Reality itself imitating in every way the nature of such a human being born in Mathurā ; because, the word under consideration, viz., Vāsudeva, is qualified by the adjective, viz., Eternal. And in other works like the Rāmāyaṇa, we find this word used as a proper name for other incarnations also of the Supreme Lord. This fact has indeed been established even by grammarians themselves.

Hence we are quite justified in saying that the purport implied by the sage for the sentence in question of the Introductory chapter is the perishable nature of everything with the single exception of the Supreme Lord and that the *Mahābhārata* as a whole is intended by him to convey the highest human value, viz., final emancipation, when the work is regarded as a scripture, and to delineate the sentiment of Quietude—whose nature is of heightened tranquillity and happiness at the cessation of desire—as the predominant sentiment in the work when it is regarded as a poem. As this purport happens to be the most essential one, it has not been stated expressly but conveyed by way of suggestion. An intrinsically essential idea acquires beauty only when it is revealed in a way other than the expressed. In polished literary

सुतरामेव शोभामावहति। प्रसिद्धिश्चेयमस्त्येव विदग्धविद्वत्परिषत्सु यदभिमततरं वस्तु व्यङ्ग्यत्वेन प्रकाश्यते, न साक्षाच्छब्दवाच्यत्वेन¹। तस्मात् स्थितमेतत् — अङ्गिभूतरसाद्याश्रयेण काव्ये क्रियमाणे नवार्थ²लाभो भवति, बन्धच्छाया³ च महती सम्पद्यते इति। अत एव च रसानुगुणार्थविशेषोपनिबन्धनमलङ्कारान्तरविरहेऽपि च्छायातिशययोगि लक्ष्ये दृश्यते। यथा—

मुनिर्जयति योगीन्द्रो महात्मा कुम्भसम्भवः।
येनैकचुलुके दृष्टौ तौ दिव्यौ मत्स्यकच्छपौ॥

इत्यादौ। अत्र ह्यद्भुतरसानुगुणमेकचुलुके मत्स्यकच्छपदर्शनं छायातिशयं पुष्णाति। तत्रह्येकचुलुके सकल⁴जलधिसन्निधानादपि दिव्यमत्स्यकच्छपदर्शनमक्षुण्णत्वादद्भुतरसानुगुणतरम्। क्षुण्णं हि वस्तु लोकप्रसिद्ध्याद्भुतमपि नाश्चर्यकारि भवति। न चाक्षुण्णं वस्तूपनिबध्यमानमद्भुतरसस्यैवानुगुणं, यावद् रसान्तरस्यापि। तद्यथा—

सिज्जइ रोमाञ्चिज्जइ वेवइ रत्थातुलग्गपडिलग्गो⁵।
सो पासो अज्जवि सुहअ⁶ जेणासि वोलीणो॥
[स्विद्यति रोमांचिज्जइ वेपते रच्छातुलग्गं।
स पार्श्वोऽद्यापि सुभग येनास्यतिक्रान्तः॥ [इति च्छाया]

एतद्गाथार्थाद् भाव्यमानाद् या रसप्रतीतिर्भवति सा त्वां स्पृष्ट्वा स्विद्यति, रोमाञ्चते, वेपते इत्येवंविधादर्थात् प्रतीयमानान्⁷मनागपि नो जायते। तदेवं ध्वनिप्रभेदसमाश्रयेण यथा काव्यार्थानां नवत्वं जायते तथा प्रतिपादितम्।

---

१. वाच्यत्वेनैव – घ. २. नवनवार्थलाभो – घ. ३. प्रबन्धच्छाया – क-ख. ४. 'सकल' घ पुस्तके नास्ति। ५. रच्छाकुलङ्ग – घ. ६. सह अतीइ – घ. ७. प्रतीयमानात्मना मनागपि – घ.

circles it has indeed become a convention of wits to communicate their best ideas only through suggestion and not at all by express words.

Therefore, the conclusion is irresistible that novelty in poetic theme as well as great beauty of construction is achieved by adopting a single sentiment as predominant in any poem as a whole. That is why compositions containing only themes in keeping with sentiment are often seen to hold out abundant charm although they may be lacking in different figures of speech. For instance—

'Victory to that sage, the foremost of ascetics,
The mighty soul who was pitcher-born ;
For he could behold both the divine Fish and Tortoisc
In the hollow af his single hand'.

and such others might be cited. The idea that, in the hollow of a single hand, one could see both the divine Fish and Tortoise heightens the sentiment of Wonderment. Further, though the idea of the whole ocean being comprised in the hollow of the sage's hand is traditional, the idea that both the divine forms of the Lord, viz., the Fish and the Tortoise were seen by him there at the same time, is most original and it heightens the sentiment mentioned, all the more. An idea which is already familiar due to wide currency among people will not cause surprise, though it might embody an element of wonder.

An original poetic theme conforms not only to the sentiment of wonder but also to the other sentiments as in the following example :—

That part of her body
Which touched the end of your balance
As you passed her along the street
Still sweats, horripilates and trembles;
O, thou handsome youth !

The sentiment apprehended by contemplating upon the verse as it is, will never be had by any express statement to the effect, 'By your touch, she sweats, horripilates and trembles'.

Thus we have demonstrated how poetic themes are rendered new by the contact of one or another major variety of *Dhvani*

गुणीभूतव्यङ्ग्यस्यापि त्रिभेदव्यङ्ग्यापेक्षया[1] ये प्रकाराः, तत्समाश्रयेणापि काव्यवस्तूनां नवत्वं भवत्येव। तत्त्वतिविस्तारकारीति नोदाहृतं, सहृदयैः स्वयमुत्प्रेक्षणीयम् ।

ध्वनेरित्थं गुणीभूतव्यङ्ग्यस्य च समाश्रयात् ।
न काव्यार्थविरामोऽस्ति यदि स्यात् प्रतिभागुणः ॥ ६ ॥

सत्स्वपि पुरातनकविप्रबन्धेषु यदि स्यात् प्रतिभागुणः, तस्मिंस्त्वसति न किञ्चिदेव कवेर्वस्त्वस्ति। बन्धच्छायाप्यर्थद्वयानुरूपशब्दसन्निवेशो[2]ऽर्थ-प्रतिभानाभावे कथमुपपद्यते। अनपेक्षितार्थविशेषाक्षररचनैव बन्धच्छायेति नेदं नेदीयः[3] सहृदयानाम् । एवं हि सत्यर्थानपेक्षचतुरमधुरवचनरचनायामपि काव्यव्यपदेशः प्रवर्तेत[4]। शब्दार्थयोः साहित्येन काव्यत्वे कथं तथाविधे विषये काव्यव्यवस्थेति चेत्—परोपनिबद्धार्थविरचने यथा तत्काव्यव्यवहारस्तथा[5] तथा-विधानां काव्यसन्दर्भाणाम् ।

न चार्थानन्त्यं व्यङ्ग्यार्थापेक्षयैव यावद्वाच्यार्थापेक्षयापीति प्रतिपाद-यितुमुच्यते—

अवस्थादेशकालादिविशेषैरपि जायते ।
आनन्त्यमेव वाच्यस्य शुद्धस्यापि स्वभावतः ॥ ७ ॥

---

१. °स्यापि प्रभेदापेक्षया – घ.　२. सन्निवेशार्थ° – घ.　३. नैतन्नेदीया – क. नैतन्नेदीयः – ख.　४. प्रवर्तते – घ.　५. यथा काव्यतद्व्यवहारः – ग. यत्काव्यत्वस्य व्यवहारस्तया – घ.

or principal suggestion. In the same way, the element of subordinated suggestion too which is threefold from the point of view of the suggested content will ensure novelty to poetic themes if adopted in the work. But we have refrained from illustrating it here in detail for fear of making the work unduly prolix. Refined critics should fancy it for themselves.

So long as these varieties of principal and subordinate suggestion are utilised in a work and so long as the poet has the gift of creative imagination (in so utilising them), there can be no dearth of poetic themes. 6

The ellipsis to be supplied in the text is 'notwithstanding the existence of several ancient poetic works' before 'so long as he has the gift of creative imagination'. But in the absence of creative imagination, the poet can certainly have no poetic theme at all. Nor can it be held justifiably that even in the absence of creative imagination directed towards vision of meanings, strikingness in style is possible of achievement; since style is nothing but employment of apt words to convey both types of meaning (viz. the expressed and the suggested). Refined critics would certainly not countenance the position that style is a mere arrangement of letters without any concern regarding the meaning to be conveyed. At that rate, every clever arrangement of sweet-sounding syllables, irrespective of meaning, should have deserved the designation of poetry. But it might be asked whether the designation of poetry is not commonly applied to all unions of words and meanings including the ones under consideration (viz. those that owe their beauty to style alone). Our reply is that such specimens are regarded as poetry only in a loose way after the analogy of a composition which is allowed to be ascribed to an imitator though it contains only ideas borrowed from another poet.

This infinitude of poetic themes is brought about not only by way of suggested content but also by way of expressed content. This is set forth in the following :—

Infinitude is achived by the expressed content also even when it remains in its pure and natural state by reason of the considerations of circumstance, place, time, etc. 7

शुद्धस्यानपेक्षितव्यङ्ग्यस्यापि वाच्यस्यानन्त्यमेव जायते स्वभावतः। स्वभावो ह्ययं वाच्यानां चेतनानामचेतनानां च[1] यदवस्थाभेदाद्देशभेदात्काल-भेदात् स्वालक्षण्यभेदाच्चानन्तता[2] भवति। तैश्च तथाव्यवस्थितैः सद्भिः प्रसिद्धा-नेकस्वभावानुसरणरूपया स्वभावोक्त्यापि तावदुपनिबध्यमानैर्निरवधिः काव्यार्थः सम्पद्यते। तथा ह्यवस्थाभेदान्नवत्वं यथा — भगवती पार्वती कुमारसम्भवे ' सर्वोपमाद्रव्यसमुच्चयेन ' इत्यादिभिरुक्तिभिः प्रथममेव परिसमापितरूपवर्ण-नापि पुनर्भगवतः शम्भोर्लोचनगोचरमायान्ती ' वसन्तपुष्पाभरणं वहन्ती ' इति मन्मथोपकरणभूतेन भङ्ग्यन्तरेणोपवर्णिता। सैव च पुनर्नवोद्वाहसमये प्रसाध्य-माना ' तां प्राङ्मुखीं तत्र निवेश्य तन्वीम् ' इत्याद्युक्तिभिर्नवेनैव प्रकारेण निरूपितरूपसौष्ठवा[3]। न च ते तस्य कवेरेकत्रैवासकृत्कृता वर्णनप्रकारा अपुनरुक्तत्वेन वा नवनवार्थनिर्भरत्वेन वा न[4] प्रतिभासन्ते। दर्शितमेव चैतद्विषमबाणलीलायाम्—

ण अ ताण घडइ ओही ण अ ते दीसन्ति कहवि पुनरुत्ता।
जे विब्भमा पिआणं अत्था वा सुकइवाणीणम्॥
[न च तेषां घटतेऽवधिः, न च ते दृश्यन्ते कथमपि पुनरुक्ताः।
ये विभ्रमाः प्रियाणामर्था वा सुकविवाणीनाम्॥ [इति च्छाया]

अयमपरश्चावस्थाभेदप्रकारो यदचेतनानां सर्वेषां चेतनं द्वितीयं रूपमभिमानित्वप्रसिद्धं हिमवद्गङ्गादीनाम्। तच्चोदितैश्चेतन[5]विषयस्वरूपयोजनयो-पनिबध्यमानमन्यदेव सम्पद्यते। यथा कुमारसम्भव एव पर्वतस्वरूपस्य हिमवतो वर्णनं, पुनः सप्तर्षिप्रियोक्तिषु[6] सचेतनतत्स्वरूपापेक्षया प्रदर्शितं,

---

१. चेतनाचेतनानां – घ. २. स्वालक्षण्यलक्षणभेदाच्चानन्तता – घ. ३. निरू-पितसौष्ठवा –घ. ४. न not found in BP and घ, but occurring in XII, 186 and No, 255 (BORI). ५. तच्चोचित BP ६. प्रियोक्तिषु (स्व) –घ.

Even the expressed content which is pure, that is to say, independent of the suggested element, will attain to infinitude in the natural course of things. It is indeed the nature of the expressed content that it becomes infinite by differences of circumstance, place and time as also by differences within itself in sentient as well as insentient objects. Even a faithful description of the several natures of such express ideas in a well known way will bring about an unlimitedness of poetic themes. To illustrate the novelty due to differences in circumstance, we may mention the description of Pārvatī in the *Kumārasambhava.* Though the description of her beauty has been completed even at the outset by the verses beginning with : *By a combination of all subjects bearing comparison, etc.*, she is once again made the subject of description in a different way as the instrument of Cupid when she comes within the range of Lord Śiva's sight in verses such as : " *Decked in the ornamental flowers of spring* ", etc., and further on, her exceeding beauty of form is described yet again at length in presenting how she was dressed up as a bride at the time of the wedding in verses beginning with : ' *Placing that damsel in her front* '. These repeated descriptions of the poet do not at all appear as tautological or as devoid of ever-fresh and rich significance. This has indeed been strikingly declared in my work (*Viṣamabāṇalīlā*):

There is no limit to them
And they will never look like repetitions;
The graces of sweethearts
And the meanings of the words of good poets.

The second variety of ' circumstance ' is this : all insentient objects such as the mountain Himavān and the river Gaṅgā are accredited with a second sentient personality that presides over their insentient form. That presiding personality of theirs lends itself to be treated in a way natural to other sentient persons and, when so treated, it will appear quite novel. For instance, in the *Kumārasambhava* itself, we have first of all a description of Himavān in his mountainous form and later on he is endowed with the nature of a sentient being and addressed persuasively by the Seven Sages. We find

तदपूर्वमेव प्रतिभाति। प्रसिद्धश्चायं सत्कवीनां मार्गः। इदं च प्रस्थानं कविव्युत्पत्तये विषमबाणलीलायां सप्रपञ्चं दर्शितम्। चेतनानां च बाल्याद्यवस्थाभिरन्यत्वं सत्कवीनां प्रसिद्धमेव[1]। चेतनानामवस्थाभेदेऽप्यवान्तरावस्थाभेदान्नानात्वम्। यथा कुमारीणां कुसुमशरभिन्नहृदयानामन्यासां च। तत्रापि विनीतानामविनीतानां च। अचेतनानां[2] च भावानामारम्भाद्यवस्थाभेदभिन्नानामेकैकशः स्वरूपमुपनिबध्यमानमानन्त्यमेवोपयाति। यथा—

हंसानां निनदेषु[3] यैः कवलितैरासज्यते कूजता-
मन्यः कोऽपि कषायकण्ठलुठनादाघर्घरो विभ्रमः।
ते सम्प्रत्यकठोरवारणवधूदन्ताङ्कुरस्पर्धिनो
निर्याताः कमलाकरेषु बिसिनीकन्दाग्रिमग्रन्थयः॥

एवमन्यत्रापि दिशानयानुसर्तव्यम्। देशभेदान्नानात्वमचेतनानां तावत् यथा वायूनां नानादिग्देशचारिणामन्येषामपि सलिलकुसुमादीनां प्रसिद्धमेव। चेतनानामपि मानुषपशुपक्षिप्रभृतीनां ग्रामारण्यसलिलादिसमेधितानां परस्परं महान् विशेषः समुपलक्ष्यते[4] एव। स च विविच्य यथायथमुपनिबध्यमानस्तथैवानन्त्यमाश्रयते[5]। तथाहि—मानुषाणामेव तावद्दिग्देशादिभिन्नानां ये व्यवहारव्यापारादिषु विचित्रा विशेषास्तेषां केनान्तः शक्यते गन्तुम्, विशेषतो योषिताम्। उपनिबध्यते च तत्सर्वमेव सुकविभिर्यथाप्रतिभम्।

---

१. सुप्रसिद्धम् – ग. २. चाचेतनानां चेतनानां – ग. ३. °रसंपु ग. ४. लक्षित – XII 186 and No. 255 (BORI). ५. °यति – BP.

novelty positively in such a description. This is indeed an established practice of poets. This principle has been shown at length in the *Viṣamabāṇalīlā* for the benefit of the poets seeking instruction.

Even among sentient themes, ' circumstances ' of age such as childhood bring about novelty. This is, in fact, commonly found in the works of poets. And even between two themes whose circumstance of age is identical, there might exist other minor circumstances conducing to difference. For example, what a world of difference is there between girls who are love-smitten and girls who are not (though they might be of the same age)! And even amongst one class of these, there might exist further variations due to their modesty or wantonness. Again, in insentient themes too, there is scope for difference in circumstances like germination, etc. Utilisation of individual differentiating circumstances like this into poetry would endow it with infinitude. Here is an example :

Such terminal sprouts of the lotus-creeper,
As compete in beauty with the peeping tusks
Of a young cow-elephant;
And by eating which a unique sweetness of sound
Is attained by the cooing swans,
Through the clearing up of their throats
By the astringency of their taste,
Have now come out in lotus ponds.

In the same way other examples too should be imagined (by the readers themselves).

Variety due to place is possible in insentient themes also. Thus winds blowing from different directions and over different places and even other objects like waters and flowers are well known to vary. In sentient objects, of course, individual differences in men, beasts and birds due to their being brought up in town, forest and water (respectively), are found to be most remarkable. If these differences are properly appreciated and embodied in a work, the scope of poetic themes will naturally become infinite. To illustrate : Among men only, there are so many differences in speech, dress, etc. between one individual and another due to the differences in their province and country that no one can recount them exhaustively. This is much more so in regard to variation in women. All this is incorporated into their works by poets according to their individual imaginations.

कालभेदाच्च नानात्वम्। यथर्तुभेदाद् दिग्व्योमसलिलादीनामचेतनानाम्। चेतनानां चौत्सुक्यादयः कालविशेषाश्रयिणः प्रसिद्धा एव। स्वालक्षण्यप्रभेदाच्च[1] सकलजगद्गतानां वस्तूनां विनिबन्धनं प्रसिद्धमेव[2]। तच्च यथावस्थितमपि तावदुपनिबध्यमानमनन्ततामेव काव्यार्थस्यापादयति[3]।

अत्र केचिदाचक्षीरन्।—यथा सामान्यात्मना वस्तूनि वाच्यतां प्रतिपद्यन्ते, न विशेषात्मना। तानि हि स्वयमनुभूतानां[4] सुखादीनां तन्निमित्तानां च स्वरूपमन्यत्रारोपयद्भिः स्वपरानुभूतरूप[5]सामान्य[6]श्रयेणोपनिबध्यन्ते कविभिः। न हि तैरतीतमनागतं वर्तमानञ्च परचित्तादि[7]स्वलक्षणं योगिभिरिव प्रत्यक्षीक्रियते। तच्चानुभाव्यानुभाव[8]कसामान्यं सर्वप्रतिपत्तृ[9]साधारणं परिमितत्वात् पुरातनानामेव गोचरीभूतम्, तस्यां[10] विषयत्वानुपपत्तेः[11]। अत एव स प्रकारविशेषो यैरद्यतनैरभिनवत्वेन प्रतीयते, तेषामभि[12]मानमात्रमेव भणितिकृतं वैचित्र्य[13]मात्रमत्रास्तीति।

तत्रोच्यते।[14] यत्तूक्तं सामान्यमात्राश्रयेण काव्यप्रवृत्तिस्तस्य च परिमितत्त्वेन प्रागेव गोचरीकृतत्वान्नास्ति नवत्वं काव्यवस्तूनामिति तदयुक्तम्। यतो यदि सामान्यमात्रमाश्रित्य काव्यं प्रवर्तते किंकृतस्तर्हि महाकविनिबध्यमानानां काव्यार्थानामतिशयः[15]? वाल्मीकिव्यतिरिक्तस्य अन्यस्य कविव्यपदेश एवं[16] वा, सामान्यव्यतिरिक्तस्यान्यस्य काव्यार्थस्याभावात्। सामान्यस्य

---

१. स्वालक्षण्याभेदाच्च – घ. २. °नमविगीतमेव – घ. ३. °स्योपपादयति – ग. ४. °भूतात्मनां – ग. ५. स्वरूपानुरूप° – घ. स्वपरानुभूतसामान्य° – क-ख. ६. °सामान्यमात्राश्रयेण – घ. ७. परिचितादि – BP. ८. °भाव्यानुभव° – BP. ९. °प्रतिपत्ति° – ग. १०. तस्य – घ. ११. तथास्य विषयस्यानुपपत्तेः – क – ख. १२. भ्रममात्रमेव – घ. १३. कृतं अभिधानवैचित्र्यं – ग. १४. तत्रोच्यते यदि सामान्याश्रयेण काव्यप्रवृत्तिस्तत्प्रदर्शितप्रकारं काव्यवैचित्र्यमवस्थादिविशेषादिकं पुनरुक्तमेवास्तु। न चेत् तथा तत्कथं न काव्यानन्त्यम्। यत्तूक्तं – घ, MB. १५. काव्यानामतिशयः – घ. १६. एव – घ.

Variety is contributed by time also. For instance, seasonal differences bring about differences in atmosphere, sky, water and such other insentient objects. With reference to sentient beings also, feelings of anxiety, etc. produced by particular times are quite common.

Equally well known is the practice of describing all objects in the world with an eye to their innate individual differences.

At this point, some might raise an objection : ' Objects are communicated only by their generic nature and not at all by their specific traits. On the basis of their own personal experiences of joy, etc. and their causes, poets universalise that the same experiences should follow from the same causes elsewhere also. Thus they embody ideas in their works only on the basis of the generic nature of experience common to them as well as to other persons. Surely, poets do not have any direct vision into the specific variations of all things in the past, present and future, like Yogins. And the generic universal of experience which is common to all experiences that are possible and which is common to men, one and all, is but restricted in scope and one can very well regard it to have been completely exhausted by the ancient poets themselves. For one cannot reasonably say that it has remained outside the ken of the ancients all along. Hence the idea of the moderners that a specific variation of an object is being presented in a novel fashion is only an empty boast. The only variation that actually exists is in the manner of presenting the (old) idea; that is all '.

This is our reply :—The statement that poetry proceeds only on the basis of generic nature and this being but limited, it must have been exhausted already and, therefore, there can be no novelty about poetic themes, is incorrect. For, if it were true that poetry proceeds on the basis of generic nature only, how could we account for the fact that the objects described by first-rate poets possess the highest beauty ? Furthermore, since there would be no matter for poetry except universals, there would be no possibility at all for a second poet to be rightly so regarded after Vālmīki, the first poet; for he will have

[1]इत्थं यथा यथा निरूप्यते, तथा तथा न लभ्यतेऽन्तः काव्यार्थानाम्। इदं तूच्यते —

अवस्थादिविभिन्नानां वाच्यानां विनिबन्धनम्[2]।

यत्प्रदर्शितं प्राक्,

भूम्नैव दृश्यते लक्ष्ये,

न तच्छक्यमपोहितुम्।

तत्तु भाति रसाश्रयात्॥ ८॥

तदिदमत्र संक्षेपेणाभिधीयते स[3]त्कवीनामुपदेशाय —

रसभावादिसम्बद्धा यद्यौचित्यानुसारिणी।
अन्वीयते वस्तुगतिर्देशकालादिभेदिनी॥ ९॥

तत्[4] का गणना कवीनामन्येषां परिमितशक्तीनाम्,

वाचस्पतिसहस्राणां सहस्रैरपि यत्नतः।
निबद्धा सा[5] क्षयं नैति प्रकृतिर्जगतामिव॥ १०॥

यथा हि जगत्प्रकृतिरतीतकल्पपरम्पराविर्भूतविचित्रवस्तुप्रपञ्चा सती पुनरिदानीं परिक्षीणापर[6]पदार्थनिर्माणशक्तिरिति न शक्यतेऽभिधातुम्। तद्वदेवेयं काव्यस्थितिरनन्ताभिः कविमतिभिरुपभुक्तापि नेदानीं परिहीयते, प्रत्युत नवनवाभिर्व्युत्पत्तिभिः परिवर्धते। इत्थं स्थितेऽपि—

संवादास्तु भवन्त्येव बाहुल्येन सुमेधसाम्।

स्थितं ह्येतत् संवादिन्य एव[7] मेधाविनां बुद्धयः। किन्तु—

---

१. 'इत्थं'–घ पुस्तके नास्ति। २. वाच्यार्थानां निबन्धनं–ग. ३. तत्कवी°–घ. ४. तत्–घ पुस्तके नास्ति. ५. निबद्धापि–घ. ६. °पर –घ. पुस्तके नास्ति। परिमित in place of परिक्षीणापर XII. 186 & No. 255 (BORI). ७. संवादिन्यो – घ.

Variety is contributed by time also. For instance, seasonal differences bring about differences in atmosphere, sky, water and such other insentient objects. With reference to sentient beings also, feelings of anxiety, etc. produced by particular times are quite common.

Equally well known is the practice of describing all objects in the world with an eye to their innate individual differences.

At this point, some might raise an objection : 'Objects are communicated only by their generic nature and not at all by their specific traits. On the basis of their own personal experiences of joy, etc. and their causes, poets universalise that the same experiences should follow from the same causes elsewhere also. Thus they embody ideas in their works only on the basis of the generic nature of experience common to them as well as to other persons. Surely, poets do not have any direct vision into the specific variations of all things in the past, present and future, like Yogins. And the generic universal of experience which is common to all experiences that are possible and which is common to men, one and all, is but restricted in scope and one can very well regard it to have been completely exhausted by the ancient poets themselves. For one cannot reasonably say that it has remained outside the ken of the ancients all along. Hence the idea of the moderners that a specific variation of an object is being presented in a novel fashion is only an empty boast. The only variation that actually exists is in the manner of presenting the (old) idea; that is all '.

This is our reply :—The statement that poetry proceeds only on the basis of generic nature and this being but limited, it must have been exhausted already and, therefore, there can be no novelty about poetic themes, is incorrect. For, if it were true that poetry proceeds on the basis of generic nature only, how could we account for the fact that the objects described by first-rate poets possess the highest beauty ? Furthermore, since there would be no matter for poetry except universals, there would be no possibility at all for a second poet to be rightly so regarded after Vālmīki, the first poet; for he will have

इत्थं[1] यथा यथा निरूप्यते, तथा तथा न लभ्यतेऽन्तः काव्यार्थानाम् । इदं तूच्यते —

अवस्थादिविभिन्नानां वाच्यानां विनिबन्धनम्[2] ।

यत्प्रदर्शितं प्राक्,

भूम्नैव दृश्यते लक्ष्ये,

न तच्छक्यमपोहितुम् ।

तत्तु भाति रसाश्रयात् ॥ ८ ॥

तदिदमत्र संक्षेपेणाभिधीयते स[3]त्कवीनामुपदेशाय —

रसभावादिसम्बद्धा यद्यौचित्यानुसारिणी ।
अन्वीयते वस्तुगतिर्देशकालादिभेदिनी ॥ ९ ॥

तत्[4] का गणना कवीनामन्येषां परिमितशक्तीनाम्,

वाचस्पतिसहस्राणां सहस्रैरपि यत्नतः ।
निबद्धा सा[5] क्षयं नैति प्रकृतिर्जगतामिव ॥ १० ॥

यथा हि जगत्प्रकृतिरतीतकल्पपरम्पराविर्भूतविचित्रवस्तुप्रपञ्चा सती पुनरिदानीं परिक्षीणापर[6]पदार्थनिर्माणशक्तिरिति न शक्यतेऽभिधातुम् । तद्वदेवेयं काव्यस्थितिरनन्ताभिः कविमतिभिरुपभुक्तापि नेदानीं परिहीयते, प्रत्युत नवनवाभिर्व्युत्पत्तिभिः परिवर्धते । इत्थं स्थितेऽपि—

संवादास्तु भवन्त्येव बाहुल्येन सुमेधसाम् ।

स्थितं ह्येतत् संवादिन्य[7] एव मेधाविनां बुद्धयः । किन्तु—

१. 'इत्थं' - प पुस्तके नास्ति । २. वाच्यार्थानां निबन्धनं - ग. ३. तत्कवी° - घ. ४. तत्-घ पुस्तके नास्ति. ५. निबद्धापि - घ. ६. °पर - घ. पुस्तके नास्ति । परिमित in place of परिक्षीणापर XII. 186 & No. 255 (BORI). ७. संवादिन्यो - घ.

Thus, the deeper we examine the nature of poetic themes, the more we will be convinced of their endlessness. This much, however, might be stated here :

We find in plenty examples of utilising the expressed content with variations of circumstances etc. But it will shine out only in the association of sentiment. **8**

The phrases ' as has been shown already ' and ' it cannot be denied that ' should be understood in the text in the latter and former half respectively of the first sentence.

Hence the following is stated in brief for the edification of good poets :—

If only the real nature of objects in the world, differing as it does according to place, time, and so on, is utilised in such a way that it is imbued with sentiment, emotion etc. and that it is in keeping with the demands of decorum; **9**

The ellipsis to be supplied in the following text is—" not to speak of human poets with limited powers ".

Like the resources of primordial Nature herself, the infinite possibilities of poetic themes can never be drained off even by a million Bṛhaspatis composing with all their might simultaneously. **10**

Though primordial Nature has been responsible for the creation of numerous worlds containing varied objects over a legion cycles of past aeons, it is not possible to say even now that her ability for the creation of new objects has diminished even by an iota. So also, the realm of poetry will not grow less, though countless poetic minds might take nourishment from it. On the countrary, it will become richer with newer and newer possibilities. All the same—

There are bound to be plenty of coincidences amongst great minds. **11 ab**

For it is a well known truth that the thoughts of great men bear strong affinities to one another.

तत्त्वस्य सारभूतस्यात्मनः सद्भावेऽन्यस्य पूर्वस्थित्यनुयाय्यपि वस्तु भातितराम्। पुराणरमणीयच्छायानुगृहीतं हि वस्तु शरीरवत् परां शोभां पुष्यति। न तु पुनरुक्तत्वेनावभासते । तन्व्याः शशिच्छायमिवाननम् ।

एवं तावत् ससंवादानां समुदायरूपाणां वाक्यार्थानां[1] विभक्ताः सीमानः। पदार्थरूपाणां च वस्त्वन्तरसदृशानां काव्यवस्तूनां नास्त्येव दोष इति प्रतिपादयितुमुच्यते—

अक्षरादिरचनेव योज्यते[2]
यत्र वस्तुरचना पुरातनी।
नूतने स्फुरति काव्यवस्तुनि
व्यक्तमेव खलु सा न दुष्यति॥ १५॥

न हि वाचस्पतिनाप्यक्षराणि पदानि वा कानिचिदपूर्वाणि घटयितुं शक्यन्ते। तानि तु[3] तान्येव उपनिबद्धानि न काव्यादिषु नवतां विरुध्यन्ति। तथैव पदार्थरूपाणि श्लेषादिमयान्यर्थतत्त्वानि। तस्मात् —

यदपि तदपि रम्यं[4]

काव्यशरीरं

यत्र लोकस्य किञ्चित्

यल्लोकस्य किञ्चित्

स्फुरितमिदमितीयं बुद्धिरभ्युज्जिहीते।

स्फुरणेयं काचिदिति सहृदयानां चमत्कृतिरुत्पद्यते ।

अनुगतमपि पूर्वच्छायया वस्तु तादृक्
सुकविरुपनिबध्नन् निन्द्यतां नोपयाति॥ १६॥

तदनुगतमपि पूर्वच्छायया वस्तु तादृक् तादृक्षं[6] सुकविर्विवक्षितव्यङ्ग्यवाच्यार्थसमर्पणसमर्थशब्दरचनारूपया बन्धच्छाययोपनिबध्नन् निन्द्यतां नैव याति।

---

१. तत्संवादानां वाक्यवेदितानां काव्यार्थानां – घ. ससंवादानां वाक्यार्थरूपाणां काव्यार्थानां° – MB. २. योक्ष्यते – ग. ३. तु–घ पुस्तके नास्ति। ४. काव्यं° – ग, MB. ५. नैव याति – MB. ६. तादृक्षं –घ पुस्तके नास्ति।

Thus, the deeper we examine the nature of poetic themes, the more we will be convinced of their endlessness. This much, however, might be stated here :

We find in plenty examples of utilising the expressed content with variations of circumstances etc. But it will shine out only in the association of sentiment. 8

The phrases ' as has been shown already ' and ' it cannot be denied that ' should be understood in the text in the latter and former half respectively of the first sentence.

Hence the following is stated in brief for the edification of good poets :—

If only the real nature of objects in the world, differing as it does according to place, time, and so on, is utilised in such a way that it is imbued with sentiment, emotion etc. and that it is in keeping with the demands of decorum; 9

The ellipsis to be supplied in the following text is—" not to speak of human poets with limited powers ".

Like the resources of primordial Nature herself, the infinite possibilities of poetic themes can never be drained off even by a million Bṛhaspatis composing with all their might simultaneously. 10

Though primordial Nature has been responsible for the creation of numerous worlds containing varied objects over a legion cycles of past aeons, it is not possible to say even now that her ability for the creation of new objects has diminished even by an iota. So also, the realm of poetry will not grow less, though countless poetic minds might take nourishment from it. On the countrary, it will become richer with newer and newer possibilities. All the same—

There are bound to be plenty of coincidences amongst great minds. 11 ab

For it is a well known truth that the thoughts of great men bear strong affinities to one another.

तत्त्वस्य सारभूतस्यात्मनः सद्भावेऽन्यस्य पूर्वस्थित्यनुयाय्यपि वस्तु भातितराम् । पुराणरमणीयच्छायानुगृहीतं हि वस्तु शरीरवत् परां शोभां पुष्यति । न तु पुनरुक्तत्वेनावभासते । तन्व्याः शशिच्छायमिवाननम् ।

एवं तावत् ससंवादानां समुदायरूपाणां वाक्यार्थानां[1] विभक्ताः सीमानः । पदार्थरूपाणां च वस्त्वन्तरसदृशानां काव्यवस्तूनां नास्त्येव दोष इति प्रतिपादयितुमुच्यते—

अक्षरादिरचनेव योज्यते[2]
यत्र वस्तुरचना पुरातनी ।
नूतने स्फुरति काव्यवस्तुनि
व्यक्तमेव खलु सा न दुष्यति ॥ १५ ॥

न हि वाचस्पतिनाप्यक्षराणि पदानि वा कानिचिदपूर्वाणि घटयितुं शक्यन्ते । तानि तु[3] तान्येव उपनिबद्धानि न काव्यादिषु नवतां विरुध्यन्ति । तथैव पदार्थरूपाणि श्लेषादिमयान्यर्थतत्त्वानि । तस्मात् —

यदपि तदपि रम्यं[4]
काव्यशरीरं

यत्र लोकस्य किञ्चित्

यल्लोकस्य किञ्चित्

स्फुरितमिदमितीयं बुद्धिरभ्युज्जिहीते ।

स्फुरणेयं काचिदिति सहृदयानां चमत्कृतिरुत्पद्यते ।

अनुगतमपि पूर्वच्छायया वस्तु तादृक्
सुकविरुपनिबध्नन् निन्द्यतां नोपयाति[5] ॥ १६ ॥

तदनुगतमपि पूर्वच्छायया वस्तु तादृक् तादृक्षं[6] सुकविर्विवक्षितव्यङ्ग्यवाच्यार्थ-समर्पणसमर्थशब्दरचनारूपया बन्धच्छाययोपनिबध्नन् निन्द्यतां नैव याति ।

---

१. तत्संवादानां वाक्यवेदितानां काव्यार्थानां – घ. ससंवादानां वाक्यार्थरूपाणां काव्यार्थानां° – MB. २. योक्ष्यते – ग. ३. तु–घ पुस्तके नास्ति । ४. काव्यं° – ग, MB. ५. नैव याति – MB. ६. तादृक्षं –घ पुस्तके नास्ति ।

So long as its vital essence is present, even a poetic theme similar to an earlier one will appear exceedingly beautiful. Just as a body appears lovely thanks to the association of even past graces, so also a poetic theme will look graceful even while it bears similarity to lovely shades of meaning in earlier works. It will never appear as tautological. The face of a lady bearing resemblance to the moon is a simile.

Hitherto different coincidences between units of whole sentences have been clearly demarcated. In the following it is shown that correspondences between individual words in poetic themes do not become flaws at all :—

Even when the already existing elements of poetic themes such as arrangements of letters etc. are utilised, it will certainly not smack of a flaw so long as the poetic theme as a whole is shining with novelty. 15

Not even a Bṛhaspati can use letters or words which are entirely new. Though the self-same letters and words which are common to all poetry are employed in present works also, their novelty does not suffer on that account. The same is true of meanings too which are conveyed by words involving *double entendre*. Therefore,

Whatever theme it might be, so long as it produces the impression in the minds of people: " Yes, this is a lovely and unique flash "; 16 ab

The meaning is ' so long as the favourable impression that it is an extraordinary flash is produced in the minds of refined critics '.

Though it might smack of earlier usages, a theme can very well be utilised by a good poet. He will never become an object of censure by so doing. 16cd

Even such a theme reflecting a shade of another earlier thought can very well be utilised by a good poet so that a new grace of construction, involving a texture of words capable of surrendering the expressed content to the intended suggestive content, is made to shine forth. He will not be open to any reproach if he does this.

So long as its vital essence is present, even a poetic theme similar to an earlier one will appear exceedingly beautiful. Just as a body appears lovely thanks to the association of even past graces, so also a poetic theme will look graceful even while it bears similarity to lovely shades of meaning in earlier works. It will never appear as tautological. The face of a lady bearing resemblance to the moon is a simile.

Hitherto different coincidences between units of whole sentences have been clearly demarcated. In the following it is shown that correspondences between individual words in poetic themes do not become flaws at all :—

Even when the already existing elements of poetic themes such as arrangements of letters etc. are utilised, it will certainly not smack of a flaw so long as the poetic theme as a whole is shining with novelty. 15

Not even a Bṛhaspati can use letters or words which are entirely new. Though the self-same letters and words which are common to all poetry are employed in present works also, their novelty does not suffer on that account. The same is true of meanings too which are conveyed by words involving *double entendre*. Therefore,

Whatever theme it might be, so long as it produces the impression in the minds of people: " Yes, this is a lovely and unique flash "; 16 ab

The meaning is ' so long as the favourable impression that it is an extraordinary flash is produced in the minds of refined critics '.

Though it might smack of earlier usages, a theme can very well be utilised by a good poet. He will never become an object of censure by so doing. 16cd

Even such a theme reflecting a shade of another earlier thought can very well be utilised by a good poet so that a new grace of construction, involving a texture of words capable of surrendering the expressed content to the intended suggestive content, is made to shine forth. He will not be open to any reproach if he does this.

NOTES

The *Bhāktavāda* carries a reference to the Mīmāṁsā-thinkers who have classified all meaning under two heads, viz. मुख्य or primary and भाक्त (गौण) or secondary. The term *bhākta* is a very old term and constantly used in several philosophical sūtras; cf. *Brahma-sutra*, II. iii. 3, II. iii. 16, II. iv. 2, and III. i. 4. We have the word used also in Śaunaka's *Bṛhaddevatā*, I. 72–3. These thinkers see no reason why the principle of meaning in poetry should be different from general principles of meaning. They think that all associated and suggested meanings can be fully explained as the handiwork of *bhakti* or *guṇavṛtti*. The later texts prefer the use of the word *lakṣaṇā* when they mean *bhakti*.

The view of treating *dhvani* as something ineffable may be taken either in a complimentary way or as a criticism. This school of objectors accepts *dhvani* as the essence of poetry and grants its existence; yet objects to the treatise because in its opinion *dhvani* is essentially indefinable —

L. 8 : सहृदय—Some scholars (Sovani, Kane; HSP, pp 191-2) have wrongly supposed that the *Kārikā-kāra*, was different from Ānandavardhana, the *Vṛttikāra*, and that the former's proper name was 'Sahṛdaya'. The present passage does not permit such wild guess-work. The word *sahṛdaya* has been used earlier not only by Vāmana but also by Udbhaṭa in his *Bhāmahavivaraṇa*. cf. सहृदयहृदयानां रञ्जकः कोऽपि पाकः। *Kāvyālaṅkāra*-sūtravṛttl, I. i. 21; सहृदयहृदयावर्जनलक्षणासहाऽप्रस्तुतप्रशंसा। Raniero Gnoli, *Udbhaṭa's commentary on the Kāvyālaṁkāra of Bhāmaha*, Roma, 1962, P. 39. Thus it is clear that the word *sahṛdaya* was long current in Kashmir literary circles as a general name for tasteful readers even before Ānandavardhana (For a fuller discussion, see-Introduction).

L. 9 : बुधैः— Since the subject-matter is poetry here, the Vṛtti explains *budha* as implying experts on poetry. But, as we saw above, this restriction in meaning does not contradict the general sense of 'grammarian' for that word. परम्परया...प्रकटितः— As pointed out by Abhinavagupta we should understand that the author presupposes only an oral tradition among experts on poetry; for we have no written records to that effect.

NOTES

The *Bhāktavāda* carries a reference to the Mīmāṁsā-thinkers who have classified all meaning under two heads, viz. मुख्य or primary and भाक्त (गौण) or secondary. The term *bhākta* is a very old term and constantly used in several philosophical sūtras; cf. *Brahma–sūtra*, II. iii. 3, II. iii. 16, II. iv. 2, and III. i. 4. We have the word used also in Śaunaka's *Bṛhaddevatā*, I. 72–3. These thinkers see no reason why the principle of meaning in poetry should be different from general principles of meaning. They think that all associated and suggested meanings can be fully explained as the handiwork of *bhakti* or *guṇavṛtti*. The later texts prefer the use of the word *lakṣaṇā* when they mean *bhakti*.

The view of treating *dhvani* as something ineffable may be taken either in a complimentary way or as a criticism. This school of objectors accepts *dhvani* as the essence of poetry and grants its existence; yet objects to the treatise because in its opinion *dhvani* is essentially indefinable —

L. 8 : सहृदय—Some scholars (Sovani, Kane; HSP, pp 191-2) have wrongly supposed that the *Kārikā-kāra*, was different from Ānandavardhana, the *Vṛttikāra*, and that the former's proper name was 'Sahṛdaya'. The present passage does not permit such wild guess-work. The word *sahṛdaya* has been used earlier not only by Vāmana but also by Udbhaṭa in his *Bhāmahavivaraṇa*. cf. सहृदयहृदयानां रञ्जकः कोऽपि पाकः। *Kāvyālaṅkāra-sūtravṛttl*, I. i. 21; सहृदयहृदयावर्जनलक्षणासहाऽप्रस्तुतप्रशंसा। Raniero Gnoli, *Udbhaṭa's commentary on the Kāvyālaṁkāra of Bhāmaha*, Roma, 1962, P. 39. Thus it is clear that the word *sahṛdaya* was long current in Kashmir literary circles as a general name for tasteful readers even before Ānandavardhana (For a fuller discussion, see-Introduction).

L. 9 : बुधैः— Since the subject-matter is poetry here, the Vṛtti explains *budha* as implying experts on poetry. But, as we saw above, this restriction in meaning does not contradict the general sense of 'grammarian' for that word. परम्परया...प्रकटितः– As pointed out by Abhinavagupta we should understand that the author presupposes only an oral tradition among experts on poetry; for we have no written records to that effect.

L. 10 : तस्य...मानस्यापि—The first and foremost evidence for the validity of *dhvani* is the felt experience of connoisseurs. And it is a landmark in the history of Sanskrit poetics. All the earlier theorists wrote more or less normative guidebooks to poets. The readers' say did not figure prominently in them.

L. 11 : अभाव...संभवन्ति—Three forms which *Abhāvavāda* might assume are posed at length in what follows : The first of these is the most formidable one and represents the conventional view of orthodox theorists. In the orthodox analysis, poetry is divisible into its elements of sound and sense. The concept of *Śabda-* and *artha- alaṅkāras* explains the beauty of both the elements. While the doctrine of *guṇas* takes into account the organisation of syllables with different poetic values. The theory of styles (*rītis*) and of *Vṛttis* also is based on *guṇas.* Thus when all the noticeable aspects of poetic beauty are accounted for, there is nothing left for a new formulation like *dhvani.*

The different *rītis, Vaidarbhī, Gauḍī* and *Pāñcālī* were noted by Vāmana while the *Vṛttis,* viz. *Upanāgarikā, Komalā,* and *Grāmyā* were codified by Udbhaṭa in his exposition of alliterative effects (Kāvyālaṅkārasaṅgraha, Chapter I).

The second form of the *Abhāvavāda* urges that a piece of composition devoid of the excellences shall *ipso facto* cease to be poetry, No amount of affirmation by a self-chosen coterie will raise the compositions with so-called *dhvani* to the level of poetry.

The third form denies the existence of anything like *dhvani* because it can at the most be a new name for old beauties.

Page 4. L. 12 : यस्मिन्नस्ति...—This quotation contains a devastating ridicule of the followers of *dhvani.* It is ascribed to Manoratha, a senior contemporary of Ānandavardhana, thus proving that there must have been some historical truth in the controversy between pro-*dhvani* and anti-*dhvani* camps before the appearance of the *Dhvanyāloka* on the scene.

Abhinavagupta takes the initial words of the second line to stand for *Śabdālaṅkāras* ; and the word '*Vakrokti*' to mean *saṅghaṭanā*, a meaning not supported by any logic. Apparently, he wants to distinguish somehow between '*alaṅkṛti*' in the first line and the '*vakrokti*' here. But even without resorting to this strained construction, we can very well take the normal meaning of it either as a specially admired individual alaṅkāra of that name or as a general principle underlying all *alaṅkāras*. Abhinavagupta's objection to such an interpretation is not convincing; because the absence of some recognised figures (as mentioned in the first line) cannot be identical with the absence of the underlying principle of all *alaṅkāras*. The possibility of unrecognised figures existing even in such an eventuality is not illogical.

L. 16 : The word गुणवृत्ति is employed here as a synonym for *bhakti*. The secondary usage of words stems from a common possession of qualities between two things. These theorists are convinced that, in all examples of linguistic usage, there are only two functions involved :—(1) primary denotation, (2) secondary or metaphorical indication. Hence, if *dhvani* is a linguistic function and different from the first, it must obviously come under the second.

L. 17 : यद्यपि च ···— Ānandavardhana turns now to the actually recorded statements of rhetoricians. No one has either mentioned the term *dhvani* or equated it with *bhakti*. But they have accorded the status of poetry to certain examples on the ground that *guṇavṛtti* figures therein. So it is, in a way, an extension of the idea implied in their procedure.

The final anti-*dhvani* stand is characterised by this author as coming from those who are too incompetent to define *dhvani*, though they may enjoy its beauty.

Page 6. L. 4 : तस्य हि ··· — The positive merits of the new doctrine are set out here. Dhvani is the quintessence of the poetry of all master-poets and is the most beautiful in itself, though undetected and left unexplained by all the writers on poetry in the past. What is more, it is widely instanced in great works like the *Rāmāyaṇa* and the *Mahābhārata*.

In this context Abhinavagupta supplies what has come to be regarded as a classic definition of a '*sahṛdaya*' :- येषां काव्यानुशीलन-वशाद्विशदीभूते मनोमुकुरे वर्णनीयतन्मयीभवनयोग्यता ते स्वहृदयसंवादभाजः

सहृदयाः। Though Ānandavardhana does not use the technical terms of Indian aesthetics, viz. तन्मयीभवन and हृदयसंवाद, one can have no doubt that he did subscribe to a theory of 'like-heartedness,' between the poet and the responsive reader.

Kārikā 2 : The reader's appreciation is always related to poetic meaning. And that alone deserves to be characterised as the soul or the essence of poetry. Now poetry is a whole; poetic meaning is also a whole. The essence of poetry cannot therefore be anything other than a whole. But it is possible to distinguish two aspects of the whole meaning, viz. the *vācya* and the *vyaṅgya.* The previous writers, in their aesthetic analysis, did not make the distinction though they were aware of it; and hence could not do justice to the specially important part contributed by suggested meaning in poetry. Ānandavardhana is very subtly introducing the basis of his aesthetic analysis here without denying the beauty of the *vācya* in poetry. The very idea of *ātman* is such that though it is figuratively used, it cannot give an equal status to any two entities denoted by it. As Abhinavagupta notes pertinently, the idea of two *ātmans* for anything is incompatible. Hence the implied relative superiority of *vyaṅgyārtha* alone is established in such a way that there is no underestimation of the *vācyārtha*, ts means.

L·11 : काव्यस्य हि···—It is often found that the 'soul of poetry' is discussed without any reference to its 'body'. It is usually taken for granted that the body consists of *śabda* and *artha.* Such a general idea does not bring out the properties of these peculiar to poetry. Ānandavardhana has unmistakenly emphasized here how his doctrine of *dhvani* as the soul does full justice to the claims of not only the body consisting of figurative beauty and guṇas in respect of artistic use of *śabda* and *artha*, but also to that of the soul whose beauty lies at the root of all harmony.

Kārikā 3 : When the above distinction from the aesthetic standpoint is made, the fact will emerge that all theories of *alaṅkāra, guṇa* etc., formulated by rhetoricians of the past are confined to an elucidation of the beauty of the *vācya* element alone. Ānandavardhana states here that he has nothing but respect for the work of the ancients; and that he will utilise the same wholeheartedly. But it is clear that the real philosophy of poetry which is concerned with the soul begins at the point where the early theories end.

Kārikā 4: That *vyaṅgya* exists over and above *vācya* in poetry is brought out with a happy simile here. The beauty of individual limbs, natural as well as embellished, is distinct from the total grace of a lovely woman.

Page 8. L. 6: स ह्यर्थो···—The province of *vyaṅgyārtha* is inclusive of (1) *vastu*, (2) *alaṅkāra* and (3) *rasādi*. The *vṛtti* labours at length to prove how each one of the types is distinct from *vācya*. L. 10: भम···—This verse is a quotation from Hāla's anthology of Prakrit lyrics, the *Gāthāsaptaśatī*; No. 175 in Weber's edition.

The readers have to imagine a proper context to grasp the intended *vyaṅgyārtha*. But for the fact that the speaker is a wanton, there would be no scope for any suggested meaning. The suggested prohibition (मा भ्रम) of the unwanted intrusion of the pious man is a *vastu* or a bare fact.

L. 15: Op. cit. No. 669. According to Prof. V. M. Kulkarni, the reading of the last word is णिमज्जिहिसि (Journal of the Shivaji University, Kolhapur, Vol. I. 1967 p. 17). Here also, the speaker is a woman of loose morals. It is a veiled invitation to the traveller to her bed. Here also the suggested is a mere *vastu* since there is no figurative touch or expression of feeling. L. 20: Op. cit. No. 944 (supplement 7). In examples like this and the following, the reader is left in doubt about the exact intent of the speaker.

Page 10. L. 4: Op. cit. No. 968. Here also the suggested import is dubious. L. 9: Abhinavagupta says that this is spoken by a clever confidant to warn her guilty mistress of the approach of the latter's husband. L. 15: द्वितीयोऽपि प्रभेदः = suggested *alaṅkāra*. अग्रे = in the second chapter. L. 16: तृतीयस्तु ...— It is the speciality of *rasādi* that it is exclusively suggested unlike *vastu* and *alaṅkāra* which can also be expressed by words. L. 18: स्वशब्द...— The only two conceivable possibilities of conveying *rasādi* are :- (1) by using their proper names; (2) by way of description of their *Vibhāvas* etc. ... पूर्वस्मिन् ... कथञ्चिदिति (p. 12, L. 5)—The first possibility is completely ruled out. Instances, positive as well as negative, are given to reject this possibility. There need be no poetry in instances where the names of *rasa* occur. There can be very good poetry in the absence of those names also. Hence, *rasādi* is by no means directly denoted by words.

P. 12. L. 5 : तृतीयोऽपि ... – *Rasādi* then, springs only from a function of language other than denotation. Abhinavagupta takes it that this might allude to *tātparya-śakti* as much as *Vyañjanā*. But Ānandavardhana has not made any such clear distinction. He seems to emphasize that what is not *vācya* must be, *ipso facto*, *vyaṅgya*.

L. 6 : अग्रे = In the third chapter. The rise of the two meanings viz. *vācya* and *rasādi* is so instantaneous that it is impossible to perceive any time sequence in them. Hence *rasādi* is called असंलक्ष्यक्रमव्यङ्ग्य.

Kārikā 5 — This is one of the most crucial *kārikās* in the text and bristles with problems of interpretation and text reading. Ānandavardhana here is citing the testimony of the famous epic-poet, Vālmīki, in support of his main thesis that *rasa-dhvani* is the soul of poetry. The wording of the *kārikā* reminds us not only of the *Rāmāyaṇa* (*Bālakaṇḍa* ii, 15) but also of the *Raghuvaṁśa* (XIV. 70). Both these passages make one think that the sorrow of the sage Vālmīki at the sight of the tragic end of one of the mating birds found a spontaneous expression in metrical form, *viz.*, मा निषाद etc. The wording of the *vṛtti* on the *kārikā* does not conclusively show whether the *śoka* in question is originally of Vālmīki or of the surviving bird. However, the additional clarification offered in the *vṛtti* " that *śoka* indeed is the *sthāyibhāva* " of *karuṇarasa* raises certain fundamental issues. Is he by chance trying to distinguish between empirical sorrow (located in the bird) from impersonal sorrow produced in the witnessing sage ? Another problem posed here is whether the specific *śloka* viz. मा निषाद etc., is the form taken by Vālmīki's *śoka* or whether it refers to the whole epic. In the *vṛtti* on IV. 5 the author openly states in so many words that the sage has 'woven' (आसूत्रित:) this *karuṇa-rasa* into the Rāmāyaṇa as a predominent content.

Some manuscripts (vide: NSP edition) construe the reference in question to be मा निषाद and quote it in the body of the *vṛtti*. But in view of other considerations noted above as well as its absence in other manuscripts, our edition has relegated it to the footnote. Even if it were held as a genuine part of the text, it would have to be understood as containing the essence of the *Rāmāyaṇa* as a whole in order to do justice to the express statement of Ānandavardhana in the fourth *Uddyota,* besides the clear implications of the present *Kārikā.*

The purpose of the present *Kārikā* is to find a poet's testimony for the thesis that *vyaṅgyārtha* alone is the soul of poetry. *Rasa* happens to be the most important element in *vyaṅgyārtha.* Vālmīki's assertion (शोकः श्लोकत्वमागतः) in the *Rāmāyaṇa* should yield the meaning—"*Karuṇa-rasa* has been transformed by me into the form of the epic-poem," if it is to be relevant in this discussion. Hence the word *śoka* should mean *karuṇa-rasa* and *śloka* should mean *Rāmāyaṇa* though it involves some stretching. The *vṛtti* has clearly indicated this by the expression शोको हि करुणस्थायिभावः. There is a likelihood of our mistaking the personal sorrow to be the *sthāyibhāva* and to think that this *sthāyibhāva* is different from *karuṇa–rasa.* But the truth is that, like the other technical terms in नाट्यशास्त्र, viz. *vibhāva* and *anubhāva, bhāva* too, whether *vyabhicāri* or *sthāyi* is applicable only in the realm of artistic representation and does not connote its empirical counterpart. Further, there is no separate entity like *rasa* other than *sthāyibhāva. Rasa* is only the name given to the *sthāyibhāva* at the point when it yields aesthetic delight.

Abhinavagupta has taken great pains to bring out this implication of Ānandavardhana. He even goes to the extent of construing the third quarter in the *Kārikā* in a very oblique way;—क्रौञ्चद्वन्द्ववियोगोत्थः=क्रौञ्चस्य साहचर्यध्वंसमहिम्ना...उद्बुद्धः. And adds that the sage has no personal sorrow like the surviving bird. The sight of the bird's sorrow excites his aesthetic contemplation of universal sorrow (शोकस्थायिभाव–करुणरस) which spontaneously overflows in metrical form. The nature of the sage's creative experience is one of pure aesthetic delight.

It has been very difficult for this editor to fix the reading of the *vṛtti* on this *Kārikā*. Most of the manuscripts consulted give the reading सन्निहितसहचरीविरहकातरक्रौञ्च. The editors of the NSP edition indicate that only ग manuscript gives निहत° for सन्निहित. (Omission of this in our footnote is by oversight). But the reading of BP as well as of KSRI is निहतसहचरी° indicating thereby that the Kerala manuscript tradition is unanimous regarding this reading. P. V. Kane holds positively that the former Kashmir reading adopted in this text is more genuine of the two (History of Sanskrit Poetics, pp. 364–365; footnote No. 1). But further studies of this editor show that the Kerala reading was perhaps known to Orissa scholars also as early as Caṇḍīdāsa, as the following extract from his काव्यप्रकाशदीपिका will show :—

......सहचरवधव्याकुलक्रौञ्च्यालोकप्रतिफलिततदीयशोकोद्बुद्धकविवदनविनिर्गतानादिरसतत्त्वपरिणामरूपादिकाव्यप्रतिफलनात्मकसहृदयहृदयानन्द...

(S. P. Bhattacharya's edition, Varanasi, 1964, page 357).

Obviously, this is a paraphrase of the relevant *Locana* passage. The word वध here possibly alludes to विरह or else it is a paraphrase of निहत. A more positive evidence in favour of the reading निहत is provided in the testimonia of the earliest reference to this *Vṛtti* passage by Rājaśekhara in his *Kāvyamīmāṁsā*—निषादनिहतसहचरीकं क्रौञ्चयुवानं... (GOS Edition. Baroda, 1934, page 7).

These extracts raise further issues. Was the bird which was shot a male or a female ? Both Ānandavardhana and Rājaśekhara assert it to be the female. This is diametrically opposed to the statement in the Rāmāyaṇa. Long before Kuppuswamy Shastri, Caṇḍīdāsa quoted above had tried to emend the text of °क्रौञ्चाक्रन्द into °क्रौञ्च्याक्रन्द, सहचरीविरह into सहचरवध (सहचारिविरह-Kuppuswami Shastri). But these are in our opinion pointless. A similar ingenious attempt by G. H. Bhaṭṭ (J. O. I, Baroda, Vol. IX, Pt. 2, pp. 148–151) to explain the compound as referring to the male bird's death is also noted and negatived effectively by Kane. His logic is this : "Supposing that निहत is the correct reading, we expect सहचरीविरहकातर-निहत-क्रौञ्च, as he must have been कातर before he was shot" (Loc. Cit.). The attempts of both Kuppuswamy Shastri (*Upalocana*) and G. H. Bhatt involve a very forced and far-fetched dissolving of the compound to yield the sense of the male as the bird shot down. This is hardly permissible in the uniformly straightforward style of the *vṛtti*. The reading सन्निहितसहचरीविरह offers an easy meaning if we understand विरह itself to mean ultimate parting due to death of the female bird in initimate embrace of the male.

As indicated above, the verse मा निषाद...may be taken to represent the essence of the Rāmāyaṇa as a whole symbolically. If Rāma and Sītā are understood by the mating birds, Rāvaṇa represents the hunter who brings pain to Sītā, the female bird. Such a symbolic interpretation has been suggested even by Paṭṭābhirāma Shastry in his notes on BP. besides P. V. Kane (op. cit.). On the other hand, if a literal meaning alone were to be understood from the verse, it would be difficult to illustrate even *karuṇa-rasa* therein. For, the verse is more an imprecation or curse hurled on the hunter by the sage in anger, and less an embodiment of sorrow or pity at the suffering bird.

Whether poetry is the expression of the poet's feelings or emotions, personal or impersonal, is a much discussed question in Western literary criticism. We have poets like Shelley (cf. *our sweetest songs are those that tell of saddest thought*) and Wordsworth who says, " poetry is the spontaneous overflow of powerful feelings; and takes its origin from emotion recollected in tranquillity; the emotion is contemploted till, by a species of reaction, the tranquillity gradually disappears, and an emotion kindred to that which was before the subject of contemplation, is gradually produced, and does itself actually exist in the mind " (*Preface to Lyrical Ballads*). There are philosophers like Bergson who confirm this :—" If the artist is able to attain the emotion, the original mood, which lies beneath the commonplace, conventional expression that conceals the individual mental state, he is a poet. By animating words with a life of their own, the poet suggests to us things that speech is not calculated to express ". (Vernon Hall, *A Short History of Literary Criticism, London*, 1964, *p*. 148).

Western classical theory also offers some parallels :—" The essence of all poetry is to be found, not in high-wrought subtlety of thought, not in pointed cleverness of phrase, but in the depths of the heart and the most sacred feelings of the men who write" (Rev. John Keble, *Lectures on Latin poetry*)." "True poetry is nothing else than each poet's innermost feeling in rhythmic language" (Ibid).

With this may be compared also the aesthetic theory of Croce that "art is not feeling in its immediacy since the poet does not totter under the emotions he sings" (Vernon Hall. A Short History of Literary Criticism, London, 1964 p. 152).

It is interesting to compare this idea of *rasa* in the creative artist with T. S. Eliot's oft-quoted dictum :— "Poetry is not a turning loose of emotion, but an escape from emotion; it is not the expression of personality, but an escape from personality". (*Points of View*, London, 1951, p. 54). The present writer has fully discussed this question in his paper : *Some aspects of T. S. Eliot's critical theory in the light of Sanskrit Poetics*, Indian Response to poetry in English, Macmillan, Madras, 1970, pp. 34–43. Pravas Jivan Chaudhury institutes a comparison between this aesthetic attitude in Indian aesthetics and Keat's "negative capability" as well as Hegel's theory of "the effacement of all idiosyncracy". (The Journal of Aesthetics and Art Criticism, Cleveland, Ohio, Vol. XXIV, No. 1., p. 200). In all these comparisons we should bear in mind that we have here only a very cryptic statement by Ānandavardhana and that we owe all the details of the aesthetic theory to Abhinavagupta's *Locana* (For a full exposition of this in particular relation to *sādhāraṇīkaraṇa*, vide :— G. Hanumantha Rao : *Sādhāraṇīkaraṇa according to Abhinavagupta*, Arts Journal of the Mysore University, Vol. XXIII (1967) pp. 18–34 ; for a short but authoritative account of it see, M. Hiriyanna, *Art Experience*, Radhakrishnan Memorial Volume, Allen & Unwin). Rabindranath's view of the creative artist's experience also bears affinity with the aesthetic attitude discussed here : "Poetry is the outcome of the desire to see with the mind what the eye sees and with the eye what the mind imagines" (*Reminiscences*, p. 240). Also : "It is necessary to remark here that merely because something has been written when feelings are brimming over, it is not therefore necessarily good. Such is rather a time when the utterance is thick with emotion. Just as it does not do to have the writer entirely *removed* from the feeling to which he is giving expression, so also it does not conduce to the truest poetry to have him too close to it... The mind of the artist must attain a degree of aloofness — the creator within must be allowed the sole control. If the subject, matter gets the better of creation, the result is a mere replica of the event, not a reflection of it through the artist's mind (*Ibid.* p. 238). Equally interesting is the parallelism in thought (noted by Rama Pisharoti in his Translation of the *Locana,* Vide, *Indian Thought,* Vol. IX, Allahabad, 1917, p. 29) in one of Hazlitt's essays who defines poetry to be the " natural impression of any object or event by its vividness exciting an involuntary movement of imagination or passion, and producing by sympathy a certain modulation of the voice or sounds expressing it ".

L. 11–12. प्रतीयमानस्य...प्राधान्यात्—This is an important point noted in the *vṛtti.* It serves to remove any possible misunderstanding in holding *vyaṅgyārtha* to be the soul of poetry and illustrating it only through *rasa* leaving out other varieties like *vastu* and *alaṅkāra. Rasādi* should be regarded as the meaning exclusively poetic and the other varieties too come to be associated with it in poetry in some form or other. It must be thus understood that a poetic *vastu* and a poetic *alaṅkāra* also are distinct from prosaic *vastu* and prosaic *alaṅkāra.* It is by the relieving touch of *rasa* that these two acquire poetic charm. The word *rasa* is a generic term here and stands for all feelings or emotive meanings classed variously by writers under heads like *bhāva* (*vyabhicāri*), *rasābhāsa, bhāvābhāsa, rasapraśama, bhāvapraśama.*

Page 14. *Kārikā* 6 : This is a poetic tribute paid to the creative genius of great poets. The word अलोकसामान्यम् (extraordinary) is reminiscent of Kālidāsa (*Kumārasambhava,* V. 75b). The rarity of great poets, like that of prophets, is well known. (cf. If thou partake the animating faith that poets, even as prophets, each with each connected in a mighty scheme of truth, have each his own peculiar faculty, Heaven's gift, a sense that fits him objects unseen before ... to perceive.

(Wordsworth, *Prelude,* Book XIII)

Among Sanskrit poets too it is a common idea; e. g. Bāṇa says—

सन्ति श्वान इवासङ्ख्या जातिभाजो गृहे गृहे ।
उत्पादका न बहवः कवयः शरभा इव ॥ *Harṣacarita*, I. 5.

For a similar idea see also :

कस्यापि शक्तिप्रभवात्प्रभावा-
दुदेति तत्काव्यमहारहस्यम् ।
क्लिष्टो गुरूणां सद्मेषु नित्यं
कश्चिद्बुधश्चेतयते न वा यत् ॥...
बह्वर्थसिद्धा परिपाकभूमिः
कस्यापि वाणी रसवत्युदेति ।

—Maṅkhuka, *Śrīkaṇṭhacarita*, II. 4, 8.

Pratibhā may be equated with what English critics mean by the word 'Imagination'. The following observations on Imagination may be of interest : "Imagination is a power intermediate between intellect and emotion, working towards both, and partaking of both...Closely connected with this is what some have called penetrative, others the interpretative power of imagination. It is that subtle and mysterious gift, that intense intuition, piercing beneath all surface appearance, goes straight to the core of an object, enters where reasoning and peddling analysis are at fault, lays hold of the inner heart, the essential life of a scene, a character, or a situation and expresses it in a few immortal words. What is the secret of this penetrative glance, who shall say? It defies analysis...The joy of imagination in its own vision, the thrill of delight, is one of the most exquisite moods man ever experiences".

—J. C. Shairp, *Aspects of Poetry*, p, 7 ff

Abhinavagupta has focussed our attention here to the views of his teacher Bhaṭṭa Tauta on *pratibhā* from the lost work *Kāvyakautuka*. Some quotations of Tauta are given below *in extenso* :—

नानृषिः कविरित्युक्तं ऋषिश्च किल दर्शनात्।
विचित्रभावधर्मांशतत्त्वप्रख्या च दर्शनम् ॥
स तत्त्वदर्शनादेव शास्त्रेषु पठितः कविः।
दर्शनाद्वर्णनाच्चाथ रूढा लोके कविश्रुतिः ॥
तथा हि दर्शने स्वच्छे नित्येऽप्यादिकवेर्मुनेः।
नोदिता कविता लोके यावज्जाता न वर्णना ॥

Quoted from Hemacandra, *Kāvyānuśāsana.*

The *pratibhā* is contagious and transports the reader all at once according to Tauṭa ; cf. नायकस्य कवेः श्रोतुः समानोऽनुभवस्ततः। (quoted in *Locana*). Many modern critics have misunderstood this quotation as related to the *rasa* experience common to the poet and the reader alike. What is really intended here is not aesthetic experience but the power of imagination or *Pratibhā*. The imaginative faculties of the poet and the reader are alike and hence the concept of *sādhāraṇīkaraṇa* becomes possible. This itself was called by the name of *bhāvakatva* or *bhāvanā-vyāpāra* by Bhaṭṭanāyaka. Vide : प्रतिपत्तॄन् प्रति सा प्रतिभा नानुमीयमाना, अपि तु तदावेशेन भासमानेत्यर्थः यदुक्तमस्मदुपाध्यायभट्टतौतेन। ... (*Locana*, before नायकस्य etc.)

That the gift of *pratibhā* is divine and its working effortless is further supported by a happy quotation from Bhaṭṭanāyaka in the *Locana* :—

वाग्धेनुर्दुग्ध एकं हि रसं यद्बालतृष्णया।
तेन नास्य समः स स्याद्दुह्यते योगिभिर्हि यः ॥

It will be seen that for the first time in the history of Sanskrit Poetics, *Pratibhā* or creative imagination has been here linked up with suggestion. Again, for the first time, relative superiority of poems is sought to be decided by the test of aesthetic suggestion.

Kārikā 7 : In India, as in the West, the traditional approach to the understanding of poetry was very much scholarly and pedantic. No special qualification of taste was laid down for a literary critic apart from general learning in different allied branches like prosody, grammar and dictionary. Even as late a commentator as Mallinātha conforms to this scholarly tradition.

to judge from the vast *Śāstra* literature asserted by him as mastered. Ānandavardhana sounds a note of warning to this school of pedantic interpreters of poetry. He declares in no uncertain terms that the central meaning of poetry has nothing to do with laborious learning, and that it can be grasped only by the few *sahṛdayas* gifted with taste. Cf.

"Two different concepts of the interpretation of literature are current :

(a) That it is simply to reveal the intention of the author by removing obstacles to understanding; i. e. to explain vocabulary idiom, and syntax, to gloss obscure allusions, to clarify arguments. It is thought that the intended meaning will then stand out clear; and the expositor's work is at an end.

(b) That a work of literature contains a latent or hidden sense that is not necessarily revealed by the simple removal of difficulties. It is the task of the critic to expound this latent meaning... "—Graham Hough. *An Essay on Criticism*, London, 1966, p. 67.

P. 14. L, 13. Correct the misprint in the text from लक्षणमिवाऽप्रगीतानाम् to लक्षणमिवाप्रगीतानाम्.

There are two readings of the text here of the word translated by us as "if they are not good musicians." The readings are प्रगीतानाम् and अप्रगीतानाम्. Abhinavagupta gives the etymological meaning of प्रगीत only; but his commentators (like Rāmasāraka, Uttungodaya and Kuppuswami Shastri) think that he is in favour of the reading अप्रगीतानाम् in the *Vṛtti*. Hermann Jocobi follows the Kavyamālā Edition and adopts the reading *pragītānām* in this German translation which reads :—

"Wie solchen, welche sur die Theorie der Musik kennen die individuellen ganzen und Zwischentone guter sanger unerkennbar sind." (ZDMG, LVI, p. 588). The word प्रगीत means "good singer" according to both Abhinavagupta and Jacobi; not "good song". The word appears with the genitive case-ending in the text and the question is whether it is to be construed with the immediately following word गान्धर्वलक्षणविदाम् or with the immediately preceding word स्वरश्रुत्यादिलक्षणम्. Jacobi adopts the latter construction and translates that those who know the theory of music only might miss the 'whole note' (semibreve) and 'middle notes' of good singers. But we have preferred the other construction in so far as it agrees on all fours with the comparison in question. The balance may be brought out as follows:

1. वाच्यवाचकलक्षणमात्रकृतश्रमाणां = गान्धर्वलक्षणविदाम्
2. काव्यतत्त्वार्थभावनाविमुखानां = अप्रगीतानाम्
   Put in apposition to above. | Put in apposition to above.
3. असावर्थः—Subject = स्वरश्रुत्यादिलक्षणम्—Subject
4. अगोचरः—Predicate = अगोचरम्—Predicate understood.

Though at first sight it might seem that the reading प्रगीत in the general sense of a song is more natural, it does not serve as an effective simile in this context. As we saw above, it involves a forced construing (as done by Jacobi) even in the sense of 'good singers'. This meaning of the word finds strange confirmation from a usage of Kālidāsa. We have in his *prastāvanā* of the Vikramorvaśīya the line किं नार्यः कलमधुराक्षरं प्रगीताः ('Have the damsels started singing sweetly?') This verse has been relegated to the foot-notes in Prof. H. D. Velankar's critical edition (Sahitya Akademi, New Delhi, 1961, p. 2) though supported by 8 Mss.

The passage is very significant as illustrative of Ānandavardhana's aesthetic attitude which surveys the other arts too like music in discussions about poetry unlike his predecessors who gave only rules of rhetoric. For the whole idea, cf :—

1. "The real danger of *dictionary understanding* is that it so easily prevents us from perceving the limitations of our understanding...In addition to directing a fairly precise thought, most language simultaneously endeavours to excite some refinement of feeling. This function of language fails at least as often as the communication of sense. And our means of discovering for ourselves whether we have or have not understood this feeling correctly are even less satisfactory than in the case of thought. As a rule, close contact with persons who are exacting in this respect can give us the necessary training...Subtleties of tone are rarely appreciated without some special training."— I. A. Richards, *Practical Criticism*, pp. 327-8.

(2) " A critic must be able to *feel* the impact of a work of art in all its complexity and its force. To do so, he must be a man of force and complexity himself, which few critics are. A man with a paltry impudent nature will never write anything but paltry impudent criticism. And a man who is *emotionally* educated is rare as a phoenix. The more scholastically educated a man is, generally, the more he is an emotional boor. "— Coombs, *Literature and Criticism*, p. 13.

Kārikā 8 : What is said of the critic in the previous *Kārikā* is here extended to the creative process of poets. The poets are exhorted to be alert in focussing all their attention on the suggestive words and meanings.

The word *pratyabhijñeya* has been so explained by Abhinavagupta as to carry the implications of the *pratyabhijñā* school of Kashmir Shaivism. But this appears far-fetched since we have no positive indication anywhere in the text, pointing to Ānandavardhana's faith in this school. These two *kārikās* (7 & 8) bring out forcefully the unique importance of *vyaṅgyārtha* in all poetry of the best order. Cf. (1) " Indeed a poet's aim may be to select and to use words so as to annul their referential expression, thus to evoke images and feelings which refer to nothing beyond themselves. " — R. W. Church, An Essay on Critical Appreciation, Allen and Unwin, 1938, p. 199–200. (2) " The business of a poet is not to clarify, but to suggest; to imply, to employ words with auras of association with a reaching out toward a vision, a probing down into an emotion, beyond the compass of explicit definition. " — Harold Hobson, New York Journal, American, Jan. 31, 1958.

P. 16. *Kārikā* 9 : The word *āloka* in this *Kārikā* could mean ' light ', as well as ' sight ' (i. e. seeing objects). We have preferred the second meaning even as Abhinavagupta does. The ultimate end served by *dīpaśikhā* or lamp-flame is the sight of objects, rather than light. But Jacobi renders it as " Helligkeit " (brightness).

Though the poet's primary concern is *vyaṅgyārtha*, he has no other go but to start with *vācyārtha*. The medium of poetry is common language ; but the poetic use of language is quite different from its referential use. That is why *Kārikā* 2 brings out how the beautiful meaning in poetry lends itself into a two-fold analysis, though it is really an undifferentiated totality. Critical function as much as the creative activity both have as the basis such an analysis. This *kārikā* emphasizes the aspect of the poet's creative activity while the next is devoted to the aspect of critical appreciation. Though inevitably a linguistic discourse is involved in the poetic activity, it is something which does not hold his exclusive attention. All his concentration as a poet is directed towards the suggested meanings only. Thus *vyaṅgyārtha* is established as the unique differentia of poetry.

Kārikā 10 : What is true of the poet is true of the critic too in his own way. All his attention and sensibility are involved only in his getting at the *vyaṅgyārtha* intended by the poet, though here too he has to start first with the comprehension of *vācyārtha*. A happy analogy is cited of *padārtha* and *vākyārtha*. The import of a sentence as a whole is the goal in all human speech. But that is rendered possible only by the means of understanding individual words and their meanings in relation. The *Locana* brings out clearly how, for a beginner in the study of language, a time interval also is possible between the understanding of the individual words and the *vākyārtha* as a whole. But, for one who is intimately familiar with the language, no time interval comes to be felt by him because the understanding of the final import is so fast. In the same way, a critic with a refined sensibility will catch the *vyaṅgyārtha* itself in a flash, almost simultaneously with the *vācyārtha*. But even then, the fact remains that the means for arriving at the *vyaṅgyārtha* is none other than the *vācyārtha* itself. Here too, a beginner could clearly notice that the understanding of the *vācyārtha* is a prelude to the understanding of the *vyaṅgyārtha*. This is the *padārtha-vākyārtha-nyāya* adduced to bring out the supremacy of the *vyaṅgyārtha* in poetry as distinguished from other modes of speech. This *nyāya* is substituted by *ghaṭa-pradīpa-nyāya* in the third chapter in order to emphasise the simultaneous awareness of both the meanings (*Vācya* and *Vyaṅgya*) in poetry. Not only the jar illumined by the lamp but also the lamp itself are simultaneously cognised. In the same way, *vācya* and *vyaṅgya* meanings admit of simultaneous comprehension.

The *padārtha-vākyārtha-nyāya* would not serve this purpose. For, when the *vākyārtha* is understood, the *padārtha* is no longer felt separately.

P. 18. *Kārikās* 11—12 : The implications of the above analogy are fully drawn out here from the point of view of the exclusive importance of *vyaṅgyārtha* in poetry. The *vṛtti* explains how though the *padārtha*, the means, is not entirely absent, its existence is not distinctly felt. In the same way, the sensitive critics are wholly and solely immersed in their appreciation of the *vyaṅgyārtha*, and the *vācyārtha* escapes their attention The *Locana* explains that the total absence of *vācyārtha* is not intended here. Though it may be present remotely in the background, it does not engage the attention of the critics prominently. So explained, there would be no opposition between the *padārtha-vākyārtha-nyāya* set out here, and the revised *ghaṭa-pradīpa-nyāya* cited in the third chapter.

Kārikā 13 : All the previous arguments are brought to a focus in the present *kārikā* which has been often regarded as the definition of *dhvani*. Every element in the *kārikā* is very significant and has given occasion to an elaborate explanation in the *Vṛtti* here and more specifically under *kārikā* 16. Though it may incidentally serve as a definition of *dhvani*, it seems to be concerned more with indicating the vast connotation of the term *dhvani* itself. If we take it as a mere definition, then *dhvani* will be the name only of a *kāvyaviśeṣa*, and the initial declaration itself, viz,. *kāvyasyātmā dhvaniḥ* would become a conundrum, since a *kāvyaviśeṣa* can by no means become the *ātman* of *kāvya*. A close reading of the *Vṛtti* under *kārikā* 16, as well as the *Locana* will leave no room for doubt that what is meant in the two *karikās* is a statement only of the vast connotation of the term *dhvani* to include :—

(i) *vācyārtha* which is *vyañjaka*;

(ii) *vācaka-śabda* which is *vyañjaka* ;

(iii) *vyaṅgyārtha*;

(iv) *vyañjanā-vyāpāra* ; and

(v) poetry as such with the above constituents. The central point in all this is the fact that the *vyaṅgyārtha* is deliberately intended by the poet to be more important and beautiful than the *vācyārtha*, and he takes all pains to see that the beauty of the *vācyārtha* is strictly kept in the background and is not allowed to outshine the beauty of the *vyaṅgyārtha*. When this is understood, it follows that the creative activity itself is none other than the deliberate use of *vyañjanā-vyāpāra*. When individual words are suggestively used with a view to charming *vyaṅgyārtha*, we have *vyañjaka-śabdas*. When the several *vācyārthas* in a sentence combine to suggest another beautiful meaning, they come under the class of *vyañjaka-arthas*. In both these cases, what s important is, that the *vācaka-śabdas* and *vācyārthas* should not attract the readers' attention to their own beauty as compared with the *vyaṅgya* beauty. Now the emergent over-all beautiful *vyaṅgyārtha* is the goal which charms the reader. It can assume three forms viz., *Vastu* (Ideas) *Alaṅkāra* (suggested figurative shade) and *Rasādi* (Emotions and sentiments). Such is indeed the soul of poetry. A poem taken as a whole and made up of these elements (*kāvyaviśeṣa*) deserves therefore to be regarded as the best specimen of poetry. The term *dhvani* is applicable thus not only to *vyaṅgyārtha* as we already saw, but also to all the constituent factors of suggestion in poetry; and ideal poetry itself can be none other than *dhvani*.

Ānandavardhana tries hard in the *vṛtti* here to justify his choice of the term *Dhvani* with wide connotations by citing the example of Vaiyākaraṇa philosophers like Bhartṛhari. Bhartṛhari propounded an idealistic philosophy of *Śabda-brahman* or *Sphoṭa* to explain meaning from language which is at the basis of all human activity (प्रक्रिया जगतो यतः, *Vākyapadīya*, I. i.). His theory, known as *Sphoṭavāda*, is primarily a semantic concept. According to this theory, meaning is revealed in a flash by the whole and indivisible aspect of speech, an aspect which underlies all distinctions of syllables or sounds. When we say 'cow', the three letters are uttered in sequence, howsover unnoticeable; and the total meaning of the animal we understand is not the result of any summation of the part-meaning of the three letters.

The words analysable into letters with varying shades of tone and pitch must have, according to this school, an abiding whole aspect, which alone can reveal a whole meaning and this aspect is termed *sphoṭa*. Since words can have meaning only in the context of a sentence, the *sphoṭa* of the sentence as a whole should be regarded as the revealer of meaning. This involves recognition of the 'revealing potency' (*vyañjakatva*) in the whole *sphoṭa* aspect of words and sentences. The sentence reveals or suggests *Sphoṭa* which in its turn reveals or suggests meaning (*artha*) in one unitary flash. The revealer (*vyañjaka*) of meaning is thus the semantic aspect of *śabda* and the revealer of this in turn is its own linguistic aspect. In this context Bhartṛhari has primarily used the term *Dhvani* to refer to the linguistic aspect of *śabda* (varṇa). He has also referred to views of grammarians which regard the semantic aspect of *śabda* also as *Dhvani*. In addition to these *vyañjakas* being called *Dhvani*, the revealed or suggested meaning as such and the process of suggestion involved are also termed *Dhvani* in some of the views cited in the *Vākyapadīya* and quoted in the *Locana*.

So Ānandavardhana found that the term *Dhvani* already enjoyed a status of prestige in the usage of *Vaiyākaraṇas*; and it was propounded to explain the mystery of meaning arising from language. In poetry too, which is nothing more than a specialised use of language, the same concept could explain all the issues with slight modifications to suit the unique poetic purpose. Here also there could be no doubt that *Dhvani* alone could be involved in the delineation of *Rasa*, the purpose unique to a poet. So with a slight extension of meaning, व्यञ्जकशब्द in poetry could be spoken of as continuing its operation even after the close of the significatory function explained by the *Vaiyākaraṇas*. That is to say, while *Sphoṭavāda* explains the व्यञ्जकत्व of शब्द with reference to वाच्यार्थ, its primary meaning only, काव्यध्वनि is concerned with the व्यञ्जकत्व of शब्द after the rise of the primary meaning towards a suggested meaning (such as *Rasa*) beyond वाच्यार्थ.

What is more, in grammar, the question of वाच्यार्थ becoming व्यञ्जक does not arise at all; while that alone is the basic issue in poetry. The वाच्यार्थ itself becomes suggestive of different ideas and feelings to the reader, depending on the uniqueness of the characters and situations described in poetry. Hence व्यञ्जक in poetry is not only शब्द in the narrow sense of Vyākaraṇa but also अर्थ (i. e. वाच्यार्थ or लक्ष्यार्थ in its wake). Since poetry is nothing but a designation given to both शब्द and अर्थ taken together, काव्य itself can be regarded as tantamount to शब्द in the ultimate sense of the grammarians.

The use of the word *Dhvani* in all these five senses indicated above follows thus as a happy extension of the fundamental philosophy of language acceptable to grammarians. This philosophical foundation was laid securely for the first time to poetic theory by Ānandavardhana in the history of Sanskrit poetics. For a further discussion of this, see : K. Krishnamoorthy, *Essays in Sanskrit Criticism* (Karnaṭak University, Dharwar, 1964), p. 41 ff.; *The Dhvanyāloka and its critics*, (Kavyalaya, Mysore 1968), Chapt. II; S. K. Ramachandra Rao, *Development of Psychological Thought in India* (Kavyalaya, Mysore, 1962), p. 161 ff.; K. V. Abhyankar, *A Dictionary of Sanskrit Grammar* (Oriental Institute, Baroda, 1961), p. 405.

Line 12. अनेन ...... दर्शितम् — A clear grasp of the above considerations will positively reveal the striking distinction between *alaṅkāras* of *vācaka-śabda* and *vācyārtha* on the one hand and the beauty of exclusive *vyaṅgyārtha* on the other. This consideration is enough to show the mistake committed by the ancient theorists when they included *rasādi* (which are exclusively *vyaṅgya*) under the head of *alaṅkāras* which are exclusively *vācya*. Had they made this important distinction between *vācya* and *vyaṅgya*, they would have been saved from what is nothing short of a blunder from the aesthetic standpoint.

Line 14. यदप्युक्तम् ...... दर्शयिष्यामः — The second variety of ध्वन्यभाववाद is now taken up for refutation. Its main contention is that anything not conforming to the classical canons ceases *ipso facto* to be poetry. Ānandavardhana points out that *dhvani* is widely familiar to readers of literature though it is unfamilar only to the theorists. The acid test which decides whether something is genuine poetry or not is only the experience of tasteful readers, and not the pronouncements of theorists.

From this new standpoint it follows that whatever is not *dhvani* in the opinion of *sahṛdayas* is not poetry at all. It may be given only a concessional admission because of its startling or pictorial properties, denoted by the term चित्र. (See third chapter for a treatment of चित्र). Rudrata treats चित्र elaborately.

P. 20. Line – 1. यदप्युक्तम् ... पातिता कृत: — The next anti-*dhvani* view is अन्तर्भाववाद and it has been refuted at length in the text. In fact, this is the most formidable charge brought by the adherents of early poetics against the new theory of *dhvani*.

No one can deny that the early theorists too were aware of the presence of *vyaṅgyārtha* in poetry as indicated by their definitions of some *alaṅkāras*. But as Ānandavardhana notes pointedly and repeatedly, they appear to have given more importance to the principle of *vācya*-beauty rather than that of *vyaṅgya*-beauty, The only underlying common ground for all *alaṅkāras* is *vācya-vācaka-cārutva* while the underlying ground for *dhvani* in all its manifestations is *vyaṅgya-vyañjaka-cārutva*. Ānanda. vardhana's accuracy of insight into the nature of *alaṅkāras* is illustrated further in his detailed exposition of this point-

L. 8. ननु ..... तस्यान्तर्भाव: — The objector might urge that *alaṅkāras* like *samāsokti* do involve an element of *vyaṅgyārtha* and *dhvani* could easily be included under them. This would be possible if a mere presence of *vyaṅgyārtha* were sufficient to raise it to the status of *dhvani*. But the fact is otherwise. *vyaṅgyārtha* becomes *dhvani* only when *vyaṅgyārtha* is also more prominent and more beautiful than the *vācyārtha*. This has been laid down as an important condition that governs Dhvani in the *Kārikā*. The वाचकशब्द and वाच्यार्थ should both be intended by the poet to be less prominent and therefore less beautiful than the *vyaṅgyārtha*. It follows that no *alaṅkāra* like *samāsokti* can explain *dhvani*.

Cf. " Subordination (as opposed to abrogation) of sense is nearly omnipresent in poetry. The poet makes a statement about something, not in order that the statement may be examined and reflected upon, but in order to evoke certain feelings, and when these are evoked, the use of the statement is exhausted. It is idle and irrelevant to consider the statement further. "— I. A. Richards, *Practical Criticism*, p. 354.

L. 14. समासोक्तौ तावत् ...— The verse उपोढरागेण etc., has been quoted from Udbhaṭa's *Bhāmaha-vivaraṇa* [Raniero Gnoli, *Udbhaṭa's Commentary on the Kāvyālaṅkāra of Bhāmaha*, Roma, 1962, p. 34]. The fragment reads :—स्पष्टं पुनरिदमुदाहरणम् समासोक्तेः– उपोढ°. We have the reading रक्षितम् there instead of लक्षितम् in the last quarter. Perhaps it is a better reading because रक्षितम् suggests the woman's inability to save her garment from slipping off inspite of her best will. The current reading लक्षितम् shows that she was unconscious of the whole thing. The emotion of bashfulness is better suggested in the former reading than in the latter.

P. 22. L. 1. इत्यादौ...वाक्यार्थत्वात् —The main theme of the verse which is relevant (प्रस्तुत) here is the beauty of the moon during twilight. It is *vācya*. The behaviour as well as emotions of lovers attributed to the personified moon and twilight is *vyaṅgya* and अप्रस्तुत. Now the *alaṅkāra* of *samāsokti* consists only in such *vyaṅgya*, adding beauty to the *vācya*. The *vyaṅgya* therefore cannot be regarded as exclusively important.

At this point the *Locana* raises the interesting question whether *rasa* is not involved in this. It is, he declares, certainly present; but at a stage later than that of *samāsokti*. *Samāsokti* transforms the bare moon and night into विभावs which in turn release *rasa* ultimately. What is called *samāsokti* is अप्रधानव्यङ्ग्य only which is a part of the figure and not the ultimate *rasa* which *samāsokti* leads up to. Vide: तेनात्र व्यङ्ग्ये प्रतीतेऽपि न प्राधान्यम्। तथाहि नायकव्यवहारो निशाशशिनावेव श्रृङ्गारविभावरूपौ संस्कुर्वाणोऽलङ्कारतां भजते, ततस्तु वाच्याद्विभावीभूताद्रसनिःष्यन्दः—*Locana*, BP. Ed. p. 11.

This is a very subtle point and unless it is realised, confusion will result in distinguishing *samāsokti* from verses like तन्वी मेघजलार्द्र..and तरङ्गभ्रूभङ्गा...cited later as brimming with *rasa* by Ānandavardhana. Both involve चेतनत्वारोप on अचेतनवस्तु. But the beauty of *samāsokti* lies more in the *vācya*, accompanied by *vyaṅgya*, while beauty in the latter is more due to the *vyaṅgya-rasa* itself. The poet's intention (विवक्षा) in the former is to describe nature primarily, whereas the poetic intention in the latter is depiction of human sentiment prominently.

L. 3. आक्षेपेऽपि काव्यशरीरम्। Turning to the next figure *Ākṣepa*, Ānandavardhana finds the same principle involved in this as in *samāsokti*. The very title of the figure *Ākṣepa*,, viz. 'Suggestive' denial reveals how the *vācyārtha* is relatively more important than the *vyaṅgyārtha*; for the suggester is *vācyārtha* itself, while the special idea suggested is *vyaṅgya*. Then he explains this further by citing Bhāmaha's definition of the figure. When there is a specific verbal negation as it were in a sentence with a view to suggesting some special idea, the expressed negation becomes the main source of charm.

L. 6. चारुत्वोत्कर्ष .... विवक्षा। This is the fundamental principle of aesthetic judgment propounded for the first time in Indian literary criticism. In all poetry there will be two elements :—the plainly stated and the suggested. The literary critic's judgment is involved in deciding which is relatively more prominent. The criterion for such judgment is provided only by his aesthetic impression of the two. That which strikes him as more beautiful will decide his characterising it as *Dhvanikāvya* or *Guṇībhūtavyaṅgya*. Whereever the *vācyārtha* is strikingly more beautiful, it is only *Guṇībhūtavyaṅgya* and this is very much true of *ākṣepa*.

L. 8. अनुरागवती ... समागमः॥ This beautiful verse is sometimes ascribed to Pāṇini in anthologies. Māṇikyacandra in *Kāvyaprakāśasaṅketa* and Hemacandra in *Kāvyānuśāsana* offer the explanation that पुरस्सर should be taken to mean 'towards her and not merely moving in front, back-turned like the vanguard of an army. The heroine Twilight must be understood to be advancing to meet her lover, the Day; and the Day, like a passionate lover, is also moving to meet her as it were. Though they thus move eagerly towards each other, they never meet. They are ever so close and ever so parted. If they were to be moving mechanically, one behind the other, as in the ranks of an army, the question of their meeting would never arise even after ages'. The context requires that it should be explained as an example of the figure *ākṣepa*. But Abhinavagupta finds it more to be of the nature of *samāsokti* (as defined by Bhāmaha), and unlike *ākṣepa* (according to Bhāmaha). So he adopts the ingenious procedure of calling it *ākṣepa* also according to Vāmana's definition of *ākṣepa* (उपमानाक्षेपश्चाक्षेपः – IV-3-27). In fact Vāmana in his main definition talks only of belittling the उपमान in order to extol the उपमेय and this has no relevance at all to this verse. Almost all the later theorists who quote this verse (e. g. Mammaṭa, IX 7 f.) follow Abhinavagupta blindly and call it *samāsokti*. Even Abhinavagupta is hesitant in taking it as a pure समासोक्ति. He is quite aware that the treatment of *ākṣepa* is not yet complete even when he calls the verse as an instance of समासोक्ति. (तेन आक्षेपप्रमेयसमर्थनमेवापरिसमाप्तमिति मन्तव्यम् । तत्रोदाहरणत्वेन समासोक्तिश्लोकः पठितः) Before concluding his remarks on this he alludes also tlo the oral explanation of his *guru* (possibly Bhaṭṭatauta) to the effect that this verse serves not only as an example of समासोक्ति according to Bhāmaha but also that of आक्षेप according to Vāmana; and that it is immaterial whether it is one or the other or both. The main point of illustration is that the suggested meaning is secondary to the beauty of the expressed in all alaṅkāras:–एषापि समासोक्तिर्वास्तु आक्षेपो वा, किमनेनास्माकम्। सर्वथाऽलंकारेषु व्यङ्ग्यं वाच्ये गुणीभवतीति नः साध्यमित्याशयोऽत्र ग्रन्थेऽस्मद्गुरुभिर्निरूपितः। (KSRI Edn., p. 200).

But as we have seen, Ānandavardhana's *vṛtti* has already completed the treatment of *samāsokti* earlier and taken up *ākṣepa* for exposition here. In the treatment of the other *alaṅkāras* too hereafter, there is an example invariably provided. If this verse is taken as *samāsokti*, *ākṣepa* would go without an example, and *samāsokti* would have a second example even in the absence of any need. That would be very unusual in a systematic writer like Ānandavardhana. Thus arises a problem of interpretation not touched by previous scholars.

Here is our attempt at a solution. The verse must be taken as an illustration of *ākṣepa* according to the definition of Bhāmaha only. The first line taken in itself fulfils the requirements of *samāsokti* completely. But that is no reason why the second line should be ignored altogether in deciding the *alaṅkāra* of this verse. The emphatic part of the verse is in the second line. It is the philosophy of life deduced by the poet by his observation of Nature (recorded in the first line). The question is whether it contains any वाच्य निषेधाभास (apparent denial stated explicitly) and whether it has any suggested implication, (विशेषाभिधित्सा) intended by the poet. 'तथापि न समागमः' does contain a **निषेध**, which cannot be anything but an **आभास** because of the fact that Day and Twilight can never physically co-exist in Nature, and it is too well known a fact to deserve any special emphasis on the part of a poet. This leads us to the conclusion that the poet must have some other purport to justify his use of verbal negation. The fancied purport which we might reconstruct may be stated in some such way as this:—

In the world of lovers and in the tradition of romantic poetry, the consummation of a couple in mutual love is nothing but union. Even when the heroine remains passive in her love, the hero's actions continue till the goal of union is achieved. There is greater joy in the result than in the quest. But this feature is reversed in the case of Day and Twilight imagined as lovers. They seem to derive greater joy in the eternal quest itself than in the momentary union. That is why the quest goes on for ever and ever ! So understood, this *vyaṅgyārtha* emphasising the desirability of the quest of lovers for the quest's sake will make the verse conform to the definition of *ākṣepa* by Bhāmaha. But the point of relative beauty between the *vācyārtha* and the *vyaṅgyārtha* remains yet to be decided. It will be easily seen that all the beauty of the verse is more centred in the *vācyārtha* which is the suggester and not in the *vyaṇgyārtha* so much. Because all its concern lies in adding beauty to the *vācyārtha* itself and thus justify its being designated as an *ākṣepa-alaṅkāra*.

Our proposed solution finds remarkable corroboration by the detailed treatment of *Ākṣepa*--varieties by Daṇḍin in his *Kāvyādarśa*. In all the varieties, the word *Ākṣepa* is used by him only in the uniform sense of *denial*. One of these varieties called **कार्याक्षेप** is explained as the denial of the occurrence of the effects though the causes required are all there :—

दूरे प्रियतमः सोऽयमागतो जलदागमः ।
दृष्टाश्च फुल्ला निचुला न मृता चास्मि किं न्विदम् ॥ II. 134.
कार्याक्षेपः स कार्यस्य मरणस्य निवर्तनात् ।
तत्कारणमुपन्यस्य दारुणं जलदागमम् ॥ II. 135.

Though there is the dreadful advent of the rainy season with blossomed trees and the lover is far away, the expected effect of the beloved's death is denied here. Similarly, Rudraṭa also considers आक्षेप to be no more than a denial of well known facts. cf. *Kāvyālaṅkāra*, VIII. 89-90. Outwardly Daṇḍin's *kāryākṣepa* which applies *in toto* to the verse अनुरागवती...is almost similar to *Viśeṣokti* of later writers. But as Rangācārya Raddy points out while commenting on Daṇḍin, the denial of the effect of a fancied cause is *Ākṣepa*, while the denial of the effect of a real cause is *Viśeṣokti.*

L. 12. यथा च...द्रष्टव्यम्—The principle explained above is strengthened by citing as proof the status of the *vyaṅgya* simile in *alaṅkāras* like *Dīpaka* and *Apahnuti.* Unless there is a suggested simile there can be no *vācyālaṅkāra* like *Dīpaka.* But they are still designated as *Dīpaka* etc. and never as *Upamā* because striking beauty relates to the former and not to the latter. This logic applies with equal force to other *alaṅkāras* also like *Ākṣepa* and *Samāsokti* considered above, and others, *Viśeṣokti, Paryāyokta* etc., which follow.

L. 15. आहूतोऽपि...शिथिलयति—In the Subhāṣitāvali and the Sarṅgadharapaddhati, the author of this verse is given as Bharcu or Bharvu (who is the guru of Bāṇa.). This example of *Viśeṣokti* too appears to have been quoted by Ānandavardhana from Udbhaṭa's *Bhāmahavivaraṇa.* For, the *Locana* expressly gives Udbhaṭa's explanation of this verse. The lethargy of the traveller to leave his bed despite reasons to the contrary is given by Udbhaṭa as the biting cold of winter, (शीतकृता खल्वार्तिरत्र निमित्तमिति भट्टोद्भटः, तदभिप्रायेणाह... ।). It also gives another possible reason for the lethargy :—

It is the eagerness of the lone traveller to have a dream-union with his beloved (कान्तासमागमे गमनादपि लघुतरमुपायं स्वप्नं मन्यमानो निद्रागमनबुद्ध्या सङ्कोचं नात्यजत् ।). In either case, it is obvious that the beauty is traceable not to the suggested reason but to the *viśeṣokti* which is *vācya,* By *Viśeṣokti* we mean here the deliberate omission of the reason itself as a source of charm.

P. 24. L. 1. पर्यायोक्तेऽपि ...... यिष्यमाणत्वात् — *Paryāyokta* has definitely *vyaṅgyārtha.* An objector might urge that it is not only present but prominently present. In such a case there would be no difference left between *vastudhvani* and *paryāyokta.*

Ānandavardhana is prepared to concede this. But the other varieties of *Dhvani* viz. *Alaṅkāradhvani* and *Rasadhvani* are left untouched and unexplained by the characteristic of a *Paryāyokta*. While the scope of *Paryāyokta* is very narrow and may at the most touch the fringe of just *vastudhvani,* the scope of the other two varieties of *Dhvani* is far wider. Hence, logic demands that *Paryāyokta* itself be brought under *vastudhvani* and not *vice versa.*

L. 3. न पुनः ...... विवक्षितत्वात् —As *Locana* observes, one might perversely urge all instances of *vastudhvani* cited earlier (भम धम्मिअ etc.) as examples of *paryāyokta.* To prevent it Ānandavardhana mentions here that only examples like the one actually cited by Bhāmaha deserve to be regarded as *paryāyokta.* The reference is to

गृहेष्वध्वसु वा नान्नं भुञ्ज्महे यदधीतिनः ।
विप्रा न भुञ्जते (तच्च रसदाननिवृत्तये) ॥ *Kāvyālaṅkāra* III. 9.

Beauty lies in the plainly stated periphrasis itself, viz. 'we won't eat either at home or on the way food which has not been first partaken of by learned brahmins' and not in the suggested part, 'since we are afraid of being poisoned'.

L. 5. See note on p. 22. L. 12.

L. 7. सङ्करालङ्कारेऽपि ...... निराकरोति — Among the ancient theorists, the concept of collocation and commingling of figures (संसृष्टि and सङ्कर) is a unique concept. It is a wide concept attempting to explain multi-faceted beauty in actual instances of poetry due to the presence of more than one tinge or shade of different *alaṅkāras.* Ānandavardhna seems to use the two words more or less as synonyms. Abhinavagupta distinguishes four types of such mixed figures :—

(i) *Sandeha-saṅkara,* where one is left in doubt as to which of the two (or more) equally applicable figures is decisive, for want of any criterion, positive or negative, to fix it one way or the other;

(ii) *Śabdārthālaṅkāra-saṅkara* or co-existence of alaṅkāras coming under different heads like *śabda* and *artha.* This itself is called *saṁsṛṣṭi* by later writers.

(iii) *Ekavākyāṁsa-saṅkara,* where more than one *arthālaṅkāra* is noticed in one and the same passage of poetry; and

(iv) *Anugrāhyānugrāhakabhāva-saṅkara,* where the relation between the two figures simultaneously applicable is that of the donor and the donee.

The last of these alternatives is taken up first for disposal. The donor which is an *alaṅkāra* is paramount by definition while the suggested *vyaṅgya* can in no wise be deemed as all important. The second and the third alternatives do not involve at all the presence of *vyaṅgyārtha* and are thus irrelevant. In the first alternative, however, reason demands that both the *alaṅkāras* applicable, one in a *vācya* way and the other in a *vyaṅgya* way, are deemed equal in importance. Yet if one were to swear that the *vyaṅgya* figure is positively more prominent than the *vācya* figures, Ānandavardhana's reply is the same as that noted in the case of *paryāyokta.* Such stray instances might by all means be brought in the realm of *vastudhvani.* But it would never be logical to include the far wider field of *Rasadhvani* in the narrow scope of any *alaṅkāra* or mixture of *alaṅkāras.* The very term *saṅkara* (commingling) used to denote figurative beauty is indicative of the fact that no element therein is preponderant over another.

L. 13. अप्रस्तुतप्रशंसायामपि ... न्यायः — In the figure *aprastuta-praśaṁsā* several types are usually distinguished depending on the *prastuta,* (which is *vyaṅgya*) and the *aprastuta* (which is *vācya*). Such relations are *sāmānya-viśeṣa* and *kārya-kāraṇa* with reference to either of them. Several beautiful examples of this figure are furnished by Ānandavardhana himself and explained in detail under III. 40. Ānandavardhana first shows how these are mutually inclusive and not exclusive. Hence, in none of these four possible alternatives of *aprastuta-praśaṁsā,* the suggested alone is exclusively prominent.

P. 26. L. 1. यदा तु ..रत्वमेव. Only we are left with the fifth variety based on the relation of similarity. Here again, if in a stray example the sensitive critic actually finds the *vācya aprastuta* less important than the *vyaṅgya prastuta* he is justified in giving it also the status of *vastu-dhvani.* Otherwise, in most of the examples, the common feature would be the greater beauty of the *vācya* only. Hence all such *alaṅkāras* involving greater beauty of the *vācya* over the *vyaṅgya* fall under the second class of poetry *Guṇībhūta-vyaṅgya*; they should not be mistaken to belong to the first class of poetry viz. *Dhvani.*

Verse 1 : In *alaṅkāras* like *Samāsokti* there is the undoubted presence of some *vyaṅgyārtha*. But this is not enough to raise them to the rank of *Dhvani* because they serve no better than handmaids to the beauty of the *vācyārtha*. Hence such *alaṅkāras* are only aspects of primary beauty in the *vācyārtha* only.

Verse 2 : From the above the rule is deduced that nothing can be *Dhvani* which is not felt as all-important. Its mere presence or assistance rendered to *vācyārtha* cannot make *vyaṅgyārtha* deserve the title of *Dhvani.*

Verse 3 : Hence we are brought to the inevitable conclusion that we have a clear instance of *Dhvani* only when all the other elements in the poem–sound as well as sense–are wholly concerned in giving greater prominence to the *vaṅgyārtha.*

L. 10. Thus the very possibility of grouping *Dhvani* under the category of any *alaṅkāra* whatsoever is completely ruled out

L. 11. इतश्च...तन्निष्ठत्वमेव—All the above discussion has been pointed towards the conclusion that *Dhvani* can never come under *alaṅkāras.* But it could possibly be urged by the *pūrvapakṣin* that *Dhvani* can well be brought under other aesthetic categor ies like *guṇa* and *vṛtti*, if not *alaṅkāra.* Ānandavardhana counters this also by emphasising how *Dhvani* is a *whole* while the other heads mentioned, *guṇa, vṛtti* etc. are only parts of the whole even like *alaṅkāras.* No wise man would ever regard a mere part torn apart as equivalent to the whole. Even if it were not to be taken apart, it would remain a part only and never become the whole. The part-whole relation is something analogous to the servant-master relation involving inherent opposition, as Abhinavagupta notes (स्वामिभृत्यवदङ्गिरूपाङ्गरूपयोर्विरोधादित्यर्थः ।). As repeatedly shown, some stray instances which might lie on the border-line could easily be accommodated under *vastudhvani*; but not *vice versa* since the scope of *Dhvani* is far wider as it includes *rasa* not touched by the rest.

L. 15. 'सूरिभिः.. °रित्युक्त :—See supra p. 322 f.

P. 28. L. 2. न चैवंविधस्य....प्रत्युक्ताः — The detailed refutation of the *pūrvapakṣin's* stand that *antarbhāva* of *Dhvani* is possible under the well known categories like *alaṅkāra* is now brought to a pointed conclusion. The main fact which has emerged in all this discussion is that the range or scope of *dhvani* is far wider than that of any other aesthetic category. The wide range is such that a space of two full chapters (II and III *uddyotas*) is rendered necessary for the treatment of the major divisions and sub-divisions of poetry infused with *Dhvani.* Now the *antarbhāva–vāda* which equates the exposition of *Dhvani* with the discovery of a new figure of speech does less than justice to the claims of *Dhvani.*

Thus the contention of the critics that *Dhvani* is no better than a fad concocted by self-styled *sahṛdayas* loses all force. To deny them their well deserved credit smacks only of envy. They are quite justified in their enthusiasm about *Dhvani.*

L. 6. अस्ति ध्वनिः...सामान्येन — It has thus been proved beyond a shadow of doubt that all poetry worth the name contains predominant suggested meaning. Unless at least a sample is given of its repeatedly asserted vastness of scope, it would be difficult to distinguish it from *bhakti* or secondary usage of words to connote an indirect meaning. Hence the primary divisions of *Dhvani* contained in chaper II are briefly mentioned and illustrated here.

L. 9 : सुवर्णपुष्पां....सेवितुम् — This is *Mahābhārata, Udyogaparvan*, XXXV, 74; also quoted in the *Pañcatantra* I. 45. The expression *suvarṇapuṣpāṁ* in this verse means literally 'flowers of gold' and is an epithet of the Earth in the verse. The primary meaning of the sentence as a whole is thus tainted with incompatibility. The earth cannot bear flowers of gold at all. Hence, resort to a metaphorical meaning through *bhakti* or *lakṣaṇā* becomes a necessity. The meaning we ultimately understand is that of the Earth 'replete with all coveted riches in an abundant measure' (सुलभसमृद्धिसंभारभाजनता — *Locana*). At the next stage we get in a flash the significance (*prayojana*) of such a metaphorical usage. It is the unique greatness of the three categories of men specified in the verse, viz. the hero, the scholar, and the servant. It is obvious that this significance is distinct from the purely secondary meaning. And it is this alone which is designated by the term अविवक्षितवाच्य - ध्वनि. The *Locana* compares the poetic charm of suggested meaning to the beauty of a noble lady's breasts hidden behind her elegant bodice (गोप्यमानं सन्नायिकाकुचकलशयुगलमिव).

L. 12. शिखरिणि .... शुकशावकः— The verse appears to be taken from a romantic play. The author is given as Dharmakīrti in the *Saduktikarṇāmṛta.* It is in the nature of a very nice compliment (चाटु) paid by a gallant to the beauty of his sweetheart. The literal meaning is not at all incompatible here, because a lover by his nature may be expected to indulge in exaggerated praise, not only of his beloved but also of natural landscape. The primary purport relates to the extraordinary good fortune of the parrot in securing a fruit as red as the lady's lips, a good fortune rhetorically conceived as the result of some extra-ordinary penance on some rare mountain. This beautiful primary meaning (of the sentence) is quite intended and hence it is *vivakṣita*, unlike the previous verse where the primary meaning is *avivakṣita.* But the *vācyārtha* leads on to the suggested idea viz., " I should like to kiss your pretty lip and I congratulate myself on my good fortune. " This is the mainly intended idea of the speaker and not the praise of the parrot alone. Hence, it is a clear example of *vastudhvani* recognised as such by later writers too like Viśvanātha (*Sāhitya-darpaṇa*, IV).

Appayyadīkṣita however, takes it as an example of *vyājastuti - alaṅkāra* (*Kuvalayānanda* 71). His *vyājastuti*, however, provides for disguised praise of one thing through the overt praise of another. And so understood, it can be an example of वाच्यालंकार also. But this does not do justice to the principle of चारुत्वोत्कर्ष laid down by Ānandavardhana. All the standard *Ālaṅkārikas* like Mammaṭa and Ruyyaka confined the limits of *Vyājastati* to disguised praise or censure involving elements of both. In their *vyājastati* the *vācyārtha* is incompatible invariably. But in *vastudhvani* it may be quite compatible as in the present instance: cf : अत एव अस्या (व्याजस्तुत्या) ध्वनेर्भेदः । स हि वाक्यार्थे वक्तृवाच्यौचित्यपर्यालोचनबलादवगम्यते । इह पुनः प्रमाणान्तराद

बाधितः सन् वाक्यार्थे स्वयमनुपपद्यमानत्वात् परत्र निन्दादौ स्वं समर्पयति । तत्रैव प्रकृतवाक्यार्थस्य विश्रान्तेः । Jayaratha's *Vimarśinī* on *Alaṅkārasarvasva*, p. 112.

So the very first condition of *lakṣaṇā* is absent in *vastudhvani* of this type. This point is brought out forcefully in the next *Kārikā*.

Kārikā 14 a : Apparently the word *dhvani* in this Kārikā, juxtaposed with *bhakti* should only mean the *vyāpāra* of *vyañjanā*. But coming as it does immediately after I. 13 which extends the application of the word *dhvani*, the *Locana* would prefer to understand all the extended meanings here also. Cf. उक्तप्रकार इति पञ्चस्वर्थेषु योज्यम् — शब्दे, अर्थे, व्यापारे, व्यङ्ग्ये, समुदाये च ।

L. 18. उपचार ... भक्तिः — उपचार is a word which comprehends the secondary function otherwise known as गुणवृत्ति and लक्षणा.

P. 30. *Kārikā* 14 b. : While Kārikā 14a denies the identity of *bhakti* and *dhvani*, this part is concerned with showing how *bhakti* cannot even be *lakṣaṇa* or a differentia of *dhvani*.

L. 4 : यत्र हि ... दृश्यन्ते — Extra-ordinary charm is the only criterion which decides what is *dhvani* in poetry. But instances of *bhakti* in poetry are possible even without any such special charm.

L. 7 : परिम्लानं ... °शयनम् — This is from Harṣa's play, the *Ratnāvalī* [II. 12]. Here the word वदति in the last line is metaphorically used to mean सूचयति. And it is thus an instance of *bhakti*, but not of *dhvani*.

L. 12 : चुम्बिज्जइ etc. : Prof. John Brough has reconstructed the second and third quarters of this Prakrit verse as follows : Second— अवरुण्डिज्जइ सहस्सहुत्तं पि । Third: विरमिअ पुणो रमिज्जइ । —*Poems from the Sanskrit*, Penguin Books, 1969, p. 146. Here the word पुनरुक्तम् is an example of only *bhakti*, not of ध्वनि.

L. 17 : कुविआओ etc. : Here the words गृहीताः and हरन्ति are metaphorically used even without any special charm associated with *dhvani*.

P. 32. L. 2 : अज्जाए etc. : The word दत्तः is figuratively used.

L. 7 : परार्थे etc. : *Bhallaṭaśataka*, V. 56. Also found in anthologies like *Śārṅgadharapaddhati* and *Saduktikarṇāmṛta*.

Kārikā 15 : Once again the *Locana* would have us understand all the five meanings of *dhvani* in the *Kārikā*. Cf. : शब्द इति पञ्चस्वर्थेषु योज्यम्। Otherwise it would refer to the *Vyañjaka-śabda* alone. The acid test of beauty in literature is the unique usage of words which baffles all attempts at a paraphrase in other words. This idea has a very striking parallel in one of the maxims attributed to his tutor by S. T. Coleridge :— " Whatever is translatable in other and simpler words of the same language, without loss of sense or dignity, is bad. " . . . . " I was wont boldly to affirm, that it would be scarcely more difficult to push a stone out from the Pyramids with the bare hand, than to alter a word, or the position of a word, in Milton or Shakespeare, (in their most important works at least), without making the poet say something else, or something worse, than he does say. " [*Biographia Literaria*, p. 4 and pp. 11-12 (Everyman's Library)]. Also cf.: ' The best poets have tried to construct a poetry that could never be reduced to the expression of a thought and so could not be translated into other terms without perishing " — Paul Valéry, *Questions de Poesie;* " The essence of prose is to perish — i. e. to be ' understood '— i. e. to be dissolved, permanently destroyed, entirely replaced by the image or the impulse which it represents according to the linguistic convention. For prose always implies the universe of experience and acts — universe in which (or *because of which*) our perceptions and our actions or emotions must, in the end, correspond or speak to one another in the same way *uniformly.* The practical universe can be reduced to a collection of *aims.* " Paul Valéry, *Au Sujet du Cimetiere Marin.* [Both these citations are taken from Laurence Lerner, *The Truest Poetry*, Hamish Hamilton, London, 1964, p. 148-9.]

Kārikā 16 : The field of *lakṣaṇā* which touches the fringe of *dhvani* is restricted to प्रयोजनवती लक्षणा only. The प्रयोजन part when beautiful may be properly brought under *dhvani.* But the fact is that it is more often than not without beauty. This applies with greater force to usage of words involving रूढिमूला लक्षणा. The example of the word लावण्य is cited in the *Kārikā*. It denotes ' loveliness ' though its etymology takes us back to the word लवण meaning ' salt '. In such examples of ' dead metaphors ', there is no question of poetic beauty or *dhvani* at all. Cf.: " when a metaphor, such as "the arm of a chair", has become so common that it is no longer recognised as such, it is called a dead metaphor." —*A Reader's Guide to Literary Terms*, Thames and Hudson, London, p. 128. Daniel H. H. Ingalls has a very illuminating note on the word लावण्य in his article *Words for Beauty in Classical Sanskrit Poetry* in *Indological Studies in Honor of W. Norman Brown* (American Oriental Society, 1962) :— "The word *lāvaṇya* appears first in classical Sanskrit, where it becomes the favourite word for referring to the beauty of women. The word is derived by Pāṇini (5·1·123) from *lavaṇa*, 'Salty', and its original meaning was 'saltiness'. The passage to beauty may strike one as strange. By way of explanation one may observe that *lavaṇa* is one of the six tastes or flavors (*rasa*) : *madhura, āmla, lavaṇa, kaṭu, tikta, kaṣāya. Lāvaṇya* is related to *lavaṇa* as *mādhurya* (sweetness) is related to *madhura* (sweet). But *lavaṇa* is the flavor (*rasa*) *par excellence*, for one adds salt and not sweetness to food to bring out its taste. Since the word *rasa* is used of everything that excites one's interest, curiosity or aesthetic sense, it is appropriate that *lāvaṇya*, as an abstraction of the chief *rasa*, should be used of a particularly striking type of beauty. .. *Lāvaṇya* then, is the physical beauty of women, although it may appeal to more than one's physical senses, which forms an additive to the real woman, who is something else and distinct."

Kārikā 17 : The author is selecting प्रयोजनवती लक्षणा and contrasting it with *dhvani*. This kind of significant metaphor does involve an element of suggestion since the significance itself is suggested and not secondarily implied. Even the first condition of *lakṣaṇā* cannot apply to the verbal function involved in the suggestion of the प्रयोजन. The condition inapplicable is स्खलद्गतित्व, or incompatibility (lit. impeded movement). The word स्खलद्गति has been used in this special sense by the earlier philosophical writer, Dharmakīrti in his *Pramāṇavārttika* ; cf.

यत्र रूढ्याऽसदर्थापि जनैः शब्दो निवेशितः ।
स मुख्यस्तत्र तत्साम्याद्गौणोऽन्यत्र स्खलद्गतिः ॥ III·37.

This idea is attributed to Bhartṛhari also by a commentary on the *Vākyapadīya*, II 267-269 :—

यो वाहीके प्रवर्तमानः शब्दस्य... । यत्रास्खलद्गतिः शब्दस्तत्र मुख्योऽर्थः, स्खलद्गतित्वे तु गौणार्थतेति बोद्धव्यम् ॥

Daṇḍin is the first rhetorician who notes the aesthetic significance of secondary usages of words and employs the term गौणवृत्ति for this usage. Cf.

निष्ठ्यूतोद्गीर्णवान्तादि गौणवृत्तिव्यपाश्रयात् ।
अतिसुन्दरमन्यत्र ग्राम्यकक्षां विगाहते ॥

[Kāvyādarśa I. 65]

तेऽमी प्रयोगमार्गेषु गौणवृत्तिव्यपाश्रयाः ।
अत्यन्तसुन्दरा दृष्टास्तदुदाहृतयो यथा ॥

[Ibid. II. 254]

The most important condition for resorting to *Lakṣaṇā* is स्खलद्गतित्व or apparent inapplicability of the word's dictionary meaning in a given context; e. g. *The boy is a lion.* The indicated meaning 'The boy is brave' removes this difficulty. But the purpose of saying 'The boy is a lion' instead of 'The boy is brave' is the idea of conveying the extraordinary nature of the boy's bravery. Now this meaning which forms the purpose is conveyed straightway by the word and indication cannot function when there is not the said incompatibility or स्खलद्गतित्व in the word. This explanation is according to Abhinavagupta, and it equates स्खलद्गतित्व with मुख्यार्थबाध. Another explanation would be to take it in a positive sense rather than in the negative sense detailed above. Positively understood, it refers to the movement of the word in signifying the intended sense. It is a convenient metaphor to explain the indirect relation between the word used and the secondary sense grasped. While the relation between the word and its meaning is direct, we can figuratively say that the word's movement or *gati* towards its sense is straight or unfaltering. But when the relation is indirect, the *gati* will be स्खलद् or faltering. The *gati* of the word then is faltering only in cases of indication and not so in cases of denotation or suggestion. Cf. also Mammaṭa's *Kāvyaprakāśa*, II. 16.

P. 34. *Kārikā* 18 : This Kārikā refutes the equation of गुणवृत्ति with ध्वनि by showing how *bhakti* leaves out of account a large number of *dhvani* instances. At this point Abhinavagupta expatiates on the different possible explanations of *lakṣaṇā* and points out how none of those possibilities can explain the unique phenomenon of *rasa* in poetry which must therefore be regarded as *dhvani.*

Kārikā 19a : At the most, all that can be conceded is that it can serve as an *upalakṣaṇa* or pointer in *some* instances of *dhvani*.

Kārikā 19b : This shows clearly that the author had no access to any written exposition on the theory of *dhvani*, though it was a wellknown concept traditionally handed down in literary circles of Kashmir. He admits here the possibility of earlier works only as a hypothesis. For a fuller discussion cf. : K. Krishnamoorthy, *Dhvanyāloka and its Critics*, Ch. II.

The plan adopted by Ānandavardhana in his treatment of *dhvani* is very well brought out by Abhinavagupta in his *Locana* on this passage. The whole of the first chapter is concerned with a general exposition (*Sāmānya-lakṣaṇa*) of *dhvani*. The general definition itself is contained in the *Kārikā* यत्रार्थः शब्दो वा etc. (I. 13). While all the preceding *Kārikās* lead upto it, the succeeding ones follow from it. But the specific treatment (विशेषलक्षण) of the types of *dhvani* in poetry is to be found only in the following chapters, from the point of view of *vyaṅgya* in the second chapter and from the point of view of *vyañiaka* in the third chapter. Even with all this if one were to say that *dhvani* is 'indescribable', it would be nothing more than a pointless criticism. It may be true only in the metaphysical sense. Nothing on earth can be exempt from such a charge. But Ānandavardhana has no quarrel with such a description of *dhvani* in case it has a complimentary sense underlining the unique beauty of *dhvani* in poetry.

P. 36. L. 5 : In some copies the word युक्ताभिधायिन एव in the text appears incorrectly as युक्ताभिधायिनं एव.

UDDYOTA II

P. 38. Ll. 1-2. This introduction in the *vṛtti* implies the common authorship of the *kārikā* and the *vṛtti* in the text. The *kārikā* here takes up for sub-division the two broad types of *dhvani* mentioned earlier in the First Uddyota only in the *vṛtti* (P. 28, l.7). The *Locana* also favours this idea if properly understood.

Kārikā 1 : These designations of *dhvani*-types are influenced by the consideration that the shades of difference in the *vyaṅgyārtha* have their origin in the *vācyārtha* itself which acts as *vyañjaka.*

In the *saṅkramita* variety the expressed sense may be felt continuing to be present, though tinged with the suggested sense. But in reality it is like the string of a flower-garland fulfilling the function of merely holding the flowers together. Whereas in the *tiraskṛta* variety the expressed sense is no more than a means to an end, disappearing once it has fulfilled its function.

Ll. 12-13. What is suggested is Rāma's experience of countless ordeals like the loss of his kingdom. It is next to impossible to recount them all expressly. Should we, by any chance, do so, they would be devoid of any special charm. When suggested, however, they lose their individual sense and come to be felt in their generality even like the taste of a sweet beverage.

ll. 8-11 : स्निग्ध... भव — This is *Mahānāṭaka*, V. 7. (JRAS, 1898, p. 296).

P. 40. Ll. 2-3. रवि...प्रकाशते This is *Rāmāyaṇa* III, xvi-13.

This is a description of winter by Rāma, when at Pañcavaṭī. Several qualities like unusual haziness, futility, etc. justify the figurative use of ' blind ' in the verse. The moon's ineptitude for illumining objects is what is suggested.

Bhaṭṭa Nāyaka misses the point when he asserts that the use of the word इव rules out any *lakṣaṇā*. For इव in the verse indicates the similarity obtaining between the moon and a mirror, not between the moon and the blind. The word ' blind ' qualifies only the mirror. To repeat the word इव in the second context may be good Mīmāṁsā, but it is bad criticism (cf. *Locana*).

It should be noted that all the examples given under *Kārikā* 1 are of individual words only, since that is the speciality of the type called अर्थान्तरसंक्रमितवाच्य. But the next *Kārikā* refers to the other type called विवक्षितान्यपरवाच्य which relates to the content of a verse or a passage as a whole. The major category of Rasa comes under this. The suggested figures of speech also represent its another aspect.

L. 9 : The word *tipsy* (मत्त) suggests those who indulge in unbecoming acts, who impose themselves etc. The word '*not proud*' suggests dependent, lacklustre, dispirited, etc. (Vide : *Locana*).

L. 12 : ध्वने:— By Dhvani here is meant Suggestion. While so far we distinguished suggestion from the point of view of *expressed sense*, now we are to do so considering the *process*. (cf. *Locana*)

L. 16 : Note that only when this variety is predominant, (अङ्गिन्), we have the *nature* of *suggestion*.

This variety must be envisaged as encompassing both *Rasādi-dhvani* and *Rasavadādi-alaṅkāras*. The first is already established. There can be no poetry in its absence. In point of fact, poetry derives its life from Rasa. Rasa, it is true, consists in an invariably charming usage. And yet it is not strange that the charming usage itself should vary when what go to make up its constituents differ in themselves. Thus we have *Bhāva-dhvani* when a *vyabhi-chāri-bhāva* that has reached its acme (in excitation) takes on the poetic charm. E. g. Purūravas' exclamation in the *Vikramor-vaśīyam* — तिष्ठेत् कोपवशात्.... In this example a variety of *Vyabhichāribhāva*, namely, वितर्क takes on a poetical charm and becomes enjoyable.

Now an objection might arise : If the poetic charm is brought about by means of *vibhāvas* or *anubhāvas*, why not call it *vibhāva-dhvani* or *anubhāva-dhvani* ? It cannot be called so because *vibhāvas* and *anubhāvas* are self-expressive. Their fruition comes to a cease in the *cittavṛtti* itself. They provide us with no delight apart from *Rasas* and *Bhāvas*. In case however they themselves are suggested, we have made room for them in *Vastu-dhvani*.

When there is a semblance of fruition due to the semblance of *vibhāvas*, *anubhāvas* etc. the kind of experience we come by is called *Rasābhāsa*; e. g. while Rāvaṇa addresses Sītā in amorous words we have *Śṛṅgārābhāsa*. Bharata, to be sure, lays down that a mimicry of *Śṛṅgāra* results in *Hāsya*. But that applies to the time following the fruition. There is no *hāsya-rasa* at the time of the fruition of दूराकर्षणमोहमन्त्र इव मे... Nor is there 'eros'

(रति) pure and simple. It is eros in disguise. Hence we must also conclude it to be *Śṛṅgārābhāsa.* Such can be the case also with other *Rasas.* In reality *Rasa-dhvani* is one. *Bhāva-dhvani* etc. are its variant forms. Though the nature of the end is uniform, the differing means may be held as criteria to distinguish it, as for instance a connoisseur in perfurmes may separate the genuine musk from the imitation although perfume itself is one and indivisible. (Vide : *Locana*).

L. 18 : Besides being predominant, the *Rasādis* can also occur as subordinate; e. g. in the figures of speech like *Rasavat*, *Preyas*, *Ūrjasvin* and *Samāhita.* That *Rasādi-dhvani* cannot be equated with *Rasavadādi alaṅkāras*, is being shown in the Kārikā 4 (cf. *Locana*).

P. 42. *Kārikās* 4-5 : These two *Kārikās* are crucial to Ānandavardhana's poetics. They represent the originality of his approach towards the relative beauty of *rasa* and *alaṅkāra* in *kāvya.* Both these terms are given a new significance in this work. Though both *rasa* and *alaṅkāra* were very familiar concepts long before Ānandavardhana, there had been no scientific or systematic distinction drawn between them. Thus Bhāmaha and Daṇḍin could regard *rasas* in poetry as forming an *alaṅkāra* viz. *rasavad.* Contrariwise, Daṇḍin could assert that *alaṅkāras* called forth *rasa* in poetic content. (cf. कामं सर्वोऽप्यलंकारो रसमर्थे निषिञ्चति। *Kāvyādarśa*). Ānandavardhana thinks that this promiscuous use of the words reveals only absence of precise thinking about the soul of poetry. In his own deeper analysis which penetrates to *dhvani*, both *rasa* and *alaṅkāra* acquire quite precise connotations. They become names of two clearly distinct levels of beauty in poetry.

Throughout the treatment of Ānandavardhana, *rasas*, or, more precisely, *rasādis* have an objective existence and are not merely subjective states of the reader, as made out by Abhinavagupta. They are different shades of emotions, feelings, moods and sentiments, depicted by the poet in relation to characters or personified nature in his poetic work, through a description of suitable *vibhāvas* etc. Besides these suggested elements, the poem is bound to have another layer of beauty in the very medium artistically handled by the poet. This latter beauty is to be clearly distinguished from the former. In Ānandavardhana's language, the former beauty is *vyaṅgya* while the latter is *vācya*. But in any given passage, which order of beauty is relatively more appealing is the question *par excellence* before the *sahṛdaya*. His literary judgement consists only in deciding in each individual case one of them as predominant (*aṅgin*) and the other as ancillary (*aṅga*). According to this *dhvani* analysis, then, that which is held as predominant decides whether one is *dhvani* or *alaṅkāra*. *Rasa*, thus, can appear not only as *dhvani* but also as *alaṅkāra*. If *rasa* is suggested and is also predominantly beautiful, i. e. if *alaṅkāras* are serving as its handmaids, it is naturally *dhvani*. But on the other hand, when, though *rasa* is suggested, it in itself becomes subordinate to the beauty of the *vācya* or *alaṅkāra*, *rasa* cannot be regarded as *dhvani*, and is functionally on a par with *alaṅkāras*, and deserves to be designated, therefore, by the name *rasavadalaṅkāra*. [For a critical exposition of *rasavadalaṅkāra*, see M. Hiriyanna's paper thereon, P. O. C. XVI.]

L. 10 : तद्यथा चाटुषु... दृश्यन्ते– Cf.

प्रेयो गृहागतं कृष्णमवादीद्विदुरो यथा ।
अद्य या मम गोविन्द जाता त्वयि गृहागते ।
कालेनैषा भवेत्प्रीतिस्तवैवागमनात् पुनः ॥

Bhāmaha's *Kāvyālaṅkāra*, III-5.

Here Vidura gives expression to his sense of supreme happiness at the arrival of Kṛṣṇa and wishes that the same may be renewed frequently.

According to Bhāmaha it is the figure of sweet flattery that predominates in verses known as *cāṭus*. *Rasādis* become subordinate to it. Bhāmaha maintains that a loving celebration of the elders, gods, kings, sons etc. is the figure of sweet flattery —

भामहेन हि गुरुदेवनृपतिपुत्रविषयप्रीतिवर्णनं प्रेयोऽलङ्कार इत्युक्तम् ।

— *Locana*.

'That embellished poem in which there is the figure of a loving celebration is प्रेयस्.' From this statement of Bhāmaha he cannot be held as saying that the figure itself is the purport of the sentence. Hence the purport of the sentence may be alternatively explained as that which is predominant. In this explanation what brings in poetic charm is that which is predominant (Vide : *Locana*).

Ll. 13-16 : Quoted by Vallabhadeva in his *Subhāṣitāvalī* [2570] anonymously. In this verse a lady in her dream encounters her smiling husband. " Since I know how cunning you are, I shall keep you chained in my arms; you shall not go," says she. ' Ruthless ' etc. refer to his faults for which he is lovingly rebuked. Her innocence is implied. As all this is the result of a dream, it disappears as soon as the lady wakes up. In this verse the lament of the widowed queens of the enemy, who meet their beloved only in a dream, is pathetic no doubt. But the pathos is made subordinate to the heroism of the king who is eulogised. Hence *Karuṇarasa* is said to be an *alaṅkāra* here.

L. 17 : The *sthāyibhāva* of *Śoka* when roused by the disappearing of the dream turns out to be the sentiment of Pathos (*Karuṇarasa*) when it comes to be felt. Since it becomes an auxiliary to the celebration of the royal mightiness, it is only a figure, viz. *Rasvadalaṅkāra*. Its poetic charm is unquestionable, especially when compared with a prosaic statement like "your foes were killed by you". The charm of the verse owes itself to the pathos. Things like ' face ' may get embellished by ' moon ' etc, thanks to similarity; in other words, similies etc. become instrumental in setting forth the beauty of things natural. In the same way, a *vastu* or a *rasa* when aided by another *rasa* becomes beautiful. Hence there is no discrepancy in a *rasa* becoming an *alaṅkāra* any more than a *vastu* becoming one. The question ' what beauty does a *rasa* add to a natural sense ? ' may be met with a counter-query ' What beauty does a simile bring in ? ' If the answer is that " a simile compares ', then the parallel reply is " *rasa* sweetens (सरस) the natural sense ". There is no room then for a specious objection like ' What does *rasa* embellish among the *vibhāvas* etc.' We have settled definitely that *prastuta-artha* itself is the *alaṅkārya;* not *vibhāvas* etc. [Vide : *Locana*].

P. 44. Ll. 3-6 : *Amaruśataka*, 2. Unlike the previous example, we have here a mixture of pathos and love, both subordinated to the chiefly intended glory of Śiva.

L. 7 : श्लेषसहितस्य — This is a double entendre because in one sense it refers to the lover and in the other sense to the fiery shaft. In the first instance the tears of the ladies are due to jealousy; in the second to chagrin as there would be no hope of reunion left.

L. 8 : अत एव...—The *rasa* which is auxiliary here is supported by a figure of speech. Hence it is not pure. Though the verse contains Pathos, the text does not speak of it in reference to *vipralambha*; because Pathos does not bring beauty in the context. Only jealousy going with *vipralambha* adds charm as an *alaṅkāra*. But it is an auxiliary; not the purport of the sentence. Had it been the purport, even a shadow of Pathos—which is a sentiment hostile to Love—could not have been brought in. *Vipralambha* being a form of Eros (रति), has hope or expectation for its basis; whereas Pathos, a form of grief (शोक) is founded on hopelessness. Hence the two are incompatible. (Vide : *Locana*).

Ll. 9f. : Whenever any *rasa* is not intended by the poet as all-important, it ceases to be *dhvani* and becomes an *alaṅkāra* even like simile etc. But if it is primarily intended, it rises to the status of *dhvani*.

यत्रहि...— That is, including simile etc. The same principle involved in rendering the simile etc. figures of speech, holds good also in the case of *Rasādis*. By principle is meant the presence of something else that has become *alaṅkārya*. That *alaṅkārya* may even be a *vastu*. For, in such a case the *vastu* itself is transformed into a *vibhāva* etc. and dissolves itself in the purport of sentiment etc. Thus, in the final analysis, it is the *Rasa-dhvani* that emerges as the 'soul' everywhere. (*Vide : Locana*).

L. 16. तस्यो...द्वारा: — The meaning is this : At first sight it would seem that a figure like simile has expressed sense for its *alaṅkārya*. But as a matter of fact, the embellishment or figure is nothing other than the capacity to signify suggestive sense. That would make *Dhvani* itself an *alaṅkārya* in reality. It is true things like ear-ring, necklace etc. become embellishments by their contact with the body. But what they embellish is not the inert body, it is rather the conscious ego or the spirit, the basis (आलम्बन) for the suggestion as to the state of the wearer's mind, or the propriety of the occasion. In the absence of the ego to be embellished, ornaments like ear-ring fail to add beauty to a dead corpse. Also things like wristlets will bring in only ridicule if a hermit wears them, for in such a case there would be an incongruity with respect to the soul, though not to the body. Thus, it is clear that it is the 'soul' that is the *alaṅkārya.* This is further borne out by a statement like 'I am adorned' (Vide : *Locana*).

P. 46. Ll. 3f. : If such a functional distinction is not made, confusion would result everywhere in distinguishing *alaṅkāra-dhvani, rasadhvani, rasavadalaṅkāra* and *upamādi alaṅkāras.* Udbhaṭa seems to have held that all human psychological behaviour is the subject of *rasavad-alaṅkāra.* Such a view would restrict the province of all the other *alaṅkāras* like simile. If the view were to be extended to include personified treatment of nature also, there would be no scope left at all for any other *alaṅkāra.* On the other hand, if *rasa* should be denied to the latter, then it would be a denial of felt beauty in all such examples. Either course would be improper. But Ānandavardhana's view which distinguishes two orders of beauty keeps in tact the contributions of *vācya alaṅkāras* as well as *vyaṅgya rasa.*

P. 59. L. 5 : तर्ह्युपमादीनां......स्यात् — The implication of the adversary is that as the insentient objects lack mind and senses and consequently sentiments etc., only figures like simile will have a place there.

Ll. 7 ff. अथ तस्यामपि...स्यात् — This is *reductio ad absurdum.* The adversary maintains that a *Rasavad-alaṅkāra* may be present only where there may also be *Rasa.* In that case, argues Ānandavardhana, a vast bulk of literature would be devoid of any sentiment (नीरस) just because it cannot have *Rasavad-alaṅkāra* [What could be a greater sin than that ?]. Whereas according to the *Dhvani*-theory lack of sentiment (नीरसत्व) is not a necessary conesequence of absence of *Rasavad-alaṅkāra. Rasa-dhvani* may as well be present there.

Ll. 10–13. Kālidāsa, *Vikramorvasīya,* IV. 28.

Ll. 15–18. „ „ IV. 38.

P. 48. Ll. 2–5. These are the words uttered by Kṛṣṇa now at far away Dvārakā, when he meets a cowherd coming from Bṛndāvana. The sight of the cowherd takes Kṛṣṇa back in memory to the shores of the Yamunā. His pangs at the separation from his beloved Rādhā are again roused as he recalls the one-time excitants of his love — those bowers on the shore (उद्दीपक विभाव) and the company of the milk-maids and Rādhā (आलम्बन विभाव).

Ll. 8–9. यस्मान्नास्त्येव...विभावत्वेन — It may be that *Sāttvika bhāvas* like stupor, and horripilation are described as effortless in their manifestation. But because they are consequent states (*anubhāvas*), they do point to a sentient being. Similarly, when the most inert objects like the moon, a garden etc. are described, their role is to act as excitants (विभाव s) of emotion; apart from this, they have no room in poetry. This is the fundamental difference between literature on one hand and science (शास्त्र) and 'history' (इतिहास) on the other. (Vide : *Locana*).

L. 11. किञ्च — An additional reason is adduced to show how *Rasa* is the object of embellishment. (Cf. *Locana*).

Kārikā 6 : This simile became the common stock of all succeeding writers on Poetics.

L. 16. तथाच — This is in answer to the query "why call sweetness (*mādhurya*) etc. qualities of *Rasādis* when they are attributes of *śabdārthas* ?"

Kārikā 7. Since Eros (रति) is present instinctively in gods, men and irrational beings, there is no one of them who cannot find delight in it. Hence, figuratively we may say Eros itself is sweet. Actually, sweetness is a quality of *Rasas* like Love. It is only by transference that we attribute it to *śabdas* and *arthas*. These last possess it in so far as they are capable of conveying the sweet *Rasa* that is Love (Vide : *Locana.*).

P. 50. L. 2 ; श्रव्यत्वं पुनः — This is the view held by Bhāmaha. Bhāmaha maintained that words which sound sweet and are not excessively compounded characterise a 'sweet' poem. This view is rejected here. Cf.

श्रव्यं नातिसमस्तार्थं काव्यं मधुरमिष्यते । *Kāvyālaṅkāra*, II 3.

L. 2. ओजसोऽपि — For, the verse 'यो यः शस्त्रं ...' is full of both 'Ojas' and sweet-sounding words.

Kārikā 8 : Love in union (सम्भोगशृङ्गार) is 'sweet'. Love in separation is sweeter; Pathos is sweeter still. Thus there are degrees in 'sweetness'. Similarly the *śabdārthas* suggesting *rasa* may be regarded as sweet, sweeter, and sweetest (Vide : *Locana.*)

L. 6. माधुर्यमेव — If 'sweetness' is to be found also in Pathos, is not the phrase शृङ्गार एव meaningless in Kārikā No. 7 ? Not so. By एव we do not mean to deny sweetness to other *rasas.* What is intended by एव is that qualities like sweetness are in reality to be found only in the *rasa* which is the soul, but by extension of meaning they may be attributed to *śabdārthas* (Vide : *Locana*).

L. 10. रौद्रादयो—like Raudra, i. e. the Heroic (वीर) and the Marvellous (अद्भुत).

Ll. 13–16 : Bhaṭṭanārāyaṇa, *Veṇīsaṁhāra* I. 21.

P. 52. Ll. 1–4 : Bhaṭṭanārāyaṇa, *Veṇīsaṁhāra* III. 32.

L. 5. At this juncture *Locana* adds :—Indignation (क्रोधं) has been let flow in यो यः शस्त्रं ..., until it has reached its climax.

Thus sweetness and excitement are rival. Their mixtures in various proportions are what we have in हास्य, भयानक, बीभत्स and शान्त Rasas. In हास्य both sweetness and forcefulness are in equal proportions. In भयानक however, forcefulness predominates; so also in बीभत्स. In *Śānta,* now one may predominate, now the other. The same mutual relationship applies to all the nine *Rasas.* (Vide : *Locana.*).

L. 9. *Locana* comments in this connection :—Thus sweetness, forcefulness and perspicuity — these are three qualities that are required and sufficient. Bhāmaha too holds on to these three only. They have a direct function to fulfil in the fruition of the *rasas*; by indication, however, they are extended to *śabdārthas* suggestive of *rasas.*

Kārikā 11 : For श्रुतिदुष्ट and other verbal flaws, see Bhāmaha, *Kāvyālaṅkāra,* I. 47 ff. Also Daṇḍin, *Kāvyādarśa,* III. 125 ff. श्रुतिदुष्ट is the flaw instanced in words that bring indecent associations; e. g. विट्, वान्त, क्लिन्न, अण्डज etc.

L. 13. शृङ्गारे — According to *Locana,* the erotic in the context should include वीर, शान्त and अद्भुत. For, the flaws mentioned above will be felt as such in these sentiments also. In बीभत्स, हास्य and रौद्र however, they may cease to be blemishes.

L. 14 : ध्वन्यात्मन्येव ... उदाहृताः — The instances quoted by Bhāmaha wherein these cease to be defects contain *rasas* other than *śṛṅgāra*. Cf.

तथा विक्लिन्नगण्डानां करिणां मदवारिभिः ।
मदक्लिन्नकपोलानां द्विरदानां चतुश्शती ॥

Kāvyālaṅkāra, I. 57 b & 58a

Hence Ānandavardhana's guess is quite brilliant.

P. 54. *Kārikā* 12 : अङ्गानां stands for 'alaṅkāras' (*Locana*).

P. 56. *Kārikā* 14—In this and the following *Kārikās* the author breaks entirely new ground. He reveals a taste which was unknown in the earlier period of decadence.

P. 58. *Kārikā* 16—In point of fact none of the दुष्कर-यमकs are conducive to any *rasas*. And yet in order to win over the large number of the blind literati who suffer from a distorted aesthetic sense, Ānandavardhana seems to reduce the domain of the blemishes to शृङ्गार, at any rate विप्रलम्भशृङ्गार. (*Locana*). Cf.

"Images, however beautiful, however faithfully copied from nature, and as accurately represented in words, do not of themselves characterise the poet. They become proofs of original genius only so far as they are modified by a predominant passion, or by associated thoughts or images awakened by that passion". Coleridge, *Biographia Literaria*. Cf. also :

"Figures naturally impart assistance to, and on the other hand, receive wonderful aid from sublime sentiments...A figure, then seems most dexterously applied when it cannot be discerned that it is a figure." *Longinus, On the Sublime*, P. 139 (Cassell's National Library Edition).

Ll. 10–13 : *Amaruśataka*. As the heroine refusing to give in sits there sighing and shedding tears, with her chin cupped in her hand, the hero would win her over artfully. While he delightedly savours the heroine's consequent states (अनुभावs) like jealousy or love-in-separation, figures like श्लेष-रूपक and व्यतिरेक flood to his mind without effort. The connoisseur too likewise would be able to enjoy the *rasa* without an obstacle (*Locana*).

According to Arjunavarmadeva, the figure of speech is *Apahnuti.* Abhinavagupta says that the figures instanced here are, " *Śleṣa, Rūpaka, Vyatireka,* and so forth. " But the existence of these figures in no way impedes a grasp of the sentiment of love.

L. 16 : यमके च...रूप: – Examples like *Ghaṭakarparakāvya, Nalodaya* and *Śiśupālavadha* XIX may be quoted in galore from Sanskrit literature. L. 20 : सेतौ = सेतुबन्धमहाकाव्ये. It is a Prakṛit art-epic by Pravarasena; sometimes ascribed to Kālidāsa.

P. 60. L. 1 : Read चैतत्, यतो रसा in the text. L. 4: रसाभासे ...*Rasābhāsa* is a technical expression whose connotation differs from writer to writer. In the eyes of later writers like Hemacandra and Viśvanātha, attribution of complete sentimental behaviour to insentient objects is *rasābhāsa.* So understood, verses referred to from the *Vikramorvaśīya* above (P. 46) will be very good instances. But Abhinavagupta thinks that incompleteness or deficiency in the subjects sentimentally described is *rasābhāsa.* He quotes a verse of his own as example wherein speech is said to be lacking in charm though equipped with all excellences and ornaments until she succeeds in winning the fascination of her dear husband, Śiva (cf. प्रियेषु सौभाग्यफला हि चारुता—Kālidāsa, *Kumārasaṁbhava,* V 1). Abhinavagupta adds that this is *rasābhāsa* because real *śṛṅgāra* is impossible so long as the heroine is lacking in excellences or ornaments as stated in the verse. In support of his view he quotes the authority (of Bharata) to the effect " Love relates to youths, gorgeously dressed, etc. (उत्तमयुवप्रकृतिरुज्ज्वलवेषात्मक:); cf. *Locana,* pp. 199-200 Kashi Sanskrit Series Edn. The precise sense in which Ānandavardhana is using the word is not clear. For a further discussion on this, see K. Krishnamoorthy, *Essays in Sanskrit Criticism,* Karnatak University, Dharwar, 1964, p. 74 ff.

P. 62. ll. 12–15 : Kālidāsa, *Śākuntala,* I. 22.

L. 16 : Others have seen in this description figures like *Rūpaka* and *Vyatireka* (*Locana*).

P. 64. ll. 2–3 : The suggested idea is that Rāhu's head was severed by the discuss of Viṣṇu, though it continued to live trunkless. Plainly stated, there is no beauty in this idea. Hence the Periphrasis which adds beauty to it. According to the

Rudraṭa's *Kāvyālaṅkāra.* But the passages adduced above go to establish that Ānandavardhana could not have used the nomenclature of उपमाश्लेष etc. at all if he had not studied Rudraṭa's text.

But here as elsewhere Ānandavardhana is also heavily indebted to Udbhaṭa in holding that संसृष्टि is the name of separable figures and that these are distinct from the varieties of inseparable figures called by the name संकर. Ānandavardhana thinks that in रक्तस्त्वं we have संसृष्टि of श्लेष and व्यतिरेक since they do not overlap. On the other hand in उद्दामोत्कलिकाम् there is a संकर of उपमा and श्लेष. The पूर्वपक्ष view quoted under रक्तस्त्वं urges that it is also a case of संकर only and hence the compound designation श्लेषव्यतिरेक applies to it. Ānandavardhana refutes this view.

But later writers like Mammaṭa and Viśvanātha hold a different opinion regarding the distinction between संकर and संसृष्टि.

ll. 14–17 : *Hanumannāṭaka*, V. 24. रक्त may mean either red or love-possessed. The red hue of the Aśoka vine works as a stimulus (उद्दीपक) for the hero's love. Hence it is हेतुश्लेष. *Sahokti*, *Upamā*, and *Hetu*—these three may favour (अनुग्राहक) a *Śleṣa* (*Locana*).

P. 66 : Ll. 12–15 : Mayūra, *Sūryaśataka*, 23.

P 68. ll. 5–8 : Yaśovarman, *Rāmābhyudaya*, cf. ZDMG. XXXVI, p. 521.

ll. 12–15 : *Amaruśataka*, 9,

L. 16. There would have been great impropriety for instance if the metaphor of the arm-noose had been prolonged by describing the lady as a tribal woman and the bed-chamber as the prison's enclosure.

P. 70. ll. 1–4 : Kālidāsa, *Meghadūta* **II.** 54.

P. 72. L. 12 : cf. Udbhaṭa, *Kāvyālaṅkārasaṅgraha* :—

एकप्रयत्नोच्चार्याणां तच्छायां चैव बिभ्रताम् ।
स्वरितादिगुणैर्भिन्नैर्बन्धः श्लिष्टमिहोच्यते ॥
अलंकारान्तरगतां प्रतिभां जनयत्पदैः ।
द्विविधैरर्थशब्दोक्तिविशिष्टं तत्प्रतीयताम् ॥

P. 76. Ll. 2–3 : Quoted also by Hemacandra as an example of *Madhyama-Kāvya* — *Kāvyānuśāsana*, Ch. II.

Ll. 6–7 : चमहिम ... Hemacandra quotes this verse and explains it as an example of figures suggesting new ideas (*vastu*). Here the metaphor of 'arm-bolts' suggests according to him that the hero does not stand in need of any military force as horses or elephants for his conquests—*Kāvyānuśāsana*. p. 79, (Bombay Edn.).

L. 12. तत्र...एव—This figure *Vakrokti* in this specific sense was not recognised by early writers like Bhāmaha, Daṇḍin, and Vāmana. But the idea is quite common in later works like Ruyyaka's *Alaṅkārasarvasva*.

But it is interesting to note that it is already traceable in Rudraṭa's *kāvyālaṅkāra* II, 14-17. Jacobi attempts to infer that Rudraṭa also could not have been earlier than Ānandavardhana and brings him under King Śaṅkaravarman of Kashmir.

Cf. WZKM, II, p. 155 and ZDMG, 56, p. 763 fn.

Hence this becomes the earliest reference to the specific figure of speech *Vakrokti* in a restricted sense.

P. 78. ll. 4-5 : Bāṇa, *Harṣacarita*, II.

ll. 7-8 : Ascribed to Śakavṛddhi in the *Subhāṣitāvali*.

ll. 10-13 : Mayūra, *Sūryaśataka*, 9.

P. 80. ll. 4-5 : Bāṇa, *Harṣacarita*, III.

ll. 11-12 : „ „ I.

P. 82. ll. 11-12 : Kālidāsa, *Kumārasambhava* VI. 84.

The divine sage referred to here is sage Aṅgiras according to Kālidāsa and as correctly explained by Mallinātha. He is not Nārada as wrongly interpreted by Jagannātha (*Rasagaṅgādhara*, vol. I. Edited Madhusudun Shastri, Benares Hindu University, 1963, p. 374) and following him by Nāgojibhaṭṭa (*op. cit.*).

J. L. Masson and M. V. Patwardhan have discussed elaborately the issue arising out of Ānandavardhana's words साक्षाच्छब्दनिवेदितेभ्यः as epithets of not only *vibhāvas* and *anubhāvas* but also of *vyabhicāribhāvas* which are admittedly *vyaṅgya* and not *vācya*. Their article is entitled—'Solution to a Long-confused issue in the Dhvanyāloka' and is published in the Journal of the Oriental Institute, Baroda, September-December 1972. pp. 48–56 :—

Abhinava is supposed to provide the solution to the seeming contradiction. "If we have correctly understood the *Locana*, he is explaining the words *Sākṣācchabdanivedita* to mean; that the apprehension of *rasa* etc. is vyavadhi-vandhyaiva i. e. it takes place without any delay, immediately. In other words, he is saying that Ānanda only intends *sākṣāt* in the *Vṛtti* to mean "immediately". One must not construe it with *Śabdaniveditebhyaḥ*. And this is in keeping with the doctrine, where *rasadhvanipratīti* must be *jhaṭiti*, "immediate". What then are we to do with *Śabdaniveditebhyaḥ*? It will apply only to the *vibhāvas* and the *anubhāvas*, which must of course always be *svaśabdavācya*. In other words, the word *sākṣāt* does *not* stand for *sva*, nor is it used in the same sense in which it is used elsewhere in the D. Āl. (e. g. p. 80 where it definitely means *svaśabdanivedita*). We admit that this is somewhat unusual and it is not *absolutely* certain that Abhinava intends to explain *sākṣāt* by *vyavadhivandhya*, **but we submit that this is the only possible solution to the problem.**" (Thick type ours). [*Op. cit.* p. 56]

In fact it is not the only possible solution and it does not explain Abhinava's stand correctly either. It reads all that Abhinava said about the general nature of *asaṁlakṣyakrama-vyaṅgya* as implied in the word *sākṣāt* without any justification. They have made a hair-splitting distinction between *sākṣāt śabdanivedita* and *svaśabdanivedita* which is unwarranted. Because Ānandavardhana himself has used an identical expression viz. साक्षाच्छब्दव्यापारविषय in explaining *rasa* as beyond the pale of direct communication [*supra*, p. 10, L. 17]. But at the same time they aver that (sākṣāt) *śabdanivedita* means *svaśabdani-vedita* with reference to *vibhāvas* and *anubhāvas* contained in the phrase *vibhāvānubhāva-vyabhicāribhyaḥ* and deny that it has that sense with reference to the third member of the same compound word ! I cannot think of a more glaring *ardhaja-ratīya*, which involves self-contradiction too !

They have ignored that Ānandavardhana has used the expression twice in the IV Uddyota again under *Kārikā* 5 while discussing the dominant *rasa* of the *Mahābhārata*. They are—

(१) ...सर्वरसगर्भत्वं न महाभारतस्य तस्मिन्नुद्देशे स्वशब्दनिवेदितत्वेन प्रतीयते।

(२) ...मोक्षस्य च सर्वपुरुषार्थेभ्यः प्राधान्यमित्येतन्न स्वशब्दाभिधेयत्वेनानुक्रमण्या दर्शितम्, दर्शितं तु व्यङ्ग्यत्वेन।

These passages leave no doubt about the meaning of *svaśabda-nivedita* which is *vācyārtha* as distinguished from *vyaṅgyārtha*. There can be no difference at all in the meanings of *śabdanivedita*, *sākṣāt-śabdanivedita*, *sva-śabdanivedita*, and *sva-śabdābhidheya* which are undoubtedly synonyms.

Is there no other solution then to the vexed problem of self-contradiction noted by me for the first time in my 'Dhvanyāloka and Its Critics' (P. 226)? Masson and Patwardhan State :—"And long before Krishnamoorthy the great commentator on the *Kāvyaprakāśa*, Śrīdhara,...found this equally disturbing", suggesting that they have first noticed it. But the fact is that I have noted it myself in my footnote to the above passage. They quote my sentence with the preface—'consternation all about!' suggesting my utter confusion, while all that I stated was "here indeed is a glaring contradiction on the face of it." Why they ignore my phrase 'on the face of it' and talk of 'consternation' is what I cannot understand.

The seeming contradiction can be solved in the light of the general philosophy of *Dhvani* itself :—*Vyaṅgyārtha* is three-fold. (1) *Vastu* (2) *Alaṅkāra* and (3) *Rasādi*. All these are *vyaṅgya*, i. e. distinct from and more strikingly beautiful than *vācya*. The first two have a *vācya* status also in addition to a *vyaṅgya* status. But *rasādis* have only one status i. e. *vyaṅgya* as they are never *vācya*. They are not *vastu* ; they arise only when they are primarily suggested through a poem. But supposing they are not primarily suggested and they are secondary to something else. Then their status is reduced from that of *Dhvani* to that of *Alaṅkāra*, though they are *vyaṅgya* incidentally. Let us suppose again that the *rasādis* are suggested neither primarily nor secondarily but are conveyed directly or indirectly like so many *vastus* in the *vācya* or the *gauṇa* way. What would be their status? They would cease to be *rasa* or *alaṅkāra* or even *vyaṅgya-vastu*. All this is from the point of view of '*vyaṅgya*' which is related to the point of view of '*vyanjaka*'. The problem under discussion relates to the *vyañjaka* standpoint vis-a-vis the *vyaṅgya*.

A subtle point in the *Dhvani* theory which is often missed is the **joint** participation of both *śabda* and *artha* in the process of *dhvani*, in its triple *vyaṅgya* possibilities. Outside poetry, *śabdas* convey only two types of *artha* or meaning viz., the *vācya* and the *lakṣya*. They do not have any *vyañjanā* or suggestive power at all concerned with beauty. But in poetry, the last alone is the most fundamental and primary consideration for the use of words. *Śabdas* can become *vyañjaka*, and *arthas* also can become *vyañjaka*. When *śabda* or *artha* is *vyañjaka* of *vastu* and *alaṅkāra*, the critic can distinguish two consecutive levels in his comprehension of the meaning, viz. the earlier *vācya* and the *vyaṅgya* following in its wake. Hence both the varieties of such *dhvani*, viz. *śabdaśaktimūla*– and *arthaśaktimūla*—are designated by the title *saṁlakśyakramavyaṅgya* and both are described as *anusvānopama* or *anuraṇanarūpa* i. e. like resonance.

But in the most important variety of *rasādivyaṅgya*, *śabda* and *artha* both contribute towards the *vyaṅgya*, so swiftly and so conjointly that it is impossible almost to distinguish any ordered sequence between the referential and the emotive meaning. As soon as the *śabda* is uttered, the *vācyārtha* is felt *along with* the *vyaṅgyārtha*. It is such a unique phenomenon which Ānandavardhana has to analyse. In his analysis, he drops the word *artha* because it is common to poetry and non-poetry and uses the word *vibhāvādi* which has exclusive reference to poetry. His usage of the word *vibhāvādi* should not mislead us into thinking that he is talking of anything other than *artha*, or to be more precise, the *vācyārtha* itself. So understood, how all examples of *asaṁlakṣyakrama-vyaṅgya-dhvani* are suggested by *vibhāvādis* which are *śabdanivedita* becomes easy to follow. In fact all these examples are *arthanivedita* in the sense that they are suggested along with the vācyartha but *arthas* are *śabdanivedita*. So in an adroit use of the langauge he apparently dispenses with *artha* altogether though he has given full recognition to it as *vibhāvādi* itself when he talks of *vyabhicāribhāvas* as *svaśabda-nivedita.* Such *vyabhicāribhāvas*, even like their associate *vibhāvādis* must end up in *rasa* at once if they are to be termed *asaṁlakṣyakrama*. That is to say, they won't permit any enjoyment of them as *vyabhicāribhāvas* distinct from *rasa*.

Ānandavardhana has never described *rasa* as *svaśabdanivedita* while he is prepared to characterise *vyabhicāribhāvas* as such. Why is it so ? This is the central point at issue. The *vyabhicāribhāvas* indeed have a dual role. As indicated clearly by Bharata in his famous *rasasūtra*, they might serve as promoters of *rasa*. Or else, they might themselves become the ultimate meaning intended by the artist when they would become primary even like *rasas* meant to be developed in a work. In the former capacity they serve merely as *means* to the *end* of *rasa*. But in the latter capacity, they become ends in themselves. This seems to be the general idea of Ānandavardhana.

Bearing this functional distinction in mind, Ānandavardhana can class the *vyabhicāribhāvas* under two heads; once under the head of *rasādi* when they are fully manifested and independently treated and then under the head of *vibhāvādis* when they serve no better purpose than suggesting *rasas*, being then as good as *vācyārthas* or *vācyavastus*. It is well known that *vibhāvādi* gets directly described in words, because, as already pointed out, *vibhāva* is identical with *artha* (cf. *Abhidheyameva*···*vibhāvādikaṁ* – *Locana*, on our text p. 12. line 4). This applies equally to *vyabhicāribhāvas*. Hence it follows that when *vyabhicāribhāvas* are on a par with the *vibhāvādis* in being *śabdanivedita* they serve as means to the suggestion of *rasa*. This is exactly why *rasa* is called *asaṁlakṣyakramavyaṅgya*. Simultaneously with *vibhāvādi* and *vyabhicāribhāvas*, *rasa* also is felt at once by the man of taste. And all men of taste get the same feeling or delight without any effort.

If on reading the verse एवं वादिनि etc. every man of taste could feel the mood of *lajjā* exclusively and pointedly without any intervening thought-process, it would also be an instance of *asaṁlakṣyakrama*. But this is not so. The *sahṛdaya's* experience is more like *vastudhvani* where out of the two or three possible explanations of the situation described that occur to him, he chooses one in preference to the others according to his taste. The process involved here is more intellectual and less emotional than in the enjoyment of *rasa.* It is nothing but emotional in the case of *rasādi.* Thus though it is comparable to inference, it is not an inference since the reasoning involved is not logical but aesthetic.

Now let us look at the verse from the *vyañjaka* standpoint of the *dhvani* theorist. We saw how the *vyabhicāribhāva* is not *śabdanivedita.* What else could it be ? Assuredly it should be *arthanivedita* or implied by sense (अभिधेयसामर्थ्याक्षिप्त to use Ānandavardhana's own expression). Such sense implications may involve more than one suggested possibility. In this instance Pārvatī's action of counting lotus petals might be as much due to her girlish pranks as to her *lajjā.* Thus *lajjā* here is not *śabdanivedita* and hence it is not an accessory of any full-fledged सम्भोगशृङ्गार. The context does not favour it. It is only an instance of *saṁlakṣyakramavyaṅgya-vastudhvani.*

We should not forget that the seemingly contradictory statements arise from his applying to one and the same example two different standpoints viz. *vyaṅgya* and *vyañjaka.* From the *vyaṅgya* standpoint to any emotive meaning, *rasa* or *bhāva,* which comes so sweepingly and overpoweringly to the *sahṛdaya* with the *vācyārtha* that he cannot distinguish the two, we must give the designation of *asaṁlakṣyakrama.* But from the *vyañjaka* point of view, if *vācyārtha* alone comes first and *vyaṅgyārtha* is an afterthought, it has to be classed as *saṃlakṣyakrama* though it may be a *bhāva.* In a given instance like एवं वादिनि the critic might apply both these standpoints and characterise it as *saṁlakṣya* or *asaṁlakṣya* as he chooses. Ānandavardhana is himself aware of this as clearly mentioned by him here (इह तु सामर्थ्याक्षिप्तव्यभिचारिमुखेन रसप्रतीतिः।) and later in the words स्वप्रभेदसंकीर्णत्वं कदाचिदनुग्राह्यानुग्राहकभावेन। यथा 'एवं वादिनि' इत्यादौ (P. 502 BP. Ed.) on which the *Locana* comments :——लज्जया हि प्रतीतयाभिलाषशृङ्गारोऽत्रानुगृह्यते व्यभिचारिभूतत्वेन.

To take an example of an *asaṁlakṣyakramavyaṅgyavyabhicāribhāva,* we may take the first two lines of the erotic verse of Amaru शून्यं वासगृहं ... (See p. 268 infra). There the *lajjā* of the *mugdhā nāyikā* directly contributes to *śṛṅgāra.* In एवं वादिनि

however, there is no such immediate association of *śṛṅgāra*, because it has to be supplied from earlier contexts in the epic. In the former we have a wholly emotive or evocative use of language, while in the latter the emphasis is on the referential side.

Bhāvas which are reduced to the level of referential facts are certainly to be distinguished from highly emotive meanings in poetry. Such a distinction has to be made even while considering *bhāvas* which are generally classed under *rasādis.*

All this lengthy discussion would serve to show how *vyabhicāribhāvas* like *lajjā* can be sometimes described as *śabdanivedita* and at other times as *arthanivedita* or *abhidheya-sāmarthayākṣipta.* The problem of Ānandavardhana was to coin a new critical vocabulary not only to give a general theory of aesthetics but also to highlight practical literary analysis. The seeming contradiction appears because he uses the same expression *śabdanivedita* to cover these two aspects. But a close study of the book should help in discovering that there is no cause for 'costernation'.

P. 84. L·3 : यथा कुमारसंभवे — The reference is to the third canto. ll. 9-10 : Cf. Kāvyādarśa II. 261.

P. 84. *Kārikā* 23 : The compound word शब्दार्थशक्त्या apparently denotes only शब्दशक्ति and अर्थशक्ति. But the *vṛtti* has explained it as including the third शब्दार्थशक्ति also. The *Locana* removes the apparent variation between the two by dissolving the compound as an एकशेष including all the three entities :— शब्दश्च अर्थश्च शब्दार्थौ चेत्येकशेषः. The *Bālapriyā* explains this as follows :—

शब्दश्च अर्थश्च शब्दार्थौ; शब्दार्थौ च शब्दार्थौ च शब्दार्थाः; तेषां शक्त्या

P. 86. ll·2-5 : Ascribed to Rudraṭa in the Subhāṣitāvalī. L·11 : See P. 76 supra for fuller citation.

P. 86. *Kārikā* 24 : The word प्रौढोक्ति is used for the first time by Ānandavardhana in the history of Sanskrit poetics. As interpreted by Abhinavagupta it means an adroit expression capable of bringing the intended matter into association with the expression. — उक्तिरपि समर्पयितव्यवस्त्वर्पणोचिता प्रौढेत्युच्यते। This explanation is something merely etymological and vague. In the context it is clear that Ānandavardhana is using the word

Prauḍhokti in sharp contrast to *svataḥ-sambhavi*, or 'naturally possible'. The subject described may be either natural or imaginative. *Prauḍhokti* refers to the latter. A subject which is true only in the poet's imagination and not to be seen in the natural world comes to be called प्रौढोक्तिमात्रनिष्पन्नशरीर. Bhoja in his *Sarasvatīkaṇṭhābharaṇa* has given a better description of *Prauḍhokti* :—

उक्तेः प्रौढः परीपाकः प्रोच्यते प्रौढिसंज्ञया। (I. 77).

Though Mammaṭa uses this word in the same sense as that of Ānandavardhana, commentators like Govinda Ṭhakkura, Nāgoji Bhaṭṭa and Vāmanāchārya Jhalakīkar wrongly take it to mean *Kavi-sampradāya* or *Kavisamaya*. Ānandavardhana has apparently distinguished this from *Kaviprasiddhi* when he says—

शब्दार्थव्यवहारे च प्रसिद्धिरेव प्रमाणम्। while commenting on a *utprekṣādhvani* in त्रासाकुलः etc. [under II·27].

Later writers, however, like Jayadeva, Appayya Dīkṣita and Jagannātha regard the *Prauḍokti* as an independent *alaṅkāra* by narrowing down its scope. Cf.

प्रौढोक्तिस्तदशक्तस्य तच्छक्तत्वावकल्पनम्।
कलिन्दजातीररुहाः श्यामलाः सरलद्रुमाः॥

(*Candrāloka, V.* 47)

Cf. also : *Kuvalayānanda* 125. and Rasagaṅgādhara; Ch. II.

The word प्रौढोक्ति is used by some *Alaṅkāra*-writers in the general sense of a hypothetical admission for the sake of argument. Cf. भट्टनायकेन तु व्यङ्ग्यव्यापारस्य प्रौढोक्त्याभ्युपगतस्य काव्यांशत्वं ब्रुवता न्यग्भावितशब्दार्थस्वरूपस्य व्यापारस्यैव प्राधान्यमुक्तम्। – Ruyyaka, *Alaṅkārasarvasva*, R. P. Dwivedi's Edition, Varanasi, 1971, p. 24. Jayaratha in his विमर्शिनी thereon brings out the force of this expression as follows :— प्रौढोक्त्येति। न पुनर्लक्षणकरणेन। अत एव उक्तेः प्रौढत्वं यल्लक्षयितुमशक्यं तस्याप्यभ्युपगमः।

That is to say, provisional acceptance of a position which defies proof. But it is accepted as an *alaṅkāra* in a technical sense by Jayadeva, Appayya Dīkṣita and Jagannātha as already noted.

They all agree that when an unreal reason is adroitly adduced by the poet to explain an effect, we get examples of प्रौढोक्ति or 'fanciful expression'. But Ānandavardhana uses it for the first time with reference to the theme of poetry. If the theme is self-existing in the world of nature, it is स्वतःसंभवि. If it exists only in the imaginative expression of the poet or the character created by the poet it is प्रौढोक्तिसिद्ध. It is merely the product of the speaker's imagination and has nothing corresponding to it outside his mind. As in the verse, सज्जेइ....the basic idea, free from all embellishment by the poet is that in spring mango blossoms come out together with tender leaves. But this idea has not got any suggestiveness until it is transformed by the speaker's imagination. The transformation consists mainly in making the spring sentient (though it is really non-sentient), cupid an archer, flowers into arrows and the young ladies into targets. Unlike *Rūpaka* or metaphor, here a whole situation is fancied by the poet. Ānandavardhana gives another verse where a similar idea is expressed without any प्रौढोक्ति, viz. सुरभिसमये (*Infra*, p. 270, Ll.16-17). What is suggested in the previous verse by the प्रौढोक्ति of the poet is here openly expressed (रागवतामुत्कलिकाः) and that accounts for the comparative dullness of this verse as Abhinavagupta puts it in his comment on the latter, शब्दस्पृष्टेऽर्थे का हृद्यता। Yet there is no *alaṅkāra* here coming under any formal pattern recognised by the writers. It is *vastu* or subject; but प्रौढोक्तिसिद्धवस्तु i. e. subject invented by the imaginative expression of the poet himself.

For a fuller discussion of this see : K. A. Subramania Iyer, The concept of Prauḍhokti in Alaṅkāra-śāstra, Journal of Oriental Research, Madras XVI, 1946-7, pp. 20-31.

P. 88 : L. 8 : See p. 28 supra for fuller citation.

Ll. 14–15 : It would be interesting to compare in this connection Aristotle's distinction of subjects into *possible* and *probable*.

L. 15 : See p. 82 supra for full citation of एवं वादिनि ...

Ll. 19–20 : Hāla, *Saptaśatī*, 173.

P. 90. L. 5 : भट्टोद्भटादिभिः —Cf.

अलङ्कारान्तरच्छायां यत्कृत्वा धीषु बन्धनम् ।
असंदेहोऽपि संदेहरूपं संदेहनाम यत् ॥

Kāvyālaṅkārasaṅgraha, VI. 3.

P. 92. Ll. 7–10 : As Abhinavagupta points out, the expressed figure here is *śleṣa*, while the suggested figure is *rūpaka*.

L. 18 : विषमबाणलीलायां — We are told by Abhinavagupta that the theme of this Prakrit art-epic of Ānandavardhana was Cupid's triumph over the three worlds.

Ll. 19–20 : Here *atiśayokti* is the figure expressed while *upamā* is the one suggested.

Ll. 24–25 : Apparently this is a citation from the lost work *Hayagrīvavadha* by Bhartṛmeṇṭha.

P. 94. L. 9 : As the *Locana* explains, the expressed meaning stops with the idea that the fruit of the Aśoka is unlike the sweet fruits of trees like the mango. But by suggestive force of the word 'fruit' we make out that the successful fruition of even royal efforts rests with Fate. That is why the suggested universal statement deriving support from the particular instance quoted is *arthāntaranyāsa*.

L. 17 : प्राक्प्रदर्शितमेव — The reference is to the verse रक्तस्त्वं... (p. 64 supra.)

P. 96. L. 9 : Cf.

मन्ये शङ्के ध्रुवं प्रायो नूनमित्येवमादिभिः ।
उत्प्रेक्षा व्यज्यते शब्दैरिवशब्दोऽपि तादृशः ॥

Daṇḍin, *Kāvyādarśa*, II. 234.

Ll. 16–19 : Māgha, *Śiśupālavadha*, V. 26.

P. 98. Ll. 2–3 : Māgha, *Śiśupālavadha*, III. 53. The question may be asked whether there is अनुरणनध्वनि in statements like the following : 'Devadatta has grown stout; but he does not eat by day'. Here the *abhidhā* does not rest with its own sense. We have अनुरणनध्वनि only when there is a change over in sense even after the *abhidhā* is complete. This general consideration is provided in the *Locana*, while discussing श्लेषध्वनि.

L. 5 : श्लेषप्रतीति...विवर्तते — Since all the attributes can apply equivocally to both terraces and women.

L. 11 : Abhinavagupta gives in his *Locana* on this several examples of other suggested figures viz. Dīpaka, Aprastuta-praśaṁsā, Apahnuti, Sasandeha, Prativastūpamā and Atiśayokti.

Kārikā 28 : This Kārikā forcefully sums up the author's attitude towards the place of figures in poetry. So long as the *alaṅkāras* are only *vācya*, they do not deserve to be regarded as part and parcel even of the external body of poetry i. e. *śabda* and *artha*. Even for those who do not recognise *dhvani*, *alaṅkāras* will be but extrinsic elements of grace (cf. काव्यस्य शोभायाः कर्तारो धर्मा गुणाः। तदतिशयहेतवस्त्वलङ्काराः—Vāmana, *Kāvyālaṅkārasūtra* III, 1–2). But if they enter into relationship with *dhvani*, they will really become intrinsic elements of charm. Here we have a strikingly novel review of the use of figures.

In this connection the *Locana* comments :— But does not the beauty-spot with which a belle marks her forehead seem distinct from her body even though somehow one with it ? Is it not a fact that however artfully a poet may strive to endow them with a naturalness, the *alaṅkāras* hardly become one with the body of poetry ? *a fortiriori*, how are they to appear as a 'part' of the soul ? The answer is that even when the suggestion plays but an ancilliary part, it invests the *alaṅkāras* with a charm untraceable in their expressed state. It is like the special status a 'King' acquires even if it be in the children's game.

P. 102. Ll. 7–8 : Hāla, *Saptaśatī*, 110.

Ll. 15–16 : Hāla, *Saptaśatī*, 874. वाणीरकुडङ्ग etc. The suggestion is that the paramour has already arrived at the rendezvous (already agreed upon). This sense is ancillary to the expressed.

Ll. 22–23 : Hāla, *Saptaśatī*, 959.

UDDYOTA III

P. 106. L. 1. एवं व्यङ्ग्यमुखेनैव...so long the nature and varieties of suggestion have been exposed from the *vyaṅgya* standpoint.

The author here introduces the discussion on the varieties of suggestion from the standpoint of ' Suggester ' (व्यञ्जक). In a sense former varieties like ' unmeant expressed ' etc. also are suggesters. The word or sense becomes subordinate when suggestion is prominent. In unmeant expressed, the expressed sense is completely neglected while in ' meant but further extending expressed sense ' (विवक्षितान्यपरवाच्य) suggestion becomes prominent (प्रधान). In that case the ' sense ' also becomes suggester. Therefore it is from the standpoint of ' suggested ' (व्यङ्ग्यमुख). The sense becomes suggested and also suggester. But the letters, words, etc. can never become suggested. They are always suggesters. Therefore, Ānandavardhana deals with those varieties here and says ' from the standpoint of suggester '. (*Locana*).

L. 7 : सत्रैताः ... श्रियः – *Mahābhārata*, V, xxxviii. 38.

L. 9 : कः संनद्धे ... जायाम् – Kālidāsa, *Meghadūta* I. 8.

L. 11. किमिव हि मधुराणाम् – Kālidāsa, *Śākuntala*, I. 15.

P. 108. L. 3–4 : या निशा ... मुनेः – *Bhagavadgītā* II. 69.

P. 110. L. 12 : सज्जेहि सुरहिमासो — See p. 88 supra, for full citation.

Ll. 17–18—Hāla, *Saptaśatī*, 951.

P. 114. *Kārikās* 3 & 4 :—Positively and negatively, facts are adduced to show how letters play a part in the portrayal of sentiments. We have the negative argument in *Kārikā* 3, and the positive argument in *Kārikā* 4. The *Locana* has taken pains to show how the words in the *Kārikā* are to be split as ते न वर्णा in *Kārikā* 3, and तेन वर्णा in *Kārikā* 4 to maintain the logical force of the argument. This has been followed in our translation. The *Locana* also refers to the significant use of the locative case in *Kārikā* 2, while enumerating the *vyañjakas* of *rasadhvani* such as *varṇa*, *pada* and so on. This indicates that they all participate in their own way in the suggestion of *rasa*. They should not be taken to imply that they can solely and wholly suggest *rasa* by themselves. The direct causes of *rasa* are only *vibhāvādis* and not letters etc.

Ll. 15–18 : Māyurāja, *Tāpasavatsarājacarita*, Act. II.

P. 118. L 1. : स्मरनवनदी etc. — Ascribed by Vallabhadeva to Narasiṁha.

Kārikās 5 & 6 : The concept of *Saṅghaṭanā* is presented and discussed at length here for the first time in the history of Sanskrit Poetics. It was only mentioned in passing in the *vṛtti* on *kārikā* I. 1. Since Bhāmaha, Daṇḍin and Vāmana do not use this word, we have to guess that Udbhaṭa must have been responsible for a full-fledged theory of *Saṅghaṭanā*, while explaining the substratum of *guṇas*. We all know that both *guṇas* and *alaṅkāras* belong to *śabda* and *artha* of *kāvya*. How to distinguish a *śabdaguṇa* from a *śabdālaṅkāra* or an *arthaguṇa* from an *arthālaṅkāra* ? Udbhaṭa thought that the beauty of *śabda* or *artha* as such is only *alaṅkāra*. But beauty due to an artistic arrangement of *śabda* or *artha* by the poet comes to be regarded as *guṇa*. This has been hinted at by Abhinavagupta in his *Locana* on the *vṛtti* of *kārikā*, I. 1 :— द्विविधं चारुत्वम् – स्वरूपमात्रनिष्ठं, सङ्घटनाश्रितश्च । तत्र शब्दानां स्वरूपमात्रकृतं चारुत्वं शब्दालङ्कारेभ्यः । सङ्घटनाश्रितं तु शब्दगुणेभ्यः । एवमर्थानां चारुत्वं स्वरूपमात्रनिष्ठमुपमादिभ्यः । सङ्घटनापर्यवसितं त्वर्थगुणेभ्यः । [NSP. Edn. 1935, P. 6]. It follows, thus, that *saṅghaṭanā* is the basis of all *guṇas* and is intimately related to them. But Ānandavardhana is concerned here not with proving whether *guṇas* are the basis of *saṅghaṭanā* or vice versa, though he dwells on both the possibilities at length. His purpose is to point out how *saṅghaṭanā* too participates in the suggestion of particular *rasas*. It is a unique speciality of the Sanskrit language that it can provide for the use of short, long or medium-sized compounds. And *saṅghaṭanā* primarily has reference to the usage of *samāsas* only with a view to artistic effect. For a fuller discussion see : K. Krishnamoorthy, *Some Thoughts on Indian Aesthetics and Literary Criticism*, Mysore University, 1969.

P. 120. Ll. 8–9 : यो यः शस्त्रं ...— See p. 52 supra for full citation.

P 124. L 11 : उत्तमदेवताविषयप्रतिषिद्धसंभोगशृङ्गार — This happy reading as against the current reading उत्तमदेवताविषयप्रसिद्ध-संभोगशृङ्गार is found in the Moodabidre manuscript used for the first time in this edition. Neither the *Bālapriyā* nor J. L. Masson and M. V. Patwardhan (*Śāntarasa and Abhinavagupta's Philosophy of Aesthetics*, BORI, Poona, 1969 P. 11, fn 1) have noticed the inadequacy of the current reading. Abhinavagupta is positive that उत्तमदेवताविषयग्राम्यशृङ्गार is a flaw, as revealed in his other statements.

The reference is obviously to Kālidāsa, *Kumārasaṁbhava*, Canto VIII.

P. 126 : L. 1. यो यः शस्त्रं ... — See p. 52, *supra* for full citation.

L. 5 : तत्र वक्ता कविः — See *supra* p. 86, l. 14 and p. 88 l. 1.

P. 128. Ll. 10–11 : यो यः शस्त्रं — See p. 52 *supra* for full citation.

P. 130. Ll. 7–8 : तथा ह्यमरुकस्य...एव—Cf. the saying अमरुककवेरेकः श्लोकः प्रबन्धशतायते । (i. e. one verse of Amaruka is as good as a whole work).

P. 134. *Kārikā* 12 : The *sandhis* are five phases in the development of the dramatic plot roughly corresponding to Introduction, Rising action, Climax, Denouement and Catastrophe. The *sandhyaṅgas* are the various intermediate stages that form a *sandhi* and are sixty-four in number. For a detailed account of these see *Nāṭyaśāstra*, XIX, 37 ff. and *Daśarūpaka*. I. 22 ff.

P. 138. Ll. 7–8. This is an important verse. This verse states the novel view of Ānandavardhana on defects. Earlier writers dealt with faults that might occur in the usage of words, sentences, and the senses conveyed in poetry. They even discussed whether defects are positive or negative. But Ānandavardhana being रसध्वनिवादिन् considers defects and merits also in relation with sentiments. So for him impropriety in the delineation of sentiment is the gravest blemish. This actually becomes the guiding principle for later writers to write on defects in poetry. *Rasabhaṅga* or hindrance to the even progress of sentiment is the gravest blemish which is a result of impropriety.

The principle of propriety is the widest and it covers each and every part of poetry as M. M. Kuppuswami Śāstri declares—

औचितीमनुधावन्ति सर्वे ध्वनिरसोन्नयाः ।
गुणालङ्कृतिरीतीनां नयाश्चानृजुवाङ्मयाः ॥

(*Highways and By-ways of literary criticism in Sanskrit*,— P. 27.)

Later on Kṣemendra develops the theory and goes to the extent of saying that it is the soul of poetry. ('काव्यस्य जीवितम्' औचित्यविचारचर्चा).

But it will be seen that propriety is decided on the basis of sentiment. It is not an independent principle like *rasa* and it would be absurd to say propriety exists even without *rasa*.

Abhinavagupta observes—

उचितशब्देन रसविषयमेवौचित्यं भवतीति दर्शयन् रसध्वनेर्जीवितत्वं सूचयति। तदभावे हि किमपेक्ष्येदमौचित्यं नाम सर्वत्रोद्घोष्यत इति भाव: ॥

Locana (P. 45, BP. Edn.)

Cf. "There can be no universal theory of poetic excellences and blemishes, [*Guṇa* and *Doṣa*] for the sole determinant of these excellences or blemishes is their function in a given context."—V. K. Chari, *The Language of Poetry*, The Indian Journal of English Studies, Vol IV. No. 1, pp. 10 f.

L. 9: अत एव च भरते — See *Nāṭyaśāstra* XVIII–10.

P. 142. L. 7: ... कवेरव्युत्पत्तिसंभावना...—Cf. Aristotle's remarks on the different provinces of the Poet and the Historian—"It is not the Poet's province to relate such things as have actually happened, but such as might have happened, such as are possible, according to probable or necessary consequence. .. The Historian and the Poet are distinguished by this that the one relates what has been, the other what might be. On this account Poetry is a more philosophical and a more excellent thing than History; for, Poetry is chiefly conversant about general truth, History about particular."—*Aristotle's Poetics*, H. Morley's translation, (Cassell's National Library) p. 32.

P. 142. Ll. 14–15 : Abhinavagupta remarks —

स्वेच्छा तेषु न योज्या, कथञ्चिद्वा यदि योज्यते तत्तत्प्रसिद्धरसविरुद्धा न योज्या । यथा रामस्य धीरललितत्वयोजनेन नाटिकानायकत्वं कश्चित् कुर्यादिति त्वत्यन्तासमञ्जसम् ॥ (*Locana*)

L. 16 : Abhinavagupta ascribes it to Yaśovarman, the author of the drama called रामाभ्युदय. The verse quoted in the *Śṛṅgāraprakāśa* is as follows —

औचित्यं वचसां प्रकृत्यनुगतं, सर्वत्र पात्रोचिता
पुष्टिः स्वावसरे रसस्य च, कथामार्गे न चातिक्रमः ।
शुद्धिः प्रस्तुतसंविधानकविधौ प्रौढिश्च शब्दार्थयोः
विद्वद्भिः परिभाव्यतामवहितैः एतावदेवास्तु नः ॥

(Quoted by Dr. V. Raghavan; *Some Concepts of Alaṅkāraśāstra*, p. 205.)

P. 144. L. 1 : यथा कालिदासप्रबन्धेषु — Abhinavagupta remarks that the chronicles which form the sources of Kālidāsa's *Raghuvaṁśa* do not relate the wedding of Aja and such incidents.

L. 2 : यथा च मदीय एवार्जुनचरिते — Abhinavagupta points out that incidents like Arjuna's conquest of the netherworld which occur in this poem are invented by the poet only and have no basis in the earlier chronicles.

Ll. 6–8 : रसादि...पेक्षया — The five stages in the action of the hero towards the achievement of his goal are called *Pañca-avasthās* by Bharata and they are — 1. Beginning (*Prārambha*), 2. Effort (*Prayatna*), 3. Possibility of goal's realisation (*Prāpteḥ sambhava*), 4. Certainty of goal's realisation (*Niyatāpti*), and 5. Realisation of goal (*Phalayoga*). The parts of the plot (*Itivṛtta-khaṇḍāḥ*) that relate to these are respectively called *mukha, pratimukha, garbha, avamarśa,* and *nirvahaṇa* according to Abhinavagupta. He also opines that the *artha-prakṛtis* or factors that ensure the intended goal, *bīja* (seed), *bindu* (unexpected extension) — *patākā* (sub-incident) and *prakarī* (mixed incident) also may come in when the hero's goal is to be secured only by the efforts of his minister — and *kārya* (attainment of goal) are included in the concept of *sandhis*. For details see Bharata's *Nāṭyaśāstra*, XXI. 20 ff.

L. 17 : दृश्यन्ते च···प्रबन्धेषु — As an example of this over-fondness for figures, at the expense of *rasa*, Abhinavagupta quotes a verse from the drama *Svapnavāsavadatta* —

स्वच्चितपक्ष्मकवाटं नयनद्वारं स्वरूपताडेन ।
उद्घाट्य सा प्रविष्टा हृदयगृहं मे नृपतनूजा ॥

But this verse is not found in Bhāsa's *Svapnavāsavadatta* published by T. Ganapati Shastri. Since the author of the thirteen Trivandrum plays is not culpable of the defect in question to any notable extent, the ascription of these to Bhāsa becomes open to doubt.

P. 146. L. 4 : तद्यथा मधुमथनविजये — Abhinavagupta quotes the relevant verse from the Prakrit poem, *Madhumathanavijaya* :—

लीलादाढा शुध्यूढ्ढासअलमहिमण्डलसच्चिअ अज्ज ।
कीस्मसुणालाहरतुज्जआइ अङ्गम्मि ॥ (?)

It may be translated as follows :—

How is it that this slender ornament of lotus-fibres is felt heavy by you who could playfully lift up at the tip of your tusks the weight of the entire earth ?

L. 5 : विषमबाणलीलायाम् — The friends in question are Spring, Youth, Malaya breeze and others. Abhinavagupta quotes one verse said by Youth :—

मिअवहण्डिअरोरो णिरङ्कुसो अविवेअरहिओ वि ।
सविण वि तुमम्मि पुणोवन्ति अ अतन्ति पंमुसिम्मि ॥ (?)

The translation is :

I do overstep limits; I am unbridled
and devoid of discrimination;
Even in dream, I shall not think of devotion
to you !

L. 6 : यथा···महाभारते — *Mahābhārata*, XII. 153. The story is very interesting. The corpse of the son just dead is taken to the cemetery by the bereaved father and relatives for purposes of funeral rites. A vulture who wants to feed upon the corpse while yet it is day tries to persuade the men to go back early —

'How terrible this cemetery is with vultures and jackals ! Everywhere there are skeletons frightening living beings. There is none who can live on for ever and escape death. Whether it is a friend or a foe, death is the natural end of all creatures... ' A jackal whose intent is to feed upon the corpse after nightfall when the vultures would not trouble him, argues with the men that they should stay at least till it gets dark — ' See, the sun is still shining ! Be affectionate yet. This moment is most unholy and the boy may yet come back to life. Oh, how his body shines like gold ! He has hardly stepped into youth. Are you like fools deserting him without a qualm on the words of a vulture ? ... '

Ll. 12–15 : *Hanumānnāṭaka*, IX. 15. Quoted also by Hemacandra (*Kāvyānuśāsana*, NSP. p. 181) and Viśvanātha.

L. 17 : तत्र ' मे यदरय: ' ... व्यञ्जकत्वम् — The references are to words in the original Sanskrit verse and cannot apply for obvious reasons to the translation.

P. 148. Ll. 10–11 : *Mahābhārata*, I. 128. 6.

Ll. 16–17 : Kālidāsa, *Meghadūta*, II. 19.

P. 150. Ll. 2–3 : Hāla, *Saptaśatī*, 706.

Ll. 8–9 : „ „ 961.

Ll. 20–21 : Kālidāsa, *Vikramorvaśīya*, IV. 10.

P. 152. Ll. 2–3 : „ *Śākuntala*, III. 23.

Ll. 6–9 : „ „ I. 14.

L. 11 : Mayūra, *Sūryaśataka*, 4.

Ll. 12—13 : मनुष्यवृत्त्या... — Abhinavagupta has given the verse in full :—

मनुष्यवृत्त्या समुपाचरन्तं स्वबुद्धिसामान्यकृतानुमानाः ।
योगीश्वरैरप्यसुबोधमीश त्वां बोद्धुमिच्छन्त्यबुधाः स्वतर्कैः ॥

' O Lord ! Thou who canst not be easily known even by the best yogins, fools are wishing to know by their intelligence, as thou art pretending the behaviour of men '.

L. 14 : अहो बतासि ... — Kālidāsa, *Kumārasambhava*.III. 20.

P. 154. L. 6 : The construction of this sentence is rather awkward. In पौनरुक्त्यं प्रयुज्यमानं शोभामावहति, the word प्रयुज्यमानं seems to be redundant. Perhaps पदं is to be understood before प्रयुज्यमानम्.

Ll. 14—15 : Hāla *Saptaśatī*, 675.

P. 156. L. 12 : उक्तमत्र ... वसरे — See *supra*, p. 83 and cf. p. 41.

L. 14 : शब्दविशेषाणाम् ... प्रदर्शितम् — By Udbhaṭa, in his *Bhūmahavivaraṇa*, according to Abhinavagupta.

P. 158. L. 2 : किमिदं सहृदयत्वं नाम —

Cf. "All the same, the principle of reader participation can be looked at in terms of the lamp and the jar — the stated meaning, when the reader makes contact with it, acts upon an existing capacity within him for response to symbolized emotion, and the suggested meaning is rendered manifest in his consciousness. Sanskrit theory, as we saw in the last chapter, assumes that when the sensuous correlates of the emotion activate one of the emotional sets latent in the reader, the supreme aesthetic response is evoked. It also assumes that only the reader whom nature or nurture has equipped with a special sensibility can respond in this way. As Lascelles Abercrombie says... '...the author must rely on his readers' ability to respond to what his language can only suggest... It is the sense of language, that makes the enjoyer of literary art'. This type of reader goes to work actively on the poem— on this showing, being illuminated is not a passive role for the jar but an energetic act of response." — Krishna Rayan, *Suggestion and Statement in Poetry*, London, 1972, p. 56.

Cf. also :— " To the majority of people aesthetic pleasure means a state of mind which is essentially indistinguishable from their ordinary behaviour. It differs merely in accidental qualities, being perhaps less utilitarian, more intense, and free from painful consequences. But the object towards which their attention and consequently, all their other mental activities, are directed is the same as in daily life : people and passions. By art they understand a means through which they are brought in contact with interesting human affairs. Artistic forms proper — figments, fantasy — are tolerated only if they do not interfere with the perception of human forms and fates. As soon as purely aesthetic elements predominate and the story of John and Mary grows elusive, most people feel out of their depth and are at a loss what to make of the scene, the book or the painting. They have never practiced any other attitude but the practical one in which a man's feelings are aroused and he is emotionally involved; a work that does not invite sentimental intervention leaves them without a cue."

— Jose Ortega Y. Gasset Weyl (Spanish writer translated by Helene), *The Dehumanization of Art*, Princeton University Press, 1968, p. 9.

P. 156, L. 17 : यत्रापि....— Abhinavagupta explains : The words like स्रक्, चन्दन etc. even though they are not suggestive of erotic sentiment in a given place, they add charm to the meaning almost suggestive of it because their suggestive capacity is familiar to us in other places. Thus in तटी तारं ताम्यति sensitive critics prefer the feminine form (तटी) to masculine and neuter forms of the word तट on the principle स्त्रीति नामापि मधुरम् :— Even names are beautiful if they are feminine.

स्रक्चन्दनादिशब्दानां तदानीं शृङ्गारादिव्यञ्जकत्वाभावेऽपि व्यञ्जकत्वशक्तेर्भूयसा दर्शनात्तदधिवाससुन्दरीभूतमर्थं प्रतिपादयितुं सामर्थ्यमस्ति। तथाहि— 'तटी तारं ताम्यति' इत्यत्र तटशब्दस्य पुंस्त्वनपुंसकत्वे अनादृत्य स्त्रीत्वमेवाश्रितं सहृदयैः 'स्त्रीति नामापि मधुरम्' इति कृत्वा।

Kuntaka quotes the whole verse तटी तारं ताम्यति and also says स्त्रीति नामैव पेशलम्। (*Vakroktijīvita* II. 22). Probably Abhinavagupta might have been acquainted with his work. A similar idea occurs in *Kāmandakīya Nītisāra* also —

नामापि स्त्रीति संह्लादि विकरोत्येव मानसम्।
किं पुनर्दर्शनं तस्या विलासोल्लासितभ्रुवः॥

But in this verse the word नाम means perhaps the name 'woman'. So it is not probable that Abhinava took the verse from Kāmandaka.

It does not appear plausible that Kuntaka quotes the verse after reading *Locana*. However we cannot say anything on the priority of Kuntaka to Abhinavagupta on this meagre evidence. Both of them might have taken it from some common source.

Pp. 158—60. *Kārikās* 17-19 : Cf. "A third sort of imperfection in the pathetic is that which Theodorus has named the Parenthyrse, or an ill-timed emotion. It is an attempt to work upon the passions, where is no need of pathos; or some excess, where modification is requisite. For some authors, as if from the efforts of intoxication, fall into passionate expressions, which bear no relation at all to their subject, but are whims of their own, or borrowed from the schools. The consequence is, as might be expected, that they meet with nothing but contempt and derision from their unmoved audience — transported themselves, whilst their hearers are calm and unexcited" — Longinus, *On the Sublime*, p. 100.

P. 166. Ll. 13—14 : यथा वा .... वर्णने — Bāṇa, *Kādambarī*, p. 146 (Ed. Peterson).

Ll. 15—16 : भ्रमिमरति — See *supra*, p. 76, for full citation.

P. 168. L. 2 : कोपात्कोमल—See *supra*, p. 68, for full citation.

L. 4 : क्षिप्तो हस्ता—See *supra*, p. 44. for full citation.

P. 172. Ll. 7–8 : *Mahābhārata*, XI 24. 19, spoken by the wives of Bhūriśravas at his death in the battle; cf. also for the description of the battle in which he fell, op. cit. VII. 142.

P. 182. Ll.5–6 : *Mahābhārata*, XII, 174. 46; 177. 51.

L. 13 : तदेवमस्ति शान्तो रसः— J. L. Masson and M. V. Patwardhan in their *Śāntarasa and Abhinavagupta's Philosophy of Aesthetics* (BORI, Poona, 1969) add the following note on this text cited by them —

> Ānanda is seriously concerned with showing that *śāntarasa* does exist. (*pratīyata eva* and *asti śānto rasaḥ*.) It is, therefore, likely that this was a controversial point in the ninth century (indeed it has remained controversial until the present day). Since the *kārikās* mention all of the eight *rasas* by name at some point or another, there is absolutely no reason why they should not have mentioned *śānta*, had *śānta* been known to their author. The fact that *Śānta* is never mentioned in a single *kārikā* leads us to believe that their author was unaware of its existence (at least of its

formal existence as a *rasa*, though there is no reason why he should not have known about *śānta* as an attitude), and most probably, therefore, lived before the time of Udbhata, the first author to mention *śānta* as a *rasa* (p. 95, fn. 6).

This is indeed a strange argument from silence. Even if the *Kārikākāra* were held to be different from Ānandavardhana, he could not have been earlier than Udbhaṭa whose views are hinted at by him. (But, for arguments supporting their identity see, K. Krishnamoorthy, *Dhvanyāloka and its Critics*. Kavyalaya, Mysore, 1968, Chapter III). We know positively that Udbhaṭa mentioned *Śānta* as a ninth *rasa* (V. Raghavan. *The Number of Rasas*, Adyar Library, Madras, 1967, p. 13) and the *Kārikākāra* could not have been ignorant of it. Masson & Patwardhan are not justified in thinking Udbhaṭa to be later than the *Kārikākāra* because the concepts of *saṅghaṭanā* and *kāvyavṛttis* (cf. III last *kārikā*) mentioned in the *kārikā* are clearly a reference to Udbhaṭa's doctrines. Further, as already noted by Raghavan, *Śāntarasa* is known under the name of *Praśānta* to an early canonical work of the Jains viz. *Anuyogadvārasūtra*, whose date is very much earlier than Udbhaṭa's (Loc. cit. p. 66).

P. 186. Ll 11–12. नाटकादिगोष्ठी ... वतारिता – cf. Bharata's *Nāṭyaśāstra*, ch. I. This well known idea is echoed by Mammaṭa in his saying–काव्यं यशसे ... कान्तासम्मिततयोपदेशयुजे ॥ *Kāvyaprakāśa*, I. 2.

Ll. 16-17 : Attributed to Vyāsa in Kṣemendra's *Aucityavicāracarcā*.

P. 188. L. 17 : कैशिक्याद्या वृत्तय: — cf. Bharata's *Nāṭyaśāstra*, ch. XX.

P. 194. L. 8 : गावो व: — See *supra*, p. 78 for full citation.

P. 198. L. 13 : व्रीडायोगा ...— See *supra*, p. 78 for full citation.

P. 200. Ll. 4--5 : यतः ... रास्थितम् — Perhaps the Sphoṭavādins are meant.

P. 200. L. 10 — घटप्रदीपन्याय: — In the words of a modern exponent of the Dhvani theory [Krishna Rayan, *Suggestion and Statement in Poetry*, London, 1972], "the 'founding metaphor ' to apply Richards' phrase [I. A. Richards, *Speculative Instruments*, London, 1955, P. 41] of the central poetic in Sanskrit — the *Dhvani* Poetic — is the lamp and the jar. The metaphor identifies the two factors of suggestion as the suggestor and the suggested. On the one hand, there is stated meaning, which is the suggestor; and on the other, there is suggested meaning. The lamp is stated meaning (*vācyārtha*); the jar is suggested meaning (*vyaṅgyārtha*), which it illuminates and reveals. The metaphor was used by Sanskrit critics, although probably not quite in the manner Richards has in mind, as an instrument for analysing and describing the relationship and comparative status of stated and suggested meanings. This, I think, is a unique enquiry; a full-length study of poetic meaning as dual and hierarchical has not been, as far as I know, undertaken elsewhere. (Pp. 52–53) ... The use of the lamp-jar metaphor as an instrument of reflection in ninth century Sanskrit Criticism yielded several insights into the behaviour of the stated and suggested components of meaning when the suggested component is emotion and the stated component is its objective correlatives. ... In the first place, *the jar was already there, the lamp only revealed it.* The lamp and the jar are a conventional formula in Indian philosophy for stating the theory of manifestation. Applied to poetry, the theory sees the process of suggestion as the revealing of what is already there rather than as the presenting of anything new (P. 55) ... The second observed feature of the lamp-jar relationship is that *the lamp continues to shine even after the jar has been illuminated* (P. 56)... (thirdly) *the lamp not only reveals the jar but reveals itself.* (P. 57)...Sanskrit theory makes the point that, strictly speaking, the suggested meaning is apprehended, despite the apparent simultaneity, *after* the stated meaning and indeed through it and is governed by it. Language, we may add, cannot suggest unless it has first stated, and then what is stated is the base which supports what it suggests. Sanskrit criticism calls this *Vācyārthāpekṣā* (dependence on stated meaning) (Pp. 57–58) ... (fourthly) *the lamp and the jar are not necessarily found together.* Inference is based on the invariable concomitance of the middle term and the major term; stated and suggested meaning have no such relationship (P. 60). "

This is indeed a very perceptive and penetrating explanation of the maxim of the jar and the lamp employed by Ānandavardhana. But colonel G. A. Jacob has misunderstood the implications of this maxim in his *Laukikanyāyāñjaliḥ*, Part II, Bombay (NSP) 1909, p. 26. He writes :—

> " *Ghaṭapradīpanyāyaḥ* — The simile of *a lighted lamp inside a vessel.* Raghunath points out that a lamp so placed illuminates only the interior of the vessel, and he applies it to one whose knowledge of Brahman is of a low order. The maxim is used very differently, however, by Ānandavardhana in his *Dhvanyāloka* as the following extract will show:—' न त्वेष...वाच्यावभासः। Abhinavagupta when explaining *Dhvanyāloka* I. 12 refers to this passage in the following words :— अत एव...न विरोधः। According to these great authorities on *alaṅkāra*, therefore, the *nyāya* teaches that as the lamp continues to burn after it has lighted up the interior of the vessel, and is indeed essential to the continuance of that illumination, so the expressed meaning of a sentence is absolutely essential as a basis for the figurative meaning which it also conveys. "

Jacob and Raghunatha are both wrong in thinking that a lighted lamp is ever placed inside a vessel. It is something inconceivable in Indian life. In Indian poetics as well as philosophy the analogy of the jar and the lamp is used in quite a different sense as seen above. They refer simply to the object illuminated (*ghaṭa*) and the light (*pradīpa*) illuminating it. That the analogy was very much in vogue in philosophical circles even before the time of Ānadavardhana is corroborated by a reference to it by Bhartṛhari in his celebrated work *Vākyapadīya* (II. 298–299). He says :—

घटादिषु यथा दीपो येनार्थेन प्रयुज्यते ।
ततोऽन्यस्यापि सान्निध्यात् स करोति प्रकाशनम् ॥
संसर्गिषु तथाऽर्थेषु शब्दो येन प्रयुज्यते ।
तस्मात् प्रयोजकादन्यानपि प्रत्याययत्यसौ ॥

[Ed. K. V. Abhyankar & V. P. Limaye, University of Poona, 1965, p. 41].

This reference is clinching and shows to what extent Ānanda-vardhana is indebted to Bhartṛhari here as elsewhere.

P. 204. L. 6 : लीलाकमल ... See *supra*, p. 82 for full citation.

P. 208. L. 17 : ... प्रिये जने नास्ति पुनरुक्तम्—See *supra*, p. 30 for full citation.

P. 210. Ll. 2-3 : सुवर्णपुष्पां ... See *supra*, p. 28 for full citation.

P. 214. Ll. 16-18 : कृत्रिमशब्दार्थ...मवतरति—Buddhist logicians also may be understood by this reference since they hold that the relation of word and its meaning is non-eternal.

P. 224. L. 1 : शब्दप्रकारेभ्यः—To be taken apparently in the sense of शब्दव्यापारेभ्यः and not in the sense of शब्दभेदेभ्यः.

P. 226. Ll. 1–2 : (1) The words 'dark lilies', 'moon', 'temples of elephant', 'plantain stems' and 'lotus stalks' suggest respectively the eyes, the face, the breasts, the thighs and the arms of the damsel that is being described. The words are literally inapplicable to the lady and hence have lost their primary meaning; but suggestively, however, they convey the idea. But these suggested meanings are subordinated to the expressed sense that she is a new ocean of Beauty. The context is a description of the woman's beauty clearly indicated by the words—'who is this maiden here' (अपरैव हि केयम्). The suggested beauty of the various expressions becomes subordinate to the expressed idea—that she is an ocean of Beauty. Hence, this is an example of the poetry of subordinated suggestion.

Abhinava strikes an important note on this—

The expressed sense becomes a विभाव for the love of the hero. Then, from the final Rasa-Dhvani point of view, even the expresed sense becomes subordinate. Further he says, it is the case in all the examples of poetry of subordinated suggestion :—

अत एवेयति यद्यपि वाच्यस्य प्राधान्यं तथापि रसध्वनौ तस्यापि गुणतेति सर्वस्य गुणीभूतव्यङ्ग्यस्य प्रकारे मन्तव्यम्।

(2) A second type of instances are found when the suggested idea becomes subordinate to expressed sense retaining its meaning. This second variety is similar to the suggestion based on primary sense (अभिधामूलध्वनि). The example अनुरागवती... illustrates this.

P. 226. L. 5 : अनुरागवती सन्ध्या ... See *supra*, p. 22 for full citation.

L. 6 : सङ्केतकाल ... See *supra*, p. 84 for full citation.

Ll. 7-8 : आधिकारिकवाक्यापेक्षया — obviously means प्रधान-वाक्यार्थापेक्षया.

L. 16-17 : लच्छी दुहिदा ... Abhinavagupta explains the suggested sense as follows :—' Lakṣmī or wealth is related to Hari and Gaṅgā on the one hand and to Moon and Nectar on the other. That is to say, wealth can be obtained through devotion to Hari and bathing in the Ganges; and once wealth is got, one can enjoy the pleasures with Moon and Nectar. In other words, the wealth is best spent on wine in the company of women on moonlit nights '. Though beautiful in itself, this suggested sense is suppressed by the contextual primary meaning, viz., ' The family of the mighty ocean is extraordinary. '

P. 230. L. 10 : प्रभामहत्या ... See Kālidāsa's *Kumārasambhava*, I. 28.

P. 230. L. 11 : तदेवं...मार्गः — If we understand the nature of the poetry of subordinated suggestion, we can understand the nature of all the poetic figures. It becomes the general definition of all the poetic figures; for, the so-called poetic figures or *alaṅkāras* deserve that name only when they are pre-eminently beautiful. And beauty is brought about only by suggestion either principal or secondary. If the underlying suggestive beauty is not recognised, we are liable to regard all comparisons as similies, all identifications as metaphors and so forth. Abhinavagupta writes a notable paragraph to illustrate this point —

मुलक्षिता इति यत्क्लिष्टं तद्विनिर्मुक्तं रूपं तत्काव्येऽभ्यर्थनीयम् । उपमा हि ' यथा गौस्तथा गवय ' इति । रूपकं ' खलेवाली यूप ' इति । श्लेषः द्विवचनेऽचीति तन्त्रात्मकः । यथासंख्यं, ' तुदीशालातुरेति ' । दीपकं ' गामश्वम् ' इति । ससन्देहः ' स्थाणुर्वा स्यात् ' इति । अपह्नुतिः ' नेदं रजतमिति '। पर्यायोक्तं ' पीनो दिवा नात्तीति '। तुल्ययोगिता ' स्थाघ्वोरिच्च ' इति । अप्रस्तुतप्रशंसा सर्वाणि ज्ञापकानि यथा पदसंज्ञायामन्तवचनम् ... ' अन्यत्र संज्ञाविधौ प्रत्ययग्रहणे तदन्तविधिर्न ' इति आक्षेपश्चोभयत्र विभाषासु विकल्पात्मकविशेषाभिधित्सया इष्टस्यापि विधेः पूर्वनिषेधनात् प्रतिषेधेन समीकृत इति न्यायात् । अतिशयोक्तिः — ' समुद्रः कुण्डिका विन्ध्यो वर्धितवानर्कवर्त्मागृह्णात् ' इति । एवमन्यत् ।

Even though they have the elements of figures enumerated above, we cannot call them poetic figures, for, they lack charm contributed by the presence of गुणीभूतव्यङ्ग्य. Figures thus become truly so only when they are helped by the underlying suggestion.

P. 232. L. 17 : स्वस्था भवन्ति ... Bhaṭṭanārāyaṇa, *Veṇısaṁhara*, I. 8.

P. 234. Ll. 2–3 : Hāla, *Gāthāsaptaśatī*, 417.

P. 236. Ll. 1-2 : Kālidāsa, *Kumārasambhava*, VII, 19. Ll. 4-5 :—Bhāravi. *Kirātārjunīya*, VIII. 14.

P. 236. L. 9. एवंवादिनि... —See *supra*, p. 82. for full citation.

P. 236. *Kārika* 40 :—This is very important. Even the instances of the poetry of subordinated suggestion assume the form of Dhvani when viewed from the standpoint of sentiment. That is, when sentiment is the main purport, then individual instances also come under Dhvani. Sentiment is the underlying principle which governs the whole. An individual part may not be very beautiful in itself while we analyse a beautiful object. But that particular part also might become beautiful when we appreciate the beauty of the whole. However this is not strictly logical.

Abhinavagupta notes a difference of opinion regarding the interpretation of the verses quoted. According to an earlier commentator (he may be Candrikākāra), in these instances, the suggested meaning is subordinated to sentiments. That is why these instances also can be called Dhvani when viewed from the Rasa standpoint. But Abhinavagupta strongly opposes that view and ridicules him.—

यस्तु त्रिष्वपि श्लोकेषु प्रतीयमानस्यैव रसाङ्गत्वं व्याचष्टे स्म स देवं विक्रीय तद्यात्रोत्सवमकार्षीत्। एवंहि व्यंङ्गयस्य या गुणीभूतता प्रकृता सैव समूलं त्रुट्येत्। रसादिव्यतिरिक्तस्य हि व्यङ्गयस्य रसाङ्गभावयोगित्वमेव प्राधान्यं नान्यत् किञ्चिदिति अलं पूर्ववंश्यैः सह विवादेन॥

P. 238. L. 3 : न्यक्कारो...—See *supra*, p. 146 for full citation.

P. 240. Ll. 4–7 : Ascribed to Dharmakīrti by Vallabhadeva also.

P. 242. Ll. 11–14 : पराथें...See *supra*, p. 32 for full citation.

P. 250. L. 13 : ...हृदयवतीषु च षट्प्रज्ञादिगाथासु ... – Dr. V. Raghavan has noted some references and discussed the meaning of the word 'Ṣaṭprajña' in his article, "*Gleanings From Somadevasūri's Yaśastilakacampū* — Gangānātha Jha Research Institute Journal, Allahabad, Vol. I, Part III, 1944, pp. 370–72. He says :—

"Somadeva continues his description of rogues. He speaks of fourteen families of rogues of which the sixth family, he says, arose from the dust of the feet of Ṣaṭprajñas.

This is an interesting reference to a community of men of society whom both Ānandavardhana and Abhinavagupta refer to in their *Dhvanyāloka* and *Locana.*

Ānandavardhana mentions these Śaṭprajñas in connection with cases of expressions where the charming *vācya* is primary '*mukhya*' and the *vyaṅgya* is subordinated 'guṇībhūta', and gives as illustrations the beautiful Prākrit verses on love composed by the Ṣaṭprajñas, Ṣaṭprajñādi-gāthās. Commenting on this in his *Locana*, Abhinavagupta says that these gāthās are called in the circles of Prākrit poets 'aaliā'; and Ṣaṭprajñas are those Sahṛdayas who, living next door to each other and being well-versed in the world, meet together and exchange expressions of wit, lyrical stanzas etc. And Abhinavagupta cites as an example a gāthā of his own Guru, Bhaṭṭendurāja.

Dhvanyāloka (p. 222) :

यदा तु चाटुषु देवतास्तुतिषु वा रसादीनामङ्गतया व्यवस्थानं, हृदयवतीषु च षट्प्रज्ञादिगाथासु कासुचिद् व्यङ्ग्यविशिष्टवाच्यप्राधान्यम् ।

Locana (pp. 222-23) :

हृदयवतीष्विति । 'अअलिया' इति प्राकृतकविगोष्ठ्यां प्रसिद्धासु त्रिवर्गोपायोपेयकुशलाः सहृदयाः षट्प्रज्ञाः प्रातिवेश्मिका उच्यन्ते । तद्गाथा यथा भट्टेन्दुराजस्य—

लंघिअगअणा फलहीलआओ होंतु त्ति वड्ढअंतीए ।
हलिअस्सासिसं पाडिवेस ... ... ॥

अथ लङ्घितगगनाः कार्पासलता भवन्त्विति हालिकस्याशिषं वर्धयन्त्या प्रातिवेश्मिकः परनिर्वृतिं प्रापित इति चौर्यसंभोगाभिलाषिणीयमित्यनेन व्यङ्ग्येन विशिष्टवाच्यमेव सुन्दरम् ।

In a gāthā in the Vajjālaggaṁ (Bib. Ind. edn., pp. 58-59, No. 281), Vidagdha-paddhati, Ṣaṭprajña is used in the sense of a Vidagdha and an adept in the art of love-making :

[जइ कहवि ताण छप्पण्णयाण तुणुयंगि गोयरे पडसि ।
ता थोरवसहदाहेक्कमंडिया दुक्करं जियसि ॥]
यदि कथमपि तेषां षट्प्रज्ञानां तन्वङ्गि गोचरे पतसि ।
तदोत्कृष्टवृषभदाहैकमण्डिता दुष्करं जीवसि ॥

In explanation of the name Ṣaṭprajña given to these gifted men, Abhinava seems to say that they are so called because of their knowledge (*prajñā*) of six (ṣaṭ) things: the *upāyas* (means) and *upeyas* (ends) pertaining to *trivarga* (*dharma*, *artha* and *kāma* — 3 × 2 = 6). Monier Williams says on the basis of some authority that six things are the four *puruṣārthas*, *lokārtha* and *tattvārtha*; and it is probably the same authority as quoted in the *Śabdakalpadruma* :

धर्मार्थकाममोक्षेषु लोकतत्त्वार्थयोरपि ।
षट्सु प्रज्ञास्ति यस्योच्चैः स षट्प्रज्ञ इति स्मृतः ॥

In Abhinava's explanation, there is the omission of Mokṣa and in Ānandavardhana too, the implication is that the Ṣaṭprajña is a man of taste and a wordly-wise man. Originally a wise man, then one with much wordly wisdom and taste, then one with a gift for fine expression and enjoyment of good things, the Ṣaṭprajña thus gradually underwent a semantic pejoration until he came to mean a Viṭa. The Prakrit verses he uttered dealt mostly with love and that of the clandestine variety. The lexicons also came to understand him so. "

Dr. A. N. Upadhye has published the text of a *Gāthākoṣa* composed by Vidagdhas and entitled *Chappaṇṇaya-Gāhāo* in the Journal of the Oriental Institute, Baroda, Vol. XI, No. 4, (June, 1962), pp. 385–402. It contains 164 verses in the Māhārāṣhtrī Prākrit, and is a Jaina recension. It has also some verses in common with the *Vajjālaggaṁ* and the *Gāthāsaptaśatī*.

P. 252. L. 8 : एवं वादिनि...See *supra*, p. 82 for full citation.

Ll. 11–12 : Hāla, *Gāthāsaptaśatī*, 983.

P. 253. L. 23. : In the English translation of the verse खणपाहुणिआ a serious mistake has crept in. Instead of " *This lady just came out to see the procession when* ", read " *This lady has come as a guest at the festival; but* "

P. 254. L. 1 : स्थिरधश्यामल — See *supra*, p. 38 for full citation.

Ll. 3 : न्यक्कारो — See *supra*, p. 146 full citation.

Ll. 5–8 : Bhaṭṭanārāyaṇa, *Veṇīsaṁhāra*, V. 26.

P. 256. L. 1 : तेषां गोपवधू...See *supra*, p. 48 for full citation.

Ll. 14–17 : Kālidāsa, *Meghadūta*, I. 32.

P. 258. Ll. 10--11 : Hāla, *Gāthāsaptaśatī*, 560.

P. 260. Ll. 7--8 : एतद्...प्रवर्तिता: — cf. Vāmana, *Kāvyālaṅkārasūtravṛtti*, I. ii. 9.

P. 262. L. 14 : ग्रन्थान्तरे — The work is *Vivṛti* or gloss on Dharmottara's *ṭīkā* or commentary (*Dharmottarī*) on Dharmakīrti's *Pramāṇa-viniścaya* according to Abhinavagupta.

UDDYOTA IV

P. 268. Ll. 2--5 : *Amaruśataka*, 82.

L. 7 : तरङ्गभ्रूभङ्ग...See *supra*, p. 46 for full citation.

L. 7 : नानाभङ्गि...—This verse is not available in full.

P. 270. *Kārikā* 4 :— John Drinkwater makes use of this very simile in writing about the limitless possibilities of genius :— " And so poetry is beautifully like life itself in seeming not to change yet always being new. Each year you see the trees covering themselves with green, the flowers in bloom...And in a way these seem to be the same trees and flowers and seasons that have been passing before men's eyes far back through the ages, and yet each year they are all marvellously new, as truly exciting discoveries for us when we see them as though there had never been such life before. And so with the poet and his poetry ". — *The Way of Poetry*. p. 27.

L. 6 : धरणीधारणायाधुना त्वं शेष: — Bāṇa, *Harṣacarita*, (NSP. Ed.) p. 127.

L. 11 : एवंवादिनि — See *supra*, p. 82 for full citation.

L. 15 : सज्जेइ...See *supra*, p 88 for full citation.

P. 272. L. 2 : वाणिअअ —See *supra*, p. 110 for full citation.

P. 274. Ll. 2-3 : शोकः श्लोकत्वमागतः — Vālmīki, *Rāmāyaṇa*, I. i. 40.

P. 276. Ll. 2-3 : प्रत्युत...प्रतीयते—cf. *Mahābhārata*, I. i. 49; ii. 238; and also I. i. 92 and ii. 385.

L. 6 : भगवान् वासुदेवश्च—*Mahābhārata*, I. i. 256.

L. 14 : स हि सत्यम्— ,, I. i. 256 ff.

L. 18 : न्यक्षेण–'न्यक्षं कात्स्न्र्यनिकृष्टयोः' — अमरकोश.

P. 284. L. 6 : सर्वोपमाद्रव्य ... — See Kālidāsa's *Kumāra-sambhava*, I. 49, for full citation.

L. 7 : वसन्तपुष्पा ... See *ibid*, III 53, for full citation.

L. 9 : तां प्राङ्मुखीम् ... ,, ,, VII 13 ,, ,, ,,

P. 290. L. 10 : read यावानयं for यावामयं.

P. 290. 15 : महमह ... This verse of Ānandavaradhana is an instance of what he calls अर्थवैचित्र्य or different shades of meaning due to peculiarities of प्रतिनियतभाषा or individual language dialects. Abhinavagupta in his *Locana* takes it as an allusion to सैन्धवभाषा. We have given the text of the verse as seen in our manuscripts. But modern Prakrit Scholars feel that the reading is too corrupt and requires major emendations. Two such attempts at emendation may be noted here :—

(i) मह महु इत्ति भणंतहो वच्चदि कालु जणस्सु ।
तोइ ण देउ जणद्दणउ गोअरीभोदि मणस्सु ॥

Dr. Bhayani, *Vidyā*, Journal of Gujarat University, Vol. XIV, No. 1 January 1971.

(ii) महु महु इत्ति भणंतहो वज्जइ कालो जणस्स ।
तोइ ण देउ जणद्दणु गोअरीभोदि मणस्स ॥

—Dr. V. M. Kulkarni, Prakrit Verses in works on Sanskrit Poetics, Journal of the University of Bombay, New Series, Arts, Vol. XL. No. 76, Oct. 1971, p. 45.

The point of illustration in this verse is the pun involved in the beginning words 'महमह', which can be derived from

Sanskrit मम मम as well as मधुमथ. It is because of this pun that there is a shade of paradox also according to Abhinavagupta. This points to the original reading महुमहु rather than महमह.

cf. *Mahābhārata*, XII. xiii. 4.

> द्व्यक्षरस्तु भवेन्मृत्युः त्र्यक्षरं ब्रह्म शाश्वतम् ।
> ममेति च भवेन्मृत्युः न ममेति च शाश्वतम् ॥

P. 294. L. 2 : read चेत् for चत्.

P. 294. *Kārikā* 14 : It is interesting to compare these ideas with the views of Alexander Pope on plagiarism:— " A mutual commerce makes poetry flourish; but then poets, like merchants, should repay with something of their own what they take from others; not, like pirates, make prize of all they meet " – Alexander Pope To W. Walsh, 2 July, 1706 [published in *Works* (1753), vii, 45].

P. 298. L. 12. इत्योम् ...— The ideas in this chapter have been elaborated by Rājaśekhara in his *Kāvyamīmāṁsā*, chs. XI, XII and XIV.

The concluding verses along with his own compositions cited as illustrations throughout the work show that Ānandavardhana was himself a poet of no mean order. [Cf. *Rājataraṅgiṇī's* reference to him as '*Kavirānandavardhanaḥ*'.]

GLOSSARY

of

Technical terms and English equivalents

अङ्ग (aṅga)	an accessory, a part
अङ्गिन् (aṅgin)	the principal, the whole
अकवि (akavi)	poetaster, a non-poet
अतिशयोक्ति (atiśayokti)	Exaggeration, Hyperbole
अतिव्याप्ति (ativyāpti)	fallacy of Too Wide
अत्यन्ततिरस्कृतवाच्य (atyantatira-skṛtavācya)	an expressed sense completely lost or concealed in the suggested
अद्भुतरस (adbhutarasa)	wonderment as a sentiment
अनित्य (anitya)	non-eternal, unstable
अनित्यदोष (anityadoṣa)	temporary or occasional defects
अनिर्देश्यत्व (anirdeśyatva)	indefinability
अनुग्राह्यानुग्राहकभाव (anugrāhy-ānugrāhakabhāva)	governor-governed relationship
अनुभव (anubhava)	experience
अनुभाव (anubhāva)	emotional reaction
अनुमान (anumāna)	inference
अनुरोध (anurodha)	a governing force, directing force
अनुवाद (anuvāda)	indirect speech or quotation
अनुस्वान (anusvāna)	resonance
अन्योन्याश्रय (anyonyāśraya)	fallacy of Circular Definition
अपशब्द (apaśabda)	solecism
अप्रस्तुत (aprastuta)	Irrelevant, extraneous
अप्रस्तुतप्रशंसा (aprastutapraśa-ṃsā)	vicarious reference, a figure of speech in Indian rhetoric
अभिधेय (abhidheya)	same as *artha* below
अभिनेयार्थ (abhineyārtha)	dramatic work, play
अर्थ (artha)	sense, meaning, content, subject, object, significance, theme, import, connotation

अर्थान्तरन्यास (arthāntaranyāsa)	exemplification (of a universal with a particular or *vice versa*) : a figure of speech in Indian Rhetoric
अर्थान्तरसङ्क्रमितवाच्य (arthāntarasaṅkramitavācya)	a literal meaning retained in the suggested; *see* atyantatiraskṛtavācya
अलङ्कार (alaṅkāra)	a figure of speech or ornament
अवमर्श (avamarśa)	one of the five major divisions of the dramatic plot roughly corresponding to denounment
अवान्तरभेद (avāntarabheda)	sub-division
अविनाभाव (avinābhāva)	integral relation
अविवक्षितवाच्य (avivakṣitavācya)	unintended literal import
अव्याप्ति (avyāpti)	fallacy of Too Narrow
अव्युत्पत्ति (avyutpatti)	imperfect education
असंभव (asambhava)	fallacy of *non esse* or *non sequitur*
असंलक्ष्यक्रम (asaṁlakṣyakrama)	of undiscerned sequentiality
अहङ्कार (ahaṅkāra)	ego
आक्षेप (ākṣepa)	a figure of speech in Indian rhetoric roughly corresponding to Paraleipsis
आख्यायिका (ākhyāyikā)	literary chronicles in prose
आत्मन् (ātman)	soul, essence, life, body, entity spirit
आधार (ādhāra)	substratum, base
आधिकारिक (ādhikārika)	the main plot
आधेय (ādheya)	the contained
आश्रय (āśraya)	same as *ādhāra* above
इतिवृत्त (itivṛtta)	theme, plot
उत्प्रेक्षा (utprekṣā)	fancied image, a figure of speech in Indian rhetoric
उत्साह (utsāha)	high-spiritedness
उपचार (upacāra)	metaphorical identification

उपनागरिका (upanāgarikā)	the urban or the refined, one of the literary *Vṛttis* or dictions in Indian rhetoric
उपलक्षण (upalakṣaṇa)	synecdoche, pointer
उपाधि (upādhi)	adventitious circumstance, extraneous condition
ओजस् (ojas)	Fieriness, forcefulness
औचित्य (Aucitya)	decorum, propriety, rightness, aptness
औपाधिक (aupadhika)	coloured by adventitious circumstances, incidental
कथा (kathā)	prose romance.
करण (karaṇa)	proximate cause
करुण (karuṇa)	the pathetic sentiment, pathos
कलापक (kalāpaka)	run-on lines up to twelve verses
कविनिबद्धप्रौढोक्तिसिद्ध (kavinibaddhapraudhoktisiddha)	Existing only in the ornate expression put into the mouth of a character created by the poet
कविप्रौढोक्तिसिद्ध (kavipraudhoktisiddha)	Existing only in the ornate expression of the poet
काकु (kāku)	ironic tone
कारिका (kārikā)	verse text, aphoristic verse
कार्य (kārya)	effect, action or plot
काव्य (kāvya)	poem, poetry, literature
काव्यप्रभेद (kāvyaprabheda)	forms of literature
कुलक (kulaka)	run-on lines running to 16 and above in poetry
कृत्रिम (kṛtrima)	conventional, natural
खण्डकथा (khaṇḍakathā)	short stories in verse, verse fables
गमक (gamaka)	pointer
गर्भ (garbha)	a division of dramatic plot corresponding to climax
गुण (guṇa)	quality, merit, excellence
गुणवृत्ति (guṇavṛtti)	indication, implication

गुणीभूतव्यङ्ग्य (guṇībhūtavyaṅgya)	poetry containing subordinated-suggestion
ग्राम्या-वृत्ति (grāmyā-vṛtti)	the soft diction
चतुरस्र (caturasra)	well-balanced, square, measured
चमत्कार (camatkāra)	strikingness, a striking effect
चाटु (cāṭu)	quatrain containing affectionate praise, eulogy
चारुत्व (cārutva)	artistic excellence, beauty
चित्तवृत्ति (cittavṛtti)	state of mind, mood
चित्र (citra)	portrait, portrait-like poetry, pictorial art
छाया (chāyā)	shade of beauty
जात्यत्व (jātyatva)	preciousness, precosity
तात्पर्य (tātparya)	purport, implication, intent, gist, content
तुल्ययोगिता (tulyayogitā)	combination of equals, a figure of speech in Indian rhetoric
दयावीर (Dayāvīra)	compassionate heroism; spirited compassion
दीपक (dīpaka)	ellipsis implying a simile making two things meaningful
दीप्ति (dīpti)	brilliance in style
दृष्टान्त (dṛṣṭānta)	analogy, a figure of speech in Indian rhetoric
दोष (doṣa)	defect, blemish, flaw
धर्म (dharma)	characteristic, speciality
धीरोदात्त (dhīrodātta)	Hero marked by nobility
धीरोद्धत (dhīroddhata)	Hero marked by hauteur
ध्वनि (DHVANI)	the function of suggestion, suggestive expression or meaning, suggested content, poetry with principal suggestion, suggestivity of expression in poetry; also words and imports pregnant with suggestivity

नित्य (nitya)	eternal, essential
नित्यदोष (nityadoṣa)	permanent defect, inherent defect
निदर्शना (nidarśanā)	corroboration, a figure of speech in Indian rhetoric
नियत (niyata)	constant
निर्वहण (nirvahaṇa)	conclusion, denouement
निषेध (niṣedha)	prohibition
नैसर्गिक (naisargika)	natural
पदार्थ (padartha)	word import, word meaning
परिकथा (parikathā)	didactic stories in verse, verse fables
परुषा-वृत्ति (paruṣā-vṛtti)	the harsh diction
पर्यायबन्ध (paryāyabandha)	several stanzas in varied or single metre on the same topic
पर्यायोक्त (paryāyokta)	a figure of speech in Indian rhetoric corresponding to periphrasis, roundabout description
प्रकृति (prakṛti)	status of characters, primordial Nature
प्रकार (prakāra)	variety, kind, type
प्रतिपत्तृ (pratipattṛ)	connoisseur, reader, responsive or tasteful critic
प्रतिपाद्य (pratipādya)	same as *abhidheya* above
प्रतिभा (pratibhā)	genius, creative imagination, vision
प्रतिमुख (pratimukha)	a major division of the dramatic plot corresponding to Rising Action
प्रतीति (pratīti)	apprehension
प्रतीयमान (pratīyamāna)	the implicit or suggested content
प्रमाण (pramāṇa)	instrument of knowledge
प्रसाद (prasāda)	perspicuity, lucidity, clarity
प्रसिद्धि (prasiddhi)	conventional usage, known usage

प्रस्थान (prasthāna)	canon, theory
प्रेयस् (preyas)	affectionate praise which is recognised as a figure of speech in Indian rhetoric
प्रौढोक्ति (prauḍhokti)	ornate or cultivated expression
बन्ध (bandha)	construction, composition
बन्धच्छाया (bandhacchāyā)	beauty of construction, structural beauty
बाध्य (bādhya)	contradicted
बीभत्स (bībhatsa)	disgust as a sentiment
भङ्गी (bhaṅgī)	an artistic turn
भणिति (bhaṇiti)	expression, utterance
भणितिवैचित्र्य (bhaṇitivaicitrya)	strikingness of expression or utterance
भयानक (bhayānaka)	fear, terror as a sentiment
भाव (bhāva)	emotion
भावना (bhāvanā)	aesthetic contemplation
महाकवि (mahākavi)	a master poet, a great poet
महाकाव्य (mahākāvya)	a great poem, epic
माधुर्य (mādhurya)	sweetness, suavity
मुख (mukha)	a major division of the dramatic plot corresponding to Introduction or Exposition
मुक्तक (muktaka)	single stanza forming a self-complete unit, epigram
यथासङ्ख्य (Yathāsaṅkhya)	Relative enumeration, a figure of speech in Indian rhetoric
युक्ति (yukti)	argument
रस (rasa)	sentiment
रसबन्ध (rasabandha)	delineation of sentiment
रसवदलङ्कार (rasavadalaṅkāra)	figurative sentiment
रसाभास (rasābhāsa)	semblance of sentiment
रीति (rīti)	style, manner
रौद्र (raudra)	the terrible, anger as a sentiment

लक्षण (lakṣaṇa)	definition, theory, defining feature
लक्षणा (lakṣaṇā)	secondary meaning
लिङ्ग (liṅga)	the *probans* of an inference
लिङ्गि (liṅgi)	the *probandum* of an inference
वक्रोक्ति (vakrokti)	artistic turn of speech, evasive speech, indirect denotation
वस्तु (vastu)	idea, subject, theme
वाक्यार्थ (vākyārtha)	purport of a sentence
वाचक (vācaka)	word
वाचकत्व (vācakatva)	the power of denotation
वाच्य (vācya)	the expressed, literal or denoted sense, explicit primary and conventional meaning
विकटबन्ध (vikaṭabandha)	affected and involved construction
विधि (vidhi)	proposal, construction, direct assertion
विप्रतिपत्ति (vipratipatti)	divergent view
विप्रलम्भशृङ्गार (vipralambha-śṛṅgāra)	the sentiment of love-in-separation, love of separated lovers as a sentiment
विभाव (vibhāva)	stimulus and stimulii provided by characters and excitants
विमति (vimati)	conflicting opinion
विरोधिन् (virodhin)	the opposite, reverse
विवक्षा (vivakṣā)	intent, intention of communication, desired or intended meaning
विवक्षितान्यपरवाच्य (vivaksitānyaparavācya)	an expressed meaning with extended signification; intended but further extending literal sense
विशेषक (viśeṣaka)	run-on lines extending up to four verses

विषय (viṣaya)	object, content, literary medium, poetic theme, instance
वृत्ति (vṛtti)	(i) procedure, (ii) literary modes of diction or ways of characters represented. (iii) gloss
व्यक्ति (vyakti)	suggestion, conveying
व्यतिरेक (vyatireka)	*Fancied contrast*, a figure of speech in Indian rhetoric
व्यपदेश (vyapadeśa)	designation
व्यभिचारिभाव (vyabhicāribhāva)	passing moods
व्याजस्तुति (vyājastuti)	veiled praise, a figure of speech
व्यापार (vyāpāra)	function or power of words
व्यञ्जकत्व (vyañjakatva)	suggestiveness or suggestivity, extended signification, suggestivity and meaningfulness
शब्द (Śabda)	sound, word, language
शब्दव्यापार (śabdavyāpāra)	the power of words to communicate meaning
शृङ्गार (śṛṅgāra)	the erotic sentiment
श्रव्यत्व (śravyatva)	sound-harmony
श्रुतिदुष्ट (śruti-duṣṭa)	Indelicacy, harshness
सकलकथा (sakalakathā)	full-fledged stories in verse, verse stories
समासोक्ति (samāsokti)	*condensed metaphor*
समुच्चय (samuccaya)	conjunction of agents with common actions, a figure of speech in Indian rhetoric
सर्गबन्ध (sargabandha)	epics running to several cantos
सहृदय (sahṛdaya)	perceptive or sympathetic critic, responsive reader, man of taste
सामर्थ्य (sāmarthya)	power of implication
सारूप्य (sārūpya)	similarity, congruency

स्थायिभाव (sthāyibhāva)	abiding emotion
स्वतःसम्भवि (svataḥsambhavi)	naturally existing, inherent
सङ्कर (saṅkara)	merging or intermingling of figures; mingled figure
सङ्घटना (saṅghaṭanā)	texture, poetic composition involving proper choice of compounds etc, stylistics
सन्दानितक (sandānitaka)	two stanzas forming a single unit with run-on lines
सन्देह (sandeha)	fancied doubt, a figure of speech in Indian rhetoric
सन्धि (sandhi)	major divisions of dramatic plot
सन्ध्यङ्ग (sandhyaṅga)	major subdivisions of dramatic plot
संलक्ष्यक्रम (saṁlakṣyakrama)	of marked sequentiality
संसृष्टि (saṁsṛṣṭi)	collocation or co-existence of figures

I. INDEX OF KĀRIKĀS

Kārikā	*Uddyota & Kārikā No.*		*Page*	*Line*
अकाण्ड एव विच्छित्तिः	III	19	160	3
अक्षरादिरचनेव योज्यते	IV	15	296	7
अतो ह्यन्यतमेनापि	IV	2	264	9
अर्थशक्तेरलङ्कारो	II	25	88	21
अर्थशक्त्युद्भवस्त्वन्यो	II	22	82	8
अर्थान्तरगतिः काक्वा	III	38	232	14
अर्थान्तरे सङ्क्रमितं	II	1	38	1
अनुस्वानोपमात्मापि	III	15	146	1
अलङ्कारान्तरव्यङ्ग्यभावे	II	30	100	10
अलङ्कारान्तरस्यापि	II	27	90	9
अलङ्कृतीनां शक्तावप्या°	III	14	136	4
अवधानातिशयवान्	III	29	184	18
अवस्थादिविभिन्नानां	IV	8	292	3
अवस्थादेशकालादि°	IV	7	282	15
अविरोधी विरोधी वा	III	34	176	13
अविवक्षितवाच्यस्य	III	1	106	3
अव्युत्पत्तेरशक्तेर्वा	II	32	104	7
असमासा समासेन	III	5	118	6
असंलक्ष्यक्रमोद्योतः	II	2	40	10
अस्फुटस्फुरितं	III	46	260	5
आक्षिप्त एवालङ्कारः	II	21	72	3
आत्मनोऽन्यस्य सद्भावे	IV	14	294	16
आलोकार्थी यथा	I	9	16	5
इतिवृत्तवशायातां	III	11	134	11
इत्युक्तलक्षणो यो	III	45	260	1
उक्त्यन्तरेणाशक्यं	I	15	32	13
उद्दीपनप्रशमने	III	13	136	1
एकाश्रयत्वे निर्दोषो	III	26	180	14
एतद्यथोक्तमौचित्यं	III	8	132	6
एवं ध्वनेः प्रभेदाः	III	44	258	17

Kārikā	Uddyota & Kārikā No.		Page	Line
कस्य चिद्ध्वनिभेदस्य	I	19	34	8
कार्यमेकं यथा व्यापि	III	23	176	1
काव्यस्यात्मा ध्वनिरिति	I	1	2	5
काव्यस्यात्मा स एवार्थः	I	5	12	7
क्रमेण प्रतिभात्यात्मा	II	20	70	14
गुणानाश्रित्य तिष्ठन्ती	III	6	118	11
चित्रं शब्दार्थभेदेन	III	42	244	17
त एव तु निवेश्यन्ते	III	4	114	11
तत्र पूर्वमनन्यात्म	IV	13	294	9
तत्र वाच्यः प्रसिद्धो यः	I	3	6	13
तद्वत्सचेतसां सोऽर्थः	I	12	18	5
तमर्थमवलम्बन्ते	II	6	48	12
तस्याङ्गानां प्रभेदा ये	II	12	54	2
दिङ्मात्रं तूच्यते येन	II	13	56	1
दृष्टपूर्वा अपि ह्यर्थाः	IV	4	270	3
ध्वनेरित्थं गुणीभूतव्यङ्ग्यस्य	IV	6	282	4
ध्वनेर्यः सगुणीभूतव्यङ्ग्यस्याध्वा	IV	1	264	4
ध्वन्यात्मभूते शृङ्गारे यमकादि°	II	15	56	10
ध्वन्यात्मभूते शृङ्गारे समीक्ष्य	II	17	60	14
निर्व्यूढावपि चाङ्गत्वे	II	19	62	8
प्रकारोऽन्यो गुणीभूत°	III	34	224	8
प्रकारोऽयं गुणीभूत°	III	40	236	11
प्रतायन्तां वाचो निमित°	IV	17	298	2
प्रतीयमानं पुनरन्यदेव	I	4	6	18
प्रधानगुणभावाभ्यां	III	41	244	15
प्रधानेऽन्यत्र वाक्यार्थे	II	5	42	6
प्रबन्धे मुक्तके वापि	III	17	158	12
प्रभेदस्यास्य विषयो	III	39	234	12
प्रसन्नगम्भीरपदाः	III	35	226	11
प्रसिद्धेऽपि प्रबन्धानां	III	21	174	9
प्रौढोक्तिमात्रनिष्पन्नः	II	24	86	12
भक्त्या बिभर्ति नैकत्वं	I	14	28	15

Kārikā	Uddyota & Kārikā No.		Page	Line
मुख्या महाकविगिरां	III	37	232	6
मुख्यां वृत्तिं परित्यज्य	I	17	32	21
यत्र प्रतीयमानोऽर्थः	II	31	102	1
यत्रार्थः शब्दो वा	I	13	18	9
यथा पदार्थद्वारेण	I	10	16	12
यदपि तदपि रम्यं	IV	16	296	14
यस्त्वलक्ष्यक्रमव्यङ्ग्यो	III	2	114	6
युक्त्यानयानुसर्तव्यो	IV	3	268	9
योऽर्थः सहृदयश्लाघ्यः	I	2	6	9
रसबन्धोक्तमौचित्यं	III	9	132	15
रसभावतदाभास°	II	3	40	15
रसभावादिसम्बद्धा	IV	9	292	9
रसाक्षिप्ततया यस्य	II	16	58	5
रसाद्यनुगुणत्वेन	III	33	188	14
रसान्तरसमावेशः	III	22	174	17
रसान्तरान्तरितयोः	III	27	182	17
रूढा ये विषयेऽन्यत्र	I	16	32	17
रूपकादिरलङ्कारवर्गो	II	92	90	2
रौद्रादयो रसा दीप्त्या	II	9	50	8
*वस्तुमात्रमपि व्यङ्ग्यं	after II	22	82	footnote
वाचकत्वाश्रयेणैव	I	18	34	4
वाचस्पतिसहस्राणां	IV	10	292	12
वाच्यवाचकचारुत्व°	II	4	42	1
वाच्यानां वाचकानां च	III	32	188	6
वाच्यालङ्कारवर्गोऽयं	III	36	288	1
*वाच्यालङ्कारशक्तेः	after II	28	98	footnote
विज्ञायेत्थं रसादीनां	III	31	186	19
विभावभावानुभाव°	III	10	134	9
विनेयानुन्मुखीकर्तुं	III	30	186	6
विरुद्धैकाश्रयो यस्तु	III	25	180	3
विरोधमविरोधं च	III	28	184	12
विरोधिरससम्बन्धि°	III	18	160	1

Kārikā	*Uddyota & Kārikā No.*		*Page*	*Line*
विवक्षा तत्परत्वेन	II	18	62	6
विवक्षिते रसे लब्धप्रतिष्ठे	III	20	164	9
विषयाश्रयमप्यन्यदौचित्यं	III	7	128	16
व्यङ्ग्यव्यञ्जकभावेऽस्मिन्	IV	5	272	11
व्यज्यन्ते वस्तुमात्रेण	II	29	100	5
शब्दतत्त्वाश्रयाः काश्चिद्	III	47	260	11
शब्दार्थशक्त्याक्षिप्तोऽपि	II	23	84	13
शब्दार्थशासनज्ञान॰	I	7	14	8
शरीरीकरणं येषां	II	28	98	14
शषौ सरेफसंयोगौ	III	3	114	9
शृङ्गारस्याङ्गिनो यत्नात्	II	14	56	5
शृङ्गार एव मधुरः	II	7	48	17
शृङ्गारे विप्रलम्भाख्ये	II	8	50	5
श्रुतिदुष्टादयो दोषाः	II	11	52	10
संवादास्तु भवन्त्येव	IV	11	292	18
संवादो ह्यन्यसादृश्यं	IV	12	294	3
सगुणीभूतव्यङ्ग्यैः	III	43	252	1
सन्धिसन्ध्यङ्गघटनं	III	12	134	13
समर्पकत्वं काव्यस्य	II	10	52	6
सरस्वती स्वादु	I	6	14	1
सर्वेष्वेव प्रभेदेषु	II	33	104	11
सुप्तिङ्वचनसम्बन्धैः	III	16	146	7
सोऽर्थस्तद्व्यक्तिसामर्थ्य॰	I	8	14	17
स्वसामर्थ्यवशेनैव	I	11	18	1

II. INDEX OF PARIKARAŚLOKAS ETC.

in the Vṛtti

Śloka	*Page*	*Line*
अनाख्येयांशभासित्वं	262	18
अनिष्टस्य श्रुतिः	112	21
अनौचित्यादृते नान्यद्	138	7
अपारे काव्यसंसारे	250	1
अव्युत्पत्तिकृतो दोषः	124	9
इति काव्यार्थविवेको	134	5
इत्यक्लिष्टरसाश्रयोचित° (concluding pen-ultimate verse)	298	13
कथा शरीरमुत्पाद्य°	142	10
काव्याध्वनि ध्वनिर्व्यङ्ग्य°	250	20
तत्परावेव शब्दार्थौ	20	8
नीरसस्तु प्रबन्धो यः	164	3
पदानां स्मारकत्वेऽपि	114	1
पूर्वे विशृङ्खलगिरः	164	5
भावानचेतनानपि	250	5
मुख्या व्यापारविषयाः	164	1
यमकादिनिबन्धे तु	60	9
यस्मिन्रसो वा भावो वा	250	18
रसभावादितात्पर्य°	44	13
रसभावादिविषय°	248	5
रसवन्ति हि वस्तूनि	60	7
रसादिषु विवक्षा तु	248	7
रसाभासाङ्गभावस्तु	60	11
वाल्मीकिव्यतिरिक्तस्य	290	7
वाल्मीकिव्यासमुख्याश्च	164	7
विच्छित्तिशोभिनैकेन	114	3
विमतिविषयो यः	224	6
व्यङ्ग्यव्यञ्जकसम्बन्ध°	20	6
व्यङ्ग्यस्य प्रतिभामात्रे	26	6
व्यङ्ग्यस्य यत्राप्राधान्यं	26	4
शृङ्गारी चेत्कविः काव्ये	250	3
सत्काव्यतत्त्वनयवर्त्म (concluding verse)	298	17
सन्ति सिद्धरसप्रख्याः	142	14
स्वेच्छाकेसरिणः (maṅgala-śloka)	2	3

III. INDEX OF QUOTATIONS*

Śloka	*Page*	*Line*
अङ्कुरितः	98	7
अञ्जाए पह्नारो	32	2
अण्णत्त वच्च	150	13
अतहट्ठिए	268	18
अतिक्रान्तसुखाः	148	10
अत्ता एत्थ	8	15
अनध्यवसिताव°	242	4
अनवरतनयनजल°	120	6
अनुरागवती सन्ध्या	22	8
अमी ये दृश्यन्ते	242	16
अम्बा शेतेऽत्र	86	7
अयमेकपदे तया	150	20
अयं स रशनोत्कर्षी	172	7
अवसर रोउं	150	2
अहिणअपओअरसिएसु	258	10
अहो बतासि	152	14
आक्रन्दाः स्तनितैः	68	5
आम्म असइओ	234	2
आहूतोऽपि सहायैः	22	15
ईसाकलुसस्स वि	96	11
उच्चिणसु पडिअ°	102	22
उत्कम्पिनी भय°	114	15
उदिह...कआमोआ	272	footnote
उद्दामोत्कलिकां	64	7
उन्नतः प्रोल्लसद्धारः	78	7
उपोढरागेण	20	15
उप्पहजाआए	244	9
एकान्तो रुअइ	176	19
एमेअ जणो तिस्सा	106	18
एवं वादिनि देवर्षौ	82, 88	11, 15 etc.
एषापि स्वयमेव	240	6
एहि गच्छ पतोत्तिष्ठ	168	8
कण्ठाच्छित्त्वाक्षमालां	178	2
कर्ता द्यूतच्छलानां	254	5
कपोले पत्राली	58	10
कमलाअरा न मलिआ	102	7
करिणीवेधव्वअरो	272	3
कस्त्वं भोः कथयामि	244	1
कस्स व ण होइ	10	9
काकार्य शशलक्ष्मणः	166	9
°किमिव हि मधुराणां	106	11
किं हास्येन न मे	42	13
कुविआओ पसण्णाओ	30	17
कृतककुपितैः	116	13
कृते वरकथालापे	270	12
कामन्त्यः क्षतकोमल°	174	1
कोपात्कोमललोल°	68	12
°कः सन्नद्धे विरहविधुरां	106	9
क्षिप्तो हस्तावलग्नः	44	3
खणपाहुणिआ देअर	252	11
खं येऽत्युज्ज्वलयन्ति	82	1
गअणं च मत्तमेहं	40	5
°गावो वः पावनानां	194	8
चक्राभिघातप्रसभाज्ञयैव	64	2
चञ्चद्भुजभ्रमित°	50	13
चन्दनासक्तभुजग°	96	4

* See Notes for sources of these where traceable.

Sloka	*Page*	*Line*
चन्दमऊएइँ णिसा	90	15
चमहिअमाणस°	76	5
चलापाङ्गां दृष्टिं	62	12
चुम्बिज्जइ सअहुत्तं	30	12
चूअंकुरावअंसं	110	6
जाएज्ज वणुद्देसे	94	19
ज्योत्स्नापूरप्रसर°	92 footnote	
झगिति कनकच्चित्रे	116	2
ण अ ताण घडइ	284	13
तद्गेहं नतभित्ति	156	1
तन्वी मेघजलार्द्र°	46	15
तरङ्गभ्रूभङ्गा	46	10
तस्या विनापि हारेण	74	4
ताला जाअन्ति गुणा	38	15
तालैः शिञ्जद्वलयसुभगैः	148	16
तेषां गोपवधूविलास°	48	2
तं ताण सिरिसहोअर°	92	19
त्रासाकुलः परिपतन्	96	16
दत्तानन्दाः प्रजानां	78	10
दन्तक्षतानि करजैश्च	258	3
दीर्घीकुर्वन् पटु मदकलं	256	14
दुराराधा राधा सुभग	236	16
देआ पसिअ	10	4
देव्वाएत्तम्मि फले	94	5
दृष्ट्या केशव गोपराग°	76	14
निद्राकैतविनः प्रियस्य	266	15
नीवाराः शुकगर्भ°	152	6
नो कल्पापायवायोः	66	12
न्यक्कारो ह्ययमेव मे	146	12
पत्युः शिरश्चन्द्रकला°	236	1
पन्थिअ न एत्थ	82 footnote	
परार्थे यः पीडामनुभवति	32, 242	7, 11

Sloka	*Page*	*Line*
परिम्लानं पीनस्तन°	30	7
°प्रभ्रश्यत्युत्तरीयत्विषि°	152	11
प्रयच्छतोच्चैः	236	4
प्रातुं धनैरर्थिजनस्य	108	17
प्राप्तश्रीरेष कस्मात्	92	2
भगवान् वासुदेवश्च	276	6
भम धम्मिअ वीसत्थो	8	10
भूरेणुदिग्धान्नव°	184	4
भ्रमिमरतिमलस°	76, 166	2, 15
मदमुखरकपोत°	152 footnote	
मनुष्यवृत्त्या	152	12
मह मह इति	290	15
मा निषाद	12 footnote	
मा पन्थं रुन्धीओ	150	7
मुनिर्जयति योगीन्द्रो	280	6
मुहुरङ्गुलिसंवृता°	152	2
यच्च कामसुखं लोके	182	5
यत्र च मत्तमातङ्गगामिन्यः	80	4
यथा यथा विपर्येति	274	10
यद्वञ्चनाहितमतिः	154	8
यस्मिन्नस्ति न वस्तु	4	12
या निशा सर्वभूतानां	108	3
या व्यापारवती रसान्	256	7
ये जीवन्ति न मान्ति	154	1
येन ध्वस्तमनोभवेन	72	8
यो यश्शत्रं बिभर्ति	120, 52	8, 1 etc.
यः प्रथमः प्रथमः	266	7
रक्तस्त्वं नवपल्लवैः	64	14 etc.
रम्या इति प्राप्तवतीः	98	2
रविसङ्क्रान्तसौभाग्यः	40	2
राजानमपि सेवन्ते	238	12

Sloka	*Page*	*Line*
रामेण प्रियजीवितेन	106	14
लच्छी दुहिदा	226	16
लावण्यकान्तिपरिपूरित	92	7
लावण्यद्रविणव्ययो	240	4
लावण्यसिन्धुरपरैव	226	1
वच्च मह व्विह	8	20
वत्से मा गा विषादं	86	2
वाणिअअ हत्थिदन्ता	110	19
वाणीरकुडङ्गोड्डीण	102	15
विसमइओ च्चिअ	108	9
विस्रम्भोत्था मन्मथाज्ञा	232	10
वीराणं रमइ	92	15
व्रीडायोगान्नतवदनया	116	7
वृत्तेऽस्मिन्महाप्रलये...	110	2
शिखरिणि क नु नाम	28	12
	88	8
शून्यं वासगृहं विलोक्य	268	2
शेषो हिमगिरिस्त्वं च	270	7
श्यामास्वङ्गं चकितहरिणी	70	1
श्लाघ्याशेषतनुं	74	10
सङ्केतकालमनसं	84	9
सत्यं मनोरमा रामाः	186	16
सज्जेहि सुरहिमासो	88	3

Sloka	*Page*	*Line*
°सप्तैताः समिधः श्रियः	106	7
°समवाय इव...	80	11
समविसमणिव्विसेसा	154	14
स वक्तुमखिलान् शक्तो	92	24
सविभ्रमस्मितोद्भेदाः	266	2
सर्वैकशरणमक्षय	80	13
स हरिर्नाम्ना देवः	66	6
साअरविइण्ण	88	10
	272	ft.note
सिज्जइ रोमाञ्चिज्जइ	280	13 ete.
सिहिपिञ्छकण्णऊरा	88	17
	112	5
सुरभिसमये प्रवृत्ते	270	16
सुवर्णपुष्पां पृथिवीं	28	9
सैषा सर्वैव वक्रोक्तिः	228	11
स्मरनवनदीपूरेणोढाः	118	1
स्वतेजःक्रीतमहिमा	266	10
स्वस्था भवन्ति मयि	232	17
स्निग्धश्यामलकान्ति	38	8
स्मितं किञ्चिन्मुग्धं	264	15
हंसानां निनदेषु यैः	286	7
हिअअट्ठाविअमण्णु	94	11

INDEX OF AUTHORS AND WORKS*

Abercrombie, Lascelles, 372
Abhyankar, K. V., 324
Alexander Pope, 385
Amaruśataka, 345, 350, 353, 359, 367, 383
Anuyogadvārasūtra, 375
Appayyadīkṣita, 335, 361
Aristotle, xxiii, 362, 368
Arjunavarmadeva, 351
Bāṇa, xxix, 315
Harṣacarita, 315, 354, 383
Bergson, xxiii
Bhagavadgītā, 365
Bhāguri, xxvii
Bhallaṭaśataka, 336
Bhamaha, xxiii, xxviii, 303, 304, 327, 328, 331, 343, 344, 349, 350, 352, 354, 366
Bhamahavivaraṇa, xxxix, 326, 330
Bharata, (*Nāṭyaśāstra*), xxii, xxvi, xxix, 341, 367, 368, 369, 375
Bhāravi, 380
Bharcu, 330
Bhartṛhari, 303, 322, 338, 377, 378
Bhartṛmeṇṭha, 363
Bhāsa, 370
Bhattacharya. B., xiii
Bhattacharya, S. P., xiin., 311
Bhat, G. H., 311, 312
Bhaṭṭanārāyṇa, 349, 380, 383
Bhaṭṭanāyaka, xviii, xx, xxvii, xxix, 316, 341, 361
Bhaṭṭa Tauta, 315
Bhaṭṭendurāja, 381
Bhavabhūti, xxix
Bhayani, Dr., 384
Bhoja, xxvii, 361
Blake, xxxv
Brahmasūtrā, 304
Bṛhaddevatā, 304
Brough, John, 336
Bühler, G., xi
Candīdāsa, 311
Caudwell. Christopher, XLi
Candrikākāra, xx, xxvii
Chari, V. K., 368
Chaudhury, P. J., 313
Church, K. W. 319
Coleridge, S. T., 337, 350
Coombes, 319
Croce, 313
Daṇḍin, xxii, xxix, 329, 330, 339, 343, 349, 352, 354, 360, 363, 366
De. S. K., x, xvii
Dhanañjaya, xxvii
Dharmakīrti, 335, 338, 380, 383
Dharmottara, 383
Drinkwater, John, 383
Dwivedi, R. P., 361
Eliot, T. S., xxiv, 313
Ganapati Shastri, T., 370
Ghaṭakarparakāvya, 351

* Names of Ānandavardhana, Abhinavagupta, *Dhvanyāloka* and *Locana* etc. which occur very frequently are not included in this Index.

Gnoli, Raniero, 326
Govinda Ṭhakkura, 361
Harṣa, 351
Hāla, 363, 364, 365, 371, 380, 382, 383
Hall, Vernon, 312, 313
Hazlitt, 314
Hanumannāṭāka, 371
Hanumantha Rao, G., 313
Haribhadra, xxvi
Hegel, 313
Hemacandra, 316, 327, 351, 354, 371
Hiriyanna, M., xi, 313, 344
Hobson, Herald, 319
Hough, Graham, 317
Hulme, xxiv
Ingalls, Daniel, H. H., xxivn, 338
Jacob, G. A., 377
Jacobi, H., xi, xvi, 317, 318, 319
Jagannātha, xxviii, 354, 361
Jayadeva, 361
Jayantabhaṭṭa, xxi
Jayaratha, 336
Jhalakikar, Vāmanācārya, 361
Jose Ortega Y. Gasset Weyl, 373
Kālidāsa, xxix, xLi, 351
Kumārasambhava, 314, 351, 354, 360, 367, 371, 379, 380, 384
Meghadūta, 353, 365, 371, 383
Raghuvaṁśa, 309, 369
Śākuntala, 351, 365, 371
Vikramorvaśīya, 315, 347, 351, 371
Kāmandaka, 373
Kāmandakīyanītisāra, 373
Kallaṭa, xxi
Kalpalatāviveka, xiv
Kane, P. V., xi, xvii, 311, 312
Kautūhala, xxvi
Kavirājamārga, xxii
Kāvyādarśa, xxii
Kāvyakautuka, 315, 316
Kāvyālaṅkāra, xxv, 348
Kāvyālaṅkārasaṅgraha, 363
Kāvyamīmāṁsā, 385
Keats, 313
Kebel, John, 313
Krishnamoorthy, K, xiiin, xviin, xxiiin., xxviiin., 324, 340, 351, 356, 366, 375
Krishna Rayan, 372, 375
Kṣemendra, 375
Kulkarni, V. M., 308, 384
Kuppuswami Shastri, xii, 311, 312, 317, 368
Kunjunni Raja, K., xvii
Kuntaka, xxvii, 373
Kuvalayamālā, xxvi
Kuvalayānanda, 335
Langer, Susan, xLi
Lerner Lawrence, 337
Līlāvatī, xxvi
Lollata, xxix
Longinus, xxx, 350, 374
Madhumathanavijaya, 370
Māgha, xxix, 363
Mahābhārata, 306, 334, 365, 370, 371, 374, 384, 385
Mahānāṭaka (See *Hanumannāṭaka*) 341, 353
Mahārthamañjarī, xvi
Mahimabhaṭṭa, xxvii
Maheśvarānanda, xvi

Mallinātha, xvii, 316, 354
Mammaṭa, xxviii, 328, 335, 339, 353, 361, 375
Māṇikyacandra, 327
Maṅkhuka, 315
Manoratha, 305
Masson J. L. and Patwardhan, M.V., xii., f. n. 354, 356, 367, 374
Mayūra, 353, 354, 371
Māyurāja, 365
Montague, C. E. xxxx
Mukherji, Ramaranjan, xii, f. n.
Nāgoji Bhaṭṭa, 354, 361
Nalodaya, 351
Nṛpatuṅga, xxii
(See *Kavirāiamārga*)
Nyāyamañjarī, xxi
Pañcatantra, 334
Pāṇini, 327
Paṇshikar W. L., xi
Pisharoti, K. R., xi, 314
Pound Ezra, xxiv
Pramāṇavārttika, 338
Pratīhārendurāja, xxvii
Pravarasena, 351
Raddi, Rangacharya, 330
Rāghavabhaṭṭa, xvii
Raghavan, V., xii, f.n. 369, 375, 381
Raghunāthā, 377
Rājaśekhara, xxi, xxvii, xLi, 311, 385
Ramachandra Rao, S. K,, 324
Ramashāraka, xii, 317
Rāmāyaṇa, 306, 309, 310, 341, 384
Ransom, J. C., xxii
Ratnāvalī, 351
Ratnaśrījñāna, xxii
Richards, I. A., xxiii, xLi, 318, 325, 376
Rudrabhaṭṭa, xxv, xxv
Rudraṭa, xxv, xxvi, xxix, 330, 352, 353, 354, 360.
Ruyyaka, 335, 354, 361
Saduktikarṇāmnrta, 335, 336
Samarāiccakahā, xxvi
Sarasvatīkaṇṭhābharaṇa, 361
Śārṅgadharapaddhati, 330, 336
Śankuka, xxix, 304
Setubandha, 351
Sankaran, A, xi
Shairp, J. C. 315
Sharma, Mukunda Madhav, xii, f. n.
Shelley, 312
Śiśupālavadha (See Māgha), 351
Somadeva, 381
Spandapradīpikā, xxi
Śrīkaṇṭhacarita, 315
Śṛṅgāraprakāśa (See Bhoja), 369
Sṛṅgāratilaka, xxv
Subhāṣitāvalī, 330, 345 354, 360
Subramania Iyer, K. A., 362
Svapnavāsavadatta, 370
Tagore, Rabindranath, 313
Tattvāloka, xxii
Udbhaṭa, xxiii, xxvii, xxix, xxxix, 303, 304, 326, 330, 352, 353, 366, 372, 375
Uddyotanasūrī xxvi
Upadhye, A. N., 382

Utpala, xxi
Uttuṅgodaya, xii, 317
Vajjālaggaṁ, 382
Vākyapadīya, 303, 321, 338
Valery, Paul, 337
Vallabhadeva, 345, 366, 380
Vālmīki, XL, 309
Vāmana, xxiii, 303, 305, 327, 352, 354, 366, 383
Velankar, H. D., 318
Vidyādhara, xxviii
Vidyānātha, xxviii
Vimarśinī, 336
Viśvanātha, xxviii, 335, 351, 353, 371,
Vyāsa, XL, 375
Wordsworth, 312, 314
Yaśovarman, 353, 369

ERRATA

Page	Line	Incorrect	Correct
41	24	For emotion	Read emotional mood
45	4	For *our*	Read *your*
61	16	*Add :* **There is nothing wrong even if assonance is deemed a fitting medium, for portraying 'semblance of sentiment** after the sentence ending with the words ... *primary in Importance.*	
83	9	*Add :* And yet which do not shine in the sky	
83	10	*Add :* And yet which outshine the lotus's colour	
124	11	Perhaps the variant प्रसिद्धं fits better than प्रतिषिद्धं if understood as *all too common portrayal of love*	
135	23 to 26	should come immediately after the first paragraph and before *suggestion with ....*	
142	f.n. 6	*Add :* घ after the dash.	
202	3	For वाक्यस्य	Read वाच्यस्य
219	9	After the word *Admitted Add :* that it is both different from the well known function of conventional denotation and yet a function of word nonetheless, and so *Before line* 10 : 'there is no cause ...	
250	6	For घ्यवहारयति	Read व्यवहारयति
272	8	For सुत्पादयति	Read मुत्पादयति
370	27	For I shall not think of devotion to you Read : I shall never forget your devotion to me For The restoring of correct readings of these two Prakrit verses, see *V.M. Kulkarni,* 'Prakrit verses in Works on Sanskrit Poetics', Bombay University Journal, Arts, Vo,. XL, No. 76 (Oct. 1971).	
401	1	Below परिम्लानं पीनस्तनं Read पाण्डु क्षामं Page 168 Line 1	